PACIFIC MEXICO
HANDBOOK

PACIFIC MEXICO
HANDBOOK

BRUCE WHIPPERMAN

MOON
PUBLICATIONS INC.

PACIFIC MEXICO HANDBOOK

Published by
Moon Publications, Inc.
P.O. Box 3040
Chico, California 95927-3040, USA

Printed by
Colorcraft Ltd.

Library of Congress Cataloging in Publication Data
Whipperman, Bruce
   Pacific Mexico Handbook / Bruce Whipperman. —1st ed.
      p.   cm.
   Includes bibliographical references and index.
   ISBN 1-56691-005-6
   1. Mexico—Guidebooks.   2. Pacific Coast (Mexico)—
Guidebooks. 3. Beaches—Mexico—Pacific Coast—Guidebooks.
I. Title.
F1209.W42   1993   93-13722
917.204'835—dc20   CIP

Editors: Mark Morris, Beth Rhudy
Copy Editors: Deana Corbitt, Asha Johnson
Production & Design: Carey Wilson, David Hurst
Cartographers: Bob Race, Brian Bardwell
Index: Mark Arends

Front cover: Puerto Vallarta, photo by Dave G. Houser
All photos by Bruce Whipperman unless otherwise noted.

Distributed in the USA by Publishers Group West

Printed in Hong Kong

Please send all comments,
corrections, additions,
amendments, and critiques to:

**PACIFIC MEXICO HANDBOOK
MOON PUBLICATIONS, INC.
P.O. BOX 3040
CHICO, CA 95927-3040, USA**

Printing History
1st edition—October 1993

To Mom, Dad and Hilda,
Peter, Sara and Kent, and Linda.

ACKNOWLEDGEMENTS

I thank the dozens of kind, unnamed Mexican people, such as the boy who stood on the road warning trucks away as I changed a tire, the men who helped me pull my car from the edge of a cliff one night atop a mountain in Oaxaca, and the staff who patiently answered my endless queries at many *turismo* offices. They all deserve credit for this book.

In Mazatlán, my special thanks go to Luis Chavez and Agustín Arellano who taught me much of Mexico.

In Manzanillo, thanks to Bart Varelman of Hotel La Posada, Susan Dearing of Underworld Scuba, and to Alfred Haslerand his tireless mechanics at SIMPSA Engineering who kept my car running.

My special thanks also go to eco-ornithologist Michael Malone in Puerto Escondido for helping me to appreciate Pacific Mexico's wildlife treasury, and to his excellent partners in agency Turismo Rodemar.

At Moon Publications, thanks to Bill Dalton, Moon's founder and former publisher, for undertaking this project with me, and to present publisher Bill Newlin for seeing it through. Also thanks to my editors Mark Morris (who coined the name "Pacific Mexico") and Beth Rhudy for their ton of work, kind encouragement and scores of suggestions that saved my manuscript. Thanks also to copy editor Deana Corbitt, whose sharp eyes caught dozens of errors, and to Bob Race and his staff for their excellent maps.

In my home town, thanks to the understanding workers at my offices-away-from home, the Coffee Connection and Espresso Roma, whose luscious *lattes, biancos,* muffins, and bagels with cream cheese were essential to the writing of this book.

Thanks and a mountain of gratitude to my mentor, writer Ken Kelley, who sweated with me to make my first travel stories readable.

Thanks also to my friends Akemi Nagafuji and Anne Shapiro, who opened my eyes to the world.

This book could not have been written if not for Halcea Valdes, my friend and business partner, to whom I am grateful for managing without me while I was on the road for nine months in Pacific Mexico.

Finally, a heap of credit is due to my sweetheart, Linda Reasin, who kept the home fires burning while I was away, came and nursed me when I got sick in Oaxaca, and was patient with everything I had to neglect back home while finishing this book.

CONTENTS

MAPS

MAP SYMBOLS

⬭ FEDERAL HIGHWAY	● HOTEL / ACCOMMODATION	▬▬ HIGHWAY / MAJOR ROAD
◯ STATE HIGHWAY	■ POINT OF INTEREST	▬▬ SECONDARY ROAD
▲ MOUNTAIN	✈ AIRPORT	— — — UNPAVED ROAD
◐ TIME ZONE	◌ WATER	—··— TRAIL
○ TOWN / VILLAGE	≜ RUIN	▬▬ RAILROAD
○ CITY / LARGE TOWN	▬ ▬ ▬ NATIONAL BORDER	→)--(← TUNNEL
🛢 GAS	▬·▬·▬ STATE BORDER	══ BRIDGE

CHARTS

SPECIAL TOPICS

ABBREVIATIONS

a/c—air-conditioned
Av.—Avenida
C—Celsius
d—double occupancy
F—Fahrenheit
Hwy.—highway
I.—*Isla* (Island)
km—kilometer

Km—kilometer marker
L.—*Laguna* (Lagoon, Lake)
R.—*Río* (River)
s—single occupancy
s/n—without a street number
t—triple occupancy
tel.—telephone number

PREFACE

Scarcely a generation ago, Mexico's tropical Pacific coast was dotted with a few sleepy, isolated towns and fishing villages, reachable only by sea or tortuous mountain roads from the interior. That gradually began to change, until, in 1984, the last link of Mexico's Pacific-coast Highway 200 was completed, creating Pacific Mexico, an entire touristic region and palmy thousand-mile path for exploring Mexico.

The choices seem endless. You can choose among resorts, some glittering and luxurious and others quiet and homey. In between the resorts stretch jungle-clad headlands, interspersed with palm-shaded, pearly strands where the fishing is good and the living easy.

When weary of lazing in the sun, visitors can enjoy a trove of ocean sports. Pacific Mexico's water is always balmy and fine to fish, swim, surf, windsurf, kayak, waterski, snorkel, and scuba dive. For nature enthusiasts, dozens of lush jungle-fringed coastal lagoons are ripe for wildlife viewing and photography.

The coastal strip would be enough but Pacific Mexico offers more: Within a hour's flight or a day's drive of the tropical shore rise the cool oak- and pine-studded highland valleys. Here, colonial cities—Guadalajara, Colima, Pátzcuaro, Taxco, Oaxaca—offer fine crafts, colorful festivals, baroque monuments, traditional peoples and the barely explored ruins of long-forgotten kingdoms.

In short, Pacific Mexico is an exotic, tropical land, easy to visit, enjoy, and appreciate, whether you prefer glamourous luxury, back-country adventure, or a little bit of both. This book will show you the way.

IS THIS BOOK OUT OF DATE?

Help from our readers is an important part of keeping the *Pacific Mexico Handbook* up to date. If you know of changes—worthy new hotels, restaurants, and "must-see" sights and attractions—please tell us about them. Furthermore, if we've omitted important information, or any of our maps needs correcting, please clue us in.

We're especially interested in hearing from female travelers, handicapped travelers, people who've traveled with children, RVers, hikers, campers, and residents, both foreign and Mexican. We welcome the comments of business and professional people—hotel and restaurant owners, travel agents, government tourism staff—who serve Pacific Mexico travelers.

We welcome submissions of unusually good photos and drawings for possible use in future editions. If photos, send duplicate slides or slides-from-negatives; if drawings, send good Xerox copies. Please include a self-addressed stamped envelope if you'd like your material returned. If we use it, we'll fully cite your contribution and give you a free new edition. Please address your responses to:

Pacific Mexico Handbook
c/o Moon Publications, Inc.
P.O. Box 3040
Chico, CA 95927-3040, USA

BOB RACE

INTRODUCTION
THE LAND AND SEA

On the map of North America, Mexico appears as a grand horn of plenty, spreading and spilling to its northern border with the United States. Mexico encompasses a vast landscape, sprawling over an area as large as France, Germany, England, and Italy combined. Besides its size, Mexico is high country, where most people live in mountain valleys within sight of towering, snowcapped peaks.

Travelers heading south of the Rio Grande do not realize the rise in elevation, however. Instead, brushy, cactus-pocked plains spread to mountain ranges on the far blue horizon. Northern Mexico is nevertheless a tableland—the *altiplano*—that rises gradually from the Rio Grande to its climax at the very heart of the country: the mile-high Bajio (BAH-heeoh) Valley around Guadalajara and the even loftier Valley of Mexico.

Here, in these fertile vales, untold generations of Mexicans have gazed southward at an awesome rampart of smoking mountains, the grand volcanic seam that stretches westward from the Gulf of Mexico to the Pacific. In a con-

tinuous line along the 19th parallel, more than a dozen volcanoes have puffed sulfurous gas and spewed red-hot rock for an eon, building themselves into some of the mightiest peaks in the Americas. Most easterly and grandest of them all is Orizaba (Citlaltépetl, the "Mountain of the Star"), rising 18,860 feet (5,747 meters) directly above the Gulf. Then, in proud succession, the giants march westward: Malinche, 14,640 feet (4,461 meters); Popocatépetl, 17,930 feet (5,465 meters); Nevado de Toluca, 15,390 feet (4,690 meters); until finally the most active of all—snowcapped Nevado de Colima—smokes 14,220 feet (4,335 meters) over the long, plumy shoreline of Pacific Mexico.

GEOGRAPHY

This sun-drenched western coastland stretches along a thousand miles of sandy beaches, palmy headlands, and blue lagoons, from Mazatlán in the north and curving southeast past Acapulco

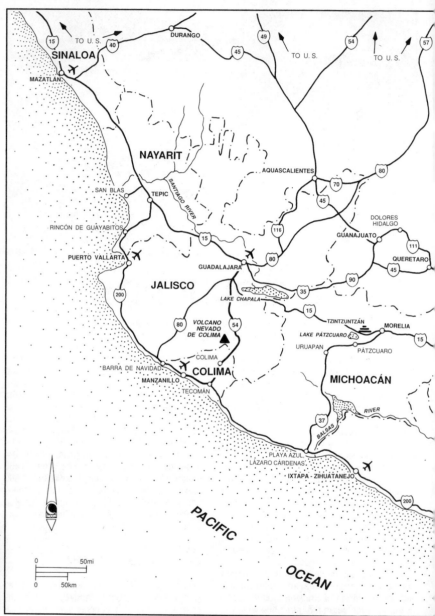

© MOON PUBLICATIONS, INC.

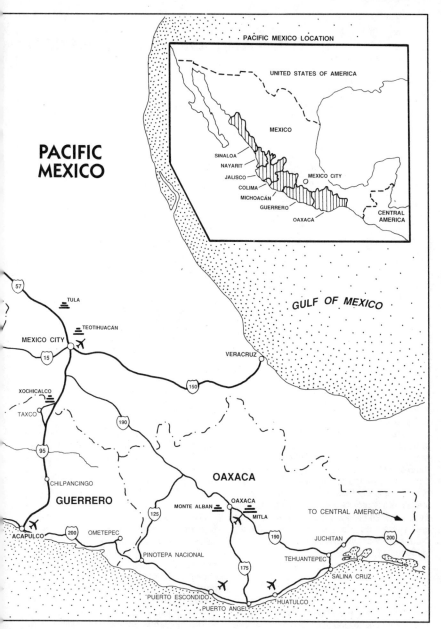

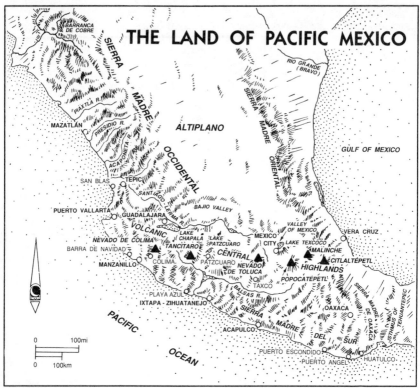

THE LAND OF PACIFIC MEXICO

to the new vacationland of Bahías de Huatulco in Oaxaca.

Pacific Mexico is a land washed by the ocean and sheltered by the western mountains: Sierra Madre Occidental and its southern extension, the Sierra Madre del Sur. Everywhere, except in the north where the coastal plain is broad, these green jungle-clad sierras rise quickly, sometimes precipitously, above a narrow coastal strip. Few rivers and roads breach these ramparts, and where roads do, they wind through deep *barrancas,* over lofty passes to temperate, oak-studded highland valleys.

CLIMATE

Elevation rules the climate of Pacific Mexico. The entire coastal strip (including the mountain slopes and plateaus up to four or five thousand feet) basks in the tropics, never feeling the bite of frost. The seashore is truly a land of perpetual summer. Winter days are typically warm and rainless, peaking at around 80-85° F (26-28° C) and dropping to 60-70° F (16-21° C) by midnight. The north-to-south variation on this theme is typically small: Mazatlán will be a few degrees cooler, Acapulco, a few degrees warmer.

Summers on the Pacific Mexico beaches are warmer and wetter. July, August, and September forenoons are typically bright and warm, heating to the high 80s (around 30° C) with afternoon clouding and short, sometimes heavy, showers. By late afternoon, however, clouds part, the sun dries the pavements, and the breeze is often balmy and just right for you to enjoy a sparkling Pacific Mexico sunset.

The highlands around Guadalajara, Pátzcuaro, Taxco, and Oaxaca experience similar, but more temperate seasons. Midwinter days are mild to balmy, typically peaking around 70° F (21° C). Expect cool, but frost-free, winter nights between 40 and 50° F (9-14° C). Highland summers are delightful, with afternoons in the 80s (27-32° C) and balmy evenings in the mid-70s to 80s (21-26° C), perfect for strolling.

May, before the rains, is often the warmest, with June, July, and August highs being moderated by afternoon showers. Many Guadalajara, Pátzcuaro, Taxco, and Oaxaca residents enjoy the best of all possible worlds: balmy summers at home and similarly balmy winters in vacation homes along the Pacific Mexico Coast.

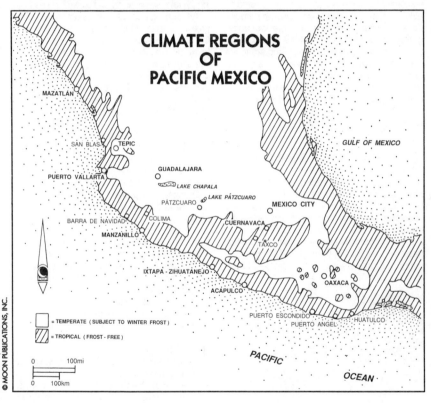

CLIMATE REGIONS OF PACIFIC MEXICO

MAZATLÁN

SAN BLAS TEPIC

GULF OF MEXICO

GUADALAJARA

PUERTO VALLARTA

LAKE CHAPALA

PÁTZCUARO LAKE PÁTZCUARO

MEXICO CITY

BARRA DE NAVIDAD COLIMA

CUERNAVACA

MANZANILLO

TAXCO

IXTAPA - ZIHUATANEJO

OAXACA

ACAPULCO

= TEMPERATE (SUBJECT TO WINTER FROST)

PUERTO ESCONDIDO

HUATULCO

PUERTO ANGEL

= TROPICAL (FROST - FREE)

PACIFIC

OCEAN

0   100mi

0   100km

© MOON PUBLICATIONS, INC.

FLORA AND FAUNA

Fascinating hothouse verdure—from delicate orchids and bulbous, fuzzy succulents to giant hanging philodendrons—luxuriates at some roadside spots of Pacific Mexico, as if beckoning admirers to notice them. Now and then visitors stop, attracted by something remarkable, such as a riot of flowers blooming from apparently dead branches, or what looks like grapefruit sprouting from the trunk of a roadside tree. More often, travelers pass long stretches of thorny thickets, viny jungles and broad, mangrove-edged marshes. A little advance knowledge of what to expect can blossom into recognition and discovery, transforming the humdrum into something quite extraordinary, even exotic.

VEGETATION ZONES

Mexico's diverse landscape and fickle rainfall have sculpted its wide range of plant forms. Botanists recognize at least 14 major Mexican vegetation zones, seven of which occur in Pacific Mexico.

Directly along the coastal highway, you often pass long sections of three of these zones: savannah, thorn forest, and tropical deciduous forest.

Lotus blossoms frequently decorate pond and lagoon edges of Pacific Mexico savannahs.

CATHY CARLSON

Savannah
Great swaths of pasturelike savannah stretch along the roadside south of Mazatlán to Tepic. In its natural state, savannah often appears as a palm-dotted sea of grass—green and marshy during the rainy summer, dry and brown by late winter.

Although grass rules the savannah, palms give it character. Most familiar is the **coconut**—the *cocotero*—used for everything from lumber to candy. Coconut palms line the beaches and climb the hillsides—drooping, slanting, rustling, and swaying in the breeze like troupes of hula dancers. Less familiar, but with as much personality, is the Mexican **fan palm,** the *palma real,* festooned with black fruit and spread flat like a señorita's fan.

The savannah's list goes on: the grapefruitlike fruit on the trunk and branches identify the **gourd tree,** or *calabaza.* The mature gourds, brown and hard, have been carved into *jicaros,* (cups for drinking chocolate) for millennia.

Orange-sized, pumpkinlike gourds both mark and name the **sandbox tree,** because they once served as desktop boxes full of sand for drying ink. The Aztecs, however, called it the exploding tree, because its ripe fruits burst their seeds forth with a bang like a firecracker.

The waterlogged seaward edge of the savannah nurtures forests of **red mangroves,** short trees that seem to stand in the water on stilts. Their new roots grow downward from above; a time-lapse photo would show them marching, as if on stilts, into the lagoon.

Thorn Forest
Lower rainfall leads to the hardier growth of the thorn forest, the domain of the pea family—the **acacias** and their cousins, the **mimosas.** Among the most common is the **long spine acacia,** with fluffy, yellow flower balls, ferny leaves, and long, narrow pods; less common, but more useful is the **fishfuddle,** with pink peaflowers and long pods, a source of fish-stunning poison. (Take care, however, around the acacias; some of the long-thorned varieties harbor nectar-feeding, biting ants.)

Perhaps the most spectacular and famous member of the thorn forest community is the

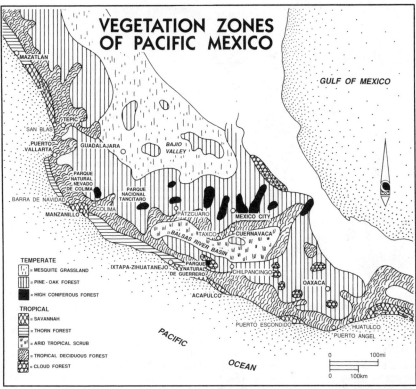

VEGETATION ZONES OF PACIFIC MEXICO

GULF OF MEXICO

MAZATLAN

SAN BLAS
TEPIC
PUERTO VALLARTA
GUADALAJARA
BAJIO VALLEY
PARQUE NATURAL NEVADO DE COLIMA
PARQUE NACIONAL TANCITARO
BARRA DE NAVIDAD
COLIMA
PÁTZCUARO
MEXICO CITY
MANZANILLO
TAXCO
CUERNAVACA
BALSAS RIVER BASIN
IXTAPA-ZIHUATANEJO
PARQUE NATURAL DE GUERRERO
CHILPANCINGO
OAXACA
ACAPULCO
PACIFIC
PUERTO ESCONDIDO
HUATULCO
PUERTO ANGEL
OCEAN

TEMPERATE
= MESQUITE GRASSLAND
= PINE - OAK FOREST
= HIGH CONIFEROUS FOREST

TROPICAL
= SAVANNAH
= THORN FOREST
= ARID TROPICAL SCRUB
= TROPICAL DECIDUOUS FOREST
= CLOUD FOREST

0   100mi
0   100km

© MOON PUBLICATIONS, INC.

morning glory tree, which announces the winter dry season's end by blooming a festoon of white trumpets atop its crown of seemingly dead branches. Its gruesome Mexican name, *palo del muerto* (tree of the dead), is exceeded only around Taxco, where folks call it *palo bobo* (fool tree) because they believe that if you take a drink from a stream near its foot, you will go crazy.

The cactuses are among the thorn forest's sturdiest and most spectacular inhabitants. In the dry Rio Balsas basin (along Hwy. 95 inland from Acapulco) the spectacular candelabra cactus *(cordón espinosa)* spreads as much as 60 feet tall and wide.

Tropical Deciduous Forest
In rainier areas, the thorn forest grades into the tropical deciduous forest. This is the "friendly" or "short-tree" forest, blanketed by a tangle of sum-

mer-green verdure whose leaves fall in the dry winter, revealing thickets of dry branches. Some trees show bright fall reds and yellows, later blossoming with brilliant flowers—spider lily, cardinal sage, pink trumpet, poppylike yellowsilk *(pomposhuti),* and mouse-killer *(mala ratón),* which swirl in the spring wind like cherry-blossom blizzards.

The tropical deciduous forest is the lush jungle coat that swathes much of coastal Pacific Mexico. And often, where the mountains rush directly down to the sea, the forest likewise spills right over the headland into the ocean. Vine-strewn thickets often overhang the highway, like the edge of some lost prehistoric world, where you might expect a last remnant allosaur to rear up at any moment.

Biological realities here, however, are nearly as exotic: a four-foot-long green iguana, looking

CATHY CARLSON

Yellow blooms of the rosa amarillo *(yellow rose) sometimes adorn forest roadsides during the winter dry season. Despite its name, its brown pods mark it as a member of the* cochlospermum *(shell seed) family.*

every bit as primitive as a dinosaur, slithers across the pavement; or at roadside, a spreading, solitary **strangler fig** stands, draped with hairy, hanging air roots (which, in time, plant themselves into the ground and support the branches). The Mexican name, *matapalo* (killer tree), is gruesomely accurate, for strangler figs often entwine themselves in a death embrace with some other, less aggressive, victim tree.

Much more benign, however, is my favorite of the tropical deciduous forest: the *guaycoyul*, or *cohune* (or Colima) palm. (*Cohune* in Pacific Mexico means "magnificent.") Capped by a proud cock-plume, it presides over the forest singly or in great, graceful swaying groves atop the headlands. Its nuts, harvested like small coconuts, yield oil and animal fodder.

Excursions by jeep or on foot along shaded, off-highway tracks through the tropical deciduous forest can yield delightful jungle scenes; unwary travelers must watch out, however, for the poison-oak-like *mala mujer*, the "bad woman" tree. The oil on its large five-fingered leaves can cause an itchy rash.

Pine-oak Forest
A couple of hours drive inland (especially on the mountain roads from the coast to Pátzcuaro, Taxco, and Oaxaca), the tropics give way to the temperate pine-oak forest, Pacific Mexico's most extensive vegetation zone. Here, most of Mexico's 112 oak and 39 pine species thrive. At the lower elevations, bushy, nut-yielding piñon pines sometimes cover the slope; then come the tall pines, often Chihuahua pine and Montezuma pine, both yellow varieties, similar to the ponderosa pine of the western United States.

Interspersed with them are oaks, in two broad classifications—*encino* (evergreen, small-leafed) and *roble* (deciduous, large-leafed)—both much like the oaks that dot California hills and valleys. Clustered in their branches and scattered in the shade are the *bellota* (acorns), which irrevocably mark them as oaks.

Arid Tropical Scrub And Cloud Forest
Pacific Mexico's two rarest and exotic vegetation zones are far from the coastal tourist centers. You can see the great cactus forests of the arid tropical scrub habitat (which occupies the wild, dry canyonland of the Rio Balsas intermountain basin) conveniently either along Hwy. 95 inland from Acapulco, or Hwy. 37 between Playa Azul and Pátzcuaro. Finally, travelers who drive to high, dewy mountainsides, beginning around 7,000 feet, can explore the plant and wildlife community of the cloud forest. The Parque Natural de Guerrero (around Corral Bravo, 50 miles west of Chilpancingo, Guerrero) preserves such a habitat, where abundant cool fog nourishes forests of tree ferns, lichen-draped pines, and oaks above a mossy carpet of orchids, bromeliads, and begonias. M. Walter Pesman's delightful *Meet Flora Mexicana* is unfortunately out of print, but libraries have copies. Also informative is the popular paperback *Handbook of Mexican Roadside Flora,* by Charles T. Mason, Jr. and Patricia B. Mason. (See the "Booklist.")

WILDLIFE

Despite continued habitat destruction—logging of forests, filling wetlands, and plowing savannahs—

CATHY CARLSON

Jaguars still hunt in remote mangrove wetlands and mountain jungles of Pacific Mexico.

Pacific Mexico still abounds with wildlife. In the temperate pine-oak forest zone of Pacific Mexico live most of the familiar birds and mammals—mountain lion, coyote, jackrabbit, dove, quail—of the American Southwest.

The tropical coastal forests and savannahs, however, are home to exotic species seen north of the border only in zoos. The reality of this often first dawns on travelers when they glimpse something exotic, such as raucous, screeching swarms of small green parrots rising from the roadside, or an armadillo or coati nosing in the sand just a few feet away at the forested edge of some isolated Pacific Mexico beach.

Armadillos, Coatis, And Spider Monkeys
Armadillos are cat-sized mammals that act and look like opossums, but carry reptilianlike shells. If you see one, remain still, and it may walk right up and sniff your foot before it recognizes you

CATHY CARLSON

Spider monkeys, once common, are now rarely seen in the wild in Pacific Mexico.

and scuttles back into the woods.

A common inhabitant of the tropics is the raccoonlike **coati** *(tejon, pisote)*. In the wild, coatis like shady stream banks, often congregating in large troupes. They are identified by their short brown or tan fur, small round ears, long nose, and straight, vertically held tail. They make endearing pets; the first coati you see may be one on a string offered for sale at a local market.

If you are lucky, you may glimpse a band of now-rare reddish brown **spider monkeys** *(monos)* raiding a forest-edge orchard. And deep in the mountain fastness of Guerrero or Oaxaca, you may find a tracker who can lead you to a view of the endangered **tapir.** On such an excursion, if you are really fortunate, you may even hear the chesty roar of or even see a **jaguar,** the fabled *tigre.*

El Tigre
"Each hill has its own *tigre,*" a Mexican proverb says. With black spots spread over a tan coat, stretching five feet (1.5 meters) and weighing about 200 pounds (90 kilograms), the typical jaguar resembles a muscular spotted leopard. Although hunted since prehistory, and now endangered, the jaguar still lives throughout Pacific Mexico, where it hunts along thickly forested stream bottoms and foothills. Unlike the mountain lion *(puma)*, the jaguar will eat any game. They have even been known to wait patiently for fish in rivers and stalk beaches for turtle and egg dinners. If they have a favorite food, it is probably the piglike wild peccary. Experienced hunters agree that no two jaguars will, when examined, have the same prey in their stomachs.

Although humans have died of wounds inflicted by cornered jaguars, there is little or no hard evidence that they are man-eaters, despite legends to the contrary.

BIRDS

The coastal lagoons of Pacific Mexico lie astride the Pacific Flyway, one of the Americas' major north-south paths for migrating waterfowl. Many of the familiar American and Canadian species, including pintail, gadwall, baldpate, shoveler, redhead, and scaup, arrive from October until January, when their numbers will have swollen into the millions. They settle near food and cover—sometimes, to the frustration of farmers—even at the borders of cornfields. Among the best places to see their spectacle is the **Marismas Nacionales** marsh complex around the Sinaloa-Nayarit border (west of coast Hwy. 15 between Mazatlán and Tuxpan).

Besides the migrants, swarms of resident species—herons, egrets, cormorants, *anhingas*, lily-walkers, and hundreds more—stalk, nest, and preen in the same lagoons.

Few spots are better for observing **seabirds** than the beaches of Pacific Mexico. Brown pelicans and huge black-and-white frigate birds are among the prime actors. When a flock of pelicans spot a school of their favorite fish, they go about their routine deliberately: singly or in pairs they circle and plummet into the waves and come up, more often than not, with a fish in their gullet. They bob and float over the swells for a minute or two, seemingly waiting for their dozen or so fellow pelicans to take their turns. This goes on until they've bagged a big dinner of 10 or 15 fish apiece.

Frigate birds, the scavengers par excellence of Pacific Mexico, often profit by the labor of the teams of fisherfolk who haul in fish right on village beaches by the netful. After the fishermen auction off the choice morsels—perch, tuna, red snapper, octopus, shrimp—to merchants and the villagers have scavenged everything else edible, the motley residue of small fish, sea snakes, skates, squids, slugs, and sharks is often thrown to a screeching flock of frigate birds. (For a discussion of fish and other shore wildlife, see ahead to "Fishing" and "Hunting" under "Sports and Recreation.") For more details of Pacific Mexico mammals and birds in general, check out A. Starker Leopold's very readable classic, *Wildlife of Mexico*, or see the "Booklist."

FISH AND MARINELIFE

Whales

At one time the gray whale *(Eschrichtius robustus)* swam the Atlantic Ocean, Baltic Sea, and North Sea as well as the Pacific, but it was decimated by Dutch, British, and American whalers in the North Atlantic by the beginning of the 19th century and now survives only in the Arctic-Pacific corridor. Currently numbering around 21,000, the grays spend their summers feeding in the Bering, Chukchi, and Beaufort seas in the vicinity of Alaska and Siberia, where the long Arctic days result in highly productive marine growth.

The gray's primary feeding grounds are in the Chirikof Basin, where they begin their annual migration south in mid-to-late fall. Swimming at an average four knots, the whales travel in pods of three to four whales and typically rest for a few hours each night. The gray's winter migration extends to the southern tip of Baja, but because their numbers are on the rise, the occasional pod strays farther south.

Female **humpback whales** get as large as 49 feet and weigh as much as 35 tons. The males average 46 feet and weigh 25 tons. These large mammals migrate from winter breeding grounds in Hawaiian and Mexican waters to summer feeding grounds in Washington and the Chukchi Sea. The Revillagigedo Islands, located 220 miles south of Baja California, offer the best viewing of the endangered humpback as well as breeding seabirds and dolphins. The volcanic Revillagigedos (pronounced ray-VEE-ya-hee-HAY-doughs), discovered in 1533, remain virtually unimpacted by tourism.

Several well-established organizations in the U.S. that operate whalewatching expeditions in Mexico are: Biological Journeys, 1696 Ocean Dr., McKinleyville, CA 95521, tel. (800) 548-7555, (707) 839-0178 (in CA); Oceanic Society Expeditions, Fort Mason Center, Bldg. E, San Francisco, CA 94123, tel. (415) 441-1106; Sven-Olof Lindblad's Special Expeditions, 720 Fifth Ave., New York, NY 10019, tel. (800) 762-0003 (outside NY), (212) 765-7740 (in NY).

Fishes

The seas along the Pacific Coast contain a truly amazing variety of marinelife. Six **billfish** species exist here in some numbers: **swordfish, sail-**

fish, and **striped blue** and **black marlin.** All are strong fighters, though the sailfish and striped marlin are generally the feistiest.

Popular varieties of **jack** include **yellowtail** (one of the most popular fishes for use in *tacos de pescado,* **Pacific amberjack,** various **pompanos, jack crevalle,** and the strong-fighting **roosterfish,** named for its tall dorsal "comb." Among the most sought-after food fish are the **dorado, mackerel,** and **tuna.**

A few types of **sea bass** can be found in the water south of the Sea of Cortez: **flag cabrilla, kelp bass,** and the **spotted sand bass.** Bottomfish, **snapper, surf fish (barred, surf perch, rubberlip surfperch,** and **sargo),** and **flatfish,** like the **California halibut** also frequent these waters.

Sharks and **rays** are quite common in the warmer offshore to inshore waters. Shark-fishing is an important activity, and **hammerhead, thresher, bonito (mako),** and **leopard shark** fillets are all very tasty. Most sharks are under two meters and are much more likely to flee from a swimmer or diver than to attack. The most dangerous is the **great white shark**—although not common, they occasionally cruise the deeper waters of the Pacific and account for most attacks. Rays can inflict a painful sting when threatened. To avoid this, swimmers do the "stingray shuffle" while walking in shallow waters. Common rays include the **butterfly ray** and **shovelnose ray.** The **mobula** and huge **Pacific manta ray** are often referred to as a "devilfish" because of their horn-like fins. The **bat ray** is often confused with the manta, but doesn't possess the horny fins.

Several varieties of **shellfish** can still be found: **oysters, mussels, scallops, clams** and **shrimp.** See pp. 30-31 for more on fish.

HISTORY

Once upon a time, maybe 50,000 years ago, the first bands of hunters, perhaps following great game herds, crossed from Siberia to the American continent. For thousands of years they drifted southward, eventually settling in the rich valleys and plains of North and South America.

Several thousand years ago, probably in Mexico, people began gathering and grinding the seeds of a hardy grass that required only the summer rains to thrive. By selecting and planting the larger seeds, their grain eventually yielded tall plants with long ears and many large kernels. This grain, which they eventually called *teocentli,* the "sacred seed," (which we call maize or corn) led to prosperity.

EARLY MEXICAN CIVILIZATIONS

Plentiful food gave rise to leisure classes—artists, architects, warriors, and ruler-priests—who had time to think and create. With a calendar, they harnessed the constant wheel of the firmament to life on earth, defining the days to plant, to harvest, to feast, to travel, and to trade. Eventually, grand cities arose.

Teotihuacán
Teotihuacán, with a population of perhaps 250,000 around the time of Christ, was one of the world's great metropolises, on a par with Rome, Babylon, and Chang'an. Its epic monu-

ments still stand not far north of Mexico City: the towering Pyramid of the Sun at the terminal of a grand 150-foot-wide ceremonial avenue faces a great Pyramid of the Moon. Along the avenue sprawls a monumental temple-court surrounded by scowling, ruby-eyed effigies of Quetzalcoatl, the feathered serpent god of gods.

Teotihuacán crumbled mysteriously around A.D. 650, leaving a host of former vassal states from the Yucatán to Pacific Mexico free to tussle among themselves. These included **Xochicalco,** not far from present-day Taxco, and the great Zapotec center of Monte Albán farther southwest in Oaxaca. From its regal hilltop complex of stone pyramids, palaces, and ceremonial ball courts, Monte Albán reigned all-powerful until it, too, was abandoned around A.D. 1000.

Quetzalcoatl
Xochicalco, however, was flourishing; its wise men tutored a young noble who was to become a living legend: in A.D. 947, Topiltzín, (literally, "Our Prince"), was born. Records recite Topiltzín's achievements. He advanced astronomy, agriculture, and architecture and founded the city-state of Tula in A.D. 968, north of old Teotihuacán.

Contrary to the times, Topiltzín opposed human sacrifice; he taught that tortillas and butterflies, not human hearts, were the food of

Mexican mothers still teach their daughters to weave with the backstrap loom exactly as did countless generations of their pre-Columbian forebears.

CODEX MENDOZA, M.N.A.H. LIBRARY

Quetzalcoatl. After ruling benignly for a generation, Topiltzín's name became so revered that the people began to know him as the living Quetzalcoatl, the plumed serpent-god incarnate.

Quetzalcoatl was not universally loved, however. Bloodthirsty local priests, desperate for human victims, tricked him with alcohol; he awoke, groggily, one morning in bed with his sister. Devastated by shame, Quetzalcoatl banished himself from Tula with a band of retainers. In A.D. 987, they headed east, toward Yucatán, leaving arrows shot through saplings, appearing like crosses, along their trail.

Although Quetzalcoatl sent word that he would reclaim his kingdom (in the 52-year cyclical calendar year of his birth, Ce Acatl) he never returned. Legends say that he sailed east and rose to heaven as the morning star.

Legends also say that Quetzalcoatl was bearded and fair-skinned. It was a remarkable coincidence, therefore, that on April 22, 1519, during the eleventh 52-year anniversary of Ce Acatl, Quetzalcoatl's birth year, that bearded, fair-skinned Castilian Hernán Cortés landed on Mexico's eastern coast.

THE CONQUEST

Cortés, then only 34, had left Cuba in February with an expedition of 11 small ships, 550 men, 16 horses, and a few small cannon. By the time he landed in Mexico, however, he was in big trouble. His men, hearing stories of the great Aztec empire west beyond the mountains, realized the impossible odds they faced and became restive.

Cortés, however, cut short any thoughts of mutiny by burning his ships. As he led his grumbling but resigned band of adventurers toward the Aztec capital of Tenochtitlán, Cortés played Quetzalcoatl to the hilt, awing local chiefs. Coaxed by Doña Marina, Cortés's wily native translator-mistress-confidante, local chiefs began to add their armies to Cortés's march against their Aztec overlords.

Moctezuma

While Cortés looked down upon the shimmering Valley of Mexico from the great divide between the volcanoes, Moctezuma, the emperor of the Aztecs, fretted about the returned Quetzalcoatl.

It is no wonder that the Spanish, approaching on horseback in their glittering, clanking armor, seemed divine to people who had never known steel, draft animals, or the wheel.

Inside the gates of the Venicelike island-city, however, it was the Spaniards' turn to be dazzled: by gardens full of animals, gold and palaces, and a great pyramid-enclosed square where tens of thousands of people bartered goods gathered from all over the empire. Tenochtitlán, with perhaps a quarter of a million people, was the great capital of an empire larger and richer than any in Europe.

Moctezuma, the lord of that empire, was frozen by fear and foreboding, however. He quickly surrendered himself to Cortés's custody. After a few months his subjects, enraged by Spanish brutality and Moctezuma's timidity, rioted and mortally wounded the emperor with a stone. With Moctezuma dead, the riot turned into a counterattack against the Spanish. On July 1, 1520, Cortés and his men, forced by sheer numbers of rebellious Mexicans, retreated along a lake causeway from Tenochtitlán carrying Moctezuma's treasure. Many of them drowned beneath their burdens of stolen Aztec gold, while others hacked a bloody path through thousands of screaming Aztec warriors to safety on the lakeshore.

MALINCHE

If it hadn't been for Doña Marina (whom he received as a gift from a local chief), Cortés may have become a mere historical footnote. Clever and opportunistic, Doña Marina was a crucial strategist in Cortés's deadly game of divide and conquer. She eventually bore Cortés a son and lived in honor and riches for many years, profiting greatly from the Spaniards' exploitation of the Mexicans.

Latter-day Mexicans do not generally honor her by the genteel title of Doña Marina, however. They call her Malinche, after the volcano—the ugly, treacherous scar on the Mexican landscape—and curse her as the female Judas who betrayed her country to the Spanish. (*Malinchismo* has become known as the tendency, which some Mexicans display, of loving things foreign and hating things Mexican.)

That infamous night, now known as Noche Triste ("Sad Night"), Cortés, with half of his men dead, collapsed and wept beneath a great *ahuehuete* cypress tree (which still stands) in Mexico City.

Cortés rallied, however. A year later, reinforced by fresh soldiers, horses, a small fleet of armed sailboats, and 100,000 *indígena* allies, Cortés retook Tenochtitlán. The stubborn defenders, led by Cuauhtémoc, Moctezuma's nephew, fell by the tens of thousands beneath a smoking hail of Spanish grapeshot. The Mexicans, although weakened by smallpox, refused to surrender. Cortés found, to his dismay, that he had to destroy the city to take it.

The triumphant conquistador soon rebuilt it in the Spanish image: Cortés's cathedral and main public buildings—the present *zócalo,* central square of Mexico City—still rest upon the foundations of Moctezuma's pyramids.

NEW SPAIN

With the Valley of Mexico firmly in his grip, Cortés sent his lieutenants south, north, and west to extend the limits of the domain that eventually expanded to more than a dozenfold the size of old Spain. He wrote his king, Charles V, that ". . . the most suitable name for it would be New Spain of the Ocean Sea, and thus in the name of your Majesty I have christened it."

The Missionaries

While the conquistadores subjugated the Mexicans, missionaries began arriving to teach, heal, and baptize them. A dozen Franciscan brothers impressed *indígenas* and conquistadores alike by trekking the entire 300-mile stony path from Vera Cruz to Mexico City in 1523. Cortés knelt and kissed their robes as they arrived.

The missionaries, interested in the welfare of the *indígena,* were a humane counterbalance to the brutal conquistadores. Missionary authorities generally enjoyed a sympathetic ear from Charles V and his successsors, who earnestly pursued Spain's Christian mission, especially when it dovetailed with their political and economic goals.

The King Takes Control

After 1525, the crown, through the Council of the Indies, began to wrest power away from Cortés and his conquistador lieutenants. Many of them had been granted rights of *encomienda:* taxes and labor of an *indígena* district. In exchange, the *encomendero,* who often enjoyed the status of feudal lord, pledged to look after the welfare and souls of his *indígena* charges.

From the king's point of view, however, tribute pesos collected by *encomenderos* translated into losses to the crown. Moreover, many *encomenderos* callously exploited their indígena wards for quick profit, sometimes selling them as slave labor in mines and on plantations. Such abuses, coupled with European-introduced diseases, began to reduce the *indígena* population at an alarming rate.

After 1530, the king and his councillors began to realize that the *indígenas* were in peril, and without their labor, New Spain would vanish. They acted decisively: new laws would be instituted by a powerful new viceroy.

Don Antonio de Mendoza, the Count of Tendilla, arrived in 1535. He set the precedent for an unbroken line of more than 60 viceroys who, with few exceptions, served with distinction until independence in 1821. Village after village along Mendoza's winding route to Mexico City tried to outdo each other with flowers, music, bullfights, and feasts in his honor.

Mendoza wasted no time. He first got rid of the renegade opportunist (and Cortés's enemy) Nuño de Guzmán, whose private army, under the banner of conquest, had been laying waste to a broad western belt of Pacific Mexico, now Jalisco, Michoacán, Nayarit, and Sinaloa. (Guzmán, during his rapacious five years in Pacific Mexico, did, however, manage to found several towns: Guadalajara, Tepic, and Culiacan being among them.)

Cortés, The Marqués Del Valle Oaxaca

Cortés, meanwhile, had done very well for himself. He was one of Spain's richest men, with the title of Marqués del Valle Oaxaca. He received 80,000 gold pesos a year from hundreds of thousands of Indian subjects on 25,000 square miles from the Valley of Mexico through Morelos, Guerrero and Oaxaca.

Cortés continued tirelessly on a dozen endeavors: an expedition to Honduras, a young wife whom he brought back from Spain, a palace (which still stands) in Cuernavaca, sugar mills, and dozens of churches, city halls, and presidios.

He supervised the exploits of his lieutenants in Pacific Mexico: Francisco Orozco subdued the Zapotecs in Oaxaca, while Pedro de Alvarado accomplished the same with the Mixtecs, then continued south to conquer Guatemala. Meanwhile, Cristóbal de Olid subjugated the Tarascans in Michoacán, then moved down the Pacific coast to Zacatula on the mouth of the Rio Balsas. There (and at Acapulco and Tehuantepec), Cortés built ships to explore the Pacific. In 1535, he led an expedition to the Gulf of California (hence the Sea of Cortés) in a dreary six-month search for treasure around La Paz.

Cortés's Monument

Disgusted with Mendoza's meddling and discouraged with his failures, Cortés returned to Spain, where he got mired in lawsuits, a minor war, and his daughter's marital troubles, all of which led to his illness and death in 1547. Cortés's remains, according to his will, were eventually laid to rest in a vault at Hospital de Jesús, which he founded in Mexico City. But in all Mexico, no monument nor statue marks his remarkable achievements. Cortés's monument, historians note, is Mexico itself.

COLONIAL MEXICO

In 1542, the Council of the Indies, through Viceroy Mendoza, promulgated its liberal New Laws of the Indies. The New Laws rested on high moral ground: the only Christian justification for New Spain was the souls and welfare of the *indígenas.* Colonists had no right to exploit the *indígenas.* Slavery, therefore, was outlawed and *encomienda* rights were to revert to the crown at the death of the original grantees.

Despite uproar and near-rebellion by the colonists, Mendoza (and his successor in 1550, Don Luis Velasco), kept the lid on New Spain. Although some *encomenderos* held on to their rights into the 18th century, chattel slavery was abolished in Mexico—300 years before Lincoln's Emancipation Proclamation.

Peace reigned in Mexico for ten generations. Viceroys came and conscientiously served, new settlers arrived and put down roots, friars preached and built country churches, and the conquistadores' rich sons and daughters played while the *indígenas* worked.

The Role Of The Church

The church, however, moderated the *indígenas'* toil. On feast days they would dress up and parade their patron saint through the streets and later eat their fill, get tipsy on *pulque,* and ooh and aah at the fireworks.

The church profited from the status quo, however. The biblical tithe—one-tenth of everything, from crops and livestock to rents and mining profits—filled church coffers. By 1800, the church owned half of Mexico. Moreover, the clergy (including lay church officers) and the military were doubly privileged. They enjoyed right of *fuero* (exemption from civil law) and could be prosecuted by ecclesiastical or military courts only.

Trade And Commerce

In trade and commerce, New Spain existed for the benefit of the mother country. Spaniards enjoyed absolute monopolies by virtue of the complete prohibition of foreign traders and goods. Colonists, as a result, paid dearly for oft-shoddy Spanish manufactures. The Casa de Contratación (the royal trade regulators) always ensured the colony's yearly balance of payments would result in deficit, which would be made up by bullion shipments from Mexican mines (from which the crown raked 10% off the top).

Despite its faults, New Spain lasted three times longer than the Aztec empire. By most contemporary measures, Mexico was prospering in 1800. The *indígena* labor force was completely subjugated and increasing, and the galleon fleets were carrying home increasing tonnages of silver and gold worth millions. Mexico, however, had changed in 300 years.

POPULATION CHANGES IN NEW SPAIN

	EARLY COLONIAL (1570)	LATE COLONIAL (1810)
peninsulares	6,600	15,000
criollos	11,000	1,100,000
mestizos	2,400	704,000
indígenas	3,340,000	3,700,000
Negroes	22,000	630,000

Criollos, The New Mexicans

Nearly three centuries of colonial rule had given rise to a burgeoning population of more than a million criollos—Mexican-born white descendants of Spanish colonists, many of them rich and educated—to whom power was denied.

High government, church, and military office had always been the preserve of a tiny but powerful minority of *peninsulares*—whites born in Spain. All but three of the 61 viceroys and all of the bishops and archbishops were *peninsulares*, although their class comprised a tiny one-half percent of Mexico's population. Criollos could only watch in disgust as unlettered, unskilled *peninsulares* (derisively called *gachupines*—"wearers of spurs") were boosted to authority over them.

Second-class citizens in their own country, criollos had to be content with minor offices or modest careers in law, teaching, parish priesthood, or business. Although the criollos stood high above the mestizo, *indígena,* and Negro underclasses, that seemed little compensation for the false smiles, the deep bows, and the costly bribes which *gachupines* demanded.

Mestizo, *Indígena,* And Negro Classes

Upper-class luxury existed by virtue of the sweat of Mexico's mestizo, *indígena,* and Negro laborers and servants. African slaves were imported in large numbers during the 17th century after typhus, smallpox, and measle epidemics had wiped out most of the *indígena* population. Although the Afro-Mexicans contributed significantly (crafts, healing arts, dance, music, drums and marimba), they arrived last and experienced discrimination from everyone.

The criollos, the class most able to ask for redress, grumbled, but mostly consoled themselves with luxury. Many sank into idleness and cynicism masked by the artificial gaiety of a busy social carousel of operas, balls, and fancy picnics in the country.

INDEPENDENCE

The chance for change came during the aftermath of the French invasion of Spain in 1808. As Napoleon Bonaparte displaced King Ferdinand VII with his brother Joseph on the Spanish throne, Mexico buzzed with excitement.

People took sides. Most Mexican *peninsulares* backed the king, while most criollos, inspired by the example of the recent American and French revolutions, talked and dreamed of independence. One such group, urged on by a firebrand parish priest, acted.

El Grito De Dolores
Viva México! Death To The *Gachupines!*

Father Miguel Hidalgo's impassioned *Grito de Dolores* (cry from the Dolores, Guanajuato church balcony) on September 16, 1810 ignited action. A mostly *indígena,* machete-wielding army of 20,000 coalesced around Hidalgo and his compatriots, Ignacio Allende and Juan Aldama. They had difficulty, however, controlling their mob, which raged through the Bajío, massacring hated *gachupines* and pillaging their homes.

Hidalgo advanced on Mexico City but, unnerved by stiff royalist resistance, retreated and regrouped around Guadalajara. His rebels, whose numbers had swollen to 80,000 criollo-officered *indígenas* and mestizos, were no match for professionals, however. On January 17, 1811, Hidalgo (now "Generalissimo") was defeated and fled before a disciplined, 6,000-strong royalist force.

Hidalgo headed north for the U.S. but was soon apprehended, defrocked, and executed. His head and those of his comrades—Aldama, Allende, and Mariano Jiménez—were hung from the walls of the Guanajuato granary (site of the slaughter of 138 *gachupines* by Hidalgo's army) for 10 years as grim reminders of the consequences of rebellion.

The 10-year Struggle

Others carried on, however. A former mestizo student of Hidalgo, José María Morelos, trained and led guerilla bands, declared independence, and wrote a model constitution. Morelos led a revolutionary shadow government in the present states of Guerrero and Oaxaca for four years until apprehended and executed in December 1815.

Morelos's heroism, however, had saved his movement. Compatriot Vicente Guerrero carried the struggle to a climax, joining forces with criollo royalist Brigadier Augustine de Iturbide. Their **Plan de Iguala** promised "Three Guarantees"—the renowned **Trigarantes**—Independence, Catholicism, and Equality, which the army (commanded by Iturbide, of course) would enforce. On September 21, 1821, Iturbide rode triumphantly into Mexico City at the head of his army of *Trigarantes.* Mexico was independent at last.

Independence, however, solved little except to expel the *peninsulares,* whom the criollo elite could no longer blame for Mexico's ills. With an illiterate populace and no experience in self-government, Mexicans began a tragic 40-year love affair with a fantasy: the general on the white horse, the gold-braided hero who could save them from themselves.

The Rise And Fall Of Augustín I

Iturbide became Augustín I, the first emperor of independent Mexico—crowned by the bishop of Guadalajara on June 21, 1822. But Augustín's charisma soon faded. In a pattern that became sadly predictable for generations of topsy-turvy Mexican politics, an ambitious garrison commander somewhere gave a *pronuncimiento,* a declaration against the government. Supporting *pronuncimientos* followed, and old revolutionary heroes Guerrero, Guadalupe Victoria, and Nicolás Bravo endorsed a "plan"—the Plan of Casa Mata (not unlike Iturbide's previous Plan de Iguala)—dethroning Iturbide in favor of a republic. Iturbide, his braid tattered and brass tarnished, abdicated in March 1822.

Antonio López de Santa Anna, the eager 28-year-old military commander of Vera Cruz, whose *pronuncimiento* had pushed Iturbide from his white horse, maneuvered to gradually replace him on Mexico's shaky political stage. After Guadalupe Victoria had miraculously managed to remain Mexico's first president for four years, the presidency bounced between liberal and conservative hands six times in three years. Meanwhile, Santa Anna had jumped to prominence by defeating a half-starved Spanish regiment that had landed abortively at Tampico in 1829. "The Victor of Tampico," people called Santa Anna.

The Disastrous Era Of Santa Anna

In 1833, the government was bankrupt; mobs demanded the ouster of conservative President Bustamante, who had executed the rebellious old revolutionary hero, Vicente Guerrero. Santa Anna gave *pronuncimiento* against Bustamante; Congress obliged, elevating Santa Anna to "Liberator of the Republic" and "Conqueror of the Spaniards," and named him president in March 1833.

Santa Anna would pop in and out the presidency like a jack-in-the-box 10 more times before 1855. Texas, Mexico's northeast frontier province, was the first of several Santa Anna disasters. Inflated by his initial success against rebellious Anglo settlers at the battle of the Alamo in February 1836, Santa Anna foolishly lost both his army and Texas two months later. He later lost his leg (which was buried with full military honors) fighting the emperor of France.

Santa Anna's greatest debacle, however, was to declare war on the United States with just 1,839 pesos in the treasury. With Mexican forces poised to defend Mexico City against a relatively small 10,000-man American invasion force, Santa Anna inexplicably withdrew his intact division. United States Marines surged into the "Halls of Montezuma" (Chapultepec Castle, where Mexico's six beloved Niños Héroes cadets fell in the losing cause) on September 13, 1847.

In the subsequent treaty of Guadalupe Hidalgo, Mexico lost two-fifths of her territory (the present states of New Mexico, Arizona, California, Nevada, Utah, and Colorado) to the United States. Mexicans have never forgotten; they have looked upon *gringos* with a combination of awe, envy, admiration, and disgust ever since.

For Santa Anna, however, enough was not enough. Called back as president for the last time in 1853, Santa Anna, now "His Most Serene Highness," financed his extravagances by selling off a part of southern Arizona (known as the Gasden Purchase) for $10 million.

The Reforms

Mexican leaders finally saw the light and exiled Santa Anna forever. While conservatives searched for a king to replace Santa Anna, liberals (whom Santa Anna had kept in jail) plunged ahead with three controversial reform laws: the Ley Juarez, Ley Lerdo, and Ley Iglesias. These Reformas, augmented by a new Constitution of 1857, directly attacked the privilege and power of Mexico's landlords, clergy, and generals: Ley Juarez abolished *fueros,* the separate military and church courts; Ley Lerdo forbade excess corporate (read: church) land holdings, and Ley Iglesias reduced or transferred most church power to the state.

Conservative generals, priests, and *hacendados* and their mestizo and *indígena* followers revolted. The resulting War of the Reform (not unlike the U.S. Civil War) ravaged the countryside for three long years until the victorious liberal army paraded triumphantly in Mexico City on New Year's Day, 1861.

Juarez And Maximilian

Benito Juarez, the leading *reformista,* had won the day. Juarez's similarity to his contemporary, Abraham Lincoln, is legend: Juarez had risen from humble Zapotec origins to become a lawyer, a champion of justice, and the president who held his country together during a terrible civil war. Like Lincoln, Juarez's triumph didn't last long, however.

Imperial France invaded Mexico in January 1862. After two costly years, the French pushed Juarez's liberal army into the hills and gave Mexican conservatives the king that they had been looking for. Austrian Archduke Maximilian and his wife Carlotta, the very models of

KAREN WHITE

President Benito Juarez, like his contemporary Abraham Lincoln, was a lawyer of humble origin who kept his country united through years of civil war.

modern Catholic monarchs, landed at Vera Cruz on May 28, 1864.

The naive archduke, crowned Emperor Maximilian I of Mexico, was surprised that some of his subjects resented his presence. Meanwhile, Juarez refused to yield, stubbornly performing his constitutional duties in a somber black carriage one jump ahead of the French occupying army. The climax came in June 1867, as Maximilian, deserted by the French, took the field himself. He watched in horror as Juarez's troops cut his army to pieces. Juarez gave no quarter. On June 17, Juarez ordered Maximilian's execution.

Juarez worked day and night at the double task of reconstruction and reform. He won reelection, but died, exhausted, in 1871. The death of Juarez, the stoic partisan of reform, signaled hope to Mexico's conservatives. They soon got their wish: General Don Porfirio Diaz, the "Coming Man," was elected president in 1876.

Pax Porfiriana

Don Porfirio is often remembered wistfully, as old Italians remember Mussolini: "He was a bit rough, but, dammit, at least he made the trains run on time."

Although Porfirio Diaz's humble Oaxaca mestizo origins were not unlike Juarez's, the resemblance stopped there. Diaz was not a democrat; as a general, his officers often took no captives; and, as president, his country police, the *rurales,* often shot prisoners in the act of "trying to escape."

Order and progress, in that sequence, ruled Mexico for 34 years. Foreign investment flowed into the country, new railroads brought the products of factories, mines, and farms to modernized Gulf and Pacific ports. Pesos flowed into government coffers; Mexico balanced its budget, repaid foreign debts, and became a respected member of the family of nations.

The price was high, however. Don Porfirio gave away more than a hundred million acres—one-fifth of Mexico's land area (including most of the arable land)—to friends and foreigners. Poor Mexicans, *indígenas* especially, suffered. By 1910, 90% of the *indígenas* had lost their *ejidos* (traditional communal land). In the spring of 1910, a smug, now-cultured and elderly Don Porfirio anticipated with relish the centennial of Hidalgo's Grito de Dolores.

THE REVOLUTION OF 1910

¡No Reelección!

Porfirio Diaz himself had first campaigned on the slogan. It was the idea that the president should step down after one term. Diaz had even stepped down (in favor of a puppet) once in 1880. But after that, he had gotten himself elected for 26 consecutive years. In 1910, Franscisco I. Madero, a short, squeaky-voiced son of rich landowners, opposed Diaz under the same banner.

Diaz had jailed Madero before the election. Madero, however, refused to quit campaigning. Fleeing to the U.S., he declared the election of 1910 null and void and called for a revolution to begin on November 20.

Not much happened. ¡No Reelección!, after all, is not much of a platform. But millions of poor Mexicans were going to bed hungry, and Diaz hadn't listened to them for years.

Villa And Zapata

The people began to stir. In Chihuahua, followers of Francisco (Pancho) Villa, an erstwhile ranch hand, miner, peddler, and cattle rustler, began attacking the *rurales,* dynamiting railroads, and raiding towns. Meanwhile, in the south, horse trader, farmer, minor official Emiliano Zapata's *indígena* guerrillas were terrorizing rich *hacendados* and forcibly recovering stolen ancestral village lands. Zapata's movement gained steam, and by May had taken the Morelos state capital, Cuernavaca. Meanwhile, Madero crossed the Rio Grande and joined with Villa's forces, who took Ciudad Juarez.

The *federales,* the government army troops, began deserting in droves, and on May 25, 1911, Diaz submitted his resignation. As Madero's deputy, General Victoriano Huerta, put Diaz on his ship of exile in Vera Cruz, Diaz confided: "Madero has unleashed a tiger. Now let's see if he can control it."

Emiliano Zapata, it turned out, was the very tiger whom Madero had unleashed. Meeting with Madero in Mexico City, Zapata fumed over Madero's go-slow approach to the "agrarian problem," as Madero termed it. By November, Zapata had denounced Madero. "¡Tierra y Libertad!" the Zapatistas cried: "The lands, woods and water that the landlords . . . have usurped will be immediately restored to the villages or citizens who hold the corresponding titles to them. . . ."

The Fighting Continues

Madero's support soon faded. The army in Mexico City rebelled; Huerta forced Madero to resign on February 18, 1913, then murdered him four days later. The rum-swilling Huerta, however, ruled like a Chicago mobster; general rebellion, led by the "Big Four"—Villa, Álvaro Obregón and Venustiano Carranza in the north, and Zapata in the south—soon broke out. Pressed by the rebels and refused U.S. recognition, Huerta fled into exile in July 1914.

The Constitution Of 1917

Control seesawed for three years between Villa and Zapata on one hand and Obregón and Carranza on the other. Finally Carranza, who controlled most of the country by 1917, got a convention together in Queretaro to formulate political and social goals. The resulting Constitution of 1917, while restating most ideas of the Reformistas' 1857 Constitution, additionally prescribed a single four-year presidential term, labor reform, and subordinated private ownership to public interest. Every village had a right to communal *ejido* land, and subsoil wealth could never be sold away to the highest bidder.

The Constitution of 1917 was a revolutionary expression of national aspirations, and, in retrospect, represented a social and political agenda for the entire 20th century. In modified form, it has lasted to the present day.

Obregon Stabilizes Mexico

On December 1, 1920, General Álvaro Obregón legally assumed the presidency of a Mexico still bleeding from 10 years of civil war. Although a seasoned revolutionary, Obregón was also a negotiator who recognized that peace was necessary to implement the goals of the Revolution. In four years, his government pacified local uprisings, disarmed a swarm of warlords, executed hundreds of *bandidos,* obtained U.S. diplomatic recognition, assuaged the worst fears of the clergy and landowners, and began land reform.

All this set the stage for the work of Plutarco Elías Calles, Obregón's Minister of Gobernación ("Interior") and handpicked successor, who won the 1924 election. Aided by peace, Mexico returned to a semblance of prosperity. Calles brought the army under civilian control, balanced the budget, and shifted Mexico's revolution into high gear. New clinics vaccinated millions against smallpox, new dams irrigated thousands of previously dry acres, and *campesinos* received millions of acres of redistributed land.

By single-mindedly enforcing the proagrarian, prolabor, and anticlerical articles of the 1917 constitution, Calles made many influential enemies, however. Infuriated by the government's confiscation of church property, closing of monasteries, and deportation of hundreds of foreign priests and nuns, the clergy refused to perform marriages, baptisms, and last rites. Militant Catholics, crying "¡Viva Christo Rey!," armed themselves, torching public schools and government property and murdering hundreds of innocent bystanders.

Simultaneously, Calles threatened foreign oil companies, demanding that they exchange their titles for 50-year leases. A moderate Mexican supreme court decision over the oil issue and the skillful arbitration of American Ambassador Dwight Morrow smoothed over both the oil and church troubles by the end of Calles's term, however.

Calles, who started out brimming with revolutionary fervor and populist zeal, became increasingly conservative and dictatorial. Although he bowed out peaceably in favor of Obregón (the constitution had been amended to allow one six-year nonsuccessive term), Obregón was assassinated two weeks after his election in 1928. Calles continued to rule for six more years through three puppet-presidents: Emilio Portes Gil (1928-30), Pascual Ortiz Rubio (1930-32), and Abelardo Rodriguez (1932-34).

For the 14 years since 1920, the Revolution had waxed and waned. Although Calles had been the first president in 40 years to succeed without violence, the presidency had changed hands six times since then. Calles and his cronies had lined their pockets while Mexico, with a cash surplus in 1930, skidded into debt as the Great Depression deepened. By slowing the Revolution to a crawl, Calles had mollified the church, landowners, and foreign corporations. In blessing his Minister of War, General Lázaro Cárdenas for the 1934 presidential election, Calles expected more of the same.

The 40-year-old Cárdenas, former governor of Michoacán, immediately set his own agenda, however. For six years, he worked tirelessly to fulfill the social prescriptions of the Revolution. While diplomats and cabinet ministers fretted in his outer office, Cárdenas ushered in delegations of *campesinos* and factory workers and sympathetically listened to their problems.

In his six years, Cárdenas moved public education and health forward on a broad front, supported strong, independent labor unions, and redistributed 49 million acres of farmland, more than any president before or since.

Cárdenas's resolute enforcement of constitution Articulo 123 brought him the most renown, however. Under this prolabor law, the government turned over a host of private companies to employee ownership and, on March 18, 1938, expropriated all foreign oil corporations.

The oil corporations had sorely neglected the wages, health, and welfare of their workers while taking the law into their own hands with ruthless private police forces. Although U.S. President Franklin Roosevelt disagreed, and Standard Oil of New Jersey cried foul, the U.S. government did not intervene. Through negotiation and due process, the U.S. oil companies eventually received $24 million plus three percent interest in compensation. In the wake of the expropriation, President Cárdenas created Petroleos Mexicanos (PEMEX), the national oil corporation, which has run all Mexican petroleum and gas operations to the present day.

Manuel Avila Camacho, elected in 1940, was the last general to be president of Mexico. His administration ushered in a gradual shift of Mexican politics, government, and foreign policy. Tourism, initially promoted by the Cárdenas administration, ballooned as Mexico allied itself with the U.S. cause during World War II. Good feeling surged as Franklin Roosevelt became the first U.S. president to officially cross the Rio Grande when he met with Camacho in Monterrey in April 1943.

In both word and deed, moderation and evolution guided President Camacho's policies. "Soy creente" ("I am a believer"), he declared to the Catholics of Mexico as he worked earnestly to bridge Mexico's serious church-state schism. Land policy emphasis shifted from redistribution to utilization as new dams and canals irrigated hundreds of thousands of previously arid acres. On one hand, Camacho established IMSS (Instituto Mexicano de Seguro Social), and on the other, trimmed the power of labor unions.

As World War II moved toward its 1945 conclusion, both the U.S. and Mexico were enjoying the benefits of four years of governmental and military cooperation and mutual trade (in the form of a mountain of strategic minerals, which had moved north in exchange for a similar mountain of U.S. manufactures south).

The Mature Revolution

During the decades after World War II, beginning with moderate President Miguel Alemán (1946-52), Mexican politicians gradually honed their skills of consensus and compromise as their middle-aged revolution bubbled along under liberal presidents and sputtered haltingly under conservatives. Doctrine required of all politicians, regardless of stripe, that they be "revolutionary" enough to be included beneath the banner of the PRI (Partido Revolucionario Institutional—the Institutional Revolutionary Party), Mexico's dominant political party.

Mexico's Revolution hasn't been very revolutionary about women's rights, however. The PRI didn't get around to giving Mexican women (millions of whom fought and died alongside their men during the revolution) the right to vote until 1953.

Adolfo Ruiz Cortines, Alemán's secretary of the interior, was elected overwhelmingly in 1952. He fought the corruption that had crept into government under his predecessor, continued land reform, increased agricultural production, built new ports, eradicated malaria, and opened a dozen automobile-assembly plants.

Women, voting for the first time in a national election, kept the PRI in power by helping to elect liberal Adolfo López Mateos in 1958. Resembling Lázaro Cárdenas in social policy, López Mateos redistributed 40 million acres of farmland, forced automakers to use 60% domestic components, built thousands of new schools, and distributed hundreds of millions of new textbooks. "La electricidad es nuestra" ("Electricity is ours"), Mateos declared as he nationalized foreign power companies in 1962.

Despite his left-leaning social agenda, unions were restive under López Mateos. Protesting inflation, workers struck; the government retaliated, arresting Demetrios Vallejo, the railway union head, and renowned muralist David Siqueros, former Communist Party secretary.

Despite the troubles, López Mateos climaxed his presidency gracefully in 1964 as he opened the celebrated National Museum of Anthropolgy, appropriately located in Chapultepec Park, where the Aztecs had first settled 20 generations earlier.

In 1964, as several times before, the outgoing president's interior secretary succeeded his former chief. Dour and conservative, Gustavo Diaz Ordaz immediately clashed with liberals in his own party, labor, and students. The pot boiled over just before the 1968 Mexico City Olympics. Reacting to a student rebellion, the army occupied the National University; shortly afterwards, on October 2, government forces opened fire with machine guns on a downtown protest, killing and wounding hundreds of demonstrators.

Despite its serious internal troubles, Mexico's relations with the U.S. were cordial. President Lyndon Johnson visited and unveiled a statue of Abraham Lincoln in Mexico City. Later, Diaz Ordaz met with President Richard Nixon in Puerto Vallarta.

Meanwhile, bilateral negotiations produced the Border Industrialization Program. Within a 12-mile strip south of the border, foreign companies could assemble duty-free parts into finished goods and export them without any duties on either side. Within a dozen years, a swarm of such plants, called *maquiladoras,* were humming with hundreds of thousands of Mexican workers assembling and exporting billions in shiny consumer goods—electronics, clothes, furniture, pharmaceuticals, and toys—worldwide.

Meanwhile, in Mexico's interior, Diaz Ordaz pushed Mexico's industrialization ahead full steam. Heavy foreign borrowing financed hundreds of new plants and factories. Primary among these was the giant Las Truchas steel plant at the new industrial port and town of Lázaro Cádenas at the Pacific mouth of the Rio Balsas.

Burgeoning prosperity and social programs boosted Mexico past most of the third world in health, education, and income standards during the post-World War II decades. In terms of calories, 1970-generation Mexicans were eating twice as well as their grandparents. During the same time, life expectancy had doubled to nearly developed-world standards, while infant mortality had dropped from a whopping 36% to 5%. Illiteracy had likewise plummeted to below 10%, and millions of Mexican families had joined the middle class, with cars, TVs, refrigerators, and children in high school and college.

ECONOMY AND GOVERNMENT

Despite huge gains, Mexico's 20th-century revolution remains incomplete. The land reform program, once thought to be a Mexican cure-all, is stalled. The *ejidos,* of which Emiliano Zapata dreamed have become mostly symbolic. The communal fields are typically small; capital for machines and fertilizers and the expertise to use them are lacking. Farms are consequently inefficient. In corn, for example, the average Mexican field produces *one-fifth* as much per acre as a U.S. farm. Mexico must consequently use its precious oil dollar surplus to import millions of tons of food annually.

Economic Trouble Of The 1980s

To make matters worse, Mexico's oil dollars haven't been as plentiful as they used to be. President Luis Echeverría (1970-76), diverted by his interest in international affairs, passed on a huge foreign debt to his successor, López Portillo. Gigantic oil discoveries and burgeoning production temporarily relieved Mexico's financial problems, however.

The world petroleum glut during the early 1980s finally burst the bubble and plunged Mexico into financial crisis. When the 1982 interest came due on its foreign debt, Mexico's largest holding company couldn't pay the US$2.3 billion owed. The peso humiliatingly plummeted more than fivefold, to 150 per U.S. dollar. At the same time, prices were doubling every year.

But by the mid-1980s, President Miguel de la Madrid (1982-88) was straining to get Mexico's economic house in order. He sliced government and raised taxes, asking rich and poor alike to tighten their belts. Despite getting foreign bankers to reschedule Mexico's debt, de la Madrid couldn't stop inflation. Prices were skyrocketing as the peso deflated to 2,500 per U.S. dollar, becoming one of the world's most devalued currencies by 1988.

All this has made life rocky for Mexican wage-earning families. With inflation rapidly eroding their income (of around US$2000 per capita), the average family has to scratch hard to make ends meet.

But in Mexico averages mean little. A primary socio-economic reality of Mexican history remains: a few Mexicans are very rich; most are very poor. Despite recent gains, the typical Mexican family owns neither car nor refrigerator. Its children do not finish elementary school, nor do their parents practice birth control.

Government And Politics

On paper, Mexico's government appears much like its U.S. model: a federal presidency, a two-house congress, and a supreme court, with their counterparts in each of 32 states. Political parties field candidates, and citizens vote by secret ballot.

Appearances, however, are sometimes deceiving. Although minority parties, such as the pro-Catholic PAN (Partido Acción Nacional) and the PMS (Partido Mexicano Socialista) mount periodic gadfly challenges, presidents and governors have been traditionally handpicked by the PRI. Political bosses and police have run roughshod over political opponents. Elections lost at the polling place have been won by faked recounts, threats, mayhem, and even murder.

Public disgust led to significant opposition during the 1988 presidential election. Billionaire PAN candidate Michael Clothier and liberal National Democratic Front candidate Cuauhtémoc Cárdenas ran against the PRI's Harvard-educated technocrat Carlos Salinas Gortari. The vote was split so evenly that all three candidates claimed victory. Although Salinas Gortari eventually won the election, his showing, barely half of the vote, was the worst ever for a PRI president.

Salinas Gortari, however, may be Mexico's "Coming Man" of the '90s. He appears serious about democracy, sympathetic to the *indígenas* and the poor, and sensitive to women's issues. His major achievement, despite significant national opposition, may eventually be the North American Free Trade Agreement (NAFTA), which he, U.S. President George Bush, and Canadian Prime Minister Brian Mulroney negotiated in 1992. If all goes as planned, NAFTA will usher in a new Mexican revolution, this time economic, in which millions of jobs in new industries and enterprises will help Mexicans finally achieve their enormous but as yet untapped human potential.

PEOPLE

Let a broad wooden chopping block represent the high plain, the *altiplano* of Mexico; imagine taking a sharp cleaver and hacking at one side of it until it is cut by a dozen grooves and pocked with voids. That fractured half resembles Mexico's central highlands, where most Mexicans, divided from each other by high mountains and yawning *barrancas,* have lived for millennia.

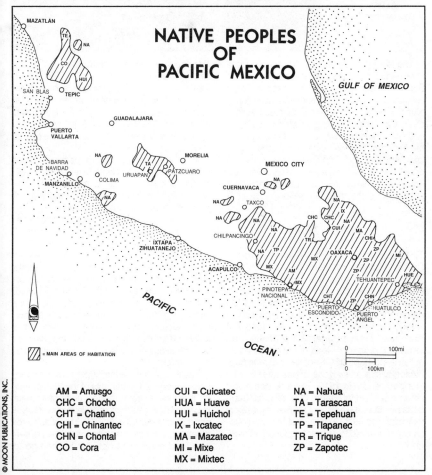

NATIVE PEOPLES OF PACIFIC MEXICO

= MAIN AREAS OF HABITATION

AM = Amusgo	CUI = Cuicatec	NA = Nahua
CHC = Chocho	HUA = Huave	TA = Tarascan
CHT = Chatino	HUI = Huichol	TE = Tepehuan
CHI = Chinantec	IX = Ixcatec	TP = Tlapanec
CHN = Chontal	MA = Mazatec	TR = Trique
CO = Cora	MI = Mixe	ZP = Zapotec
	MX = Mixtec	

© MOON PUBLICATIONS, INC.

Rich colors, graceful designs, and fine quality draw streams of visitors to Teotitlán del Valle weaving village near Oaxaca.

The Mexicans' deep divisions, in large measure, led to their downfall at the hands of the Spanish conquistadores. The Aztec empire Cortés conquered was a vast but fragmented collection of tribes. Speaking more than a hundred mutually alien languages, those original Mexicans viewed each other suspiciously, as barely human barbarians from strange lands beyond the mountains. And even today the lines that Mexicans still draw between themselves—of caste, class, race, and wealth—result, to a significant degree, from the realities of their mutual isolation.

POPULATION

The Spanish colonial government and the Roman Catholic religion provided the glue that over 400 years, has welded Mexico's fragmented people into a nation. Mexico's population, more than 81 million by the 1990 national census, is exploding. This was not always so, however. Historians estimate that European diseases, largely measles and smallpox, probably wiped out as many as 20 million—perhaps 95%!—of the *indígena* population within a few generations after Cortés stepped ashore in 1519. The Mexican population dwindled to a mere one million inhabitants by 1600. It wasn't until 1950—more than four centuries after Cortés—that Mexico's population recovered to its preconquest level of 25 million.

Mestizos, *Indígenas,* Criollos, And Negroes

Although by 1950 Mexico's population had recovered, it was completely transformed. The mestizo, a Spanish-speaking person of mixed blood, had replaced the pure Native American, the *indígena* (een-DEE-hay-nah), as the typical Mexican.

The trend continues. Perhaps three of four Mexicans would identify themselves as mestizo, that class whose part-European blood elevates them, in Mexican mind, to the level of *gente de razón*—people of "reason" or "right."

And there's the rub. The *indígenas* (or, mistakenly but commonly, Indians), by usual measures such as income, health, or education, squat at the bottom of the Mexican social ladder.

The typical *indígena* family lives in a little adobe house in a remote valley, subsisting on the corn, beans, and vegetables from its small unirrigated *milpa* (cornfield). Often there are chickens, a few pigs, and sometimes a cow, but no electricity; even if there is, however, the few hundred dollars a year cash income isn't enough to buy even a small refrigerator, much less a truck.

The typical mestizo family, on the other hand, enjoys many of the benefits of the 20th century. It usually owns a modest concrete house in town. The furnishings, simple by developed-world standards, will often include an electric refrigerator, washing machine, gas stove, television, and a car or truck. The children go to school every day, and the eldest son sometimes even looks forward to college.

Sizable Negro communities, descendants of 18th-century African slaves, live in the Gulf states and along the Guerrero-Oaxaca coastline of Pacific Mexico. Last to arrive, the Negroes experience discrimination at the hands of everyone else and are integrating very slowly into the mestizo mainstream.

Above the mestizos, a tiny criollo (Mexican-born white) minority, a few percent of the total population, inherits the privileges—wealth, education, and political power—of colonial Spanish ancestry.

THE *INDÍGENAS*

Although anthropologists and census takers classify them according to language groups (such as Nahuatl, Mixtec, and Zapotec) *indígenas* typically identify themselves as residents of a particular locality rather than by language or ethnic grouping. And although, as a group, they are referred to as *indígenas* (native, or aboriginal),

INDIGENOUS POPULATIONS OF PACIFIC MEXICO

For the seven states of Pacific Mexico (from north to south), the 1990 government census totals were:

STATE	INDIGENOUS POPULATION (over five years of age)	TOTAL POPULATION (over five years of age)	PERCENT OF TOTAL
Sinaloa	31,000	1,924,000	1.6%
Nayarit	24,000	712,000	3.4%
Jalisco	25,000	4,585,000	0.5%
Colima	1,500	372,000	0.4%
Michoacán	106,000	3,037,000	3.4%
Guerrero	299,000	2,228,000	13.4%
Oaxaca	1,018,000	2,603,000	39.1%

The same government sources tabulate indigenous peoples by language groupings. Although such figures are probably low, the 1990 figures revealed significant populations in many areas of Pacific Mexico:

LANGUAGE	POPULATION (1990)	IMPORTANT CENTERS
Zapotec	402,000	East and South Oaxaca (Tlacolula)
Mixtec	387,000	North, West, and Coastal Oaxaca (Nochixtlán)
Mazatec	168,000	North Oaxaca
Mixe	95,000	East Oaxaca
Chinantec	104,000	Oaxaca-Guerrero (Ometepec)
Tarasco	95,000	Michoacán (Pátzcuaro, Tzintzuntzán)
Tlapanec	69,000	East Guerrero (Tlapa de Comonfort)
Chatino	29,000	South Oaxaca (Miahuatlán)
Amusgo	28,000	Oaxaca-Guerrero (Xochistlahuaca)
Chontal	24,000	Southwest Oaxaca (Tequisistlán)
Huichol	20,000	Nayarit (San Andres)
Trique	15,000	Central Oaxaca
Chocho	13,000	North Oaxaca (Telixtlahuaca)
Cuicatec	13,000	Southwest Oaxaca
Cora	12,000	Nayarit (Acaponeta)
Huave	12,000	Southeast Oaxaca (Rincón Juarez)

individuals are generally made uncomfortable (or may even feel insulted) by being labeled as such.

While the mestizos are the emergent self-conscious majority class, the *indígenas,* as during colonial times, remain the invisible people of Mexico. They are politically conservative, socially traditional, and tied to the land. On market day, the typical *indígena* family might make the trip into town. They bag up some tomatoes, squash, or peppers, and tie up a few chickens or a pig. The rickety country bus will often be full, and the mestizo driver may wave them away, giving preference to his friends, leaving them to trudge stoically along the road.

Their luck has been slowly improving, however. *Indígena* families often now have access to a local school and a clinic. Improved health has led to large growth of their population. (Official census figures, however, are probably low. *Indígenas* are traditionally suspicious of government people snooping around, and census takers, however conscientious, seldom speak the local language.)

Recent figures nevertheless indicate that about eight percent of Mexicans are *indígenas*—that is, they speak one of Mexico's 50-odd native languages. Of those, about a quarter speak no Spanish at all. These fractions, moreover, are changing only slowly. Many *indígenas* prefer the old ways. If present trends continue, the year 2019 (500 years after the Spanish conquest) or thereabouts will mark the return of the Mexican indigenous population to the preconquest level of roughly 25 million.

Indian Language Groups

The Maya speakers of Yucatán and the aggregate of the Nahuatl (Aztec language) speakers of the central plateau are Mexico's most numerous *indígena* groups, totaling roughly three million (one million Maya, two million Nahua).

Indigenous population centers, relatively scattered in the north of Pacific Mexico, concentrate in the southern states of Guerrero and Oaxaca. The groups are not evenly spread, however. The language map of Oaxaca, for example, looks like a crazy quilt, with important Zapotec, Mixtec, and other centers scattered along the coast and through the mountains surrounding Oaxaca city.

Dress

Maps and figures, however, cannot describe the color of a fiesta or market day. Many country people, especially in Oaxaca, still wear the traditional cottons, which blend the Spanish and native styles. Men usually wear the Spanish-origin straw sombrero (literally, "shade-maker") on their heads, baggy white cotton shirt and pants and leather huaraches on their feet. Women's dress is often more colorful. This can include a *huipil* (long, sleeveless dress), often embroidered in bright floral and animal motifs, and a handwoven *enredo* (wrap-around skirt that identify the wearer with a particular locality.) A *faja,* (waist sash), and, in the winter, a *quechquémitl* (shoulder cape) complete the costume.

RELIGION

"God and Gold" was the two-pronged mission of the conquistadores. Most of them concentrated on gold, while missionaries tried to shift the emphasis to God. They were famously successful: more than 90% of Mexicans profess to be Catholics.

Catholicism, spreading its doctrine of equality of all persons before God and incorporating native gods into the church rituals, eventually brought the *indígenas* into the fold. Within a hundred years, nearly all Mexicans accepted the new religion, which raised the universal God of all humankind over local tribal deities.

The Virgin Of Guadalupe

Conversion of the native Mexicans was sparked by the vision of Juan Diego, a simple farmer. On the hill of Tepeyac north of Mexico City in 1531, Juan Diego saw a brown-skinned Virgin Mary enclosed in a dazzling aura of light. She told him to build a shrine in her memory on that spot, where the Aztecs had long worshipped their "earth mother," Tonantzín. Juan Diego's brown Virgin told him to go to the cathedral and relay her instruction to Archbishop Zumárraga.

The archbishop, as expected, turned his nose up at Juan Diego's story. The vision returned, however, and this time Juan Diego's brown Virgin realized that a miracle was necessary. She ordered some roses to be grown (a true miracle, since roses had been previously unknown in the vicinity) and taken to the archbishop. Juan Diego wrapped the roses in his rude fiber cape, returned to the cathedral, and placed the wrapped roses at the archbishop's feet. When he opened the offering, Zumárraga gasped: imprinted on the cape was an image of the Virgin herself—proof positive of a genuine miracle.

In the centuries since Juan Diego, the brown Virgin—La Virgen Morena, or Nuestra Señora La Virgen de Guadalupe—has blended native and Catholic elements into something uniquely Mexican. In doing so, she has become the virtual patroness of Mexico, the beloved symbol of Mexico for *indígenas,* mestizos, Negroes, and criollos alike.

Every Mexican city, town, and village celebrates the cherished memory of their Virgin of Guadalupe on Dec. 12. This celebration, however joyful, is but one of the many fiestas Mexicans, especially the *indígenas,* live for. Each village holds its local fiesta in honor of their patron saint, who is often a thinly veiled sit-in for some local preconquest deity. Themes often appear Spanish—Christians vs. Moors, devils vs. priests—but the native element element is strong, sometimes dominant. During Semana Santa (Holy Week) at Pinotepa Nacional in coastal Oaxaca, for example, Mixtec people, costumed as Jews, shoot arrows skyward, simultaneously reciting traditional Mixtec prayers.)

SPORTS AND RECREATION

BEACHES

It's easy to understand why many vacationers stay right at the beach. And not just at the famous crystalline stretches of Mazatlán, Puerto Vallarta, Manzanillo, Ixtapa, Acapulco, and Puerto Escondido. Many flee the big resorts and spread out along the whole coast—gathering at small beach resorts such as San Blas, Rincón de Guayabitos, Playa Azul, and Puerto Ángel—while others set up camp and enjoy the solitude and rich wildlife of hundreds of miles of pristine strands. Shorelines vary from mangrove-edged lagoons and algae-decorated tidepools to shoals of pebbles and sand of dozens of colors and consistencies.

Sand makes the beach, and Pacific Mexico has plenty, from hot, black mica dust to cool, velvety, white coral. Some beaches drop steeply to turbulent, close-in surf, fine for fishing. Others are level, with gentle, rolling breakers, made for surfing and swimming.

Beaches are fascinating for the surprises they yield. Pacific Mexico's beaches, especially the hidden strands near resorts and the hundreds of miles of wilderness beaches and tidepools, yield troves of shells and treasures of flotsam and jetsam for those who enjoy looking for them. **Beachcombing** is more rewarding during the summer storm season, when big waves deposit acres of fresh shells—among them, conch, scallop, clams, combs of Venus, whelks, limpets, olives, cowries, starfish, and sand dollars.

Beaches near rivermouths during the rainy season are often fantastic outdoor galleries of wind- and water-sculpted snags and giant logs deposited by the downstream flood.

Viewing Wildlife

Wildlife watchers should keep quiet and always be on the alert. Animal survival depends on them seeing you first. Occasional spectacular offshore sights, such as whales, porpoises, and manta rays, or an on-shore giant constrictor, beached squid or octopus, crocodile (caimán), or even a jaguar looking for turtle eggs are the reward of those prepared to recognize them.

(Don't forget your binoculars and your Peterson's Field Guide to Mexican Birds.)

For extensive notes on good hiking, tidepooling, wildlife-viewing, and shell-browsing spots, see each chapter's "Sights" section.

WATER SPORTS

Swimming, surfing, windsurfing, snorkeling, scuba diving, kayaking, sailing, and jet-skiing are Pacific Mexico's water sports of choice. For details in local favorite spots, conditions, rental shops, and equipment, see "Sports and Recreation" in each travel chapter.

Safety First

As viewed from Pacific Mexico beaches, the Pacific Ocean usually lives up to its name. Many protected inlets, safe for child's play, dot the coastline. Unsheltered shorelines, on the other hand, can be deceiving. Smooth water in the calm forenoon often changes to choppy in the afternoon; calm ripples that lap the shore in March can grow to hurricane-driven walls of water in November. Such storms can wash away sand, changing a wide, gently sloping beach into a steep one, plagued by turbulent waves and treacherous currents.

Undertow, whirlpools, crosscurrents, and occasional oversized waves can make ocean swimming a fast-lane adventure. Getting unexpectedly swept out to sea or hammered onto the beach bottom by a surprise breaker are major hazards.

Never attempt serious swimming when tipsy or full of food; never swim alone where no one can see you. Always swim beyond the breakers (which come in sets of several, climaxed by a big one, which breaks highest and farthest from the beach). If you happen to get caught in the the path of such a breaker, avoid it by diving under and letting it roll harmlessly over you. If you do get caught by a serious breaker, try to roll and tumble with it (as football players tumble) to avoid injury.

Now and then swimmers get a nettlelike jellyfish sting. Be careful around coral reefs and

BRUCE WHIPPERMAN

Balmy water and gentle conditions make afternoon sailing a breeze in many of Pacific Mexico's protected coves and bays.

beds of sea urchins; corals can sting (like jellyfish) and you can get infections from coral cuts and sea-urchin spines. Shuffle along sandy bottoms to scare away stingrays before stepping on one. If you're unlucky, its venomous tail-spines may inflict a painful wound. (See "Staying Healthy" under "Other Practicalities" for first-aid measures.)

Snorkeling And Scuba Diving

Many exciting clear-water sites, such as Puerto Vallarta's Los Arcos, Zihuatanejo's Playa Las Gatas, Isla Roqueta at Acapulco, and Playa Estacauite at Puerto Ángel await both beginner and expert skin divers. Veteran Pacific Mexico divers usually arrive during the dry winter and early spring when river outflows are mere trickles, leaving offshore waters clear. In the major tourist centers, professional dive shops rent equipment, provide lessons and guides, and transport divers to choice sites.

While convenient, rented equipment is often less than satisfactory. To be sure, serious divers bring their own gear. This should probably include wetsuits in the winter, when many swimmers begin to feel cold after an unprotected half-hour in the water.

Surfing And Windsurfing

In addition to several well-known surfing beaches, such as Matanchén at San Blas, Puerto Vallarta's Punta Mita, and Boca de Apiza south of Manzanillo, Pacific Mexico has the country's acknowledged best surfing beach at Puerto Escondido.

The surf everywhere is highest and best during the July-November hurricane season, when big swells from storms far out at sea cause an inundation of surfers at the favored beaches (except at crowded Acapulco Bay, where surfing is off-limits).

Windsurfers, sailboaters, and kayakers—who, by contrast, require tranquil waters—do best in the Pacific Mexico winter or early spring. It is then that they gather to enjoy the near-ideal conditions at many coves and inlets near the big resorts.

While beginners can have fun with the equipment available from rental shops, serious surfers, windsurfers, sailboaters and kayakers should pack their own gear.

POWER SPORTS

Acapulco and other big resorts have long been centers for waterskiing, parasailing, and jet-skiing. In parasailing, a motorboat pulls while a parachute lifts you, like a soaring gull, high over the ocean. After ten minutes they deposit you gently back on the sand. Jet-ski boats are like snowmobiles except that they operate on water, where, with a little practice, even beginners can quickly learn to whiz over the waves.

Although the luxury resorts generally provide experienced crews and equipment, crowded conditions increase the hazard to both participants and swimmers. You, as the paying patron, have a right to expect that your

FISH

A bounty of fish dart, swarm, jump, and wriggle in Pacific Mexico's surf, reefs, lagoons and offshore depths. While many make for a delicious dinner (albacore, red snapper, pompano) others are tough (sail-fish), bony (bonefish), and even poisonous (puffers). Some grow to half-ton giants (marlin, jewfish), while others are diminutive reef-grazers (parrot fish, damselfish, angelfish) whose bright colors are a delight to snorkelers and divers.

ENGLISH NAME	SPANISH NAME	AVERAGE SIZE	COLORS	EDIBILITY	OCCURRENCE
albacore	*albacora, atún*	two to four feet	blue	excellent	deep
angelfish	*angel*	one foot	yellow, orange, blue	*	reef
barracuda	*barracuda, picuda*	two feet	brown	good	deep
black marlin	*marlin negro*	six feet	blue-black	good	deep
blue marlin	*marlin azul*	eight feet	blue	poor	deep
bobo	*barbudo*	one foot	blue, yellow	fair	surf
bonefish	*macabi*	one foot	blue, silver	poor	inshore
bonito	*bonito*	two feet	black	good	deep

barracuda

angel fish

bonito

butterfly fish	*muñeca*	six inches	black, yellow	*	reef
chub	*chopa*	one foot	gray	good	reef
croaker	*corvina*	two feet	brownish	rare and protected	inshore bottoms
damselfish	*castañeta*	four inches	brown, blue, orange	*	reef
dolphin fish, mahimahi	*dorado*	three feet	green, gold	good	deep
grouper	*garropa*	three feet	brown, rust	good	offshore reefs
grunt	*burro*	eight inches	black, gray	*	rocks, reefs
jack	*toro*	one to two feet	bluish-gray	good	offshore
jewfish	*mero*	three feet	brown	good	rocky reef bottoms

providers and crew are well-equipped, sober, and cautious.

Beach Buggies And ATVs

Some visitors enjoy racing along the beach and rolling over dunes with beach buggies and ATVs (All-Terrain Vehicles—*motos* in Mexico), balloon-tired, three-wheeled motor scooters. While certain resort rental agencies cater to the growing use of such vehicles, limits are in order. Of all the proliferating high-horsepower beach pastimes, these are the most intrusive. Noise, exhaust and gasoline pollution, injuries to operators and bystanders, scattering of wildlife and destruction of their habitats has led (and I hope will continue to lead) to the restriction of dune buggies and ATVs on beaches.

mackerel	*sierra*	two feet	gray with gold spots	good	offshore
mullet	*lisa*	two feet	gray	good	sandy bays
needlefish	*agujón*	three feet	blue-black	good	deep
parrot fish	*perico, pez loro*	one foot	green, pink, blue, orange	*	reef
pompano	*pápano*	one foot	gray	excellent	inshore bottoms
puffer	*botete*	eight inches	brown	poisonous	inshore
Pacific porgy	*pez de pluma*	one to two feet	tan	good	sandy shores
red snapper	*huachinango, pargo*	one to two feet	reddish pink	excellent	deep
roosterfish	*pez gallo*	three feet	black, blue	excellent	deep
sailfish	*pez vela*	five feet	blue-black	poor	deep
sardine	*sardina*	eight inches	blue-black	good	offshore
sea bass	*cabrilla*	one to two feet	brown, ruddy	good	reef crevices
shark	*tiburón*	2-10 feet	black to blue	good	in- and offshore
snook	*robalo*	two to three feet	black-brown	excellent	brackish lagoons
spadefish	*chambo*	one foot	black-silver	*	reefs, sandy bottoms
swordfish	*pez espada*	five feet	black to blue	excellent	deep
triggerfish	*pez puerco*	one to two feet	blue, rust, brown, black	*	reef
wahoo	*peto, guahu*	two to five feet	green to blue	excellent	deep
yellowfin tuna	*atún amarilla*	two to five feet	blue, yellow	excellent	deep
yellowtail	*jurel*	two to four feet	blue, yellow	excellent	offshore

damselfish

*reef fish are generally too small to be considered edible

sailfish

ERIC SCHNITTIGER / ERIN DWYER

TENNIS AND GOLF

Most Mexicans are working too hard to be playing much tennis and golf. Although there are almost no public courses or courts, Pacific Mexico's resort centers enjoy excellent private facilities. If you are planning on a lot of golf and tennis, check into one of the many hotels with these facilities. See the travel chapter "Sports and Recreation" and "Accommodations" headings for plenty of golf and tennis listings.

FISHING

Experts agree that Pacific Mexico is a world-class deep-sea and surf fishing ground. Sportspersons routinely bring in dozens of species from among the more than 600 which have been hooked in Pacific Mexico waters.

Surf Fishing

Most good fishing beaches away from the immediate resort areas will typically have only a few locals (mostly with nets) and fewer visitors.

Mexicans typically do little sportfishing. They either make their life from fishing, or they do none at all. Consequently, few shops sell sportfishing equipment in Mexico, so you should bring your own surf-fishing equipment, including hooks, lures, line, and weights.

Your best general information source before you leave is a good shop around home. Tell them where you're going, and they'll often know the best lures and bait to use and what fish you can expect to catch with them.

In any case, the cleaner the water, the more interesting will be your catch. On a good day, your reward might be *sierras, cabrillas, porgys,* or *pámpanos* pulled from the Pacific Mexico surf.

You can't have everything, however. Foreigners cannot legally take Mexican abalone, coral, lobster, pismo clams, rock bass, sea fans, seashells, shrimp, or turtles. Neither are they supposed to buy them directly from fishermen.

Deep-sea Fishing
Mazatlán and Manzanillo are renowned spots for the big prize marlin and sailfish, while Zihuatanejo, Puerto Vallarta, and Acapulco run close behind.

A deep-sea boat charter generally includes the boat and crew for a full or half day, plus equipment and bait for two to six persons, not including food or drinks. The full-day price depends upon the season. Around Christmas and New Year and before Easter (when advance reservations will be mandatory) a boat can run $300 at Mazatlán or Manzanillo. At lesser-known resorts, or even at the big resorts during low season you might be able to bargain a captain down to as low as $150.

Big boats are not the only choices. Business is sometimes so brisk at big resorts that agencies make reservations for individuals at about $60 per person per day.

Pangas, outboard launches seating four to six are available for as little $50, depending on the season. (Once in Barra de Navidad six of my friends hired a *panga* for $50, had a great time, and came back with a boatload of big tuna, jack, and mackerel. A restaurant cooked them up as a banquet for a dozen of us in exchange for the extra fish. I discovered for the first time how heavenly fresh *sierra veracruzana* can taste.)

Bringing Your Own Boat
If you're going to be doing lots of fishing, your own boat may be your most flexible and economical option. One big advantage is that you can go to the many excellent fishing grounds that the charter boats do not frequent. Keep your equipment simple, scout around, and keep your eyes peeled and ears open for local regulations and customs, plus tide, wind, and fish-edibility information.

Fishing Licenses
Anyone 16 or over who is either fishing or riding on a fishing boat in Mexico is required to have a fishing license. Although Mexican fishing licenses are obtainable from certain travel and insurance agents or at Oficinas de Pesca in Pacific Mexico ports, save yourself trouble and get your fishing licenses ahead of time by mail from the U.S. offices of the Mexican Department of Fisheries, 2550 Fifth Avenue, Suite 101, San Diego, CA 92103-6223, tel. (619) 233-6956.

Call them a month before you leave and find out the license fee (which depends on the period of validity and the fluctuating exchange rate). Write a letter, including names (exactly as they appear on their passports) of persons requesting licenses. Send a cashier's check or a money order for the exact amount along with a stamped, self-addressed envelope.

HUNTING

Game, especially winter-season waterfowl, doves, rabbits, deer, and wild pigs are plentiful in Pacific Mexico. Bag limits and seasons, however, are carefully controlled by the government Secretariat of Development and Urban Ecology (Secretaria de Desarollo y Ecologia Urbano), SEDUE. They and the Mexican consular service jointly issue the various required permits through a time-consuming and costly procedure, which, at minimum, runs months and hundreds of dollars.

Private fee agencies, however, will do all the tedious footwork. Among the most experienced are the **Mexican Hunting Association,** 3302 Josie Ave, Long Beach, CA 90808, tel. (310) 421-1619, and the **Wildlife Advisory Service,** P.O. Box 76132, Los Angeles, CA 90076, tel. (213) 385-9311, fax (213) 385-0782.

Both of these agencies also arrange guides and accommodations.

BULLFIGHTING

It is said that there are two occasions for which Mexicans arrive on time: funerals and bullfights.

Bullfighting is a recreation, not a sport. The bull is outnumbered seven to one and the outcome is never in doubt. Even if the matador (literally, "killer") fails in his duty, his assistants will entice the bull away and slaughter him in private beneath the stands.

La Corrida De Toros

Mexicans don't call it a "bullfight"; it's the Corrida de Toros, during which six bulls are customarily slaughtered, beginning at 5 p.m. (4 p.m. in the winter). After the beginning parade, the first bull rushes into the ring in a cloud of dust. Three clockwork *tercios* (thirds) define the ritual: the first, the *puyazos,* or "stabs," requires

Bullfights, more correctly corridas de toros, *are highly stylized rituals whose outcome is never in doubt.*

that two *picadores* on horseback thrust lances into the bull's shoulders, weakening him. During the second *tercio,* the *bandilleras* dodge the bull's horns to stick three long, streamered darts into his shoulders.

Trumpets announce the third *tercio* and the appearance of the matador. The bull—weak, confused, and angry—is ready for the finish. The matador struts, holding the red cape, daring the bull to charge. Form now becomes everything. The expert matador takes complete control of the bull, who rushes at the cape, past his ramrod-erect opponent. For charge after charge, the matador works the bull to exactly the right spot in the ring—in front of the judges, a lovely señorita, or perhaps the governor—where the matador mercifully delivers the precision *estocada* (killing sword thrust) deep into the drooping neck of the defeated bull. (Benito Juarez, as governor during the 1850s, got bullfights outlawed in Oaxaca. In his honor, they remain so, making Oaxaca unique among Mexican states.)

FESTIVALS AND EVENTS

Mexicans love a party. Middle- and upper-class families watch the calendar for midweek national holidays that create a *puente,* or "bridge" to the weekend and allow them to squeeze in a three- to five-day minivacation. Visitors should likewise watch the calendar. Such holidays (especially Christmas and Semana Santa pre-Easter week) often mean packed buses, roads, and hotels, especially in Pacific Mexico's beach resorts.

Country people, on the other hand, await their local saint's day for an excuse to dress up in their traditional best, sell their wares, join a procession, get tipsy, and do a little dancing in the plaza.

MIKE WELLINS

FIESTAS

Here's a list of of national and local Pacific Mexico fiestas. If you happen to be where one of these is going on, get out of your car or bus and join in!

Jan. 1: ¡ Año Nuevo! (New Year's Day; national holiday)

Jan. 6: Día de Los Reyes ("Day of the Kings"; traditional gift exchange)

Jan. 17: Día de San Antonio Abad (decorating and blessing animals)

Jan. 18: Fiesta de Santa Prisca, (in Taxco, Guerrero; dances and fireworks)

Jan. 23-Feb. 2: Fiesta de la Virgen de la Salud (in Colima, Colima; processions, food, dancing, and fireworks)

Feb. 2: Día de Candelaria (plants, seeds, and candles blessed, processions, and bullfights)

Feb. 5: Constitution Day (national holiday)

Feb. 5: a Tarascan fiesta begins in Zitacuaro, Michoacán

Feb. 7-23: Fiesta de la Villa Alvarez (in Colima, Colima; bullfights, rodeos, and carnival)

Feb. 24: Flag Day (national holiday)

Feb.: The week before Ash Wednesday, usually in late Feb., many towns, especially Mazatlán and around Pinotepa Nacional, Oaxaca, stage Carnaval—Mardi Gras—extravaganzas.

March 21: Benito Juarez (the "Lincoln of Mexico") national holiday, especially in Oaxaca, Juarez's birthplace

April 9: native dances in Santiago de Las Penas, Oaxaca

April: Santa Semana (pre-Easter Holy Week, culminating in Domingo Santa, Easter national holiday)

May 1: Labor Day (national holiday)

May 2-10: Tarascan dances, processions, and a fair take place in Morelia, Michoacán

May 3: Día de la Cruz ("Day of the Cross")

May 5: Cinco de Mayo (defeat of the French at Puebla in 1862, national holiday)

May 10: Mother's Day (national holiday)

May 18-25: local fiesta in Juchitán, Oaxaca (Chontal, Huave dances and fair)

June 13-29: local fiesta in Uruapan, Michoacán (Tarascan dances)

June 29: local fiesta in Guadalajara, Jalisco

July 8: Zapotec dances and fair in Teotitlán del Valle, Oaxaca

July: Lunes del Cerro (in Oaxaca city; a two-week extravaganza of native dances, events, and fairs, beginning on the first Monday after July 16; among the most colorful in Mexico)

Sept. 14: Charro Day (cowboy day all over Mexico; rodeos)

Sept. 16: Independence Day (Father Hidalgo's 1810 Grito de Dolores sparked the revolt against Spain; a national holiday.)

Oct. 12: Día de la Raza (Columbus Day; national holiday)

Late October-early November: Fería de Mexicanidad (in Nayarit state)

Nov. 1: Día de Todos Santos ("All Souls' Day", in honor of the souls of children. The departed descend from heaven to eat sugar skeletons, skulls, and treats on family altars; all Mexico.)

Nov. 2: Día de los Muertos ("Day of the Dead"; in honor of ancestors. Families visit graveyards and decorate graves with flowers and favorite foods of the deceased.)

Nov. 7-30: Fería de la Nao de China (In Acapulco; a fair celebrating the galleon trade, which linked colonial Acapulco with the Orient.)

Nov. 20: Revolution Day (Anniversary of the Revolution of 1910-17; national holiday)

Dec. 1: Inauguration Day (national government changes hands every six years: 1994, 2000, 2006, etc.)

Dec. 12: Día de Nuestra Señora de Guadalupe (festival of the Virgin of Guadalupe, patroness of Mexico; processions, music, and dancing nationwide)

Dec. 16-24: Christmas Week (week of *posadas* and piñatas; midnight mass on Christmas Eve)

Dec. 25: Navidad ("Christmas Day"; Christmas trees and gift exchange; national holiday)

Dec. 31: New Year's Eve

ACCOMMODATIONS AND FOOD

ACCOMMODATIONS

Pacific Mexico has thousands of lodgings to suit every style and pocketbook: world-class resorts, small beachside hotels, homey *casas de huéspedes* (guesthouses), palm-shaded trailer parks, and hundreds of miles of pristine camping beaches. The high seasons, when reservations are generally recommended, are from mid-December through March, during pre-Easter week, and the month of August.

The hundreds of accommodations described in this book are positive recommendations—checked out in detail—good choices, from which you can pick, according to your own taste and purse.

Guesthouses And Local Hotels
Most coastal resorts began with an old town, which expanded to a new "zona hotelera" hotel strip, where big hostelries rise along a golden strand. In the old town, near the piquant smells, sights and sounds of traditional Mexico, are the *casas de huéspedes,* where families rent out rooms around their plant-decorated patio.

Guesthouses vary, from scruffy to spic and span, and from humble to luxurious. Typically, you can expect a plain room, a shared toilet and hot-water shower and plenty of atmosphere for your money. Rates average around $10, depending upon amenities. Discounts are often available for long-term stays. *Casas de huéspedes* will rarely be near the beach, unlike many local hotels.

Locally owned and operated hotels make up the most of the recommendations of this book. Many veteran travelers find it hard to understand why people come to Mexico and spend $200 a day for a hotel room when excellent alternatives run as little as $20. Most local hotels can be phoned directly for information and reservations; and like the big resorts, many even have U.S. and Canada toll-free 800 information numbers. Always ask about money-saving packages and promotions when reserving.

Many such locally run hostelries are right on the beach, sharing the same velvety sand and golden sunsets as their much more expensive neighbors. Local hotels, which depend mostly on Mexican tourists, generally have clean, large rooms, often with private view balconies, and toilet and hot water bath or shower. What they often lack are the plush amenities—air-conditioning, cable TV, phones, tennis courts, exercise gyms, and golf courses—of the resort hotels.

Guests commonly enjoy swimming pools, even in modest Pacific Mexico lodgings.

BRUCE WHIPPERMAN

RESORT 800 NUMBERS

These hotel chains have branches at Mazatlán (MZ), Guadalajara (GD), Puerto Vallarta (PV), Manzanillo (MN), Ixtapa (IX), Acapulco (AC), Bahías de Huatulco (BH), and other Pacific Mexico locations.

(** = outstanding, * = recommended)

RESORT	PHONE NUMBER	LOCATIONS
Club Med	(800) CLUBMED	Playa Blanca, IX, BH
Club Maeva	(800) GOMAEVA	PV, MN*, BH**
Fiesta Americana	(800) FIESTA-1	GD, PV**, Los Angeles Locos*, AC*
Hilton	(800) 445-8667	PV, AC
Holiday Inn	(800) 465-4329	GD, BH
Hyatt	(800) 233-1234	GD, PV, AC*
Krystal	(800) 231-9860	PV**, IX*
Radisson	(800) 333-3333	Nuevo Vallarta, MN**, AC
Sheraton	(800) 325-3535	PV, IX*, AC, BH*
Stouffer	(800) 468-3571	IX, Oaxaca*
Westin	(800) 228-3000	MZ, PV*, IX**

Luxury Resorts

Pacific Mexico has many beautiful, well-managed international-class resorts. They spread along the pearly strands of Mazatlán, Puerto Vallarta, Manzanillo, Ixtapa, Acapulco, and Bahías de Huatulco. Their super-deluxe amenities, moreover, need not be overly expensive. During the right time of year you can vacation at many of the big-name spots—Sheraton, Westin, Stouffer, Hilton, Radisson, Hyatt, Holiday Inn—for surprisingly little. While high-season room tariffs ordinarily run $100-200, low-season (May-November, and to a lesser degree, Jan.-Feb.) packages and promotions can cut these prices significantly. Shop around for savings via your Sunday newspaper travel section, travel agents, and by calling the hotels directly through their toll-free 800 numbers.

Condominiums And Apartments

For longer stays, many Pacific Mexico vacationers prefer the economy and convenience of a condominium or apartment rental. Options vary from Spartan studios to luxurious suites with all resort amenities. Local agents in all Pacific Mexico resorts list and rent units, many of which enjoy beachfront locations for very reasonable prices. Rates can run as low as $400/month, especially during the low May-Nov. season, for a one-bedroom air-conditioned beachfront kitchenette apartment. One place to start looking is the Sunday travel section of a metropolitan daily, such as the Los Angeles *Times*. Vacation rentals might also be located through your local real estate agents, such as Century 21, who specialize in nationwide and foreign contacts. In this book , see the listing agent information for Puerto Vallarta, Bucerías, Manzanillo, and Ixtapa-Zihuatanejo.

Camping

Beach camping is common among middle-class Mexican families, especially during the Christmas-New Year week and during Semana Santa, the week before Easter.

Other times, tenters and RV campers usually find beaches uncrowded. The best spots typically have a shady palm grove for camping and a palapa (palm-thatched) restaurant that serves drinks and fresh seafood. (Heads up for falling coconuts, especially in the wind. Cost for parking and tenting is often minimal; typically only the price of food at the restaurant.

Days are often perfect for swimming, strolling, and fishing; nights are usually balmy—too warm for a sleeping bag, but fine for a hammock (which allows more air circulation than a tent). Good tents, however, keep out mosquitos and other pesties, which should be further discouraged with good bug repellent. Tents are generally warm inside, however, requiring only a sheet or very light blanket for cover.

As for camping on isolated beaches, opinions vary, from dire warnings of "bandidos" to bland assurances that all is peaceful along the coast. The truth is probably somewhere in between. Trouble is most likely to occur in the vicinity of resort towns, where a few local thugs sometimes harass isolated campers.

When scouting out a campsite, a good general rule is to arrive early enough in the day to get a feel for the place. Buy a soda at the palapa or store and take a stroll up the beach. Say "buenos dias," to the people along the way; ask if the fishing is good: "¿Pesca buena?" Use your common sense. If the people seem friendly, ask if it's *seguro* (safe). If so, ask permission: "¿Es bueno acampar aca?" ("Is it okay to camp around here?"). You'll rarely be refused.

Trailer Parks

Campers who prefer company to isolation usually stay in trailer parks. Dozens of them dot Pacific Mexico's beaches. The most luxurious have electricity, water, and sewer hookups and many amenities, including restaurants, recreation rooms, and swimming pools; the humblest are simple palm-edged lots beside the beach. Virtually all of them have good swimming, fishing, and beachcombing. Prices run to a maximum of about $14 per night, including air-conditioning power, down to a few dollars for a tent space only. Significant discounts are generally available for weekly and monthly rentals.

Palapas

Some palapas (thatched beach houses) are still rented in small coastal resorts. Amenities typically include beds or hammocks, a shady, thatched porch, cold running water, a kerosene stove, and shared toilets and showers. You usually walk right out your front door onto the sand, where surf, shells, and seabirds will be there to entertain you. (Palapa rentals are common in Barra de Nexpa, Puerto Escondido, and Zipolite.)

FOOD AND DRINK

Some travel to Pacific Mexico for the food. True Mexican food is old-fashioned, home-style fare that requires many hours of loving preparation. Such food is short on meat and long on corn,

---

MEXICAN FOOD

Tortillas y frijoles refritos: (tortillas and refried beans) cooked brown or black beans, mashed and fried in pork fat, rolled into a tortilla with a dash of vitamin-C-rich salsa (to form a near-complete combination of carbohydrate, fat, and balanced protein)

Tacos or *taquitos:* tortillas served open or wrapped around any ingredient

Enchiladas and *tostadas:* Variations on the filled-tortilla theme, except that enchiladas are usually stuffed with meat, cheese, olives, or beans and covered with sauce and baked, while tostadas are served on a crisp, open-faced tortilla.

Quesadillas: resemble tostadas, except that they're made from soft flour tortillas, rather than corn, and always contain melted cheese

Tamales: As Mexican as apple pie is American. This savory mixture of meat and sauce embedded in a shell of corn dough and baked in a wrapping of corn husks is rarely known by the singular, however. They are so yummy that one *tamal* invariably leads to more tamales.

Chiles Rellenos: Fresh roasted green chiles, stuffed usually with cheese, but sometimes fish or meat, coated with batter and fried. They provide a piquant, yummy contrast to tortillas.

Moles: (MOH-lays) Uniquely Mexican specialties. *Mole poblano,* a spicy-sweet mixture of chocolate, chiles, and a dozen other ingredients, is cooked to a smooth sauce then baked with chicken (or turkey, a combination called *mole de pavo),* so *típica* that it is widely regarded as the national dish.

Guacamole: This luscious, everywhere-available avocado-onion-tomato-lime-salsa mixture remains the delight which it must have seemed to its Aztec gourmet-inventors centuries ago.

Sopas: (soups) Usually vegetables in a savory chicken broth, an important part of both *comida* (afternoon) and *cena* (evening) Mexican meals. *Pozole,* a rich steaming stew of hominy, vegetables, and pork or chicken, often constitutes the prime evening offering of small side-street shops.

Tortas: the Mexican sandwich, with most anything good, usually hot meat and fresh tomato and avocado, stuffed between two halves of a crisp *bolillo* (boh-LEE-yoh) Mexican bun

beans, rice, tomatoes, onions, eggs, and cheese.

Mexican food is the unique end-product of thousands of years of native tradition. It is based on corn—*teocentli,* the Aztec "holy food"—called *maíz* (mah-EES) by present-day Mexicans. In the past, a Mexican woman spent much of her time grinding and preparing corn: soaking the grain in limewater (which swells the kernels and removes the tough seed-coat) and grinding the bloated seeds into meal on a stone *metate.* Finally, she would pat the meal into tortillas and cook them on a hot, baked mud griddle.

Sages (men, no doubt) have wistfully imagined that gentle pat-pat-pat of women all over Mexico to be the heartbeat of Mexico, which they feared would someday cease. Fewer women these days make tortillas by hand. The gentle pat-pat-pat has been replaced by the whir and rattle of automatic tortilla-making machines in myriad *tortillerías,* where women and girls line up for their family's daily kilo-stack of tortillas.

Tortillas are to the Mexicans as rice is to the Chinese and bread to the French. Mexican food is invariably some mixture of sauce, meat, beans, cheese, and vegetables wrapped in a tortilla, which becomes the culinary be-all: the food, the dish, and the utensil all wrapped into one. If a Mexican man has nothing to wrap in his tortilla, he will content himself by rolling a thin filling of *salsa* (chile sauce) into his lunchtime tortilla.

Hot Or Not?

Much food served in Mexico is not "Mexican." Eating habits, as most other Mexican customs, depend upon social class. Upwardly mobile Mexicans typically shun the corn-based *indígena* fare in favor of the European-style food of the Spanish colonial elite: chops, steaks, cutlets, fish, clams, omelettes, soups, pasta, rice, and potatoes.

Such fare is often as bland as Des Moines on a summer Sunday afternoon. "No picante"— not spicy—is how the Mexicans describe bland food. *Caliente,* the Spanish adjective for "hot" weather or water, does not, in contrast to English usage, also imply spicy, or *picante.*

Vegetarian Food

Strictly vegetarian cooking is rare in Mexico, as are macrobiotic restaurants, health-food stores,

and organic produce. Meat is such a delicacy for most Mexicans that they can't understand why people would give it up voluntarily. If vegetable-lovers can manage with corn, beans, cheese, eggs, *legumbres* (vegetables), and fruit and not be bothered by a bit of pork fat *(manteca de cerdo),* Mexican cooking will suit them fine.

Seafood

Early chroniclers wrote that Moctezuma employed a platoon of runners to bring fresh fish 300 miles every day to his court from the sea. In Pacific Mexico, fresh seafood is fortunately much more available from thousands of shoreline establishments, ranging from thatched beach palapas to five-star hotel restaurants.

Pacific Mexico seafood is literally there for the taking. When strolling on the beach, I have

---

CATCH OF THE DAY

Ceviche: (say-VEE-chay) A chopped raw fish appetizer that seems to be as popular on Mexico beaches as sushi is on Tokyo side streets. Although it can contain anything from conch to octopus, the best ceviche is made of diced young shark or mackerel *(tiburón* or *sierra)* fillet, plenty of fresh tomatoes, onions, garlic, and chiles, all doused with lime juice.

Pescado frito: (pays-KAH-doh FREE-toh) Fish pan-fried whole; if you don't specify that it be cooked lightly *(a medio),* the fish will arrive well done, like a big crunchy french fry.

Filete de pescado: (fish fillet) popularly fried gently with butter and garlic—*(al mojo,* "ahl-MOH-hoh")

Pescado veracruzana: A favorite everywhere: it's best with red snapper *(huachinango),* smothered in a savory tomato-onion-chile-garlic sauce. *Pargo* (snapper), *mero* (jewfish), *cabrilla* (sea bass), and others are also popularly used in this and other specialties.

Shellfish also abound: *ostiones* (oysters) and *almejas* (clams) by the dozen; plates of *langosta* and *langostina* (lobster and crayfish) *asado* (broiled), *al vapor* (steamed), or fried; and pots of fresh-boiled *camarones* (shrimp) are sold on the street by the kilo, which cafes will make into *cóctel,* or cook *en gabardinas* (breaded), at your request.

A TROVE OF FRUIT AND NUTS

Besides the usual temperate varieties, *jugerías,* and especially markets, are sources of a number of exotic (*) varieties:

anona—*anona:* greenish-pink and creamy, like a Southeast Asia custard apple

avocado—*aguacate* (ah-wah-KAH-tay): Aztec aphrodisiac

banana—*platano:* many kinds—big and small, red and yellow

chirimoya*—*chirimoya:* green scales, white pulp

coconut—*coco:* coconut "milk" is *agua coco*

grapes—*uva:* Aug.-Nov. season

guanabana*—*guanabana:* looks (but doesn't taste) like a green mango

guava—*guava:* great juice; widely available canned

lemon—*lima* (LEE-mah): uncommon and expensive, use lime instead

lime—*limón* (lee-MOHN): douse salads with it

mamey*—*mamey:* brown skin, red, puckery fruit, like persimmon

mango—*mango:* king of fruit, in a hundred varieties June-Nov.

orange—*naranja* (nah-RAHN-ha): greenish skin, but sweet and juicy

papaya—*papaya:* said to aid digestion and healing

peanuts—*cacahuates* (kah-kah-WAH-tays): home roasted and cheap

pear—*pera:* fall season

pecan—*nuez:* for a treat, try freshly ground pecan butter

pineapple—*piña:* huge, luscious, and cheap

strawberry—*fresa* (FRAY-sah): local favorite

tangerine—*mandarina:* common around Christmas

watermelon—*sandía* (sahn-DEEAH): perfect on a hot day

zapote*—*zapote* (sah-POH-tay): said to induce sleep

---

often seen well-fed, middle-class local vacationers breaking and eating oysters and mussels right off the rocks. In the summer on the beach at Puerto Vallarta, fish and squid sometimes swarm so thickly in the surf that tourists can pull them out by hand. Villagers up and down the coast use small nets (or bare hands) to retrieve a few fish for supper, while communal teams haul in big netfuls of silvery, wriggling fish for sale right on the beach.

Despite the plenty, Pacific Mexico seafood prices reflect high worldwide demand, even at the humblest seaside palapa. The freshness and variety, however, make the typical dishes seem bargains at any price.

Fruits And Juices

Squeezed vegetable and fruit juices (*jugos,* HOO-gohs), including fresh peanut and pecan butter, are among the widely available thousand delights of Pacific Mexico. Among the many establishments—restaurants, cafes, and *loncherías*—willing to supply you with your favorite *jugo,* the juice bars (*jugerías*) are often the most fun. Colorful fruit piles usually mark the

jugerías; if you don't immediately spot your favorite, ask anyway; it might be hidden in the refrigerator.

Besides your choice of pure juice, a *jugería* will often serve *liquados.* Into the juice, they whip powdered milk, your favorite flavoring, and sugar to taste for a creamy afternoon pick-me-up or evening dessert. One big favorite is a cool banana-chocolate *liquado,* which comes out tasting like a milk shake (minus the calories).

Alcoholic Drinks

The Aztecs usually sacrificed anyone caught drinking alcohol without permission. The later, more lenient, Spanish attitude toward getting *borracho* (soused) has led to a thriving Mexican renaissance of native alcoholic beverages: tequila, mescal, Kahlua, pulque, and *aguardiente.* Tequila and mescal,distilled from the fermented juice of the maguey (century) plant, originated in Oaxaca, where the best are still made. Quality tequila and mescal come 76 proof (38% alcohol) and up. A small white worm, endemic to the maguey plant, is added to each bottle of factory mescal for authenticity.

Pulque, although also made from the sap of the maguey, is locally brewed to a small alcohol content, between beer and wine. The brewing houses are sacrosanct preserves, circumscribed by traditions which exclude both women and outsiders. The brew, said to be full of nutrients, is sold to local *pulquerías* and drunk immediately. If you are ever invited into a *pulquería,* it will be an honor you cannot refuse.

Aguardiente, by contrast, is fiery Mexican "white lightning," a locally distilled, dirt-cheap ticket to oblivion, notably for poor Mexican men.

While pulque comes from age-old Indian tradition, beer is the beverage of modern mestizo Mexico. Full-bodied and tastier than "light" U.S. counterparts, Mexican beer enjoys an enviable reputation.

Those visitors who indulge usually know their favorite among the many brands, from light to dark: Superior, Corona, Pacifico, Tecate (served with lime), Carta Blanca, Modelo, Dos Equis, Bohemia, Tres Equis, and Negra Modelo.

Nochebuena, a flavorful dark brew, becomes available only around Christmas.

Mexicans have yet to develop much of a taste for *vino* (wine), although some domestic wines (such as the Baja California labels Cetto and Domecqu) are quite drinkable.

Bread And Pastries

Excellent locally baked bread is a delightful suprise to many first-time visitors to Pacific Mexico. Small bakeries everywhere put out trays of hot, crispy-crusted *bolillos* (rolls) and sweet *panes dulces* (pastries). They range from simple cakes, muffins, cookies, and donuts to fancy fruit-filled turnovers and puffs. Half the fun occurs before the eating: perusing the goodies, tongs in hand, picking out the most scrumptious. With your favorite dozen or two finally selected, you take your tray to the cashier, who deftly bags everything up and collects a few pesos (a dollar or two) for your whole mouth-watering selection.

GETTING THERE

BY AIR

From The U.S. And Canada

The vast majority of travelers reach Pacific Mexico by air. Flights are frequent and reasonably priced. Competition sometimes shaves prices down as low as $300 or less for a Mazatlán or Puerto Vallarta roundtrip from Los Angeles, Denver, or Dallas.

Travelers can save even more money by shopping around. Don't be bashful about trying for the best price. Make it clear to the airline or travel agent that you're interested in a bargain. Ask the right questions: Are there special incentive, advance-payment, night, midweek, tour-package, or charter fares? Peruse the ads in your Sunday newspaper travel section for bargain-oriented travel agencies. An agent costs you no money (although some don't like discounted tickets because their fee depends on a percentage of ticket price). But, some agents will work to get you a bargain.

Although few airlines fly directly to Pacific Mexico from the northern U.S. and Canada, many **charters** do. In locales near Vancouver, Calgary, Ottawa, Toronto, Montreal, and Minneapolis, consult a travel agent. Northern folks can also fly to San Francisco, Los Angeles, Denver, Dallas, or Houston and connect to direct flight to Pacific Mexico.

AIRLINES TO PACIFIC MEXICO FROM NORTH AMERICA

The busiest air carriers are Mexicana, Aeromexico, Delta, Alaska, American, Continental, and Canadian Holidays (charter) airlines.

Destination key: MZ = Mazatlán, PV = Puerto Vallarta, MN = Manzanillo, GD = Guadalajara, IX = Ixtapa-Zihuatanejo, AC = Acapulco, MX = Mexico City.

MEXICANA   (tel. 800-531-7121)

from Los Angeles	to MZ PV GD MN MX IX
from San Francisco	to MZ PV GD MX
from San Jose	to GD
from Tijuana	to GD
from Denver	to PV GD MX MZ
from Dallas	to PV GD
from Chicago	to PV GD AC
from Miami	to MZ

AEROMEXICO   (tel. 800-237-6639)

from Los Angeles	to MZ PV GD MN
from Tijuana	to MZ PV GD MN
from New York	to MX
from Miami	to MX
from Houston	to MX GD IX AC
from Tucson	to MZ

DELTA   (tel. 800-221-1212)

from Los Angeles	to MZ PV GD MX IX AC
from Dallas	to MX AC
from Atlanta	to MX

ALASKA   (tel. 800-426-0333)

from Seattle	to MZ PV GD
from San Francisco	to MZ PV GD
from Los Angeles	to MZ PV GD

AMERICAN   (tel. 800-433-7300)

from Dallas	to PV GD MX AC

CONTINENTAL   (tel. 800-231-0856)

from Houston	to PV GD MX AC

CANADIAN HOLIDAYS (charter)
(tel. 800-661-8881)

from Toronto	to MZ PV AC
from Vancouver	to MZ PV AC
from Calgary	to MZ PV AC

Less-frequented Pacific Mexico destinations, such as Oaxaca, Puerto Escondido, Puerto Ángel, and Bahías de Huatulco are air-accessible by connection through Mexico City.

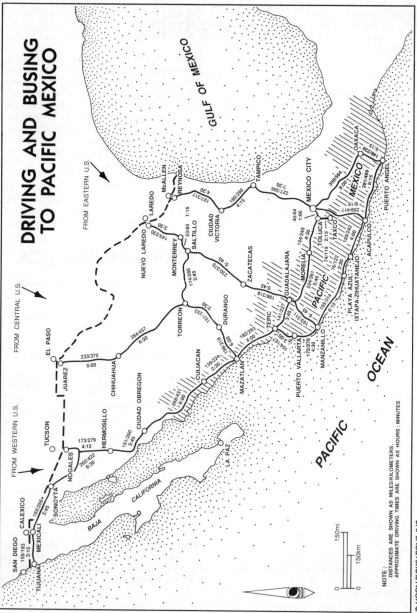

DRIVING AND BUSING TO PACIFIC MEXICO

NOTE:
DISTANCES ARE SHOWN AS MILES/KILOMETERS.
APPROXIMATE DRIVING TIMES ARE SHOWN AS HOURS : MINUTES

© MOON PUBLICATIONS, INC.

From Europe, Australasia, And Latin America

Few, if any, airlines fly across the Atlantic or Pacific directly to Mexico. Travelers from Australasia and Europe generally transfer at New York, Chicago, Dallas, San Francisco, or Los Angeles for Pacific Mexico destinations.

A number of Latin American flag carriers fly directly to Mexico City. From there, easy connections are available via Mexicana or Aeromexico Airlines to all Pacific Mexico air destinations.

BY BUS

As air travel rules in the U.S., bus travel rules in Mexico. Hundreds of sleek, first-class buses with names such as Red Arrow ("Flecha Roja"), Three Stars of Gold ("Tres Estrellas de Oro"), and White Star ("Estrella Blanca") roar out daily from the border, headed toward Pacific Mexico.

First-class bus service in Mexico is generally much cheaper and better than in the United States. Tickets for comparable trips in Mexico cost a small fraction (as little as $20 for a 1,000-mile trip, compared to perhaps $100 in the United States).

In Mexico, as on U.S. buses, you have to take it like you find it. Seat reservations, tickets, and information usually must generally be obtained in person at the bus station, and credit cards and traveler's checks are not generally accepted. There are no refunds, so don't miss the bus. On the other hand, plenty of buses roll south almost continuously.

Bus Routes To Pacific Mexico

From California and the west, cross the border to **Tijuana, Mexicali,** or **Nogales,** from where you can ride one of three bus lines to Mazatlán and points south: Tres Estrellas de Oro, Transportes del Pacifico, or Transportes Norte de Sonora. From Mazatlán, you can continue to Puerto Vallarta and Manzanillo. The trip requires approximately a full 24-hour day to Mazatlán.

From the midwest and the east cross the border from El Paso to **Juarez** and ride Estrella Blanca via Chihuahua and Durango; or cross at **Reynosa** and ride Transportes del Norte or Estrella Blanca via Monterrey and Durango to Mazatlán.

Travelers who instead want to head directly to Acapulco and the Pacific Mexico south should ride from the border directly to **Mexico City.** At the main southern Mexico City terminal (Terminal Central del Sur), you can continue south by either Flecha Roja or Estrella de Oro to Acapulco, thence Ixtapa-Zihuatanejo or Puerto Escondido-Puerto Ángel. From the U.S. border, allow two days travel for Acapulco and Zihuatanejo, and half a day more for Puerto Escondido-Puerto Ángel. (See the chart "What Buses Go Where" above for more details on Mexican bus travel.)

BY TRAIN

In contrast to airplanes and buses, the train is the leisurely, nostalgic route to Pacific Mexico. Trains roll into sleepy little stations and pass scenery far from the highway clutter and bustle. Instead of being wedged into a cramped seat, you can walk around, go to the restroom, or practice your Spanish with your aisle-mates.

Trains are not for people on a tight time budget, however. Delays are frequent; the train will sometimes stop and sit inexplicably for many minutes, then back up, and sit again before finally rolling ahead once more.

Mexican railroads are all government-subsidized, and tickets are consequently economical. A first-class coach seat runs only around $110 for a U.S. border-Mazatlán roundtrip. Second-class seating, service, and sanitation, although cheaper, are poor and dirty. Better go by bus if you're trying to save money.

The rail route of choice to Pacific Mexico is the Pacific route, which runs from Mexicali through Nogales, then south to Los Mochis, Mazatlán, Guadalajara, and Mexico City. Passengers headed for Manzanillo can transfer at Guadalajara and continue through Colima to the coast; connections are likewise available at Morelia, Michoacán, for Pátzcuaro, continuing to Lázaro Cárdenas (near Playa Azul) on the coast. Oaxaca-bound passengers can similarly transfer at Mexico City and continue through Puebla to Oaxaca. Buses connect from these points to Puerto Vallarta, Acapulco, Ixtapa-Zihuatanejo, and Puerto Ángel-Escondido.

A spectacular alternative is to ride the train south from Juarez and transfer at Chihuahua to the renowned Barranca de Cobre (Copper

Canyon) route to Los Mochis. This traverses the spectacular canyonland home of the Tarahumara people. Only finished in the early 1960s, the route hugs the labyrinthine Barranca de Cobre, a canyon so deep its climate varies from Canadian at the top to tropical jungle at the bottom.

Mexico by Rail (P.O. Box 3508, Laredo, TX 78044-3508), a private U.S.-based agency, arranges first-class rail, tour, and hotel reservations along the Mexican National Railway routes. For more information, call their toll-free number, (800) 228-3225, or local number (210) 727-3814 (Mon.-Fri. 9-5).

BY CAR OR RV

If you're adventurous and enjoy going to out-of-the-way places, or want to have all the comforts of home, you may enjoy driving your car or RV to Pacific Mexico. On the other hand, consideration of cost, risk, wear on both you and your vehicle, and the congestion hassles in towns may change your mind.

Mexican Auto Insurance
Mexico does not recognize foreign insurance. When you drive into Mexico, Mexican auto in-

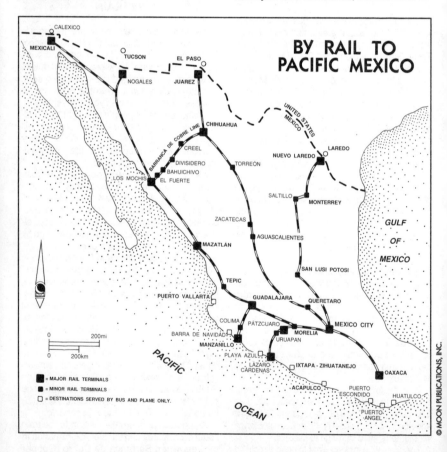

surance is at least as important as your passport. At the busier border crossings, you can get it at insurance "drive-ins" just inside the border. The many Mexican auto insurance companies (AAA and National Automobile Club agents recommend La Provincial and Tepeyac insurance, respectively) are government-regulated; their numbers keep prices and services competitive.

Sanborn's Mexico insurance, one of the best known, certainly seems to be trying hardest. One of their spokespersons, "Mexico Mike" Nelson, drives 20,000-plus miles of Mexico highway each year, gathering information for their lively consumer-oriented newsletter, books, and services (RV campground list, road map, *Travel With Health* book, *Smile-by-mile Travelog* guide to "every highway in Mexico," hotel discounts, and a trip-share listing service) available to members of "Sanborn's Mexico Club." (Contact them through their toll-free tel. 800-222-0158, or by writing Sanborn's Mexico Insurance, P.O. Box 310, McAllen, TX 78502.)

Mexican insurance runs from a bare-bones liability-only rate of about $2 a day to a more typical $8 a day for complete coverage ($50,000/$40,000/$80,000 public liability/property damage/medical payments) on a vehicle worth $10,000-15,000. On the same scale, insurance for a $50,000 RV and equipment runs about $16 a day. These daily rates decrease sharply for one-year policies, which run about $100 for the minimum to $400-$800 for complete coverage.

If you get broken glass, personal effects, and legal expenses coverage with these rates, you're lucky. Mexican policies don't usually include them.

You should get something for your money, however: the deductibles should be no more than $200-400, the liability should be about double the minimum ($25,000/$25,000/$50,000 required), and you should be guaranteed to get your car fixed in the U.S. and receive payment in U.S. dollars for losses. If not, shop around.

A Sinaloa Note Of Caution

Although bandidos no longer menace Mexican roads, be cautious in the infamous drug-growing region of Sinaloa state north of Mazatlán. Do not stray from Hwy. 15 between Culiacán and Mazatlán and Hwy. 40 from Mazatlán to Durango. Curious tourists have been assaulted in the hinterlands adjacent to these roads. (The same is true, to a lesser degree, in rural areas of Michoacán, Guerrero, and Oaxaca.)

The Green Angels

The Green Angels have answered many motoring tourists' prayers in Mexico. Bilingual teams of two, trained in auto repair and first aid, help distressed tourists along main highways. They patrol fixed stretches of road twice daily by truck. If, furthermore, you have to leave your vehicle on the roadside, don't leave it unattended. Hire a local teenager or adult to watch it for you. Un-

---

DISASTER AND RESCUE ON A MEXICAN HIGHWAY

My litany of Mexican driving experiences came to a climax when, south of Mazatlán one night, I hit a cow at 50 miles per hour head on. Poor cow. She went flying about 150 feet down the road, while I and my two friends went on an impromptu roller-coaster ride.

All was well that ended well, however. Two buses stopped and forty men got out and lifted my severely wounded van to the shoulder. Meanwhile, the cow's owner came along and carted off the remains of his property in a jeep. Then the police (a man and his wife in a VW bug) stopped. "Pobrecita camioneta" (poor little van), the woman said, as she took one look at my vehicle, which resembled an oversized, rumpled accordion. They gave us a ride to Mazatlán, found us a hotel room and made sure that we were okay.

If I hadn't had Mexican auto insurance, I would have been in deep trouble. Mexican law—based on the Napoleonic Code, which presumes guilt and does not bother with juries—would have kept me in jail until all damages were settled. The insurance agent I saw in the morning took care of everything. He called the police station (where I was dismissed from damages the next day when the cow's owner failed to show), and got my car towed to a repair shop, where they banged it into good-enough shape to drive home a week later. Bound to stay in one place, my friends and I enjoyed the most relaxed time of our entire three months on the road in Mexico. The *pobrecita camioneta*, all fixed up a few months later, lasted 14 more years.

SAFE RULES OF THE ROAD

Hundreds of thousands of tourists enjoy safe Mexican auto vacations every year. Their success is due in large part to frame of mind: drive defensively; watch everything—the side roads, the shoulders, both the car in front of you and far down the road—anticipate and adjust to danger before it happens.

Don't drive at night. Animals, sand piles, pedestrians, one-lane bridges, and drunk drivers are doubly hazardous at night.

Although speed limits are rarely enforced, don't break them. Mexican roads have many hazards. Poor markings and macho drivers who pass on curves are best faced at a speed of 40 miles per hour rather than 75.

Even with four-wheel drive, you will eventually get stuck if you do too much driving on sand. When the tide comes in, who will get your car out?

Slow down at the *topes* (speed bumps) at the edge of towns and for *vados* (dips), which may be dangerously full of water.

Yielding the courtesy of the road goes hand in hand with safe driving. Both courtesy and machismo are more infectious in Mexico; on the highway, it's much safer to spread the former than the latter.

attended vehicles on Mexican highways are quickly stricken by a mysterious disease, the main symptom of which is rapid loss of vital parts.

Mexican Gasoline
Pemex, short for Petroleos Mexicanos, the government oil monopoly, markets only two grades of gasoline: Nova (or "no va", which translates as "no go") leaded 82 octane, and 92 octane Magna Sin plomo (without lead). Magna Sin is good gas, yielding performance similar to U.S.-style "super-unleaded" gasoline. It's expensive, however, running typically about $.35 a liter (or about $1.40 a gallon.)

On main highways, Pemex makes sure that some major stations (typically spaced about 100 miles apart) stock Magna Sin. Since Mexicans typically use leaded gas, local stations, especially in outlying areas, do not stock Magna Sin.

Gas Station Thievery
Kids who hang around gas stations to wash windows are notoriously light-fingered. When stopping at the *gasolinera*, make sure that your cameras, purses, and other movable items are out of sight and reach.

Also, as you pull up to the pump, **immediately make certain that the pump reading is zeroed** before the attendant pumps the gas. Sad, but true, such overcharging for gas and oil is common, especially among teenage gas-station workers.

A Healthy Car
Preventative measures spell good health for both you and your car. Get that tune-up (or that long-delayed overhaul) *before,* rather than after you leave.

Carry a stock of spare parts, which will be probably be both more difficult to get and more expensive in Pacific Mexico than at home. Carry an extra tire or two, oil and gas filters, fan belts, spark plugs, a tune-up kit, points, and fuses. Carry basic tools and supplies, such as screwdrivers, pliers (including Vice-Grip), lug wrench and jack, adjustable wrenches, tire pump and patches, pressure gauge, steel wire, and electrical tape. For breakdowns and emergencies, carry a folding shovel, a husky rope or chain, a gasoline can, and flares. (For much more information, and entertaining anecdotes of car and RV travel in Mexico, consult Carl Franz's *The People's Guide to Mexico.* (See the "Booklist.")

Bribes *(Mordidas)*
The usual meeting ground between visitors and Mexican police is in their car on the highway or downtown street. To tourists, such encounters sometimes appear as mild harassment, accompanied by vague threats of having to go to the police station, or having their car impounded for such-and-such violation. The tourists often go on to say, "It was all right, though . . . we paid him five dollars and he went away. Mexican cops sure are crooked, aren't they?"

And, I suppose, if people want to go bribing their way through Mexico, that's their business.

But calling the Mexican cops crooked isn't exactly fair. Police, like most everyone else in Mexico, have to scratch for a living, and they have found that many tourists are willing to slip them a five-dollar bill for nothing. Rather than crooked, I would call them hungry and opportunistic.

BY FERRY

The ferry from La Paz at the tip of Baja California across to Los Mochis or Mazatlán in Pacific Mexico is a tempting option, especially for travelers without cars. If you have a car, however, you may get "bumped" by the large volume of commercial traffic (regardless of your reservation). You may end up stuck in La Paz with no way to get to the mainland except by a thousand-mile detour up the Baja Peninsula. The auto fare, moreover, is very high: a minimum of $200 to Mazatlán; about half that to Los Mochis.

Moreover, the ferry situation often changes. For numbers to call for updated information and for addresses and numbers to contact for ferry reservations, try calling Mexican tourism's information number, 800-44-MEXICO. Better still, call "Mexico Mike" Nelson (at Sanborn's Mexico Insurance, P.O. Box 310 McAllen, TX 78502, tel. 800-222-0158), who makes it his business to know about volatile ferry schedules.

TOURS AND CRUISES

Travel agents will typically have a stack of different Pacific Mexico tour and cruise brochures. The main question you should ask yourself, however, is whether you are the type who would enjoy a tour. If you get impatient standing in line, are a loner, or like acting on impulse and initiative, you probably should stay away from tours. If, on the other hand, you are shy about speaking Spanish, aren't very aggressive, enjoy being in a group, like planned vacations, or are concerned about your health, a tour or cruise may be just the thing for you.

While some tours can save you money, cruises generally are very expensive. People who like being pampered and don't mind paying for it generally have great fun on cruises. Accommodations on a typical 10-day Pacific Mexico winter cruises run as little as $200 to as much as $1,000 or more (per day per person, double occupancy).

If you want to get to know Pacific Mexico, a cruise would not be for you. On-board food and entertainment are the main events of a cruise; shore sightseeing excursions, which generally cost extra, are a sideshow.

Special Tours And Study
In Pacific Mexico

Travelers looking for an unusual tour might enjoy going along with Lorena Havens and Carl Franz, the authors of *The People's Guide to Mexico*. Their culture and crafts-oriented tours usually cover Indian areas of Oaxaca and Chiapas. Contact People's Tours of Mexico, P.O. Box 179, Acme, WA 98220.

Mayan Adventure Tours conducts tours of Zapotec and Mixtec archaeological sites and present-day crafts villages in the Valley of Oaxaca, continuing to colorful markets around Cuernavaca and Mexico City. Contact Mayan Adventure Tours, P.O. Box 15204, Wedgewood Station, Seattle, WA 98115-15204, tel. (206) 523-5309.

The American Institute for Foreign Study (AIFS) arranges academic study programs in arts, economics, history and government, psychology, language, and culture at the University of Guadalajara. Write or call for their information and catalog: AIFS, 102 Greenwich Ave., Greenwich, CT 06830, tel. (203) 869-9090.

GETTING AROUND

BY AIR

Mexicana and Aeromexico (and smaller carriers Aero California, Aeromorelos, and Aerocaribe) connect the main destinations of Pacific Mexico: Mazatlán, Puerto Vallarta, Guadalajara, Manzanillo-Barra de Navidad, Ixtapa-Zihuatanejo, Acapulco, Puerto Escondido, Puerto Ángel-Huatulco, and Oaxaca. Although much pricier than first-class bus tickets, domestic air fares are on a par with U.S. prices.

Travelers may book tickets by contacting agencies in the destination cities. (See destination chapters for airlines' local agency phone numbers.)

For planning, get the airlines' handy *itinerarios de vuelo* (flight schedules) booklets at your arrival airport counter. Flight changes, however, make a printed flight schedule simply a guide, rather than a bible.

Flying Tips

Mexican airlines have operating pecularities that result from their tight budgets: Don't miss a flight; you will lose half the ticket price. Adjusting your flight date may cost 25% of the ticket price. Get to the airport an hour ahead of time. Last-minute passengers are often "bumped" in favor of early-bird waitees. Conversely, go to the airport and get in line if you must catch a flight the airlines have claimed to be full. You might get on anyway. Keep your luggage small so you can carry it on. Lost luggage victims receive scant compensation in Mexico.

BY BUS

The first-class bus is the king of the Mexican road. Dozens of lines connect virtually every town in Pacific Mexico.

Tickets, Seating, And Baggage

Mexican bus lines do not usually publish schedules or fares. You have to ask someone (such as your hotel desk clerk) who knows, or call (or have someone call) the bus station. Few travel agents handle bus tickets. If you don't want to spend the time to get a reserved ticket yourself, hire someone trustworthy to do it for you. Another way of doing it all is to get to the bus station early enough on your traveling day to ensure that you'll get a bus to your destination.

First-class bus tickets are sold for cash and marked, usually on the back, with a specific seat number *(numero de asiento)*. If you miss the bus, you lose your money. Furthermore, airline-style computerized reservations have not yet arrived at many Mexican bus stations. You can generally buy first-class reserved tickets only at the local departure *(salida local)* station. The agent at Mazatlán, for example, cannot sell a ticket on a bus that originates from Puerto Vallarta, hundreds of miles down the road.

Request a seat number, if possible, around the middle or front *(en medio o delante de)* of the bus. The rear seats are often occupied by smokers, drunks, and general rowdies. At night, you will sleep better on the right side, away from the glare of oncoming vehicles.

Baggage is generally secure on Mexican buses. Label it, however. Overhead racks are cramped and will not usually accommodate airline-size carry-ons. Carry a small bag of your crucial items on your person; pack clothes and other less essential items in your checked luggage. For peace of mind, watch the handler put your checked baggage on the bus and watch to make sure that it is not mistakenly taken off the bus at intermediate stops.

If, somehow, your baggage gets misplaced, remain calm. Bus employees are generally competent and conscientious; if you are patient, recovering your luggage will become a matter of honor for many of them. Baggage handlers are at the bottom of the pay scale; a tip for their mostly thankless job would be very much appreciated.

On long trips, carry food, drinks, and toilet paper. Station food will sometimes be dubious and the sanitary facilities may be ill-maintained.

If you are waiting for a first-class bus at an intermediate *salida de paso* (passing station), you often have to trust to luck that there will be an empty seat. If not, your best option may be to

WHAT BUSES GO WHERE

DESTINATIONS	BUS LINES
Acapulco, Guerrero	EB EO FR
Barra de Navidad, Jalisco	TCL TEO
Colima, Colima	AO OM TEO
Guadalajara, Jalisco	AO AP EB OM TEO TP TNS
Ixtapa-Zihuatanejo, Guerrero	EB EO FR
Lázaro Cárdenas, Michoacán	EB FA FR GA TEO
Manzanillo, Colima	AO FA GA TCL TEO TNS
Mazatlán, Sinaloa	TC TEO TNS TP
Oaxaca, Oaxaca	ADO CC
Pátzcuaro, Michoacán	AO GA TEO
Pinotepa Nacional, Oaxaca	EB FR
Puerto Ángel, Oaxaca	CC EB
Puerto Escondido, Oaxaca	CC EB
Puerto Vallarta, Jalisco	TCL TEO TNS TP
Rincón de Guayabitos, Nayarit	TP
San Blas, Nayarit	EB TEO TNS
Bahías de Huatulco, Oaxaca	EB CC
Taxco, Guerrero	EO FR
Tepic, Nayarit	EB TEO TNS TP

BUS KEY

ADO	Autobuses del Oriente
AO	Autobuses del Occidente
AP	Autocamiones del Pacifico
CC	Cristóbal Colón
EB	Estrella Blanca
EO	Estrella de Oro
FA	Flecha Amarilla
FR	Flecha Roja
GA	Galeana
OM	Omnibus de Mexico
TC	Transportes Chihuahuenses
TCL	Transportes Cihuatlán
TN	Transportes del Norte
TNS	Transportes Norte de Sonora
TP	Transportes del Pacifico
TEO	Tres Estrellas de Oro

See "Getting There and Getting Away" in travel chapters for more detailed bus information. See also "Second-class Buses" below.

ride a (usually much more frequent) second-class bus.

Second-class Buses

Second-class bus seating is unreserved. In some parts of Pacific Mexico, there are lower classes of buses than second class, but given the condition of many second-class buses, it usually seems that third-class buses wouldn't run at all. Second-class buses are the stuff of travelers' legends: the recycled old GMC, Ford and Dodge schoolbuses that stop everywhere and carry everyone and everything to the smallest villages tucked away in the far mountains. As long as there is any kind of a road to it, such a bus will most likely go there.

Now and then you'll read a newspaper story of a country bus that went over a cliff somewhere in Mexico, killing the driver and a dozen unfortunate souls. The same newspapers, however, never bother to mention the half-million safe passengers trips that same bus probably provided during the 15 years prior to the accident.

Second-class buses are not for travelers with week knees or stomachs. Half the time you will have to start off standing cramped among a crowd of *campesinos*. They are warmhearted but poor people, so don't tempt them with open, dangling purses or wallets bulging in back pockets. Stow your money safely away. After a while, you will probably be able to sit down. Such a privilege comes with obligation, however, such as holding an old lady's bulging bag of carrots or a toddler on your lap. But if you accept your burden with humor and equanimity, who knows what favors and blessings may flow to you in return.

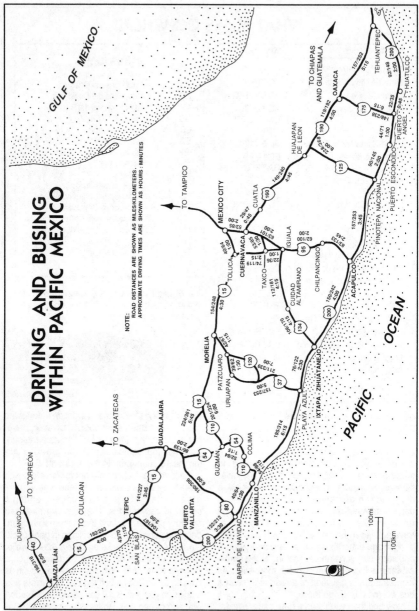

DRIVING AND BUSING
WITHIN PACIFIC MEXICO

NOTE:
ROAD DISTANCES ARE SHOWN AS MILES/KILOMETERS;
APPROXIMATE DRIVING TIMES ARE SHOWN AS HOURS : MINUTES

GULF OF MEXICO

PACIFIC OCEAN

© MOON PUBLICATIONS, INC.

ROAD SIGNS

STOP

RAILROAD CROSSING

YIELD RIGHT OF WAY

ONE WAY

TWO WAY

PARKING

NO PARKING

DIP (across arroyo)

DIP (across arroyo)

BUS STOP

KEEP TO THE RIGHT

BY TRAIN OR CAR

Although trains connect several points in Pacific Mexico, they are slow and the routes circuitous. And even if you decide on a train option, you often will have to take long bus rides to make connections to get to the places where the train doesn't go. Better take the bus in the first place.

Driving your car in Mexico may or may not be for you. See "By Car or RV" in the "Getting There" section above.

BY RENTAL CAR, TAXI, AND HITCHHIKING

Car rentals are an increasingly popular transportation option in Pacific Mexico. They offer mobility and independence for local sightseeing and beach excursions. In the resorts, the gang's all there: Hertz, National, Avis, Budget, and a host of local outfits. They generally require drivers to have a valid driver's license and passport, a major credit card, and may require a minimum age of 25. Some local companies do not accept credit cards, but offer lower rates in return.

Base prices of international agencies, such as Hertz, National, and Avis, are not cheap. They cost more than in the U.S., with a 10% "value added" tax tacked on. The cheapest possible rental car, usually a stick-shift VW Beetle, runs $30 per day or $180 per week and up, depending on location and season. Prices increase during post-Christmas and Carnaval (especially in Mazatlán).

Car insurance (medical, property damage, and public liability) is a must with your rental car. If you get into an accident without insurance, you will be in deep trouble, probably jail. Driving in Mexico is more hazardous than back home. For many hints, including insurance requirements, see "By Car or RV" in "Getting There" above.

Taxis

The high prices of rental cars make taxis a viable option in Pacific Mexico. Cars are luxuries, not necessities, for Mexican families. Visitors might profit from the Mexican money-saving practice of piling everyone in a taxi for Sunday park, beach and fishing outings. You may find that an all-day taxi and driver (who, besides relieving you of driving, will become your impromptu guide) will cost less than a rental car.

The magic Mexican word for saving money by taxi is *colectivo:* a taxi you share jointly with other travelers. Your first place to practice getting a taxi will be at the airport, where *colectivo* tickets are routinely sold from booths at the terminal door.

If, however, you want your own private taxi, ask for a *taxi especial,* which will probably run about three or four times the individual tariff for a *colectivo.*

Your airport experience will prepare you for in-town taxis. Pacific Mexico taxis rarely have meters, so you must establish the price before getting in. Bargaining is expected in Mexico, so don't shrink from it, even though it seems a hassle. If you get into any taxi without an agreed-upon price, you are letting yourself in for a more serious, potentially nasty hassle later. If your driver's price is too high, he'll probably come to his senses as soon as you hail another taxi.

After a few days getting taxis around town will be a cinch. You'll find that you don't have to take the high-ticket taxis lined up in your hotel driveway. If the price isn't right, walk toward the street and hail a regular taxi.

In town, if you can't seem to find a taxi, it may be because they are all hanging around waiting for riders at the local stand, called a taxi *sitio.* Ask someone to direct you to it: Say: "Excúseme. ¡Donde está el sitio taxi, por favor?" ("Excuse me. Where is the taxi stand, please?)

Hitchhiking

Most everyone agrees that hitchhiking is not the safest mode of transport. If you're unsure, don't do it. Hitchhiking doesn't make a healthy steady travel diet, nor should you hitchhike at night. The recipe for trouble-free hitchhiking requires equal measures of luck, savvy, and technique. The best places to catch rides are where people are arriving and leaving anyway, such as bus stops, highway intersections, gas stations, RV parks, and on the highway out of town.

Male-female hitchhiking partnerships seem to net the most rides (although it is technically illegal for women to ride in commercial trucks). The more gear you and your partner have, the fewer rides you will get. Pickup and flatbed truck owners often pick up passengers for pay. Before hopping onto the truck bed, ask how much the ride will cost.

OTHER PRACTICALITIES

TOURIST CARDS AND VISAS

For U.S. and Canadian citizens, entry by air into Mexico for a few weeks could hardly be easier. Airline attendants pass out tourist cards on the plane and an officer makes them official by glancing at passports and stamping the cards at the immigration gate.

Otherwise, Mexican consulates, Mexican government tourist offices, offices of airlines serving Mexico, border immigration authorities, auto clubs (AAA and National Auto Club), and certain travel agencies issue free tourist cards to all travelers 15 years old or over who present proper identification. Rules state that U.S. citizens must show either birth certificate, valid U.S. passport, or military I.D., while naturalized citizens must show naturalization papers or valid U.S. passport.

Canadian citizens must show a valid passport or birth certificate. Nationals of other countries may be subject to different regulations; they should check with their local Mexican tourist information office or consulate for the details.

More Options

For more complicated cases, get your tourist card early enough to allow you to consider the options: Tourist cards can be issued for multiple entries and a maximum validity of 180 days; photos are often required. If you don't request multiple entry or the maximum time, your card will probably be stamped single entry, valid for some shorter period, such as 90 days. If you are not sure how long you'll stay in Mexico, request the maximum and bring passport photos. (One hundred eighty days is the absolute maximum for a tourist card; long-term foreign residents routinely make semiannual "border runs" for new tourist cards.)

Student And Business Visas

A visa is a notation stamped and signed into your passport showing the number of days and entries allowable for your trip. Apply for visas at the consulate nearest your home well in advance of your departure. One year renewable

student visas are available (often with considerable red tape). Check with you local Mexican consulate for details; an ordinary 180-day tourist card may be the easist option, if you can manage it.

Your Passport

Your passport (or birth or naturalization certificate) is your positive proof of national identity; without it, your status in any foreign country is in doubt. Don't leave home without one. United States citizens may obtain passports at local post offices.

Don't Lose Your Tourist Card

If you do, present your passport at the police station and get an official police report detailing your loss. Take the report to the nearest federal *oficina de turismo* (in major Pacific Mexico vacation centers) and ask for a duplicate tourist card. (Savvy travelers carry copies of their tourist cards with them, while leaving the originals safe in their hotel room.)

Car Permits

If you drive to Mexico, you will need a permit for your car. Show proof of ownership (state title certificate, or a notarized bill of sale), current license plates, and a current driver's license at the border. **The fee is $10, payable only by Mastercard, Visa, or American Express credit cards.** (The credit-card-only requirement discourages those who sell or abandon U.S.-registered cars in Mexico without paying customs duties.)

The resulting car permit becomes part of the owner's tourist card and receives the same length of validity. Cars being purchased under finance contracts must be accompanied by a notarized written permission from the finance company. Vehicles registered in the name of an organization or other person must be accompanied by a notarized affidavit authorizing the driver to use the car in Mexico for a specific time.

Accessories, such as a small trailer, boat less than six feet, CB radio, or outboard motor may be noted on the car permit and must leave Mexico with the car.

MEXICAN INFORMATION OFFICES AND CONSULATES

In North America

For simple questions and Mexico information brochures, call Mexican tourist information in the U.S. and Canada toll-free (800) 44-MEXICO. The U.S. has dozens of Mexican government tourist information offices and consulates. Consulates generally handle questions of Mexican nationals in the U.S., while tourist information offices service tourists heading for Mexico. Your home location and need determines which you should contact. Consult your closest regional Mexican **tourist information office** for guidance:

Los Angeles: 10100 Santa Monica Blvd., Suite 224, Los Angeles CA 90067, tel. (310) 203-8191

Houston: 2707 N. Loop W., Suite 450, Houston, TX 77008, tel. (713) 880-5153

Chicago: 70 E. Lake St., Suite 1413, Chicago, IL 60601, tel. (312) 565-2786

Miami: 128 Audubon Ave., Coral Gables, FL 33134, tel. (305) 443-9160

Washington: 1911 Pennsylvania Ave. NW, Washington, DC 20006, tel. (202) 728-1750

New York: 405 Park Ave. 10th floor, New York, NY 10022, tel. (212) 421-6655

In Canada, contact the tourist information offices in:

Montreal: 1 Place Ville-Marie, Suite 1526, Montreal, PQ H3B 2B5, tel. (514) 871-1052

Toronto: 2 Bloor St. W., Suite 1801, Toronto, ON M4W 3E2, tel. (416) 925-0704

In Europe And Japan

Mexico also maintains tourist information offices in Europe:

London: 7 Cork St., London W1X1PB, tel. (441) 734-1058

Frankfurt: Weisenhüttenplatz 26, 6000 Frankfurt-am-Main 1, tel. (4969) 25-3441

Paris: 4 rue Notre-Dame-des Victoires, 75002 Paris, tel. (331) 40-2734

Madrid: Calle de Velázquez 126, Madrid 28006, tel. (341) 561-3120

Rome: Via Barberini 3, 00187 Rome, tel. (396) 474-2986

Mexico's Japan tourist information office is in:

Tokyo: 2-15-2 Nagata-cho, Chiyoda-ku, Tokyo 100, tel. (813) 580-2961

The owner cannot leave the country without the car unless he or she gets permission from local customs authorities, usually the *aduana*, (customs house) or the *oficina federal de hacienda* (federal treasury office.) For local details, see "Immigration and Customs" sections in the destination chapters below.

Separate motorized vehicles carried or towed (motorcycles, another car, a boat) by your car may require their own separate permits, subject to the same rules as automobiles.

Since Mexico does not recognize foreign automobile insurance, you must purchase Mexican automobile insurance. (For more information on this and other details of driving in Mexico, see "Getting Around.") Also see "Sports and Recreation," about Mexican fishing and hunting licenses.

Entry For Children

Children under 15 can be included on their parents' tourist card, but complications occur if the children (by reason of illness, for example) cannot leave Mexico with both parents. Parents can avoid such possible red tape by getting a passport and a Mexican tourist card for each of their children.

In addition to a passport or birth certificate,

minors (under age 18) entering Mexico without parents or legal guardians must present a notarized letter of permission signed by both parents or legal guardians. Even if accompanied by one parent, a notarized letter from the other must be presented. Divorce or death certificates must also be presented, when applicable.

Pacific Mexico travelers should hurdle all such possible delays far ahead of time in the cool calm of their local Mexican consulate rather than the hot, hurried atmosphere of a border or airport immigration station.

Pets

A pile of red tape stalls the entry of many dogs, cats, and other pets into Mexico. Veterinary health and rabies certificates are required to be stamped by a Mexican consul responsible for a specific foreign zone (such as Texas, or southern California, for example). Contact your closest Mexican Tourist Information Office for assistance. (See the chart "Mexican Information Offices and Consulates" above.)

MONEY

Traveler's checks, besides being refundable, are widely accepted in Pacific Mexico. Before you leave, purchase enough of a well-known brand, such as American Express or Visa, of U.S. dollar traveler's checks to cover your Mexico expenses. (Canadian traveler's checks and currency are not widely accepted; European and Asian even less so.) Unless you like signing your name or paying lots of per-check commissions, buy denominations of US$50 or more.

The Peso: Down And Up

Overnight in early 1993, the Mexican government shifted its monetary decimal point three places and created the "new" peso worth about three per U.S. dollar. (Although they still accept the "old" 3,000-per-dollar peso bills, they won't forever, so exchange them without delay.) Also, since the corresponding old and new notes resemble each other, pay heed when you receive change. **Note:** Because of the recent rapid inflation of the peso, all prices in this book are given in U.S. dollars.

Since the new peso has acquired respectable value, the centavo (one-hundredth new peso),

now appears in coins of five, 10, 20, and 50 centavos. (Incidentally, in Mexico the dollar sign, "$," also marks Mexican pesos.) New peso bills, in denominations of one, two, five, 10, 20, and 100 pesos are common. Banks like to exchange your traveler's checks for a few crisp large bills, rather than the often-tattered smaller denominations, which are much more useful for everyday purchases. (A 100-peso note, while common at the bank, looks awfully big to a small shopkeeper, who might be hard-pressed to change it.) Ask the bank teller who changes your traveler's checks to break at least one of those big peso bills into a handful of five- or 10-peso notes.

Mexican Banks are traditionally open Mon.-Fri. 9 a.m.-1:30 p.m. (although money exchange services may be shorter than this). Some banks, notably the Banco Nacional de Mexico (Banamex), are opening longer hours and staffing special after-hours money exhange windows in resort centers. Banamex traditionally posts the dollar exchange rate in the lobby like this: *Tipo de cambio: venta 3.154, compra 3.202,* which means that they will sell pesos to you at the rate of 3.154 per dollar, and inversely buy them back from anyone else for 3.202 per dollar. All of which means that you get 315.40 pesos for each of your $100 traveler's checks.

You don't necessarily have to go to the trouble of changing your money at a bank. Merchants, hotels, and restaurants also change money, usually at much less favorable rates, however. Consequently, money-exchange lines (on Monday mornings especially) at Banamex are often long. In such cases, look for a less-crowded (such as Bancomer, Banco Serfin, and Banco Confia) bank around the corner. Small money-exchange offices *(casas de cambio)* are the most convenient, offering long hours and faster service for a pittance (sometimes as little as 25 pennies on $100) more than the banks.

Credit cards, such as Visa, MasterCard, and to a lesser extent, American Express, are widely honored in the hotels, restaurants, craft shops, and boutiques that cater to foreign tourists. You will generally get better bargains, however, in shops that depend on local trade and do not so readily accept credit cards. Such shops sometimes offer discounts for cash sales.

Whatever the circumstance, your travel money will usually go much farther in Pacific Mexico than back home. Despite the national

BRUCE WHIPPERMAN

Pottery making is a time-honored Pacific Mexico pastime. Here a potter of Comala, near Mazatlán, works in his family shop.

10% ("value added" IVA) sales tax, local lodging, food, and transportation prices will often seem like bargains compared to the developed world. Outside of the pricey high-rise beachfront strips, pleasant, palmy hotels often run $30 or less.

Bargaining

Bargaining will stretch your money even farther. It comes with the territory in Mexico and needn't be a hassle. If done with humor and moderation, bargaining can be an enjoyable path to encountering Mexican people and gaining their respect, even friendship. The local crafts market is where bargaining is most intense. For starters, try offering half the asking price. From there on, it's all psychology: content yourself with not having to have the item. (Otherwise, you're sunk; the vendor will probably sense your need and stand fast.) After a few minutes of good-humored bantering, ask for *el último precio* (the final price); if it's close, you may have a bargain.

Keeping Your Money Safe

In Pacific Mexico, as everywhere, thieves circulate among the tourists. Keep valuables in your hotel *caja de seguridad* (security box). If you don't particularly like the desk clerk, carry what you cannot afford to lose in a money belt.

Pickpockets love crowded markets, buses, terminals, and airports, where they can slip a wallet out of a back pocket or dangling purse in a wink. Guard against this by carrying your wallet in your front pocket, and your purse, waist pouch, and daypack (which thieves can go so far as to slit open) on your front side.

Don't attract crooks; don't display wads of money or flashy jewelry. Don't get drunk; if so, you may become a pushover for a sober, determined thief.

Don't leave valuables untended on the beach; share security duties with some of your trustworthy-looking neighbors, or leave a bag with a shopkeeper nearby.

Tipping

Without their droves of foreign visitors, Mexican people would be even poorer. Devaluation of the peso, while it makes prices low for visitors, makes it rough for Mexican families to get by. The help at your hotel typically gets paid only a few dollars a day. They depend on tips to make the difference between dire and bearable poverty. For good service, tip 15%. Give your chambermaid *(camarista)* and floor attendant a couple of new pesos every day or two. And whenever uncertain of what to tip, it will probably mean a lot to someone, maybe a whole family, if you err on the generous side.

In restaurants and bars, Mexican tipping customs are similar to U.S. and Europe: tip waiters, waitresses and bartenders about 15% for satisfactory service.

COMMUNICATIONS

Telephone

In resort cities and larger towns, direct long-distance dialing is the rule—from hotels, public phone booths, and efficient private telephone offices. Since the Mexican government imposes heavy taxes on international calls, generally the most economical way to call home is **collect** (dial 09 for the English-speaking international operator.)

For **station-to-station** calls to the U.S. and Canada, dial 95 plus the area code and the local number. For other international calls, see the directions in the local Mexican telephone directory.

In smaller towns, long-distance phoning is done in the *larga distancia* (local phone office). Typically staffed by a young woman and often connected to a cafe, the *larga distancia* often becomes an informal community social center as people pass the time waiting for their connections to arrive.

To call Mexico direct from the U.S., first dial 011, then 52, followed by the area code and local number. Consult your local telephone directory or operator for more details.

Post And Telegraph

Mexican *correos* (post offices) operate similarly to their counterparts all over the world. Mail services include *lista de correos* (general delivery; address letters "a/c lista de correos,") *servicios filatelicas* (philatelic services), *por avión* (airmail), *giros* (money orders), and Mexpost fast delivery service.

Telegrafos (telegraph offices), usually near the post office, send and receive *telegramas* (telegrams) and money orders *(giros)*. *Telecommunicaciones,* the shiny high-tech telegraph offices, add telephone and public fax to the available services.

Electricity And Time

Mexican electric power is supplied at U.S.-standard 110-volts, 60-cycles. Plugs and sockets are generally two-pronged, non-polar, like the old pre-1970s U.S. plugs and sockets. Bring adaptors for your appliances with two-pronged polar or three-pronged plugs. (Hint: A two-pronged "polar" plug has different prongs, one of which is generally too large to plug into an old-fashioned non-polar socket.)

Pacific Mexico operates on **Central Time** except for the states of Sinaloa and Nayarit, which operate on Mountain Time.

STAYING HEALTHY

In Pacific Mexico, as everywhere, prevention is the best remedy for illness. For those visitors who confine their travel to the beaten path, a

---

MEDICAL TAGS AND AIR EVACUATION

Travelers with special medical problems might consider wearing a medical identification tag. For a reasonable fee, Medic Alert (P.O. Box 1009, Turlock CA 95381, tel. 800-344-3226) provides such tags, coupled with an information hot line that will provide doctors with your vital medical background information.

For life-threatening emergencies, Critical Air Medicine (Montgomery Field, 4141 Kearny Villa Road, San Diego CA 92123, tel. 619-571-0482; from the U.S. toll-free 800-247-8326, from Mexico 24 hours toll-free 95-800-010-0268) furnishes high-tech jet ambulance service from any Mexican locale to the United States. For a fee running typically around $20,000, they promise to come and fly you to the right U.S. hospital in a hurry.

---

few basic common sense precautions will ensure vacation enjoyment.

Resist the temptation to dive headlong into Mexico. It's no wonder that some people get sick—broiling in the sun, gobbling peppery food, downing beer and margaritas, then discoing half the night—all in their first 24 hours. Instead, they should give their bodies time to adjust.

Travelers often arrive tired and dehydrated from travel and heat. During the first few days, they should drink plenty of bottled water and juice and take siestas.

Traveler's Diarrhea

Traveler's diarrhea (known in Southeast Asia as "Bali Belly" and in Mexico as "Turista," or "Moctezuma's Revenge") persists even among prudent vacationers. You can even suffer turista for a week after simply traveling from California to New York. Doctors say that the familiar symptoms of runny bowels, nausea, and sour stomach result from normal local bacterial strains to which newcomers' systems need time to adjust. Unfortunately, the dehdydration and fatigue from heat and travel reduce your body's natural defenses and sometimes lead to a persistent cycle of sickness at a time when you least want it.

Time-tested protective measures can help your body either prevent or break this cycle. Many doctors and veteran travelers swear by

Pepto-Bismol for soothing sore stomachs and stopping diarrhea. Acidophilus (yogurt bacteria), widely available in the U.S. in tablets, aids digestion. Warm chamomile (*manzanilla*) tea, used widely in Mexico (and by Peter Rabbit's mother), provides liquid and calms upset stomachs. Temporarily avoid coffee and alchohol, drink plenty of *manzanilla* tea, and eat bananas and rice for a few meals until your tummy can take regular food.

Although powerful antibiotics and antidiarrhea medications such as Lomotil and Imodium are readily available over *farmacia* counters, they may involve serious side effects and should not be taken in the absence of solid medical advice. If in doubt, see a doctor.

Sunburn

For sunburn protection, use a good sunscreen with a sun protection factor (SPF) of 10 or 15 or more, which will reduce burning rays to one-tenth or one-fifteenth or less of direct sun. Better still, take a shady siesta-break from the sun during the most hazardous three or four midday hours. If you do get burned, however, use a moisturizing lotion (or maybe one of the "-caine" creams for numbing the pain) for healing.

Safe Water And Food

Although municipalities have made great strides in sanitation, food and water are still major potential sources of germs in Pacific Mexico. Do not drink Mexican tap water. Drink bottled water only. Hotels, whose success depends vitally on their customers' health, generally provide purified bottled water (*agua purificada*). If, for any reason, water is doubtful, add Halazone water purification tablets (*hidroclonazone* in Mexico) or a few drops of household chlorine bleach (*blanqueador*) or iodine (*yodo* from the *farmacia*) per quart.

Pure bottled water, soft drinks, beer, and pure fruit juices are so widely available that it is easy to avoid tap water, especially in restaurants. Ice and *paletas* (iced juice-on-a-stick) can be risky, especially in small towns.

Washing hands before eating in a restaurant is a time-honored Mexican ritual, which visitors should religiously follow. The humblest Mexican eatery will generally provide a basin for washing hands (*lavar los manos*). If it doesn't, don't eat there.

Hot, cooked food is generally safe, as are peeled fruits and vegetables. Milk and cheese these days in Mexico are generally processed under sanitary conditions and sold pasteurized (ask: "¿pasteurizado?") and are typically safe. Mexican ice cream used to be both bad tasting and of dubious safety, but national brands available in supermarkets are so much improved that it's no longer necessary to resist ice cream in resort towns.

Salad lovers must eat with caution, however. In restaurants, you'd best avoid lettuce and cabbage unless you're sure they've been washed with purified water. If you must have a fresh salad, tomatoes, carrots, cucumbers, onions, and green peppers doused in vinegar or lime juice entail less risk. (The safest raw Mexican vegetables are those you buy, wash, and peel yourself.)

Medications And Immunizations

A good physician can recommend the proper preventatives for your Pacific Mexico trip. If you are going to stay pretty much in town, your doctor will probably suggest little more than updating your basic typhoid, diphtheria-tetanus, and polio shots.

For camping or trekking in remote tropical areas—below 4,000 feet or 1,200 meters—of Pacific Mexico, doctors recommend a gamma-globulin shot against hepatitis A and a schedule of chloroquine pills against malaria. In order to discourage mosquitoes (and fleas, blackflies, ticks, no-see-ums, and other tropical pesties) from biting you in the first place, use pure DEET (N,N diethylmetatoluamide—"jungle juice") mixed 1:1 with rubbing (70% isopropyl) alcohol. (100% DEET, although super-effective, dries and irritates skin.)

If You Get Hurt

While snorkeling or surfing, you may get an occasional coral scratch or jellyfish sting. Experts advise that you should wash the afflicted area with ocean (not fresh) water and pour alcohol (rubbing alcohol or tequila), if available, over the wound, then apply hydrocortisone cream from your first-aid kit or the *farmacia*.

Sea Creatures, Scorpions, And Snakes

Injuries from sea urchin spines and stingray barbs are both painful and sometimes serious. Physicians recommend similar first aid for both:

First remove the spines or barbs manually or with tweezers, then soak the injury in hot-as-possible fresh water to weaken the toxins and provide relief. Get medical help immediately.

While camping or staying in a thatched palapa or other "rustic" accommodation, watch for scorpions, especially in your shoes (whose contents you should dump out every morning). Scorpion stings and snakebites are rarely fatal to an adult, but are potentially very serious to a child. Get the victim to a doctor calmly but quickly.

First-aid Kit
In the tropics, ordinary cuts and insect bites are much more prone to infection and should receive immediate first aid. A first-aid kit (with a minimum of: aspirin, rubbing alcohol, hydrogen peroxide, Halazone tablets or bleach for water, swabs, Band-Aids, gauze, adhesive tape, an Ace bandage, chamomile, Pepto-Bismol, acidophilus tablets, antibiotic ointment, hydrocortisone cream, mosquito repellent, a knife, and tweezers) is a good precaution for any traveler and a top priority for campers.

Medical Care
For medical advice and treatment, let your hotel (or if you're camping, the closest *farmacia)* refer you to a good doctor, clinic, or hospital. Mexican doctors, especially in medium-size and small towns, practice like private doctors in the U.S. and Canada once did before health insurance, liability, and group practice. They will come to you if you request; they often keep their doors open even after regular hours, and charge very reasonable fees.

You will receive generally good treatment at one of the many good local hospitals in Pacific Mexico's tourist centers. See individual destination chapters for details. For many more useful details of health and safety in Mexico, consult Dr. William Forgey's *Mexico, A Guide to Health and Safety* (Merrillville, Indiana: ICS Books, 1991), or Dr. Dirk Schroeder's *Staying Healthy in Asia, Africa, and Latin America* (Chico, California: Moon Publications, Inc., 1993).

CONDUCT AND CUSTOMS

Safe Conduct
Mexico is an old-fashioned country where people value traditional ideals of honesty, fidelity, and piety. Crime rates are low; visitors are often safer in Mexico than in their home cities.

Even though three generations have elapsed since Pancho Villa raided the U.S. border, the image of a Mexico bristling with *bandidos* persists, nevertheless. And similarly for Mexicans: despite the century and a half since the *yanquis* invaded Mexico City and took half their country, the communal Mexican psyche still views *gringos* (and, by association all white foreigners) with revulsion, jealousy, and wonder.

Fortunately, the Mexican love-hate affair with foreigners in general does not necessarily apply to individual visitors. Your friendly "buenos dias" or "por favor," when appropriate, is always appreciated, whether in the market, the gas station, or the hotel. The shy smile you will most likely receive in return will be your small, but not insignificant, reward.

Women
Your own behavior, despite low crime statistics, largely determines your safety in Mexico. For women traveling solo, it is important to realize that the double sexual standard is alive and well in Mexico. Dress and behave modestly and you will most likely avoid embarrassment. Whenever possible, stay in the company of friends or acquaintances; find companions for beach, sightseeing, and shopping excursions. Ignore strange men's solicitations and overtures. A Mexican man on the prowl will invent the sappiest romantic overtures to snare a *gringa*. He will often interpret anything except silence or a firm "no" as a "maybe," and a "maybe" as a "yes."

Men
For male visitors, on the other hand, alcohol often leads to trouble. Avoid bars and cantinas, and if (given Mexico's excellent beers) you can't abstain completely, at least maintain soft-spoken self-control in the face of challenges from macho drunks.

The Law And Police
While Mexican authorities are tolerant of alcohol, they are decidedly intolerant of other substances such as marijuana, psychedelics, cocaine, and heroin. Getting caught with such drugs in Mexico usually leads to swift and severe results.

MACHISMO

I once met a man in Acapulco who wore five gold wristwatches and became angry when I quietly refused his repeated insistences that I get drunk with him. Another time on the beach near San Blas, two drunk *campesinos* nearly attacked me because I was helping my girlfriend cook a picnic dinner; a third time near Taxco I nervously sat for an hour behind a bus driver who insisted on speeding down the middle of the two-lane highway, honking aside oncoming automobiles.

Despite their wide differences (the first was a rich criollo, the *campesinos* were *indígenas,* and the bus driver, mestizo), their common affliction was **machismo,** a habit that possesses most Mexican men: a sometimes reckless obsession to prove their masculinity, to show how macho they are.

Men of many nationalities (Japan's *bushido* samurai code is but one extremely macho example) share the instinct to prove themselves. Mexican men, however, often seem to try the hardest.

Male visitors, when confronted by a Mexican braggart, should (unless they themselves are trying to prove something) be careful and controlled. If your opponent is yelling at you, be polite, cool, and soft-spoken; try to withdraw as soon as possible. On the highway, be courteous and unprovocative; don't try to use your car to spar with a macho driver.

Drinking often leads to problems. It's best to stay out of bars or cantinas, unless you are prepared to deal with the consequences. Polite refusal of a drink may be taken as a challenge by your macho bar-stool neighbor. If you go to a bar with Mexican friends or acquaintances, be warned that you may be heading for a no-win choice of either a drunken all-night *borrachera* (binge) or insulting your friends' honor by refusing.

Machismo's flip side requires extreme femininity for women. In Mexico, women's liberation is long in coming. Few women hold positions of power in business or politics. (One woman, Rosa Luz Alegría, did attain the rank of Minister of Tourism during the former Portillo administration; she was the president's mistress.)

Machismo requires that female visitors obey the rules or suffer the consequences. Keep a low profile; wear bathing suits and brief shorts only at the beach. Follow the example of your Mexican sisters: make a habit of going out (especially at night) in the company of friends or acquaintances. Mexican men believe that an unaccompanied woman, regardless of what she says, wants to be picked up. Ignore such offers; any response, even refusal, might even be taken as a "maybe."

If, on the other hand, there is a Mexican man whom you would genuinely like to meet, the traditional way is to arrange an introduction through family or friends. (Mexican families, as a source of protection and friendship, should not be overlooked—especially on the beach or in the park, where, among the gaggle of kids, grandparents, aunts and cousins, there is often room for one more.)

Equally swift is the punishment for nude sunbathing, which is both illegal in public and offensive to Mexicans. Confine your nudist colony to very private locations.

Traffic **police** in Pacific Mexico's resorts watch foreign cars with eagle eyes. Officers seem to inhabit busy intersections and one-way streets, waiting for confused tourists to make a wrong move. If they whistle you over, stop immediately or you really will get into hot water. If guilty, say "lo siento" (I'm sorry), and be cooperative. Although he probably won't mention it, the officer is usually hoping that you'll cough up a $20 *mordida* (bribe) for the privilege of driving away.

Don't do it. Although he may hint at confiscating your car, calmly ask for an official *boleto* (written traffic ticket, if you're guilty) in exchange for your driver's license (have a copy), which the officer will probably keep if he writes a ticket. If no money appears after a few minutes, the officer will most likely give you back your driver's license rather than go to the trouble of writing the ticket. If not, the worst that will usually happen is that you will have to go to the *palacio municipal* (city hall) the next morning and pay the $20 to a clerk in exchange for your driver's license.

Pedestrian Hazards
Although Pacific Mexico's many pavement and sidewalk holes won't land you in jail, one of them might send you to the hospital if you don't watch your step, especially at night. "Pedestrian beware" is doubly good advice on Mexican streets (where it is rumored that some drivers speed up rather than slow down when they spot

a tourist stepping off the curb). Falling coconuts, especially frequent on windy days, constitute additional hazards to unwary campers and beachgoers.

Cars can get you both in and out of trouble in Mexico. Driving Mexican roads, where slow carts block lanes, *campesinos* stroll the shoulders, and cattle wander at will, is hazardous, and doubly so at night.

SPECIALTY TRAVEL

Bringing The Kids

Children are treasured like gifts from heaven in Mexico. Traveling with your kids (or your neighbors' if you don't have any to bring) will ensure your welcome most everywhere. On the beach, make sure they are protected from the sun. Children often adjust slowly to Mexican food. (Eggs, cheese, *hamburguesas,* milk, oatmeal, corn flakes, bananas, cakes, and cookies are always available, however.

A sick child is no fun for anyone. Fortunately, excellent doctors and clinics are available even in small towns. When in need, ask a storekeeper or a pharmacist, "¿Donde hay doctor, por favor?" (DOHN-day eye doc-TOHR por fah-VOHR?). In most cases within five minutes you will be in the waiting room of the local hospital or clinic. For more details on traveling with children, see Maureen Wheeler's excellent *Traveling With Children* (Lonely Planet Publications).

Travel For The Handicapped

Mexican airlines and hotels are becoming increasingly aware of the needs of handicapped travelers. Open, street-level lobbies, large, wheelchair-accessible elevators and rooms are available in many Pacific Mexico resort hotels.

Certain organizations both encourage and provide information about handicapped travel. Contact the **Society for the Advancement of Travel for the Handicapped** at 347 Fifth Ave., Suite 610, New York NY 10016, tel. (212) 447-7284; also **Mobility International USA,** P.O. Box 3351, Eugene, Oregon 97403, tel. (503) 343-1284. You can also consult the excellent book, *Traveling Like Everybody Else,* by Jacqueline Freedman and Susan Gerstein.

Travel For Senior Citizens

Age, according to Mark Twain, is a question of mind over matter: If you don't mind, it doesn't matter. Mexico is a country where whole extended families, from babies to great-grandparents, still live together. Elderly travelers will generally benefit from the resulting respect and understanding that Mexicans accord to older people. Besides these encouragements, consider the number of retirees already in havens in many Pacific Mexico towns. A number of organizations, furthermore, support senior travel. For more information, contact **Elderhostel,** 80 Boylston St., Suite 400, Boston, MA 02116, tel. (617) 426-7788. Additionally, the **American Association of Retired Persons (AARP),** in cooperation with American Express, arranges cruises and tours that cater to senior needs. Contact the AARP Travel Experience, P.O. Box 37580, Louisville, KY 40233-7580, toll-free tel. (800) 745-4567.

WHAT TO TAKE

For evening wear, one of Pacific Mexico's classiest hotels suggests that "men wear pants, ladies be beautiful," reflecting the very casual dress styles common in tropical Mexico. Men can gracefully do with only slacks and sportshirts; women, with simple skirts and blouses.

Loose-fitting, hand-washable, easy-to-dry clothes make for troublefree tropical vacationing. Synthetic, or cotton-synthetic blend shirts, blouses, pants, socks, and underwear will fit the bill everywhere in coastal Pacific Mexico. For breezy nights, bring a lightweight windbreaker. If you're going to the highlands (Guadalajara, Pátzcuaro, Taxco, Oaxaca), add a medium-weight jacket.

In all cases, leave showy, expensive clothes and jewelry at home. Stow items that you cannot lose in your hotel safe or carry them with you in a sturdy zippered purse or waist pouch on your front side.

Packing

What you pack depends on how mobile you want to be. If you're staying the whole time at a self-contained resort, you can take the two suitcases and one carry-on that airlines generally allow. If you're going to be moving around a lot, best condense everything down to one easily carryable bag that doubles as luggage and a soft backpack. Experienced travelers routinely accomplish this by packing prudently and tightly, choosing items which will do double- or triple-duty (such as a Swiss army knife, for example.)

Campers will have to be super-careful to accomplish this. Fortunately, camping along the tropical coast requires no sleeping bag. Simply use a hammock (buy it in Mexico) or a sleeping pad and a sheet for cover. In the winter, at most, you may have to buy a light blanket. A compact tent, which you and your partner can share, is a must against bugs, as is mosquito repellent. Additionally, a first-aid kit is absolutely neccessary.

PACKING CHECKLIST

Necessary (*) And Useful Items For Everyone
* keys, tickets
* traveler's checks, money checkbook, credit cards
* tourist card, visa
  passport
  vaccination certificate
* purse, waist-belt carrying pouch
* guidebook, reading books
  address book
* swimsuit
* clothes, hat
* windbreaker
* toothbrush, toothpaste
  dental floss
* prescription medicines and drugs
  first-aid kit
* mosquito repellent
  birth control
* prescription eyeglasses, contact lenses

razor
earplugs
* comb
* sunglasses,
* sunscreen
  flashlight, batteries
* inexpensive watch, clock
* camera, film (expensive in Mexico)
  lightweight binoculars
  travel booklight
  immersion heater

For Campers
* single-burner stove with fuel
* water purifying tablets or iodine
* first-aid kit
* insect repellent
* Swiss army knife
* Sierra Club cup, fork, and spoon
  plastic plate
  hot pad

* matches in waterproof case
* two nesting cooking pots
* wire grate for barbecuing fish
* potscrubber-sponge
* dish soap
  dish cloths
  instant coffee, tea, sugar, powdered milk
  short candles
* towel, soap
* lightweight tent
* hammock (buy in Mexico)
* tarp
* nylon cord
* sheet or light blanket
* toilet paper
* plastic bottle, quart
* collapsible gallon plastic bottle
  poncho
* lightweight hiking shoes
  moleskin (Dr. Scholl's)
  compass
  whistle

BOB RACE

MAZATLÁN

INTRODUCTION

The Pearl Of The Pacific

Mazatlán (pop. 500,000) spreads for 15 sun-splashed miles along a thumb of land that extends southward into the Pacific just below the Tropic of Cancer. Mazatlán thus marks the beginning of the Mexican tropics: a palmy land of perpetual summer, refuge from winter cold for growing numbers of international vacationers.

Mazatlán's beauty is renowned. Sprinkled by islands beckoning offshore from miles of golden beaches and blue lagoons, it aptly deserves its title as "Pearl of the Pacific."

Despite its popularity as a tourist destination, Mazatlán owes its existence to local industry. As well as being a leading manufacturing center in the state of Sinaloa, Mazatlán is home port for a huge commercial and sportfishing fleet, whose annual catch of shrimp, tuna, and swordfish amounts to thousands of tons.

Mazatlán, consequently, lives independently of tourism. The vacationers come and frolic on the beach beside their "Golden Zone" hotels, while in the old town at the tip of the peninsula,

life goes on in the old-Mexico style: in the markets, the churches, and the shady plazas scattered throughout the traditional neighborhoods.

HISTORY

Pre-Columbian

For Mexico, Mazatlán is not an *old* city. Most of its public buildings have stood for less than a hundred years. Evidence of local human settlement dates back before history, however. Scientists reckon that petroglyphs found on offshore islands may be as much as 10,000 years old.

During the 1930s archaeologists began uncovering exquisite polychrome pottery, with elaborate black and red designs, indicative of a high culture. Unlike their renowned Tarascan, Aztec, and Toltec highland neighbors, those ancient potters, known as the Totorames, built no pyramids and left no inscriptions. They had been gone a dozen generations before conquistador

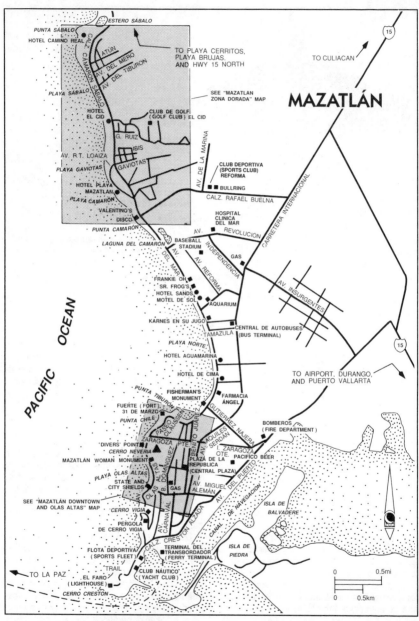

hieroglyph of
Mazatlán ("Place of
the Deer")

Nuño de Guzmán burned his way through
Sinaloa in 1531.

Colonial

The rapacious Guzmán may have been responsible for the name "Mazatlán," which, curiously, is a name of Nahuatl (Aztec language),
rather than local, origin. Since Aztecs rarely
ventured anywhere near present-day Mazatlán,
the name Mazatlán ("Place of the Deer"), presents an intriguing mystery. Historians speculate that a Nahuatl-speaking interpreter with
Guzmán may have translated the name from
the local language.

Mazatlán was first mentioned in 1602 as the
name of a small village, San Juan Bautista de
Mazatlán (now called Villa Union), 30 miles
south of present-day Mazatlán, which was un-
settled at the time.

English and French pirates soon discovered
Mazatlán's benefits, however. They occasionally used its hill-screened harbor as a lair from
which to pounce upon the rich galleons that
plied the coast. The colonial government replied
by establishing a small *presidio* on the harbor
and watchtowers atop the *cerros*. Although the
pirates were gone by 1800, legends persist of
troves of stolen silver and gold buried in hidden
caves and under windswept sands, ripe for
chance discovery along the Mazatlán coast.

Independence

Lifting of foreign trade restrictions in 1820 and Independence in 1821 seemed to bode well for the
port of Mazatlán. Cholera, yellow fever, and
plague epidemics, however, and repeated foreign occupations (the U.S. Navy in 1847, the

French in 1864, and the British in 1871), slowed
the growth of Mazatlán during the 19th century.
It nevertheless served as the capital of Sinaloa
from 1859 to 1873, with a population of several
thousands.

The "Order and Progress" of dictator-Presi-
dent Porfirio Diaz (1876-1910) gave Mazatlán
citizens a much-needed spell of prosperity. The
railroad arrived, the port and lighthouse were
modernized, and the cathedral was finished.
Education, journalism, and the arts blossomed.
The Teatro Rubio, completed in the early 1890s,
was the grandest opera house between Baja
California and Tepic.

The opera company of the renowned diva,
Ángela Peralta, the "Mexican Nightingale," arrived and gave a number of enthusiastically received recitals in Mazatlán in August 1883. Trag-
ically, Peralta and most of her company fell victim to a disastrous yellow fever epidemic, which
claimed more than 2,500 Mazatlán lives.

The revolution of 1910-17 literally rained down
destruction on Mazatlán. In 1914, the city gained
the dubious distinction of being the second city
in the world to suffer aerial bombardment.
(Tripoli, Libya, was the first.) General (later President) Venustiano Carranza, intent upon taking
the city, ordered a biplane to bomb the ammunition magazine atop Nevería Hill, adjacent to
downtown Mazatlán. But the pilot missed the
target and dropped the crude leather-wrapped
package of dynamite and nails onto the city
streets instead. Two citizens were killed and
several wounded.

Modern Mazatlán

After order was restored in the 1920s, Mazatlán
soared to a decade of prosperity, followed by the
deflation and depression of the 1930s. Recovery
after World War II, however, led to port im-
provements and new highways, setting the stage
for the tourist "discovery" of Mazatlán during
the 1960s and 1970s. The city limits expanded to include the strand of white sand (Playa
Norte) north of the original old port town. High-
rise hotels sprouted in a new "Golden Zone"
tourist area, which, coupled with Mazatlán's traditional fishing industry, provided thousands of
new jobs for an increasingly affluent population, which, by the early '90s, was climbing past
half a million.

ÁNGELA PERALTA

ERIC SCHNITGER

Diva Ángela Peralta (1845-83) was thrilling audiences in Europe's great opera houses by the age of 16, when a Spanish newpaperman dubbed her the "Mexican Nightingale." On May 13, 1863, she brought down the house at La Scala in Milan with an angelic performance of *Lucia de Lammermoor*.

During Peralta's second European tour she charmed maestro Guiseppi Verdi into bringing his entire company across the Atlantic so she could sing *Aida* in Mexico City. With Verdi conducting, Peralta inaugurated the 1873 Mexico City season on a pinnacle of fame.

Legends abound of the fiercely nationalistic Peralta. She once got the last word in a *tête á tête* with Europe's most famous Italian soprano of the time. In an unforgettable joint recital, Peralta courteously extended first bows to the haughty Italian diva, who remarked of her own performance, "that is the way we sing in Italy." Not to be outdone, Peralta rejoined: "Mine was the way we sing in heaven."

Not content with mere performance, Ángela Peralta went on to excel as a composer, librettist, and impresario, organizing her own opera companies. Her success and outspoken ways earned her enemies in high places, however. In 1873, Mexico City bluebloods were shocked to find out that she was having an affair with her lawyer, Julian Montiel y Duarte. (It didn't seem to matter that Peralta was widowed and Montiel was single at the time.) Much of Mexico City's high society boycotted her performances; when that didn't work, they sent hecklers to harass her. Liberals, however, defended her, and Peralta finally regained her audience in the early 1880s with a heartrending performance of *Linda de Chamounix*. She kept her vow, however, to never sing again in Mexico City.

Her star-crossed life came to an early end on August 30, 1883. Touring with her company in western Mexico, a Mazatlán yellow fever epidemic claimed her life and the lives of 76 (of 80) of her company. On her deathbed, she married Montiel y Duarte, the only man she ever loved. Her remains were removed to Mexico City in 1837, where they now lie enshrined at the Rotunda de Hombres Ilustres (Rotunda of Illustrious Men).

SIGHTS

Getting Oriented

Mazatlán owes its life to the sea. The city's main artery, which changes its name five times as it winds northward, never strays far from the shore. From beneath the rugged perch of **El Faro** lighthouse at the tip of the Mazatlán peninsula, the *malecón* (seawall) boulevard curves past the venerable hotels and sidewalk cafes of the **Olas Altas** ("High Waves") neighborhood. From there it snakes along a succession of rocky points and sandy beaches, continuing through the glitzy lineup of **Zona Dorada** ("Golden Zone") beach hotels and restaurants. After that, the hotels thin out as the boulevard continues miles northward, past grassy dunes and old coconut groves to a sheltered cove beneath **Punta Cerritos** hill, 15 miles from where it started.

Getting Around

A welter of little local buses run to and fro along identical main-artery routes. From the downtown central plaza they head along the *malecón*, continuing north through the Zona Dorada to various north-end destinations, scrawled on the windshields. Fares should run from about $.10 to $.30.

Small open-air taxis, called *pulmonías*, seating two or three passengers, provide quicker and more convenient service. The average *pulmonía* (pneumonia, directly translated) ride should total no more than a dollar or two. Agree on the price before you sit down, and if you think it's too high, hail another *pulmonía* and your driver will usually come to his senses. The same rules apply to taxi rides, which run about double the price of *pulmonías*.

A Walk Around Old Mazatlán

Let the towering double spire of the **Catedral Basílica de la Purísima Concepción** guide you to the very center of old Mazatlán. Begun by the Bishop Pedro Loza y Pardave in 1856, the cathedral was built on the filled lagoon-site of an original Indian temple. Mazatlán's turbulent history delayed its completion until 1899 and final elevation in 1937 to the status of a basílica.

Inside, the image of the city's patron-saint, the Vírgen de la Purísima Concepción ("Virgin of the Immaculate Conception") stands above the gilded, baroque main altar, beneath soaring, rounded Renaissance domes and pious, pointed gothic arches. On the left, as you exit, pause and notice the shrine to the popular **Virgin of Guadalupe.** (The cathedral is open daily 6 a.m.-1 p.m and 4-8 p.m.)

In front of the cathedral, the verdant tropical foliage of the central **Plaza de la Republica** encloses the traditional wrought-iron Porfirian bandstand. To the right is the **Palacio Municipal** (city hall) where on the eve before Independence Day, September 16, the *presidente municipal* (county mayor) shouts the traditional "Grito de Dolores" from the balcony above a patriotic, tipsy crowd.

After enjoying the sights and aromas of the colorful **Mercado Central** (central market) two blocks behind the cathedral, reverse your path and head down Juarez. Turn right at Constitución, one block to **Plazuela Machado,** Mazatlán's original central plaza. It was named in honor of Juan Nepomuceno Machado, a founding father of Filipino descent who donated the land. The venerable Porfirian buildings and monuments clustered along the surrounding streets include the **Teatro Ángela Peralta,** completed around 1890 and later dedicated to Ángela Peralta. At the west end of the Plazuela, along Calle Heriberto Frías, walk beneath the **Portales de Cannobio,** the arcade of the old estate house of apple grower Luis Cannobio, a 19th-century Italian resident.

Olas Altas

Continue west a few blocks toward the ocean from Plazuela Machado along Calle Sixto Osuna and step into the small **Museo Arqueologia** (Sixto de Osuna 76, tel. 853-502, open Tues.-Sun. 10 a.m.-1 p.m. and 4-6 p.m.) to peruse its well-organized exhibits outlining Sinaloan prehistory and culture. The displays include case after case of petroglyphs, human and animal figurines, and the distinctive red- and black-glazed ancient polychrome pottery of Sinaloa.

Continue west a couple of blocks to the *malecón* and **Av. Olas Altas.** This cafe-lined stretch of boulevard and adjacent beach was at one time *the* tourist zone of Mazatlán. It extends several shorefront blocks from the **Monumento al Venado** ("Monument to the Deer," north end, past La Siesta Hotel) to the **Escudos de Sinaloa y Mazatlán** ("Sinaloa State and Mazatlán City Shields") in front of the distinguished 1889 school building at the foot of Cerro Vigia, the steep hill to the south.

BRUCE WHIPPERMAN

Children play beneath the Monument to the Mazatlán Woman.

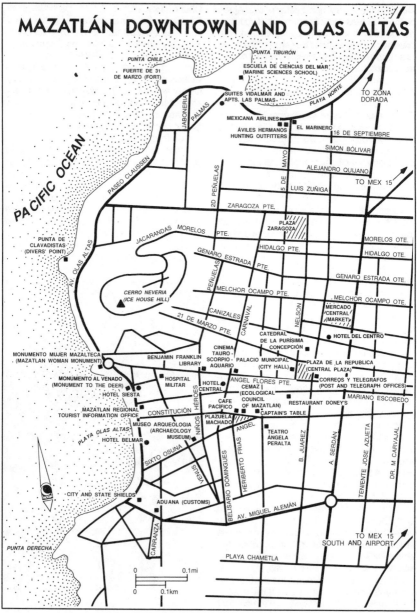

MAZATLÁN DOWNTOWN AND OLAS ALTAS

PUNTA CHILE
PUNTA TIBURÓN
FUERTE DE 31 DE MARZO (FORT)
ESCUELA DE CIENCIAS DEL MAR (MARINE SCIENCES SCHOOL)

JABONERIA
PALMAS

SUITES VIDALMAR AND APTS. LAS PALMAS
PLAYA NORTE
TO ZONA DORADA

MEXICANA AIRLINES
EL MARINERO
16 DE SEPTIEMBRE
ÁVILES HERMANOS HUNTING OUTFITTERS
SIMON BÓLIVAR

PASEO CLAUSSEN

5 DE MAYO
ALEJANDRO QUIJANO
TO MEX 15
LUIS ZUÑIGA

PACIFIC OCEAN

2D PEÑUELAS
ZARAGOZA PTE.

PLAZA ZARAGOZA

JACARANDAS
MORELOS PTE.
HIDALGO PTE.
MORELOS OTE.
HIDALGO OTE.

PUNTA DE CLAVADISTAS (DIVERS' POINT)

AV. OLAS ALTAS

GENARO ESTRADA PTE.

PEÑUELAS

GENARO ESTRADA OTE.

MELCHOR OCAMPO PTE.
MELCHOR OCAMPO OTE.

CERRO NEVERIA (ICE HOUSE HILL)

CANIZALES
21 DE MARZO PTE.

CARNAVAL

NELSON

MERCADO CENTRAL (MARKET)

CATEDRAL DE LA PURÍSIMA CONCEPCIÓN
HOTEL DEL CENTRO

MONUMENTO MUJER MAZALTECA (MAZATLAN WOMAN MONUMENT)

CINEMA TAURO - SCORPIO - AQUARIO

BENJAMIN FRANKLIN LIBRARY

PALACIO MUNICIPAL (CITY HALL)

PLAZA DE LA REPUBLICA (CENTRAL PLAZA)

MONUMENTO AL VENADO (MONUMENT TO THE DEER)

HOSPITAL MILITAR

HOTEL CENTRAL

ANGEL FLORES PTE.

CORREOS Y TELEGRAFOS (POST AND TELEGRAPH OFFICES)

HOTEL SIESTA

CEMAZ (ECOLOGICAL COUNCIL OF MAZATLAN)

MARIANO ESCOBEDO

CAFE PACIFICO

RESTAURANT DONEY'S

MAZATLAN REGIONAL TOURIST INFORMATION OFFICE

CONSTITUCIÓN

CAPTAIN'S TABLE

PLAYA OLAS ALTAS

MUSEO ARQUEOLOGIA (ARCHAEOLOGY MUSEUM)

PLAZUELA MACHADO

ANGEL

TEATRO ÁNGELA PERALTA

HOTEL BELMAR

SIXTO OSUNA

NIÑOS HEROES

HERIBERTO FRIAS

B. JUAREZ

A. SERDÁN

TENIENTE JOSE AZUETA

DR. M CARVAJAL

CITY AND STATE SHIELDS

VENUS

BELISARIO DOMINGUES

ADUANA (CUSTOMS)

CARRANZA

AV. MIGUEL ALEMÁN

PUNTA DERECHA

TO MEX 15 SOUTH AND AIRPORT

PLAYA CHAMETLA

0   0.1mi
0   0.1km

© MOON PUBLICATIONS, INC.

Cerro Vigia

Now, unless, you're in the mood for a hike, bargain for a *pulmonía* to take you up **Paseo Centenario,** the southern extension of Av. Olas Altas, to the **Pergola de Cerro Vigia** viewpoint at the top of the hill. There, next to the old cannon (stamped by its proud London maker, "Vavaseur no. 830, 1875") you get the sweep of the whole city.

To the south rises Mazatlán's tallest hill, **Cerro Creston,** topped by the **El Faro** lighthouse, whose 515-foot (157-meter) elevation qualifies it as the world's highest natural lighthouse. Along the jetty-landfill that connects Cerro Creston to the mainland lie the docks and anchored boats of the several **flotas deportivas** (sport fleets). Every morning they take loads of tourists out in search of big fighting marlin and sailfish.

Across the deep-water harbor entrance looms the bulk of **Isla de la Piedra** ("Stone Island"), actually a peninsula. Its southern beach stretches to the horizon in a narrowing white thread, beneath the dark green plumes of Mexico's third-largest coconut grove.

Cerro Vigia is the spot where, according to tradition, the colonial soldiers of the old Mazatlán presidio maintained their 200-year vigil, scanning the horizon for pirates. Step across the little hilltop plaza and down to the **Cafe El Mirador** and enjoy lunch, a drink, and the view; open daily noon-9 p.m.

Turning north, you'll see the rounded profile of **Cerro Nevería** ("Icehouse Hill") rising above above the patchwork of city streets. Its unique label originated during the mid-1800s, when the tunnels that pock the hill served for storage of ice imported from San Francisco. Now the hilltop holds a number of radio and microwave beacons.

The curving white ribbon of sand north of the downtown area traces the *malecón* northward to **Punta Camarón** and the Golden Zone, marked by the cluster of shoreline high-rise hotels.

From Cerro Vigia, the three islands—**Chivos** ("Rams") and **Venados** ("Deer"), appearing together, and **Pájaros** ("Birds") near the horizon—seem to float offshore, like a trio of sleeping whales.

Along Paseo Claussen

Back downhill on Av. Olas Altas, pass the Statue of the Deer in the middle of the intersection where the *malecón* becomes Paseo Claussen. Named for the rich German immigrant who financed the blasting of the scenic drive, Paseo Claussen continues around the wave-tossed foot of Cerro Nevería. First, you will pass a striking bronze sculpture, the **Monumento Mujer Mazalteca,** nearly erotic in its intensity. Nearby, a yawning cave (plugged by heavy bars), pierces the hill. Known by local people as the **Caverna del Diablo** ("Devil's Cave"), it served as an escape route for soldiers guarding the ammunition stored in caves farther up the hill.

Not far ahead, a four-story platform at the **Punta de Clavadistas** ("Divers' Point") towers above the wave-swept tide pools. The divers—(professionals, who take their work very seriously, especially at low tide, when their dives must coincide with the arrival of a big swell)—perform a number of times daily, more frequently on Sundays and holidays.

Continue on past the old fort, **Fuerte 31 de Marzo** (now a maritime office), named in honor of the heroic stand of the local garrison, which repelled a French invasion on March 31, 1864. The fort was built in 1892 to deter such attacks on Mazatlán.

BEACHES

Olas Altas To Punta Camarón

Exploration of Mazatlán's beaches can start at Av. Olas Altas, where narrow **Playa Olas Altas** offers some water sports opportunities. The strip is wide and clean enough for wading, sunning, bodysurfing, and boogieboarding. Swimmers take care: the waves often break suddenly and recede strongly. Locally popular intermediate surfing breaks angle shoreward along the north end. Bring your own equipment, since there's rarely any for rent on this largely locals-only beach.

For fly- and bait-casting—although the beach surf is too murky to catch much of interest—casts from the rocks on either end may yield rewards worth the effort.

Continuing around Paseo Claussen, past the fort, you'll come to a wave-tossed cove adjacent to the modern Ciencias del Mar (Marine Sciences) college. Although the narrow strand here is suitable for no more than wading, the rocks provide good casting spots, and the left-

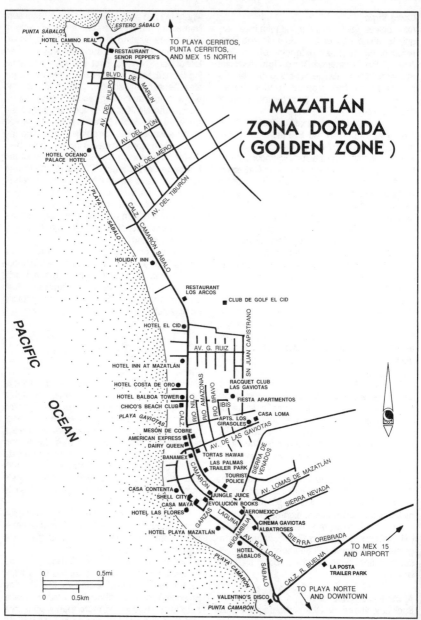

MAZATLÁN ZONA DORADA (GOLDEN ZONE)

breaking swells challenge beginning and intermediate surfers.

Next comes the small boat cove, where **Playa Norte** begins. Unfortunately, the first one-mile stretch is too polluted for much more than strolling (due to the waste from the fleet of fishing *lanchas*) along the beach.

A mile farther north, however, beginning around the oafish-looking **Monumento al Pescador** ("Fisherman's Monument"), where Paseo Claussen becomes Av. del Mar, a relatively wide, clean white strand extends for three miles. This stretch is popular with local families and is uncrowded except during holidays. On calm days the waves break gently and gradually; other times they can be rough. If so, stick by a lifeguard if you see one.

Beginning and intermediate surfers congregate at the north end of this beach, on both flanks of **Punta Camarón** (marked by Valentino's disco), where the swells break gradually left. For fisherfolk, the rocks on the point provide good spots for casting.

Zona Dorada Beaches

At Punta Camarán, Av. del Mar becomes Calzado Camarón Sábalo, which winds northward through the clutter of Zona Dorada streetside eateries, crafts shops, travel agencies, and banks.

The way to enjoy and understand the Zona Dorada is not on the boulevard, but on the beach a few blocks away. The lineup of successful high-rise hotels immediately north of Punta Camarón testifies to the beauty of **Playa Camarón** and **Playa Gaviotas.** These shining strands—with oft-gentle, rolling waves, crystal sand, and glowing, island-silhouetted sunsets—give meaning to the label "Golden Zone": golden memories for visitors and gold in the pockets of the Mazatlán folks lucky enough to own or work in the Zona Dorada. (Sometimes it seems as if half the town *is* trying to work there. During the low-season months of September and October, beach-front crafts and food vendors often outnumber the sunbathers.)

Although the Playas Camarón and Gaviotas are often lumped together, the beaches themselves contrast sharply. Playa Camarón, the more southerly, is narrow and steep, with coarse, yellow sand. Its waves often break suddenly and recede strongly. At such times, body-

Playa Gaviotas, where visitors enjoy some of Pacific Mexico's softest, silkiest sand, curves past the Hotel Cid tower in the background.

surfing on Playa Camarón is a thrilling, but potentially hazardous, pastime.

Despite the popularity of this strip, small shells, such as lovely rust-brown-mottled little clams, and mother-of-pearl, are sometimes plentiful.

About 500 yards north of the point, near the Las Flores Hotel, Playa Camarón becomes Playa Gaviotas. There, the beach changes to Playa Gaviotas' silky smooth sand and lazy slope. Waves usually roll in gently and always for a long distance. They are not good for surfing, since they head straight into the beach and tend to break all at once along a long front, rather than angling left or right.

After about another quarter mile (at around Hotel El Cid), Playa Gaviotas becomes its identically lovely northward extension, **Playa Sábalo,** which stretches another mile to Punta Sábalo at the Hotel Camino Real.

Past the rocks of Punta Sábalo, the waters of the shallow, serene **Estero Sábalo** tidal lagoon ebb through a narrow, creek-like channel. The lagoon itself is clean, shallow, and round as a full moon, with a sandy beach on one side, perfect for toddlers' water games. Automobiles can access this spot via a driveway from the beach boulevard, there called Calz. Sábalo Cerritos.

Northern Beaches

The strand north of Punta Sábalo, called **Playa Cerritos,** begins to look like a wild beach along its largely undeveloped northern stretch. Grass sways atop the dunes, flocks of sandpipers probe the wave-washed sand, pelicans and frigate birds glide overhead, and shells and driftwood accumulate.

At the northern end of Playa Cerritos, just south of the hill that marks Punta Cerritos, the beach becomes **Playa Brujas** (for the *brujas,* female witch doctors, who used to perform their rituals there). If you're thirsty or hungry by the time you've gone this far, a seafood restaurant at the end of the beach will gladly accommodate you.

On the other side of Punta Cerritos, two more seafood restaurants perch at the very end of the beach boulevard. On the left, a rocky, tidepool-shelf juts out into the waves, forming a protected cove. This, some say, is the best **fishing** spot in Mazatlán. It appears so; half a dozen *lanchas* are usually pulled up on the rocky beach, while offshore, one or two divers hunt for oysters in the clear, calm waters.

Hikes

The best hike in Mazatlán leads right along the beach. Just walk any of your favorite stretches. You could do the whole thing (or just part of it) starting anywhere—Olas Altas, Playa Norte, Playa Gaviotas—and walk as far north (to avoid having the sun in your eyes) as you want. Other than a hat and sunscreen, you won't have to carry anything along; beach restaurants and stores along the way will provide the goodies. Neither will you have to walk back; just grab the bus or a *pulmonía* back to town whenever you decide you've walked enough.

Another good hike leads to the summit of **Cerro Creston** and provides a close, interesting look at **El Faro** lighthouse. The trail begins at the foot of the hill, at the end of the pavement past the *flotas deportivas* (sportfishing fleet) docks. Wear a hat, and take some insect repellent, water, and maybe food for a breezy summit picnic.

Follow the initially wide track as it zigzags up the hill. Sometimes overhung by vines, leafy trees, and gnarled cacti, the trail narrows to a rocky path about halfway to the summit. Nearing the top, you wind your way beside rocky outcroppings until you come to the fence around the lighthouse. If your group is small, the keeper may let you in for a look around and to sign his book. He claims the lighthouse is 400 years old.

If you arrive around dusk (bring a flashlight), you will see the beacon in action. The dazzling 1.5-million-watt beacon rotates gradually, like the spokes of a heavenly chariot, with several brilliant wheeling pencils of light focused by the great antique Fresnel lens atop the tower.

PRACTICALITIES

ACCOMMODATIONS

You can nearly predict the room price of a hotel by its position on a Mazatlán map. The farther north, away from the old downtown, the newer and more expensive it's likely to be.

Downtown Hotels

At one time, all Mazatlán hotels were downtown. The plush new hotels and condos on the Playa Norte-Zona Dorada luxury beach strip have drawn away practically all the high-ticket vacationers, leaving the old Olas Altas tourist zone to a few old-timers, a handful of budget travelers seeking the charms of traditional Mexico, and Mexican families on holiday outings. The exception to this is the week after Christmas, the week before Easter, and, most of all, Carnaval (Mardi Gras, in late Feb. or March), when Olas Altas is awash with merrymakers.

The popular **Hotel Siesta** is tops for enjoying the flavor of the Olas Altas neighborhood. For balcony views of Carnaval, or lovely sunsets

---

MAZATLÁN HOTELS

Mazatlán hotels, in order of increasing approximate double-room price. (area code 69, postal code 82000, unless otherwise noted)

DOWNTOWN AND OLAS ALTAS

Hotel del Centro, Canizales 18, 812-673, $18

Hotel Siesta, Av. Olas Altas 11, 812-640, $20

Hotel Belmar, Av. Olas Altas 166, 851-111, $20

Hotel Central, Calle Belisario Dominguez 2 Sur, 821-888, $24

Suites Vidalmar and Apts. Las Palmas, Calle Las Palmas 15, 812-190, $26

PLAYA NORTE

Hotel Sands, Av. del Mar 1910 (P.O. Box 309), 820-000, $27

Motel del Sol, Av. del Mar s/n (P.O. Box 400), 851-103 $33

Hotel de Cima, Av. del Mar s/n (P.O. Box 350), 827-300, $50

Hotel Aguamarina, Av. del Mar 110 (P.O. Box 301), 817-080, (800) 528-1234, $52

ZONA DORADA

Fiesta Apartmentos, Calle Ibis 502, postal code 82110, 835-355, $15

Hotel Tropicana, Av. R.T. Loaiza 27, (P.O. Box 501), postal code 82110, 838-000, $25

Racquet Club Las Gaviotas, Calle Ibis at Bravo (P.O. Box 173), 835-939, $30

Apts. Girasoles, Av. Gaviotas 709, postal code 82110, 835-288, $30

Holiday Bungalows, Calz. Sábalo Cerritos s/n (P.O. Boxes 682 and 202), postal code 82110, 832-578, $33

Casa Contenta, Av. R.T. Loaiza s/n, 834-976, $44

Hotel Las Flores, Av. R.T. Loaiza 212 (P.O. Box 583), 835-011, $60

Hotel Playa Mazatlán, Av. R.T. Loaiza 202 (P.O. Box 207), postal code 82110, 834-444, $64

Hotel Inn at Mazatlán, Calz. Camarón Sábalo 6291 (P.O. Box 1292), postal code 82110 835-500, $58

Hotel El Cid, Calz. Camarón Sábalo s/n (P.O. Box 813), 833-333, $100

any time of the year, reserve one of the several oceanfront rooms. Added bonuses include the classy, Revolutionary-decor La Cantina piano bar. Best of all, however, is the inner patio, decorated by the colorful umbrellas of the El Shrimp Bucket restaurant and shaded by ancient, leafy trees festooned with hanging air-roots. A combo plays traditional Latin melodies on the patio (weather permitting) most nights till around 11 p.m. At Av. Olas Altas 11, Mazatlán, Sinaloa 82000, tel. (69) 812-640, (69) 812-334; 57 rooms with TV, a/c, and phones. From about $20 d, somewhat higher during holidays, credit cards accepted.

A few blocks away stands the venerable six-story oceanfront **Hotel Belmar,** faded but still welcoming the long-timers who remember when it was *the* hotel in Mazatlán. Although now a bit tattered, its old amenities remain: pool, sidewalk restaurant, and many ocean-view rooms, some carpeted and modern (and some so old and makeshift that they're quaint). Located at Av. Olas Altas 166, Mazatlán, Sinaloa 82000, tel. (69) 851-111; 200 rooms, with a/c, phones and parking, from about $20 d, credit cards accepted.

About a half mile north, where Paseo Claussen bends around Cerro Nevería, a big sign on the hill above the Ciencias del Mar (Marine Sciences) college marks **Suites Vidalmar.** The modern stucco apartment complex clusters artfully above a blue designer swimming pool with a sweeping view of the nearby rocky bay and northward-curving shoreline. Ten one-bedroom suites—all spacious, tastefully furnished, with kitchenettes—can accommodate four in two double beds. One airy, two-story suite accommodates five. This is a place for those who want a restful vacation while enjoying quiet pursuits: cooking, basking in the sun, reading, and watching sunsets from the comfort of their own home in Mazatlán. For the high winter season, be sure to reserve early: Calle Las Palmas 15, Mazatlán, Sinaloa 82000, tel. (69) 812-190 or (69) 812-197, a/c, phones, parking, pool, kitchenette; rates are about $26 for two, $33 for four, and $40 for the big five-person suite, credit cards accepted.

The same management operates **Apartmentos las Palmas,** a stack of apartments and a penthouse, across the street. Although not nearly as luxurious as Suites Vidalmar, the apartments are large, modern, and Spartan but thoughtfully furnished, and sleep up to four. Residents have access to the pool across the street. Same address and phone as Suites Vidalmar; the 11 one-bedroom apartments rent from about $26 d; the penthouse about $40, a/c, no parking, credit cards accepted. Bargain for lower low-season rates.

If you want to be near the center of colorful downtown bustle, try the no-frills **Hotel del Centro,** within sight of the cathedral, right around the corner from the market. (The hotel's street-front, although busy, is too narrow for buses, and is consequently not too noisy.) Here you pay only for what you want: a/c $2, TV another $2. There's not much in the (clean) rooms but the basics. No matter, however; the attraction of this part of town is what's outside the door. Their 24 rooms rent for about $15 d low season, $18 high; Canizales 18, Mazatlán, Sinaloa 82000, tel. 69-812-673.

For a little more luxury in the downtown district, walk about four blocks to the opposite (quieter) side of the cathedral to the **Hotel Central.** Past the upstairs lobby you'll find a small restaurant (a friendly place for meeting other travelers) and three floors of cool, clean, modern-style rooms. On Calle Belisario Dominguez 2 Sur at Calle Ángel Flores, Mazatlán, Sinaloa 82000, tel. (69) 821-888. The rates for their 40 rooms, with a/c, TV, and phones, are from about $24 d low season, higher during holidays.

Playa Norte Hotels
During the 1960s Mazatlán burst its old city limits at the end of Paseo Claussen and spilled northward along the long sand crescent called Playa Norte. Now, a three-mile string of '60s-style hotels and motels lines the breezy beachfront (extension of Paseo Claussen) Av. del Mar. Unfortunately, however, the wide, busy thoroughfare intervenes between the hotels (save one, below) and the beach.

The one exception is the dignified **Hotel de Cima,** a few blocks north of the Fisherman's Monument. Its tunnel beneath Av. del Mar leads directly to the hotel's beachfront seafood palapa restaurant. Back inside, the staff try hard to live up to the hotel's "We Only Look Expensive" motto, maintaining a cool, relaxed restaurant, pool, nightclub, bars, and keeping the spacious, comfortable rooms (all with ocean view) spotless. Reserve at Av. del Mar s/n, P.O. Box 350, Mazatlan, Sinaloa 82000, tel. (69) 827-300 and (69) 827-400. Their 150 rooms, all with two double beds, are from about $50 d low season, with a/c, cable TV, phones, parking, tennis, and limited wheelchair access; credit cards accepted.

About two blocks farther north stands **Hotel Aguamarina,** Best Western's very worthy representative in Mazatlán. With a low-rise stucco motel facade, built around a pool-patio, its rooms (either ocean or garden view) are large and gracefully decorated with *indígena*-style handmade wood furniture. The wall art hangs tastefully on colonial-style textured white interiors. Contact them at Av. del Mar 110, P.O. Box 301, Mazatlán, Sinaloa 82000, tel. (69) 817-080 or 816-909 or fax 824-624. The 101 rooms rent for about $52 d standard, $66 d deluxe, with a/c, cable TV, phones, parking, an airy, high-ceilinged restaurant, and pool; credit cards accepted. From the U.S. and Canada, reserve through the Best Western toll-free number, (800) 528-1234.

Farther north a few blocks (just past the Pizza Hut) appears the smallish facade of the **Motel del Sol.** A few steps from the streetfront reception, however, you will find that the Motel del Sol is larger than it looks. Its rooms cluster around an inviting pool-patio where, on one corner, a plaster Donald Duck squirts water from his mouth. Inside, tasteful wood furniture, white walls, and spotless tile floors decorate the spacious rooms. Thirteen of the 21 rooms are equipped with modern kitchenettes. Contact them at Av. del Mar s/n, P.O. Box 400, Mazatlán, Sinaloa 82000, tel. (69) 851-103. Rooms run about $33 d with kitchenette, $25 without, with a/c, phones, some TV, and parking.

Finally, next to the popular Restaurant Señor Frog's, comes the best-buy **Hotel Sands.** It's clean and with everything for a restful beach vacation: sea-view rooms with balconies overlooking an inviting pool-patio, a/c, phones, and TV. At Av. del Mar 1910, P.O. Box 309, Mazatlán, Sinaloa 82000, tel. (69) 820-000. Their 100 rooms rent from about $27 d low season, higher during the winter and holidays.

Zona Dorada
Budget-to-moderate Lodgings

Along a six-mile strip of golden sand rise Mazatlán's newest, plushest hotels. But unlike some other world-class resorts, the Zona Dorada is not wall-to-wall high-rises. In the breezy, palm-fringed spaces between the big hotels, there are many excellent moderately priced hotels and apartment complexes.

For one of the most charming budget accommodations in Mazatlán, try **Fiesta Apartmentos,** a complex of studios and one-bedroom apartments within a jungle-garden blooming with bushy guavas, hanging vines, squawking parrots and slinking iguanas. Hardworking owner-manager Yolanda Olivera and her carpenter spouse built the place from the ground up while raising a family during the '60s and '70s. Their units are each uniquely furnished with husband-made wooden chairs and tables, toilet, hot shower, and a double bed. Larger units have an additional bed, a sofa or two, and a kitchenette. While you may have to do some initial cleaning up, the price and ambience are certainly right. They're three blocks directly inland from beachside landmark Balboa Tower, at Calle Ibis 502, Fraccionamiento Gaviotas, Mazatlán, Sinaloa 82110, tel. (69) 835-355. Their 11 studio and one-bedroom apartments rent from about $10/day ($200/month), while larger units with kitchenettes go for about $15/day ($300/mo). All apartments come with fans and parking; reservations are mandatory during the winter.

Right next door is the less personal, but equally unique, **Racquet Club Las Gaviotas,** a complex of bungalow-apartments and condominiums spread around a spacious palm-shaded swimming-pool garden. While a good, moderately priced vacation lodging for anyone, this is a paradise for tennis buffs on a budget, with its row of seven well-maintained (three clay and four hard) courts. The bungalows themselves are spacious, one- and two-bedroom units with a living room/dining room furnished in Spanish-style tile and wood and equipped with modern kitchenettes. Reservations are mandatory year-round. On Calle Ibis at Bravo, P.O. Box 173, Mazatlán, Sinaloa 82000, tel. (69) 835-939. The 20 units rent from about $500/month for a one-bedroom bungalow and $700 for two bedrooms (with higher daily and weekly rates, fans and daily cleaning service included). Lower units are wheelchair-accessible.

Even lovelier (but minus the tennis courts) is the nearby **Los Girasoles,** a stucco apartment complex built around an inviting pool garden, fringed with banana trees (whose fruit, when ripe, becomes available to guests). Inside, the airy Mexican-style wood and tile kitchenette apartments are comfortably furnished and spotless. They're at Av. Gaviotas 709, Mazatlán, Sinaloa 82110, tel. (69) 835-288 or 813-835, five blocks from the beach at the end of Gaviotas, next to Restaurant Casa Loma. The 22 apartments (both one- and two-bedroom) rent for $30/day or $750/month. Low-season discounts may be available. Rental includes fans, parking, and daily cleaning service; credit cards are accepted.

On Mazatlán's most beautiful beach stand a number of small, moderately priced lodgings along Av. R.T. Loaiza (which, at the Dairy Queen corner, branches right, one way) away from busy Calz. Camarón Sábalo. Among the best is **Casa Contenta,** a comfortable two-story complex that lives up to its name. Step past the off-street parking and you will find seven roomy, tastefully furnished kitchenette apartments tucked behind a luxurious family house, all within a manicured garden. Besides the beach and a small pool in their backyard, Casa Contenta residents can enjoy good restaurants and the entertainment of plush hotels within a few minutes' walk. Reserve early: Playa Las Gaviotas, Av. R.T. Loaiza s/n, tel. (69) 834-976, from about $44/day for an apartment, $130 for the house, with a 10% discount for one-month rental. Rental includes daily cleaning service, a/c, and parking. Credit cards are accepted, and lower-level units have limited wheelchair access.

The **Hotel Tropicana** shares virtually everything—beach, shopping, restaurants and nightlife—with Zona Dorada luxury hotels except prices. For many savvy vacationeers, the hotel's other big plusses—spacious rooms, private ocean-view balconies, big marble baths—far outweigh the sometimes worn furnishings, the dirt in the corners, and the half-block walk to the beach. To assure yourself of the best room (top floor, beach side) reserve early: R.T. Loaiza 27, P.O. Box 501, Mazatlán, Sinaloa 82110, tel. (69) 838-000. Rooms go for about $14 s, $25 d (families $10/person) any time except Dec. 25-Jan. 1 and Feb. and March, when prices are somewhat higher (but still a bargain). Amenities include a/c, phones, a pool, beach club, restaurant-bar, and full wheelchair access; credit cards accepted.

On the beachfront nearby is the **Hotel Las Flores,** very popular with North American winter package vacationers. In the standard-grade (but less than spotless) rooms, bright orange-red bedspreads blend with ruddy brick wall highlights. The deluxe rooms, in contrast, feature soothing blue and white decor and kitchenettes. All units enjoy expansive ocean views. Downstairs, the lobby spreads to an attractive restaurant, pool-bar, and tables beneath beachside palapas. At R.T. Loaiza 212, P.O. Box 583, Mazatlán, Sinaloa 82110, tel. (69) 835-011 or 835-100, fax 843-422. During high season, their 119 rooms rent from about $60 d standard, $70 w/kitchenette, $80 deluxe w/kitchenette. You should never have to pay this, however. A few months before departure, shop around among agents for an air-hotel promotional package; also, monthly and weekly rates are often much cheaper. Rentals include a/c, TV, phones, and parking. Credit cards are accepted.

Zona Dorada Luxury Hotels

A few blocks farther south along Loaiza stands the landmark of the Zona Dorada—the first hotel built (despite many doubters) on what was once an isolated sand-strip far from the city center. Even in the September and October "low" months (when many Zona Dorada hotels and restaurants are virtually empty) everyone—Mexicans and foreigners alike—still flock to the **Hotel Playa Mazatlán.** The band plays every night, the Fiesta Mexicana buffet show goes on every Saturday, and the fireworks boom and flash above the beach every Sunday night. To enjoy the Playa Mazatlán, you don't have to stay there; just order something at the beachside palapa-terrace restaurant and enjoy the music, the breeze, and the same ocean view shared by all its luxurious rooms. In the heart of the Zona Dorada at Av. R.T. Loaiza 202, P.O. Box 207, Mazatlán, Sinaloa 82110, tel. (69) 834-444 and 834-455, fax 840-366. The 425 rooms go for about $64 d standard low season, $73 deluxe one-bedroom suite—$90 and $100 high season, respectively; with a/c, TV, phones, pool, jacuzzi, tennis, parking, and full wheelchair access; credit cards accepted.

For the classiest tropical retreat in town, step into the **Hotel Inn at Mazatlán.** Although mostly a time-share (buy a room for a specified week or two each year), they do rent out their vacant units, hotel-style. All guests, furthermore, whether owners or one-time renters, receive the same tender loving service. Every lovely feature of the Inn at Mazatlán shines with care and planning, from the excellent inside-outside beachview restaurant and the artistically curved pool to the palms' sunset silhouettes and the spacious, luxuriously appointed sea-view rooms. Right on silky Playa Camarón at Camarón Sábalo 6291, P.O. Box 1292, Mazatlán, Sinaloa 82110, tel. (69) 835-500; their 126 rooms rent about $58 d low season, $81 high. For $127 all-season you can have a one-bedroom suite sleeping six including kitchenette. All rentals enjoy a/c, phones, refrigerators, and parking. For recreation there is tennis but no TV. Reservations are generally necessary; credit cards are accepted.

No discussion of Mazatlán hotels would be complete without mention of the **Hotel El Cid** "mega resort", the hotel that tries to be everything. The huge complex, which sprawls over the north end of Calz. Camarón Sábalo, claims to be the biggest in Mexico—with 1,000 rooms in three separate hotels, 15 separate bars and restaurants, a health club, a giant glittering disco, and a country club subdivision with a world-class 18-hole golf course and 17 tennis courts. Size, however, gives El Cid a definite institutional feeling—as if everyone, the 2,000 employees and 2,000 guests alike, were simply numbers. On the other hand, the El Cid's saving grace (besides its velvet-sand beachfront) may be its huge pool. It meanders among the three hotels, a palm-fringed blue lagoon complete with a fake (albeit very clever fake) rock waterslide, waterfall, and diving platform straight from an old Tarzan movie. But this doesn't seem to matter to the poolside crowd of guests, from ages four to 90, who enjoy watching each other slipping, sliding, and jumping into the cool water. On Camarón Sábalo s/n, P.O. Box 813, Mazatlan, Sinaloa 82000, tel. (69) 833-333; room rates are from about $100 d with everything, including complete wheelchair access. They often offer cheaper low-season promotions, obtainable through travel agents or their reservations office.

Beyond The Zona Dorada

Vacationers who hanker for a more rustic beach atmosphere enjoy the **Holiday Bungalows** (not to be confused with the plush Zona Dorada Hotel Holiday Inn) on quiet Playa Cerritos, about five miles north of the Zona Dorada. Administered by the trailer park office across the boulevard, the 20 whitewashed bungalows laze beneath a swaying coconut palm grove. The clean, modern, tile-kitchenette units, in parallel rows facing the ocean, sleep two to four. The more heavily used beachfront row enjoys sweeping ocean views, while the others lie sheltered beneath the palms behind the dune. During the winter season you can enjoy plenty of friendly company at the pool with the trailer park residents across the street. Stores and restaurants are within a short drive nearby. Reserve at Calz. Sábalo Cerritos s/n, P.O. Boxes 682 and 202, Mazatlán, Sinaloa 82110, tel. (69) 832-578. The 19 bungalows rent from about $33/day (or $600/month) high season to about $27 low, with a/c, parking, and limited wheelchair access.

Homestay Program

Besides offering Spanish classes, the privately owned **Centro de Idiomas** (Language Center) also runs a homestay program. Participants live with a Mexican family (shared room around $120/week, private room around $150/week, including three meals). Contact them in the U.S. at Mazatlán Connection, 344 Wyatt Way, Bainbridge Island, WA 98110, tel. (206) 842-1800, or in their downtown school on Belisario Dominguez 1908, upstairs, tel. (69) 822-053.

RV And Trailer Parks

Mazatlán beachfront trailer space is an increasingly scarce commodity, victim to rising land values. If you're planning on a winter stay, phone or mail in your reservation and deposit by September or you may be out of luck, especially for the choice spaces.

One trailer park owner who is determined never to sell out is Gabriela, of **Mar Rosa Trailer Park**. Besides being the on-the-spot manager, she's Mazatlán's informal one-woman welcoming committee and information source. "I will never sell. The people who come here are my friends . . . like my family." If you ask if she has a pool, she will probably point to the beach a few feet away, and say, "one big pool." She's north of the Hotel Holiday Inn at Calz. Camarón Sábalo 702, P.O. Box 435, Mazatlán, Sinaloa, 82000, tel. (69) 836-187; 55 mostly unshaded spaces, all hookups, from $11/day, with toilets and hot showers; near markets and restaurants, leashed dogs okay.

Another popular close-in (Zona Dorada, two blocks from the beach) trailer park is the **Las Palmas,** in a big, palm-shaded lot off Camarón Sábalo, about half a block south of the Dairy Queen. Address is Calz. Camarón Sábalo 333, tel. (69) 835-310; shaded spaces, all hookups, toilets, showers, leashed dogs okay, camping available, near everything.

Nearby (on Calz. R. Bueina, two blocks inland from Valentino's Disco) the **Trailer Park La Posta** spreads beneath the shade of a banana, mango, and avocado grove (all-you-can-eat in season). Residents enjoy a plethora of facilities, including all hookups, showers and toilets, a big pool and sundeck, shaded picnic palapas, a small store, and the beach two blocks away. Their 180 spaces rent for about $10/day or $275/month; add $2 daily for a/c power. Early winter reservations are generally necessary: P.O. Box 362, Mazatlán, Sinaloa 82000, tel. (69) 835-310.

In the quieter country on northside Playa Cerritos the **Holiday Trailer Park** spreads for acres beneath a lazy old coconut grove. Residents enjoy direct access to the long, uncrowded beach across the road and to nearby supermarkets and restaurants. They can also stay in the trailer park's Holiday Bungalows across the street (Calz. Sábalo Cerritos s/n, P.O. Box 682 or 202, Mazatlán, Sinaloa 82110, tel. 69-832-578). The 200 spaces are $12/day or $300/month, all hookups, big saltwater pool, rec room, hot showers, toilets, leashed dogs okay.

Camping

Although there is no established public campground in Mazatlán, camping is allowed for a fee in the **La Posta, Las Palmas,** and **Holiday** trailer parks.

If, however, you prefer solitary beach camping there are plenty of empty grassy dunes on the northerly end of **Playa Cerritos** that appear ripe for tenting. If you are uncertain about the safety or propriety of a likely looking spot, inquire locally.

Other, more isolated spots (be sure to bring water) lie along the long curve of sand on the south shore of **Stone Island** (ride the launch across from the Stone Island dock on Playa Sur), and **Isla Venados** (a mile off Playa Sábalo, ride the boat from the El Cid beachfront). On Isla Venados, don't set up your tent on the narrow beach; it's under water at high tide.

For wilderness beach camping, try **Playa Delfin,** the pearly sand crescent north of Punta Cerritos. Get there by taking the signaled right fork toward Highway 15 about a mile before the northern end of end of Calz. Sábalo Cerritos. Pass Mazagua water park, continue about another mile and turn left at the gravel road just before the railroad track. This soon leads past the big white El Delfin condo complex, which marks the beginning of Playa Delfin, a 10-mile breezy strip of sand, unused except by occasional local fishermen. There's little of civilization here (not even any trees)—simply sand, surf (steep beach: beware of undertow), seabirds, and a seemingly endless carpet of shells.

FOOD

Mazatlán abounds in good food. The competition is so fierce that bad eateries don't survive. The best are easy to spot because they have customers even during the quiet fall Sept.-Nov. low season.

Snacks, Stalls, And Market

With care, you can do quite well right on the street downtown. An afternoon cluster of folks around a streetside cart piled with oyster shells and shrimp is your clue that their fare is fresh, tasty, and very reasonably priced. These carts usually occupy the same place every day and, for most of them, the quality of their food is a matter of honor. One of the best is **El Burro Feliz,** which occupies a spot on Calle Sixto Osuna (outside of their family house near the Archaeological Museum). Try their dozen-oyster cocktail, enough for two, $5.

For dessert, an elderly gentleman runs a shaved (literally, with a hand tool) ice stand across the street, from which he serves the best old-fashioned (safe ice) snowcones in Mazatlán.

If you're cooking your own meals, or simply hanker for some fresh fruit and vegetables, the best place to find the crispest of everything is the **Central Market,** (open daily 6 a.m.-6 p.m.), on the corner of Calles Benito Juarez

MAZATLÁN RESTAURANTS

In approximate ascending order of price:

DOWNTOWN AND OLAS ALTAS

Captain's Table, Plazuela Machado, noon-11 p.m., European
Restaurant Doney's, Calle Mariano Escobedo 610, 812-651, 8 a.m-10 p.m., Mexican
El Shrimp Bucket, Av. Olas Altas 11, 816-350, 6 a.m.-11 p.m., seafood

PLAYA NORTE

El Marinero, Claussen and Cinco de Mayo, 817-682, noon-11 p.m., seafood
Karnes en Su Jugo, Av. del Mar 550, 821-322, 1 p.m-1 a.m., Mexican
Señor Frog's, Av. del Mar s/n, 851-110, noon-midnight, international

ZONA DORADA

Dairy Queen, Calz. Camarón Sábalo 500, 861-522, 10 a.m-11 p.m., hamburgers
Tortas Hawaii, Calz. Camarón Sábalo at Gaviotas, 841-600, 9 a.m.-10 p.m., Mexican sandwiches
Mesón de Cobre, Calz. Camarón Sábalo 1540, 841-101, 7 a.m.-11 p.m., Mexican
El Pancho, Av. R.T. Loaiza s/n, 840-911, 8 a.m.-11 p.m, international
Terraza Playa, at the Hotel Playa Mazatlán, Av. R.T Loaiza 202, 834-455, 7 a.m.-11 p.m., international
Papagayo, at Hotel Inn at Mazatlán, Calz. Camarón Sábalo 6291, 835-500, ext. 1235, 7 a.m.-10 p.m., international
Restaurant Los Arcos, Calz. Camarón Sábalo s/n, 839-577, noon-10 p.m., seafood
Casa Loma, Av. Gaviotas 104, 835-398, 6 p.m.-11 p.m., closed July-Sept., international
Señor Pepper's, Calz. Camarón Sábalo, north end, 831-111, 6 p.m.-midnight, international

and Melchor Ocampo, two short blocks behind the cathedral.

After an hour of hard market bargaining, you may be in the mood for a cool, restful lunch. If so, step one block down Juarez and enter the air-conditioned interior of **Pastelería Panamí** (Av. Juarez, corner of Canizales, tel. 851-853, open daily 8 a.m.-10 p.m) and try one of their tasty lunch specials or treat yourself to their excellent *helado chocolate* (chocolate ice cream).

Afterwards, just outside the door, you may see the *churro* cart that always seems to be parked at that corner. Try three of these uniquely Mexican, foot-long thin sugar doughnuts for $1.

Although macrobiotic fare is a novelty in Mexico, downtown Mazatlán has **Tienda Naturalista**, its own small natural food store-*lonchería* (a minute's walk west of the central plaza at Ángel Flores 208 Pte.). They often feature an economical lunch special, which may include exotic-sounding dishes, such as Frijoles Charros and Salad Tricolor, in addition to the more pedestrian rice water and vegetarian tacos and enchiladas.

Downtown And Olas Altas Restaurants

(Complete Meal Price Key: Budget = under $7, Moderate = $7-14, Expensive = over $14). **Restaurant Doney's,** (two blocks from the central plaza at Calle Mariano Escobedo 610, tel. 812-651, open daily 8 a.m-10 p.m., credit cards accepted) one of Mazatlán's "must" eateries, is a labor of love of the owners, Sr. and Sra. Alfonso T. Velarde (one or both of whom usually can be seen occupying one of the side tables an hour before closing). For a relatively new (started in 1980) location, the cool, airy ambience—towering arched brick ceiling, Victorian chandelier, old Mazatlán photos—is refreshingly traditional. The mostly local, upper-class patrons enjoy a broad menu of home-style Mexican food, such as chorizo (spiced sausage) various *antojitos,* (small tacos, tostadas, tamales), Mazatlán's regional specialty, *asado* (spicy beef stew), and a scrumptious selection of homemade pies and cakes. Moderate.

From the central plaza, walk three blocks away from the cathedral along Juarez. At Constitución turn right one block to the small **Captain's Table** restaurant on a corner of the intimate, old-world Plazuela Machado (Plazuela Machado, open daily noon-11 p.m., credit cards accepted). More like a pub than a restaurant, you would think it was a ship chandler's shop if you didn't know otherwise: a big fish tank on one side, diving gear in a corner, flags draped and ropes strung from walls to ceiling. At first glance, the menu reads as if the fare were typically Mexican seafood—but the style of cooking is more like Basque or Spanish. Moderate.

If you're in a festive mood, **El Shrimp Bucket**—hung with a riot of taffeta flowers and balloons inside, with the marimba combo humming away by dinnertime in the tropical patio outside—is a party waiting to happen (Av. Olas Altas 11, bottom floor of Hotel La Siesta, tel. 816-350, open daily 6 a.m.-11 p.m., credit cards accepted). This is especially true when you call for their bounteous bucket of shrimp ($16, enough for two or three), which they will fix—breaded, grilled, steamed, barbecued—exactly as you wish. Moderate.

Playa Norte Restaurants

It's hard to imagine a restaurant closer to the source than **El Marinero,** located right where the boats bring the fish in every morning (Paseo Claussen and Cinco de Mayo, open daily noon-11, tel. 817-682). The cooking shows it: Marinero's is to Mazatlán as Alioto's #9 is to San Francisco (but at half the price, with mariachis every night except Sunday). In true Mexican style, they augment many of their dishes with a number of flavorful sauces, which range from a mild Salsa Oriental (onions, celery, and a bit of soy) to a peppery Salsa Ranchero. Pick your favorite and have them serve it with their recommended catch of the day.

Heading north along the *malecón,* a bright sign marks **Karnes en Su Jugo** (Av. del Mar 550, tel. 821-322, open daily 1 p.m-1 a.m., credit cards accepted), the unique culinary contribution of personable owner Jorge Perez (who, with his red hair, looks more like a Swede than most Swedes do). If he's there, let him place your order: a bounteous table, likely set with a plate of savory roast beef in juice, hot melted Chihuahua white cheese, refried beans, and enough salsa and hot corn tortillas for a dozen yummy tacos and tostadas. Moderate.

A stay in Mazatlán wouldn't be complete without a trip to **Señor Frog's,** the second (El Shrimp Bucket was the first), and perhaps the best, creation of late owner Carlos Anderson's worldwide chain (Av. del Mar s/n, next to Frankie Oh's disco, tel. 851-110, open daily noon-midnight, credit cards accepted). Many adjectives, mostly extremes—brash, bold, loud, risqué, funny, far-out—have been used to describe the waiters, patrons, and the music at Señor Frog's. Most everyone agrees that the ribs are the best and the margaritas the most potent in town. Expensive.

Zona Dorada Restaurants

Despite their "Golden Zone" locations, Zona Dorada restaurant tariffs needn't be excessive. For excellent food with a flair, crisp service, *tipico* decor, including feisty parrots and a colorful, intriguing wall mural, try **Mesón de Cobre** (Camarón Sábalo 1540, across the street from American Express, tel. 841-101, open daily 7 a.m.-11 p.m., credit cards accepted). Their delicious breakfasts include fresh fruit, eggs any style, home-fried potatoes, refried beans, toast and all the coffee you can drink for $2! For lunch or dinner, try the regional *molcajete* (big three-legged stone bowl) laid with strips of grilled meat and tender *nopale* (cactus), cooked scallions, and filled with savory, steaming broth. Moderate.

When you're in a sweat from shopping, sunburn, and street vendors and you're ready to escape to from Mexico, escape into Mexico's first **Dairy Queen** instead (Camarón Sábalo 500, corner of R.T. Loaiza, tel. 861-522, open daily 10 a.m.-11 p.m.). The regular hamburgers and the associated soft ice-cream goodies will taste better than home. When you emerge, you'll feel like staying another couple of months. Budget.

For fast food, Mexican style, step across the street from Dairy Queen to **Tortas Hawaii** (Camarón Sábalo s/n, at Gaviotas, tel. 841-600, open daily 9 a.m.-10 p.m.). Hawaii, however, seems to have little relation to their food except for the pineapple in some of their huge sandwiches. These include your choice of ham, roast pork, or chicken, with Chihuahua or Oaxaca cheese on a big *bolillo* bun—enough for a light lunch for two—from $3. Budget.

For more serious eaters, the big beach-view **Terraza Playa** restaurant at Hotel Playa Mazatlán is so popular that tables are sometimes hard to get (R.T Loaiza 202, tel. 834-455, open daily 7 a.m-11 p.m., credit cards accepted). This is frequently true Sunday nights when families begin to arrive two hours early for the free eight o'clock fireworks show. The Terraza Playa offers many excellent entrees, such as pescado veracruzana (fish veracruz) for between $5 and $10. Moderate.

A spectacular beachfront view, cool breezes, snappy service and fresh salads, sandwiches and seafood at reasonable prices keep patrons coming to restaurant **El Pancho** year-round (at the beach end of the small complex across from Shell City, tel. 840-911, open daily 8 a.m.-11 p.m.). During the winter season, when vacationers crowd in, come early. The dozen tables can fill by noon. Moderate.

Outside **Restaurant Los Arcos,** as at Señor Frog's, the patrons line up during the high season (Camarón Sábalo s/n, look for big palapa across the street between Holiday Inn and El Cid, tel. 839-577, credit cards accepted, open daily noon-10). Los Arcos claims to specialize in "the secret flavor which the sea has confided," meaning piquant sauces, many of them peppery hot. Specify *pica* (spicy) or *no pica* before you order your shrimp, oysters, smoked swordfish, snapper, or whatever—they'll all be good. Moderate.

For impeccable service and tranquil, palm-framed sunsets, **Papagayo** restaurant at the Hotel Inn at Mazatlán is hard to beat (Camarón Sábalo 6291, low-rise behind wall and trees between Hotels El Cid and Costa de Oro, tel. 835-500, ext. 1235, open daily 7 a.m.-10 p.m., credit cards accepted). Their menu caters to the tastes of their mostly North American clientele, with salad bar and reasonable complete dinner specials (notably, a mouth-watering chicken-rib combo). Moderate.

One of the most successfully exclusive restaurants in town is **Casa Loma** which, besides tucking itself behind a wall on a quiet dead-end street, manages to close July-October (Gaviotas 104, at end of street, tel. 835-398, open 6-11 p.m., credit cards accepted, reservations recommended). The Casa Loma secret: a secluded location, subdued tropical atmosphere, excellent service, and a selection of tasty international specialties that continues to attract a club-by list of affluent patrons. Expensive.

The low-key facade of **Señor Pepper's** gives little hint of what's inside: a flight of fancy away from Mexico to some Victorian polished brass, mirror, and wood-paneled miniplanet, more San Francisco than San Francisco ever was (Camarón Sábalo, north end, across from Hotel Camino Real, tel. 831-111, open daily 6 p.m.-midnight, credit cards accepted, reservations recommended). When you sit down at a table and ask for a menu, the tuxedo-attired waiter will probably do a double take, scurry away, and return with a small tray of a few thick steaks, a pork chop huge enough for two, and a big lobster. You choose one of these as the basis for your dinner. The meal proceeds from there like a Mozart symphony, through each delectable course, until dessert served with coffee, which one of your three waiters will rush to your table in polished silver and pour with a determined flourish. You look up at him, convinced that he *believes* in his mission; and by the time you exit the front door, comfortably satisfied, you will probably be convinced of his mission, also. Expensive.

ENTERTAINMENT AND EVENTS

Just Wandering Around

A good morning place to start is the little beach at the beginning of **Playa Norte,** at the north end of Av. Cinco de Mayo, where the fishermen sell their daily catches. Besides the cluster of buyers busily bidding for the choicest tuna, shrimp, mahimahi, and mackerel, a flock of pelicans and seagulls will be scurrying after the leftovers.

Come back later, around supper time, to enjoy the end-product of what you just witnessed: fresh-cooked seafood (for example, try Restaurant El Marinero or Mariscos Cancún), accompanied by the tunes of one of many strolling mariachi bands—perhaps even one of the famous Sinaloan-style brass bands. If someone else is paying, just sit back and enjoy, especially the tuba solo. If you are paying, however, make sure that you agree upon the price, usually around $2 per selection, before the performance begins.

Around noon, the area around the central plaza (Juarez and Ángel Flores) downtown is equally entertaining. Take a seat beneath the shade of the big trees and have your shoes polished (about $1).

Shady Plazas

Downtown Mazatlán has a number of neighborhood squares within strolling distance of the central plaza. Five blocks north along Calle Guillermo Nelson lies **Plaza Zaragoza** and its colorful row of little flower shops.

West of the central plaza, two short blocks behind the *palacio municipal,* is the **Plazuela de Los Leones** (Calles Ángel Flores and Niños Héroes), marked by a pair of brass lions guarding the city library. Upstairs, you can peruse the venerable collection of the all-English **Benjamin Franklin Library.**

In a southerly direction from the cathedral, stroll along Juarez three blocks; at Constitución turn right one block to **Plazuela Machado,** the gem of old Mazatlán. Depending upon the time, you may want to stop for a light lunch in the charming Captain's Table at one corner, or a drink and a round of pool at the friendly, elegantly Victorian (or, in Mexico, Porfirian, after former President Porfirio Diaz) Cafe Pacifico at the other. Across the square, in the midafternoons on school days, you can take a park bench seat and listen to the violin lessons going on in the upstairs chambers of the **Academia Ángela Peralta.**

Sidewalk Cafes

A few blocks west, on beachfront **Av. Olas Altas,** watch the passing parade from a table at one of the shady sidewalk cafes clustering around the old **Hotel Belmar.** If it's summer and you're lucky, you may get a chance to enjoy a Pacific Mexico rainstorm. It usually starts with a few warm drops on the sidewalk. Then the wind starts the palms swaying. Pretty soon the lightning is crackling and the rain is pouring as if from a million celestial faucets. But no matter; you're comfortably seated, and even if you happen to get a little wet it's so warm that you'll dry off right away.

Late afternoons on Olas Altas yield up a feast of quiet people-watching delights. Perch yourself on the old *malecón* seawall and watch the sunset, the surfers tackling the high waves *(olas altas)* offshore, and the kids, old folks, and loving couples strolling along the sidewalk.

Old-fashioned Shops

During your wanderings around old Mazatlán be sure to step into some of the traditional *pa-*

pelerías, dulcerías, and *ferreterías* (stationery, candy, and hardware stores) that still sell the quaint dime-store style of goods that only grandparents back home remember. For starters, try the Dulcería La Fiesta (two blocks north of the cathedral at Melchor Ocampo 13-A Pte.), for enough candy to fill a truck, plus a delightful selection of huge Minnie Mouse, Donald Duck, and Snow White piñatas.

Special Cultural Events

Mazatlán's nearly 100-year-old **Carnaval** is among the world's renowned Mardis Gras. The merrymaking begins the week before Ash Wednesday (usually late February or early March, when the faithful ceremoniously receive ash-marks on their foreheads), beginning the period of fasting called Lent. Mazatlán Carnaval anticipates all this with a vengeance in a week-long series of folk dances, balls, ballets, literature readings, beauty contests, and "flower" games. The celebration climaxes on Shrove Tuesday (the day before the beginning of Lent) with a parade of floats and riotous merrymakers (which by this time includes everyone in town), culminating along Av. Olas Altas. If you'd like to join in, reserve your hotel room (streetfront rooms at the Hotels Siesta and Belmar are best located for Carnaval) at least six months in advance.

Other unique local celebrations include the Dec. 8 **Feast of the Immaculate Conception** and the **Cultural Festival of Sinaloa,** a statewide (but centering in Mazatlán) month-long feast of concert, sports, and cultural events in November. Check with the tourist information office (see "Information" below) for details.

Bullfights, Rodeos, And Baseball

Every Sunday from around mid-December through Easter, bullfights (not really "fights"), called **Corridas de Toros,** are held at the big bullring, Plaza Monumental (Av. R. Buelna at Av. de la Marina), about a mile from the beach. The ritual begins at 4 p.m. sharp. Get your tickets through a travel agency or at the bullring.

Once or twice a year the Mazatlán professional association of *charros* (cowboys) holds a rodeo-like *charreada.* Some events (such as jumping from one racing, unbroken horse to another, or trying to flatten an angry steer by twisting its tail!) make the garden-variety North American rodeo appear tame by comparison.

Los Venados ("The Deer"), Mazatlán's entry in the Mexican Pacific Coast Baseball (Beisbol) League (AAA), begins its schedule in early October and continues into the spring. Get your tickets at the stadium (Estadio Teodoro Mariscal), whose night lights you can't help but see a few hundred yards from Av. del Mar when the team is home. Baseball fever locally heats up to epidemic proportions when Culiacan, Los Venados's arch-rival, is in town.

Tourist Shows
While a number of hotels present folkloric song and dance shows, the Hotel Playa Mazatlán's **Fiesta Mexicana** remains the hands-down favorite. The entire three-hour extravaganza, including a sumptuous buffet, begins at 7 p.m. every Tuesday, Thursday, and Saturday during high season (Saturday only during low). Call the hotel (tel. 834-455) or a travel agent for tickets, which run about $25 per person. If you miss Fiesta Mexicana on Saturday, you can get in on the free beach fireworks show the next evening at 8 p.m. It's popular, so arrive an hour early to ensure yourself a seat.

Others are trying harder. Two blocks away, at the **Casa Maya** fine leather emporium, owner C. Roberto Soto Robles has built a stage including an entire replica Mayan pyramid, where his company puts on **Show Maya.** In three hours, beginning at 7:30, guests enjoy dinner with an open bar, then in succession the famous Yaqui deer dance, the Mayan fire dance and human sacrifice, a Totonac ritual human Ferris wheel, and finally, the Voladores of Papantla—four feather-clad warriors swinging, in 13 revolutions (one for each of the Maya months), from a 50-foot pole to the ground. For a schedule and tickets, see a travel agent or inquire at Casa Maya, R.T. Loiaza 414, next to Shell City, no phone.

Movies
A number of Mazatlán cinemas screen first-run Hollywood movies. Try **Cinemas Gaviotas y Albatroses** (Camarón Sábalo 218, a few blocks north of Valentino's disco); call 837-554 for programs. On the other hand, you can sample popular Mexican movies at the triple cinema **Tauro, Scorpio, and Aquario** downtown, where in one afternoon you can enjoy the pot bubble and simmer through epics such as *Born to Die* or *Flight of the Intruder,* each accompanied by complementary Disney cartoons (at Ángel Flores and Belisario Dominguez, four short blocks past the *palacio municipal* from the central plaza, $1.70 per movie, tel. 812-526, open daily, 4 p.m.-midnight).

Nightlife
It's difficult not to enjoy the sunset in Mazatlán, especially on the beach, where the sun ends most days with a spectacular show. And with your evening having been properly begun, you have your choice of entertainment in dozens of dances, discos, clubs, and bars.

Dance music is plentiful in Mazatlán. You can start out by enjoying drinks or dinner with the medium-volume, '50s- and '60s-style bands that play nightly at around 8 p.m. at the larger hotels and restaurants, such as the **Playa Mazatlán, El Cid, Los Sábalos, Costa de Oro,** and **El Shrimp Bucket.**

Then, at around 11 p.m. or midnight, while the Mazatlán night is still young, you can go out and jump at one of several local discos. **Valentino's** (tel. 836-212) jumble of white spires and turrets perched on Punta Camarón inspires intense curiosity, if not wonder, among newcomers. Its three separate dance floors have the requisite flashing lights and speakers varying from loud, louder, and the loudest (with a booming bass audible for a couple of miles up and down the beach).

On the other hand, what **El Caracol** (tel. 833-333) at El Cid lacks on the outside, it makes up on the inside. There is one huge dance floor beneath two upper levels, which patrons can exit to the lower by sliding down a chute or slithering down a brass firehouse pole.

Another very popular disco, **Frankie Oh's** (tel. 825-800) combines with Señor Frog's on Av. del Mar next door to jam traffic for a mile on Saturday and Sunday. Frankie Oh's attracts huge young local crowds to its weekend live performances, which are announced on its sign above Av. del Mar.

The discos, which charge a cover of about $5-10 and expect you to dress casually but decently (slacks and shirts, dresses or skirts and blouses, and shoes), open around 10 p.m. and go on until four or five in the morning.

Bars And Hangouts
Mazatlán has several romantic, softly lighted piano bars. Besides the **Cantina** (tel. 812-640)

at Hotel La Siesta, try the friendly **Mikonos** piano bar (right next to Valentino's at Camarón Sábalo and Rafael Buelna), or the smooth sophistication of **Señor Pepper's** (tel. 831-111) piano bar across from the Hotel Camino Real at the north end of Camarón Sábalo.

For high-volume '70s rock and beer-and-popcorn camaraderie, **Jungle Juice** restaurant's upstairs bar (tel. 833-315) is literally wall-to-wall customers during the high season (on a side street off R.T Loaiza one block from Hotel Playa Mazatlán). The same is true for open-air cantina **Gringo Lingo,** around the corner, except there's more room and more air.

Child's Play

When your kids get tired of digging in the sand and playing in the pool, take them to the **Aquarium,** Mexico's largest, with many big, well-maintained fish tanks—of flinty-eyed sharks, comical wide-bodied box-fish, and shoals of luminescent damselfish (Av. de Los Deportes 111, tel. 817-815, admission $3 adults, $1.50 kids, open daily 10-6, just off Av. del Mar about a mile south of Valentino's; watch for the "Acuario" sign). Outside, don't miss the exotic tropical botanical garden, where you'll find a pair of monstrously large alligators. Time your arrival to take in one of the three daily sea lion shows at 11 a.m., 1 p.m., or 3 p.m. For details of the Aquarium's very worthy **ecological efforts,** see the "Information" section of this chapter.

For a different type of frolic, take the kids to **Aquatico Mazagua** water park, where they'll be able to slip down the hundred-foot-long Kamikaze slide, swish along the toboggan, loll in the wave pool, or simply splash in the regular pool. Located at Playa Cerritos s/n, tel. 840-622, open daily 10-6, $9 entry for everyone over three, restaurant, snack bar; follow the right fork toward Hwy. 15 near the north end of Calz. Camarón Sábalo and you'll immediately see the water park on the left.

During the adult fun and games of Carnaval, there's no reason your kids have to feel left out if you take them to the **"Carnival"** (as known in North America). You'll find it by looking for the Ferris wheel near the bus terminal on Calle Tamazula and Hwy. 15 (four blocks behind the Sands Hotel on Av. del Mar).

SPORTS AND RECREATION

Walking And Jogging

The Mazatlán heat keeps walkers and joggers near the shoreline. On the beaches themselves, the long, flat strands of **Playa Norte** (along Av. del Mar), **Playa Gaviotas** (north from about the Hotel Los Flores), and the adjoining **Playa Sábalo** (north from about El Cid), provide firm stretches for walking and jogging. If you prefer an even firmer surface, the best uncluttered stretch of the *malecón* seaside sidewalk is along **Av. del Mar** from Valentino's disco south about three miles to the Fisherman's Monument.

Swimming And Surfing

During days of calm water, you can safely swim beyond the gentle breakers, about 50 yards off **Playa Gaviotas** and **Playa Sábalo.** Heed the

Tough-eating sailfish and black marlin (above) are often discarded after they are brought in. Progressive captains encourage anglers to turn them loose when caught.

usual precautions. (See "Watersports" in the main "Introduction.")

On rough-water days, however, you'll have to do your laps in a hotel pool, since there is no public pool in Mazatlán. If your hotel has no pool, many of the big hotels don't seem to mind if you use theirs.

There are several challenging intermediate surfing spots along the Mazatlán shoreline, mostly adjacent to rocky points, such as **Pinos** (next to Ciencias del Mar off Paseo Claussen), **Punta Camarón** (at Valentino's disco), and **Punta Cerritos** at the far north end of the *malecón*. (For more details, see "Beaches" above.)

Bodysurfing and boogieboarding are popular on calm days on Mazatlán's beaches. Boogieboards are rentable for about $3/hr on the beachfronts of some Zona Dorada hotels, such as (from south to north) Los Sábalos, Playa Mazatlán, El Cid, Oceano Palace, and Camino Real.

Snorkeling And Scuba Diving

The water near Mazatlán's beaches is generally too churned up for good visibility. Serious snorkelers and divers head offshore to the outer shoals of Isla Venados and Isla Chivos. A number of shops along the Zona Dorada beaches arrange such trips. The best equipped is **El Cid's Aqua Sports Center** (tel. 833-333, ext. 341), marked by the clutter of equipment on the beach, on the south side of Hotel El Cid. A three-hour snorkeling or scuba excursion, including equipment and instructor, runs from about $50-$70 per person. Snorkel, mask, and fins only rent for about $7 per day.

Chico's Beach Club (tel. 840-777, next to Balboa Tower) and **Ocean Sports Center** (beachfront, Hotel Camino Real, tel. 831-111) also make similar arrangements and rentals.

Sailing And Windsurfing

Aqua Sports Center, Chico's Beach Club, and Ocean Sports Center (locations and details above), rent Hobie Cats for around $20 per hour (three-person limit) for sailing from the beach.

Windsurfing is possible nearly anywhere along Mazatlán's beaches. An especially good, smooth spot is the protected inlet at the north end of Av. Sábalo Cerritos. Bring your own equipment, however, for there's little windsurfing rental gear available in Mazatlán.

Jet-skiing And Parasailing

The highly maneuverable snowmobile-like jet-ski water beetles have completely replaced waterskiing at Mazatlán. Three or four of them can usually be seen tearing up the water, hotdogging over big waves, gyrating between the swells and racing each other far offshore. For a not-so-cheap thrill, rent one of them at Aqua Sports Center at El Cid (tel. 833-333, ext. 341), which has the best and most equipment, for about $30 per half hour for one, $45 for two persons.

Parasailing chutes are continually ballooning along high over Zona Dorada beaches. For about $25 for a 10-minute ride, you can fly like a bird through arrangements made at any one of the above-listed beach rental shops.

Tennis And Golf

If you're planning on playing lots of tennis in Mazatlán, best check into one of the several hotels, such as **Playa Mazatlán, Inn at Mazatlán** or **El Cid** (which charges $10/hr even for guests), all of which have courts. If your lodging does not provide courts, you can rent one at **Gaviotas Racquet Club** (tel. 835-939, three clay, four hard courts, some lighted) for $10/hour. They're popular and likely to be crowded during the winter season, however. Otherwise, try **Club Deportiva Reforma** (Rafael Buelna s/n, tel. 831-200, with six lighted courts next to the bullring, about a mile from the beach).

Mazatlán golf is even more exclusive. The 18-hole course at **El Cid** is the only one within the city limits, and they allow only their (and Hotel Camino Real's) guests to play. On top of this, the greens and caddy fees total $26. (Double this if you're merely from the Camino Real.)

There is a more egalitarian, although mediocre, nine-hole course at the **Club Campestre** (tel. 847-494, $10 for one/$15 for two) next to the Coca-Cola factory on the airport highway just past the south edge of town.

Sportfishing

Good captains and long experience have made Mazatlán among the world's leading billfish (the marlin, swordfish, and sailfish with the sharp killing "bill") ports. The several licensed *flotas deportivas* (sports fleets) line up along the jetty road beneath the El Faro lighthouse point. They vary, mostly in size of fleet; some have two or three boats, others have a dozen. Boats generally return with about three big fish—one of them a whopping marlin or sailfish—per day.

The biggest is the **Bill Heimpel Star Fleet,** owned and operated by personable Bill Heimpel, a descendant of a German immigrant family. During the high season he sends out around a hundred customers a day. He organizes the groups so that you can fish without having to rent a whole boat. One day's fishing runs about $60 per person, complete. Entire boats for about eight passengers (six of whom can fish at a time) rent for around $300 per day, complete. May-Oct., reservations are not generally necessary; call them in Mazatlán (tel. 823-878) for information. During the high (Nov.-April) season, however, prepaid reservations at Star Fleet's Texas booking office are mandatory. (For more details, contact Star Fleet, P.O. Box 290190, San Antonio, Texas 78280, tel. 800-426-6890, fax 512-377-0454.)

There are smaller fleets equally as competent, however. Heimpel's neighbor is **Mike Maxemin Sportfishing Marina,** whose office is invitingly plastered with yellowing "big catch" photos (Mazatlán's record fish was a half-ton, 13-foot black marlin) beneath huge stuffed marlin and sailfish trophies. Like Heimpel, Maxemin (who has 10 boats) accepts individual reservations. His prices are about $5 less per person for a completely supplied fishing outing. (Be at the dock at 6 a.m. sharp; expect to return before 3 p.m.) Phone Mike Maxemin for information and reservations at (59) 812-824 or (69) 824-977, or write him at P.O. Box 235, Mazatlán, Sinaloa 82000.

A bit farther down the scale, you can check out some of the local boats, such as **Flota El Dorado,** run by "Fishing Is Our Business" Federico Castro. He rents out a big 38-foot boat with skipper, bait, and poles for billfish for six people ($135 low season, $175 high). He'll also furnish a group of four with a launch and skipper, fully equipped for half a day to catch smaller fry, such as 30-pound tuna or *sierra,* for around $70. (Contact him at the dock, or call 69-816-204; P.O. Box 1286, Mazatlán, Sinaloa 82000.)

You can also negotiate with one of the fishermen on **Playa Norte** (at the foot of Cinco de Mayo at Paseo Claussen) to take you and a few friends out in his *panga* for half a day. He'll supply lines and bait enough to hook several big mahimahi and red snapper for a total price of about $50.

Boat Launching

If you have your own boat, there are a couple of official launching ramps in Mazatlán. One ramp is at the **Ciencias del Mar** college (on the point just past the boat cove on Paseo Claussen). The school office (tel. 828-656) inside sells tickets for about $17 to use the ramp for one day 7 a.m.-6 p.m. The tariff for a one-month permit is only double that. That would entitle you to anchor your boat, among a dozen neighbors, in the sheltered Playa Norte cove for a month. No facilities are available except the ramp.

The other boat ramp is at **Club Nautico** (Explanada del Faro s/n, Mazatlán, Sinaloa 82000, tel. 815-195) at the far end of the line of sportfishing docks. A one-day launching permit runs about $20. They have a first-class yacht harbor with hoists, a repair shop, and gasoline, but unfortunately no room for outsiders to store boats, either in or out of the water. You may, however, be able to get permission to park your boat and trailer on the road outside the gate.

Hunting Outfitters And Guides

The best outfitters in town are the Aviles Hermanos (Aviles Brothers) at 5 de Mayo and Paseo Claussen. Their business peaks during the winter duck season; their other options include an airplane, which will take you anywhere to legally hunt most anything else. Contact them at their office on Paseo Claussen between El Marinero Restaurant and Mexicana Airlines, tel. 813-728 or 816-060 or 843-130.

SHOPPING

Judging from the platoons of racks in the Zona Dorada and in the Central Market, T-shirts would seem to be the most popular sale item in Mazatlán. Behind the racks, however, Mazatlán's curio shops stock an amazing bounty of goods from all over the country. The best route to quality purchases at reasonable prices is first to look downtown for the lowest prices, next search the Zona Dorada for the best quality, and then make your choice.

Central Market Shopping

The market occupies one square block near the cathedral, between Calles Juarez, Ocampo, Serdan, and Valle. Here, bargaining is both expected and essential unless you don't mind paying $20 for a $5 item. (See the bargaining hints in the main "Introduction.")

Although the colorful mélange of meat and vegetable stalls occupies most of the floor space, dozens of small curio shops are tucked inside on the Juarez and Valle (west and south) sides and along all four outside sidewalks.

Perhaps the most unusual of the outside shops is **Artesanías Marina Mercante,** a dusty clutter of handmade accessories, including big Zapatista-style sombreros from Oaxaca, wallets and belts from Guadalajara, and locally made hammocks (on the market southeast corner, at Valle and Serdan).

Nothing more typifies Mexico than *huaraches.* One of Mazatlán's best selections is at **Huarachería Internacional** on the outside market sidewalk at Ocampo and Juarez. Their Michoacán goods are all authentic and, with bargaining, very reasonably priced (tel. 202-729, open daily 9-8).

For a big, air-conditioned selection of everything, from hardware and cosmetics to film and groceries, local people and tourists flock to Mexico's K mart look-alike, **Gigante** (on R. Buelna, about a mile from Valentino's disco, tel. 836-011, open daily 9-9).

Zona Dorada Shopping

The Zona Dorada presents a bewildering variety of curio shops—in small shopping centers, hotel malls, and at streetside along Calz. Camarón Sábalo. Nearly everything you're looking for,

however, probably can be found in the concentration of many good and unusual shops along the one-way south-heading side street Av.R.T. Loaiza, which forks off from Calz. Sábalo at the Dairy Queen. Following are a few highlights, moving south on Loaiza.

Shell City is not only a store, it's a virtual museum of shells (and perhaps the reason they've become so scarce on Mazatlán's beaches). Constellations of pearly curios—swirling conches, iridescent abalones, bushy corals (and in one single deviation, whimsical coconut faces)—fill Shell City's seeming acres of displays (Av. R.T. Loaiza 407, tel. 831-301, open daily 9-8, credit cards accepted).

Pardo Jewelry, adjacent to Shell City, specializes in unusually fine gems and jewelry (411 Av. R.T. Loaiza, tel. 843-354, open Mon.-Sat. 9:30-5:30, closed Sun., credit cards accepted). Their glittering silver- and gold-set diamonds, rubies, emeralds, lapis, opals, and amethysts are worth a look whether you're buying or not.

Across the street stands **Mazatlán Art Gallery,** focusing on fine impressionist-style Mexican landscapes and folk scenes (in Tres Islas Plaza, 404 Av. R.T. Loaiza, open daily 9-7). They also carry the near-surrealistic paintings of artist Paul Modlin.

The **Casa Maya** fine leather store is unmissable because of its replica Mayan pyramid (for details on their excellent tourist show, see "Tourist Shows" preceding) looming above the street (open 10-6, closed Sun., no phone). Like Pardo Jewelry nearby, many of Casa Maya's

A worker crafts one of dozens of styles of ornaments for sale at Shell City.

one-of-a-kind leathercraft items—boots, coats, jackets, shoes, purses, stuffed animals, and Indian motifs—are interesting as works of art alone.

Among the finest of Mazatlán's art galleries is **Sí Como No**, on Garzas, one short block off R.T. Loaiza, across from Evolución Bookstore. Specializing in prints and originals of famous Latin painters, a plethora of hard-to-find Orozcos, Dalis, Ertés, and Viejos decorates its walls and windows. Open 10-6, closed Sundays and the months of September and October.

Back on R.T. Loaiza around the corner, next to Gringo Lingo Restaurant, is the big bargain-basement **Mercado Viejo**, enclosing an acre of all-Mexico crafts (R.T. Loaiza 315, tel. 836-366, open daily 9-9). If you can name it they probably have it: giant ceramic trees of life, a zoo of onyx animals, black Oaxaca pottery, carved and gilded wooden fish—the items so common in stores here that they seem ordinary—until you take them back home, where, on your bookshelf they gradually become precious mementos.

SERVICES

Money Exchange

Obtain the most pesos for cash and traveler's checks at the **Banco Nacional de Mexico** (Banamex). In the Zona Dorada (Camarón Sábalo 424, tel. 838-101, across the corner from Dairy Queen) they have a special extra-hours cashier (outside, to the right of the regular bank) open Mon.-Fri. 8:30-1 and 3-5:30 (8:30-11:30 only for Canadian money), closed weekends. The downtown main branch (at the central plaza, corner of Juarez and Ángel Flores, tel. 827-733) changes money during its extended hours, Mon.-Fri. 8:30-11:30 and 3:30-5:30 (Canadian 8:30-11:30 only), closed weekends.

After bank hours, change money at one of the many of *casas de cambio* along Av. del Mar and Calz. Camarón Sábalo (such as the counter at the north end of R.T. Loaiza, across from Dairy Queen, open daily 9-7, Sun. 9-5, tel. 839-209). The **Hotel Playa Mazatlán** (R.T. Loaiza 202, tel. 834-444) reception money-exchange counter services both outside customers and guests daily 6 a.m.-10 p.m.

American Express maintains a full-service money counter and travel agency on Camarón Sábalo (half a block from Dairy Queen, tel. 830-600, open Mon.-Fri. 9-5, Sat. 9-12), which gives bank rates for American Express U.S. dollar traveler's checks (no others accepted, however).

Post Office, Telegraph, And Telephone

For routine mailings, use one of the several **post boxes** *(buzónes)* at the big hotels, such as Los Sábalos, Playa Mazatlán, El Cid, Camino Real, and others.

Otherwise, the **Post Office** (Correos) is adjacent to the central plaza downtown, corner of Juarez and Ángel Flores (tel. 812-121, open Mon.-Fri. 8-5:45, Sat. 9-1, philatelic services in the morning only).

The **Telegraph Office** (Telégrafos), tel. 812-220, open Mon.-Fri. 8-5:30, Sat. 8-11, is also in the post office building; enter half a block along Ángel Flores from the corner at Juarez.

Operator-assisted **long-distance telephone** service is generally available from telephones in Mazatlán. For calls within Mexico, dial 02; for international calls, dial 09. (For other hints on using telephones in Mexico, see the main "Introduction.")

Mazatlán also has Computel, an efficient computer-assisted *larga distancia* (long distance) and **fax** service: in the Zona Dorada (tel. 860-268) on Camarón Sábalo a few doors from Dairy Queen; at the bus terminal (tel. 853-930) at Calle Tamazula and National Hwy. 15; and downtown (tel. 851-480) at Aquiles Serdán 1512. A call to the U.S. runs about $2.50 per minute (although the bus station office sometimes offers discounts).

Immigration And Customs

For visa extensions up to 180 days total (or more, in cases of real emergency) or loss of tourist card (make copy beforehand and get a report from the tourist police) go to **Migración** at Aquiles Serdán and Playas Gemelas (on the south side of downtown, near the ferry dock, tel. 813-813). They are open Mon.-Fri. 9-3 for business, and until 8 p.m. for information only, closed weekends. For general hints on Mexican immigration and customs procedures, see the main "Introduction."

For customs matters, such as leaving your car behind in Mexico while you leave the country temporarily, contact the **Aduana** (tel. 812-059, corner of Calles Carranza and Cruz in the

Olas Altas district, one block from the U.S. Consulate).

Consulates
The **United States Consulate** (Circunvalación 120 Pte., two short blocks from Av. Olas Altas, tel. 852-205, 852-207, 852-208), conducts business Mon.-Fri. 8-1 and 2-5. For outside-of-hours emergencies, contact the 24-hour duty officer by phone (unless the consulate is shut down; in such case, call the nearest consulate in Hermosillo, tel. 62-172-375)

The **Canadian Consulate** (on Av. R.T. Loaiza, just outside the Hotel Playa Mazatlán, tel. 837-320), is open Mon.-Fri. only, 9-12. For real emergencies, call Consul Norbert James Gibson any time at 835-951 or 853-243.

Language Courses And Lessons
The downtown Centro de Idiomas (Language Center), owned and operated by American resident Dixie Davies, offers good beginning to advanced Spanish courses. Tuition runs about $80/week for small, two-hour daily classes. Contact them in the U.S.A. and Canada at 344 Wyatt Way, Bainbridge Island, WA 98110, tel. (206) 842-1800, or in downtown Mazatlán at Belisario Dominguez 1908, upstairs, tel. 822-053.

A very knowledgeable and personable Spanish tutor, José Luis Chavez (tel. 839-173 at home, or 860-839 at the Evolución bookstore), gives individual or small-group lessons at very reasonable rates.

Arts And Music Classes
The **Centro Municipal de Artes Ángela Peralta** offers continuous-enrollment ballet, instrumental music, and other performance-arts classes for adults and children. Their sessions are conducted in the airy old-world buildings that cluster around the charming downtown Plazuela Machado. For more information, contact the English director, Mrs. Jane Abreu, at Teatro Ángela Peralta, Plazuela Machado.

Afternoons and evenings, the halls of the **Academia de Artes Centro Francisco Martines Cabrera** echo with the cheerful sounds of students and their violins, guitars, and dancing feet. They offer many semester courses (beginning Sept. and Jan.), including instrumental music, dance, painting, and theater, for children and adults. (For more information, drop in and talk to the friendly director, Prof. José Guadalupe L. Sánchez, 4-9 p.m. at the old landmark school building at the south end of Av. Olas Altas, adjacent to the streetside city and state shields monument.

Special Tours
Augustin Arellano Tirado, a very knowledgeable local college teacher and guide, leads special-interest individual and small-group ecological, archaeological, and sacred-sites tours. Contact him through the Francisco Iriarte Conde Tour Guides Association, P.O. Box 1144, Mazatlán, Sinaloa 82000, fax (69) 840-708, or home tel. 839-438.

Massage
The Centro de Massage of Mazatlán provides massage therapy (around $10/hour) using a variety of techniques, such as Swedish, water, and sport massage, acupressure, and foot reflexology (open afternoons 2-5, Sat. 12-6, in the small shopping center in front of the Coral Reef Hotel on Av. R.T. Loaiza, tel. 837-666). A sign in their window, announcing the "Land of the Deer Healing Center," quotes a Yaqui proverb: "In gentleness there is great strength." Local hotels refer many customers there.

Film And Photofinishing
Although many big hotels develop and sell film, their services are limited and expensive. Competition lowers the prices on "photo row," Calle Ángel Flores downtown, just west of the central plaza. For reasonable one-hour developing and jumbo printing, try **Photo Arauz** (Ángel Flores 607, tel. 822-015, open daily 8-8). They do 35mm rolls for about $12. Very reasonable Konica color print film is often available at **Photo Makoto** (Ángel Flores 508, tel. 821-182, open daily 8:30-7:30), half a block away across the street.

INFORMATION

Tourist Information Office
The combined federal-state **Mazatlán Regional Tourist Information Office** is in the big Banamex bank plaza (Av. Olas Altas 1300, corner of Mariano Escobedo, tel. 851-220, 851-221 open Mon.-Fri. 8-3 and 4-6)

where clerks dispense a number of useful maps and brochures. If you have a difficult problem, or need more than the usual information, ask for Benito, Adalberto, or Señora Aguilar, the very able, English-speaking administrative secretary.

Hospitals And Pharmacies

Its 24-hour duty staff of specialists earns the **Hospital Militar** (in the Olas Altas district at Malpica and Venus, tel. 812-079, one block from the Hotel Siesta) high recommendations. Despite its exclusive-sounding title, anyone can receive treatment at the Hospital Militar.

Another good place to be sick is the **Sanitorio del Divina Providencia** (tel. 824-011, 824-022, downtown at Galeana 22 Pte., four blocks from the central plaza). They have an ambulance service and a highly recommended heart attack-treatment center.

Closer to the Golden Zone is the respected **Hospital Clinica del Mar** (tel. 831-636, 831-777, and 831-524) at Revolución 5 (at Insurgentes), about half a mile from Av. del Mar and the beach. They offer 24-hour emergency care and a mile-long list of on-call specialists.

The **Cruz Roja** (private Red Cross, tel. 813-690, 851-451) operates ambulances and is usually called to auto accidents when the victims are incapacitated. The Cruz Roja hospital is not highly recommended, however. Tell them to take you to Militar, Divina Providencia or Clinica del Mar if you can manage it.

If you must have a bona fide American-trained doctor, try Surgeon Dr. Gilberto Robles Guevara's **Clinica Mazatlán** (office tel., 812-917, home 851-923) at Zaragoza and Cinco de Mayo, on the downtown "doctors' row."

Farmacias in Mexico are allowed wide latitude to diagnose illnesses and dispense medicines. For a physician and pharmacy all in one right on the *malecón,* try **Farmacia Ángel,** run by Dr. Ángel Avila Tirado, who examines, diagnoses, prescribes, and rings up the sale on the spot. (tel. 824-746, 816-831, Av. del Mar s/n, one block from the Fisherman's Monument, open daily 8 a.m.-8:45 p.m.)

Another good pharmacy (with bookstore to boot) is in the shopping center in front of the Hotel Playa Mazatlán: **Farmacia Playa,** R.T. Loaiza 202, tel. 834-016, open daily 8 a.m.-8:45 p.m.

Police And Fire Emergencies

For police emergencies in the Zona Dorada, the special **Policía Turística** police force (which patrols the Zona Dorada exclusively) can respond quickly. Call 848-444 or go to their headquarters in bottom-floor Suite 9 of the "Centro Commercial Las Palmas" shopping center on Camarón Sábalo near the Las Palmas Hotel.)

For **downtown police emergencies,** contact the *preventiva* police, in the *palacio municipal* (city hall) on the central plaza, tel. 813-919.

In case of **fire,** call the *servicio bomberos* (fire station), tel. 839-920 and 812-769.

Books, Newspapers, And Magazines

The most bountiful English-language bookracks in town are at the bookstore-pharmacy at the Hotel Playa Mazatlán. (Farmacia Playa, tel. 834-016, open daily 8 a.m.-8:45 p.m.) They stock a few hundred titles, mostly thick popular novels, a raft of U.S. popular magazines, and a small but solid collection of Mexico travel, folklore, art, history, and language books. They also sell the *L.A. Times,* and *U.S.A. Today,* (which arrive around 4 p.m.) and the daily English-language Mexico City *News.*

You will usually find the same three newspapers, plus the *New York Times* (Oct.-March only), many U.S. magazines, and the excellent *Pemex Highway Atlas* of Mexico at the **Kioskito de Tin Marin** corner newsstand (on Camarón Sábalo across from the Dairy Queen).

The unique new age **Evolución Bookstore** stocks many English-language occult/self-help/meditation/music/astrology titles, along with used assorted paperbacks, cards, Mexico state and city maps, crystals, incense, and oils. The small natural-foods deli (with fresh-ground coffee and macrobiotic muffins) and the quiet, friendly air-conditioned ambience invite lingering.

They also rent their fax machine for $6.95 per copy and allow local calls on their phone for $.30 each. Evolución is open daily 10-9 and located between R.T. Loaiza and Camarón Sábalo next to Jungle Juice restaurant, tel. 860-839.

Public Library

Mazatlán's respectable public library is downtown, at **Plazuela de Los Leones,** two short blocks behind the *palacio municipal.* Of special interest is the upper-floor **Benjamin Franklin Library:** row upon row of venerable volumes of classic American literature. Open Mon.-Fri. 8-8, Sat. 9-12.

Ecology And Volunteer Work

Mazatlán has a small but growing ecological movement, which has coalesced under the acronym **CEMAZ,** Ecological Council of Mazatlán. Their main focus has been on education by example—cleaning up and restoring Mazatlán's offshore islands and lagoons. Operating out of a small city-financed office on Plazuela Machado (Constitución 511, tel. 852-552), they occasionally need volunteers for projects. Drop in and let them know you're around.

The Mazatlán **Acuario** (Aquarium) is another center of ecological activity. Mainly through school educational programs, they are trying to save the marine turtles that come ashore to lay eggs along local beaches during the summer and early fall. They may be able to use volunteers to help with such efforts. Check with their public-relations officer for more details (Av. de Los Deportes, one block off Av. del Mar about a mile south of Valentino's disco—watch for the signs; tel. 817-815, 817-816, 817-818, open daily 10-6).

GETTING THERE AND GETTING AWAY

By Air

A number of reliable U.S. and Mexican airlines connect Mazatlán with many destinations in Mexico and the United States.

Alaska Airlines flights connect daily with Los Angeles, San Francisco, and Seattle. Their local reservations/information offices are at the airport, tel. 852-730.

Mexicana Airlines flights connect daily with Los Angeles, San Francisco, Denver, Miami, Monterrey, Puerto Vallarta, Mexico City, Guadalajara, and Los Cabos. Their local reservations/information offices are on the *malecón* (tel. 837-722 at Paseo Claussen #101B, corner Belisario Dominguez), and in the Zona Dorada (tel. 836-202, 835-554 in the Balboa Tower Commercial Center).

Aeromexico flights connect daily with Los Angeles, Tucson, Tijuana, Mexico City, Aguascalientes, Durango, Hermosillo, Leon, and Los Mochis. Their local reservations/information offices are in the Zona Dorada (at Calz. Camarón Sábalo #310, tel. 841-111, 841-609), and at the airport, tel. 823-444.

Delta Airlines flights connect daily with Los Angeles. Their local reservations/information offices are at Hotel El Cid, ground floor, tel. 832-709, and at the airport, tel. 821-349.

Canadian Holiday Airlines charter flights connect with Toronto, Vancouver, and Calgary. For information, call their agent at the Hotel Playa Mazatlán, tel. 134-444.

Mazatlán Airport Arrival And Departure

For arrivees, the Mazatlán Airport (code-designated MZT, officially the General Rafael Buelna Airport) unfortunately lacks many basic services. There are neither money exchange, tourist information, nor hotel-booking services. Car-rental (Budget, National, Hertz, and the local "AIAI" agency) clerks try to help, but independent travelers should have their first-night hotel reservations and guidebook in hand when they arrive. (Otherwise, they'll be at the mercy of their taxi driver, who will most likely collect a commission from the hotel where he deposits them.)

Taxi and *colectivo* (collective van) transportation for the 15-mile (25-km) ride into town is, by contrast, well organized. Booths sell both kinds of tickets *(colectivo* about $5 per person, taxi about $14 per car). No public bus runs from town to the airport.

For departure, *colectivos* are harder to find around hotels than are departing tourists. Share a regular taxi and save on your return to the airport.

The **airport-departure tax** runs $12. If you've lost your tourist card and haven't had time to get a duplicate (see "Immigration and Customs," in the main "Introduction"), you may be able to avoid the $20 departure fine by presenting a police report of your loss. See the Zona Dorada Tourist Police (tel. 848-444) on Camarón Sábalo (in the Centro Comercial Las Palmas shopping center near the Hotel Las Palmas) for such a report.

By Car Or RV

There are three highway routes to Mazatlán: from the U.S. through Nogales and Culiacan; from the northeast, through Durango, and from the southeast, from Guadalajara or Puerto Vallarta through Tepic.

The quickest and safest way to drive to Mazatlán from the U.S. border is by **Mexico National Hwy. 15,** which connects with U.S. Interstate 19 from Tucson, at Nogales, Mexico. A four-lane superhighway for most of the 743-mile (1,195-km) route, Hwy. 15 allows a safe, steady 55 mph (90 km/hour) pace. Although the tolls total about $15 for a car (more for trailers and big RVs) the safety and decreased wear and tear are well worth it. Take it easy and allow yourself at least two days travel to or from Nogales.

Heading to Mazatlán from the northeast, the winding (but spectacular) two-lane **National Hwy. 40** crosses the Sierra Madre Occidental from Durango. Steep grades over the 7,350-foot (2,240-meter) pass will stretch the trip into the better part of a day, even though it totals only 198 miles (318 km). During the winter, snow can temporarily block the route.

From the southeast, heavy traffic slows progress along the mostly two-lane narrow **National Hwy. 15,** which connects with Guadalajara (323 miles, 520 km) via Tepic. Allow at least a full day for this trip.

The same is true of the two-lane route from Puerto Vallarta. Each leg, first **National Hwy. 200** (104 miles, 167 km) to Tepic, thence **National Hwy. 15** (182 miles, 293 km), is sometimes slowed by heavy traffic and will require at least a full day.

By Bus

The **Central de Autobuses** (Central Bus Terminal) is at the corner of Hwy. 15 and Calle Tamazula, about two miles north of downtown and four blocks from Playa Norte behind the Sands Hotel.

The terminal, efficiently divided into *primera-* and *segunda-clase* (first- and second-class) sections, has big suitcase lockers (about $5/day), a number of clean snack stands and stores where travelers can purchase food, pure water, and drinks. Stock up before you leave.

Several well-equipped bus lines provide frequent local departures. Go first-class whenever possible. The service, speed, and reserved seats *(asientos reservados)* of first-class buses far outweigh their small additional cost. All connections listed below are first-class and depart locally *(salidas locales)* unless otherwise noted.

Tres Estrellas de Oro (TEO, tel. 813-680) buses connect with southeast destinations of Tepic, Guadalajara, and Mexico City and intermediate points. *Salidas de paso* (buses passing through) connect en route south to Tepic and Puerto Vallarta. Buses connect with northwest destinations of Culiacan and Los Mochis (hourly), Nogales (two per day), and Tijuana (three per day), including intermediate points.

Every two hours, **Transportes Norte de Sonora** (TNS, tel. 813-846) connects northwest with Culiacan and Tijuana and southeast with Tepic, Guadalajara, Mexico City and intermediate points.

Transportes Chihuahuaenses (TC, tel. 812-335) buses connect twice a day with the north via Durango, Chihuahua, Juarez, and intermediate points. **Transportes del Norte** buses (TN, operating out of the same office) connect (nine per day) northeast with Durango, Torreon, Monterrey, and Nuevo Laredo.

Transportes del Pacifico (TP, tel. 820-577) salidas de paso connect hourly en route northwest to Tijuana and southeast to Tepic, Guadalajara, Mexico City and intermediate points. You can change buses at Tepic, however, and continue to Puerto Vallarta.

Estrella Blanca (EB, tel. 815-381) and its subsidiary carrier, **Rojo de los Altos,** connect with the north via Durango, Torreon, and Juarez. They also connect with the east via Fresnillo, Zacatecas, and San Luis Potosi. To the southeast, buses connect with Tepic (thence to Puerto Vallarta), Guadalajara, and Mexico City.

By Train

The first-class (coach only) accommodation is so cheap (the Mexicali-Mazatlán fare is less than $50 for 1,100 miles) that it doesn't make sense to most folks to go any lower class. The **Estrella** is the only train that runs the long Ferrocarilles del Pacifico (Pacific Railroad) line from Mexicali to Guadalajara. Two trains run per day, one north, one south. The northbound train leaves Guadalajara at around 9 a.m., stops in Tepic, and arrives at Mazatlán around 6 p.m. It chugs out of Mazatlán around 7 p.m., heading for Culiacan, continuing overnight, rolling into Nogales next morning around eleven. It finally gets to Mexicali about 32 hours after it left Guadalajara, at around 5 p.m.

The next day, the Estrella turns around and moves out of Mexicali around 9 a.m. It rolls into Mazatlán about 22 hours later, around 6 a.m. It departs Mazatlán around 7 a.m., bound for Tepic and Guadalajara, where it arrives at around 6 p.m. (If you think the Estrella is slow, reflect on this: the second-class train that used to make this same trip was called El Burro.)

Make your reservations by phone (tel. 846-710) and verify times at the Mazatlán train station. You can buy tickets at the station booth an hour before departure. The station is called Colonia Esperanza, for the east-side district where it's located. (Since you're saving so much on the train, invest in a *pulmonía* to the station.)

By Ferry

The only ferry runs to and from **La Paz,** Baja California, leaving daily sometime between 3 and 5 p.m. from the terminal at the foot of Av. Carnaval. Passenger and vehicle tickets (cars, from around $100, big RVs and trailers much more) are sold at the terminal ticket office, open daily 8-12. Save yourself *mucho* trouble, however, and reserve your ferry tickets through a travel agent, such as Marza Tours (in the Hotel Puesta del Sol, tel. 840-708).

You cannot remain in your vehicle during the 16-hour trip. There there are four kinds of accommodations: salon (sitting room, $17/person), tourist (four-person cabin with beds, $34/person), cabin (for four with bath, $40/person), and special (suite, $51/person).

Feo (ugly) is the local description of the La Paz ferry. Besides poor service and dirty facilities, drivers must typically wait days, even a week or more, for vehicle space during the high winter season. Commercial vehicles receive priority, so private cars and RVs (even *with* reservations) often get "bumped" for days on end.

SOUTH TO PUERTO VALLARTA AND INLAND TO GUADALAJARA

ALONG THE ROAD TO SAN BLAS

National Highway 15 winds southward from Mazatlán through a lush, palm-dotted patchwork of pasture, fields, and jungle-clad hills. To the east rise the sculpted domes of the Sierra Madre Occidental, while on the west, a grand, island-studded marshland stretches to a virtually unbroken barrier of ocean sand.

Although a few scattered fishing villages edge this 150-mile (250-km) coastline, it remains mostly wild, the domain of hosts of shorebirds and waterfowl, and, in the most remote mangrove reaches, jaguars and crocodiles. Its palmy, driftwood-strewn beaches invite adventurous trekkers, RV campers, and travelers who enjoy Pacific Mexico beaches at their untouristed best.

PLAYA CAIMANERO

A cluster of beachside palapa restaurants marks the southern end of Playa Caimanero, a 20-mile barrier dune that blocks Laguna Caimanero from the sea. (The salinity of Laguna Caimanero, however, is a mystery to local people, who speculate that the salt water migrates under the dune.)

Besides most of the low-key beach pastimes, both Playa Caimanero and its lagoon are a bird-lover's heaven (bring your bird book, binoculars, and repellent). The broad, shallow **Laguna Caimanero** is less than a mile from the beach along any one of a dozen little tracks through the

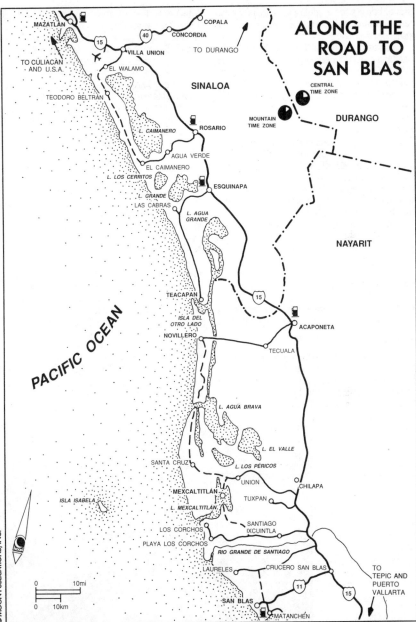

ALONG THE ROAD TO SAN BLAS

MAZATLAN

TO CULIACAN AND U.S.A.

VILLA UNION

40
CONCORDIA
COPALA
TO DURANGO

CENTRAL TIME ZONE

DURANGO

MOUNTAIN TIME ZONE

EL WALAMO

SINALOA

TEODORO BELTRAN

L. CAIMANERO

ROSARIO

15

AGUA VERDE

EL CAIMANERO

L. LOS CERRITOS

ESQUINAPA

L. GRANDE

LAS CABRAS

L. AGUA GRANDE

NAYARIT

15

TEACAPAN

ISLA DEL OTRO LADO

NOVILLERO

ACAPONETA

TECUALA

PACIFIC OCEAN

L. AGUA BRAVA

L. EL VALLE

SANTA CRUZ

L. LOS PÉRICOS

UNION

CHILAPA

ISLA ISABELA

MEXCALTITLAN

L. MEXCALTITLAN

TUXPAN

LOS CORCHOS

SANTIAGO IXCUINTLA

PLAYA LOS CORCHOS

RIO GRANDE DE SANTIAGO

LAURELES

CRUCERO SAN BLAS

TO TEPIC AND PUERTO VALLARTA

0   10mi
0   10km

11

15

SAN BLAS

MATANCHEN

© MOON PUBLICATIONS, INC.

grove. Local people could probably point you to a boatman who could take you on a bird-watching excursion.

Besides birds, Playa Caimanero is a prime hatching ground for endangered species of sea turtles. They crawl ashore, especially during the later summer and fall, when volunteers patrol the sand, trying to protect the eggs from poachers and predators.

Beach Activities

Playa Caimanero offers many possibilities, from a scenic, one-day excursion out of Mazatlán or a side loop from Highway 15, traveling either north or south, to a weeklong trekking-camping-fishing and wildlife-watching adventure. (Swimmers, however, must be careful of the rough waves and undertow.)

Although no beach facilities exist save the rustic seafood palapas at El Caimanero, small stores at two or three villages behind the dune carry basic food supplies. Water, however, is scarce along the beach; campers, bring your purification tablets or filter and some big plastic bottles to fill at the villages. If you get tired of walking, a truck bumps along the beach road every five or ten minutes; stick out your thumb.

Getting There

At Villa Union, 15 miles (24 km) south of Mazatlán, stock up on gas and supplies. Then head west (or ride the local bus) another 15 miles along Sinaloa Highway 5-14 through the dusty little town of El Walamo to beachside

Teodoro Beltrán village. The paved road ends a few miles before Beltrán, but improves within a mile to graded gravel and continues atop the beach dune for about 12 miles (20 km) to the seafood palapas at El Caimanero. The pavement resumes at the south end (where the road becomes Sinaloa 5-19), heading along the southeastern edge of the lagoon through Agua Verde and rejoining Hwy. 15 at Rosario. The reverse, northward-bound, trip could be done just as easily from Rosario.

TEACAPAN

The downscale little beach resorts of Teacapan and Novillero have not yet been "discovered." They remain quiet retreats for lovers of sun, sand, simple lodgings, and super-fresh seafood. Trucks travel from all over Sinaloa and Nayarit to buy their shrimp and fish.

Although Teacapan and Novillero are only a few miles apart, the rivermouth that divides Sinaloa from Nayarit also divides Teacapan from Novillero. Novillero's peninsula is identified by Teacapan residents as simply Isla Del Otro Lado ("Island on the Other Side").

The small town of Teacapan (pop. 5,000) lies along the sandy northeast edge of the estuary, which most residents know only as la boca, the river "mouth." Tambora, Teacapan's broad beach, borders a towering old palm grove on the open ocean a couple of miles north of the town.

Wildlife-rich Laguna Caimanero invites exploring by boat.

The shimmering expanse of the Marismas Nacionales ("National Marshes") wetlands spreads west from Hwy. 15 south of Mazatlán.

Most lodgings and restaurants, however, are on the estuary, a lazy place, where people walk very slowly. Here, a crumbling old dinghy returns to the sand; there, native-style *canoas* lie casually beneath the palms.

Accommodations And Food

A few restaurants line the estuary beach; the best is seafood **Restaurant Wayne** (from the name of an American friend of the enterprising Mexican owner). He employs his own fisherman to bring the best *pargo, robalo,* and *mero* to the barbecue every afternoon.

Oldest of the town's three accommodations is the very laid-back **Motel-Trailer Park Oregon.** The trailer section (right on the estuary) has about 15 shadeless pads with all hookups, which rent for about $7 per night or $200 per month. They also rent a pair of motel-style tiled rooms with onyx baths, ceiling fans, and screen doors and windows against bugs for about $17 d per night. At Calle Reforma 50, Teacapan, Sinaloa, tel. (695) 310-76, ext. 166. Get there by turning right at the sign before the town plaza. Ask for owner Vicki Sambrano, or her brother Vicente.

Across the street is a 20-unit motel so new that it has no name. The rooms, spacious, with fans and baths, encircle an inner pool-patio and rent for about $20 a night.

Beneath a palm grove on the town's outskirts is the **RV Park Las Lupitas,** owned and operated by a friendly refugee from L.A. smog, Hugh Thompson, and his Mexican wife. They, along with many other longtime Teacapan residents,

lament the overfishing of the estuary. "When I arrived in the fifties," Hugh reports, "they were pulling big turtles out of the lagoon by the truckloads." There are now no turtles or oysters left from the many acres of original beds, and precious few fish, which the local fishermen must now dive for with spearguns.

Hugh and his wife have 20 shady spaces a quarter-mile from Tambora beach that rent for $8.50/day, tents $4. Their address is simply Teacapan, Sinaloa 82560; no phone, all hookups, showers with hot water, a satellite dish available if you have your own lead-in and connectors, discounts available for monthly rentals and self-sufficient units, reservations generally not necessary.

Beach Activities

Fortunately, **ocean fishing** remains good off Tambora beach. Watch for the sign on the right about two miles before town. You can rent a *lancha,* or launch your own boat right on the beach.

Tambora is a very broad silky sand beach where the waves normally roll in gently from about a hundred yards out, breaking gradually both left and right for **surfing. Windsurfing** would also be good here, although the water is too sandy for snorkeling. Various **clam, cowrie,** and **cockle shells** turn up at seasonal times. A permanent beachside palapa restaurant serves fresh seafood and drinks. Other food and supplies are available in stores back in town.

Camping is customary most anywhere, either on the sand or beneath the big palm grove that edges the shoreline, curving south back to the estuary. To the north, the beach stretches, wild and breezy, for several miles.

Services
Along the main street back in town, residents enjoy the services of a doctor, a pharmacy, a fairly well-stocked grocery, and a long-distance telephone office.

Getting There
Teacapan is accessible from Hwy. 15 by Sinaloa Highway 5-23 from Esquinapa. Ride the local *urbano* or red Transportes Escuinapa buses from in front of the cathedral or the Pemex gas station at the Highway 15-Teacapan highway junction. The all-paved 24 miles (38 km) passes quickly, through bushy thorn forest and past shallow lagoons dotted with waterbirds and rafts of wild lotus. Palm groves and broad fields of *chiles* (chile peppers, which make Sinaloa one of Mexico's top chili-producing states) line the roadside.

Esquinapa (pop. about 60,000), a busy farm town, has a good overnight hotel, the IQ de Esquinapa (with restaurant), half a block from the downtown plaza (Gabriel Leyva 7 Sur, tel. 695-304-71, 695-307-82). The 30 luxurious rooms around an enclosed courtyard rent for about $25 d, with TV, a/c, phones, and parking; credit cards accepted.

NOVILLERO

Little Novillero (pop. about 1,000) enjoys one of the longest (55 miles, 90 km), smoothest stretches of sand in Mexico. The waves roll in gently from a hundred yards out and swish lazily along a velvety, nearly level beach. Here, all of the ingredients for a perfect beach stay come together: palapa seafood restaurants, hotels, a big palm grove for RV or tent camping, ocean fishing, and a broad creamy strand for beachcombers and wilderness campers stretching from both ends of town.

Accommodations And Food
Foremost among the several lodgings is the aging, 40-room **Hotel Playa Novillero** beside the palm grove about two blocks from the beach (P.O. Box 56, Tequala, Nayarit 63440, no

phone). The hotel encloses a bushy green garden and patio with a spacious, well-maintained pool. The tile-floored rooms are simple, but comfortable. Carved dark hardwood doors and tight shutters add a homey touch of class and keep out bugs. A wide, screened-in porch furnished with plants, big wooden rockers, and rustic chairs and tables provides a shady setting for reading and relaxing. Rates run $10 for one, $20 for two to four; ceiling fans, restaurant in season, credit cards accepted. It's popular with North Americans and Europeans, winter reservations necessary.

If you must stay right on the beach, however, the **Hotel Paraiso de Novillero** can accommodate you (same owner, address, and prices as Hotel Playa Novillero, 24 rooms, a pool, parking, credit cards accepted). This lodging's air-conditioned Motel 6-style ambience would appeal most to families busily heading for the pool or beach.

If both of these are full, you can try fourth-choice **Hotel Miramar** across the street, or third-choice **Bungalows** on the beach dirt road past the grove on the north edge of town.

For food, Novillero offers a number of choices: a well-stocked country grocery (here called the "super") and half a dozen palapa restaurants accustomed to serving a generation of vacationers. Try the big beachside **Hotel Miramar** palapa, or look into Lola's **La Gaera,** on the town street two blocks south, where Lola has built a palapa supported entirely by front-yard trees and furnished by a rainbow assortment of chairs and oilcloth-covered tables. Her son usually arrives about nine o'clock and belts out gratis serenades for customers on his guitar.

MEXCALTITLÁN

Mexcaltitlán (pop. 2,000), the "House of the Mexicans," represents much more than just a scenic little island town. Archaeological evidence indicates that Mexcaltitlán may actually be the legendary island-town of Aztlán ("Place of the Herons") where, in 1091, the Aztecs (who called themselves the Mexica—"MAY-shi-kuh") began their generations-long migration to the Valley of Mexico.

Each year in late October, residents of Mexcaltitlán and surrounding villages dress up in

BRUCE WHIPPERMAN

Mexcaltitlán children pose before the town mural, which depicts the traditional story of the migration of their Aztec ancestors to the Valley of Mexico.

feathered headresses and jaguar robes and breathe life into their tradition. As part of the patriotic, all-Nayarit **Fería de Mexicanidad,** they start off by boat, winding through the coastal mangrove channels, picking up costumed brother-participants at each village along the way. At nearby Santiago Ixcuintla, the procession swells to many hundreds, continuing by foot 60 miles all the way to its climax at Tepic, usually in mid-November.

Getting There

The southbound Hwy. 15 turnoff for Mexcaltitlán is 136 miles (219 km) miles south of Mazatlán, four miles (six km) south of the village of Chilapa. Northbound, turn off 38 miles (60 km) north of Tepic, on to the signed road to Santiago Ixcuintla.

The 30-mile (50-km) southbound side trip passes its last half along a rough gravel road-dike through the marsh, edged by bushy mangroves and lotus ponds and inhabited by constellations of waterbirds and water-lily-munching cattle.

Sights

At the road's-end **Embarcadero,** a boatman will row you across to the island-village, many of whose inhabitants have never crossed the channel to the mainland. The town itself is not unlike many Mexican villages, except more civilized and tranquil, due to the absence of motor vehicles.

Mexcaltitlán is getting ready for tourists, however. They have put together a small museum and have painted all their houses a spiffy red and white.

Occasionally the streets, which radiate from the central plaza, are flooded like Venice-style canals. At the watery lagoon-ends of these streets, men set out in canoes and boats for the open-ocean fishing grounds, where, armed with kerosene lanterns, they attract the shrimp into their nets.

At the central plaza stands the proud village **church,** flanked by the city hall, where a mural showing the Aztecs' struggle to found their empire spreads around the inner courtyard wall.

Food And Accommodations

Opposite the church stands the attractive **El Camarón** seafood restaurant, and, at the view-edge of the lagoon nearby, is Mexcaltitlán's first **hotel,** yet to be named. More like a guesthouse than a hotel, its four clean, comfortable, tiled rooms with bath, some with a/c, rent from about $20 d. Write to the manager, Emilio Beltrán, Mexcaltitlán, Nayarit 63560, for reservations.

SAN BLAS AND VICINITY

San Blas (pop. about 6,000) is a little town slumbering beneath a big coconut grove. No one seems to care that the clock on the crumbling plaza church remains stuck at 5:28. Neither is there anyone who remembers San Blas's glory days, when it was Mexico's burgeoning Pacific military headquarters and port, with a population of 30,000. Ships from Spain's Pacific-rim colonies crowded its harbor, silks and gold filled its royal countinghouse, and noble Spanish officers and their mantilla-graced ladies strolled the plaza on Sunday afternoons.

Times change, however. Politics and San Blas's pesky *jejenes* (hey-HEY-nays, invisible "no-see-um" biting gnats) have always conspired to deflate any temporary fortunes of San Blas. The *jejenes'* breeding ground, a vast hinterland of mangrove marshes, may, paradoxically, someday give rise to a new, prosperous San Blas. Those thousands of acres of waterlogged mangrove jungle and savannah are a nursery-home for dozens of Mexico's endangered species. This rich trove is now protected by ecologically aware governments and admired (not unlike the game parks of Africa) by increasing numbers of eco-tourists.

HISTORY

Conquest And Colonization
San Blas and the neighboring, southward-curving Bay of Matanchén were reconnoitered by gold-hungry conquistador Nuño de Guzmán in May of 1530. His expedition noted the protected anchorages in the bay and the Estero El Pozo adjacent to the present town. Occasionally during the 16th and 17th centuries, Spanish explorers and galleons (and pirates lying in wait for them) would drop anchor in the estero or the adjacent Bay of Matanchén for rendezvous, resupply or cargo-transfer.

By the latter third of the 18th century, New Spain, reacting to the Russian and English threats in the North Pacific, launched plans for the colonization of California through a new port called San Blas. The town was officially founded atop the hill of San Basilio in 1768. Streets were

surveyed; docks were built. Old documents record that more than a hundred pioneer families received a plot of land and "a pick, an adze, an axe, a machete, a plow . . . a pair of oxen, a cow, a mule, four she-goats and a billy, four sheep, a sow, four hens and a rooster."

They multiplied, and soon San Blas became the seat of Spain's eastern Pacific naval command. Meanwhile, simultaneously with the founding of the town, the celebrated Father Junípero Serra set out for California with 14 missionaries-brothers on the *La Concepción,* a sailboat built on Matanchén beach just south of San Blas.

Independence
New Spain's glory, however, crumbled in the bloody 1810-21 war for independence, taking San Blas with it. In December 1810, the *insurgente* commander captured the Spanish fort atop San Basilio hill and sent 43 of its cannon to fellow rebel-priest Miguel Hidalgo to use against the loyalists around Guadalajara. After independence, fewer and fewer ships called at San Blas; the docks fell into disrepair, and the town slipped into somnolence, then complete slumber when president Lerdo de Tejada closed San Blas to foreign commerce in 1872.

SIGHTS

Getting Oriented
The overlook atop the **Cerro de San Basilio** is the best spot from which to orient yourself to San Blas. From that breezy point, the palm-shaded grid of streets stretches to the sunset-side **El Pozo** estuary and lighthouse-hill beyond it. Behind you, to the east, the mangrove-lined **San Cristobal** estuary meanders south to the **Bay of Matanchén.** Along that south shore, the crystalline white line of San Blas's main beach, **Playa El Borrego,** ("Sheep Beach") stretches between the two estuary-mouths.

Around Town
While you're atop the hill, take a look around the old *contaduria* countinghouse and fort (built in 1770) where the riches were tallied and stored

THE BELLS OF SAN BLAS

Henry Wadsworth Longfellow (1807-82), America's favorite romantic poet, visited San Blas in the early 1870s, just after San Blas's door had been closed to foreign trade. With the ships gone, and not even the trickle of tourists it now enjoys, Longfellow's San Blas was even dustier and quieter than it is today.

Ten years later, his visit must have loomed important to him. Ill and dying, Longfellow hastened to complete *The Bells of San Blas*, which became his very last poem, nine days before he passed away on March 24, 1882. Longfellow writes of the silent bells of the old Nuestro Señora del Rosario ("Our Lady of the Rosary") church that still stands atop the Cerro San Basilio, little changed since his day.

THE BELLS OF SAN BLAS
by Henry Wadsworth Longfellow

What say the Bells of San Blas
To the ships that southward pass
From the harbor of Mazatlan?
To them it is nothing more
Than the sound of surf on the shore,—
Nothing more to master or man.

But to me, a dreamer of dreams,
To whom what is and what seems
Are often one and the same,—
The Bells of San Blas to me
Have a strange, wild melody,
And are something more than a name.

For bells are the voice of the church;
They have tones that touch and search
The hearts of young and old;
One sound to all, yet each
Lends a meaning to their speech,
And the meaning is manifold.

They are a voice of the Past,
Of an age that is fading fast,
Of a power austere and grand;
When the flag of Spain unfurled
Its folds o'er this western world,
And the Priest was lord of the land.

The chapel that once looked down
On the little seaport town
Has crumbled into the dust
And on oaken beams below
The bells swing to and fro,
And are green with mould and rust.

"Is then, the old faith dead,"
They say, "and in its stead
Is some new faith proclaimed,

That we are forced to remain
Naked to sun and rain,
Unsheltered and ashamed?

"Once in our tower aloof
We rang over wall and roof
Our warnings and our complaints;
And round about us there
The white doves filled the air,
Like the white souls of the saints.

"The saints! Ah, have they grown
Forgetful of their own?
Are they asleep, or dead,
That open to the sky
Their ruined Missions lie,
No longer tenanted?

"Oh, bring us back once more
The vanished days of yore,
When the world with faith was filled;
Bring back the fervid zeal,
The hearts of fire and steel,
The hands that believe and build.

"Then from our tower again
We will send over land and main
Our voices of command,
Like exiled kings who return
To their thrones, and the people learn
That the Priest is lord of the land!"

O Bells of San Blas, in vain
Ye call back the Past again!
The Past is deaf to your prayer;
Out of the shadows of night
The world rolls into light;
It is daybreak everywhere.

en route to Mexico City, the Philippines, or China. Several of the original great cannons still stand guard at the viewpoint, like aging sentinels waiting for long-dead adversaries.

Behind and a bit downhill from the weathered stone arches of the *contaduria* stand the gaping portals and towering, moss-stained belfry of the old church of **Nuestra Señora del Rosario,** built in 1769. Undamaged by war, it was still an active church in 1872, when visiting poet Henry W. Longfellow was captivated by the melancholy tolling of its aging bells.

Historic houses and ruins dot San Blas town downhill. The old hotels **Bucanero** and **Flamingos** on the main street, Juarez, leading past the central plaza, preserve some of their original charm. (See "Hotels" below.) Just across the street from the Hotel Flamingos you can admire the crumbling yet monumental brick colonnade of 19th-century **ex-Aduana,** now supplanted by a nondescript new customshouse at the foot of Av. Juarez.

At that shoreline spot, gaze across El Pozo estuary. This was both the jumping-off point for Father Junipero Serra's colonization of the Californias and the anchorage of the silk- and porcelain-laden Manila Galleon and the bullion ships from the northern mines.

The palapa restaurant and spring (background) at La Tovara reward visitors with refreshment after the boat tour through the jungle from San Blas.

El Faro lighthouse across the estuary marks the top of **Cerro Vigia,** the southern hill-tip of Isla del Reye (actually a peninsula). There, the first beacon shone during the latter third of the 18th century.

Although only a few local folks ever bother to cross over to the island, it is nevertheless an important pilgrimage site for Huichol people from the remote Nayarit and Jalisco mountains. Huichols have been gathering on the Isla de Los Reyes for centuries to make offerings to Aramara, their goddess of the sea. (A not-so-coincidental shrine to a Catholic virgin-saint stands on an offshore sea rock, visible from the beach-endpoint of the Huichol pilgrimage a few hundred yards beyond the lighthouse.)

A large cave, sacred to the Huichols, at the foot of Cerro Vigia was sadly demolished by the government during the early 1970s for rock for a breakwater. Fortunately, however, President Salinas de Gortari partly compensated for the insult by deeding the sacred site to the Huichols during the early '90s.

Two weeks before Easter, they begin arriving by the hundreds, the men decked out in their flamboyant feathered hats. On the ocean beach, 10 minutes' walk straight across the island, anyone can respectfully watch them perform their rituals: elaborate marriages, feasts, and offerings of little boats laden with arrows and food, consecrated to the sea-goddess to ensure good hunting, crops, and many healthy children.

La Tovara Jungle River Trip

On the downstream side of the bridge over Estero San Cristobal, launches-for-hire will take you up the Tovara River, a side channel that winds into the jungle about a mile downstream.

The channel quickly narrows into a dark tree-tunnel, edged by great curtainlike swaths of mangrove roots. Big snowy egrets *(garza)* peer out from leafy branches; startled turtles slip off their soggy perches into the river, while big submerged roots, like gigantic pythons, bulge out of the inky water. Riots of luxuriant plants—white lilies, green ferns, red *romelia* orchids—hang from the trees and line the banks.

Finally you reach Tovara Springs, which wells up from the base of a verdant cliffside. On one side, a bamboo-sheltered palapa restaurant serves refreshments, while on the other, families picnic in a hillside pavilion. In the middle, everyone jumps in and paddles in the clear, cool water.

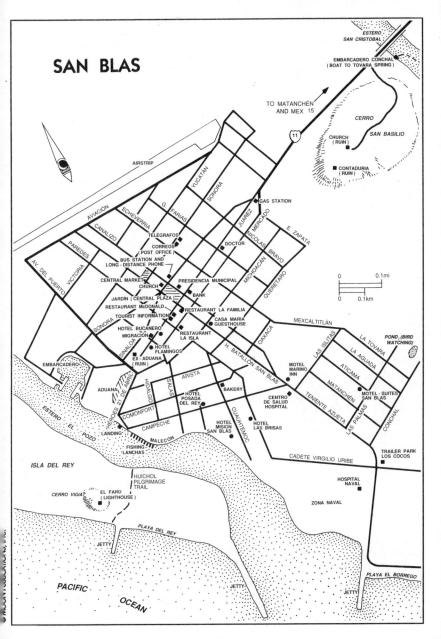

You can enjoy this trip either of two ways: the longer, three-hour excursion as described (for about $30 per boatload of six to eight) from Conchal landing on the estuary, or the shorter version (two hours, about $24/boatload) beginning upriver at road-accessible Aguada landing (near Matanchén village—take the hourly Matanchén bus from the San Blas central plaza).

The more leisurely three-hour trip allows more chances (especially in early morning) to spot a jaguar or crocodile, or a giant boa constrictor hanging from a limb (no kidding). Many of the boatmen are very professional; if you want to view wildlife, tell them, and they'll go slower and keep a sharp lookout. For one of the better boatmen, ask for Elias Partida.

Isla Isabel

Isla Isabel is a two-square-mile offshore bird and wildlife study area 40 miles (65 km—three hours) north by boat. It is home for a small government station of eco-scientists and a host of nesting boobies, frigate birds, and white-tailed tropic birds. Fish and sea mammals, especially dolphins, and sometimes whales, abound in the surrounding clear waters. Although not a recreational area, serious visitors can get permission (from the local office of SEDUE, Secretariat for Urban Development and Ecology; you must also pay a small fee at the City Hall) for a few days of camping, snorkeling, scuba diving, and birdwatching. (See Mike Vasquez, manager of the Motel Posada del Rey and the Pato Loco store, who outfits trips and obtains permits, boat and equipment, including scuba tanks and lessons.)

Birdwatching

Although San Blas's extensive mangrove and mountain jungle hinterlands are renowned for their birds and wildlife, rewarding birdwatching can start in the early morning right at the edge of town. From Motel-Suites San Blas, walk one block to Calle Conchal. Turn left and continue a few blocks to a small pond on the left. With binoculars, you might get some good views of local species of cormorants, flycatchers, grebes, herons, jacanas, and motmots. A handy copy of Peterson's *A Guide to Mexican Birds* will assist in further identification.

Profitable birdwatching is also possible on the **Isla del Rey.** Bargain for a launch (from the foot of Juarez, about $2 roundtrip) across to the opposite shore. (Watch for wood, clapper, and Virginia rails, and boat-billed herons near the estuary shore.) Then follow the track across the island (look for warblers and a number of species of sparrows) to the beach where you might enjoy good views of plovers, terns, Heerman's gulls, and rafts of pelicans. In early morning, look around the hillside cemetery and the ruins atop **Cerro San Basilio** for good views of hummingbirds, falcons, owls, and American redstarts.

You can include serious birdwatching with your boat trip through the mangrove channels branching from the **Estero San Cristobal** and **La Tovara River.** (Especially if you obtain the services of the extremely knowledgeable English-speaking guide, Manuel Lomelli, home tel. 321-505-58, afternoons and evenings.

For many more details on birdwatching and hiking around San Blas, get a copy of the booklet *Where to Find Birds in San Blas, Nayarit* by Rosalind Novick and Lan Sing Wu, at the shop at the Las Brisas Hotel for around $4, or order from them directly at 178 Myrtle Court, Arcata, CA 95521. The American Birding Association Bookstore, P.O. Box 6599, Colorado Springs, CO 80934, and the Los Angeles and Tucson Audubon Society bookstores also stock it.

Beaches And Activities

San Blas's most convenient beach is **Playa Borrego,** at the south end of Calle Cuauhtémoc about a mile south of town. With a lineup of palapas for food and drinks, the mile-long, broad, fine-sand beach is ripe for all beach activities except snorkeling (due to the murky water). The gradual-breaking waves provide **boogieboarding** and intermediate **surfing** challenges, however. Bring your own equipment for no one rents any on the beach (although the Pato Loco beachware shop on Juarez across the street from Restaurant McDonald in town rents surfboards and boogieboards for $9 a day).

Shoals of shells—clams, cockles, mother-of-pearl—wash up on Borrego Beach during storms. **Fishing** is often good, especially by casting from the jetty and rocks at the north and south ends.

ACCOMMODATIONS

Hotels
San Blas has several hotels, none of them big, but all with personality. They vary from luxurious to seedy, and during the high winter season, even the seedy ones are likely to be full.

At the low end, the family-run *casa de huéspedes* (guesthouse) **Casa Maria** makes a reality of the old Spanish saying, "mi casa es tu casa" (Heroico Batallón 108, San Blas, Nayarit 63740, at Michoacán, two blocks from the plaza). With 10 rooms around homey, cluttered patios on opposite sides of the street, they offer to do everything for the guests except give them baths (which they would probably do if someone got sick). Not too clean, but very friendly and with kitchen privileges. Rooms rent for about $10 s, $12 d with bath; $7 and $9 without; ceiling fans, hot water, dinner for $3.

The **Hotel Flamingos** seems like a vision out of old San Blas (Juarez 105, San Blas, Nayarit 63740, three blocks down Juarez from the plaza). Once the German Consulate, it looks scarcely changed since the day it opened in 1863. A leafy jungle blooms in the patio, enfolded by shaded porticoes. The best 12 of the 20 rooms are airy, high ceilinged, and graceful; others are tiny and dark. Look before you put your money down. The 20 rooms run about $15 s, $20 d, with hot water and ceiling fans.

Half a block along Juarez, the **Hotel Bucanero** appears to be living up to its name (Juarez 75, San Blas, Nayarit 63740, a block from the plaza, tel. 321-501-01). A stanza from the *Song of the Pirate,* emblazons one wall, a big stuffed crocodile bares its teeth beside the other, and a crusty sunken anchor and cannons decorate the shady patio. Despite peeling paint the rooms retain a bit of spacious, old-world charm, with high-beamed ceilings under the ruddy roof tile. (High, circular vent windows in some rooms cannot be closed, however. Use your mosquito net.) Outside, the big pool and leafy old patio-courtyard provide plenty of nooks for daytime snoozing and socializing. A noisy nighttime (winter-spring seasonal) bar, however, keeps most guests without earplugs jumping till about midnight. Their 32 rooms are about $14 s, $17 d; credit cards accepted.)

SAN BLAS HOTELS

San Blas hotels, in order of approximate double-room price (area code 321, postal code 63740)

Casa Maria, H. Batallón 108, $12
Hotel Bucanero, Juarez 75, 501-01, $17
Hotel Misión San Blas, Cuauhtémoc 197, 500-23, $18
Hotel Flamingos, Juarez 105, $20
Motel-Suites San Blas, Aticama and Las Palmas, $25
Hotel Posada del Rey, Campeche 10, 501-23, $27
Motel Marino Inn, H. Battalón s/n, 503-03, $30
Hotel Las Brisas, Cuauhtémoc 106 Sur, 501-12, $60

San Blas's more modern hotels are nearer the water. The lively, family-operated **Hotel Posada del Rey** seems to be trying hardest (Campeche 10, San Blas, Nayarit 63740, tel. 321-501-23). It encloses a small but inviting pool-patio beneath a top-floor viewpoint bar (and high-season-only restaurant), which bubbles with continuous soft rock and salsa tunes. Friendly owner Mike Vasquez, who splits his day between his Pato Loco everything-for-the-beach store and his bar at night, also arranges tours and fishing, snorkeling and diving excursions to nearby coastal spots. His hotel rooms, while nothing fancy, are comfortable. The rates for their 12 rooms are about $20 s, $27 d with fan; a/c $6 extra, credit cards accepted.)

San Blas's only waterfront lodging is the slightly run-down **Hotel Misión San Blas** (Cuauhtémoc 197, San Blas, Nayarit 63740, tel. 321-500-23—formerly Posada Casa Morales), whose surrounding chain-link fence unfortunately sullies its view of the nearby estuary and boat-filled beachline. This is not true, however, of a pair of upstairs rooms, the best of the lot. Request "cuartos arriba, por favor." Amenities include a pool-patio and palapa-bar with food and drinks during holidays and high season. Their 20 rooms, rent for about $15 s, $18 d, credit cards accepted; with fans, TV, and parking.

In the palm-shadowed, country fringe of town not far from Playa Borrego is the **Motel-Suites San Blas** (Calles Aticama and Las Palmas, San Blas, Nayarit 63740, left off H. Batallón a few blocks after the Motel Marino). Its pool-patio, playground, game room, and spacious (but slightly worn) suites with kitchenettes (dishes and utensils *not* included) are nicely suited for active families. The 23 suites include 16 singles for two adults and kids renting for about $25, and seven doubles accommodating four adults with kids for about $30; credit cards accepted, fans.

Although the facilities list of the four-star **Motel Marino Inn** looks fine on paper, the place is generally unkempt. Its tattered amenities—from the bare-bulb reception and cavernous upstairs disco to the mossy pool-patio and mildewed rooms—sorely need scrubbing and a modicum of care (Av. H. Batallón s/n, San Blas, Nayarit 63740, tel. 321-503-03). The 60 rooms go for about $25 s, $30 d, all with a/c and private balconies; seasonal restaurant, credit cards accepted.

In fortunate contrast is San Blas's best, **Hotel Las Brisas** (Cuauhtémoc 106 Sur, San Blas, Nayarit 63740, south end of town, two blocks off H. Batallón, tel. 321-501-12 and 321-504-80). The careful management of its family-owners shows everywhere: manicured palm-shaded gardens, crystal-blue pool, immaculate sun deck, and centerpiece restaurant. The cool, air-conditioned rooms are tiled, tastefully furnished, and squeaky clean. Their 40 rooms go for about $50 s, $60 d, with a good breakfast included, credit cards accepted; a gift shop and travel agency are on the premises.

Trailer Park
San Blas's only trailer park, the **Los Cocos,** is a two-minute walk from the wide, yellow sands of Playa Borregos. Friendly management, spacious, palm-shaded grassy grounds, pull-throughs, unusually clean showers and toilet facilities, a laundry next door, good fishing, and a good, air-conditioned bar with satellite TV all make this place a magnet for RVers and tenters from Mazatlán to Puerto Vallarta. The biting *jejenes* require a good repellent for residents to enjoy the balmy evenings, however. Los Cocos is at H. Batallón s/n, San Blas, Nayarit 63740, tel. 321-500-55. The 100 spaces rent for about $7/day for two persons, $1 for each additional,

with all hookups. Monthly rates run $130 low season, $190 high; pets okay.

Camping
The *jejenes* and occasional local toughs and Peeping Toms make camping on close-in Borrego Beach a marginal possibility only. On the other side of town, however, **Isla del Rey** (accessible by *lancha* from the foot of Calle Juarez) presents possibilities for prepared trekker-tenters. The same is true for eco-sanctuary **Isla Isabel,** two hours by hired boat from San Blas. For those less equipped, the palm-lined strands of **Playa Islitas, Playa Matanchén,** and **Playa Cocos** on the Bay of Matanchén are ripe for camping. (For details on all these, see "Beaches and Activities," above, and "Around the Bay of Matanchén," below.)

FOOD

Snacks, Stalls, And Market
During the mornings and early afternoons try the fruit stands, groceries, *fondas,* and *jugerías* in and around the **Central Market** (behind the plaza church). Late afternoons and evenings, many semipermanent streetside stands around the plaza, such as the **Taqueria Las Cuatas** (corner of Canalizo and Juarez), offer tasty *antojitos* and drinks.

For sit-down snacks every day till midnight, drop into the **Lonchería Ledmar** (also at the Canalizo-Juarez corner), for a hot *torta,* hamburger, quesadilla, tostada, or freshly-squeezed *jugo* (juice).

Get your fresh cupcakes, cookies, and crispy *bolillos* rolls at the **bakery** at Comonfort and Cuauhtémoc (around the uptown corner from Hotel Posada del Rey, closed Sundays).

Restaurants
(Complete Dinner Price Key: Budget = under $7, Moderate = $7-14, Expensive = more than $14.) Family-managed **Restaurant McDonald** is one of the gathering places of San Blas (36 Juarez, tel. 504-32, half a block from the plaza, open daily 7 a.m-10 p.m.). Their eclectic menu features soups (cream of asparagus $2), meat (pork chops $5), and seafood (shrimp $7, fish fillet $5), plus a hamburger that beats no-relation U.S. McDonald's by a mile). Budget to moderate.

For TV with dinner, the **Restaurant La Familia** is just the place (H. Batallón between Juarez and Mercado, open 5-10 p.m., closed Sunday). American movies, serape-draped walls, and colorful Mexican tile supply the ambience while a reasonably priced seafood and meat menu furnishes the food. For dessert, step into their luminescent-decor bar next door for giant-screen American baseball or football. Moderate.

For subdued marine atmosphere and good fish and shrimp, both local folks and visitors choose **Restaurant La Isla** (Mercado and Paredes, tel. 504-07, open daily 2-9). As ceiling fans whir overhead and a guitar strums softly in the background, the net-draped walls display a museum-load of marine curiosities, from antique Japanese floats and Tahitian shells to New England ship models. Moderate.

The classiest restaurant in town is the **El Delfin** at the Hotel Las Brisas (Cuauhtémoc 106, tel. 501-12, open daily 8-10 a.m. and 4-8:30 p.m., credit cards accepted). Balmy evening air and leafy planter-dividers enhance the refined tropical atmosphere of this large garden (but *jejene*-screened) dining room-in-the-round. Meticulous preparation and service, bountiful breakfasts, savory dinner soups, and fresh salad, seafood, and meat entrees keep customers returning year after year. Moderate to expensive.

ENTERTAINMENT

Sleepy San Blas's entertainment is mostly of the local, informal variety. Visitors usually content themselves with strolling the beach (or riding the waves) by day, and reading, watching TV, listening to mariachis, or dancing at a handful of clubs by night.

Nightlife

Owner-manager Mike McDonald works hard to keep **Mike's Place** (on the second floor, above his family's restaurant) the classiest club in town. He keeps the lights flashing and the small dance floor thumping with blues, Latin music, and '60s-style rock tunes from his own guitar, accompanied by his equally excellent drum- and electronic-piano partners (Juarez 36, tel. 504-32, live music Fri., Sat., and Sun. nights and holidays 9 p.m.-midnight, small cover, reasonable drinks).

Another spot with an upstairs view for sunsets and that offers satellite TV and an occasional live combo is the **El Mirador** bar above the Hotel Posada del Rey (Campeche 10, tel. 501-23).

A few other places require nothing more than your ears to find. Every weekend night music booms out of **Los Ponchos** dance hall (down H. Batallón, a couple of blocks past the Marino Inn), and the **Hotel Bucanero** (at Juarez 75, tel. 501-01, open seasonally only).

SPORTS

Walking And Jogging

The cooling sea breeze and the soft but firm sand of **Playa Borrego** at the south end of H. Batallón make it the best place around town for a walk or jog. Arm yourself against *jejenes* with repellent and long pants, especially around sunset.

Water Sports

Although some intermediate- and beginner-level surfing breaks roll in at Borrego Beach, nearly all of San Blas's action goes on at world-class surfing mecca Matanchén Beach. (Please see "Around the Bay of Matanchén," below, for details.)

The mild offshore currents and gentle, undertow-free slope of Borrego Beach are nearly always safe for good swimming, bodysurfing, and boogieboarding. Wind and water are often right for good windsurfing. Bring your own equipment, however; no rentals are available.

Sediment-fogged onshore water limits snorkel and scuba possibilities around San Blas to offshore eco-preserve Isla Isabel. See "Sights" above for details.

Sportfishing

Tony Aguayo is one of the best local contacts for boat, tackle and bait rentals for offshore fishing trips. Tony's "office" is the palapa-shelter to the left of the little dock at the foot of Calle Juarez. Expect to pay about $70 for a complete six-hour excursion for four people. Otherwise, simply bargain for a *lancha* with any one of the owners of the dozen-odd craft pulled up on the nearby estuary shoreline.

SHOPPING

San Blas visitors ordinarily spend little of their time shopping. For basics, however, the stalls at the **Central Market** offer lots of good tropical fruits, meats and staples (open daily 6 a.m.-2 p.m.). For used clothes and a little bit of everything else a **flea market** operates on Calle Canalizo a block past the bus station (away from the *jardín*) each Saturday morning and early afternoon.

One or two permanent *artesanís* (handicrafts) shops are on the block (behind the church) of Calle Sinaloa between Paredes and H. Batallón San Blas.

The plaza-corner **Comercial de San Blas** store (corner of Juarez and H. Batallón, open Mon.-Sat. 9-2 and 5-9) offers an unique mix of everything from film and development service to fishing poles, hooks, sinkers, and line.

INFORMATION

Tourist Information Office
The local branch of Nayarit state-federal tourism (83 Juarez, by Restaurant McDonald) is open Mon.-Fri. 9-3 except when officer-in-charge Enedina Toscano Fuerte has to be out of the office on business. In emergencies, you can reach her at home, tel. 504-09, however.

Health And Police
One of San Blas's most highly recommended physicians is **Dr. Alejandro Davalos,** three blocks east of the plaza at Juarez 202 Ote. (corner of Gomez Farías, tel. 503-31). San Blas has a respectable local hospital: the government **Centro de Salud** (health center, tel. 503-32) at Yucatán and H. Batallón (across the street from the Motel Marino Inn). The **Botica Mexicana** pharmacy (tel. 501-22, open daily 8:30-1:30 and 5-9), on the plaza opposite the church, stocks a large variety of medicines, along with a bit of everything, including film.

For **police** emergencies, contact the headquarters in the Palacio Municipal (city hall, tel. 500-28) on Canalizo, east side of the central plaza).

Books, News, And Magazines
English-language reading material in San Blas is as scarce as tortillas in Nome. The **newsstand,** on the plaza opposite the church, regularly sells *Time, Newsweek,* and *People* magazines, however. The **Hotel Las Brisas** shop stocks a few books, and **Pato Loco** shop across from

Restaurant McDonald has a shelf of used English and American paperbacks.

SERVICES

Bank And Moneychanger
Banamex (one block off the plaza at Juarez 36 Ote., tel. 500-30, 500-31) exchanges U.S. dollar traveler's checks and cash weekday mornings 8:30-10:30 only. After hours, try your hotel desk.

Post Office, Telegraph, And Telephone
The *Correos* (post office) and *Telégrafos* stand side by side at Sonora and Echeverróa (one block behind, one block east of the plaza church). The post office (tel. 509-25) is open Mon.-Fri. 9-1 and 3-5, Sat. 9-1; Telégrafos (tel. 501-15) is open Mon.-Fri. 8-2.

Efficient computer-assisted *larga-distancia* (long-distance) telephone service is available daily 6 a.m-9:30 p.m at the bus station on the plaza corner adjacent to the church. San Blas's area code is 321.

Immigration And Customs
Migración, at Juarez 150 (tel. 501-78, open weekdays 8-3) across from Hotel Bucaneros will help you if you lose your tourist card. The **Aduana** at the end of Juarez, tel. 503-54, will assist you with the necessary paperwork if you have to temporarily leave Mexico without your car.

GETTING THERE AND AWAY

By Car Or RV
Two paved roads connect San Blas to main-route National Hwy. 15. From the northeast, National Highway 11 winds 19 miles (31 km) downhill from its junction 161 miles (260 km) south of Mazatlán and 22 miles (35 km) north of Tepic. From the turnoff (marked by a Pemex gas station), the road winds through a forest of vine-draped trees and tall palms. (Go slowly; the road lacks a shoulder, and cattle or people may appear unexpectedly around any blind, grass-shrouded bend.)

From the southeast, Nayarit Hwy. 28 leaves Highway 15 at its signed "Miramar" turnoff at the northern edge of Tepic. The road winds downhill 3,000 feet (1,000 meters) through a wild mountain forest to **Santa Cruz del Miramar.** It continues along the **Bahía de Matanchén** shoreline to San Blas, a total of 34 miles (76 km) from Tepic. Although this route generally has more shoulder than Hwy. 11, frequent pedestrians and occasional unexpected cattle nevertheless necessitate caution.

By Bus
The San Blas bus terminal stands adjacent to the plaza church, at Calles Sinaloa and Canalizo. **Tres Estrellas de Oro** (TEO) first-class buses connect with southeast destinations of Tepic and Guadalajara once a day, departing San Blas in the afternoon. Second-class **Transportes Norte de Sonora** (TNS) buses connect several times a day with Tepic, some continuing to Guadalajara, departing San Blas between 6:30 a.m. and 5 p.m. First-class **Camiones de Los Altos** (a subsidiary of Estrella Blanca) buses also connect to Tepic in the afternoon.

AROUND THE BAY OF MATANCHÉN

The shoreline of the Bahía de Matanchén sweeps southward from San Blas, lined with an easily accessible, pearly crescent of sand, ripe for beachcombers. The villages of Matanchén, Aticama, Los Cocos, and Santa Cruz del Miramar dot this strand with palapa restaurants and stores offering food and basic supplies for camping. For noncampers, a few lodgings (one of which is excellent, see below) can provide basic accommodations.

Beaches, Activities, Food, And Accommodations
The beaches of **Matanchén** and **Las Islitas** make an inseparable pair. Las Islitas (if heading south, turn right at the Matanchén village junction) is dotted by little outcroppings topped by miniature jungles of swaying palms and spreading trees. One of these is home for a colony of surfers waiting for the Big Wave, the Holy Grail of surfing. The Big Wave is one of the occasional gigantic 20-foot breakers that rise off Playa Las Islitas and carry surfers as much as a mile and a quarter (an official Guin-

ness world record) to the soft sand of Playa Matanchén.

For camping, the scenic, intimate protected curves of sand around Playa Islitas are ideal. Although few facilities exist (save for a few winter-season food palapas), the beachcombing, swimming, fishing from the rocks, shell-collecting, and surfing are usually good even without the Big Wave. The water, however, isn't clear enough for for good snorkeling. Campers, be prepared with plenty of good insect repellent.

In season (around Nov.-March) the Team Banana and other palapa-shops open up at Matanchén and Las Islitas to rent surfboards and sell what each of them claims to be the "world's original banana bread."

Getting There
Drive or ride the Santa Cruz del Miramar-bound bus, which departs several times a day from the San Blas central plaza. The Matanchén-Santa Cruz del Miramar road branches south (right) after the estuary bridge, about two miles from the central plaza.

South From Matanchén
Bending south from Playa Islitas past a lineup of beachfront palapa restaurants, the super-wide and shallow (like a giant kiddie-pool) Playa Matanchén stretches to a palm-fringed, sand-ribbon washed by gentle rollers and frequented only by occasional fisherfolk. Past a marine sciences school a couple of miles south of Matanchén village, the sand gives way to rocky shoals beneath a jungly headland.

South of **Aticama** village (small stores and restaurants) the road continues along a shoreline coconut grove, name-source of the bordering Playa Los Cocos. Unfortunately, however, the ocean is eroding the beach, leaving a crumbling, ten-foot embankment along a mostly rocky shore. A winter-only oceanfront trailer park (with lush grass beneath the palms) and a pair of small motels could provide accommodation.

Far better, however, is the idyllic shoreline retreat, **Casa Mañana,** at the south end of Playa Los Cocos (about six miles from Matanchén). Owned and managed by an Austrian man, Reinhardt, and his Mexican wife Lourdes, Casa Mañana's double-storied tier of rooms rises over a homey, spic-and-span beach-view

roadside sign at Matanchén, near San Blas

BRUCE WHIPPERMAN

restaurant. Very popular with Europeans and North Americans seeking south-seas tranquility on a budget, Casa Mañana offers fishing, beachcombing, hiking, swimming, and volleyball right in the palm-tufted front yard, and RV- and tent-camping next door (P.O. Box 49, San Blas, Nayarit 63740; 14 rooms, about $20 d with kitchenette, $13 without, longer-stay discounts negotiable, RV or tents $5; winter reservations strongly recommended).

A couple of miles farther south, above rocky **Playa La Manzanilla,** a mile north of Santa Cruz del Miramar village, follow the roadside sign to the big garden-palapa **Restaurant La Playa Manzanilla.** From there, atop Manzanilla headland, you can feast on seafood and the cloud-tipped vista of the broad blue bay, enfolded by its verdant mountain hinterland (open Mon.-Fri. 8-5, Sat. and Sun. 8-7).

Waterfall Hikes
A number of pristine creeks tumble down boulder-strewn beds and foam over cliffs as waterfalls *(cataratas)* in the jungle above the Bay of Matanchén. Some of these are easily accessible and perfect for a day of hiking, picnicking, and swimming. Don't hesitate to ask local directions: say "¿Donde está la senda a [path to] la catarata, por favor?" If you would like a guide, ask "¿Hay guia, por favor?" One (or all) of the local crowd of kids may immediately volunteer.

You can get to within walking distance of the waterfall near **Tecuitata** village either by car or the Tepic-bound bus a few miles out of Santa Cruz del Miramar along Nayarit Hwy. 28. Half a mile uphill past the village, a sign "Balneario Nuevo Chapultepec" marks a dirt track heading downhill half a mile to a creek and a bridge. Cross over to the other side ($1 entrance), where you'll find a palapa restaurant and a hillside waterslide and small swimming pool.

Continue upstream along the right-hand bank of the creek for a much rarer treat, however. Half the fun are the sylvan jungle delights— flashing butterflies, pendulous leafy vines, gurgling little waterfalls—along the meandering path. The other half is at the end, where the creek spurts through a verdure-framed fissure and splashes into a cool, broad pool, festooned with green, giant-leafed *chalata* (taro in Hawaii, tapioca in Africa) plants. Both the pool area (known locally as Arroyo Campiste, popular with kids and women who bring their washing) and the trail have several possible campsites. Bring everything, especially your water purification kit and insect repellent.

Another waterfall, the highest in the area, near the village of **El Cora,** is harder to get to but the reward is even more spectacular. Again, on the west-east Santa Cruz del Miramar-Tepic Hwy. 28, a negotiable dirt road to El Cora branches south just before Tecuitata. At road's end, after about five miles, you can park by a banana loading platform. From there, the trail is under an hour on foot, climaxed by a steep descent to the rippling, crystal pool at the bottom of the waterfall. Best ask someone to guide you.

TEPIC

Tepic (elev. 3,001 feet, 915 meters) basks in a lush highland valley beneath a trio of giant mountains: 7,000-foot Sanganguey and Tepetiltic in the east and south, and the brooding Sierra de San Juan in the west. The waters that trickle from those cool wooded slopes have nurtured green valley fields and gardens for millennia. The city's name itself reflects its fertile surroundings: from the Nahuatl *tepictli,* meaning "land of corn."

Although it resembles a prosperous U.S. county seat, Tepic (pop. 150,000) is the Nayarit state capital, concentrating the services of an entire region. Local people flock to deposit in its banks, shop in its stores, and visit its diminutive main-street state legislature.

The **Huichol** Indians are among the many who come to trade in Tepic. The Huichol fly in from their remote mountain villages, loaded with crafts—yarn paintings, beaded masks, ceremonial gourds, God's eyes—which they sell to local handicrafts stores. Tepic has thus accumulated a few troves of their intriguing ceremonial art, whose peyote-induced animal and human forms symbolize the Huichol's animistic world view.

HISTORY

Historians believe that, around A.D. 1160, the valley of Tepic was a stopping place for a generation of the México (Aztecs) on their way to the Valley of Mexico. By the eve of the conquest, however, Tepic was ruled by the kingdom of Xalisco (whose capital occupied the same ground as the present-day city of Jalisco, a few miles south of Tepic).

In 1524, the expedition headed by the Great Conquistador's nephew, Francisco Cortés de San Buenaventura, explored the valley in peaceful contrast to those who followed. The renegade-conquistador Nuño de Guzmán, bent on accumulating gold and *indígena* slaves, arrived in May 1530 and seized the valley in the name of King Charles V. After building a lodging-house for hoped-for future immigrants, Guzmán hurried north, burning a pathway to Sinaloa. He returned a year later and founded a settlement near Tepic, which he named, pretentiously, Espíritu Santo de la Mayor España.

Guzmán's excesses soon caused him serious trouble. The king ordered his settlement's name changed to Santiago de Compostela in 1532 (which it remains today—Nayarit's oldest municipality, 23 miles south of present-day Tepic). Soon, immigrants began colonizing the countryside of Nueva Galicia (the sprawling new province, which included the modern states of Jalisco, Nayarit, and Sinaloa). Guzmán managed to remain as governor until 1536, when the viceroy finally had him arrested and sent back to Spain in chains.

With Guzmán gone, Nueva Galicia began to thrive. The colonists settled down to raising cattle, wheat, and fruit; the padres founded churches, schools, and hospitals. Explorers set out for new lands: Coronado to New Mexico in 1539, Legazpi and Urdaneta across the Pacific in 1563, Vizcaíno to California and Oregon in 1602, and Father Kino to Arizona in 1687. Father Junípero Serra stayed in Tepic for six months en route to the Californias in 1761. Excitement rose in Tepic when a troupe of 200 Spanish dragoons came through, on their way to establish the new port of San Blas nearby, in 1768.

San Blas's glory days, like Spain's, were numbered, however. Insurgents captured its fort cannons and sent them to defend Guadalajara in 1810, and finally President Lerdo de Tejada closed the port to foreign commerce in 1872.

Now, however, trains, jet airplanes, and a seemingly interminable flow of giant diesel trucks carry mountains of produce and goods through Tepic to Pacific Mexico and the United States. Machines hum in suburban factories, and business thrives at banks, stores, and shops around the plaza, where the aging colonial cathedral church remains a brooding reminder of the old days that few have time to remember.

SIGHTS

Getting Oriented

Tepic has two main plazas and two main highways. If you're only passing through, stay on

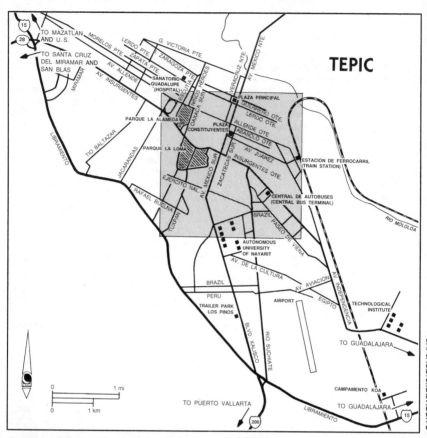

the **Libramiento**, which bypasses the city's western side. At the south end, the Libramiento splits east to Guadalajara via Hwy. 15 and south to Puerto Vallarta via Hwy. 200. On the north end, a similar interchange directs traffic either west to Santa Cruz del Miramar and San Blas via Nayarit Hwy. 28 or north toward Mazatlán and the U.S. via Hwy. 15.

Most travelers also enter town by either of those interchanges, which connect with the old thoroughfares, **Av. Insurgentes** on the north side and to **Blvd. Xalisco** on the south.

Av. Mexico, Tepic's main downtown street, angles off Av. Insurgentes just south of big **Parque La Loma** and heads north though the downtown, passing the main plazas, Plaza

Constituyentes and Plaza Principal, about half a mile farther on.

A Walk Around Downtown

The **cathedral,** adjacent to Av. Mexico, at the east side of the Plaza Principal, marks the center of town. The cathedral, dedicated to the Purísima Concepción ("Immaculate Conception") was completed in 1750. Its twin neo-Gothic bell towers rise somberly over everything else in town, while inside, by contrast, cheerier neo-classic gilded arches lead toward the main altar. There, a sculpture of the Virgin de la Asunción stands piously, flanked by choirs of cherubs.

The workaday **Palacio Municipal** (city-county hall) faces the plaza opposite the cathedral, while behind it (and half a block north on Zacatecas Nte.) the **Museo Amado Nervo** occupies the house where the renowned poet was born on August 27, 1870. The four-room permanent exhibition displays photos, original works, a bust of Nervo, and paintings donated by artists J.L. Soto, Sofía Bassi, and Erlinda T. Fuentes (open Mon.-Fri. 9-1 and 3-7, Sat. and Sun. 9-1).

Return to the plaza and join the shoppers beneath the arches in front of the Hotel Fray Junípero Serra on the plaza's south side, where a block-long platoon of shoeshiners ply their trade.

Head around the corner, south, along Av. Mexico. After two blocks you will reach the venerable 18th-century **Casa de los Condes de Miravalle,** which houses the Regional Anthropology and History Museum (Av. 91 Nte., open daily 9 a.m-6:45 p.m., tel. 219-00). The palatial residence was built with profits from silver and gold mined (at great human cost) by the rich merchant-family of Don Carlos Rivas. Its downstairs rooms now house a host of charming, earthy, pre-Columbian pottery artifacts, including dancing dogs, a man scaling a fish, a boy riding a turtle, a dog with a corncob in its mouth, and a very unusual explicitly amorous couple. In another room, displays illustrate the Huichol symbolism hidden in the Cicuri ("Eye of God") yarn

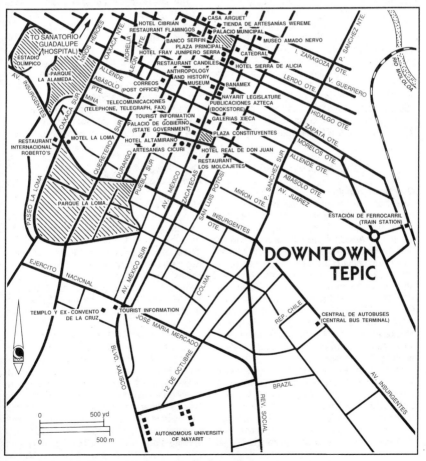

sculptures, yarn paintings, ceremonial arrows, hats, musical instruments, and other tokens.

Continue south along Av. Mexico; pass the state legislature across the street on the left and the federal-state **tourist information office** on the right just before **Plaza Constituyentes.**

On your right, along the west side of the plaza, spreads the straightlaced Spanish classical (as if transported directly from 18th-century Madrid) facade of the State of Nayarit **Palacio de Gobierno.** Inside, in the center, rises a cupola with a 1975 collection of paintings by artist José Luis Soto. In a second, rear building, a mural by the same artist portrays the struggles of the Independence and the 1910-17 Revolution.

Continuing about a mile south of Plaza Constituyentes past Insurgentes, where Av. Mexico crosses Ejercito Nacional, you will find the **Templo y Ex-convento de la Cruz de Zacate,** ("Church and Ex-convent of the Cross of Grass"). This aging but restored monument has two claims to fame: the miraculous cross in the sanctuary (dating from 1540 and made of a paste from a local wild grass) and the rooms where Father Junípero Serra stayed for several months during the 1760s en route to California.

ACCOMMODATIONS

Downtown Hotels

Tepic has a pair of good deluxe and several acceptable moderate downtown hotels. Starting in the north, near the Plaza Principal, the **Hotel Cibrian,** on Amado Nervo, a block and a half behind the Palacio Municipal, offers clean, no-frills rooms with baths, ceiling fans, telephones, parking, and a pretty fair local restaurant at reasonable prices (Amado Nervo 163 Pte., Tepic, Nayarit 63000, tel. 321-286-98. The 46 rooms go for about $18 s, $22 d; credit cards are accepted). The Cibrian's only apparent drawback is the noise that might filter into your room through louvered windows facing the tile (and therefore sound-reflective) hallways.

Right on the Plaza Principal stands the five-story tower of the **Hotel Fray Junípero Serra** (Lerdo 23 Pte., Tepic, Nayarit 63000, tel. 321-225-25). It offers spacious, tastefully furnished view rooms with deluxe amenities, efficient service, convenient parking, and an air-conditioned restaurant-bar that overlooks the plaza. The 90

rooms run about $40 s and $45 d and have satellite TV, a/c, and phones; no pool, limited wheelchair access, credit cards accepted.

On Av. Mexico, a few steps to the right (south) of the cathedral, the **Hotel Sierra de Alicia** remains a long-time favorite of Tepic business travelers (Av. Mexico 180 Nte., Tepic, Nayarit 63000, tel. 321-203-25, fax 321-213-09). Polished wood paneling downstairs and its plain but comfortable rooms upstairs reflect the Sierra de Alicia's solid unpretention. The 60 rooms are about $27 s, $30 d with fan; $30 s, $34 d with a/c, credit cards accepted; satellite TV, phones, and parking.

The new **Hotel Real de Don Juan** on Plaza Constituyentes is trying to establish itself as Tepic's class-act hotel. A gleaming, plush lobby and adjoining restaurant-bar matches the luxury of the king-size beds, thick carpets, marble baths, and soft pastels of the rooms (Av. Mexico 105 Sur, Tepic, Nayarit 63000; 48 rooms for about $70 s or d, with a/c, TV, phones, parking, and limited wheelchair access).

Nearby (on Mina, half a block from the Av. Mexico plaza corner), the **Hotel Altamirano** offers basic bare-bulb rooms with baths and moderate rates. The hotel, although clean, is nondescript to the point of shabbiness (Mina 19 Pte., Tepic, Nayarit 63000, tel. 321-271-31. The 31 rooms cost about $17 s, $20 d; fans and parking).

Motels, Trailer Parks, And Camping

If you prefer not to stay downtown, try the **Motel La Loma,** (across Av. Insurgentes from the north side of La Loma Park). One of the few Tepic lodgings with a pool, it has a standard two-story layout of 40 clean, tastefully furnished rooms, some with air-conditioning (Paseo La Loma 301, Tepic, Nayarit 63000, tel. 321-322-22 and 321-320-52). Rooms run about $35 d, credit cards accepted; restaurant, TV, and phones, pets okay.

Farther south, on Blvd. Xalisco about a mile before the south-end Puerto Vallarta interchange, the friendly **Trailer Park Los Pinos** offers, besides trailer and camping spaces, six large kitchenette rooms and plenty of homey atmosphere, contributed by the grandmotherly on-site owner. The 25 pine-shaded concrete trailer pads, with all hookups and good drinkable well water, spread in two rows up a gradual, hillside slope (P.O. Box 329, Tepic, Nayarit

63000, tel. 321-312-32). The rooms cost about $20 low season, trailer spaces about $10/night, camping is $5, with discounts for weekly and monthly rentals; showers, toilets.

Further out of town still, the **Campamento KOA** is located off Guadalajara Hwy. 15 about two miles past the south-end interchange (Carretera Mexico-Nogales, Km 899, tel. 321-331-13). Follow the cobblestone road just past the Lázaro Cárdenas tobacco plant. They offer about 70 trailer spaces (about half with all hookups, the others with electricity and water) in a large country lot. Spaces run about $10/night; recreation hall, grocery, camping, pets okay.

FOOD

(Complete Dinner Price Key: Budget = under $7, Moderate = $7-14, Expensive = more than $14.) Annoying traffic noise and exhaust smoke sometimes spoil the atmosphere in many downtown restaurants. The **Hotel Fray Junípero Serra** restaurant however, does not suffer such a drawback (Lerdo 23 Pte., tel. 225-25, open daily 7 a.m.-9 p.m., credit cards accepted). It's on the second floor, overlooking the plaza. Moderate.

A much humbler, but good and relatively quiet lunch or supper spot is the plaza favorite **Loncheria Flamingos,** where a trio of friendly female chefs puts out a continuous supply of steaming tortas, tostadas, tacos, *liquados,* and *hamburguesas.* The Torta Ahogado, however, is their supreme specialty. Here, the question is: "Are you big enough for the Torta Ahogado?" Budget. On Puebla Nte., behind the Palacio Municipal, open Thurs.-Tues. 10 a.m.-10:30 p.m.

On Av. Mexico, a block south of the Plaza Principal (near the corner of Hidalgo), the **Restaurant Candiles** offers a bit of atmosphere with your *huevos mexicanos, ensalata de chef,* or chiles rellenos (Av. Mexico 139 Nte., open daily 8 a.m.-10 p.m.). Moderate.

Farther down Av. Mexico, just past the Plaza Constituyentes, the very popular **Restaurant Los Molcajetes** names itself after one of its specialties: a big *molcajete* (stone bowl) of steaming leeks with meat in spicy broth, served with succulent cooked cactus leaves (Mexico 133 Sur, open daily 10 a.m.-midnight, tel. 364-59). Moderate.

One of the fancier spots, popular with both travelers and some locals, is **Restaurant Internacional Roberto's** (Paseo La Loma, near the corner of Insurgentes, adjacent to La Loma Park, open daily 1 p.m.-midnight, tel. 330-05). Their tasty menu entrees are divided between standard North American and Mexican favorites. Moderate to expensive.

Another good spot, especially for an early American-style breakfast, or late-night salad and spaghetti, is the restaurant of the **Motel La Loma,** across Insurgentes from Roberto's (north end of La Loma Park, open daily 6 a.m.-11 p.m., tel. 322-22. Moderate to expensive.

SHOPPING

Its for-sale collections of Huichol art provide an excellent reason to stop in Tepic. At least four downtown shops specialize in Huichol goods, acting as agents for more than just the commissions they receive. They have been involved with the Huichol for years, helping them preserve their religion and traditional skills in the face of expanding tourism and development. Starting near the Plaza Principal, the **Casa Arguet** (on Nervo, a block behind the Palacio

Common charms that Huichol pilgrims carry with them include a rattle and a small gourd for collecting peyote.

THE HUICHOL

The Huichol, having retained more of their culture than perhaps any other indigenous Mexicans, are a yet-open window to the lives and beliefs of dozens of now-vanished Mesoamerican peoples. Huichol art contains representations of prototype deities—Grandfather Sun, Grandmother Earth, Brother Deer, Mother Maize—that once guided the lives of many North American peoples.

The Huichols' natural wariness and their isolation in rugged mountain valleys have saved them from being swallowed up by modern Mexico. Despite increased tourist, government, and mestizo contact, prosperity and better health swelled the Huichol population to around 15,000 by the 1990s.

Although many have migrated to the coast and cities such as Tepic and Guadalajara, several thousand Huichol remain in their ancestral heartland—a roughly 50-mile-square centering about 50 miles northeast of Tepic. They mostly cultivate corn and raise cattle on about 400 *rancherías* dotting five country municipalities not far from the winding Altengo River valley: Guadalupe Ocotán, in Nayarit, and Tuxpan de Bolanos, San Sebastián Teponahuaxtlán, Santa Catarina, and San Andrés Cohamiata, in Jalisco.

Although studied by a procession of researchers since Carl Lumholtz's seminal 1890s work, the Huichol and their religion remain enigmatic. Lumholtz analyzed it long ago:

Religion to them is a personal matter, not an institution and therefore their life is religion—from the cradle to the grave, wrapped up in symbolism.

Perhaps, as some believe, the only way to really understand the Huichol is to be Huichol.

Hints of what it means to be Huichol, however, come from their art. It blooms with tangible religious symbols, from green-faced Mother Earth Tatei Urianaka and the dripping rain goddess, Tatei Matiniera, to Tayau, the ray-festooned Father Sun and antlered folk hero Brother Kauyumari, forever battling the evil sorcerer Kieri.

The Huichol are famous for their use of the hallucinogenic peyote, their bridge to the divine. Peyote (eaten in the gathered buds—"buttons"—of a humble cactus) contains mescaline and a score of other vision-inducing ingredients and grows in the Huichol's Elysian land of Wirikuta, in the San Luis Potosí desert 300 miles east of their homeland, near the town of Real de Catorce. To the Huichol, going to Wirikuta is a danger-frought trip to heaven. Preparations—innumerable prayers, ceremonies, and the crafting of a festoon of votive feathered arrows, bowls, gourds, and paintings for the gods who live along the way—go on for weeks. Only the chosen, such as village shamans, temple elders, or those fulfilling vows or seeking visions may go. Each participant, in effect, becomes a god, whose identity (and very life) is divined and protected en route to Wirikata by the shaman. (For more details, see *Art of the Huichol Indians,* edited by Kathleen Berrin.)

The fertility goddess symbolically gives birth in a Huichol yarn painting.

Municipal) has an upstairs attic-museum of Huichol curios (132 Amado Nervo, open Mon.-Sat. 9-2 and 4-8, Sun. 9-2, tel. 241-30). The founder's son, personable Miguel Arguet, knows the Huichol well. His copy of *Art of the Huichol Indians* furnishes authoritative explanations of the intriguing animal and human painting motifs.

The government handicrafts store, **Tienda de Artesanías Wereme** (corner Nervo and Mérida, next to the Palacio Municipal), has a limited selection of Huichol and other handicrafts. The staff, however, does not appear to be as knowledgeable as the private merchants. Open Mon.-Fri. 9-2 and 4-7, Sat. 9-2.

Several blocks south on Av. Mexico, half a block from Plaza Constituyentes, the **Galerias Xiecá** displays a galaxy of museum-quality Huichol *cuadra* yarn paintings, masks, gourds, shamanistic tokens, and much more (Av. Mexico 39 Sur, tel. 227-76; open daily 9-2 and 4-9). The owner, José Ramon Mercado Acuña, a local Huichol authority, gives frequent lectures and leads discussions on Huichol folkcrafts, costumes, culture, and religion. His shop also operates an adjacent coffeehouse, a pleasant place for a bit of cake or a sandwich to go with your conversation and cappuccino.

The **Artesanías Cicuri** nearby (on Av. Mexico, near the corner of Mina) names itself after the renowned Cicuri, the "Eye of God" of the Huichol. Although not as extensive as some others, their collection is particularly fine, especially the eerie beaded masks (Av. Mexico 110 Sur, open Mon.-Sat. 9-2 and 4-8, tel. 237-14 and 214-16).

EVENTS

Tepic's big festival is the all-Nayarit **Fería de Mexicanidad,** held during the latter half of October and early November. The fair is a semi-patriotic celebration of *Mexicanidad,* "Mexican-ness," featuring the accomplishments of past and present Mexican generations. Consisting of a busy schedule of sporting, cultural, musical, and dramatic performances, the fair climaxes each year with the reenactment of the Aztec migration. With fireworks and great fanfare, Aztec-costumed pilgrims arrive after two weeks on foot from the small estuary and island communities near original Aztec "home" of Mexcaltitlán.

SERVICES

For the best **money exchange** rates, go to a bank, such as the main Banamex branch on Av. Mexico and Zapata. Open 9-11 a.m. for U.S. dollar cash and traveler's check exchange only. If the lines at Banamex are too long, go to the Banco Serfin on the main square next to the Palacio Municipal (Merida 184 Nte., open for U.S. dollar money exchange Mon.-Fri. 8:30-10:30 a.m.). After hours, try one of two *casas de cambio* (money exchange counters) nearby: the Cerdana, at Av. Mexico 139 Nte., corner of Hidalgo (open Mon.-Fri., 8-8) or Lidor, just north of Plaza Constituyentes at Av. Mexico Sur 44 (open Mon.-Sat. 8:30-2 and 4-8 p.m., tel. 233-84).

Tepic has two **post offices.** The main branch is downtown at Durango Nte. 27, about two blocks west and three blocks south of the Plaza Principal; the other is at the Central de Autobuses (central bus terminal) on Av. Insurgentes about a mile east (Guadalajara direction) from downtown.

Telecomunicaciones, which provides telegraph, telephone, and public fax services, likewise has a downtown branch (Allende Pte. 123, corner Puebla, tel. 217-11), one block north and two blocks west of Plaza Constituyentes, and a Central de Autobuses branch (tel. 323-27). The area code is 321.

INFORMATION

Tepic's downtown branch **Tourist Information Office** is near the north corner of Av. Mexico and the Plaza Constituyentes (Av. Mexico 34 Sur, tel. 295-47). The main office is at the Ex-Convent de la Cruz, about a mile south of downtown (Av. Mexico and Ejercito, tel. 392-03).

English books and magazines are scarce in Tepic. Newsstands beneath the plaza portals (just west of the Hotel Fray Junípero Serra) and bookstore Publicaciones Azteca (open daily 8 a.m.-midnight, Av. Mexico, corner Morelos) usually have the *News* from Mexico City, however.

If you need a **doctor,** contact the Sanitorio Guadalupe (Juan Escuita 68 Nte., tel. 294-01, 227-13) seven blocks west of the Plaza Principal, which has a 24-hour emergency room and a group of specialists on call. A fire department paramedic squad is also available by calling 318-09.

For **police** emergencies, dial 06, or for the municipal police station, call 201-23. For **fire** emergencies, call the *servicio bomberos* (fire station) at 316-07.

GETTING THERE AND AWAY

By Car Or RV

Main highways connect Tepic with Mazatlán in the north, Guadalajara in the east, Puerto Vallarta in the south, and San Blas in the west. From **Mazatlán,** traffic, towns, and rough spots slow progress along the 182-mile (293-km) two-lane stretch of National Hwy. 15. Expect four or five hours of driving time under good conditions.

The same is true of the winding, 141-mile (227-km) continuation of Hwy. 15 eastward over the Sierra Madre Occidental to Guadalajara. Fortunately, a toll superhighway at the summit eliminates an hour of driving time. Allow about four hours.

Two-lane Hwy. 200 from Puerto Vallarta is in good condition for its 104-mile (167-km) length. Curves, traffic, and the 3,000-foot Tepic grade, however, usually slow the northbound trip to about three hours, a bit less southbound.

A pair of routes (both about 43 miles, 70 km) connect Tepic with San Blas. The most scenic of the two takes about an hour and a half, heading south from San Blas along the Bay of Matanchén to Santa Cruz del Miramar, then climbing 3,000 feet west to Tepic via Nayarit Hwy. 28. The quicker route leads west from San Blas along National Hwy. 11, climbing through the tropical forest to Hwy. 15, where four lanes guide traffic rapidly to Tepic.

By Bus

The shiny, modern **Central de Autobuses,** on Insurgentes Sur, about a mile south of downtown has many services, including left-luggage lockers, a cafeteria, and post, telephone, public fax, and telegraph offices. First-class ticket windows occupy the left side of the terminal as you enter, second-class the right.

Both **Transportes del Pacifico** (tel. 323-20) and **Transportes Norte de Sonora** (tel. 323-15) have many local departures, connecting with San Blas, Puerto Vallarta, Guadalajara, Mazatlán, and the U.S. border at Tijuana and Nogales. **Tres Estrellas de Oro** (tel. 323-26), in addition to connecting with Mazatlán, the U.S. border, Guadalajara, and Puerto Vallarta, connects southward with Barra de Navidad and Manzanillo. **Camiones de Los Altos** (tel. 323-17) connects with many other destinations, including San Blas, with a local departure daily at 5:30 p.m.

By Train

The Estación de Ferrocarril (railway station, tel. 348-61 for tickets and schedule confirmation) is also on the south side of town (prolongation of Av. Allende Ote.). **Estrella,** two first-class coach trains headed in opposite directions, pass through daily: at around 2 p.m. for Guadalajara and around 3 p.m. for Mazatlán and the U.S. border. At Guadalajara, connections are available for Mexico City and Pacific Mexico destinations of Colima, Manzanillo, Pátzcuaro, and Playa Azul (Lázaro Cárdenas).

(previous page) Guadalajara's main market, Mercado Libertad; (this page, top) dyeing and drying, Teotitlán del Oaxaca; (bottom) pre-Columbian-motif onyx masks, Taxco, Guerrero (photos by Bruce Whipperman)

GUADALAJARA

Pacific Mexico people often go to Guadalajara (pop. 3,000,000, elev. 5,214 feet, 1590 meters), the capital of Jalisco, for the same reason Californians frequently go to Los Angeles: to shop and choose from big selections at correspondingly small prices.

But that's only part of the fascination. Although Guadalajarans like to think of themselves as different (calling themselves, uniquely, "Tapatíos,") their city is renowned as the "most Mexican" of cities. Crowds flock to Guadalajara to bask in its mild, spring-like sunshine, savor its music, and admire its grand monuments.

HISTORY

Before Columbus

The broad Atemajac Valley, where the Guadalajara metropolis now spreads, has nurtured humans for hundreds of generations. Discovered remains date back at least 10,000 years. The Rio Lerma-Santiago (Mexico's longest river, which meanders across six states) has nourished Atemajac Valley corn fields for at least three millenia.

Although they built no pyramids, high cultures were occupying western Mexico by A.D. 300. They left sophisticated animal- and human-motif pottery in myriad bottle-shaped underground tombs of a style found only in Jalisco, Nayarit, Colima (and, intriguingly, in Colombia and Ecuador).

During the next thousand years, waves of migrants swept across the Atemajac Valley. Aztecs came from the west, the Toltecs from the northeast. As Toltec power declined during the 13th century, the Tarascan civilization took root in Michoacán to the south and filled the power vacuum left by the Toltecs. On the eve of the Spanish conquest, semiautonomous local chiefdoms, tributaries of the Tarascan Emperor, shared the Atemajac Valley.

Conquest And Colonization

The fall of the Aztecs in 1520 and the Tarascans a few years later made the Atemajac Val-

ley a plum ripe for the picking. In the late 1520s, while Cortés was absent in Spain, the opportunistic Nuño de Guzmán vaulted himself to power in Mexico City on the backs of the native peoples and at the expense of Cortés's friends and relatives. Suspecting correctly that his glory days in Mexico City were numbered, Guzmán cleared out three days before Christmas in 1529, at the head of a small army of adventurers seeking new conquests in western Mexico. They raped, ravaged, and burned for half a dozen years, inciting dozens of previously pacified tribes to rebellion.

Hostile Mexican attacks repeatedly foiled Guzmán's attempts to establish his western Mexico capital, which he wanted to name after his Spanish hometown, Guadalajara (from the Arabic wad al hadjarah, "River of Stones"). Ironically, it wasn't until the year of Guzmán's death in 1542 (in Spain, six years after his arrest by royal authorities) that the present Guadalajara was founded. At the downtown Plaza de los Fundadores, a panoramic bronze frieze (see "Sights" below) shows cofounders Doña Beátriz de Hernández and governor Cristóbal de Oñate christening the soon-to-become capital of the "Kingdom of Nueva Galicia."

The city grew; its now-venerable public buildings rose at the edges of sweeping plazas, from which expeditions set out to explore new lands. In 1563, Legazpi and Urdaneta sailed west to conquer the Philippines; 1602 saw Vizcaino sail for the Californias and Oregon. In 1687, Father Kino left for 27 years of mission-building in Arizona and New Mexico; finally during the 1760s, Father Junipero Serra and Captain Gaspar de Portola began their arduous trek to discover San Francisco Bay and found a string of California missions.

During Spain's Mexican twilight, Guadalajara was a virtual imperial city, ruling all of northwest Mexico, plus California, Arizona, New Mexico, and Texas—an empire twice the size of Britain's 13 colonies.

Independence

The cry, "Death to the gachupines, Viva México" by insurgent priest Miguel Hidalgo ignited re-

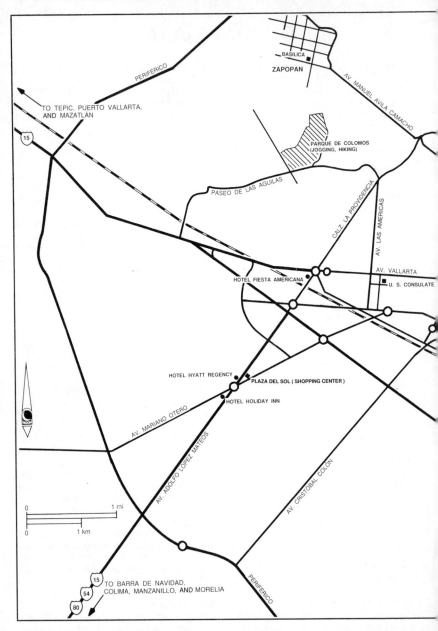

METROPOLITAN GUADALAJARA

TO ZACATECAS

AV. ALCALDE

CIRCUNVALACIÓN

CALZ. INDEPENDENCIA NTE.

PERIFERICO

AV. FEDERALISMO

AV. ALCALDE

CALZ. INDEPENDENCIA

BELISARIO DOMINGUEZ

PLAZA DE TOROS (BULLRING)

CALZ. OBREROS

TEATRO
DEGOLLADO
HOSPICIO CABAÑAS
TEDRAL
PLAZA
PLAZA TAPATÍA
LIBERACION
MERCADO LIBERTAD
JUÁREZ

JUAN DE DIOS ROBLEDO

CENTRAL CAMIONERA ANTIGUA
(OLD BUS STATION)

PARQUE AGUA AZUL

CALZ

AV. REVOLUCION

STACION DE
ERROCARRIL
RAILWAY STATION)

CALZ. OLIMPICA

TLAQUEPAQUE

BALNEAFIO LINDO
MICHOACAN
(SWIMMING)

CALZ. J. GONZALES GALLO

AV. INDEPENDENCIA

PLAZA
AV. HIDALGO

TLAQUEPAQUE

AV. NIÑOS
HEROES

HOTEL EL PARADOR
CENTRAL CAMIONERA
(LONG - DISTANCE BUS STATION)

TONALÁ

SUNDAY
MARKET
PLAZA

PERIFERICO

AUTOPISTA
ZAPOTLANEJO (TOLL)

CARRETERA TONALÁ (FREE)

TO AIRPORT AND LAKE CHAPALA

TO MEXICO CITY

© MOON PUBLICATIONS, INC.

bellion on September 16, 1810. Buoyed by a series of quick victories, Hidalgo's huge ragtag army advanced on Mexico City. But, facing the punishing fusillades of a small but disciplined Spanish force, Hidalgo lost his nerve and retreated to Guadalajara instead. Loyalist General Felix Calleja pursued and routed Hidalgo's forces on the bank of the Lerma, not far east of Guadalajara. Although Hidalgo and Allende escaped, they were captured in the north a few months later. It wasn't for another dozen bloody years that others—Iturbide, Guerrero, Morelos—realized Hidalgo's dream of independence.

Guadalajara, its domain reduced by the new republican government to the new state of Jalisco, settled down to corn, cattle, and tequila. The railroad came, branched north to the U.S. and south to the Pacific, and by 1900, Guadalajara's place as Mexico's second city was secure.

Modern Guadalajara

After the bloodbath of the 1910-17 Revolution, Guadalajara's growth far outpaced the country in general. From a population of around 100,000, Guadalajara ballooned to 3,000,000 by 1990. People were drawn from the countryside by jobs in a thousand new factories, making everything from textiles and shoes to chemicals and soda pop.

Handicraft manufacture, always important in Guadalajara, zoomed during the 1960s when waves of jet-tourists came, saw, and bought mountains of blown glass, leather, pottery, and metal finery. During the 1980s, Guadalajara put on a new face that preserved the best part of its old downtown. An urban-renewal plan of visionary proportions created Plaza Tapatía—acres of shops, stores, and offices beside fountain-studded malls—incorporating Guadalajara's venerable theaters, churches, museums, and government buildings into a single grand open space.

SIGHTS

Getting Oriented

Although Guadalajara sprawls over a hundred square miles, the treasured mile-square heart of the city is easily explorable on foot. The cathedral corner of north-south **Av. 16 de Septiembre** and **Av. Morelos** marks the center of town. A few blocks south, another important artery, east-west **Av. Juarez,** runs above the subway line through the main business district, while a few blocks east **Av. Independencia** runs beneath Plaza Tapatía and past the main market to the railway station a couple of miles south.

A Walk Around Old Guadalajara

The twin steeples of the **Catedral** serve as an excellent starting point to explore the city-center plazas and monuments. The cathedral was dedicated to the Virgin of the Assumption at its founding in 1561; it was finished about 30 years later. A potpourri of styles—Moorish, Gothic, Renaissance, and classic—make up its spires, arches, and facades. Although an earthquake demolished its steeples in 1818, they were rebuilt and resurfaced with cheery canary yellow tiles in 1854.

Inside, gold-encrusted altars and white facades climax at the principal altar, built over a tomb containing the remains of several former clergy (including the mummified heart of renowned Bishop Cabañas). The main attraction, however, is the **Virgin of Innocence,** the image to the left of the principal altar. The figure contains the bones of a 12-year-old girl who was martyred in the third century, forgotten, then rediscovered in the Vatican catacombs and shipped to Guadalajara during the 1800s. The legend claims that she died protecting her virginity; it is equally likely that she was martyred for refusing to recant her Christian faith.

Outside, broad plazas surround the cathedral: the **Plaza Laureles,** in front (west) of the cathedral, then moving counterclockwise, the **Plaza de Armas** to the south, **Plaza Libertad** to the east (behind), and **Plaza de los Hombres Ilustres** to the north of the cathedral.

Across Av. Morelos, the block-square Plaza de los Hombres Ilustres is bordered by 15 sculptures of Jalisco's eminent sons. Their remains lie beneath the stone rotunda in the center.

Adjacent, east of the plaza, the colonial building behind the lineup of horse-drawn *calandrias* housed the Seminario de San José for six generations, beginning with its construction in 1696. During the 1800s it served variously as a barracks, a public lecture hall, and, since 1918, has housed the **Museo Regional de Guadalajara** (60 Liceo, open Tues.-Sun. 9-3:45).

Inside, tiers of rooms around a tree-shaded interior patio illustrate local history, from as early as the Big Bang and continuing with a hulking mastodon skeleton and whimsical animal and human figurines recovered from the bottle-shaped tombs of Jalisco, Nayarit, and Colima. Upstairs rooms contain life-size displays of contemporary (but traditional) fishing at nearby Lake Chapala and costumes and culture of regional Cora, Huichol, Tepehuan, and México peoples.

Back outside, head east two blocks down Av. Hidalgo, paralleling the expansive **Plaza Liberación** behind the cathedral. On your left pass the baroque facades of the Congreso del Estado (state legislature) and the Palacio de Justicia (state supreme court). Ahead at the east end of the plaza rises the timeless silhouette of the **Teatro Degollado.**

The theater's classic facade climaxes in a panorama from Dante's *Divine Comedy,* complete with its immortal cast—Julius Caesar, Homer, Virgil, Saladin—and the robed and wreathed author himself in the middle. The Degollado's equally resplendent interior is said to rival the gilded refinement of Milan's renowned La Scala. The Degollado (named for the millionaire who financed its construction) opened with appropriate fanfare on September 13, 1866, with a production of *Lucia de Lammermoor,* starring Ángela Peralta, the "Mexican Nightingale." (An ever-changing menu of artists still graces the Degollado's stage. These include an excellent local folkloric ballet troupe every Sunday morning. See "Entertainment and Events" below.)

Walk behind the Degollado, where a modern bronze frieze, the **Frisa de Los Fundadores,** decorates its back wall. Appropriately, a mere two blocks from the spot where the city was founded, the 68-foot sculpture shows Guadalajara's cofounders facing each other on opposite sides of a big tree. Governor Cristóbal de Oñate strikes the tree with his sword, while Doña Beátriz de Hernández holds a fighting cock, symbolizing her determination (and that of dozens of fellow settlers) that Guadalajara's location should remain put.

Plaza Tapatía

Turn around and face east. The 17 acres of the Plaza Tapatía Complex extends ahead for several blocks across sub-plazas, fountains, and malls. At the sub-Plaza de Los Fundadores, the Tapatía Complex narrows between a double

row of shiny shops and offices. It then widens into a broad esplanade and continues beside a long pool-fountain that leads to the monumental, domed Hospicio Cabañas, a third of a mile away. Along the Tapatía's lateral flanks, a pair of long malls—continuations of Avs. Hidalgo and Morelos—parallel the central sub-mall, Paseo Degollado, for two blocks.

The eastern end of the Morelos side climaxes with the striking bronze **Escudo** ("Coat of Arms") of Guadalajara. Embodying the essence of the original 16th-century coat of arms authorized by Emperor Charles V, the Escudo shows a pair of lions protecting a pine tree. The lions represent the warrior's determination and discipline, and the solitary pine symbolizes noble ideals.

Continue east, to where the Plaza Tapatía widens, giving berth for the sculpture-fountain **Imolación de Quetzalcoatl,** designed and executed by Víctor Manuel Contreras in 1982. Four bronze serpent-birds, representing knowledge and the spirit of humankind, stretch toward heaven at the ends of a giant cross. In the center, a towering bronze spiral represents the unquenchable flame of Quetzalcoatl, transforming all that it touches. (Local folks call the sculpture the "big corkscrew," however.)

At this point, Av. Independencia runs directly beneath Plaza Tapatía, past the adjacent sprawling **Mercado Libertad,** built in 1958 on the site of the traditional Guadalajara *tianguis* (open-air market) known since pre-Columbian times. Follow the elevated pedestrian walkway to explore the Libertad's produce, meat, fish, herb, food, and handicrafts stalls. (See "Food" and "Shopping" below.)

On Independencia, just beyond the market, musicians at the **Plaza de Los Mariachis** continue the second century of a tradition born when mariachi (cowboy troubadour) groups first appeared during the 1860s in Guadalajara. The musical hubbub climaxes Saturday nights and Sunday afternoons, as musicians gather, singing while they wait to be hired for serenades and parties. (See "Entertainment and Events" below for more details.)

Behind the long pool-fountain at the east end of Plaza Tapatía stands the domed neoclassic **Hospicio Cabañas,** the largest, and one of the most remarkable colonial buildings in the Americas. Designed and financed by Bishop Juan Ruiz de Cabañas, construction was complete

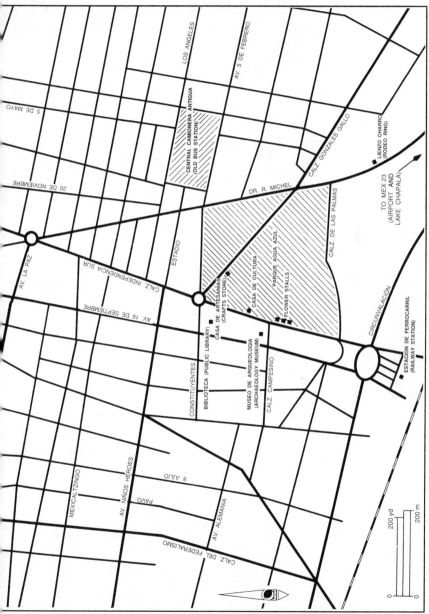

© MOON PUBLICATIONS, INC.

An ice cream vendor waits for customers on Tlaquepaque's main shopping street, Av. Independencia.

BRUCE WHIPPERMAN

in 1810. The purpose of the "Guadalajara House of Charity and Mercy," as the good bishop originally named it, as a home for the sick, helpless, and homeless, was fulfilled for 170 years. Although it was still successfully serving as an orphanage during the 1970s, time had taken its toll on the Hospicio Cabañas. The city and state governments built a new orphanage in the suburbs, restored the old Hospicio, and changed it to the **Instituto Cultural Cabañas,** a multi-purpose center for the arts (Cabañas 8, open Tues.-Sat. 10-6, Sun. 10-3, tel. 540-008, 540-129). Public programs include classes, films, and instrumental, chorale, and dance concerts. (For details, see "Entertainment and Events" below.)

Inside, seemingly endless ranks of corridors pass dozens of sculpture-decorated patios. Practice rooms resound with the clatter of dancing feet and the halting strains of apprentice violins, horns, and pianos. Exhibition halls and studios of the José Clemente Orozco Art Museum occupy a large fraction of the rooms, while the great muralist's brooding work spreads over a corresponding fraction of the walls. Words such as dark, fiery, nihilistic, even apocalyptic, would not be too strong to describe the panoramas that Orozco executed (1938-39) in the soaring chapel beneath the central dome. On one wall, an Aztec goddess wears a necklace of human hearts; on another, armored, automaton-soldiers menace Indian captives, while in the cupola overhead, Orozco's "Man of Fire," wreathed in flame, appears to soar into a hellishly red-hot sky.

Out-of-downtown Sights

The former villages of Zapopan, Tlaquepaque, and Tonalá—now parts of metropolitan Guadalajara—are ideal for leisurely side-trips from the city center.

Zapopan, about six miles northwest of downtown, is famous for its soaring baroque (1730) basilica, home of the renowned Virgin of Zapopan. The legendary image, a one-foot blue and white statue, won the hearts of Tapatíos by aiding the city in time of disaster and war. From October 13, when she returns home from the downtown cathedral, to June, you can see the Virgin in the basilica (see "Bullfights, Rodeos, and Fiestas" below). Afterwards, look over the displays of Huichol Indian handicrafts in the adjacent museum-shop Artesanías Huichola. Sale items include fascinating beaded masks, mystical yarn paintings, and intriguing Ojos de Dios ("Eyes of God") yarn sculptures. Outside, browse for bargains among the handicrafts stalls in front of the Basilica. Zapopan-bound buses leave from the Camionera Antigua, the Old Bus Terminal, at the end of Av. Estadio, just north of Parque Agua Azul.

Tlaquepaque and **Tonalá,** in the southeast suburbs, are among Mexico's renowned handicrafts villages. Tlaquepaque (now touristy, but still interesting), about five miles from the city center, is famous for fine stoneware and blown glass; Tonalá, another five miles farther, retains plenty of sleepy, colorful country ambience. Shops abound in its celebrated ceramic, brass, and papier mâché animal figurines. The most exciting (but crowded) time to visit is during the

Sunday market. (For many more Tlaquepaque and Tonalá details, see "Shopping" below.)

ACCOMMODATIONS

Downtown Hotels

Several good hotels, ranging from budget to plush, dot the center of town, mostly in the Av. Juarez business district, a few blocks from the cathedral and plazas. Downtown hotels farthest from the cathedral plazas are generally the most economical.

The **Posada La Plata,** one block off Juarez (on Lopez Cotillo, near the corner of Calle 8 Julio) is about 10 blocks from the cathedral (Lopez Cotillo 619, Guadalajara, Jalisco 44100, tel. 69-149-146). Its plain but clean rooms with baths spread around a light but otherwise lackluster central patio. Tightly managed by the on-site owner, La Plata's prices are certainly right. Try for a room away from the noisy street. The 12 rooms rent for about $10 s, $13 d, with fans.

On the same street, on the other side of Calle 8 Julio one block closer in, is the equally well-managed but very plain **Posada España** (Lopez Cotillo 594, Guadalajara, Jalisco 44100, tel. 69-135-377). The clean but unadorned rooms with bath circle the well-lighted interior patio. For maximum peace and quiet, get a room away from the street. Their 12 fan-equipped rooms run about $9 s, $10 d, and $12 t.

Smack in the downtown business center (across from the Hotel Fenix), a short walk from everything, the second-floor **Hotel Posada Regis** offers both economy and a bit of old-style charm (171 Corona, Guadalajara, Jalisco 44100, tel. 69-133-026 and 69-148-633). Its very clean and comfortable rooms with baths enclose a spacious lobby-patio. Evening videos, a leisurely, friendly atmosphere, and a good budget breakfast-lunch lobby restaurant provide opportunities for relaxed exchanges with other travelers. The 19 rooms cost $17 s, $22 d, credit cards accepted; with phones and fans.

Central location, near-deluxe rooms and moderate prices explain the popularity of the nearby **Hotel Universo,** corner of Cotilla and Degollado, just three blocks from the the Teatro Degollado (Lopez Cotilla 161, Guadalajara, Jalisco 44100, tel. 69-132-815). Guests enjoy very clean, carpeted and draped air-conditioned rooms with wood furniture and ceiling-to-floor tiled bathrooms. The 137 rooms and suites go for about $23 s, $25 d, suites from $27; TV, phones, and parking; credit cards accepted.

Guests of the **Hotel Calinda,** one block away (on the corner of Degollado and Juarez), enjoy luxurious amenities—plush lobby, shiny restaurant-bar, elegant rooftop garden and pool—usually available only at much pricier hostelries (Av. Juarez 170, Guadalajara, Jalisco 44100, tel. 36-148-650, fax 36-130-557). The 150 rooms cost about $33 s, $36 d; suites from about $65;

GUADALAJARA HOTELS

Guadalajara hotels, in order of increasing approximate double-room price (area code 36, postal code 44100)

Posada España, Lopez Cotillo 594, 135-377, $10
Posada La Plata, Lopez Cotillo 619, 149-146, $13
Hotel El Parador, Carretera Zapotlanejo 1500, 590-142, $20
Hotel Posada Regis, 171 Corona, 133-026, $22
Hotel Universo, Lopez Cotilla 161, 132-815, $25
Hotel Calinda, Juarez 170, 148-650, fax 130-557, (800) 221-2222, $36
Hotel Frances, Maestranza 35, 131-190, $55
Hotel Mendoza, V. Carranza 16, 134-646, fax 137-310, $72
Hyatt Regency, López Mateos and Moctezuma, 227-778, fax 229-877, (800) 233-1234, $143
Holiday Inn, López Mateos Sur 2500, 340-650, fax 481-562, (800) 465-4329, $170

TV, phones, a/c, parking $1, credit cards accepted, limited wheelchair access). Some rooms, although clean and comfortable, are small. Look before moving in. In the U.S. and Canada, reserve through the toll-free Quality Inns number (800) 221-2222.

The three-story baroque **Hotel Frances** (1610), Guadalajara's first hotel, rises among its fellow monuments on a quiet side street within sight of the Teatro Degollado (Maestranza 35, Guadalajara, Jalisco 44100, tel. 69-131-190 and 69-130-917). Guadalajara's most traditional-style lodging, the Frances has been restored to its original splendor. The rooms, all with bath, glow with polished wood, bright tile, and frosted cut-glass windows. Downstairs, an elegant chandelier illuminates the dignified, plant-decorated interior patio and adjacent restaurant. Rooms cost about $45 s, $55 d, and $64 t, credit cards accepted, discounts sometimes available; fans only, no parking.

The big colonial-facade **Hotel Mendoza,** on the north side of the Teatro Degollado, is a long-time favorite of Guadalajara repeat visitors (V. Carranza 16, Guadalajara, Jalisco 44100, tel. 36-134-646, fax 36-137-310, 100 rooms and suites). Elegant traditional embellishments— neo-Renaissance murals and wall portraits, rich dark paneling, glittering candelabras—grace the lobby, while upstairs, carpeted halls lead to spacious, comfortable rooms furnished with tasteful dark decor, including large baths, thick towels and many other extras. Room prices begin at about $60 s, $72 d, with American cable TV, phones, a/c, a small pool, pricey restaurant, parking, credit cards accepted, and limited wheelchair access.

Plaza Del Sol Hotels

During the 1980s the Plaza del Sol, a large American-style hotel, shopping, and entertainment complex, mushroomed on west-side Av. Adolfo López Mateos. The Holiday Inn and the Hyatt Regency, the pair of plush hostelries that anchor the development, have drawn many of the high-ticket visitors away from the old city center to the Plaza del Sol's shiny shops, restaurants, and clubs.

The **Hyatt Regency** occupies the giant glass tower right across the boulevard from the Plaza del Sol (Av. López Mateos and Moctezuma, Guadalajara, Jalisco 45050, tel. 36-227-778 and 36-226-688, fax 36-229-877). Inside, life fills the plush, cool lobby. Vacationers, convention-goers, and tour groups stroll to and fro; conversation overflows from the bar, where the band plays every evening. Outside, during the days, people sun themselves by the pool; at night they dance in the disco till three. The 346 rooms with everything cost from about $143 s or d; with health spa, gym, complete wheelchair access; from the U.S. and Canada, call toll-free (800) 233-1234 for reservations.

The **Holiday Inn,** a quarter mile south on López Mateos (past the traffic circle), offers much of the same, but in a more relaxed resort setting (Av. López Mateos Sur 2500, Guadalajara, Jalisco 45050, tel. 36-340-650, fax 36-481-562). The rooms, most with private view balconies, rise in a 10-story tower above the pool and garden. Their luxurious furnishings, in soothing earth tones, include spacious, marble-accented baths. The 285 rooms rent from about $170 s or d, with everything; spa, sauna, gym, children's area, miniature golf, tennis courts, wheelchair access; from the U.S. and Canada, call toll-free (800) 465-4329 for reservations and information.

Hotel El Parador

The big long-distance Central Camionera bus station is at Guadalajara's far southeast edge, at least 20 minutes by taxi from the center. Some bus travelers find it convenient to stay at the huge two-pool (but moderately priced) modern **Hotel El Parador** adjacent to the sprawling terminal (Carretera Zapotlanejo 1500, Guadalajara, Jalisco 45625, tel. 36-590-142). The rooms, all with baths, are tidy and comfortable. Bus and truck noise, however, may be a problem. Ask for a quiet *(tranquilo)* room. The place is impersonal, so be prepared to show your receipts. The 600 rooms rent for about $17 s, $20 d; there is a restaurant.

FOOD

Breakfast And Snacks

Local folks flock to the acres of *fondas* (permanent foodstalls) on the second floor of the **Mercado Libertad** (east end of Plaza Tapatía, open daily about 7 a.m.-6 p.m.). Hearty homestyle fare, including Guadalajara's specialty, *birria—*

pork, goat, or lamb in savory, spiced tomato-chicken broth—is at its safest best here. It's hard to go wrong if you make sure that your choices are hot and steaming. Market stalls, furthermore, depend on repeat customers and are generally very careful that their offerings are wholesome. Be sure to douse fresh vegetables with plenty of lime *(limón)* juice, however.

Downtown Guadalajara is not overloaded with restaurants, and many of them close early. For round-the-clock breakfast or supper, however, you can always rely on **Denny's** (corner Juarez and 16 Sept., tel. 140-219), which has the same food, prices, and 1950s vinyl-stainless steel ambience as Denny's restaurants everywhere.

For a local variation, head upstairs to **Restaurant Esquina** (same corner as Denny's, open 7 a.m.-10:30 p.m.), or **Sanborn's** across the street (open daily 7:30 a.m.-11 p.m.). Besides a fair-to-middling North American coffee shop, Sanborn's has a big gift and bookstore, offering maps, guidebooks, and loads of fairly priced handicrafts.

For a light breakfast or snack, try the baked goods and coffee at **Croissants Alfredo** (on Plaza Liberación, south side, between Maestranza and Degollado, open daily 8 a.m.-9:30 p.m.).

Downtown Restaurants

(Complete Dinner Price Key: Budget = under $7, Moderate = $7-14, Expensive = more than $14.) Moving from the Plaza Tapatía, west across the downtown, first comes the airy, Victorian-style **Restaurant Rinconada** (86 Morelos, across the plaza behind the Teatro Degollado, Mon.-Sat. 1-9 p.m., tel. 139-914). The mostly tourist and upper-class local customers enjoy Rinconada for its good meat-fish-fowl entrees plus the mariachis who wander in from the Plaza Mariachis nearby. By 4 p.m. many afternoons, two or three groups are filling the place with their melodies. Moderate to expensive.

Customers at the **Restaurant Cópa de Leche,** one of Guadalajara's acknowledged best restaurants, enjoy an open-air view of the passing Av. Juarez scene (Juarez at Galeana, two blocks south and two blocks west of the Cathedral, open daily 7:30 a.m.-10 p.m.). Cool salads and tasty regional entrees, plus prompt service by dinner-jacketed waiters, continue to

satisfy a legion of repeat customers. Moderate to expensive.

Continue west along Juarez to **Restaurant La Gran China,** (Juarez 590, between Martinez and 8 Julio, open daily noon-10:30) where the Cantonese owner-chef puts out an array of dishes, authentic and tasty enough even for San Francisco. Despite the reality of La Gran China's crisp bok choy, succulent spareribs, and savory noodles, they nevertheless seem a small miracle here, half a world away from Hong Kong. Budget to moderate.

Continue about a mile west of the cathedral (at the west end of Parque Revolución) to **Restaurant Copenhagen 77,** one of Guadalajara's classiest institutions. Its brand of unpretentious elegance—polished 1940s decor, subdued background jazz, correct, attentive service—will never go out of style. The conclusion: tasty entrees, presented invitingly (and enjoyed afternoons and evenings to live virtuoso jazz) are no less than one would expect. Moderate to expensive. At 140 Z. Castellanos; follow Juarez nine blocks west of Av. 16 Sept., to the west end of Parque Revolución; open Mon.-Sat. 8 a.m.-midnight, Sun. 7-7; live jazz afternoons 3-4 and nights 8-12.

ENTERTAINMENT AND EVENTS

Just Wandering Around

Afternoons any day (and Sundays especially) are good for people-watching around Guadalajara's many downtown plazas. If you're lucky (or time it right) you can enjoy the band concert in the Plaza de Armas adjacent to the cathedral (Sundays at 7 p.m.), or take in an art film at the Hospicio Cabañas (Mon.-Sat. 4 p.m., 6 p.m., and 8 p.m.). If somehow you miss these, climb into a *calandria* (horse-drawn carriage) for a ride around town (on Liceo, between the rotunda and the history museum, just north of the cathedral, $17/hour).

Parque Agua Azul

Some sunny afternoon, hire a taxi (about $2 from the city-center) and find out why Guadalajara families love Parque Agua Azul. The entrance is on Independencia, about a mile south of Plaza Tapatía. It's a green shaded place where you *can* walk (roll, sleep, or lie) on the grass.

When weary of that, stroll to the bird park, admire the banana-beaked toucans and squawking macaws, and continue into the aviary where free-flying birds flutter overhead. Nearby, duck into the butterfly aviary and enjoy the flickering rainbow-hues of a host of *mariposas*. Continue to the orchids in a towering hothouse, festooned with growing blossoms and misted continuously by a rainbow spray from the center. Before other temptations draw you away, stop for a while at the open-air band or symphony concert in the amphitheater. Open Tues.-Sun. 10-6.

Music And Dance Performances

The Teatro Degollado hosts world-class opera, symphony, and ballet events. Ask at your hotel desk, or while you're in the Plaza Liberación, drop by the theater box office and ask for a *lista de eventos*. For something very typically Mexican, attend one of the regular Sunday morning University of Guadalajara folkloric ballet performances. They're immensely popular; get tickets at the box office in advance.

If you miss a Teatro Degollado performance, try the **Instituto Cultural Cabañas** instead. They sponsor many events, both experimental and traditional, including frequent folkloric ballet performances. For more information, ask at the Hospicio Cabañas admission desk (see "Sights" above). Open Tues.-Sat. 10-6, Sun. 10-3, tel. 540-008, 540-129.

Local **jazz** mecca Restaurant Copenhagen 77 presents Maestro Carlos de la Torre and his group nightly Mon.-Sat. 8-12 and afternoons 3-4. At 140 Z. Castellanos, tel. 252-803, at Parque Revolución, about 10 blocks west of the cathedral.

Nightlife

The big westside hotels are among the best spots in town for **dancing and discoing.** Moving west from the cathedral-center of town, the **Hotel Fiesta Americana** is just past the Minerva traffic circle (about four miles along Avs. Juarez and Vallarta). Groups play for dancing in the lobby-bar nightly from about 7 p.m. and in the nightclub Caballo Negro from about 9:30 p.m. (Call 253-434 to doublecheck the times.)

Another two miles southwest on the right side of Av. López Mateos rises the big glass tower of the **Hotel Hyatt Regency.** The group in the lobby bar plays for dancing nightly from about 8 p.m. while the disco Iceberg fires up Tues.-Sun. from about 10 p.m. (For info, call 227-778.)

The **Holiday Inn** (a quarter-mile farther, past the traffic circle) also has a live trio in the lobby-bar La Cantera for dancing in the afternoons and evenings (happy hour 5-8 p.m.), and another trio (Thurs.-Sat. from about 9) at the Bar La Fiesta. Also, the Da Vinci disco booms away Thurs.-Sat. from 10 p.m. (Call 340-650 for confirmation.)

Bullfights, Rodeos, And Fiestas

Winter is the main season for **Corridas de Toros,** or "bullfights." The bulls charge and the crowds roar "Olé" (oh-LAY) Sunday afternoons at the Guadalajara Plaza de Toros (bullring, on Calz. Independencia about two miles north of the Mercado Libertad).

Local *charros* (gentleman cowboys) stage rodeo-like Sunday *charreadas* at the main Lienzo Charro ("Rodeo Ring") just beyond the southeast side of Parque Agua Azul (near the end

The strum of guitars is pleasantly common, especially weekend afternoons and evenings near the Plaza Tapatía.

MIKE WELLINS

of Calz. de Las Palmas). In addition to the usual bull-roping and bronco-busting, Guadalajara *charreadas* often end with the "Escaramuza Charra," a show of riding skill by beautifully dressed *charras* (cowgirls). Watch for posters, or ask at your hotel desk or the Tourist Information Office (see below) for bullfight and rodeo details and dates.

Although Guadalajara people always seem to be celebrating, the town really heats up during its three major annual festivals. Starting the second week in June, the southeast neighborhood (formerly a separate village) of Tlaquepaque hosts the **National Ceramics Fair.** Besides its celebrated stoneware (see "Shopping" below), a riot of ceramics and folkcrafts from all over Mexico stuff its shops and stalls, while cockfights, regional food, folkdances, fireworks, and mariachis fill its streets.

A few months later, the whole city, Mexican states, and foriegn countries get into the **Festival of October.** For a month, everyone contributes something, from ballet performances, plays, and soccer games to selling papiermâché parrots and sweet corn in the plazas. Concurrently, Guadalajarans celebrate the traditional **Festival of the Virgin of Zapopan.** Church plazas are awash with merrymakers enjoying food, mariachis, dances (don't miss the Dance of the Conquest), and fireworks. The merrymaking peaks on Oct. 12, as the virgin returns from the downtown cathedral to Zapopan. The crowd often swells to a million faithful, who escort the Virgin, accompanied by ranks of costumed saints, devils, Spanish conquistadores, and Aztec chiefs.

SPORTS

Walking, Jogging, And Exercise Gyms

Walkers and joggers enjoy several spots around Guadalajara. Close in, the **Plaza Liberación** (behind the cathedral) provides a traffic-free (although concrete) jogging and walking space. To avoid crowds, work out during the mornings. If you prefer grass underfoot, try **Parque Agua Azul** (entrance $3) on Calz. Independencia about a mile south of the Libertad market. An even better jogging-walking park is the **Parque de los Colomos,** hundreds of acres of greenery, laced by special jogging trails. The park is four

miles northwest from the center, before Zapopan; take a taxi or bus 51C from the old bus terminal, at the end of Av. Estadio, east of the traffic circle at north edge of Parque Agua Azul.

A number of Guadalajara hotels have good exercise gyms open to the public. The Hotel Fiesta Americana (Av. López Mateo Sur 110, tel. 253-434 ext. 3001, third floor) has the usual machines plus a jacuzzi and steam rooms. One-time use runs about $12. The Hyatt Regency (tel. 226-688 and 227-778) and the Holiday Inn (tel. 340-650) have similar facilities. (See "Plaza del Sol Hotels" above for location details.)

Tennis, Golf, And Swimming

Guadalajara has no public tennis courts. However, the Hotels Fiesta Americana (tel. 253-434, Av. López Mateos 110 Sur) and Holiday Inn (tel. 340-650) rent their tennis courts by appointment to the public.

The 18-hole **Club de Golf Atlas** welcomes nonmembers from dawn to dusk Tues.-Sun. Greens fee runs $50 Tues.-Fri. and $60 Sat. and Sunday. Clubs and carts rent for about $14 and $23; a caddy will run about $12. Get there via Chapala Hwy. 23, the south-of-town extension of Calz. J. Gonzales Gallo. The golf course is at Km 6.5, past the edge of town, near Parque Montenegro.

Nearly all the plush hotels (see "Plaza del Sol Hotels" above) have swimming pools. One of the prettiest pools, however, perches atop the moderate Hotel Calinda in the heart of town (corner Juarez and Degollado, see "Downtown Hotels" above). If somehow you can't get into any of the hotel pools, go to the very popular public pool and picnic ground at Balneario Lindo Michoacán (Rio Barco 1614, corner Calz. J. Gonzalez Gallo, tel. 359-399) about two miles along Gallo southeast of Parque Agua Azul.

SHOPPING

Downtown

The sprawling **Mercado Libertad** (south end of Plaza Tapatía) has several specialty areas distributed through two main sections. Most of the handicrafts are in the eastern, upper half. While some stalls carry guitars and sombreros, leather predominates—in jackets, belts, saddles, and the most huaraches you'll ever see under one roof. Here, bargaining *es la costumbre*. Competition, furthermore, gives buyers the advantage. The upper floor also houses an acre of foodstalls, many of them excellent. (See "Breakfast and Snacks" above.)

A central courtyard leads past a lineup of bird-sellers and their caged charges to the Mercado Libertad's lower half, where produce, meat, and spice stalls fill the floor. (Photographers, note the photogenic view of the produce floor from the balcony above.) Downstairs, don't miss browsing intriguing spice and herb stalls, which feature mounds of curious dried plants, gathered from the wild, often by village *brujos* (shamans or witch-doctors). Before you leave, be sure to look over the piñatas, which make colorful gifts.

Outside of Mercado Libertad, two downtown government stores have excellent, reasonably priced selections of both local and national folkcrafts. The closest, the **Casa de las Artesanías Normal** is at Av. Alcalde 1211 (from the front of the cathedral, walk several blocks north). Here, you can find everything—brilliant stoneware, endearing ceramic, brass, and papier mâché animals, and handsome gold and silver jewelry—without actually going to Tonalá, Tlaquepaque and Taxco. The very similar alternate store, the Casa de Artesanías Agua Azul, is at Calz. Gonzales Gallo 20, in Parque Agua Azul (off of Independencia, a mile south of the Libertad market). Both stores are open Mon.-Sat. 10-7, Sun. 10-2.

Tlaquepaque

Tlaquepaque was once a sleepy village of potters miles from Guadalajara. Attracted by the quiet of the country, rich families built palatial homes there during the 19th century. Now, entrepreneurs have moved in and converted them into upscale restaurants, art galleries, and showrooms, stuffed with quality Tonalá and Tlaquepaque ceramics, glass, metalwork and papier-mâché. In spite of having been swallowed by the city, Tlaquepaque still has the feel of and look of a small colonial town, with its cathedral and central square leading westward onto the mansion-decorated main street, now mall, Av. Independencia.

Although generally a bit pricier than Tonalá, Tlaquepaque still has bargains. Proceed by finding the base prices at the crafts stalls edging Independencia and Calles Madero and P. Sanchez, around the central plaza, then price out the tonier merchandise in the galleries of the next three blocks west along Independencia. For super-fine examples of Tlaquepaque and Tonalá crafts, be sure to stop by the **Museo Regional de Ceramica y Arte Popular** before they close (237 Independencia, open Tues.-Sun 10-3).

From the Museo, cross the street to the **Sergio Bustamante** store, upscale outlet for the famous sculptor's arresting, whimsical studies in juxtaposition. Bustamante supervises an entire Guadalajara studio-factory of artists who put out hundreds of one-of-a-kind variations on a few human, animal, and vegetable themes. Prices seem to depend mainly on size; rings and bracelets may go for as little as $200, while a three-foot humanoid chicken may cost $2,000. Don't miss the restroom. (Open daily 10-7.)

Next to Bustamante, at 232 Independencia, **La Rosa Cristal** is one of the few spots where (until 2 p.m. daily) visitors may see glassblowers practicing their time-honored Tlaquepaque craft. Samples of their work—clutches of big red, green, blue, and silver glass balls—decorate the room (open Mon.-Sat. 10-7, Sun. 10-2, tel. 397-180).

Not far west, at the intersection of Independencia and Alfarareros ("Potters"), a pair of regally restored former mansions, now galleries, enjoy a dignified retirement facing each other. **La Casa Canela** (Independencia 258, open Mon.-Fri. 10-2 and 3-7, Sat. 10-3, tel. 571-343) takes pride in its museum-quality lace, cloth, pottery, blown glass, and classic, blue-on-white Tlaquepaque stoneware. Across the street, **Antigua de Mexico** (Independencia 255, tel. 353-402, open daily except Sun.) specializes in baroque gilt wood antiques and reproductions, being one of the few studios in Mexico that manufactures fine 17th-century-style furniture.

Getting to Tlaquepaque: Take a taxi (about $10) or ride the usually crowded city bus 275A ($.50) from the 16 Sept.-Morelos Cathedral corner. By car from the center of town, drive Av. Revolución southeast about four miles to the Niños Héroes traffic circle. Continue right along Av. Niños Héroes about a mile to the west end of the Av. Independencia on the left.

Tonalá

About five miles east past Tlaquepaque, Tonalá perches at Guadalajara's country edge. When the Spanish arrived in the 1520s, Tonalá was dominant among the small kingdoms of the Atemajac Valley. Tonalá's widow-queen and her royal court were adorned by the glittering handiwork of an honored class of silver and gold craftsmasters. Although the Spaniards carted off the valuables, the tradition remains today. To the visitor, everyone in Tonalá seems to making something. Whether it be pottery, stoneware, brass, or papier mâché, Tonalá family patios are piled with their specialties.

Right at the source, bargains couldn't be better. Dozens of shops dot Tonalá's few blocks around the central plaza corner at Av. Hidalgo (north-south) and Av. Juarez (east-west). For super bargaining opportunities and *mucho* holiday excitement and color, visit the Sunday market, which spreads along the tree-lined *periférico* highway about four blocks west of the Tonalá plaza.

Under any circumstances, make the **Museo de Ceramicas** (104 Constitución, at Morelos, two blocks north, one block west of the plaza, open Tues.-Fri 10-5, Sat. 10-3, Sun. 10-2) one of your first Tonalá stops. If you arrive before 2 p.m., you may get to see someone turning out a classic vase or painting the smile on a Tonalá cat.

Several Tonalá shops stand out. Moving south along Hidalgo toward the town plaza from Constitución, **Artesanías Garay,** one of several *fábrica* (factory) shops that retail directly, offers

The mágico sol, *worshipped universally in preconquest Mexico, continues as a popular pottery and metalwork motif.*

a plethora of Tonalá motifs. They're especially proud of their fine floral-design stoneware (Hidalgo 86, open Mon.-Sat. 10-3 and 4-7, Sun. 10-3, tel. 830-019, credit cards accepted).

El Bazar de Sermel (Hidalgo 67, open Mon.-Fri. 9-6:30, Sat. 9-2, Sun. 10-3), diagonally across the street, has stretched the Tonalá papier-mâché tradition to the ultimate. Stop in and pick out the life-size flamingo, pony, giraffe, or zebra you've always wanted for your living room.

La Hacienda (13 Hidalgo, corner of the plaza, open Mon.-Sat. 10-6, Sun. 12-3) offers an interesting assortment from Tonalá and other parts of Mexico. These include Huichol Indian yarn paintings and God's Eyes, painted tin Christmas decorations from Oaxaca, and Guanajuato papier-mâché clowns.

Around the corner, a few steps west on Juarez, **Artesanías Nuño** (Juarez 59, open daily 10-7) displays a fetching menagerie, including parrots, monkeys, flamingos, and toucans, in papier-mâché, brass, and ceramics. Bargain for very reasonable buys.

Continue south past the Juarez plaza corner (where Hidalgo becomes Madero) one block to **La Antigua Tonalá** (Madero 50, tel. 830-200, open Mon.-Sat. 10-2 and 4-7, Sun. 10-3). There you'll find a store full of hand-hewn tables, chairs, and chests, complete with the Tonalá stoneware place settings to go with them. They ship.

Getting to Tonalá: Taxi (about $20 roundtrip) or ride the oft-crowded city bus 275B from the downtown cathedral corner of 16 de Septiembre and Morelos. By car, drive Av. Revolución about six miles southeast of the city-center to the big Plaza Camichines interchange. Continue ahead along the Carretera Tonalá *libre* (free) branch. (Avoid forking onto the Hwy. 90 Carretera Zapotlanejo *cuota* toll road.) The Carretera Tonalá continues due east for about three more miles, passing under the Carretera Zapotlanejo. Continue across the arterial *periférico* (peripheral highway); three blocks farther, turn left and within a few more blocks you'll be at the Tonalá central plaza.

Photo And Department Stores

The several branches of the **Laboratorios Julio** chain offer quick photofinishing and a big stock of photo supplies and film, including professional 120 transparency and negative rolls. Their big downtown branch is at Colon

125 (between Juarez and Cotilla, open Mon.-Sat. 10-2 and 4-8, Sun. 10-2, tel. 142-850). Their Plaza del Sol store is in Zone F, local #6, tel. 215-359.

For convenient, all-in-one shopping, try **Gigante,** downtown on Juarez, corner of Martinez. (Open Mon.-Sat. 8-9, Sun. 8-3, tel. 138-638. For even more under one air-conditioned roof, try the big **Comercial Mexicana** at Plaza del Sol (Av. Lopez Mateos Sur 2077, open daily 9-9, tel. 225-192 and 225-619).

SERVICES AND INFORMATION

Change more types (U.S., Canadian, German, Japanese, French, Italian, and Swiss) of money at the best rates at the downtown streetfront **Banamex** office (Juarez, corner of Corona, open Mon.-Fri. 9-5).

The **U.S. Consulate** is at Progreso 175 (between Cotillo and Libertad) about a mile west of the town-center (open Mon.-Fri. 8 a.m.-4 p.m., tel. 252-700). The **Canadian Consulate** is in the Hotel Fiesta Americana at Aurelio Acedes 225 (near the intersection of Av. López Mateos and Av. Vallarta, tel. 253-434, ext. 3005, open Mon.-Fri. 10 a.m.-1 p.m.).

For **police** emergencies, call the radio patrol (dial 06) or the police headquarters at 176-060 and 180-260. In case of **fire,** call the *servicio bomberos* fire station at 195-241 or 230-833. If you need a doctor, the **Hospital Mexico Americano** (Colomos 2110, tel. 413-141, 424-520, ambulance emergency 427-152) has specialists on call.

The local **Tourist Information** office is on Paseo Degollado (the mall behind the Teatro Degollado between Avs. Morelos and Hidalgo). Their hours are Mon.-Fri. 9-9 and Sat. 9-1 (tel. 140-606, ext. 114).

For books and newspapers, try the good bookstore in the **Hotel Fenix** (Av. Corona at Cotilla, open daily 8-9:30) downtown. They stock dozens of U.S. magazines, a rack of paperback bestsellers, and newspapers, such as the Mexico City *News,* and *USA Today.*

For many arts, crafts, history, and cultural books on Mexico, try the bookstore at the **Instituto Cultural Cabañas,** east end of Plaza Tapatía (Cabañas 8, open Tues.-Sat. 10-6, Sun. 10-3, tel. 540-008, 540-129).

GETTING THERE AND AWAY

By Air

Several jet carriers connect Guadalajara International Airport (code-designated GDL, about 12 miles, 19 km southeast of downtown) with many U.S. and domestic destinations.

Mexicana Airlines (tel. 472-222) has daily connections with Los Angeles, San Francisco, San Jose, Denver, San Antonio, Dallas, Chicago, Puerto Vallarta, Mazatlán, Manzanillo, and other domestic destinations.

Aeromexico (reservations tel. 156-565, flight info tel. 890-163) connects daily with Los Angeles, Houston, Tijuana, Mazatlán, Manzanillo, Acapulco, and other domestic destinations.

Alaska Airlines (tel. 890-386) connects daily with Los Angeles, San Francisco, and Seattle.

American Airlines (tel. 164-090) connects twice daily with Dallas.

Delta Airlines (reservations tel. 303-530 and 303-113, flight info tel. 890-048) connects twice daily with Los Angeles.

Airport arrival is simplified by money exchange and major car rental booths. Ground transportation is likewise well organized, with minibuses (about $2 per person), *colectivos* (shared VW van taxis, about $13 total for one to four persons), and individual taxis for about $15 for one to four persons. International departure tax runs $19 ($12 federal tax plus a local $7) cash per person (no credit cards, no traveler's checks).

By Car Or RV

Three major routes connect Guadalajara with the Pacific coast. From **Tepic-Compostela-Puerto Vallarta** in the west, Hwy. 15 winds about 141 miles (227 km) over the Sierra Madre Occidental crest. The two lanes are narrow, sometimes congested, and in only fair condition. A toll superhighway at the pass saves an hour, however. For safety, allow around four hours from Tepic or Compostela. Add three hours for the winding, sometimes steep 104-mile (167-km) Hwy. 200 leg to/from Puerto Vallarta.

From Barra de Navidad in the southwest, traffic bumps, curves, and climbs along Hwy. 80 for 190 miles (306 km) to/from Guadalajara. Allow around five or six hours. For an easier route, see below.

From Manzanillo (or Barra de Navidad) in the south, combined *autopistas* (superhighways) 200, 110, and 54 safely allow an easy 55 mph (90 km/hour) most of the way for this 192-mile (311-km) trip. Allow about four hours either way. Add another hour for the additional 38 miles (61 km) of Hwy. 200 to/from from Barra de Navidad.

By Bus

The long-distance Guadalajara Camionera Central (Bus Terminal) is at least 20 minutes by taxi (about $7) from the city center. The huge, clean, and modern complex sprawls past the southeast-sector intersection of the old Tonalá Highway (Carretera Antigua Tonalá) and the new Zapotlanejo Autopista (freeway) Hwy. 90. The Camionera Central is sandwiched between the two highways. Tell your taxi driver where you want to go, and he'll drop you at one of the terminal's seven sections.

To and from **western** and **northwestern destinations,** such as Puerto Vallarta, Tepic, Mazatlán, and the U.S. western border, go Transportes Norte de Sonora (TNS, tel. 576-202, section 3), Tres Estrellas de Oro (TEO, 576-969, section 3), or Transportes Pacifico (TP, 574-668, section 3).

To and from **southern destinations,** such as Barra de Navidad, Manzanillo, Colima, and Ixtapa-Zihuatanejo, ride Tres Estrellas de Oro (see above), Estrella Blanca (EB, tel. 576-030, section 6), or Autocamiones del Pacifico (AP, tel. 574-805), which goes to Barra and Manzanillo via Hwy. 80.

By Train

The rail terminal (for ticket and exact schedule details, tel. 500-826) fronts the end of Calz. Independencia, about a mile south of the city-center. The subsidized seat prices are extremely reasonable. Three major passenger lines branch out from Guadalajara: **northwest** to Tepic, Mazatlán, and the U.S. border, **south** to Colima and Manzanillo, and **east** to Morelia and Mexico City.

The first-class coach **Estrella** leaves Guadalajara at around 9:30 a.m., stopping en route at Tepic (around 3 p.m.) and Mazatlán (around 7 p.m.), arriving in Mexicali (or Nogales) on the U.S. border about 35 hours later. (The opposite number Estrella train departs Mexicali also in the morning, arriving in Guadalajara after 35 hours.)

The southern-line pair of trains (known perfunctorily only as "nos. 91 and 92,") are lowly second-class diesels. Number 92 leaves Guadalajara at around 9 a.m., rolling downhill to Colima by about 4 p.m. and Manzanillo an hour later. Number 91 starts out at 6 a.m. from Manzanillo, arriving in Colima an hour later. It continues, chugging uphill to Guadalajara, arriving by the late afternoon.

The crack first-class sleeper-equipped **Tapatío** heads out from Guadalajara about 9 p.m., stopping in Morelia (from which connections to Pátzcuaro and Lázaro Cárdenas on the coast may be made). The Tapatío continues overnight, arriving in Mexico City the next day around 8:30 a.m. A two-person sleeper on the Tapatío runs about $40 per person; coach seats, while much cheaper, are correspondingly less comfortable.

ALONG THE ROAD TO PUERTO VALLARTA

The lush, hundred-mile stretch between Tepic and Puerto Vallarta is a Pacific Eden of flowery tropical forest and pearly palm-shaded beaches, largely unknown to the outside world. The gateway Mexican National Highway 200 is still new; the traffic and development that will inevitably follow have barely begun. Only a few roadside villages, pastures, tobacco fields, and tropical fruit orchards encroach upon the vine-strewn jungle.

PLAYAS CHACALA AND CHACALILLA

Side roads off Hwy. 200 often provide exotic, close-up glimpses of Nayarit's tangled, tropical woodland, but rarely will they lead to such a delightful surprise as the green-tufted golden crescent of Playa Chacala and its diminutive neighbor, Playa Chacalilla.

Two miles south of Las Varas, follow the six-mile cobble and gravel road to the great old palm grove at Chacala. Beyond the line of venerable palapa seafood restaurants lies a heavenly curve of sand, enfolded on both sides by palm-tipped headlands.

A mile farther on, the road ends at Chacalilla, Chacala's miniature twin, with its own sandy beach, grove, and palapa where, on holidays, someone will show up to sell barbecued fish and drinks to beach-camping families.

Beach Activities

Chacala's oft-gentle surf is good for close-in bodysurfing and boogieboarding, swimming, and beginning-to-intermediate surfing. Furthermore, the water is generally clear enough for snorkeling off the rocks on either side of the beach. If you bring your equipment, windsurfing and sailing would also be possible. Fishing is so good that local people make their living at it. Chacala Bay is so rich and clean that tourists eat oysters right off the rocks.

Food And Accommodations

Supplied by the beachside restaurants and the stores in the village of Chacala (on the headland between the beaches), either of these two strands are ideal for tent or small RV **camping.** The sometimes rough, steep, and narrow entry road, however, appears too difficult for most big trailers and motorhomes.

Mar De Jade

The Mar de Jade, a holistic-style living center at the south end of Playa Chacala, offers an alternative to camping. Laura del Valle, Mar de Jade's

Roadside stalls at Las Varas offer a trove of local fruit. Sometimes more exotic varieties, such as guanabanas, shown, are available.

physician-founder, has worked hard since the early 1980s, building living facilities and a learning center, while simultaneously establishing a local health clinic. By 1990, Mar de Jade was offering Spanish-language and work-study programs for people who like the tropics but want to do more than laze in the sun. The main thrust is interaction with local people. Spanish, for example, is the preferred language at the dinner table.

Their thatched, cool, and clean adobe and brick cabins (with concrete floors, showers, restrooms, and good water) nestle among a flowery, palm-shaded garden of fruit trees. Stone pathways lead to the main complex, which consists of a dining room, kitchen, offices, library, and classroom overlooking the sea.

While Mar de Jade's purpose is earnest and serious, they have nothing against visitors who *do* want to laze in the sun. They invite travelers to make reservations (or simply drop in) and stay as long as they like for $30 a day per adult, three meals included. If, on the other hand, guests want to camp on the property, they would probably negotiate such an arrangement for a reasonable fee.

For more information on their course schedule and fees, write to them at P.O. Box 81, Las Varas, Nayarit 63715, or call the clinic (officially, the Casa Clínica de la Mujer Campesina) Mon., Wed., or Fri. 10-1 in Las Varas at 327-200-42 (or telex FEDEME 065552, Puerto Vallarta).

RINCÓN DE GUAYABITOS
AND LA PEÑITA

Rincón de Guayabitos (pop. about 4,000 permanent, maybe 8,000 in the winter) lies halfway between Tepic and Puerta Vallarta, at the tiny south-end *rincón* (wrinkle) of the broad, mountain-rimmed Bay of Jaltemba. The full name of Rincón de Guayabitos's sister town, La Peñita (Little Rock) de Jaltemba, comes from its perch on the sandy edge of the bay.

Once upon a time, Rincón de Guayabitos (or simply, Guayabitos, meaning "Little Guavas"), lived up to its diminutive name. During the 1970s, however, the government decided that Rincón de Guayabitos was to become both a resort and one of the three places in Pacific Mexico (the other two were to be Bucerías and Nuevo Vallarta near Puerto Vallarta) where foreigners could own property outright. So now Rincón de Guayabitos is a summer, Christmas, and Easter haven for Mexicans and a winter haven for Canadians and Americans weary of big, pricey resorts.

SIGHTS

Getting Oriented

Guayabitos and La Peñita (pop. around 15,000) comprise practically a single town. Guayabitos has the hotels and the sleepy scenic ambience while, two miles north, La Peñita's main street, Emiliano Zapata, bustles with stores, restaurants, a bank, and a bus station.

Guayabitos's main street, **Avenida del Sol Nuevo,** curves lazily for about a mile parallel to the beach. From the *avenida,* several short streets and *andandos* (walkways) lead to a line of *retornos* (cul-de-sacs). Nearly all of Guayabitos's community of small hotels, bungalow complexes, and trailer parks lie on these *retornos,* within a block of the beach.

Isla Islote

From every spot along the bay, the rock-studded humpback of Isla Islote beckons a few miles offshore. A flotilla of wooden glass-bottomed launches plies the Guayabitos shoreline, ready to whisk visitors across to the island. For about $25 an hour you can view the fish through the boat bottom and see the colonies of nesting terns, frigate birds, and boobies on Islote's guano-plastered far side. Often dolphins will play in your boat's wake, and occasionally a pod of whales will spout and dive not far away.

Beaches And Activities

The main beach, Playa Guayabitos-La Peñita, curves two miles northerly from the rocky Guayabitos point, growing wider and steeper at La Peñita. The shallow Guayabitos cove, lined by palapa restaurants and dotted with boats, is a favorite of Mexican families on Sundays and holidays. They play in the one-foot surf, ride the boats, eat barbecued fish, and throw everything on the sand. During busy times, the place can get a bit polluted from the people, boats, and fishing.

Farther along toward La Peñita, however, the beach broadens and becomes much cleaner, with surf good for swimming, bodysurfing and boogieboarding. Afternoon winds are often brisk enough for sailing and windsurfing with your own equipment (none is available locally). Scuba and snorkeling are good near offshore Isla Islote, accessible via rental boat from Guayabitos. Local stores sell inexpensive but serviceable masks, snorkels, and fins.

Just past the palm-studded headland a mile north of La Peñita (where another long, inviting beach begins) the waves angle in, offering good chances for beginning and intermediate surfing.

Playa Los Muertos And Playa Los Ayala

Follow the road to Los Ayala (over the headland adjacent to Guayabitos cove) and you will see a dirt road that forks right downhill through a cemetery (thus Los Muertos, "The Dead") to Playa Los Muertos, where the graves come right down to the beach.

Ghosts notwithstanding, this is a scenic little sandy cove, where on fair days you can get your fill of safe swimming, sunning on the beach, or tidepooling amongst the oysters and mussels that cluster and the crabs that skitter on the rocks nearby.

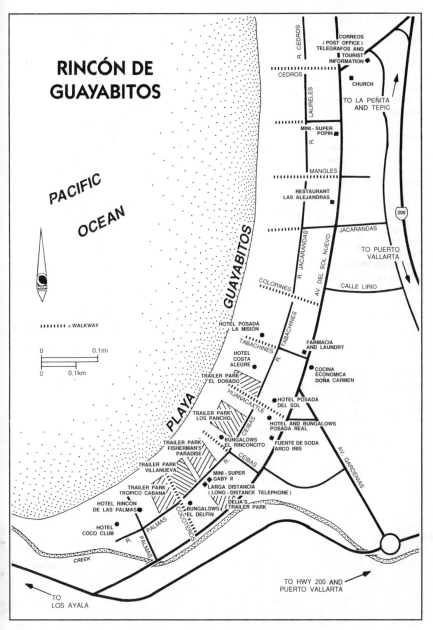

Continue along the road about a mile farther and you'll reach the tiny rustic settlement and half-mile yellow strand of Playa Los Ayala. With no facilities other than a dusty little store and a lineup of beachside palapas, Los Ayala retains its Sunday and holiday popularity among local families because of its long, lovely beach. All of the beach sports possible at Guayabitos are possible here, with the added advantage that, away from the fishing cove, the beach is much cleaner.

Like Guayabitos, Los Ayala also has its secluded south-end cove. Follow the path up the palmy, beach-end headland. Ten minutes' walk along a tropical forest trail leads you to the romantic little jungle-enfolded sand crescent called **Playa Del Beso** ("Beach of the Kiss"). Except during holidays, few if any people come here for hours on end.

Playa La Raza

The road to Playa La Raza, while not long, requires a maneuverable high-clearance vehicle. The reward is a long wild beach, perfect for beachcombing and camping. Bring everything, including water.

Three miles south of Guayabitos along Hwy. 200, turn off at Monteon; pass through the village, turn right just before the pavement ends, and follow the rough road through the creek and over the ridge north of town. At the summit, stop and feast your eyes on the valley view below, then continue down through the near-virgin jungle, barely scratched by a few poor cornfields. Halfway to the beach, stop to see if the seasonal hillside restaurant is open.

At the bottom of the steep grade, the track parallels the beach beneath big trees; sandy trails run through the brush to the beach. (Experienced sand drivers only; it's very easy to get stuck.) You have two miles straight of pristine, jungle-backed sand virtually to yourself.

The beach itself slopes steeply, with the resulting close-in crashing waves and undertow. The water would be fine for splashing, but swimmers be careful. With its jungle hinterland, birds and other wildlife are plentiful here. Bring your repellent, binoculars, and identification books.

Turtles also arrive (marked by obvious tracks in the sand) periodically in late summer and fall to lay eggs here. They attract predators—cats, iguanas, birds, and human poachers. If you find an egg nest, keep watch over it; your reward may be to witness the birth and return to the ocean of dozens of baby turtles.

ACCOMMODATIONS

Guayabitos Hotels

Guayabitos has more hotels than any other town in Nayarit, including the capital, Tepic. Competition keeps standards high and prices low. During the low season (Aug.-Nov.) most places are only half full and ready to bargain. The livelier part of town is at the south end, where most of the foreigners, mostly Canadians and Americans, congregate during the winter. Guayabitos has many lodgings that call themselves "bungalows." This generally implies a motel-type kitchenette-suite with less service than a hotel.

Perhaps the cheapest good lodging in town is the friendly 32-room **Hotel and Bungalows Posada Real,** built around a cobbled jungly courtyard parking lot with squawking parrots and snoozing crocodiles. The bungalow units are on the ground floor in the courtyard; the hotel rooms are stacked in three plant-decorated tiers above

---

RINCÓN DE GUAYABITOS HOTELS

Guayabitos hotels, in order of increasing approximate double-room price (area code 327 unless otherwise noted, postal code 63726)

Hotel and Bungalows Posada Real, Retorno Ceibas s/n, 401-77, $14

Hotel Posada La Misión, Retorno Tabachines 6, 400-18, $33

Hotel Rincón de Las Palmas, Retorno Palmas s/n, 401-90, $35

Bungalows El Delfin, Retorno Ciebas s/n, 403-85, $36

Hotel Costa Alegre, Retorno Tabachines s/n, 402-43, $38

Bungalows El Rinconcito, Retorno Ceibas s/n (P.O. Box 19), 402-29, $40

Hotel Posada del Sol, Retorno Tabachines s/n, (321) 401-52, $30

the good restaurant-bar in front. At Retorno Ceibas s/n and Andando Guanacaste, Rincón de Guayabitos, Nayarit 63726, tel. (327) 401-77. Their 19 four-person bungalows w/kitchenettes rent for about $16/day, $105/week, $420/month; 13 two-person hotel rooms, about $14/day, $91/week, $360/month; with fans, a small pool, racquetball, free bicycle use, parking, restaurant; one block from the beach, credit cards accepted.

One of the most charming off-beach Guayabitos lodgings is **Bungalows El Delfin**, built around an intimate banana- and palm-fringed pool-patio, with deck recliners and umbrellas for resting and reading. Chairs on the shaded porch-walkways in front of the three room-tiers invite quiet relaxation and conversation with neighbors. The pastel-walled four-person suites are large and plainly furnished, with basic stove, refrigerator and utensils, rear laundry porches, and big tiled toilet-showers. At Retorno Ciebas and Andando Cocoteros s/n, Rincón de Guayabitos, Nayarit 63726, tel. (327) 403-85. The 15 bungalows w/kitchenettes sleep four and rent for about $36, $7 per extra person; with fans, pool, pets okay, parking.

Right-on-the-beach **Bungalows El Rinconcito** is one of the best buys in Guayabitos (Retorno Ceibas s/n and Calle Ceibas, P.O. Box 19, Rincón de Guayabitos, Nayarit 63726, tel. 327-402-29). The smallish whitewashed complex, set back from the street, offers large, tastefully furnished units with yellow and blue tile kitchens and solid, Spanish-style dark-wood chairs and beds. Its oceanside patio opens to a grassy garden overlooking the surf. They rent three two-bedroom bungalows for about $50, and seven one-bedroom bungalows for about $40, with fans and parking.

One of the fancier Guayabitos lodgings is the colonial-style **Hotel Posada La Misión**, whose centerpiece is a beachside restaurant-bar-garden nestled beneath a spreading, big-leafed *hule* (rubber) tree (Retorno Tabachines 6, Rincón de Guayabitos, Nayarit 63726, tel. 327-400-18). Extras include a luxurious, shady garden-veranda and an inviting azure pool patio, thoughtfully screened off from the parking. Their rooms are high-ceilinged and comfortable except for their unimaginative bare-bulb lighting; bring your favorite bulb-clip lampshades. Doubles rent for $33 high season, $23 low; quadruples,

$50 and $35; suites sleeping six, $45 and $60. Two kitchenette bungalows go for $63; pool, good restaurant, ocean-view bar, fans, and parking; credit cards accepted.

Travelers who prefer an air-conditioned, modern-style lodging (and who want to play tennis) pick the compact, sparklingly white motel-patio ambience of the **Hotel Rincón de Las Palmas** near the south end. With an airy beach-view restaurant-bar for sitting and socializing, this is a lodging for those who want company. Guests often have a hard time *not* getting acquainted. The smallish rooms are packed in two double parallel breezeway tiers around a pool-patio above the beach. Right outside your room during the high season you will probably have your pick of around 50 sunbathing bodies to gaze at and meet.

This hotel is operated by its big neighbor Hotel Coco Club, which handles reservations (call 327-401-90, -91, and -92), which are mandatory during the winter (Retorno Palmas s/n at Calle Palmas, Rincón de Guayabitos, Nayarit 63726, tel. 327-403-50). The 40 rooms rent for about $35 d; some with two double beds and kitchenette, $50; a/c, pool, TV, good tennis court, restaurant-bar, parking; credit cards accepted.

Just as modern but less cramped is the more family-oriented **Hotel Costa Alegre,** where the Guayabitos beach widens out (Retorno Tabachines s/n at Calle Tabachines, Rincón de Guayabitos, Nayarit 63726, tel. 327-402-43, 73 rooms). Its pluses include a big, blue, palm-shaded pool-patio on the street side and a broad, grassy, ocean-view garden on the beach side. Although the rooms are adequate, they radiate a motel-institutional feel. Some of them are off to the side, with no view but the back of neighboring rooms. The best choices are the several upper-tier oceanfront rooms, all with kitchenettes and sliding glass doors leading to private view balconies. Rates for the 30 smaller rooms are $38 for one to four persons; the 43 rooms with views and kitchenettes go for $46; a/c, a pool, parking, restaurant-bar; credit cards accepted.

Guayabitos Trailer Parks

All but one of several Guayabitos trailer parks are wall-to-wall RVs all winter. Some old-timers have painted and marked out their spaces for years of future occupancy. The best spaces of the bunch are all booked by mid-October. And although the longtime residents are polite enough, many of them are clannish and don't go out of their way to welcome new kids on the block.

This is fortunately not true at **Delia's,** Guayabitos's funkiest trailer park (Retorno Ceibas 4, Rincón de Guayabitos, Nayarit 63726, tel. 327-403-98). Friendly realtor-owner Delia Priske has 15 spaces, a good number of which are unfilled even during the high season. Her place, alas, is not right on the beach, nor is it as tidy as some folks would like. On the other hand, Delia offers a little store, insurance, long-distance phone service, and a small cafe, Abel's Lonchería, with good breakfasts, right next to the premises. She also rents two bungalows for about $300 a month. Spaces run $7/night, $180/month with all hookups, room for big rigs, pets okay, showers, toilets.

The rest of Guayabitos's trailer parks line up right along the beachfront. Moving from south to north, first comes **Trailer Park Tropico Cabana,** built with boats and anglers in mind. One old-timer, a woman, the manager says, has been coming for 20 years running. It must be for the avocados—bulging, delicious three-pounders that hang from a big shady tree. Other extras are a boat launch and storage right on the beach, with an adjacent fish-cleaning sink and table. This is a prime, very popular spot; get your reservation in early (Retorno Las Palmas, P.O. Box 3, Rincón de Guayabitos, Nayarit 63726). The 39 cramped spaces, six 38-footers, and 22 33-footers rent for about $11/day with all hookups, discounts for longer stays; showers, toilets, barbecue, pets okay.

The single Guayabitos trailer park that celebrates a traditional Christmas-eve *posada* procession is the family-run **Trailer Park Villanueva** (Retorno Ceibas s/n, Rincón de Guayabitos, Nayarit 63726, tel. 327-403-70). Allowing for 30 spaces (including three drive-throughs), they can still stuff in some big rigs, although room is at a premium. Shade, however, is not: lovely palms cover the entire lot. Moreover, their romantic palapa restaurant is very popular with Guayabitos long-timers. Spaces go for $12/daily, with all hookups; restaurant, showers, toilets, boat ramp, pets okay.

Trailer Park Los Pancho is Guayabitos's

newest RV park (Retorno Ceibas s/n, Apdo. 42, Rincón de Guayabitos, Nayarit 63726.). Its all-concrete (and consequently sterile and shade-less) spaces are wide and long enough for 40-foot rigs. A palmy yard with a designer bar-restaurant fronts the beach. The 19 spaces rent for $11/day with all hookups; showers, toilets, fish-cleaning facility, boat ramp, pets okay.

Residents of **Trailer Park El Dorado** enjoy shady, grass-carpeted spaces beneath a rustling old palm grove, the result of the tender loving care of the friendly on-site owner-manager (Retorno Tabachines s/n, Rincón de Guayabitos, Nayarit 63726, Guadalajara tel. 321-401-52). Extras include a pool and recreation palapa across the street in **Hotel Posada Del Sol** (14 tastefully furnished bungalows around a palmy garden-patio, from about $30 d, $500/month). Rate for the 21 spaces is $11/day, with all hookups, add $2 for a/c; showers, toilets, pets okay.

La Peñita Trailer Park

The **Trailer Park Hotelera La Peñita** enjoys a breezy oceanview location one mile (at the big red-and-white-cross highway sign) north of La Peñita. Their spaces spread over a grassy tree-dotted hillside park overlooking a golden beach and bay. Write for reservations to P.O. Box 22, La Peñita, Nayarit 63726. The 120 spaces run $11/day, most with all hookups; pool, terrace club, restaurant, showers, and toilets; good for tenting, surfing, and fishing.

FOOD

Fruit Stands And Mini-supermarkets

The farm country along Hwy. 200 between Tepic and Puerto Vallarta offers a feast of tropical fruits. Roadside stands, especially at Las Varas and to a lesser extent, Guayabitos and La Peñita, offer mounds of papayas, mangos, melons, and pineapples in season. Also watch out for more exotic species, such as the *guanabana,* which looks like a spiny mango, but whose pulpy interior looks and smells much like its Asian cousin, the jackfruit.

A number of small Guayabitos mini-supermarkets supply a little bit of everything. Try **Mini-Super Gaby II** on the south end (Retorno Ceibas by Bungalows El Delfin, open daily 7-

12:30 and 4-7:30) for vegetables, a small deli, and general groceries. Competing nearby is **Mini-Super Juan de Dios** (open daily 7 a.m.-8 p.m.). On the north end, **Mini-Super Popin** (Av. del Sol Nuevo and Laureles, open daily 8 a.m.-9 p.m.) stocks more, including fresh-baked goods.

For larger, fresher selections of everything, go to one of the number of large main-street supermarkets, such as **Supermercado Lorena** (tel. 402-55, open daily 8 a.m.-8 p.m.).

Restaurants

(Complete Dinner Price Key: Budget = under $7, Moderate = $7-14, Expensive = more than $14.) Several Guayabitos restaurants offer good food and service during the winter, spring, and early summer. Hours and menus are often restricted during the low Aug.-Oct. rainy season, however. La Peñita, on the other hand, has a number of dependable eateries that do not depend so heavily on tourist trade and consequently offer steadier, year-round service.

At the low end, the family-run **Cocina Economica Doña Carmen** puts out hearty tacos, enchiladas, spicy *pozole* (shredded pork roast and hominy vegetable stew), and the catch of the day at rock-bottom prices (Av. del Sol Nuevo at Andando Tabachines, open every day from early morning till nine or ten year-round). Budget.

Across the street not far away, the **Fuente de Sodas Arco Iris** claims to be Guayabitos's all-in-one "fast food" restaurant (Av. del Sol Nuevo, open daily 8:30 a.m.-9 p.m.). The friendly owner-family offers hot dogs, hamburgers, tortas, Mexican-style beef stew, and many fruit juices and *liquados*. They usually feature an economical afternoon special dish. Budget to moderate.

Two long blocks north, the very clean, modern-decor **Restaurant Las Alejandras** offers a good general Mexican-style menu (Av. del Sol Nuevo, open 8-8 in season). Moderate.

Abel's Lonchería, near the south end, serves a North American-style menu, including pancakes, French toast, eggs any style, and sandwiches. With a small, shady front patio between a minimarket and the long-distance telephone office, Abel's is a popular Guayabitos gathering and people-watching place (Retorno Ceibas

across from Trailer Park Villanueva, open daily 7 a.m.-9 p.m. in season). Budget.

The restaurant at the **Hotel Posada la Misión** is a favorite of the semipermanent North American trailer colony. The menu features bountiful salad, fresh seafood, meat, and Mexican plates (Retorno Tabachines 6 at Calle Tabachines, tel. 403-57, open 8 a.m.-9 p.m. in season, credit cards accepted). Moderate.

Another "best" of Guayabitos is the restaurant at **Trailer Park Villanueva.** Within their romantic oceanfront palapa-patio they offer a menu specializing in caught-in-the-bay fresh seafood (south end of Retorno Ceibas, at Andando Cocoteros, open daily 8 a.m-9 p.m. in season). Moderate.

For a change of pace (or if your favorite Guayabitos restaurants are seasonally closed), try **Chuy's,** La Peñita's local and tourist favorite. It offers a broad, reasonably priced menu within a *tipica* Mexican patio setting (on Calle Bahía Punta Mita, just off Emiliano Zapata, about five blocks from Hwy. 200, open daily till around nine). Moderate.

SPORTS AND ENTERTAINMENT

Nightlife

Although Guayabitos is a resort for those who mostly love peace and quiet, there is at least one night spot. The liveliest place in town is **Hotel Coco Club** (the high-rise at the very south end, Retorno Palmas, tel. 401-90), where a Canadian and American crowd gyrates to rock most winter nights till the wee hours.

Sports

Aquatic sports center around the south end of Guayabitos beach, where launches ply the waters, offering banana (towed-tube) rides, **snorkeling** at offshore Isla Islote, and **sportfishing** launch rentals along the beach. If you want to launch your own boat, ask one of the trailer parks if you can use their ramp. For many more beach sports details, see specific beaches described above.

For **tennis,** check into the Hotel Rincón de Las Palmas or its oversize brother Hotel Coco Club, which maintain one good tennis court for guests only.

SERVICES AND INFORMATION

The well-informed, friendly local officer of Nayarit State Tourism is **Francisco Javier,** who maintains an information office (no phone, open Mon.-Fri. approx. 9-11, 1-4) in the tree-shaded municipal plaza at the highway-beginning of Av. del Sol Nuevo behind the church. The **Correos** (post office, open Mon.-Fri.9-1 and 3-6) and **Telégrafos** (open Mon.-Fri. 8-2) are next door.

Guayabitos has no money-exchange agency. In La Peñita, however, the **Bancomer** branch (E. Zapata 22, tel. 402-37) changes U.S. dollar traveler's checks (Mon.-Fri. 8:30-11 a.m., closed weekends).

Guayabitos has no hospital. For serious medical consultations and emergency treatment, drive or taxi 14 miles (22 km) south to the general hospital in San Francisco ("San Pancho," as known locally). They offer X-ray, laboratory, gynecological, pediatric, and internal medicine services both during regular office hours (weekdays 10:30-12 and 4-6) and on call.

For less urgent medical matters, Jorge Castuera, the well-informed, veterinarian-owner of the **Farmacia** (Av. del Sol Nuevo at Tabachines, tel. 404-46 and 404-00, open 8-2 and 4-8) can recommend medicines or put you in contact with a doctor if you're sick. (While Jorge handles the pharmacy, his wife does washing at the **laundry** on the same premises.)

The *larga-distancia* (long-distance) telephone office next to Abel's Lonchería on Retorno Ceibas opens (mornings and afternoons till about nine) in season, but maintains shorter hours otherwise. They also have a shelf of used mostly English paperbacks for two-for-one exchange or purchase.

Getting There And Away

Puerto Vallarta- and Tepic-bound Transportes Pacifico (TP) second-class buses routinely stop (about once each daylight hour, each direction) on the main highway entrance to Guayabitos Av. del Sol Nuevo. Several first-class buses pick up Puerto Vallarta- and Tepic-bound passengers at the Transportes Pacifico station (tel. 400-25) at the main street highway corner in La Peñita.

The Guayabitos coast is easily accessible by bus or taxi from the **Puerto Vallarta International Airport,** a busy terminal for flight connections with U.S. and Mexican destinations. Buses and taxis cover the 39-mile (62 km) distance to Guayabitos in less than an hour. For details, see "Puerto Vallarta Airport Arrival and Departure" in the Puerto Vallarta chapter.

SOUTH OF GUAYABITOS

Playa Lo De Marco

Drive (or ride a second-class green Transportes Pacifico bus) about eight miles (13 km) south of Guayabitos to the signed Lo de Marco ("That of Marco") turnoff. Continue about a mile through the town to the beach lineup of palapa restaurants. Playa Lo de Marco is popular with Mexican families; on Sundays and holidays they dig in the fine golden sand and frolic in the gentle, rolling waves. The surf of the nearly level, very wide Playa Lo de Marco is good for most aquatic sports except surfing, snorkeling, and diving (for which you can rent boats, however, to take you to the offshore Isla Islote). The south end has a rocky tidepool shelf, fine for bait-casting.

Lo de Marco has an excellent trailer park-bungalows complex, **El Caracol,** owned and operated by German expatriate Gunter Maasan and his wife. Their nine luxuriously large, "little bit of Europe in the tropics" motel-bungalows-beneath-the-palms sleep four to six persons with all the comforts of Hamburg. With a/c, fans, and complete kitchenettes, they rent for about $45 for four, $65 for six.

Their trailer park is correspondingly luxurious, with concrete-pad spaces (up to 40 feet) in a palm- and banana-shaded grassy park right on the beach. With all hookups and immaculate hot showers and toilet facilities, the 15 spaces rent for $10/day (air-conditioning power extra), pets okay. It's popular, so get your winter reservations in by September (write P.O. Box 89, La Peñita de Jaltemba, Nayarit 63726).

Camping is possible at or adjacent to the former trailer park Pequeña Paraiso ("Little Paradise") beside the jungle headland at the south end of the beach. Stores in town can furnish basic supplies.

Continuing south along the Lo de Marco beach road, you will soon come to two neighboring miniature pearly-sand paradises, **Playa las Minitas** and **Playa El Venado.** Bring your swimsuit, picnic lunch, and, if you crave isolation, your camping gear.

Playa San Francisco

The idyllic beach and hotel at the little mango-processing town of San Francisco ("San Pancho," as locals say) remains another of Nayarit's best-kept secrets. Exit Hwy. 200 at the road sign 14 miles (22 km) south of Guayabitos (or 25 miles, 40 km north of the Puerto Vallarta airport) and continue straight through the town to the beach.

The broad, golden-white strand, enclosed by palm-tipped green headlands, extends for half a mile on both sides of the town. Big open-ocean waves (take care—undertow) pound the beach for nearly its entire length. Offshore, flocks of pelicans dive for fish while frigate birds sail overhead. At night during the rainy months, sea turtles come ashore to lay their egg clutches, which a determined group of nearby volunteers is trying to protect from poachers. (Ask for Jessie Hencky if you want to help.)

A sign on the right a couple of blocks before the beach marks the bumpy road to the **Costa Azul Adventure Resort**. In-hotel activity centers around the beach and palm-shaded pool-bar-restaurant patio. Further afield, the owner-manager John Cooper and his assistants guide guests on kayaking, biking, surfing, snorkeling, and horseback adventures in nearby coves, beaches, and jungle trails. The hotel itself, located on a hillside beneath a magnificent colima palm grove, has 20 large, comfortable rooms (suites), six one-bedroom villas, and a pair of two-bedroom villas (all with fans only), which rent for $52, $65, and $75, respectively. Make reservations (mandatory in winter) through their Vista (San Diego, California) booking agent: (714) 493-6043.

Sayulita

Sayulita (17 miles, 27 km south of Guayabitos, 22 miles, 35 km north of the Puerto Vallarta airport) is what Guayabitos used to be before the hotels came: a fishing village along a palm-tufted curve of sand that curls to a rocky little kink at the south end—an untouristed retreat for those who hanker for quiet pleasures and the local color of Mexico. Sayulita's clean waters are fine for swimming, bodysurfing, and fishing, while stores, a homey restaurant, a palm-shadowed trailer park-campground, and a bed-and-breakfast provide food and lodging.

Accommodations and Food: Adrienne Adams, owner-manager of the bed-and-breakfast **Villa de la Buena Salud** rents six luxurious rooms (about $35 d, including breakfast for two) in her airy, art-draped, three-story house, a few steps from the Sayulita beach. Get your winter reservations in early; Adrienne enjoys dozens of repeat customers. Adrienne's daughter Lynn (at 1754 Caliban Dr. Encinitas California 92924, tel. 619-942-9640), handles reservations year-round. Adrienne also takes reservations Nov.-June in Sayulita; write P.O. Box 5, La Peñita de Jaltemba, Nayarit 63726. You can contact Adrienne quickly by calling the local operator, tel. 327-045-65, and asking for "Tia Adriana," (Auntie Adriana), as she is known locally. The operator will summon Adrienne, who will be waiting for your second call ten minutes later.

For RVs and tent camping, visitors love the **Sayulita Trailer Park** in a big shady, sandy lot with about twenty hookups right on the beach. Guests enjoy just about everything—good clean showers and toilets, electricity, water, a bookshelf, concrete pads, and dump station; pets okay—rates are about $11/day, with discounts for extended stays.

Vegetables, groceries and baked goods are available at a pair of stores by the town plaza; cuisine is supplied by a good plaza taco stand weekend nights, a few *loncherías,* and best of all, **Amparo,** an elderly woman who cooks for a few dinner guests a day. Ask for directions (Amparo's house is only a couple of blocks from the plaza) and drop by a day ahead of time to tell her you're coming. The next day, don't eat much lunch. At dinnertime you will be ready for Amparo's bountiful table of homemade enchiladas, chiles rellenos, tacos, and perhaps tamales, plus rice, beans, and all of the hot tortillas you can eat for about $12 per person.

Beach Hike: Lovers of the outdoors enjoy the four-mile beach and jungle walk between Sayulita and San Francisco. Besides the birds, flowers, and plants of the palmy forest wilderness and beach in between, your reward at trail's end will be the pool and restaurant at Costa Azul Adventure Resort. Wear walking shoes and a hat for sun, and carry insect repellent and water. Allow a whole day for strolling both ways and lingering at the hotel.

Head out north along the beach at Sayulita. After about a mile the beach ends at some rocks, but you can continue along a dirt road above the beach to the right. After about a hundred yards, cut to the left, parallel to the beach, and take several steps across a small meadow (marshy in the wet season) to another dirt road (which dead-ends at a beachfront house on the left). Follow the palm-shaded jungle track about another mile, bearing left downhill to a wild beach. (If you come to a house with a fence and barking dogs, you haven't gone far enough.) Continue north beneath shady, spreading *kukui*-nut trees (as they're called in Hawaii) to a long, driftwood-strewn beach beneath a towering jungle headland.

Past a cliffside spring (good water in the rainy season), you will soon see a big palapa-roofed house on the rocky point ahead. This is the former home of President Luis Echeverría (1970-76). At the end of the beach, continue up the stone stairs and straight ahead to San Francisco beach on the other side. In another mile, past the lagoon and palapa restaurants, you will arrive at the hotel. If you prefer not to walk back to Sayulita, hire a taxi in San Francisco.

BOB RACE

PUERTO VALLARTA AND THE BAY OF BANDERAS

PUERTO VALLARTA

The city of Puerto Vallarta (pop. 300,000) perches at the most tranquil recess of one of the Pacific Ocean's largest, deepest bays, the Bay of Banderas. The city owes its prosperity, in good measure, to this most fortunate location. The sun, the golden sand, the bay's rich blue waters and the seafood they nurture are magnets for a million seasonal visitors. On the map of Pacific Mexico, the Bay of Banderas looks as if it was gouged from the coast by some vengeful Aztec god (perhaps in retribution for the conquest) with a single 20-mile-wide swipe of his giant hand, just sparing the city of Puerto Vallarta.

Time, however, has healed that great imaginary cataclysm. The jagged mountains, Sierra Vallejo on the north and Sierra Cuale on the south, have acquired a green coat of jungly forest on their slopes, and a broad river, the Ameca, winds serenely through its fertile vale to the bay.

Furthermore, sand has accumulated on the great arc of the Bay of Banderas, where fisherfolk have built little settlements: Punta Mita, Cruz de Huanacaxtle, and Bucerías north of Puerto Vallarta; and Mismaloya, Boca de Tomatlán, and Yelapa to the south.

Taking a look at the city proper, visitors find that Puerto Vallarta is really two cities in one—a new town strung along the hotel strip on its northern beaches, and an old town nestled beneath jungle hills on both sides of a small river, the Rio Cuale, which rushes from a deep gap in the hills.

Travelers arriving from the north, whether by plane, bus, or car, see the new Puerto Vallarta first, however—a parade of luxury hotels, condominiums, apartments, and shopping centers. Such visitors could stay for a month in a slick new Vallarta hotel, sun on the beach every day, disco half of every night, and return home, never having experienced the old Puerto Vallarta, which lives beside the Rio Cuale.

NIGHT OF THE IGUANA:
THE MAKING OF PUERTO VALLARTA

The idea to film Tennessee Williams's play *Night of the Iguana* in Puerto Vallarta was born not in Puerto Vallarta, but in the bar of the Beverly Hills Hotel. In mid-1963, director John Huston (whose movies had earned a raft of Academy Awards) was meeting with Guillermo Wulff, a Mexican architect and engineer. Wulff proposed Mismaloya, an isolated cove south of Puerto Vallarta where, on leased land, Wulff would build the movie set and cottages for staff housing, which he and Huston would later sell for a profit as tourist accommodations. Most directors would have been scared away by the Mismaloya jungle (no road, no phones, no electricity). But, according to Alex Masden, his biographer, Huston loved Mismaloya: "To me, *The Night of the Iguana* was a picnic, a gathering of friends, a real vacation."

A "gathering of friends," indeed. The script required most of the cast to be either dissolute, mentally ill, or both: A blonde nymphet tries to seduce an alcoholic defrocked minister while his voluptuous, hard-drinking former lover keeps a clutch of vulturous biddies from destroying his last bit of self-respect— all while an iguana chained to a jungle tree screams pathetically for its freedom.

Huston's casting was perfect. The actors simply played themselves. Richard Burton (the minister) came supplied with plenty of booze. Burton's lover, Elizabeth Taylor (who was not part of the cast but was still married to singer Eddie Fisher) accompanied him. Sue Lyon (the nymphet) came with her lover, whose wife was rooming with Sue's mother; Ava Gardner (the voluptuous former lover) became the toast of Puerto Vallarta while romping with her local beach boyfriend; Tennessee Williams (advising the director) came with his lover Freddy, while Deborah Kerr (who acted the only prim main role) jokingly complained that she was the only one not having an affair.

With so many temperamental characters isolated together in Mismaloya, the international press flew to Puerto Vallarta in droves to record the expected fireworks. Huston gave each of the six stars a velvet-lined case containing a gold Derringer with five bullets, each engraved with the names of the others. Unexpectedly (and partly due to Huston's considerable charm) none of the bullets was used. Bored by the lack of major explosions, the press corps discovered Puerto Vallarta instead.

As Huston explained later to writer Lawrence Grobel: "That was the beginning of its popularity, which was a mixed blessing." Huston, nevertheless, stayed on until his death in 1987; Burton and Taylor bought Puerto Vallarta houses, got married and also stayed for years. Although his Mismaloya tourist accommodations scheme never panned out, Guillermo Wulff became wealthy building dozens of the luxurious houses and condominiums that now dot Puerto Vallarta's jungly hillsides and golden beaches.

HISTORY

Before Columbus

For centuries prior to the arrival of the Spanish, the coastal region that includes present-day Puerto Vallarta was subject to the Indian kingdom of Xalisco, centered at the modern Nayarit city of Jalisco (founded around A.D. 600 by the Toltecs), near Tepic. The Xalisco civilization was ruled by chiefs who worshipped a trinity of gods: foremost, Naye (a legendary former chief elevated to a fierce god of war), followed by the more benign Teopiltzin, god of rain and fertility, and finally by wise Heri, the god of knowledge.

Recent archaeological evidence indicates another influence: the Aztecs, who probably left Nahuatl-speaking colonies along the southern Nayarit coastal valleys during their centuries-long migration to the Valley of Mexico.

Conquest And Colonization

Some of those villages still remained when the Spanish conquistador Francisco Cortés de Buenaventura, nephew of the Hernán Cortés, arrived on the Jalisco-Nayarit coast in 1524. In a broad mountain-rimmed green valley, an army of 20,000 warriors, their bows decorated by myriad colored cotton banners, temporarily blocked the conquistador's path. So impressive was the assemblage that Cortés called that fertile vale of the Ameca River north of present Puerto Vallarta the Valle de las Banderas ("Valley of the Banners") and thus the great bay later became known as the Bahía de Banderas.

The first certain record of the Bay of Banderas itself came from the log of conquistador Don Pedro de Alvarado, who sailed into the bay in 1541 and disembarked (probably at Mismaloya) near some massive sea rocks. He named these Las Peñas, undoubtedly the same as the present "Los Arcos" rocks that draw daily boatloads of snorkelers and divers.

For 300 years the Bay of Banderas slept under the sun. Galleons occasionally watered there; a few pirates hid in wait for them in its jungle-fringed coves.

Independence

The rebellion of 1810-21 freed Mexico, and finally, a generation later, the lure of gold and silver led (as with many of Mexico's cities) to the settlement of Puerto Vallarta. Enterprising merchant Don Guadalupe Sanchez made a fortune, paradoxically not from gold, but from salt (for ore processing), which he hauled from the beach to the mines above the headwaters of the Rio Cuale. Don Guadalupe and his wife soon built a hut and brought their family. Their tiny trading station grew into a little town, Puerto de Las Peñas, at the mouth of the river.

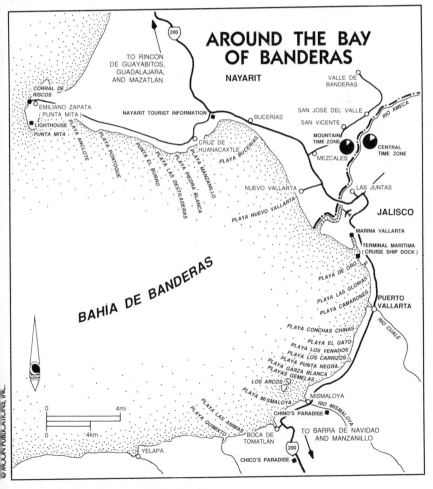

AROUND THE BAY OF BANDERAS

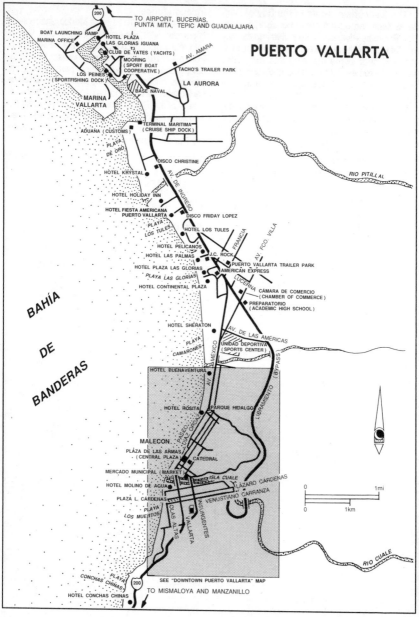

PUERTO VALLARTA

TO AIRPORT, BUCERIAS,
PUNTA MITA, TEPIC AND GUADALAJARA

BOAT LAUNCHING RAMP
MARINA OFFICE
HOTEL PLAZA
LAS GLORIAS IGUANA
CLUB DE YATES (YACHTS)
MOORING
(SPORT BOAT
COOPERATIVE)
LOS PEINES
(SPORTFISHING DOCK)
AV. AMARA
TACHO'S TRAILER PARK
LA AURORA
BASE NAVAL

MARINA
VALLARTA

ADUANA (CUSTOMS)
TERMINAL MARITIMA
(CRUISE SHIP DOCK)

PLAYA
DE ORO

RIO PITILLAL

DISCO CHRISTINE

HOTEL KRYSTAL
AV. DE INGRESO

HOTEL HOLIDAY INN

HOTEL FIESTA AMERICANA
PUERTO VALLARTA
DISCO FRIDAY LOPEZ
PLAYA
LOS TULES
HOTEL LOS TULES
AV. FCO. VILLA
FRANCIA
HOTEL PELICANOS
J.C. ROCK
HOTEL LAS PALMAS
PUERTO VALLARTA TRAILER PARK
HOTEL PLAZA LAS GLORIAS
AMERICAN EXPRESS
PLAYA LAS GLORIAS
LUCERNA
HOTEL CONTINENTAL PLAZA
CAMARA DE COMERCIO
(CHAMBER OF COMMERCE)
PREPARATORIO
(ACADEMIC HIGH SCHOOL)

HOTEL SHERATON
AV. DE LAS AMERICAS

PLAYA
CAMARONES
AV. MEXICO
UNIDAD DEPORTIVA
(SPORTS CENTER)

BAHÍA
DE
BANDERAS

HOTEL BUENAVENTURA

LIBRAMIENTO (BYPASS)

HOTEL ROSITA
PARQUE HIDALGO

PASEO DIAZ ORDAZ

MALECON
PLAZA DE LAS ARMAS
(CENTRAL PLAZA)
CATEDRAL
MERCADO MUNICIPAL (MARKET)
ISLA CUALE
LÁZARO CARDENAS
HOTEL MOLINO DE AGUA
VENUSTIANO CARRANZA
PLAZA L. CARDENAS
PLAYA
LOS MUERTOS
OLAS ALTAS
VALLARTA
INSURGENTES

0   1mi
0   1km

CONCHAS CHINAS
PLAYA
SEE "DOWNTOWN PUERTO VALLARTA" MAP
HOTEL CONCHAS CHINAS
TO MISMALOYA AND MANZANILLO

RIO CUALE

© MOON PUBLICATIONS, INC.

(top) in the valley of the the River Purificación, Jalisco;
(bottom) guest palapas at Lo Cosmico Zipolite Beach, Puerto Ángel (photos by Bruce Whipperman)

(top left) comblike *peineta* blossom, Oaxaca coast; (top right) *flamboyán* (royal poinciana) tree decorates a village near San Blas; (bottom left) coffee berries, Colima; (bottom right) *ahuehuete* (Mexican cedar) (photos by Bruce Whipperman)

Later, the local government founded the present municipality, which, on May 31, 1918, officially became Puerto Vallarta, in honor of the former governor of Michoacán, Ignacio L. Vallarta. The mines, however, had gradually petered out, and Puerto Vallarta, isolated, with no road to the outside world, slumbered again.

Modern Puerto Vallarta
But not for long. Passenger planes began arriving sporadically from Tepic and Guadalajara in the 1950s; a gravel road was pushed through from Tepic in the 1960s. The International Airport was built, the highway was paved, and tourist hotels sprouted on the beaches. Meanwhile, in 1963, director John Huston, at the peak of his creative genius, arrived with Richard Burton, Elizabeth Taylor, Ava Gardner, and Deborah Kerr to film *Night of the Iguana*. Huston, Burton, and Taylor stayed on for years, waking Puerto Vallarta from its long slumber. It hasn't slept since.

SIGHTS

Getting Oriented
Puerto Vallarta is a long beach town, stretching about five miles from the Riviera-like Conchas Chinas condo headland at the south end. Next, heading north, comes the popular Playa Los Muertos beach and the intimate old Rio Cuale neighborhood, which join, across the river, with the busy central *malecón* (seawall) shopping and restaurant (but beachless) bayfront. North of there, the beaches resume again at Playa Camarones and continue past the Zona Hotelera string of big resorts to the Marina complex, where tour boats and cruise liners depart from the Terminal Maritima dock. In the Marina's northern basin lie the Peines (pay-EE-nays) sportfishing and Club de Yates yacht docks. A mile farther north, the city ends at the bustling International Airport.

One basic thoroughfare serves the entire beachfront. Called **Avenida de Ingreso** as it conducts express traffic south past the Zona Hotelera, it changes names three times. Narrowing, it becomes the cobbled **Av. de Mexico,** then **Paseo Diaz Ordaz** along the seafront *malecón* tourist restaurants, clubs, and shops, changing finally to **Av. Morelos** before it passes the Palacio Municipal (city hall) and central plaza.

When southbound traffic reaches Isla Rio Cuale, the tree-shaded, midstream island where the city's pioneers built their huts, traffic slows to a crawl and finally dissipates in the colorful old neighborhood on the south side of the river.

There being little traffic south of the Cuale, people walk everywhere, and slowly, because of the heat. Every morning men in sombreros lead burros down to the mouth of the river to gather sand. Little *papelerías, miscelaneas,* and streetside *taquerías* serve the local folks

The Chino's Paradise restaurant palapa perches in the jungle canyon above the clear, rushing Mismaloya River.

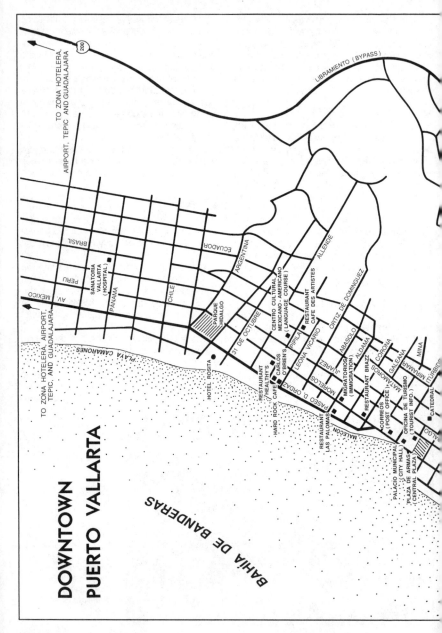

DOWNTOWN
PUERTO VALLARTA

BAHÍA DE BANDERAS

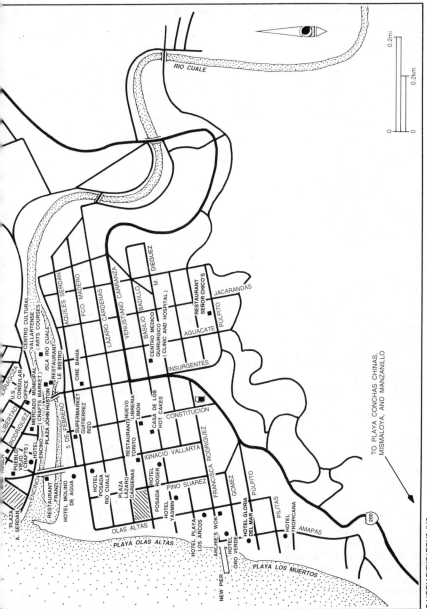

RIO CUALE

0.2mi
0.2km
0

PLAZA
CARRAZA
LIBERTAD
RODRIGUEZ
U.S. CONSULAR
OFFICE
CENTRO CULTURAL
VALLARTENSE
(ARTS COURSES)
MERCADO MUNICIPAL
(CRAFTS MARKET)
ISLA RIO CUALE
RESTAURANT
LE BISTRO
CINE BAHIA
AQUILES SERDAN
FCO. MADERO
LAZARO CARDENAS
VENUSTIANO CARRANZA
BASILIO BADILLO
M. DIEGUEZ
RESTAURANT
SEÑOR CHICOS
JACARANDAS
CENTRO MEDICO
QUIRURGICO
(CLINIC AND HOSPITAL)
AGUACATE
PULPITO
INSURGENTES
PUEBLO
VIEJO
(CRAFTS)
ENCINO
HOTEL
ENCINO
PLAZA JOHN HUSTON
RESTAURANT
FRANZI
HOTEL MOLINO
DE AGUA
5 DE FEBRERO
SUPERMARKET
GUTIERREZ
RIZO
RESTAURANT
TORITO
NUEVO
LIBRERIA
LIMON
CASA DE LOS
HOT CAKES
CONSTITUCION
A. SERDAN
ENCINO
HOTEL
POSADA
RIO CUALE
PLAZA
LAZARO
CARDENAS
POSADA
ROGER
HOTEL
ROGER
IGNACIO VALLARTA
FRANCISCA RODRIGUEZ
GOMEZ
PULPITO
OLAS ALTAS
HOTEL
YASMIN
PINO SUAREZ
PLAYA OLAS ALTAS
HOTEL PLAYA
LOS ARCOS
ARCHIE'S WOK
HOTEL
ORO VERDE
NEW PIER
HOTEL GLORIA
DEL MAR
PILITAS
HOTEL
TROPICANA
AMAPAS
PLAYA LOS MUERTOS
200
TO PLAYA CONCHAS CHINAS,
MISMALOYA, AND MANZANILLO

© MOON PUBLICATIONS, INC.

while small restaurants, hotels, and clubs serve the visitors.

Getting Around

Since nearly all through traffic flows along one thoroughfare, Puerto Vallarta transportation is a snap. Simply hop on one of the frequent (but usually crowded) city buses (fare $.15-.30), virtually all of which end up at Plaza Lázaro Cárdenas on Av. Olas Altas a few blocks south of the river. Northbound, the same buses retrace the route through the Zona Hotelera to one of several destinations scrawled across their windows. Taxis, while much more convenient, are all individual and rather expensive (about $3-4 per trip within the city limits; don't get in until the price is settled).

Drivers who want to quickly travel between the north and the south ends of town often take the Libramiento bypass (see the map "Downtown Puerto Vallarta") and avoid the crowded downtown traffic.

A Walk Around Isla Cuale

Start at the **Museo Rio Cuale**, a joint government-volunteer effort near the very downstream tip of Isla Rio Cuale. Inside is a small but fine collection of paintings by local artists as well as locally excavated pre-Columbian artifacts (open Mon.-Sat. when volunteers are available, no phone).

Head upstream beneath the bridge and enjoy the shady *paseo* of shops and restaurants. For fun, stroll out on one of the two quaint **suspension bridges** over the river. Evenings, these are the coolest spots in Puerto Vallarta. A river of cool night air often funnels down the Cuale valley, creating a refreshing breeze along the length of the clear, tree-draped stream.

The Rio Cuale is not always so clean. Once upon a time, a few dozen foreign residents, tired of looking down upon the littered riverbank, came out one Sunday and began hauling trash from the riverbed. Embarrassed by the example, a neighborhood crowd pitched in. The river has been clean ever since.

Farther upstream, on the adjacent riverbank, stands the **Mercado Municipal Rio Cuale,** a honeycomb of stalls stuffed with crafts from all over Mexico. Continue past the upriver (Av. Insurgentes) bridge to **Plaza John Huston,** marked by a smiling bronze likeness of the renowned Hollywood director who helped put Puerto Va-

llarta on the map with his filming of Tennessee Willams's *Night of the Iguana* in 1963.

A few steps farther on, stop in at the small gallery of the **Centro Cultural Vallartense.** On Sunday mornings, beginning around eleven, a crowd of artists, art students, and anyone else interested gathers for several pleasant hours exchanging ideas and painting techniques. Bring your paints, easel, canvas, and brushes, or just come and watch.

A few more steps upstream you will pass the round stucco headquarters and practice room of the **Escuela Municipal de Musica.** They, along with the Centro Cultural Vallartense, offer courses to the general public. See "Language, Arts, and Music Courses" below.

At the boulder-strewn upstream point of the island, a cadre of women wash clothes. Many of them are professionals who practice their craft on special rocks, perfectly positioned for a day of productive washing. Their clean handiwork stretches out to dry—on rocks, on grass, on bushes—in rainbow arrays beneath the sun.

Gringo Gulch

The steep, villa-dotted hillside above the island's upper end is called Gringo Gulch, for the colony of rich *norteamericanos* who own big homes there. It's an interesting place for a stroll.

Back at the Insurgentes bridge, head right, toward the center of town, bear right to the end of one-block Calle Emilio Carranza and continue up a steep, bougainvillea-festooned staircase to Calle Zaragoza one block above.

At Zaragoza and the upper level of Emilio Carranza, you are at the gateway to Gringo Gulch. Wander through the winding, hillside lanes and enjoy the picturesque scenes that seem to appear around each rickety-chic corner. For example, note the luxurious palapa perched atop the tall villa on Carranza, half a block above Zaragoza.

During your meanderings, don't miss the Gringo Gulch centerpiece mansion at Zaragoza 446, once owned by Elizabeth Taylor. (You'll scarcely be able to miss it, for it has a pink passageway arching over the street.) The house was a gift to Taylor from Richard Burton. After they were married, they also bought the house on the other side of Zaragoza, renovated it, and built a pool; thus the passageway became necessary. It is now a private residence.

The **Club Internacional de la Amistad** (Friendship Club) conducts seasonal tours through some of Puerto Vallarta's showplace homes on weekends, beginning at the central plaza. (See "Volunteer Work" below.)

On The *Malecón*

Head back down Zaragoza, and let the church belfry be your guide. Named **La Parroquia de Nuestra Señora de Guadalupe**, for the city's patron saint, the church is relatively new (1951) and undistinguished except for the very unusual huge crown atop the tower. Curiously, it was modeled after the crown of the tragic 19th-century Empress Carlota, who went insane after her husband was executed. On the church steps, an *indígena* woman frequently sells textiles, which she weaves on the spot with a traditional backstrap loom (in Spanish, *tela de otate*, "loom of bamboo," from the Nahuatl *otlatl*, "bamboo").

Continue down Zaragoza past the Palacio Municipal at one side of the central Plaza de Armas, straight toward the Los Arcos (the Arches), right at the water's edge. They form a backdrop for frequent free weekend evening music and dance performances. From there, the *malecón* seawall-walkway stretches north toward the Zona Hotelera hotels, which you can see along the curving northern beachfront.

The *malecón* marks the bay's innermost point. From there the shoreline stretches and curves westerly many miles on both sides, adorned by dozens of sandy beaches until it reaches its wave-washed extremities at Punta Mita (on the distant horizon, at the bay's northwest extremity) and Punta La Iglesia to the far southwest.

BEACHES

Playa Los Muertos

Generations ago, when Puerto Vallarta was a small, isolated town, there was only one beach, Playa Los Muertos, the strand of yellow sand that stretches for a mile south of the Cuale River. Old-timers still remember the Sundays and holidays when it seemed as if half the families in Puerto Vallarta had come south of the Río Cuale, to Los Muertos Beach especially, to play in the surf and sand.

This is still largely true, although now droves of winter-season North American vacationers and residents have joined them. Fortunately, Playa Los Muertos is much cleaner than during the polluted 1980s. The fish are coming back, as evidenced by the flocks of diving pelicans and the crowd of folks who drop lines every day from the **New Pier** (foot of Francisca Rodriguez).

Fishing is even better off the rocks on the south end of the beach. *Lisa* (mullet), *sierra* (mackerel), *pargo* (snapper), and *torito* are commonly caught anywhere along close-in beaches. On certain unpredictable occasions, fish (and one memorable time even giant 30-pound squids) swarm offshore in such abundance that anyone can pick them out of the water barehanded.

Gentle waves and lack of undertow make Playa Los Muertos generally safe for wading and good for **swimming** beyond the close-in breakers. The same breakers, however, eliminate Los Muertos for bodysurfing, boogieboarding, or surfing (except occasionally at the far south end).

Playas Conchas Chinas

Playa Conchas Chinas ("Chinese Shells Beach") is not one beach but a series of small sandy coves dotted by rocky outcroppings beneath the condo-clogged hillside that extends for about a mile south of Playa Los Muertos. A number of streets and driveways lead to the beach from the Manzanillo Hwy. 200 (the extension of Insurgentes) south of town. Drive (or taxi, or ride one of the many the minibuses marked "Mismaloya" or "Boca," which leave the from Olas Altas's Plaza Lázaro Cárdenas, corner Carranza and Suarez) or hike along the tidepools from Los Muertos Beach.

Fishing off the rocks is good here; the water is even clear enough for some **snorkeling**. Bring your gear, however, as there's none for rent. The usually gentle waves, however, make any kind of surfing very doubtful.

Beach Exploring

Beach lovers can spend many enjoyable days poking around the many little beaches south of town. Drive, taxi, or take a "Mismaloya"- or "Boca"-marked minibus from Plaza Lázaro Cárdenas.

Just watch out the window and when you see a likely spot, ask the driver to stop. Say "Pare (PAH-ray) por favor." The location will most likely be one of several lovely *playas:* **El Gato** ("Cat"), **Los Venados** ("Deer"), **Los Carrizos** ("Reeds"), **Punta Negra** ("Black Point"), **Garza Blanca** ("White Heron"), or **"Gemelas"** (Twins).

Although many of these little sand crescents have big hotels, it doesn't matter, because beaches are public in Mexico up to the high-tide line. There is always some path to the beach used by local folks. Just ask "¿Donde está el camino (road, path) a la playa?" and someone will probably point the way.

Mismaloya And Los Arcos
If you ride all the way to Playa Mismaloya, you will not be disappointed, despite the oversize Hotel Mismaloya crowding the beach. Follow the dirt road just past the hotel to the intimate little curve of sand and lagoon where the cool, clear Mismaloya stream meets the sea. A rainbow array of fishing *lanchas* lie beached around the lagoon's edges, in front of a line of beachside palapa restaurants.

Continue a few hundred yards past the palapas to the ruins of the movie set of the *Night of the Iguana.* Besides being built for the actual filming, the rooms behind those now-crumbling stucco walls served as lodging, dining, and working quarters for the hundreds of crew who camped here for those eight busy months in 1963.

North, offshore beyond the Mismaloya cove, rise the green-brushed **Los Arcos** sea rocks, a federal underwater park and eco-preserve. The name comes from the arching grottoes that channel completely through the bases of some of the rocks. Los Arcos is one of the best snorkeling grounds around Puerto Vallarta. Get there by hiring a glass-bottomed boat in the lagoon.

Snorkeling near the wave-washed Los Arcos is a Puerto Vallarta "must do." Swirling bunches of green algae and branching ruddy corals attract schools of grazing parrot, angel-, butter-fly, and goat fish. Curious pencil-thin cornet fish may sniff you out as they pass, while big croakers and sturgeon slowly drift, scavenging along the coral-littered depths.

Fishing (especially casting from the rocks beneath the movie set) and every other kind of beach activity are good at Mismaloya, except surfing and boogieboarding, for which the waves are generally too gentle.

Stop for food (big fish fillet plate, any style, with all the trimmings, $6, breakfast eggs from their own hens) or a drink at the **Restaurant Las Gaviotas** palapa behind the lagoon.

For still another treat, visit nearby **Chino's Paradise.** Follow the riverside, lower road which forks upstream at the north end of the bridge across the road from the hotel. Arrive in the late morning (around eleven, or around three in the late afternoon) to avoid the tour-bus rush. Chino's streamside palapas nestle like big mushrooms on a jungle hillside above a cool, cascading creek. Adventurous guests enjoy sliding down the cascades (be careful—some have injured themselves seriously), while others content themselves with lying in the sun or lolling in sandy-bottomed, clear pools. Beneath the palapas, they serve respectable but uninspired seafood and steak plates and Mexican *antijitos.* (Be wary of their very bold parrots, however; open daily 11-5.)

Beaches Farther South
Three miles south of Mismaloya is the very tranquil, jungle-fringed beach and bay of **Boca de Tomatlán,** where you can rent boats and head out for the pristine paradises of **Las Animas, Quimixto,** and **Yelapa** farther south. Las Animas has seafood palapas, an idyllic beach, and snorkeling; the same is true for Quimixto, which also has a waterfall nearby for splashing.

Yelapa, a settlement nestled beneath verdant, palm-crowned hills beside an aquamarine cove, is home for perhaps a hundred local families and a small colony of foreign expatriates. For visitors, it offers a glimpse of south seas life as it was before the automobile. Accessible only by sea, Yelapa's residents get around on foot or horseback. A waterfall cascades through the tropical forest above the vil-

hieroglyph of Mismaloya

lage, and a string of palapa restaurants lines the beach. Lodging is available in the palapa-roofed cabañas of the rustic **Hotel Lagunitas.** Rooms run about $25 d, and reservations are generally not necessary, but you can try writing the hotel (no phone in paradise, of course) at simply Hotel Lagunitas, Yelapa, Jalisco, Mexico.

Cruises to Las Animas, Quimixto, and Yelapa: Most Puerto Vallarta visitors reach these little southern beaches by a different route than by Boca Tomatlán. They usually go by one of several all-day tourist cruises, which leave (around nine and return by four) from the dock at the Puerto Vallarta Maritime terminal.

One of the most popular and least expensive of these excursions is aboard the big *Princess Yelapa,* a tripled-decked white steel tub with room for 400. The cruise follows the coastline past Los Arcos, Mismaloya, Las Animas, and Quimixto. Passengers disembark at Yelapa for two hours, just long enough for the short waterfall hike (or by horseback, if desired) and lunch at a beach palapa. This no-frills ($15) trip includes a no-host bar and restrooms.

The *Princess Vallarta,* a scaled-down version of the *Princess Yelapa,* offers a more luxurious, all-inclusive ($33/person) cruise, with on-board continental breakfast, live music for dancing, and open bar. They head out, enjoying views of the town, beaches, and hills, stopping at Los Arcos for snorkeling. Continuing past Mismaloya and Tomatlán, they arrive at Las Animas for lunch, relaxing on the beach, and snorkeling for a couple of hours before returning.

The *Vagabundo,* a smaller but comfortable 50-person sportfishing-type motor yacht, heads straight across the bay, as guests enjoy drinks from the open bar. They anchor at Yelapa for two hours, enough time for the waterfall hike. On the way back, a modest buffet lunch is served as the cruise continues to Los Arcos for snorkeling. Then they return, enjoying views of intimate rocky beaches, green jungle-strewn hills, and a procession of palm-fringed shoreline hotels ($28 per person, includes restrooms).

The *Buenaventura,* a 40-foot double-decker, offers a deluxe ($45 per person) cruise, which includes continental breakfast, a stop at Los Arcos for snorkeling, open bar all the way, and lunch at Las Animas Beach. From there they continue to the beach and waterfall at Quimixto, then return.

If you tend toward seasickness, fortify yourself with Dramamine before these cruises. Destination disembarkation is by motor launch and can be difficult for the physically handicapped.

You may buy tickets for any of these cruises from travel agents. Try Servicios Turisticos Miller, with headquarters at Hotel Krystal (tel. 411-97, 412-97, and 413-97) and branches at hotels Playa Los Arcos, Vidafel, Melia, Plaza Las Glorias, and Sheraton.

North-end (Zona Hotelera) Beaches

These are Puerto Vallarta's cleanest, least crowded, in-town beaches, despite the many hotels that line them. Beginning at the Hotel Rosita at the north end of the *malecón, playas* **Camarones, Las Glorias, Los Tules,** and **de Oro** form a continuous three-mile strand to the Marina. Stubby rock jetties about every quarter-mile have succeeded in retaining a fifty-yard-wide strip of golden-cream sand most of the way.

The sand is midway between coarse and fine, the waves are gentle, breaking right at the water's edge, and the ocean past the breakers is relatively clear (10- or 20-feet visibility) and blue. Stormy weather occasionally dredges up clam, cockle, limpet, oyster, and other shells from the offshore depths.

Fishing by pole, net, or simply line is common along here. Surfing, bodysurfing, and boogieboarding, however, are not. All other beach sports, especially the high-powered variety, are available at nearly every hotel along the strand. (See "Sports" below.)

Beach Hikes

A pair of good close-in hikes are possible. For either of them don't forget a sun hat, sunscreen, repellent, a shirt, and some light shoes. On the south side, walk from **Playa Los Muertos** about a mile and a half along the little beaches and tidepools to **Playa Conchas Chinas.** Start at either end and take half a day swimming, snorkeling, sunning, and poking among the rocks.

More ambitiously, you can hike the entire three-mile beach strip from the northern end of the *malecón* to the Marina. If you start by nine you'll enjoy the cool of the morning with the sun at your back. Stop along the way at the showplace pools and beach restaurants of hotels such as the Sheraton, the Plaza Las Glorias, the Fiesta Americana Vallarta, and Krystal. Walk back, or opt for a return by taxi or city bus.

ACCOMMODATIONS

In Puerto Vallarta you can get any type of lodging you want at nearly any price. The location sets the tone, however. The relaxed, relatively tranquil but interesting neighborhood south of the Rio Cuale (especially around Av. Olas Altas) has many budget and moderately priced hotels within easy walking distance of restaurants, shopping, and services. Many of them are very close, if not right on, lively Los Muertos Beach.

Hotels: Rio Cuale And South
Although landmark **Hotel Molino de Agua** ("Water Mill") occupies two riverfront blocks right on the beach, many visitors miss it completely. (Ignacio Vallarta and Aquiles Serdan, Puerto Vallarta 48380, tel. 322-219-07, 322-219-57, fax 322-260-56) Its very tranquil colony of rustic-chic cabañas hides in a jungle-garden of cackling parrots, giant-leafed vines, and gigantic, spreading trees. Most of the cabañas are at ground level and unfortunately don't feel very private inside (unless you close the shutters—which seems a shame in a tropical garden). The very popular beachside upstairs units, however, remedy this dilemma. The hotel's 40 garden rooms rent from about $40 d low season, $62 high, while the upstairs beachside rooms go for a $56 d low season, $80 high, credit cards accepted; two pools, a restaurant, and a/c, reserve toll-free (800) 826-9408 from the U.S. and Canada, (800) 423-5512 from California.

Just across the river bridge from the Molino de Agua stands the renovated old **Hotel Encino** (Av. Juarez 122, Puerto Vallarta, Jalisco 48300, tel. 322-200-51, 322-202-80, fax 322-225-73). The entrance lobby opens into a pleasant, tropical fountain-patio, enfolded by tiers of rooms. Inside, the rooms are tastefully decorated in blue and white, many with ocean or city-hill views. They also offer many large, similarly appointed kitchenette suites in a nearby building. The hotel climaxes at the rooftop pool-sun deck, where guests enjoy a panoramic view of the surrounding green jungly hills above the white-stucco-and-tile old town, spreading to the blue,

mountain-rimmed bay. The 75 rooms and suites rent for about $25 d low season, $33 high; one- and two-bedroom kitchenette suites begin at about $39 low season, $45 high; all a/c, phones, security boxes, restaurant-bar.

Head along I. Vallarta south, back across the river to the corner of Aquiles Serdan. There, the diminutive **Hotel Posada Rio Cuale** packs lots of hotel into a small space (Av. Aquiles Serdan 224, P.O. Box 146, Puerto Vallarta 48300, tel. 322-204-50, 322-211-48). Good management is the key to this picturesque warren of rooms that clusters beside its good restaurant-bar and small but pleasant pool-patio. Tasteful brown and brick decor makes the rooms somewhat dark, especially on the ground floor. Artful lighting, however, improves on this. Unless you like diesel-bus noise, try to avoid getting a room on the busy Av. Vallarta side of the hotel. The 41 a/c rooms rent for about $25 d low season, about $42 high; credit cards accepted.

The **Hotel Posada Roger** nearby (on Basilio Badillo at Vallarta) is a longtime favorite with budget travelers. Its three stories of rooms enclose an inviting vine-decorated courtyard with plenty of quiet nooks for reading and relaxing. The Tucan, the hotel's breakfast cafe (open daily 8 a.m.-2 p.m.), provides yet another setting for relaxed exchanges with other travelers. A small pool-patio on the roof adds a bit of class to compensate for the many rather drab, cramped, fan-only rooms that Roger offers for his increased prices (Basilio Badillo 237, Puerto Vallarta, Jalisco 48380, tel. 322-208-36). The 50 rooms run about $20 d low season, $28 high, add $5 for air-conditioning; three blocks from beach, credit cards accepted.

The **Hotel Yasmin** nearby offers a viable budget-lodging alternative. The Yasmin's main attractions are its two short blocks to the beach and its verdant, plant-festooned inner patio. The three tiers of fan-only rooms are clean, but small and mostly dreary. Inspect before you pay. You can compensate by renting one of the lighter, more private upper rooms (Basilio Badillo 168, at Piño Suarez, Puerto Vallarta, Jalisco 48380, tel. 322-200-87). Rates for all 30 rooms run about $17 d low season, $23 high.

Head downhill toward the beach and left around the Av. Olas Altas corner and you are in the popular Olas Altas neighborhood. At the hub of activity is the **Hotel Playa Los Arcos**

PUERTO VALLARTA HOTELS

Puerto Vallarta hotels, in order of increasing approximate high-season double-room price (area code 322, postal code 48300, unless otherwise noted)

HOTELS: RIO CUALE AND SOUTH

Hotel Yasmin, B. Badillo 168, postal code 48380, 200-87, $23

Hotel Posada Roger, B. Badillo 237, postal code 48380, 208-36, $28

Hotel Costa Alegre, F. Rodriguez 168, 247-93, (800) 221-6509, $31

Hotel Encino, Juarez 122, 200-51, fax 225-73, $33

Hotel Fontana del Mar, M. Dieguez 171, postal code 48380, 207-12, (800) 221-6509, $38

Hotel Gloria del Mar, Amapas 114, postal code 48380, 251-43, fax 217-67, $39

Hotel Tropicana, Amapas 214, postal code 48380, 209-12, $40

Hotel Posada Rio Cuale, A. Serdan 224 (P.O. Box 146), 204-50, $42

Hotel Playa Los Arcos, Olas Altas 380, postal code 48380, 205-83, (800) 221-6509, $48

Hotel Playa Conchas Chinas, P.O. Box 346, 201-56, fax 207-63, $57

Hotel Oro Verde, R. Gómez 111, postal code 48380, 215-55, fax 224-31, (800) 878-4484 in U.S., (800) 458-6888 in Canada, $60

Hotel Molino de Agua, Ignacio Vallarta at A. Serdan, postal code 48380, 219-07, fax 260-56, (800) 826-9408 in the U.S. and Canada, (800) 423-5512 in California, $62

Hotel Camino Real, P.O. Box 95, 301-23, fax 300-70, (800) 228-3000, $150

HOTELS: NORTH OF THE RIO CUALE

Hotel Rosita, Diaz Ordaz 901 (P.O. Box 32), 210-33, $27

Buenaventura, Mexico 1301 (P.O. Box 8B), postal code 48350, 237-37, $78

Hotel Las Palmas, Av. de Ingreso Km 2.5, 406-50, fax 405-43, $85

Hotel Plaza Las Glorias, Plaza Las Glorias s/n, 444-44, fax 465-59, (800) 342-AMIGO, $86

Hotel Krystal, Av. de las Garzas s/n, 402-02, fax 402-16, (800) 231-9860, $130

Hotel Continental Plaza, Av. de Ingreso Km 2.5, Plaza Las Glorias, 401-23, fax 452-36, (800) 635-8483, $135

Fiesta Americana Puerta Vallarta, P.O. Box 270, 420-10, fax 421-08, (800) FIESTA-1, $170

(between Calles M. Diegez and F. Rodriguez), a best-buy favorite of a generation of savvy American and Canadian winter vacationers. The Playa Los Arcos is the flagship of a triad, which includes the nearby **Hotel Fontana del Mar** and the **Hotel Costa Alegre,** whose guests are welcome to enjoy all of the Playa Los Arcos's attractive facilities (in exchange for even more reasonable tariffs than the Playa Los Arcos itself).

All three of these hotels have swimming pools and comfortable, tastefully decorated, air-conditioned rooms with TV, phones, and even some mini-refrigerators in the Fontana and Alegre. The mecca, however, is the deluxe Playa Los Arcos, with its palm- and vine-decorated inner pool-patio sun deck, restaurant with salad bar, a live combo every night, and beach chairs in the sand beneath shady palms or golden sun—take your pick. The Hotel Playa Los Arcos is at Olas Altas 380, Puerto Vallarta, Jalisco 48380, tel. (322) 205-83, (322) 215-83, toll-free (800) 221-6509, fax (322) 205-83. The 135 rooms rent from about $41 d low season, about $48 high, and credit cards are accepted.

The Hotel Fontana del Mar is around the corner at M. Dieguez 171, Puerto Vallarta, Jalisco 48380, tel. (322) 207-12 or toll-free (800) 221-6509. Its 42 rooms rent from about $27 d low season, to about $38 high, credit cards accepted. A block away is the Hotel Costa Alegre, at Francisco Rodriguez 168, Puerto Vallarta, Jalisco 48380, tel. 322-247-93 or toll-free (800) 221-

6509. Tariffs for its 30 rooms run about $22 d low season, about $31 high, credit cards accepted. The Playa Los Arcos, Fontana, and Costa Alegre may be booked through travel agents or the U.S. and Canada toll-free number (800) 221-6509. In all three, two kids under 12 are free when sharing with parents. They often offer discounts, such as: during April, May, and June, fourth night free, while during Sept. and Oct., both the sixth and seventh nights are free.

Vacationers who require an ocean view with their luxury often pick the Los Arcos's Swiss-managed beachside neighbor, the **Hotel Oro Verde** (Rudolfo Gómez 111, Puerto Vallarta, Jalisco 48380, tel. 322-215-55, 322-230-50, fax 322-224-31). The Oro Verde's soaring palapa-restaurant patio opens to a palmy ocean-view pool courtyard and sundeck. Occupants of all of the marble-floored, pastel- and white-decor rooms enjoy city, mountain, or ocean views. The 160 rooms and suites rent for about $45 d low season, about $60 high; ocean-view suites about $60 low and $85 high; with a/c, radio, phones, bar, two restaurants. For reservations, call toll-free (800) 878-4484 from the U.S.; (800) 458-6888 from Canada.

Farther south on Playa Los Muertos, the **Hotel Tropicana** and its nearby brother, condo-style Hotel Gloria del Mar (both near Amapas and Pulpito), offer ocean-view lodgings at bargain prices. The guests at the seven-story beachfront **Hotel Gloria del Mar** (which has no pool or beach facilities) are invited to enjoy all of the Tropicana's facilities instead. Additionally, Gloria del Mar adds the option of 50 spacious, bright kitchenette suites, many with sweeping ocean views (Amapas 114, Puerto Vallarta, Jalisco 48380, tel. 322-251-43, fax 322-217-67). For a hill-view suite, expect to pay about $24 low season, $39 high; for ocean-view, $32 and $50. Monthly rents run about $450 low season, $600 high, with phones and a/c. Credit cards are accepted.

The Tropicana, although large, is easy to miss, because the beach-level lobby is street-accessible only by an unobtrusive downward staircase. From there, however, the hotel's popular beachfront facilities—pool, sun deck, restaurant, palapas shading the sand, volley-ball—spread all the way to the surf. Upstairs, most of the several tiers of not fancy, but comfortable, rooms enjoy private balconies and

ocean vistas (Amapas 214, Puerto Vallarta, Jalisco 48380, tel. 322-209-12, 322-209-52, 250 rooms). Rates run about $33 d low season, about $40 high; a/c, security boxes, credit cards accepted.

Follow the Manzanillo Hwy. 200 (the southward extension of Insurgentes) about two miles south of town and your reward will be the **Hotel Playa Conchas Chinas,** one of Puerto Vallarta's most charming hotels at any price. The stucco and brick complex rambles down a palm-shaded hillside several levels (no elevator) to an intimate cove on Conchas Chinas Beach. Here, a series of intimate sandy crescents nestles between tidepool-dotted sandstone outcroppings.

Standard-grade rooms are spacious, decorated in Mexican traditional tile-brick, and furnished in brown wood with kitchenettes and tub baths, and most have ocean views. Superior- and deluxe-grade rooms have all that plus luxurious spas and ocean-view patio-balconies. The Playa Conchas Chinas is very popular, reserve early, especially during high season (P.O. Box 346, Puerto Vallarta, Jalisco 48300, tel. 322-201-56, 322-206-66, fax 322-207-63). Of their 39 rooms, the standard grade run $35 d low season, $57 high, while superior and deluxe rooms begin at about $42 d low season, $76 high; with a/c, phones, and the romantic "El Set" sunset restaurant; no pool, credit cards accepted.

Another mile south, you can enjoy the extravagant isolation of the Westin **Camino Real** at correspondingly extravagant prices. A totally self-contained resort on a secluded (sometimes seasonally narrow) strip of golden-white sand, the twin-towered Camino Real offers everything—luxury jacuzzi, rooms with view, all water sports, restaurants, bars, and live music every night (P.O. Box 95, Playa de Los Estacas, Puerto Vallarta, Jalisco 48300, tel. 322-301-23, fax 322-300-70). The 250 rooms of the "Main" tower begin at about $150 d, while the 150 jacuzzi-equipped rooms of the "Royal Beach Club" tower go for about $240 d, with everything, including wheelchair access; for reservations, call a travel agent or the toll-free Westin Hotels and Resorts number, (800) 228-3000.

Hotels North Of The Rio Cuale

Hotels generally get more luxurious and expensive the farther north of the Rio Cuale you look. Most of the central part of town, which stretches for a mile along the *malecón*, has no beach to speak of and is too noisy and congested for comfortable lodgings.

Around the north end of the *malecón*, however, where the beach resumes at Playa Camarones, so do the hotels. They continue, dotting the tranquil, golden strands of Playa Las Glorias, Playa Los Tules, and Playa de Oro. These beaches have plush hotels (actually, self-contained resorts) from which you must have wheels to escape for shopping, restaurants, and the piquant sights and sounds of old Puerto Vallarta back downtown.

At the north end of the *malecón* (at 31 de Octubre), stands one of Puerto Vallarta's popular old mainstays, the friendly, beachfront **Hotel Rosita** (Diaz Ordaz 901, P.O. Box 32, Puerto Vallarta, Jalisco 48300, tel. 322-210-33, 322-221-71). The Rosita centers on a grassy, palm-shadowed ocean-view pool-patio and restaurant, with plenty of space for relaxing and socializing. About half of the spacious rooms, of *tipica* Mexican tile and white-stucco and wood, look down upon the tranquil patio scene, while others, to be avoided if possible, border the noisy, smoggy main street. An unfortunate wire security fence mars the ocean view from the patio. Egress to the beach, Playa Camarones, is through a side door. The Rosita's 90 rooms range from about $23 d low season with fan, $27 high, to about about $31 d low season with a/c, $38 high; security boxes, bar.

The **Buenaventura**, on the beach several blocks farther north (between Calles San Salvador and Nicaragua, where the airport boulevard becomes cobblestone), is one of Puerto Vallarta's few close-in luxury hotels (Av. Mexico 1301, P.O. Box 8B, Puerto Vallarta, Jalisco 48350, tel. 322-237-37). The lobby rises to an airy wood-beamed atrium then opens toward the beach through a jungle walkway of giant hanging leafy philodendrons and exotic palms. At the beachfront Los Tucanes Beach Club, a wide, palm-silhouetted pool-patio borders a line of shade palapas along the whitish yellow sand beach. Most of the smallish rooms, tastefully decorated in wood, tile, and earth-tone drapes and bedspreads, open to small private ocean-facing balconies. The 206 rooms go for about $44 d low season, $78 high; with a/c, phones, restaurant, bar, entertainment nightly, and credit cards accepted.

Zona Hotelera Luxury Hotels

Puerto Vallarta's plush hostelries vary widely, and higher tariffs do not guarantee quality. Nevertheless, some of Pacific Mexico's best-buy luxury gems glitter among the twenty-odd hotels that line Puerto Vallarta's north-end Zona Hotelera beaches. The selection below hopefully includes the gems and eliminates the duds. The prices listed are "rack rates"—prices paid by walk-in customers. Much cheaper (as much as 50% discount) air fare-lodging packages are often available, especially during low season (May-July, Sept.-Nov.). Get yourself a good buy by shopping around among travel agents several weeks before departure.

Continuing north, the **Hotel Continental Plaza,** (formerly the Fiesta Americana Plaza Vallarta) buzzes all day with activities: tennis in the eight-court John Newcombe Tennis Club, aerobics, water polo and volleyball in the big pool, and parasailing, jet-skiing, and windsurfing from the golden Playa Las Glorias beach. Happy hours brighten every afternoon, and live music fills every balmy evening. The luxurious but not large rooms, decorated in soothing pastels, open to balconies overlooking the broad, palmy patio (Av. de Ingreso Km 2.5, Zona Hotelera, Plaza Las Glorias, Puerto Vallarta, Jalisco 48300, tel. 322-401-23, fax 322-452-36). The Continental Plaza's 434 room tariffs run about $105 d low season, $135 high; with a/c, all sports, restaurants, bars, sauna, jacuzzi, exercise room, wheelchair access, and parking. Reserve from the U.S. and Canada by calling toll-free (800) 635-8483.

The **Hotel Plaza Las Glorias** next door is as Mexican and relaxed as the Continental Plaza is *norteamericano* and busy. At Plaza Las Glorias, a blue swimming pool meanders beneath a manicured patio-grove of rustling palms. The rooms, behind the Spanish-style stucco, brick, and tile facade, overlook the patio and ocean from small view balconies. Inside, the luxurious rooms are tile-floored, in dark wood, white stucco, and blue and pastels. (Plaza Las Glorias s/n, Puerto Vallarta, Jalisco 48300, tel. 322-444-44, fax 322-465-59.) The 237 rooms rent for about $77 d low season, $86 high; with a/c, TV, phones, two pools, bars, restaurants, use of tennis courts next door at John Newcombe Tennis Club, all beach sports, and parking. Credit cards are accepted; for U.S. reservations, call (800) 342-AMIGO.

The **Hotel Las Palmas,** a quarter-mile further north, is a scaled-down, less luxurious version of the Plaza Las Glorias. A towering, rustic palapa covers the lobby, which continues to a lovely beachside pool-patio. Here, on the wide and clean Playa Las Glorias, opportunities for aquatic sports are at their best, with the Silent World Diving Center (which also offers all other water sports besides diving) right on the beachfront. Rooms, while comfortable, are not deluxe. (Av. de Ingreso Km 2.5, Puerto Vallarta, Jalisco 48300, tel. 322-406-50, 322-43-37, fax 322-405-43). Its 114 rooms run about $51 d low season, $85 high; with a/c, phones, TV, restaurant, snack bar, bars, pool, parking, credit cards accepted.

The **Fiesta Americana Puerto Vallarta,** another half-mile north, is, for many, the best hotel in town. The lobby-palapa, the world's largest, is an attraction all in itself. Its 10-story palm-thatch chimney draws air upward, creating a continuously cool breeze through the open-air reception area. Outside, the high-rise rampart of ocean-view rooms overlooks a pool-garden of earthly delights, with a gushing pool fountain, water volleyball, a swim-up bar, and in-pool recliners. Just roll off your recliner and you're in the water. Beyond that spreads a 150-foot-wide strip of wave-washed yellow sand. (P.O. Box 270, Puerto Vallarto, Jalisco 48300, tel. 322-420-10, fax 322-421-08.) The 291 view rooms sometimes go for as low as $90 d low season, and rise to $170 during the high, credit cards accepted; with a/c, TV, phones, all sports, three restaurants, a huge pool, three bars, a disco, wheelchair access, and parking. In the U.S. or Canada call call 800-FIESTA-1 for reservations.

The **Hotel Krystal** (a quarter-mile south of the Maritime Terminal) is more than a hotel, it's a palmy, manicured resort-village, exactly what a Mexican Walt Disney would have built (Av. de las Garzas s/n, Puerto Vallarta, Jalisco 48300, tel. 322-402-02, fax 322-402-16). The Krystal is one of the few Puerto Vallarta ultra-luxury resorts designed by and for Mexicans. Scores of deluxe low-rise garden bungalows, opening into private pool-patios, spread over its 34 beachside acres. A Porfirian bandstand stands proudly at the center, while nearby a colonial-style aqueduct gushes water into a pool at the edge of a serene, spacious, palm-shaded

park. Guests who prefer a more lively environment can have it—in the lobby where dancing and shows go on every night, or beside the huge, meandering beachside pool, where the music is anything but serene. The Krystal's 460 rooms and suites rent from about $90 d low season, $130 high; with a/c, phones, TV, 44 pools—no joke—six restaurants, all sports, including donkey polo; for reservations, call toll-free 800-231-9860 in the U.S. and Canada.

Apartments And Condos

Sept.-Nov., comfortable condominiums and apartments right on (or within a block from) Los Muertos Beach rent for as low as $400 per month ($13-14/day) and about twice that during high season. Agencies handle daily, weekly, or monthly advance rentals by phone or mail. Among the best known in the Los Muertos Beach area is **Promotura Olas Altas,** Amapas 192, Colonia Emiliano Zapata, Puerto Vallarta 48380 (tel. 322-249-78, fax 322-247-46).

Trailer Parks And Camping

Puerto Vallarta has two trailer parks, both of them good. Closest in is the friendly, shady **Puerto Vallarta Trailer Park,** two blocks off the highway at Francia and Lucerna, a few blocks north of the *libramiento* downtown bypass fork. (Francia 141, Puerto Vallarta, Jalisco 48300, tel. 322-428-28). Their 65 spaces rent for $10 d, with one free day per week, one free week per month; with all hookups, laundromat, showers, toilets, and long-distance phone, three blocks from beach, pets okay. Luxury hotel pools and restaurants are nearby.

Larger **Tacho's Trailer Park** (half a mile from Hwy. 200 on Av. Amara, the road that branches inland across from the harbor naval compound), offers a large grassy yard with some palms, bananas, and other trees for shade (P.O. Box 315, Puerto Vallarta, Jalisco, 48300, tel. 322-421-63). Although their 100 spaces run a steep $12/day, they offer one free week for a monthly rental; with all hookups, showers, toilets, laundry room, pool, shuffleboard, some bricked spaces; pets are okay.

Other than the trailer parks, Puerto Vallarta has precious few camping sites within the city limits. Plenty of camping possibilities exist outside the city, however. (See "Around the Bay of Banderas" below.)

FOOD

Puerto Vallarta is brimming with good food. Dieters beware, however: "light" or "nouveau" cuisine, crispy vegetables, and bountiful salads are the exception here, as in all Mexico. In the winter, when the sun-hungry vacationers crowd in, a table at even an average restaurant may require a reservation. During the low season, however, Puerto Vallarta's best eateries are easy to spot. They are the ones with the customers.

Stalls, Snacks, And Breakfast

Good Puerto Vallarta eating is not limited to sit-down restaurants. Many foodstalls offer wholesome, inexpensive snacks to hosts of loyal repeat customers. It's hard to go wrong with hot, prepared-on-the-spot food. Each stand specializes in one type of fare—seafood, tortas, tacos, hot dogs—and occupies the same location daily. For example, a number of them concentrate along **Av. Constitución** just south of the River Cuale; several others cluster on the side-street corners of **Av. Olas Altas** a few blocks away.

A number of such foodstalls have graduated to storefronts. **Rickey's Tamales** capitalizes on the general Mexican belief that tamales (like Chinese food in the U.S.) are hard to make and must be bought, take-out style. Big rolls of husk-wrapped, lime-soaked cornmeal, stuffed and baked with beef, chicken, or pork, are three for $2. (At 325 Basilio Badillo, open Mon.-Fri. 6-10 p.m.)

If you're lusting for a late-night snack, drop into the no-name *lonchería* and *jugería,* a few doors from the Cinema Bahía (Insurgentes 153, open daily 7 a.m.-midnight). Try their luscious *tortas de pierna* (roast leg of pork smothered in avocado on a bun, $1.50) and a banana *liquado* (like a milkshake, minus the calories), with a touch of *(un poquito de)* chocolate.

The only do-it-yourself taco stand in Puerto Vallarta (and maybe in all Mexico) is **La Cocina Deli-Mex,** at the nightclub crossroads (near Banana Max and Torito's) of Av. I. Vallarta and L. Cárdenas (open Wed.-Mon. 11 a.m.-1 a.m.). You start with steamed *tacos al vapor* (bean, chicken, or beef, three for a dollar), to which you add any of several delectable sauces.

Some of the most colorful, untouristed places to eat in town are, paradoxically, at the tourist-mecca **Mercado Municipal** on the Rio Cuale, at the Insurgentes upper bridge. The *fondas* tucked on the upstairs floor (climb the streetside staircase) specialize in steaming, home-style soups, fish, meat, tacos, *moles,* and chiles rellenos. Point out your order to the cook and take a seat at their cool, river-view seating area (open daily 7-6).

For breakfast, **La Casa de los Hot Cakes,** skillfully orchestrated by personable owner Memo Barroso, has quickly become a Puerto Vallarta institution (Basilio Badillo 289, between Vallarta and Constitución, open Tues.-Sun. 8 a.m.-2 p.m.). Besides bountiful Mexican and North American style breakfasts (orange juice or fruit, eggs, toast, and hash browns for $3.25), Memo offers an indulgent list of pancakes. Try his nuts-topped, peanut butter-filled "O. Henry" chocolate pancakes, for example. Add his bottomless cup of coffee and you'll be buzzing all day.

Restaurants South Of Rio Cuale

(Complete Dinner Price Key: Budget = under $7, Moderate = $7-14, Expensive = more than $14.) **Archie's Wok** is the founding member of a miniature "gourmet ghetto," which is appearing in the Olas Altas neighborhood (Francisca Rodriguez 130, between Av. Olas Altas and the beach, tel. 204-11, open Mon.-Sat 1-10, Visa accepted). The friendly Asian-trained owner, John Huston's longtime personal chef, often shares anecdotes of old times in Puerto Vallarta with his mostly resident American customers. As for food, it's hard to go wrong with his varied vegetable, fish, meat, and noodle menu. Favorites include Thai Coconut Fish, Barbecued Ribs Hoi Sin, and Spicy Fried Thai Noodles. Make up a party of three or four, and each order your favorite. Arrive early; there's usually a line by 7:30. Moderate.

Right next door to Archie's spread the inviting outdoor tables of **Restaurant Santos** (Francisca Rodriguez 136, tel. 256-70, open Tues.-Sun. 4-midnight, credit cards accepted). The all-fresh, carefully prepared salads and entrees, such as leg of pork, spaghetti al pesto, and whole broiled fish, together with a carefully chosen wine selection (try the excellent Baja California Cetto-label varietals) reflect Santos's graceful continental ambience. Moderate.

PUERTO VALLARTA RESTAURANTS

Restaurants, in approximate ascending order of price:

RIO CUALE AND SOUTH

Tres Huastecas, Olas Altas 44, 8 a.m.-8 p.m., Mexican

Los Arbolitos, Camino Rivera 184, 8 a.m.-11 p.m., Mexican

da Franco, Olas Altas and Gomez, 246-65, Mon.-Sat. 4-11, Italian

Archie's Wok, F. Rodriguez 130, 204-11, Mon.-Sat 1-10, Asian

Franzi's, Isla Cuale 33, 8 a.m.-11 p.m., international

Restaurant Santos, F. Rodriguez 136, 256-70, Tues.-Sun 4-midnight, international

Restaurant Puerto Nuevo, B. Badillo 284, noon-11 p.m., seafood

Le Bistro, Isla Cuale 16A, 202-83, Mon.-Sat. 9 a.m.-11:30 p.m., international

Señor Chico's, Pulpito 377, 235-70, 5-11, international

NORTH OF RIO CUALE

Healthy's, Morelos 803, Mon.-Sat. 8 a.m.-10 p.m., natural

Las Palomas, Malecón at Aldama, 236-75, 8 a.m.-midnight, Mexican

Restaurant Brazz, Morelos 518, 203-24, noon-11 p.m., Mexican-international

Chef Roger, Av. Rodriguez, 259-00, Mon.-Sat. 6:30-11, international

Cafe des Artistes, G. Sanchez 740, 232-28, Mon.-Sat. 7 p.m.-midnight, international

Another of Olas Altas's low-profile gourmet gems, the **da Franco** Italian restaurant, lies tucked away in the little shopping square behind Santos and Archie's (Centro Comercial Costa Alegre 16, at Olas Altas and Gomez, next to the Hotel Oro Verde, tel. 246-65, open Mon.-Sat. 4-11, credit cards accepted). The Brindisi-born owner-chef personally directs preparation of every dish, old-country style. His favorites are Lobster Franco, Shrimp de

Mancuso, and Filete Rossini. For an extra treat, leave room for his scrumptious apple strudel. Moderate.

Restaurant Tres Huastecas is among the most interesting of Puerto Vallarta's dozens of one-room, local-style eateries (Olas Altas 44, at R. Gomez, no phone, open daily 8-8). The charming, unassuming owner, of pure Huastec blood (who calls himself "El Querreque") while others call him the "Troubadour of Puerto Vallarta"), is behind it all. His poetry, together with sentimental Mexican country scenes, covers the walls, while everything from soft-boiled eggs and toast to frog's legs and enchiladas Huastecas fills the tables. Budget to moderate.

Los Arbolitos, way upstream along the River Cuale, remains very popular, despite its untouristed location (Camino Rivera 184; bear right at the upper end of Av. Lázaro Cárdenas; open daily 8 a.m.-11 p.m.). Here, home-style Mexican specialties reign supreme. The house pride and joy is the Mexican plate ($7), although they serve a good T-bone steak for $8. Colorful decor, second-floor river-view location, and attentive service spell plenty of satisfied customers. Moderate.

Someday when you're lusting for seafood, visit **Restaurant Puerto Nuevo** on Basilio Badillo, across from Casa de los Hot Cakes, for a gourmet's gourmet seafood dinner (Basilio Badillo 284, no phone, open daily noon-11, credit cards accepted). Completely without pretention, owner-chef Roberto Castellon brings the customers in with his ingeniously variable list of specialties. For a real party for four, try his (guaranteed) bottomless seafood dinner, served course by course, including clams, oysters, lobster, scallops, and red snapper-stuffed chiles rellenos thrown in for good measure. For dessert, he recommends either his Kahlua cheesecake or fried ice cream (what?). Moderate to expensive.

Finally, your stay in Puerto Vallarta would not be complete without a visit to **Señor Chico's** for sunset cocktails and dinner beneath the stars (Pulpito 377, reservations recommended, tel. 235-70, open daily 5-11). Although presented with a flair, the food is only average. The atmosphere, however—soft guitar solos, flickering candlelight, pastel-pink tablecloths, balmy night air, and the twinkling lights of the city below—is memorable. Expensive.

Isla Rio Cuale Restaurants

For ambience, the showplace **Le Bistro** is tops (Isla Rio Cuale 16A, just upstream from the Av. Insurgentes bridge, reservations recommended, tel. 202-83, open Mon.-Sat. 9 a.m.-11:30 p.m., credit cards accepted). The river gurgles past outdoor tables, plants festoon the greenhouse roof, a tree trunk twists upward into a leafy tree canopy, while recorded jazz plays so realistically that you look in vain for the combo. All this creates the impression of life at the bottom of some fantastic, giant, show-biz terrarium. Dieters, furthermore, encounter serious dilemmas at Le Bistro. Many of the short menu of intriguingly labeled and skillfully served entrees, such as Steak Lena, Brubeck Brochette, and Mignon Ellington, come with gobs of cheese, butter, or cream. Expensive.

Low-key **Franzi's,** by contrast, features live virtuoso jazz or guitar Tues.-Sun. 8-10:30 p.m. (Isla Rio Cuale 33, just below the downstream Av. Vallarta bridge, no telephone, book exchange, open daily 8 a.m.-11 p.m., credit cards accepted). Their extensive, straightforward menu is skillfully served and artfully presented, the atmosphere elegantly simple. Seating is both inside, near the music, or outside in a shady, riverside patio. Moderate.

Restaurants North Of Rio Cuale

Chef Roger, arguably the best restaurant in Puerto Vallarta, is among the least visible (Av. Rodriguez, between Hidalgo and Juarez, one block down from the Rio Cuale Market, reservations mandatory, tel. 259-00, open Mon.-Sat. 6:30-11, credit cards accepted). A legion of satisfied customers, however, is the Swiss owner-chef's best advertisement. Heated dinner plates, chilled beer and white wine glasses, candlelight, etchings hung on the pastel stucco walls, guitars strumming softly, and an eclectic list of exquisitely executed continental dinner entrees keep the faithful coming year-round. Moderate to expensive.

With its air-conditioned restaurant section glass-partitioned from its airy concert-bar, **Restaurant Brazz** offers something for everyone (Morelos 518, at the bend in the *malecón* at Galeana, tel. 203-24, open daily). During the high winter season, it is usually open for lunch (good sandwich plates), during the low season, dinner only, specializing in steaks

and seafood. After dinner, guests often stay to enjoy the live mariachi concerts 9-11 nightly. Moderate.

Right in the bustle of the *malecón* tourist row stands the longtime favorite **Las Palomas** (Malecón and Aldama, tel. 236-75, open daily 8 a.m.-midnight, credit cards accepted). Its graceful, Mexican-style decor—colonial-style wall portraits and exquisite pottery plates—all beneath a towering big-beamed ceiling affords a restful contrast to the sidewalk hubbub just outside the door. The entrees (nearly all Mexican) are tasty and bountiful. Budget to moderate.

Downtown, the striking castle-tower of **Restaurant Cafe des Artistes** rises above the surrounding hillside neighborhood (740 Guadalupe Sanchez at Vicario, tel. 232-28, open Mon.-Sat. 7 p.m.-midnight). Only romantics need apply here. Candlelit tables, gently whirring ceiling fans, soothing music, and gourmet international cuisine all set the luxurious tone. Expensive.

Farthest out in both location and food is the Mexican-macrobiotic **Healthy's,** with the requisite knotty-pine all-wood decor to match (Morelos 803 at Pipila, open 8 a.m.-10 p.m. high season, 10-7 low, closed Sundays). This petite, two-story cafe is one of a small but growing chain, owned and operated in partnership with the employees by the Blum family of Puerto Vallarta. They know what they are doing: Their all-fresh, hearty offerings include *cocina integral* (whole-food) versions of everything, including omelettes, cereals, sandwiches (both veggie and non), pasta, and many fruit juices and *liquados.* Not fancy, but give them five stars for wholesome food. Budget to moderate.

Supermarkets, Bakery, And Health Food

The acknowledged best national supermarket chain is **Comercial Mexicana,** Mexico's K mart with groceries. The quality is generally good to excellent, and the prices match those in the U.S. and Canada. Comercial Mexicana maintains two Puerto Vallarta branches, both in the north-side suburbs: at **Plaza Marina** (Km 6.5, Hwy. 200, just before the airport, beneath the McDonald's sign, tel. 100-53, 104-90); and three miles closer in, at **Plaza Genovese** (Km 2.5, Hwy. 200, near the John Newcombe Tennis Club, tel. 464-44). Both are open daily 9-9.

Much closer to downtown is the big local **Supermarket Gutierrez Rizo,** a remarkably well-organized dynamo of a general store (Constitución and Vallarta, just south of the Rio Cuale, tel. 202-22, open 6:30-10, 365 days of the year). Besides vegetables, groceries, film, socks, spermicide, and sofas, they stock one of the largest racks of English-language magazines (some you'd be hard pressed to find back home) outside of Mexico City.

Panadería Mungía is nearly worth the trip to Puerto Vallarta all by itself (Downtown at Juarez and Mina, tel. 220-90, open Mon.-Sat. 7-9). Big, crisp cookies, flaky fruit tarts, hot, fresh rolls, and cool cream-cakes tempt the palates of visitors, locals, and resident foreigners alike.

If you've run out of *salvado* (oat bran), stock up at **La Buena Vida** health food store (Morelos 799 at Pipila, tel. 213-48, open Mon.-Sat. 9-2 and 4-8). Their shelves are packed with a thousand additional items, such as soya milk, vitamins, aloe vera cream, and tonics (purported to cure everything from warts and gallstones to impotence).

ENTERTAINMENT AND EVENTS

Wandering Around
The *malecón,* where the sunsets seem the most beautiful in town, is a perfect place to begin the evening. Make sure you eventually make your way to the downtown central plaza by the Palacio Municipal (city hall). On Fridays and Saturdays, the city often sponsors free music and dance concerts beginning around eight at the bayside **Los Arcos** amphitheater. Later, you can join the crowds who watch the **street artists** painting plates, watercolors, and fanciful outer-galaxy spray-can scenery.

If you miss the weekend Los Arcos concert, you can usually console yourself with a balloon, *palomitas* (popcorn), and sometimes a band concert in the plaza. If you're inconsolable, however, buy some peanuts, a roasted ear of sweet corn, or a hot dog from a vendor. After that, cool down with an *agua* or *jugo* fruit juice from the *juguería* across the bayside plaza corner, or a cone from Bing ice cream on the other.

A tranquil south-of-Cuale spot to cool off evenings is the **Muelle Nuevo** (New Pier) at the foot of Francisca Rodriguez (beach side of Hotel Playa Los Arcos, open daily till around eleven, entrance fee $.30). On a typical evening you'll find a few dozen folks—men, women, and kids—enjoying the breeze, the swish of the surf, and, with nets or lines, trying to catch a few fish for sale or dinner.

Special Cultural Events
Some of the very professional local **Fiesta Mexicana** tourist shows are as popular with Mexican tourists as foreigners. The evening typically begins with a sumptuous buffet of salads, tacos, enchiladas, seafood, barbecued meats, and flan (custard) and pastries for dessert. Then begins a non-stop program of music and dance from all parts of Mexico: a chorus of revolutionary *soldaderas* and their *zapatista* male compatriots; raven-haired señoritas in flowing, flowered Tehuantepec silk dresses; rows of dashing Guadalajaran *charros* twirling their fast-stepping Chinas Poblanas sweethearts, all climaxed by enough fireworks to swab the sky red, white, and green.

The south-of-Cuale **Restaurant Iguana** (Calle Lázaro Cárdenas 311, between Insurgentes and Constitución, tel. 201-05) stages a very popular such show on Tuesdays and Sundays around seven. Another safe bet is the **Hotel Krystal** show (tel. 402-02), Tuesdays and Saturdays at seven.

Local folks and visitors alike enjoy Puerto Vallarta's *severa; regular folkloric dance shows.*

MIKE WELLINS

Fireworks-stuffed paper-mâché bulls provide exciting finales to local fiestas.

BOB RACE

Other such shows are held seasonally at the **Holiday Inn** (northern Hotel Zone, tel. 416-00), the **Playa Los Arcos** (Av. Olas Altas, tel. 215-83), and the **Buenaventura** (midtown, Av. Mexico 1301, tel. 237-37).

The tariff for these shows typically runs around $30 per person. During holidays and the high winter season reservations (either directly or through a travel agent) are generally necessary.

Movies
Puerto Vallarta's "art" movie house is the **Cinema Elizabeth Taylor** (Cinco de Febrero 19, just south of the River Cuale, tel. 206-67). The afternoon and evening programs tend toward the mild exotic-erotic, but also include films on the classic themes of honor, love, virtue, and revenge, which Mexican audiences love.

The **Cine Bahía** nearby (Insurgentes 189, between Madero and Serdan, tel. 217-17), a typical fifties-style small-town movie house, runs a mixture of Mexican and American pop horror, comedy, and action, such as *Silence of the Lambs, American Ninja,* and *Teenage Mutant Ninja Turtles.*

Get into the Puerto Vallarta mood and make a night of it at **Hotel Mismaloya,** which shows a video of *Night of the Iguana* nightly at seven (tel. 243-72, restaurant reservations recommended, at Mismaloya Beach, seven miles (12 km) south of town, take the Mismaloya or "Boca" marked minibus van from south-of-Cuale Plaza Lázaro Cárdenas).

Music And Dancing
Cover charges are not required at the hotel lobby-bars, many of which offer nightly live music and dancing. For example, the **Krystal Vallarta** (tel. 402-02) band plays Mexican-romantic-pop daily from around eight to midnight adjacent to the reception area at the Hotel Krystal.

The **Hotel Continental** (tel. 401-23) tropical music group is guaranteed to brighten the spirits of any vacationer after a hard day on the beach.

The **Hotel Playa Los Arcos** (tel. 205-83) combo in the palapa-restaurant bar offers a little bit of everything (8-11 evenings, daily) from "Yellow Bird" and "Yesterday" to "La Bamba," with requests thrown in.

Discoing
Discos get started around ten and go on till about five in the morning. They have dress codes that require shoes, shirts and long pants for men, and blouses and skirts or pants, or modest shorts for women. Often they serve only soft drinks. Discos that cater to tourists (all of the following) generally monitor their front doors very carefully; consequently they are pleasant and, with ordinary precautions, secure places to have a good time. In order of roughly increasing volume:

The mostly young, genteel customers at the south-of-Cuale **Centro Nocturno XC** (I. Vallarta, between Badillo and Carranza, tel. 207-19) enjoy the usual flashing lights and mostly medium-volume seasonally live Latin-style pop for their $7 entrance fees.

Approximately the same is true at **J.C. Rock** on the north side of town in front of the Hotels Los Pelicanos and Las Palmas.

Less than a quarter mile north, one of the most amicable (although a bit smoky) discos in Puerto Vallarta is **Friday Lopez** (tel. 420-10, at the Hotel Fiesta Americana Puerto Vallarta). The youngish crowd pays a $7 entrance tariff for live, medium-volume, mostly Latin rock and rap on a small, crowded dance floor. The room, however, is high ceilinged and well lighted, and the atmosphere is congenial.

Another half mile north stands **Christine,** the showplace of Puerto Vallarta discos (in front of Hotel Krystal, tel 402-02, ext. 878, $10 cover). They entice customers to come early (at eleven) to see their display of special fogs, spacy gyrating colored lights, and sophisticated woofers and tweeters which, even when loud as usual, are supposed to leave you with minimum hearing impairment.

Malecón Bars And Hangouts
One of the simplest Puerto Vallarta entertainment formulas is to walk along the *malecón* until you hear the kind of music at the volume you like.

Traditionalists like the big bar at **Brazz** (Morelos 518 at Galeana, tel. 203-24), where a crowd of regulars fills the leather chairs around nine to enjoy the nightly mariachi concert. (See "Restaurants North of Rio Cuale" above for more details.)

Four blocks north, the African safari-decorated **Mogambo** (tel. 234-76, *malecón* between Ortiz and Abasolo) restaurant-bar offers the repertoire of a piano and bass jazz duo evenings, year-round.

Many popular *malecón* spots regularly pound out a continous repertoire of heavy-metal recorded rock. Since nearly all of them are trying to imitate the **Hard Rock Cafe,** you might as well go right to the source (*malecón* at Pipila, tel. 302-99, no cover).

The other place that tries to imitate no one (except for its many brother-establishments around the world) is **Carlos O'Brien's Restaurant** (tel. 214-44, right next door to Hard Rock). Deafening recorded music, Revolutionary wall-photos, zany mobiles, zingy margaritas, and "loco" waiters often lead patrons to dance on the tables by midnight.

Bars And Hangouts South Of Cuale
Besides romantic, riverside atmosphere and good food, **Franzi's** (see under "Isla Rio Cuale Restaurants" above) offers very smooth, very professional live jazz or guitar Tues.-Sun. 8-10:30 p.m. (no phone).

Three more blocks along Av. Vallarta, a bustling little entertainment block between Carranza and Badillo has some lively spots, among

them **Banana Max** bar-restaurant (medium-volume non-heavy metal live pop till the wee hours).

Across the street, the longtime favorite, friendly **Toritos** (tel. 237-84) has good ribs, reasonable prices, and a seasonal live music from nine to midnight, bar open till around 5 a.m.

Many folks' nights wouldn't be complete without stopping in at the **Andale** Mexican pub (so-so restaurant upstairs, tel. 210-54, Olas Altas 425, open till around 4 a.m.), whose atmosphere is so amicable and lively that few even bother to watch the nonstop TV.

SPORTS

Jogging And Walking
Puerto Vallarta's cobbled streets, high curbs (towering sometimes to six feet!), and "holey" sidewalks make it tricky walking around town. The exception is the *malecón,* which can provide a good two-mile roundtrip jog when it is not crowded. Otherwise, try the beaches or the big public sports field, **Unidad Deportiva,** on the airport boulevard across from the Sheraton.

Swimming, Surfing, And Bodysurfing
While Puerto Vallarta's calm waters are generally safe for swimming, they are too tranquil for much surfing, bodysurfing, or boogieboarding. The only exception is at the mouth of the **Ameca River** (north of the airport) during the rainy summer season, when the large river flow helps create bigger than normal waves. (Surfing is common at **Bucerías** and **Punta Mita,** however. For details, see under "Around the Bay of Banderas" below.

Sailing And Windsurfing
Island Sailing International offers sailboat rentals and lessons from their Marina Vallarta dockside in front of the Hotel Plaza Las Glorias Iguana. Their boats, all with keels, range from Optimist dinghies for kids to Impulse 21's for serious ocean sailing ($125/day). Their lessons vary from a two-hour ($40) introduction to an entire 12-hour ($200) American Sailing Association certification course. Call them for more information at (322) 108-80, or drop by at their hotel office, open Mon.-Fri. 9-1 and 4-6. Directions: One mile north of the Maritime Terminal

cruise-ship berth, a phony lighthouse at a gate marks the entrance to the Isla Iguana development. Ask the gatekeeper to direct you toward the Hotel Plaza Las Glorias Iguana.

A small but growing nucleus of local windsurfing enthusiasts practice their sport from Puerto Vallarta's beaches. They hold a **windsurfing tournament** during the citywide Fiesta de Mayo during the first week in May. Check with Island Sailing International (see above) for details.

Windsurfing lessons and equipment rentals are available at the **Club de Playa Iguana,** the beach club of the Hotel Plaza Las Glorias Iguana. Complete 12-hour courses run $70, windsurfing rigs rent (to those who know how to use them) for $10/hour. For more details, contact Island Sailing International (see above).

The **Silent World Diving** water sports center (tel. 406-50, ext. 626, open daily 9-5), headquartered on the Las Palmas Hotel beachfront, also offers windsurfing lessons and equipment ($40 for a two-hour minimum lesson). Additionally, they rent simple-to-operate Hobie Cat sailboats (no lessons required) for $30/hour.

Snorkel And Scuba

The biggest scuba instructor-outfitter in town is **Chico's Dive Shop,** on the *malecón* at Diaz Ordaz 770 (between Pipila and Vicario, tel. 322-218-95, fax 322-254-39, open daily 9-9). They offer complete lessons, arrange and lead dive trips, and rent scuba equipment to qualified (bring your certificate) divers. A beginning scuba pool lesson runs $14, after which you'll be qualified to dive at **Los Arcos.** (A day boat trip, including one 40-minute dive costs $46, complete. Snorkelers on the same trip pay $25.) Chico's takes certified divers only to the **Marietas Islands,** the best site in the bay (for $75, two dives; snorkelers go for $42).

Other shops which offer similar services are **Silent World Diving Center** at the Las Palmas Hotel (see above), and **Paradise Divers** at Av. Olas Altas 443 (between Dieguez and Rodriguez, tel. 240-04, open daily 9-9).

Jet-skiing, Waterskiing, And Parasailing

These are available right on the beach at a number of the northside resort-hotels, such as the Sheraton, Hotel Continental Plaza, Hotel Las Palmas, Fiesta Americana Puerto Vallarta, and Krystal.

Parasailing and waterskiing are often also available on Playa Los Muertos, in front of the Hotels Playa Los Arcos and Tropicana.

Expect to pay about $25 per half hour for a jet-ski boat, $70/hour for waterskiing, and $20 for a 10-minute parasailing ride.

Tennis And Golf

The eight (four night-lit outdoor clay, four indoor) courts at the **John Newcombe Tennis Club** (Hotel Continental Plaza, tel. 401-23) rent all day for $11/hour. They also offer massage, steam baths, equipment sales and rentals, and professional lessons ($30/hour).

The several night-lit courts at the **Hotel Krystal** (tel. 402-02) rent for $9/hour. They also offer equipment sales, rentals, and professional lessons. Other hotels, such as the **Sheraton** (tel. 304-04), **Los Tules** (tel. 429-90) and **Holiday Inn** (tel. 416-00) customarily rent tennis courts.

The 18-hole, par-71 **Marina Vallarta Golf Course,** designed by architect Joe Finger, is one of Mexico's best. It is open, however, only to club members and guests of the Hotels Marriot, Vela Vallarta, Quinta Real, Camino Real, Plaza Las Glorias, Sheraton, and Marina del Rey. The $60 greens fee includes caddy and cart. Open daily 7:30 to dusk (tel. 101-71).

The green, palm-shaded 18-hole Los Flamingos Golf Course (at Km 145 Hwy. 200, eight miles, 13 km north of the International Airport, tel. 802-80) offers an attractive alternative, however. Open to the public daily 7 a.m.-4:30 p.m., the Los Flamingos services/facilities include carts ($22), caddies ($10), club rentals ($14), a pro shop, restaurant, and locker rooms. The greens fee runs $25. Their shuttle bus leaves daily from the Zona Hotelera (front of the Sheraton) at 6:30, 9:30, and 11:30 a.m., returning at 1, 3, and 5 p.m.

Gyms

Puerto Vallarta has a number of good exercise gyms. The **European Health Spa** (say "ays-PAH") at the Marina (Tennis Club Puesta del Sol, tel. 107-70) has 40 machines, complete weight sets, professional advice, aerobics workouts, and separate men's and women's facilities. The **Spa Fiesta Americana** (tel. 444-46, at the Hotel Continental Plaza, $10/day, $46/week) offers aerobics, Nautilus, massage, saunas, and professional personnel.

Sportfishing

You can hire *pangas* (outboard launches) with skippers on the beach in front of several hotels, such as Los Arcos (on Playa Los Muertos), the Buenaventura and Sheraton (Playa Los Camarones), the Plaza Las Glorias, Las Palmas, and Fiesta Americana Puerto Vallarta (Playa Las Glorias) and Krystal (Playa de Oro). Expect to pay about $25/hour for a two- or three-hour trip that might net you and a few friends some five-pound jack, bonito, toro, or dorado for dinner. Ask your favorite restaurant to fix you a fish banquet with them.

Another good spot for panga rentals is near the **Peines** ("pay-EE-nays") docks, where the fishermen keep their boats. You may be able to negotiate a good price, especially if you or a friend speaks Spanish. Access to the Peines is along the dirt road to the left of the Isla Iguana entrance (at the fake roadside lighthouse a mile north of the Marina cruise-ship terminal). The fishermen, 16 members of the Cooperativa de Deportes Aquaticos Bahía de Banderas, have their boats lined up along the roadside channel a few hundred yards from the highway.

At the end-of-road dock complex (the actual Peines) lie the big-game sportfishing boats, which you can reserve only through agents back in town or at the hotels. For sailfish and marlin, call **Miller Travel Agency,** 411-97, for individual reservations on their 40-foot boats. They go out mornings at 7:30 and return about eight hours later with an average of about one big fish per boat. The tariff is about $63 per person; food and drinks available but extra. Boats generally have space for 10 passengers, about half of whom can fish at any one time. If not a big sailfish or marlin, most everyone usually gets something. Call Miller's main office, in front of Hotel Krystal, at 411-97, 412-97, and 413-97, or contact their subsidiary branches at the Hotels Playa Los Arcos, Sheraton, Plaza Las Glorias, Melia, and Vidafel.

Miller also rents entire 40-foot boats for $300 per day (50-foot, $350) for about 10 passengers, food and drinks extra. Another agency that rents big sportfishing boats is the **Sociedad Cooperativa Progreso Turistico,** which has 10 boats, ranging from 32 to 40 feet. You can talk to them and make reservations at their office on the north end of the *malecón* (at 31 de Octubre, across the street from the Hotel Rosita).

It's best to talk to the manager, Hilarion Rodriguez, who is usually there Mon.-Fri. 4-8 p.m.

If you'd like to enter the Puerto Vallarta **Sailfish Tournament,** held annually (1993 marks the 38th) in November, call the tournament office at the Club de Yates, tel. 107-40 or 108-40 or write Puerto Vallarta Torneo de Pez Vela (sailfish tournament), P.O. Box 212, Puerto Vallarta, Jalisco 48300. The registration fee runs about $400 per person, which includes the welcome dinner and the closing awards dinner. The five grand prizes include automobiles. The biggest sailfish caught was a 168-pounder in 1957.

At present rates of attrition, sailfish and marlin will someday disappear from Pacific Mexico. Some captains and participants have fortunately seen the light, and are letting the fish go after they are hooked.

Yachting And Boat Launching

The superb 350-berth **Marina Vallarta** has all possible hookups, including certified water, metered 110-220 volts, phone, fax, showers, toilets, laundry, dock lockers, trash collection, pumpout, and 24-hour security. With a yacht club and complete repair yard, it is surrounded by luxurious condominiums, tennis courts, a golf course, and dozens of shops and offices. Slip rates run about $.52 per foot per day (minimum charge: about $16 per day) for up to six days. Prices are lower for longer stays and during the low (June-Oct.) season. For more information, write P.O. Box 350-B, Puerto Vallarta, Jalisco 48300, or telephone 322-102-75, or fax 322-101-41.

The Marina has a **public boat-launching ramp** where you can float your craft into the Marina's sheltered waters for free. (Access: follow the unnamed street toward the water, one block south of the main Marina Vallarta entrance, about a mile north of the cruise-ship terminal.)

SHOPPING

Although Puerto Vallarta residents make very few folkcrafts themselves, they import tons of good—and some very fine—pieces from the places where they *are* made. Furthermore, Puerto Vallarta's scenic beauty has become an inspiration for a growing community of artists and discerning collectors who have opened shops filled with locally crafted sculpture, painting, and museum-grade handicrafts gathered from all over Mexico.

Shopping Along The River: Mercado Municipal And Pueblo Viejo

For the more ordinary, yet attractive, Mexican handicrafts, start any day except Sunday (when most shops are closed) in the **Mercado Municipal** at the upstream Rio Cuale bridge. Here, most shops begin with prices two to three times higher than the going rate. You should counter with a correspondingly low offer. If you don't get the price you want, always be prepared to find another seller. If your price is fair, however, the shopkeeper will usually give in as you begin to walk away. (Theatrics, incidentally, are less than useful in bargaining, which should merely be a straightforward discussion of the merits, demerits, and price of the article in question.)

The Mercado Municipal is a two-story warren of dozens upon dozens of shops filled with jewelry, leather, papier-mâché, T-shirts, and everything in between. The congestion can make the place hot; after a while, take a break at a cool river-view seat at one of the *fonda* restaurants on the second floor.

One of the most unusual Mercado Municipal stalls is **Cabaña del Tío (Uncle) Tom,** whose menagerie of colorful papier-mâché parrots are priced a peg or two cheaper than at the tonier downtown stores.

It's time to leave when you're too tired to distinguish silver from tin and Tonalá from Tlaque-paque. Head downstream to the **Pueblo Viejo** complex (on Calle Augustin Rodriguez between Juarez and Morelos) near the Av. Vallarta lower bridge. This mall, with individual stores rather than stalls, is less crowded but pricier than the Mercado Municipal. Some shopkeepers will turn their noses up if you try to bargain. If they persist, take your business elsewhere.

Ric jewelry, Pueblo Viejo's most unusual store, has cases of unique designs in sterling and gold by owner Erika Hult de Corral (tel. 301-43, open daily 9-8).

Downtown Shopping: Along Juarez And Morelos

The majority of Puerto Vallarta's best handicrafts and fine arts stores lie along the first six blocks of Av. Juarez downtown.

Galería La Indígena, in the second block of Juarez, features Huichol ceremonial yarn paintings (flying animals, oak and pine trees, cornstalks) and beadwork. An eclectic treasury of rare ritual masks, skulls, and sculptures lines the walls. At Juarez 168, tel. 230-07, open Mon.-Sat. 10-2 and 5-9.

Conventional but elegant, the **Joyería La Azteca II** sells many classic designs of jeweled silver and gold earrings, bracelets, and necklaces. They also exclusively carry the whimsical, fairy-tale-like art of Hector Manzo, a former student of Sergio Bustamante (Juarez 244, tel. 243-03, open Mon.-Sat. 10-2 and 5-8).

On the adjacent corner, **La Bamba,** Puerto Vallarta's only specialty bathing suit store, some-

The renowned black barra pottery from Colotepec village near Oaxaca is available in shops all over Pacific Mexico.

BRUCE WHIPPERMAN

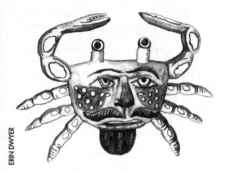

Mexican maskmaking traditions live on, especially in rural areas of Michoacán, Guerro, and Oaxaca.

times offers designer buys at big discounts. Good items can go for as little as $12 (Juarez 252, tel. 237-99, open Mon.-Sat. 10-2 and 4-8).

Art lovers Barbara and Jean Peters collected so many Mexican handicrafts over the years that they had to find a place to store their finds. **Galería Vallarta,** a museum of singular paintings, ceremonial masks, lampshades, art-to-wear, and more, is the result (Juarez 263, tel. 202-90, open Mon.-Sat. 10-9).

The store of renowned **Sergio Bustamante** (who lives in Guadalajara) contains so many unique sculptures that it is hard to figure out how a single artist could be so prolific. (The answer: he has a factory-shop full of workers who execute his fanciful, sometimes even unnerving, studies in juxtaposition.) Bustamante's more modest faces on eggs, anthropoid cats, and double-nosed clowns go for as little as $200; the largest, most flamboyant, for $10,000 or more. (Juarez 275, tel. 211-29, open Mon.-Sat. 9-9).

An adjacent pair of stores, the **Queribines** ("Cherubs") and **La Rejas** ("Grillwork"), display their excellent traditional merchandise—riots of papier-mâché fruit, exquisite blue pottery vases, gleaming pewter, clay trees of life, rich Oaxaca and Chiapas textiles, shiny Tlaquepaque handpainted pottery—so artfully that they are simply fun to walk through (Juarez 501 and 501B; Queribines, tel. 234-75, is open Mon.-Sat. 9-9; La Rejas, tel. 222-72, is open Mon.-Sat. 9-2 and 4-8).

Gary Thompson, the personable owner of **Galería Pacifico,** displays a varied inside collection of fine oils and watercolors on consignment from artists all over Mexico. Outside, in a pleasant patio shaded by a huge tree, he has a number of intriguing sculptures (Juarez 519, tel. 267-68, open Mon.-Sat. 10-9).

Around the corner downhill, on Morelos, **Galería Uno** is one of Puerto Vallarta's longest-established fine art galleries. Their collection of expensive work by mostly internationally recognized artists tends toward the large, the abstract, and the primitive (Morelos 561, tel. 209-08, open Mon.-Sat 10-9).

Step into the **Onix and Silver Factory** on the *malecón* by the post office and you may have to shop for jewelry no longer. They have what seems like acres of gold and silver. Their very reasonable prices are largely determined simply by weight (Morelos 434, tel. 224-87, open Mon.-Sat. 10-10).

Huichol ritual yarn painting depicts a pilgrim praying to the sea gods.

Department Stores
The best department stores in Puerto Vallarta are the two branches of the big **Comercial Mexicana** chain, and the equally excellent local store, **Guitierrez Rizo**. For details, see "Supermarkets, Bakery, and Health Food" under "Food" above.)

Photofinishing, Cameras, And Film
Although a number of downtown stores do one-hour developing and printing for U.S. prices, **Laboratorios Oscar,** owned and operated by professional photographer Gonzalo Ramirez, is one of the few in town that develop slides and black-and-whites. (Hidalgo 363, across from the church, open daily 9-8:30, tel. 240-33).

Lab Vallarta nearby stocks the most film of any downtown store: lots of Fuji and Kodak color negative (print) film in many speeds and sizes plus transparency, professional 120 rolls, and black-and-white. (Libertad 335, tel. 215-58, open 9-10 Mon.-Sat., 10-8 Sunday).

Cameras are an import item in Mexico, and consequently very expensive. Even the simplest point-and-shoot cameras cost as much as three times what they would in the U.S. or Canada. Bring your own.

SERVICES

Money Exchange
The **National Bank of Mexico** (Banamex), on the central plaza, changes U.S. and Canadian cash and traveler's checks at the best rates in town (corner of Juarez and Zaragoza, tel. 219-98, 209-11, money exchange open Mon.-Fri. 9-1). If the lines at Banamex are too long, try **Bancomer** two blocks north (at Juarez and Mina, tel. 208-78, 250-50, money exchange hours Mon.-Fri. 9-12), or **Banco Serfin** across the street.

Scores of little *casas de cambio* (exchange booths) dot the old town streetsides, especially along the *malecón* and Av. Juarez downtown, and along Av. Olas Altas and Insurgentes south of the Rio Cuale. Although they offer about $2 per $100 less than the banks, they compensate with long hours (often 9-9, daily). In the big hotels, cashiers will generally exchange your money at rates comparable to the downtown exchange booths.

The local **American Express** agency offers high bank exchange rates for American Express traveler's checks and full member travel services, such as check cashing (up to $1000, every 21 days). Bring your checkbook, your ID or passport, and your American Express card (Centro Comercial Valla Vallarta H-6, on the airport highway, beach side, three blocks north of the *libramiento* downtown bypass fork, tel. 468-77, 468-76, open Mon.-Fri. 9-2:30 and 4-6, Sat. 9-1).

Post Office, Telegraph, Telephone
Puerto Vallarta has a number of branch post offices. The smallish main **Correos** (post office), on the *malecón* (Morelos 444, at Mina, tel. 218-88), is open Mon.-Fri. 8-7:30, Sat. 9-1, and Sun. 9-12. The branch at the Edificio Maritima (Maritime building) at the cruise liner dock is open Mon.-Fri. 8-3. The airport branch, on the ground level check-in floor, is open 9-7 Mon.-Fri., 9-1 Sat. (After hours they have a mailbox outside the door.)

Telegraph, fax, telex, and money orders *(giros)* are available at the **Telecomunicaciones** at Hidalgo 582 (five blocks north of the central plaza, tel. 202-12, open Mon.-Fri. 9-5:30).

Nearly all Puerto Vallarta (area code 322) hotels have *larga distancia* (long-distance telephone service.) Lacking this (or if you don't like their extra charges), go to one of the many *casetas de larga distancia* (long-distance telephone offices) sprinkled all over town. For example, south of Rio Cuale, the Tres Estrellas de Oro bus terminal, Calle V. Carranza 322, (at Av. Constitución, tel. 249-13) has efficient Computel computer-assisted service daily from 6 a.m. till past midnight. In the center of town, try the little offices at Juarez 124 (below the bridge by the Hotel Encino, tel. 247-13, open Mon.-Sat. 9-2 and 4-7) or at Aldama 180 (five blocks north of the central plaza, tel. 301-99, open Mon.-Sat. 9-9).

Immigration, Customs, And Consulates
If you need an extension to your tourist card, you can get it (up to 180 days total) at the **Migratorios** at 600 Morelos (at Aldama, tel. 214-78, open Mon.-Fri 8-3). If you lose your tourist card, however, go first to the Tourist Information Office (see "Information" below).

If you have to temporarily leave your car in Mexico, take your tourist card, car permit (with copies), and your car papers to the **Aduana** (customs, tel. 406-60, open Mon.-Fri. 9-3 in the Maritime Building, Edificio Maritima) at the cruise-liner dock. (The Aduana presently hasn't the room to store cars, so until they do you don't have to take your car to them as is customary in many Mexican cities.)

The small local **United States Consular Office,** supervised by consular agent Jenny McGill, issues passports and does other essential legal work for U.S. citizens (P.O. Box 462, Puerto Vallarta, Jalisco 48300, tel. 200-69, fax 300-74, open Mon.-Fri. 9-1, in the little second-story office, marked by the U.S. flag, on the uphill side of the Av. Insurgentes Rio Cuale bridge). In true emergencies, you may phone any time.

The **Canadian Consular Officer,** Nicole Vasquez, performs similar services for Canadian citizens at 236 Hidalgo, between Libertad and Guerrero (tel. 253-98, open Mon.-Fri. 9-1).

Language, Arts, And Music Courses

The private, volunteer **Centro Cultural Vallartense** conducts theater, modern dance, aerobics, martial arts, and photography courses for adults and children. Every Sunday morning from about eleven they also have a working art exposition at their gallery-information center (upstream end of Rio Cuale, see "Sights" above) where you can watch painters work, exchange ideas, and even do your own (P.O. Box 218, Puerto Vallarta 48300, tel. 218-66, at the Plaza del Arte near the upstream end of Isla Rio Cuale).

Sharing the Plaza de Arte is the round **Escuela Municipal de Musica** building, where, late weekday afternoons, you may hear the strains of students practicing the violin, guitar, piano, flute, and pre-Columbian instruments. Such lessons are open to the general public; apply in person during the late afternoons or early evening.

The excellent language school, **Centro Cultural Mexicano Americano,** offers tutorial and small group instruction in Spanish for reasonable fees. Besides formal instruction, they sponsor social get-togethers and a live-in study program. (Av. Pipila 213, Puerto Vallarta, Jalisco 48300, tel. 322-234-88, 322-248-10).

INFORMATION

Tourist Information Offices

The joint federal-state Oficina de Turismo (tel. 202-42, open Mon.-Fri 9-8, Sat. 9-1) is at the street-level (Juarez and central plaza) corner of the Palacio Municipal. They provide assistance and information, and dispense whatever maps and pamphlets they happen to have. If you've lost your tourist card, tell them and they'll fill out a loss report, which you then take to Migratorios (see "Services" above) to get a duplicate. One of their most knowledgeable staff, Luis Rodriguez, handles the front information desk after about three most afternoons (after working mornings in the local U.S. consular office).

This Oficina de Turismo is also a good spot to contact members of the Puerto Vallarta **Asociación Cooperativo de Guias** (Guides Association Cooperative, Av. Niza 153, Colonia Diaz Ordaz, tel. 455-35, 449-39), who can arrange out-of-the-ordinary cultural, ecological, and historical tours and treks.

Another good source of local information office is the Puerto Vallarta branch of the **Camara Nacional de Comercio** (chamber of commerce), which publishes the excellent *Directorio Comercial Turistico* directory to everything you might be likely to need in Puerto Vallarta (Morelia 138, 2nd floor, tel. 427-08, one block off the *libramiento* downtown bypass boulevard, four blocks from the airport highway).

Health, Police, And Emergencies

One of the most respected hospital-clinics in town is the **CMQ (Centro Medico Quirurgico)** south of the River Cuale at 305 Basilio Badillo (the hospital section, tel. 260-61, is at no. 364 on the same street), between Insurgentes and Aguacate, tel. 308-78, 235-72, 243-95.

A respected midtown hospital is the **Sanatorio Vallarta** (tel. 209-33, at Brasil and Panama, five blocks along Av. Mexico north of the end of the *malecón* to Panama, then right (east) three blocks to Brasil).

Farther north in the Hotel Zone stands the generally respected hospital-clinic of **Servicios Médico de la Bahía** (at Km 1 on the airport boulevard across from the Sheraton, tel. 226-27, 251-52).

For a **police** emergency, call headquarters (tel. 201-23) at the City Hall at the central plaza;

in case of a **fire** emergency, call the bomberos at the fire station (tel. 266-13 at Bolivia 1321, in the neighborhood a quarter mile north of the end of the *malecón).*

The **Farmacia Roma** fills prescriptions around the clock (Francisco Villa 518, tel. 455-17, just off the *libramiento* downtown bypass, in front of the *preparatorio* high school).

Books, Newspapers, Magazines, And Library
New books in English are not common in Puerto Vallarta. However, **Nuevo Librería Limón,** the best bookstore in town, regularly sells *USA Today,* the *Los Angeles Times, Wall Street Journal,* and a few dozen popular U.S. magazines. In addition, they have a collection of used English-language paperback novels and some local, state, and national maps. At 310 Carranza, between Vallarta and Constitución, tel. 224-52, open daily 8-9.

The **Supermercado Gutierrez Rizo,** corner Constitución and F. Madero, open daily 6:30 a.m.-10 p.m., offers the best American magazine selection in town.

Vallarta Today, an unusually informative tourist daily, is handed out free at the airport and hotels all over town. Besides detailed information (much of it non-commercial) on hotels, restaurants, and sports, they include a local events calendar and good historical, cultural, and personality feature articles. Call them if you can't find a copy; tel. 429-28, Merida 118, Colonia Versalles.

The local **public library** has a small general collection, including Spanish-language reference books and a dozen shelves of English-language paperbacks (at Parque Hidalgo, one block north of the end of the *malecón,* in front of the church, open Mon.-Fri. 8-8, Sat. 9-5).

Women's Organization
The **Asociación Femenil Vallartense,** an organization of mostly professional women, maintains active civic programs. One major project is fund-raising for construction of a new orphanage. They welcome exchanges with visitors. You can reach them through Sara Diaz de Nuño, president, tel. 203-66; or Lucila Nuño de Lopez, secretary, tel. 221-91.

Volunteer Work
The **Club Internacional de la Amistad** (International Friendship Club), an all-volunteer service club, sponsors many medical, educational, and cultural projects. One of the best ways to find out about their work is on the popular Tour of Puerto Vallarta Homes, which begins at the central plaza, near the bandstand, Saturday or Sunday mornings during the Nov.-April high season. Contact the Tourist Information Office, tel. 202-42, seasonal, for details.

GETTING THERE AND GETTING AWAY

By Air
Several major carriers connect Puerto Vallarta by direct flights with many United States and Mexican destinations.

Mexicana Airlines flights connect daily with Los Angeles, Denver, Chicago, Mexico City, Guadalajara, and Monterrey. Mexicana flights also connect with San Francisco (four flights/week), and Dallas (three flights/week). In Puerto Vallarta, telephone 250-00 for reservations, 112-66 for airport flight information.

Continental Airlines flights connect daily with Houston, Denver, and San Diego; tel. 110-96 or 110-25.

Aero California flights connect daily with San Diego and Guadalajara, and with Phoenix (four flights/week); tel. 414-99 reservations, 114-44 airport flight information.

Aeromexico flights connect daily with Los Angeles, Tijuana, Guadalajara, and Mexico City; tel. 112-04 or 110-55.

Alaska Airlines flights connect daily with Los Angeles, San Francisco, and Seattle; tel. 113-50, 113-52 or 303-50.

American Airlines flights connect daily with Dallas-Ft. Worth; tel. 117-99 or 119-27.

Delta Airlines flights connect daily with Los Angeles; tel. 119-19 or 110-32.

Canadian Holidays Airlines charter flights connect with Toronto, Vancouver, and Calgary (mostly during the winter). Call their agent at 437-36 for information.

Puerto Vallarta Airport Arrival And Departure
Air arrival at Puerto Vallarta Airport (code-designated PVR, officially the Gustavo Diaz Ordaz International Airport) is generally smooth and simple. After the cursory (if any) customs check,

arrivees can avail themselves of **money-exchange counters** (open daily 9-9, rate about $2 per hundred less than bank rate), a lineup of **car rental booths** (Budget, National, Avis, Odin, and Hertz), and the arrival desk of the **Association of Travel Agents** (whose main job is to meet tours, but who will call specific hotels for reservations if they have time).

Transportation to town is easiest by *colectivo* (VW van collective taxi) or *taxi especial* (individual taxi). Booths sell tickets at curbside. The *colectivo* fare runs about $3 per person to the northern hotel zone, $3.50 to the center of town, and $4 or more to Mismaloya and other beaches south of town. Individual taxis run about $7, $12, and $17 for the same rides. Taxis to more distant northern destinations, such as Rincón de Guayabitos (30 miles, 50 km) and San Blas or Tepic (100 miles, 160 km), run about $50 and $130, respectively. A much cheaper alternative is to ride one of the second-class Transportes del Pacifico (green and white) northbound buses. Wave them down across the highway outside the airport gate. The Guayabitos fare should run less than $2, Tepic less than $5. They are often crowded; don't tempt poor people with a dangling open purse or a bulging wallet pocket.

Airport departure is as simple as arrival. Save by sharing a taxi with departing fellow hotel guests. Agree on the fare with the driver before you get in. If the driver seems too greedy (see inbound fares above) hail another taxi. Once at the airport, you can do last-minute shopping at a number of airport shops, or mail a letter at the airport post office (open Mon.-Fri. 9-7, Sat. 9-1).

If you've lost your tourist card, be prepared to pay a fine (roughly $20) unless you've gotten a duplicate at the Tourist Information Office. (See "Information" above.) In any case, be sure to save enough pesos to pay your **$12 departure tax.** They don't accept credit cards.

By Car Or RV
There are three road routes to Puerto Vallarta: from the north through Tepic, from the east through Guadalajara, and from the south through Barra de Navidad and Manzanillo. They are all two-lane roads, requiring plenty of caution.

From Tepic, Mexican National **Hwy. 200** is all-asphalt and in good condition most of its 104 miles (167 km) to Puerto Vallarta. Heavy trucks and buses sometimes slow traffic over a few low passes, but traffic is ordinarily light to moderate, except for the 10 miles around Puerto Vallarta. Allow three hours for the southbound trip (and half an hour longer in the reverse direction for the 3,000-foot climb to Tepic).

The story is similar for Mexican National Hwy. 200 along the 172 miles (276 km) from Manzanillo via Barra de Navidad (134 miles, 214 km). Going may be slow while climbing the 2,400-foot Sierra Cuale summit south of Puerto Vallarta, but light traffic should prevail along other stretches. Allow about four hours from Manzanillo, three from Barra de Navidad, and the same in the opposite direction.

The Guadalajara route is slower and more complicated. From Guadalajara, follow **Mexican National Hwy. 15** to Chapalilla. Heavy traffic usually lengthens the 112-mile (179-km) stretch to about three hours, even *including* the *cuota* toll superhighway cutoff over the 7,000-foot summit. At Chapalilla, breathe a sigh of relief as you fork left onto the 22-mile (36-km) toll cutoff to Compostela. At Compostela, head left (south) on Hwy. 200 and sail the remaining 80 miles (129 km) in two hours. Grand total to Puerto Vallarta: 214 miles (344 km), five hours, either way.

By Bus
Many bus lines run through Puerto Vallarta, and they each have their own small stations, all clustering south of the Rio Cuale on or near Av. Insurgentes. All departures listed are local *(salidas locales)* unless otherwise noted as *(salidas de paso):*

First-class **Tres Estrellas de Oro** (TEO, Av. V. Carranza 322, tel. 266-66) buses connect with Guadalajara and intermediate points about a dozen times a day. A few daily *salidas de paso* connect en route with southern destinations of Manzanillo and Lázaro Cárdenas and northern destinations of Tepic, Mazatlán, Tijuana, and intermediate points.

Second-class **Transportes del Pacifico** (TP, Insurgentes 160, tel. 210-15) buses connect every half hour with Tepic. Several first-class buses connect with Guadalajara via La Peñita, Compostela, and Ixtlán.

First-class **Transportes Norte de Sonora** (TNS, Madero 343, tel. 216-50) buses *(salidas de paso)* connect with Barra de Navidad and

Manzanillo in the south and Tepic, Mazatlán, and the U.S. border in the north. Several first-class buses connect daily with Guadalajara and Mexico City in the east.

Transportes Cihuatlán (tel. 234-36, corner Madero and Constitución) provides the most

frequent connections with southern cities of Barra de Navidad, Manzanillo and intermediate points. Three super-first-class "Primera Plus" buses per day connect with Manzanillo, while many second-class buses travel the same route, stopping everywhere.

AROUND THE BAY OF BANDERAS

Puerto Vallarta is a tourist city with all the convenient services, food, and good accommodations that a resort can supply. What Puerto Vallarta sometimes cannot supply, however, is peace and quiet.

But an out exists. The diadem of villages and sandy beaches around the Bay of Banderas can provide a retreat—for a day, a week, or a month—from the tourist rush.

The Southern Arc:
Mismaloya And Beyond
The southern-arc beach gems of **Mismaloya, Boca de Tomatlán, Las Animas, Quimixto,** and **Yelapa** are described under "Sights" above.

The Northern Arc: Nuevo Vallarta, Bucerías, And Punta Mita
The northern curve of the Bay of Banderas begins as Hwy. 200 crosses the Ameca River and enters the state of Nayarit, where clocks shift from Central to Mountain time. (Heading north, set your watch back one hour.)

NUEVO VALLARTA

The Nuevo Vallarta development, just north of the river, is Nayarit's design for a grand resort, comparable to the Zona Hotelera 10 miles south. The plans turned out to be premature, however. For years, miles of boulevard-parkways, dotted with street lights and nested with cul-de-sacs, remained empty, waiting for the homes, condos, and hotels to be built.

A spurt of activity in the early '90s, however, seemed to promise that the potential of Nuevo Vallarta would someday be realized. The **Club de Playa Nuevo Vallarta,** the core of the original development, is a pretty place—perfect for a relaxing beach afternoon. Get there by turning left at Av. Nuevo Vallarta about five miles, eight

km, north of the airport (one mile past the north end of the Ameca bridge) at the Jack Tar Village sign. At the end of the 1.4 mile driveway entrance you will come to the Club de Playa—a parking lot, a small regional (art and artifacts) museum, a pool, a snack bar, and a seemingly endless pearly strand.

The miles-long beach is the main attraction. Its wide, nearly level golden-white sand is perfect for beachcombing, surf fishing, swimming, body-surfing, and boogieboarding. Even some beginning or intermediate surfing might be possible if you bring your own board.

For those who enjoy isolation, beach camping would be good during the temperate winter on the endless dune past the north end of Paseo Cocoteros beach boulevard. Bring everything, including water and a tarp for shade.

Nuevo Vallarta Hotels
For nightlife lovers, however, Nuevo Vallarta shuts down at sunset—unless you are staying in one of the hotels. Adjacent to the Club de Playa is the big Club Med-style **Jack Tar Village,** which often invites the public to drop in on their continuous party, including sports, crafts, games, food and drink, for about $40 per person per day. If you're staying, the all-inclusive lodging and activities run from about $160 per day for two, and can only be reserved through their Texas office at 5949 Sherry Lane, Suite 1800, Dallas TX 75225. Call toll-free numbers (800) 999-9182 in the U.S. and (800) 952-2582 in Mexico; from Canada, call (214) 987-4909)

A more tranquil possibility is the Best Western **Las Camelinas,** the high-rise a quarter-mile north of the Jack Tar along the Cocoteros beach boulevard (Retorno Cancun and Av. Cocoteros Lot 34, Villa 8, Nuevo Vallarta, Nayarit 70112, tel. 322-701-12, 322-700-33, fax 322-700-51). For peace and quiet in luxury, this may be just the ticket. Their deluxe kitchenette apartments provide all the comforts of home, with sweeping ocean views to boot. Their big kitchenette apartments rent from about $50 d low season, about $100 high; with TV, phones, a/c, a pool, restaurant, long, lovely beach, and limited wheelchair access; credit cards accepted; from the U.S. and Canada, reserve through the toll-free Best Western number (800) 528-1234.

BUCERÍAS

The scruffiness of the Bucerías roadside clutter (12 miles, 19 km north of the Puerto Vallarta airport) is deceiving. Bucerías ("Place of the Divers") has the longest, creamiest sand beach on the Bay of Banderas. Local people flock there on Sundays for beach play and fresh seafood in any one of a dozen seaside palapa restaurants.

Bucerías (pop. around 5,000) offers many options. It is basically a country town of about four long streets running for a couple of miles parallel to the beach. Small businesses and grocery stores and at least a dozen local-style restaurants can supply services and food. Bucerías, furthermore, has lots of old-fashioned local color, especially in the evenings around the lively market at the south end of the business district.

The beach—seemingly endless and nearly flat, with slowly breaking waves and soft, light gold sand—is good for everything, with shells for the taking, swimming, bodysurfing, boogie-boarding, beginning and intermediate surfing, and surf fishing. Beyond the edges of town, tent camping is customary, especially during Christmas and Easter holidays.

Bucerías Accommodations

At Bucerías's serene north end is the Playas de Huanacaxtle subdivision of big flower-decorated homes of rich Mexicans and North Americans. Sprinkled among the intimate, palm-shaded *retornos* (cul-de-sacs) are a number of good bungalow-style beachside lodgings.

The family-style **Bungalows Princess,** a lineup of luxurious beach cabañas, looks out on the blue Bay of Banderas beneath the rustling fronds of lazy coco palms (Retorno Destiladeras, Playas Huanacaxtle, Bucerías, Nayarit 63732, tel. 322-801-00, 322-801-10, fax 322-800-68). Their two-story beachfront bungalows provide all the ingredients for a restful beachside vacation for a family or group of friends. Behind them, past the swimming pools, a stone's throw from the beach, a motel-style lineup of suites fills the economy needs of couples and small families. They have a total of 36 bungalows and suites. The big beach bungalows rent from about $75 d; off-beach suites, from about $60 d. Bargain for discounts and for long-term rates, especially during low Jan.-Feb., May-June and Sept.-Nov. months; TV with HBO, phones, a/c, a minimarket, and two pools; credit cards accepted.

Nearby **Bungalows Picos** shares the same palm-shadowed Bucerías beachfront (Av. Los

at Bucerías on the Bay of Banderas

Pico and Retorno Pontoque, Playas Huanacaxtle, Bucerías, Nayarit 63732, tel. 322-804-
70, 322-801-31). A rambling, Mexican family-
style complex, Bungalows Pico clusters around
a big inner pool-patio, spreading to a second
bungalow tier beside a breezy beachside pool
area. These units, which enjoy ocean views,
are the most popular. During low season, the
management offers promotions, such as three
nights for the price of two. Discounts for long-
term rentals are also generally available. Bargain
under all conditions. Their 47 bungalows, many
with kitchenettes, run from about $45 d; four
small units rent for about $27, with TV, a/c, and
two pools; credit cards accepted)

Sharing the same plumy beachside as Bungalows Pico and Princess is **Suites Atlas,** a
Spanish-style tile and stucco villa built around a
luxurious beachside pool-patio garden (Retorno
Destiladeras, Bucerías, Nayarit 63732, tel. 322-
802-35, 322-800-659). The units are huge and
deluxe, sleeping about six, with fully equipped
kitchenettes, all with a/c. Try for one of the
choice upstairs front units, which enjoy private
balconies and ocean vistas. The 11 units rent
from around $100/day; the special $1200/month
rate is generally available during low seasons of
Jan.-Feb., May-June, and Sept.-November.

Casa Blanca, on the opposite, south side of
town (corner Galeana and Cárdenas) is a similarly elegant Spanish-style villa of large, tastefully furnished kitchenette apartments beside an
elegant beachside pool-patio-garden. Amenities
include a palm-thatched view house perched in a
lush green rubber tree right above the beach.
Get your reservation in early for one of the three
upper units, which enjoy palm-silhouetted ocean
sunset vistas. The Casa Blanca units are
rentable, preferably monthly, through the rep-
utable and friendly agents Mina Sánchez de Gonzales and her husband Carlos, whose office is on
the highway at the south edge of town. If Casa
Blanca is full, Mina and Carlos will do their best to
find you something just as good (Gonzales Real
Estate, P.O. Box 95 Aeropuerto, Puerto Vallarta
48300, Jalisco, tel. 322-802-94, 322-801-27).
The nine luxury suites with kitchenettes rent for
about $1000/month; with TV, phones, and a/c; a
boat-launch ramp is on the street.

In a big, palm-shaded grassy lot right near
the beach, **Bucerías Trailer Park** (on Calle
Lázaro Cárdenas, a quarter-mile south of the

business district) would be just fine even if it
hadn't once been owned by Elizabeth Taylor.
That, however, makes it even better, because
Mayo and Fred, the present owners, have converted the luxurious living room of the former
residence into a homey restaurant-social room,
which they call Restaurant Pira-pa. Ask them
what it means. Get your winter reservation in
early (P.O. Box 39-A Aeropuerto, Puerto Vallarta, Jalisco 48300, tel. 322-802-65). Their 48
spaces rent for about $12/day, with all hookups,
showers, toilets, a boat ramp nearby, and good
drinkable well water.

Pie In The Sky
Even if only passing through Bucerías, don't
miss Pie In the Sky, the little living room-bakery
of Don and Teri Murray, entrepreneurs who
have developed a thriving business soothing
the collective sweet tooth of Puerto Vallarta's
expatriate and retiree colony. Their chocolate-nut
cookies have to be tasted to be believed. Near
the highway, watch for their sign (Av. Los Picos
13, Playas de Huanacaxtle, Bucerías, Nayarit,
next to big Motel Los Picos, tel. 803-06, open
Mon.-Fri. 9-5).

PUNTA MITA COUNTRY

A few miles north of Bucerías, slow down at the
intersection where the Punta Mita Hwy. forks
west from Hwy. 200 and stop at the local office
of the **Nayarit State Tourist Information Office**
(Mon.-Fri. 9-1 and 3-5). The officer in charge,
friendly, knowledgeable, and locally born, Jose
D. Elizondo, can answer most any question
about the Nayarit half of the Bay of Banderas.

Drivers, mark your mileage at the Hwy. 200
turnoff before you head west along the Punta
Mita Highway. Within a mile you'll see the little
town of **Cruz de Huanacaxtle** drowsing downhill above its little fishing harbor. Although it has
stores, a few simple lodgings, and a protected
boat and yacht anchorage, Cruz de Huanacaxtle has no good beach.

Half a mile (at around Mile 2, Km 3) further on,
however, a left side road leads to beautiful **Playa
Manzanillo** and the Hotel and Trailer Park
Piedra Blanca. The beach itself, a carpet of fine,
golden-white coral sand, stretches along a little
cove sheltered by a limestone headland, thus

Piedra Blanca, "White Stone." This place was made for peaceful vacationing, with a long list of good low-key beach activities: snorkeling at nearby **Playa Piedra Blanca** (on the opposite side of the headland), fishing from the beach or rocks, or by boat (which you can launch on the beach or hire in the harbor at Cruz de Huanacaxtle), camping by RV or tent in the trailer park or in the adjacent grassy dunes.

The **Hotel** is a small, friendly, family-managed resort. The best of the big (not luxurious, but comfortable), suites enjoy upstairs ocean views. All the ingredients—a good tennis court, a shelf of used novels to read, and a rustic palapa restaurant beside an inviting beach-view pool-patio seem perfect for tranquil relaxation. The 31 suites with kitchenettes rent from about $40 d low season, $220 weekly, $670 monthly, or $60 high, with a/c; credit cards accepted, reserve by writing directly (P.O. Box 48, Bucerias, Nayarit 63732) or phoning their Guadalajara agent: tel. 36-176-031.

The hotel also manages the **trailer park** in the beachside (but largely unshaded) lot next door. Although the trailer park residents aren't supposed to be able to use the pool, the hotel management doesn't seem to mind. This is a popular winter park, so get your reservation in early. Their 26 spaces rent for about $12/day, $70/week, $240/month, with all hookups, showers, and toilets; pets okay.

Past Piedra Blanca, the highway winds for 12 miles (19 km) to Punta Mita through the bushy green jungle country at the foot of the Sierra Vallejo, empty except for a few scattered ranchos. Side roads draw adventurous travelers, often to hidden little beaches, for a day (or a week) of tranquil swimming, snorkeling, and beachcombing. Precautions: Get out and walk before your vehicle gets stuck on these side roads. Campers bring everything, including plenty of drinking water. If in doubt about anything, don't hesitate to inquire locally, or ask Jose Elizondo in the little information office back at Hwy. 200.

Rock coral, the limestone skeleton of living coral, becomes gradually more common on the beaches (thus tinting the water aqua and the sand white). As the highway approaches Punta Mita the living reef offshore becomes intact and continuous.

Playa Las Destiladeras

Marked (at Mile 5, Km 8) by a pair of palapa restaurants at the beginning of a mile of white sand, Playa Las Destiladeras is a beach-lover's heaven. Nearly flat, its two- to five-foot waves roll in gently, giving good bodysurfing and boogieboarding rides. Surfing gets better the closer you get to the end-of-beach **Punta El Burro** (known also as Punta Veneros) headland, where good left-breaking waves make it popular with local surfers.

The intriguing label *destiladeras* (seepage) originates with the fresh water that oozes from the cliffs past Punta El Burro, which often col-

sea cucumbers out to dry at Corral de Riscos, near Punta Mita at the northwest tip of the Bay of Banderas

lects in freshwater pools right beside the ocean. (Campers, if you happen upon one of these seepage pools, it will probably solve your water problem.)

Playa Pontoque And Playa Anclote

A "Restaurante Paraiso Escondido" sign (Mile 8, Km 13) marks the downhill, vine-draped forest road to Playa Pontoque, an intimate jungle-backed crescent of coral-white sand. Here, the living reef lies offshore, ripe for snorkeling and fishing (red snapper and toro). Surfing, boogieboarding, and bodysurfing are fine when the snorkeling isn't.

The restaurant, specializing in seafood and steaks, caters to tourist tastes. Relatively few Mexican families come here. The owner says that they prefer a continuous shoreline to Pontoque's scenic, outcropping-dotted sand and offshore reef. The people who do come seem to have a great time, strolling, swimming, snorkeling, and tidepooling. Acacia boughs overhang the upper edge of the sand, forming shady nooks, perfect for lazing away the day and night. If you decide to camp, bring water, as the restaurant has none to spare.

Playa Anclote ("Anchor Beach"), farther west (Mile 13, Km 21), gets its name from the galleon (or pirate) shipwreck anchor that one of the beachside palapa restaurants displays. Playa Anclote is a broad, half-mile-long curving strand of soft, very fine, coral sand. The water is shallow for a long distance out and the waves are gentle and long-breaking, good for surfing, boogieboarding, and bodysurfing.

Tent **camping** is also a good possibility under big trees at both ends of the beach. Stores in the small town of Emiliano Zapata (half a mile away, commonly known as Punta Mita) can furnish the necessities, including drinking water.

Punta Mita

The Punta Mita Hwy. ends at **Corral del Riscos,** an islet-enfolded aqua lagoon, bordered by a long coral-sand beach. A few folks relax beneath a lineup of restaurant palapas; boats rest at the edge of the water, while fishermen talk and laugh as they mend their nets.

The two bare-rock islets **Isla del Mono** and **Isla de las Abandonadas** shelter the lagoon. The former name comes from a *mono* (monkey) face that people see in one of the outcroppings; the latter label springs from the legend of the fishermen who went out to sea, never to return. "Las Abandonadas" were their wives who waited on the islet for years, searching the horizon for their lost husbands.

The local fisherfolk have organized themselves into a cooperative whose representative, friendly Jesus Casilla, welcomes tourists in the parking lot daily 9-6. Jesus rents boogieboards, snorkel gear, and surfboards (all $5 for two hours). He can also arrange sportfishing launches (three-hour trip, about $65 complete) and snorkeling and wildlife viewing boat-tours to the pristine offshore wildlife sanctuaries, **Islas Las Marietas.** During a typical half-day trip, visitors may glimpse dolphins, sea turtles, sometimes whales, and visit breeding grounds for brown and blue-footed boobies, Heerman's gulls, and many more birds.

When he is not working, Jesus follows his love, surfing, for which he is an instructor. He says that the best surfing in the Bay of Banderas are the left-breaks off Isla del Mono, and off the lighthouse point, about a quarter-mile to the south.

Plenty of open land nearby with trees provides breezy **camping** sites, while a clean basic store, **Abarrotes Las Palmeras,** can supply milk, cheese, juice, some meats, groceries, and fruit (in addition to the bountiful coconut grove in the back yard).

Getting There

Transportes Pacifico (Insurgentes 282, tel. 210-15) buses leave Puerto Vallarta for Tepic via Nuevo Vallarta (highway only) and Bucerías about once an hour. In addition, a small local Transportes Pacifico bus completes the Punta Mita roundtrip a few times daily.

A larger **Auto Transportes Medina** bus also completes daily roundtrips between their Punta Mita and their Puerto Vallarta station at 1279 Brasil (tel. 269-43, at Honduras, one block south of the Buenaventura Hotel and three blocks away from the beach).

SOUTH TO MANZANILLO

ALONG THE ROAD
TO BARRA DE NAVIDAD

The country between Puerto Vallarta and Barra de Navidad is as unsullied as the new road that traverses it. Development has barely begun to penetrate its vast tracts of mountainous jungle, tangled thorny scrub, and pine-clad summit forests. Footprints rarely mark mile after mile of its curving, golden strands.

This is a landscape ripe for adventurers—traveling by thumb, by bus, or by car or RV—who enjoy getting away from the tourist track. Fortunately, everyone who travels south of Puerto Vallarta doesn't have to be a Daniel Boone. The coastal strip within a few miles of the highway has aquired some comforts—stores, trailer parks, campgrounds, hotels, and a scattering of small resorts—enough to become well known to Guadalajara people as The Costa Alegre, "The Happy Coast."

This modicum of amenities makes it easy for all travelers to enjoy what local people have for years: plenty of sun, fresh seafood, clear blue water, and sandy beaches, some of which stretch for miles, while others are tucked away in little rocky coves like pearls in an oyster.

Heading Out

If you're driving, note your odometer mileage (or reset it to zero) as you pass the Pemex station at kilometer marker 214 on Hwy. 200 at the south edge of Puerto Vallarta. In the open country south of there, mileage and roadside kilometer markers are a useful way to remember where your little paradise is hidden.

If you're not driving, simply hop onto one of the many southbound Transportes Cihuatlán second-class buses that depart from their little station at the corner of Madero and Constitución. Let the driver know a few minutes beforehand where along the road you want to get down.

CHICO'S PARADISE

The last outpost on the Puerto Vallarta tour-bus circuit is Chico's Paradise in the lush jungle country 13 miles (22 km, at Km 192) from the south edge of Puerto Vallarta. Here, the clear, cool Rio Tuito cascades over a collection of smooth, friendly granite boulders. Chico's restaurant itself is a big multilevel palapa which overlooks the entire lovely scene—deep green pools for swimming, flat warm rocks for sunning, and gurgling gentle waterfalls for splashing.

A few homesteads and a couple of down-scale rival restaurants dot the streamside near-by, but the original Chico's still dominates (although their reputation rests mainly on the beauty of the setting rather than the quality of their rather expensive menu).

But pay no mind, as the place is unforgettably lovely, a perfect spot to shed the cares of the world for a few days. Although there are no formal lodgings, there are a number of good **camping** spots up and down the river. **Stores** at Boca de Tomatlán, three miles downhill, can provide supplies. Local guides offer horseback rides along the river and into the hills. They could lead you on day or overnight treks into the wildlife-rich **Sierra Lagunillas,** which rise above both sides of the river.

CABO CORRIENTES COUNTRY

El Tuito

The town of El Tuito, at Km 170 (27 miles, 44 km from Puerto Vallarta) appears from the highway as nothing more than a bus stop. It doesn't even have a gas station. Most visitors pass by without even giving a second glance. This is a pity, because El Tuito (pop. about 3,000) is a friendly little place that spreads along a long main street to a pretty square about a mile from the highway.

El Tuito enjoys at least two claims to fame: besides being the **mescal** capital of western Jalisco, it's the jumping-off spot for the seldom-visited coastal hinterland of Cabo Corrientes, the southernmost lip of the Bay of Banderas. This is pioneer country, a land of wild beaches and forests, unpenetrated by electricity, phone, or paved roads. Wild creatures still abound: Turtles come ashore to lay their eggs, hawks soar, parrots swarm, and the faraway scream of the jaguar can yet be heard in the night.

The rush for the *raicilla,* as local connoisseurs call El Tuito mescal, begins on Saturday when men crowd into town and begin up-ending bottles around noon, without even bothering to sit down. For a given individual, this cannot last too long, so the fallen are continually replaced by fresh arrivals all weekend.

Flat, friendly rocks decorate the clear River Tuito, which flows beneath the palapa at Chico's Paradise.

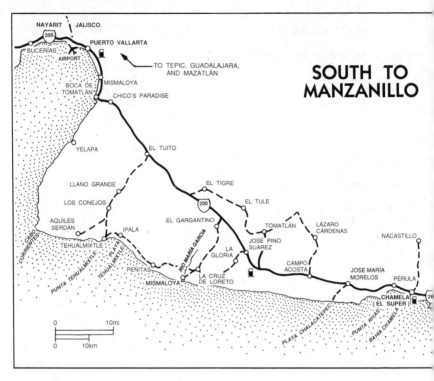

NAYARIT | JALISCO
PUERTO VALLARTA
BUCERÍAS
AIRPORT
TO TEPIC, GUADALAJARA,
AND MAZATLÁN
BOCA DE
TOMATLÁN
MISMALOYA
CHICO'S PARADISE

**SOUTH TO
MANZANILLO**

YELAPA
EL TUITO
LLANO GRANDE
EL TIGRE
LOS CONEJOS
EL TULE
AQUILES
SERDÁN
EL GARGANTINO
IPALA
TOMATLÁN
LÁZARO
CÁRDENAS
NACASTILLO
TEHUALMIXTLE
CABO CORRIENTES
PLAYA TEHUALMIXTLE
PUNTA TEHUALMIXTLE
RÍO MARÍA GARCÍA
LA
GLORIA
JOSÉ PINO
SUAREZ
PEÑITAS
LA CRUZ
DE LORETO
CAMPO
ACOSTA
JOSÉ MARÍA
MORELOS
PÉRULA
MISMALOYA
CHAMELA
(EL SUPER)
PLAYA CHALACATEPEC
PUNTA RIVAS
BAHÍA CHAMELA

0   10mi
0   10km

Although El Tuito is famous for the *raicilla,* it is not the source. *Raicilla* is made from the sweet sap of the maguey plants (a close relative of the cactus-like "century plant," which blooms once then dies) of the *ejido* (cooperative farm) of Cicatan, six miles out along the dirt road that heads to the coast west of town.

Along The Road To Aquiles Serdán
You can get to the coast with or without your own wheels. If you're driving, it should be a strong, high-clearance vehicle (pickup, jeep, very maneuverable RV, or VW van, filled with gas); if you're not driving, trucks and VW taxi-vans *(kombis* or *colectivos)* make daily trips. Their destinations include the coastal hamlet of Aquiles Serdán, the storied fishing cove of Tehualmixtle, and the agricultural village of Ipala beside the wide Bahía de Tehualmixtle. The fare runs about $5 per person; inquire at the Hwy. 200 crossing, or the west end of the El

Tuito central plaza, where the road heads into the country.

Getting there along the bumpy, rutted, some-times steep 28-mile (45-km) dirt track is half the fun of Aquiles Serdán (pop. around 200). About six miles (10 km) from Hwy. 200, you'll pass through the lands of the mescal cooperative, Cicatan, marked only by a whitewash-and-thatch *bodega* (storage house) in front of a tiny school on the right. On the left, you'll soon glimpse a field of maguey in the distance. A few dozen families (who live in the hills past the far side of the field) quietly go about their business of tending their maguey plants and extracting, fer-menting, and distilling the precious sap into their renowned *raicilla.*

The road dips up and down the rest of the way, over sylvan hillsides dotted with oak *(ro-bles),* through intimate stream valleys perfect for parking an RV or setting up a tent, and past the hardscrabble rancho-hamlets of Llano

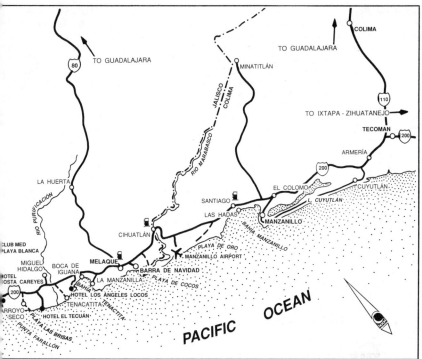

Grande ("Broad Plain"; 15 miles, 24 km, a small store) and Los Conejos ("The Rabbits"; 21 miles, 34 km).

You can't get lost, because there's only one route until a few miles past Los Conejos, where a fork (26 miles, 42 km) marks your approach to Aquiles Serdán. The left branch continues to Maito and Tehualmixtle. A mile and a half along the right branch you will arrive at the Rio Tecolotlán. Aquiles Serdan is on the far bank, across 100 yards of watery sand. Fortunately, however, the riverbed road is concrete-bottomed, allowing you to drive right across any time other than after a storm.

Aquiles Serdán

The Aquiles Serdán villagers see so few outsiders that you will become their attraction of the week. Wave and say hello, buy a *refresco*, stroll around town, and, after a while, the kids will stop crowding around and the adults will stop

staring when they've found out that you, too, are human. By that time, someone may even have even invited you (accept, of course) into their tree-branch-walled, clean dirt-floor house for some fresh fish-fillet tacos, fresh tomatoes, and beans.

Aquiles Serdán basks above the lily-edged river lagoon, which during the June-Oct. rainy season usually breaks through the beach-sand-bar and drains directly into the surf half a mile below the town. During the dry season, however, the lagoon wanders lazily up the coast for a few miles. In any case, the white sand beach is accessible only by boat (which you can borrow or hire at the village).

If you do, you'll have miles of untouched white sand and surf all to yourself for days of camping, beachcombing, shell collecting, surf fishing, wildlife viewing and, if the waves permit, swimming, surfing, boogieboarding, and snorkeling. The town's two stores can provide your necessities.

Tehualmixtle

Back at the fork (26 miles, 42 km from the highway) continue along the left branch about three miles through Maito (pop. around 100, one store) to another fork (29 miles, 47 km). The right branch goes steeply up and then down a rough track to the right, which soon levels out on the cliff above the idyllic fishing cove of Tehualmixtle. It's a blue nook behind a headland, where a few launches float, tethered and sheltered from the open sea. To one side, swells wash over a submerged wreck, while an ancient, moss-stained warehouse crumbles above a rocky little beach. At the end of the road downhill, a beachside palapa invites visitors with drinks and fresh-out-of-the-water oysters, lobster, dorado, and red snapper.

Owner-operator Candelario is the moving force behind this pocket-sized paradise. After your repast, and a couple more bottles of beer for good measure, he might tell you his version of the history of this coast—of legends of sunken galleons, or of the days when the old warehouse stored cocaine for shipment to the United States. (Coca-Cola, by the way, got its name from the cocaine that, generations ago, was legally added to produce "the pause that refreshes.")

Nowadays, however, Tehualmixtle serves as a resting point for occasional sailboats, travelers, fisherfolk, and those who enjoy the rewards of clear-water snorkeling and scuba diving around the sunken shrimp trawler and the rocky shoreline nearby. Several level spots beside the cove invite camping or RV parking. Candelario will gladly supply you with your stomach's delight of choice seafood and drinks.

Southeast Of Tehualmixtle

Returning back up the road above the cove, glimpse southward toward the azure Bay of Tehualmixtle washing its gently curving white-sand ribbon, the Playa de Tehualmixtle. The village of **Ipala,** three miles down the road, is supply headquarters for the occasional visitors drawn by the good fishing, beachcombing, and camping prospects of the Playa de Tehualmixtle. Being on the open ocean, its waves are usually rough, especially in the afternoon. Experienced swimmers who can judge undertow and surf should act as lifeguards for anyone else who's thinking of swimming.

From Ipala (32 miles, 52 km), you can either retrace your path back to the highway at El Tuito, or continue down the coast (where the road gets rougher before it gets better) through the hamlet and beach of **Peñitas** (39 miles, 63 km, a few stores, restaurants), past **Mismaloya** (49 miles, 79 km), the site of a University of Guadalajara turtle-hatching station (turn right onto the dirt trail just before the concrete bridge over the broad Río María Garcia).

From Mismaloya, return to the bridge, continue over the river three miles, and you will soon be back to the 20th century at **La Cruz de Loreto** (52 miles, 84 km, many stores, sidewalks, electric lights and phones). From there, a snappy 13 miles along the gravel, graded road through La Gloria brings you to José Piño Suarez (65 miles, 105 km) at Km 124, 28 miles south of where you started at El Tuito.

PLAYA CHALACATEPEC

Playa Chalacatepec lazes in the tropical sun just six miles from the highway at Km 88. Remarkably few people, however, seem to know of its charms except a handful of local youths and the occasional families who come on Sunday outings.

Playa Chalacatepec, with three distinct parts, has something for everyone: on the south side, a wild, arrow-straight miles-long strand with crashing open-ocean breakers; in the middle, a low, wave-tossed, rocky point; and on the north, a long, tranquil, curving fine-sand beach.

The north beach, shielded by the point, has gently rolling breakers good for surfing, body-surfing, and safe swimming. Shells seasonally carpet its gradual white slope, and visitors have even left a pair of palapa shelters. These seem ready-made for camping by night and barbecuing fish by day with the plentiful driftwood lying around for the taking.

The point, Punta Chalacatepec, which separates the two beaches, is good for pole fishing on its surf-washed flanks and tidepooling in its rocky crevices. Folks with RVs can pull off and park either along the approach road just above the beach or along tracks (beware of soft spots) downhill in the tall acacia scrub that borders the sand.

One of the few natural amenities that Playa Chalacatepec lacks is water, however. You'll have bring your own from the town back on the highway.

How To Get There

At kilometer marker 88, just as you're entering little José María Morelos (pop. about 2,000), turn toward the beach at the corner with the auto-parts store marked with a big Bardahl sign. Besides oil and batteries, the store sells a few snack-groceries. A number of better-stocked stores nearby sell water and more substantial supplies.

The road, although steep in spots, is easily negotiable by passenger cars and small-to-medium RVs. Owners of big rigs should should do a test run, however. On foot, the road is an easy two-hour hike (all of which probably won't be necessary because of the many farm pickups that pass that way).

Mark your odometer at the highway. Continue over brushy hills and past fields and pastures until Mile 5.2 (Km 8.4) where the road forks sharply right. You take the left track, however, and pass a gate (close it after yourself). Atop the dune, glimpse the mangrove lagoon (bring a kayak or rubber boat for wildlife-watching) distance to the left. Downhill, at Mile 6.0 (Km 9.7) you will be at Playa Chalacatepec.

CHAMELA BAY

Most longtime visitors know Jalisco's Costa Alegre through Barra de Navidad and two big, beautiful, beach-lined bays: Tenacatita and Chamela. Tranquil Bahía de Chamela, the most northerly of the two, is broad, blue, dotted with islands, and lined by a strip of fine, honey-yellow sand.

Stretching five miles south from the sheltering Punta Rivas headland near Perula village, Chamela Bay is open but calm. A chain of intriguingly labeled rocky *islas,* such as Cocinas ("Kitchens"), Negrita ("Little Black One"), and Pajarera ("Place of Birds"), scatters the strong Pacific swells into gentle billows by the time they roll onto the beaches.

Besides its natural amenities, Chamela Bay has three bungalow complexes, one mentionable motel, two trailer parks and an unusual campground. The focal point of this low-key resort area is the Km 72 highway corner (88 miles, 142 km, from Puerto Vallarta, 46 miles, 74 km, to Barra de Navidad). This spot, marked "Chamela" on many maps, is known simply as **El Super** by local people. (The supermarket and neighboring bank have closed, and are filled with the owner's antique car collection. El Super, nevertheless, lives on in the minds of the local folks.)

Beaches And Activities

Chamela Bay's beaches are variations on one continous strip of sand, from Playa Rosadas in the south, through Playa Chamela in the middle to Playas Fortuna and Perula at the north end.

Curving behind the sheltering headland **Playa Perula** is the broadest and most tranquil beach of Chamela Bay. It is best for children and a snap for boat launching, swimming, and fishing from the rocks nearby. A dozen pangas usually line the water's edge, ready to take visitors on fishing excursions (figure $15 per hour) and

Accommodations are often available (drop in only) to the public at Centro Vacational Chamela, the Chamela Bay teacher's resort.

snorkeling around the offshore islets. A line of seafood palapas provides the food and drinks for the fisherfolk and mostly Mexican families who know and enjoy this scenic little village-cove.

Playas Fortuna, Chamela, and Rosadas: Heading south, the beach gradually changes character. The surf roughens, the slope steepens, and the sand narrows from around 200 feet at Perula to perhaps 100 feet at the south end of the bay. Civilization also thins out. The dusty village of stores, small eateries, vacation homes, and beachfront palapa restaurants that lines Playa Fortuna has given way to farmland and scattered houses at Playa Chamela. Two miles farther on, grassy dunes above trackless sand line Playa Rosada, frequented only by occasional strollers.

The gradually varying vigor of the waves and the isolation of the beach determine the place where you can most indulge your own favorite pastimes: For bodysurfing and boogieboarding, Rosada and Chamela are best; and while windsurfing is usually possible anywhere on Chamela Bay most of the time, it will be generally best beyond the tranquil waves at La Fortuna. For surf fishing, best try casting beyond the vigorous, breaking billows of Rosada. And likewise, Rosada, being the most isolated, will be the place where you'll most likely find that beachcombing and shell-collecting treasure you've been wishing for.

Beach Hiking, Jogging, and Bicycling: The five-mile curving strand of Chamela Bay is perfect for a morning hike from Rosada Beach (to get there, ride a Transportes Cihuatlán second-class bus to around the Km 65 marker, where a dirt road heads a half mile to the beach.) With the sun comfortably at your back, you can walk all the way to Perula if you want, stopping for refreshments at any one of a dozen palapas along the way.

The firm sand of Chamela Bay beaches is good for jogging, even for bicycling, provided you don't mind cleaning the sand out of the gears afterwards.

Accommodations

The El Super corner is hard to miss. Far removed from his homeland, an understandably forlorn Polynesian god stands in continuous vigil across from the corner, silently directing people down the side road to Chamela Beach and Villa Polinesia one mile away.

Villa Polinesia's owners, who live in Guadalajara, call it a "camping club." The description fits. It is the only place in Mexico, they say, "to allow you to meet nature." The beach and bay certainly set the mood: soft, golden sand, island-silhouetted sunsets, tranquil surf, abundant birds and fish; sometimes dolphins, and occasionally great manta rays, leap from the water offshore.

For a campground, Villa Polinesia's facilities are luxurious. The lovely, palm-shadowed complex has two tall, elaborate palapa restaurant-bars, a minimarket, drinkable water, hot water, communal showers, toilets, and a laundry.

They offer four kinds of accommodations. Most luxurious are a dozen open-air oceanfront Swiss Family Robinson-style **cabañas,** each with a cooking-eating area, a toilet and shower downstairs, and a pair of thatch-roofed bedrooms with soft floor-sleeping pads upstairs.

There is much more. Besides half an acre of space for **camping,** they have about three dozen concrete "tents," each with a pair of soft sleeping pads, electricity, and a small screened ventilation window inside. These may be a bit hot for sleeping during the warm half of the year; bring your own tent, which is easier to adjust for temperature than their clever concrete installations. In addition, they have a pleasant, shady 15-space **trailer park** with all hookups, right next to the communal showers and toilet.

A minor drawback to all this, besides there being no pool, is their somewhat steep rates: the open-air cabañas go for the same price as an economical hotel room: about $27 for four, $18 for one or two; the trailer spaces go for about $14 per day; tent spaces rent for $5/day per person. These prices, however, are subject to bargaining and discounts any time other than peak holidays. Their address is simply Carretera 200, Km 72, Barra de Navidad a Puerto Vallarta, Chamela, Jalisco, no phone; for more info and reservations, write, or call Guadalajara tel. 36-223-940, or Mexico City tel. 5-5101-464.

Right next door to the Villa Polinesia stands **Bungalows Mayar Chamela,** perhaps the most attractive moderate accommodation between Puerto Vallarta and Barra de Navidad. The spacious, well-maintained units surround a palmy, banana-fringed pool and patio, gleaming with loving care. With the beach just steps away, no wonder people come from all over the world to stay here for months on end. Get your winter reservation in early (Km 72, Carretera Puerto Vallarta, Chamela, Jalisco, no phone; 18 kitchenette-bungalows, about $25 for two, $42 for four, about $500 per month, fans only; write the reservations manager, Arturo Javier Yañez G. at Obregon 1425 S.L., Guadalajara, Jalisco, tel. 36-440-044 and 36-439-318).

A Motel, A Trailer Park, And Two More Bungalows

At Km 76, a sign marks a dirt road to Playas Fortuna and Perula. About two miles downhill, right on the beach, you can't miss the bright yellow stucco **Bungalows Playa Dorada,** the biggest building on Chamela Bay. More a motel than bungalows, its three tiers of very plain rooms and kitchenette-suites are nearly empty except on weekends and Mexican holidays.

Playa Dorada's two saving graces, however, are the beach, which curves gracefully to the scenic little fishing nook of Perula, and the motel's inviting palm-fringed pool patio. The best-located rooms (which could be quite habitable at times other than the raucous Christmas and Easter holidays) are on the top floor, overlooking the ocean. With bargaining, you might be able to stay there most any time for a song (Perula, Jalisco, Km 76, Carretera 200 Melaque-Puerto Vallarta, Jalisco, no phone; 18 units with kitchenettes sleeping four, about $47, 18 rooms sleeping two to three, about $20, parking).

Nearby is the funky **Punta Perula Trailer Park,** with about 16 usable spaces (out of 20) right on the beach a few blocks north of the hotel, with all hookups, a fish-cleaning sink, and showers and toilets. Although it lacks shade and it's not fancy, Playa Perula Trailer Park residents enjoy stores nearby, good fishing, and a lovely beach for a front yard (Perula, Km 76, Carretera Puerto Vallarta, Jalisco; rates are low, but indefinite—although one of the residents said he was paying a monthly rate that amounted to about $5 a day)

The **Centro Vacacional Chamela** is a teachers' vacation retreat that rents its unoccupied units right on pristine Rosada Beach to the general public. The building itself is a modern, two-story apartment house with a well-maintained pool and patio. An outdoor palapa stands by the pool and another open room invites cards and conversation. The units themselves are large,

bright, and airy one-bedrooms, sleeping four, with sea views and kitchens. (They rent for about $35, drop-in only; on nonholiday weekdays the place is often nearly empty. Have a look by following the upper of two side roads at the big concrete "47" monument near the Km 66 marker. Within a mile you'll be there. Ask one of the teachers to explain the significance of the "47."

If the teachers' retreat turns you away, try next door at the **Club Playa Chamela,** perhaps the most downscale time-share in Mexico, if not the world. For a one-time $1000 fee, you can get one idyllic week for each of 20 years there. In the meantime, while the units (about 10 funky nondescript stucco kitchenette cottages that sleep four in a young palm grove, no pool, palapa sometimes-restaurant) are being sold, the owner is renting them out. Contact Jose Santana, at Venezuela 719, Guadalajara, tel. 36-101-103, or 36-103-487 for information and reservations. The manager wasn't saying how much they rent for, but the 20 weeks for a $1000 amounts to $50 a week; you might expect to pay double that, with bargaining.

Camping

For RVs, the best spots are the trailer parks at **Villa Polinesia** and the **Perula Trailer Park** (see above). Car-camping sites are likewise available at the Villa Polinesia for $10 per day for two.

If you can walk in, however, you can set up a tent anywhere along the bay you like. One of the best places would be the grassy dune along pristine Playa Rosada a few hundred yards north of the Centro Vacacional (Km 66, see above). They have water.

Playa Negro, the pristine little sand crescent that marks the southern end of Chamela Bay, offers still another picnic or camping possibility. Get there by following the dirt road that angles downhill from the highway at the south end of the bridge between Km 63 and Km 64. Turn left at the Chamela village stores beneath the bridge, continue about two miles, bearing left to the end of the road, where the palapa of an old restaurant stands at beachside. This is the southernmost of two islet-protected coves flanking the low Punta Negro headland. With clear, tranquil waters and golden-sand beaches, both coves are great for fishing from the rocks, snorkeling, windsurfing, and swimming. The south-end beach is unoccupied and has plenty of room for tenting and RV parking; a house sits back from the north-end beach about a quarter-mile away on the far side of the point. If you want to camp there, ask them if it's okay: "¿Es bueno campar aca?"

Food
Supplies are available at stores near the **El Super** corner (Km 72) or in the villages of **Perula** (on the beach, turn off at Km 76) and **Chamela** village (follow the side road at the south end of the bridge between Km 64 and 63).

Hearty country Mexican food and hospitality are available at the **Tejaban** restaurant (open daily from breakfast time till 10 or 11 p.m.) at the El Super corner. Two popular local roadside seafood spots are the **La Viuda** ("The Widow," Km 64) and **Don Lupe Mariscos** (Km 63). They both have their own divers who go out daily for fresh fish ($6), octopus *(pulpo)* ($6), conch, clams, oysters, and lobster ($12). Open daily 8 a.m. until around 9 p.m.

Services, Information, And Emergencies
The closest **bank** is 34 miles north at Tomatlán (Km 116, local tel. 322-125, 322-126). A *casetas de larga distancia* (long-distance telephone office) operates at the El Super corner (daily 8-3 and 4-9) and at Pueblo Careyes, the village behind the soccer field at Km 52.

The **Pemex** at El Super usually has unleaded Magna Sin gas. Fill up because the next ónes are 33 miles north at José Piño Suarez (Km 124) and 45 miles south at Melaque (Km 0).

If you get sick, go to your hotel desk. If you're not staying at a hotel, the closest clinic is in Perula (Km 76, four blocks south of the village plaza, no phone) or at Pueblo Careyes at Km 52 (tel. 333-701-57, doctors available daily 8-8). Local **police** (known as the Policia Auxiliar del Estado) are stationed in a pink roadside house at Km 46, no phone.

HOTEL COSTA CAREYES

The Hotel Costa Careyes, one of the little-known gems of Pacific Mexico, is really two hotels in one. After Christmas and before Easter it brims with well-to-do Mexican families letting their hair down. The rest of the year the hotel is a tranquil, tropical retreat basking at the edge of a pristine, craggy cove.

The natural scene sets the tone: a majestic palm grove opens onto a petite sandy beach, set between rocky cliffs. Offshore, the water, deep and crystal clear, is home for dozens of kinds of fish. Overhead, hawks and frigate birds soar, pelicans dive, and boobies and terns skim the waves. At night nearby, turtles carry out their their ancient ritual by silently depositing their precious eggs on the beach where they were born.

As if not to be outdone by nature, the hotel itself is a charming repository of personal touches—shops filled with one-of-a-kind handicrafts, boutiques selling art-to-wear, corridors decorated with stone turtles, whimsical cats and birds, and a toothy wooden crocodile. At night, the grounds glimmer with the lacy shadows of myriad shaded lamps. They illuminate the tufted grove, light the path to a secluded beach, and lead the way up through the cactus-sprinkled hillside thorn forest to a romantic restaurant high above the bay.

Hotel Activities
You can enjoy the delights of Hotel Costa Careyes even if you don't stay overnight. It'll cost you something, but the tariff is quite fair. The gateman sells tickets for about $20/person, completely redeemable for food and drink at the hotel's classy restaurant-bar. You can swim in the pool, sun on the beach, and after dinner you can dance to the combo, which plays nightly.

Overnight guests, on the other hand, can enjoy the use of the hotel's 4,000-foot airstrip, polo field, tennis courts, riding stables, game room, TV room, and aquatic sports shop (snorkeling, kayaks, sailing, deep-sea fishing, boat excursions for picnics, birdwatching, and turtle nesting in season).

Playa Careyes
Careyes is the name of an endangered species of sea turtle that used to lay eggs on the little beach of Careyitos in front of the hotel. Saving the turtles at nearby (Km 52) Playa Careyes, accessible only through hotel property, has now become a major hotel mission. They do allow serious visitors access during hatching times (no camping, please). Check with the hotel desk for information and permission.

SAVING TURTLES

Sea turtles, recognized by their big, strong front flippers, were once so common on Pacific Mexico beaches that trucks were needed to haul away the catches. Times have changed, however. Now, determined corps of hardy volunteers are literally camped out on lonely Pacific Mexico beaches, trying to save the turtles from extinction. This is tricky business, because their poacher-opponents are invariably poor and sometimes armed. Since turtle tracks lead right to the eggs, the trick is to get there before the poachers. If so, the turtle-savers dig up the eggs and hatch them themselves or bury them in a secret location, where hopefully the eggs will hatch unmolested. Whichever the case, the sight of hundreds of new hatchlings returning to the sea—*vale la pena*—is worth the pain for this new generation of Mexican eco-activists.

Once featured on a thousand restaurant menus from Puerto Angel to Mazatlán, turtle meat, turtle soup, and turtle eggs are now illegal. Someday such menus may return, but hopefully not until the sea turtles who once swarmed ashore to lay eggs in the warm sands reappear in comparable numbers.

Although not extinct, Pacific Mexico's three sea turtle species—green, hawksbill, and leatherback—out of seven species worldwide have dwindled to a tiny fraction of previous numbers.

The **green turtle**, *Chelonia mydas,* known locally as the *tortuga verde,* or *caguama* (kah-WA-mah), is named for the color of its fat. Although officially threatened, the prolific green turtle remains relatively numerous. Females sometimes return to shore up to eight times during a year, depositing an aggregate of 500 eggs in a single season. When not

mating or migrating, the vegetarian greens can most often be spotted in lagoons and bays (especially in the Bay of Banderas) nipping at seaweed (sea turtles have no teeth) with their beaks. Adults, usually around three or four feet long and weighing 100-200 pounds, are easily identified out of water by the four big plates on either side of their shells. Green turtle meat was once prized as the main ingredient of turtle soup.

The endangered **hawksbill**, *Eretmochelys imbricata,* has vanished from many Pacific Mexico beaches. Known locally as the *tortuga carey,* (kah-RAY) it was the source of both meat and the lovely translucent "tortoiseshell," which fortunately has been largely supplanted by plastic. Adult *careys,* among the smaller of sea turtles, usually run two to three feet in length and weigh 30-100 pounds. Their usually brown shells are readily identified by their shingle-like overlapping scales. During the late summer and fall (Aug.-Nov.) females come ashore to lay clutches of around 100 eggs in the sand. *Careys,* although preferring fish, mollusks, and shellfish, will eat most anything, including seaweed. When attacked, they can be plucky fighters, inflicting bites with their eagle-sharp "hawksbills."

You will be fortunate indeed, if you ever get a glimpse of the rare **leatherback**, *Dermochelys coriacea,* the world's largest turtle. The leatherback, or *tortuga de cuero,* isn't even known well enough for experts to firmly determine how endangered it is. Tales have been told of fisherfolk netting seven- or eight-foot leatherbacks weighing nearly a ton. If you see even a small one you will recognize it immediately because, instead of shell, its back is of smooth, tough skin, creased with several lengthwise ridges.

Hotel Information
For reservations and more information, write or phone the hotel at Km 53.5 Carretera Barra de Navidad-Puerto Vallarta, Jalisco, tel. (333) 700-50, (333) 700-10, fax (333) 701-07. Rates: 74 rooms, suites, bungalows, and villas, from about $100 low season d, $130 high; one-bedroom suites go for about $130 low, $175 high; two-

bedroom, about $210 low, $265 high; a/c, parking, credit cards accepted, 100-person meeting room.

Getting There
The Hotel Costa Careyes is a few minutes' drive down a cobbled entrance road (bear left all the way) at Km 53.5 (100 miles, 161 km

from Puerto Vallarta, 34 miles, 55 km from Barra de Navidad, and 52 miles, 84 km from the Manzanillo International Airport).

PLAYA LAS BRISAS

For a tranquil day, overnight, or weeklong beach adventure consider Playa Las Brisas, a few miles by the dirt road (turnoff sign near Km 36) through the village of Arroyo Seco.

About two miles long, Playa Las Brisas has two distinct sections: first comes a very broad, white sandy strand decorated by pink-blossomed verbena and pounded by wild, open-ocean waves. For shady tenting or RV parking, a regal coconut grove lines the beach. Before you set up there, however, you should offer a little rent to the owner-caretaker, who may soon show up on a horse. Don't be alarmed by his machete, however; it's merely for husking and cutting the fallen coconuts.

To see the other half of Playa Las Brisas, continue along the road past the little beach-side vacation home subdivision (with a seasonal store and snack bar). You will soon reach an open-ocean beach and headland, backed by a big, level, grassy dune, perfect for tent or RV camping. (Take care not to get stuck in soft spots, however.)

The headland borders the El Tecuán Lagoon, part of the Rancho El Tecuán, whose hilltop hotel and airstrip you can see on the far side of the lagoon. The lagoon is an unusually rich fish and wildlife habitat; see "Hotel El Tecuán" below for details.

Getting There

You reach the village of Arroyo Seco, where stores can furnish supplies, 2.3 miles (3.7 km) from the highway (at Km 36). At the central "plaza," a dirt lot occupied only by what look like ramshackle ex-market stalls, turn left, then immediately right at the Conasupo rural store, then left again, heading up the steep hillside dirt road. In the valley on the other side, bear right at the fork at the mango grove, and soon you will be in the majestic beach-bordering palm grove.

HOTEL EL TECUÁN

Little was spared in perching the Hotel El Tecuán above its small kingdom of beach, lagoon, and palm-brushed rangeland. It was to be the centerpiece of a sprawling vacationland, with marina, golf course, and hundreds of houses and condos. Although those plans have yet to materialize, the hotel still stands, with an ambience more like an African safari lodge than a Mexican beach resort.

Masculinity bulges out of its architecture. Its corridors are lined with massive, polished tree trunks, fixed by brawny master joints to thick, hand-hewn mahogany beams. The view restaurant is patterned after the midships of a Manila Galleon, complete with a pair of varnished tree-trunk masts reaching into inky darkness, as if stretching to the night sky above. If the restaurant could only sway, the illusion would be complete.

The rooms are comfortable and, as expected, pleasantly masculine. The best have private balconies, which, in addition to a luxurious ocean vista, overlook the elegantly manicured grounds and blue pool and palapa-patio a hundred feet below.

Hotel Activities

It is perhaps fortunate that the hotel and its surroundings, part of the big **Rancho Tecuán,** may never be developed. Being private, public access has always been limited, so the Rancho has become a de facto habitat-refuge for the rapidly diminishing local animal population. Wildcats, ocelots, small crocodiles, snakes, and turtles hunt in the mangroves that edge the lagoon and the tangled forest that climbs the surrounding hills. The lagoon itself nurtures hosts of water birds and shoals of snook *(robalo)* and snapper *(pargo)*.

Guests can enjoy the hotel's wildlife-viewing opportunities, first by simply walking down to the lagoon, where big white herons and egrets perch and preen in the mangroves. Don't forget your binoculars, sun hat, mosquito repellent, telephoto camera, and identification book. If you hire a boat (only during the high winter-spring season) or bring your own inflatable raft or canoe you could mount an even more rewarding wildlife-viewing outing.

If interested in fishing, you can, of course, hire boats or launch your own in the lagoon. Be sure to talk to the manager, Paul Siliceau, before you do, however; he'll tell you what's biting and how to hook them.

Hotel El Tecuán offers plenty of jogging and walking opportunities. For starters, stroll along the lagoonside entrance road and back (three miles) or south along the beach to the Rio Purificación and back (four miles; take water, mosquito repellent, sunscreen, a hat, and something to carry your beachcombing treasures in). There are plenty of fish in the river, so you might want to take your fishing rod, too.

Besides swimming in the pool or the lagoon, you can enjoy the hotel's excellent tennis (bring your own racquet and balls) and volleyball courts. Rent a bicycle (or ride your own) along miles of ranch roads and the long beach airstrip.

Tecuán Beach

The focal point of the long, wild, white-sand Playa Tecuán is at the north end, where, at low tide, the lagoon's waters rush into the sea. Platoons of water birds—giant brown herons, snowy egrets, and squads of pelicans, ibises, and grebes—stalk and dive for fish trapped in the shallow, rushing current.

On the beach nearby, the sand curves southward beneath a rocky point, where the roiling surf strews rainbow carpets of limpet, clam, and snail shells. There the waves rise sharply, angling shoreward with good intermediate and advanced surfing breaks. Casual swimmers stay out, however; the surf is much too powerful for safety.

Hotel Information

For more information, contact the hotel at Km 33.5, Carretera 200, Jalisco (tel. 333-70-132; 36 rooms and suites, from $63 d, $75 t, suites $75 and up; a/c, a restaurant, 4,000-foot paved airstrip, bar, long-distance phone; credit cards accepted, discounts during low season). For advance reservations, contact Promotora El Tecuán, Garibaldi 1676, Sector Hidalgo, Guadalajara, Jalisco 44680, tel. (36) 160-085 and (36) 160-183.

Getting There

The Hotel El Tecuán is six miles (10 km) along a paved entrance road marked by a white light-house at Km 33 (112 miles, 181 km, from Puerto Vallarta, 22 miles, 35 km, from Barra de Navidad, and 40 miles, 64 km, from the Manzanillo International Airport).

PLAYA TENACATITA

Imagine an ideal Pacific Mexico paradise: free camping on a long curve of clean white sand, right next to a lovely little coral-bottomed cove, with all the beer you can drink and all the fresh seafood you can eat. That describes Tenacatita, a place that old Pacific Mexico hands refer to with a sigh: Tenacatitaaahhh. . . .

Folks usually begin to arrive sometime in November; by Christmas, some years, there's only room for walk-ins. Which anyone who can walk can do: carry in your tent and set it up in one of the many RV-inaccessible spots.

Tenacatita visitors enjoy three distinct beaches: the main one, Playa Tenacatita, the little one, Playa Mora, and Playa Maravierta, a breezy, palm-bordered sand ribbon stretching two miles north to the mouth of the Rio Purificación.

Playa Tenacatita's strand of fine white sand curves from north-end Punta Tenacatita along a long, tall packed dune to Punta Hermanos, a total of about two miles. The dune is where most folks (nearly all North Americans) park their RVs. The water is clear with generally gentle waves, fine for swimming and windsurfing. Being so calm, it's easy to launch a boat for fishing—common catches are red snapper (*huachinango*), and sea bass (*cabrilla*)—especially at the very calm north end.

That sheltered north cove is where a village of palapas has grown to service the winter camping population. One of the veteran establishments is **El Puercillo,** run by long-timer José Bautista. He and several other neighbors take groups out in his launches ($50 total per half day, complete, bring your own beer) for offshore fishing trips and excursions.

Tenacatita may be headed for changes, however. The federal government has sold out to a foreign corporation to develop a hotel at Tenacatita. The trouble, however, is that the 50-odd squatter-operators of the Tenacatita palapas refuse to leave. One night in November 1991, after giving the squatters plenty of warning, federal soldiers and police burned and smashed the palapas. The squatters, however, backed by Rebalcito *ejido*, the traditional owner of Tenacatita, have vowed to have their day in court. Meanwhile, the squatters have rebuilt their palapas.

Playas Mora And Maravierta

Jewel of jewels Playa Mora is accessible by a dirt road running north from the Tenacatita palapas. The beach itself, salt-and-pepper black sand dotted with white coral, is washed by water sometimes as smooth as glass. Just 50 feet from the beach the reef begins. Corals, like heads of cauliflower, some brown, some green, and some dead white, swarm with fish: iridescent blue, yellow-striped, yellow-tailed, some silvery, and other brown as rocks. (Careful: Moray eels like to hide in rock crannies; they bite. Don't stick your hand anywhere you can't see.)

If you get to Playa Mora by mid-November you may be early enough to snag one of the roughly half-dozen car-accessible camping spots. If not, plenty of tenting spaces exist, and a few abandoned palapa thatched huts are usually waiting to be resurrected.

Playa Maravierta is the overflow campground for Tenacatita. It's not as popular because of its rough surf and steep beach. Its isolation and vigorous surf, however, make Maravierta the best for driftwood, beachcombing, shells, and surf fishing.

Wildlife Viewing

Tenacatita's hinterland is a spreading, wildlife-rich mangrove marsh. From a landing behind the Tenacatita dune you can float a rowboat, rubber raft, or canoe for a wildlife-viewing excursion. Local guides also lead trips from the same spot. Take your hat, binoculars, camera, telephoto lens, and plenty of repellent.

Tenacatita Bugs

That same marshland is the source for swarms of mosquitos and *jejenes*, "no-see-um" biting gnats, especially around sunset. At that time no one sane at Tenacatita should be outdoors without having lathered up with good repellent.

Food, Services, And Information

The village of **Rebalcito**, a mile and a half away, is Tenacatita's supply and service center.

It has two or three fair *abarróterias* (groceries), which carry meat and vegetables, a *caseta de larga distancia*, a *gasolinera*, which sells leaded regular from drums, a water *purificadora*, which sells drinking water retail, and even a tiny bus station. A single Transportes Cihuatlán bus makes one run a day between Rebalcito and Manzanillo, leaving Rebalcito at the crack of dawn (inquire locally) and returning from the Manzanillo central bus station, leaving at 3:30 p.m.

If you want a diversion from the fare of Tenacatita's seafood palapas and Rebalcito's single restaurant, you can drive or thumb a ride seven miles (11 km) to **Restaurant Yoly** in Miguel Hidalgo (Km 30 on Hwy. 200) for some country-style enchiladas, tacos, chiles rellenos, tostadas, and beans (open daily 7 a.m.-8 p.m.).

Getting There

Leave Highway 200 at the Tenacatita sign (Km 28) just south of the big Rio Purificación bridge. Rebalcito is 3.7 miles (6.0 km), Tenacatita 5.4 miles (8.7 km), by a wide, level dirt road.

HOTEL FIESTA AMERICANA LOS ANGELES LOCOS

In spite of its name, the Hotel Fiesta Americana Los Angeles Locos has nothing to do with crazy people from Los Angeles. Once upon a time, a rich family built an airstrip and a mansion by a lovely little beach on pristine Tenacatita Bay and began coming for vacations by private plane. The local people, who couldn't fathom why their rich neighbors would go to so much trouble and expense to come to such an out-of-the-way place, dubbed them *los angeles locos*, "crazy angels," because they always seemed to be flying.

The beach is still lovely and Tenacatita Bay, curving around Punta Hermanos south from Tenacatita Beach, is still pristine. Now the Hotel Los Angeles Locos makes it possible for droves of sun-seeking vacationers to enjoy it en masse.

Continuous music, an open bar, bottomless buffets, and endless activities set the tone at Los Angeles Locos—the kind of place for folks who want a hassle-free week of fun in the sun. The guests are typically working-age couples and singles, mostly Mexicans during the summer, Canadians and some Americans during the winter. Very few children seem to be among the guests, however.

Hotel Activities
Although all sports and lessons—including tennis, snorkeling, sailing, windsurfing, horseback riding, volleyball, aerobics, exercises, waterskiing—plus dancing, disco, and games cost nothing extra, guests can, if they want, do nothing but soak up the sun. Los Angeles Locos simply provides the options.

A relaxed attitude will probably allow you to enjoy yourself the most. Don't try to eat, drink, and do too much in order to make sure you get your money's worth. If you do, you're liable to arrive back home a week later in need of a vacation.

Although people don't come to the tropics to stay inside, Los Angeles Locos' rooms are quite comfortable—completely private, in pastels and white, air-conditioned, each with cable TV, phone, and private balcony overlooking either the ocean or the palmy pool-patio.

Hotel Information
For information and reservations, contact the hotel at P.O. Box 7, Melaque-San Patricio, Jalisco, tel. (333) 702-20, fax (333) 702-29, or in the U.S. and Canada toll-free at (800) 223-2332. Rates for the 201 rooms and suites are about $85 per person per day d, $105 per day, s; for a bigger, better-view junior suite, add $30 per room; prices include everything except transportation.

Getting There
The Hotel Fiesta Americana Los Angeles Locos is about four miles (six km) off Highway 200 along a signed cobbled entrance road near the Km 20 marker (120 miles, 194 km from Puerto Vallarta, 14 miles, 23 km, from Barra de Navidad, and 32 miles, 51 km, from the Manzanillo International Airport).

If you want to simply look around the resort, don't drive up to the gate unannounced. The guard won't let you through. Instead, call ahead and make an appointment for a "tour." After your guided look-see, you have to either sign up or mosey along. They don't accept day guests.

PLAYA BOCA DE IGUANAS

Plumy Playa Boca de Iguanas curves for six miles along the tranquil inner recess of the Bay of Tenacatita. The cavernous former Hotel Bahía Tenacatita, which slumbered for years beneath the grove, is being reclaimed by the jungle and the mosquitos and gnats that swarm out of the nearby mangrove marsh.

The beach, however, is as enjoyable as ever: wide, level, with firm white sand, good for hiking, jogging, and beachcombing. Offshore, the gently rolling waves are equally fine for bodysurfing and boogieboarding. Beds of oysters, free for those who can dive for them, lie a few hundred feet offshore. A rocky outcropping at the north end invites fishing and snorkeling while the calm water beyond the breakers invites windsurfing. Bring your own equipment, however.

Accommodations
The pocket paradise, **Camping and Trailer Park Boca de Iguanas** (follow a signed gravel road at Km 17 for 1.5 miles, 2.4 km), seems to be succeeding where the old hotel failed. Instead of fighting the jungle, the manager is trying to coexist with it. A big crocodile lives in the mangrove-lined lotus marsh at the edge of the trailer park. "When the crocodile gets too close to my ducks," the manager says, "I drive him back into the mangrove where he belongs. This end of the mangrove is ours, the other side is his."

The trailer park offers 40 sandy, shaded spaces for tents and RVs, including electricity, well water for showering, flushing, and laundry, bottled water for drinking, and a dump station. The manager runs a minimarket, which supplies the necessities for a relaxed week or month on the beach. Many American and Canadian regulars stay here all winter. The trailer park includes a funky bungalow with kitchen, which sleeps four for $45/day. Reservations are generally needed only during Christmas or Easter week. Address: Km 16.5 Carretera Melaque-Puerto Vallarta, P.O. Box 93, Melaque, Jalisco. Rates are $5 per person, $4 for kids under 10.

The neigboring **Camping Tenacatita Trailer Park** also has 40 camping and RV spaces shaded beneath a majestic, rustling grove. Although their layout is not so developed as their senior neighbor's, friendly owners Michel and Bertha (he's French, she's Mexican) are trying harder. Their essentials are in place, however: electricity, water, showers, toilets, and 20 spaces with sewer hookups. Much of their five acres is undeveloped and would be fine for tenters who prefer privacy, but with the convenience of fresh water, a small store, and congenial company around a driftwood campfire at night. Address: Km 16.5 Carretera Melaque-Puerto Vallarta, P.O. Box 18, Melaque, Jalisco; Guadalajara tel. 36-414-284. Rates: $9 per RV, including two people, $3 per extra person, camping $3.50.

A third lodging, the nearby **Hotel and Campamento Entre Palmeras** ("Between the Palm Groves") is situated, unfortunately, close to the mangrove swamp. Their camp, however, appears to be under water only during the rainy, summer-fall low season. They have six apartment-bungalows, much camping space, electricity, showers, toilets, and a swimming pool. Their bungalows would do for a night if you used plenty of repellent and a mosquito coil *(espiral)*. It would be better to use your tent or borrow one and camp away from the bugs.

PLAYA LA MANZANILLA

The little fishing town of La Manzanilla (pop. about 3,000) shares the same long strip of sand that begins at the Boca de Iguanas trailer parks. At Playa de Manzanilla the beach is as broad and flat and the waves are as gentle, but the sand has become several shades darker. Probably no better fishing exists on the entire Costa Alegre than at La Manzanilla. A dozen seafood palapas on the beach exist on the local weekend and holiday patronage alone.

One basic hotel, the **Hotel Posada del Cazador** ("The Hunter") accommodates guests in its 11 rooms and bungalows. Get there by following the signed paved road at Km 13 for one mile (Maria Asunción 183, La Manzanilla, Jalisco, tel. 333-702-14, 333-703-30, about $13 d, $27 for suite sleeping four with kitchenette, $57 for suite sleeping eight with kitchenette, fans, long-distance phone).

BARRA DE NAVIDAD, MELAQUE, AND VICINITY

THE BAR OF CHRISTMAS

The little country beach town of Barra de Navidad, Jalisco (pop. 5,000), whose name literally means "Bar of Christmas," has unexpectedly few saloons. (In this case, "Bar" has nothing to do with alcohol; it refers to the sandbar upon which the town is built.) That lowly spit of sand forms the southern perimeter of the blue Bay of Navidad, which arcs to Barra de Navidad's twin town of San Patricio de Melaque (pop. 10,000) five miles to the north.

Barra and San Patricio de Melaque, locally known as Melaque (May-LAH-kay) are twin, but distinct, towns. Barra has the cobbled, shady lanes and friendly country ambience; Melaque is the metropolis of the two, with most of the stores and services.

HISTORY

The sandbar is called "Navidad" because the Viceroy Antonio de Mendoza, the first, and arguably the best, viceroy Mexico ever had, disembarked there on December 25, 1540. The occasion was auspicious for two reasons. Besides being Christmas Day, Don Antonio had arrived to personally put down a bloody rebellion raging through western Mexico, which threatened to burn New Spain off the map. Unfortunately for the thousands of Indians who were torched, hung, or beheaded during the brutal campaign, Don Antonio's prayers on that day were soon answered. The rebellion was smothered, and the lowly sandbar was remembered as Barra de Navidad from that time forward.

A generation later, Barra de Navidad became the springboard for King Philip's efforts to make the Pacific a Spanish lake. Shipyards built on the bar launched the vessels that carried the expedition of conquistador Miguel López de Legazpi and Father André de Urdaneta in search of God and gold in the Philippines. Urdaneta came back a hero one year later, in 1565, having discovered the great circle route followed by a dozen subsequent generations of the renowned Manila Galleon.

By 1600, however, the Manila Galleon was landing in Acapulco, with much quicker land access to the capital for their priceless Oriental cargoes. Barra de Navidad went to sleep and and didn't wake up for more than three centuries.

Now, however, Barra de Navidad only slumbers occasionally. The town welcomes crowds of beachgoing Mexican families during national holidays, and during the winter a steady procession of North American and European budget vacationers.

SIGHTS

A Walk Around Barra

Nearly all hotels and the fancier restaurants in Barra lie on one oceanfront street (named, uncommonly, after a conquistador), Miguel López de Legazpi. Barra's only other main street, Vera Cruz, one short block inland, has most of the businesses, groceries, and small family-run eateries.

Head south along Legazpi toward the steep Cerro San Francisco in the distance and you will soon be on the palm-lined walkway that runs atop the famous sandbar of Barra. On the right, ocean side, the Playa Barra de Navidad curves to the hotels of Melaque spread like white pebbles at the far end of the strand. The great blue water expanse beyond the beach, bordered on the north and south horizons by jagged, rocky sea stacks, is the **Bahía de Navidad.**

Opposite the ocean, on the other side of the bar, lies the *panga* (fishing launch) dock adjacent to the tranquil, mangrove-bordered expanse of the **Laguna de Navidad,** which forms the border with the state of **Colima,** whose mountains (including nearby Cerro San Francisco) loom beyond it.

The calm appearance of the Laguna de Navidad is deceiving, for it is really an *estero* (estuary), an arm of the sea, which ebbs and flows through the channel beyond the rock **jetty** at

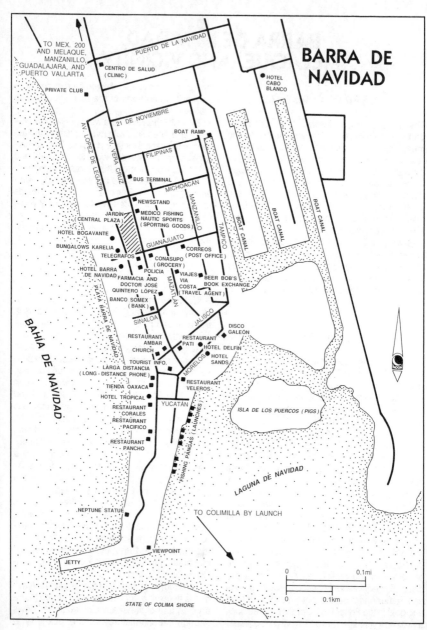

TO MEX. 200 AND MELAQUE, MANZANILLO, GUADALAJARA, AND PUERTO VALLARTA

PUERTO DE LA NAVIDAD

BARRA DE NAVIDAD

CENTRO DE SALUD (CLINIC)

HOTEL CABO BLANCO

PRIVATE CLUB

21 DE NOVIEMBRE

AV. LOPEZ DE LEGAZPI

AV. VERA CRUZ

BOAT RAMP

FILIPINAS

BUS TERMINAL

MICHOACAN

NEWSSTAND

MANZANILLO

JARDIN (CENTRAL PLAZA)

MEDICO FISHING NAUTIC SPORTS (SPORTING GOODS)

HOTEL BOGAVANTE

BUNGALOWS KARELIA

TELEGRAFOS

GUANAJUATO

TAMPICO

BOAT CANAL

BOAT CANAL

BOAT CANAL

CORREOS (POST OFFICE)

CONASUPO (GROCERY)

HOTEL BARRA DE NAVIDAD

POLICIA

FARMACIA AND DOCTOR JOSE QUINTERO LÓPEZ

VIAJES VIA COSTA (TRAVEL AGENT)

BEER BOB'S BOOK EXCHANGE

BANCO SOMEX (BANK)

MAZATLAN

PLAYA BARRA DE NAVIDAD

SINALOA

JALISCO

DISCO GALEÓN

BAHÍA DE NAVIDAD

RESTAURANT AMBAR

CHURCH

RESTAURANT PATI

HOTEL DELFIN

HOTEL SANDS

TOURIST INFO.

LARGA DISTANCIA (LONG-DISTANCE PHONE)

MORELOS

RESTAURANT VELEROS

TIENDA OAXACA

HOTEL TROPICAL

YUCATÁN

RESTAURANT CORALES

RESTAURANT PACIFICO

ISLA DE LOS PUERCOS (PIGS)

RESTAURANT PANCHO

FISHING PANGAS (LAUNCHES)

LAGUNA DE NAVIDAD

NEPTUNE STATUE

TO COLIMILLA BY LAUNCH

VIEWPOINT

JETTY

STATE OF COLIMA SHORE

0   0.1mi

0   0.1km

© MOON PUBLICATIONS, INC.

the end of the sandbar. (Because of this natural flushing action, untreated sewage is unfortunately still dumped into the lagoon. Twentieth-century waste treatment may, hopefully, arrive in the Laguna de Navidad before the 21st century. Until then, best not swim in its inviting waters.)

Beaches And Activities

Although a continuous strand of medium-fine golden sand joins Barra with Melaque, it changes character (and names) along its gentle, five-mile arc. At Barra de Navidad, where it's called **Playa de Navidad,** the beach is narrow and steep, and the waves are sometimes very rough. Those powerful swells, however, often provide good intermediate **surfing** breaks just north of the jetty. **Fishing** by line or pole is also popular from the jetty rocks.

Most mornings are calm enough to make the surf safe for **swimming** and splashing, which, along with the fresh seafood of beachside palapa restaurants, make Barra a popular Sunday and holiday picnic ground for local Mexican families. The relatively large number of folks walking the beach, however, makes for slim pickings for shell collectors and beachcombers.

As the beach curves northwesterly toward Melaque, the restaurants and hotels give way to dunes and pasture. At the outskirts of Melaque, civilization resumes, and the broad beach, now called **Playa Melaque,** has billows as gentle as child's play.

Continuing past the town, a lineup of rustic palapas and *pangas* pulled up on the sand decorate the tranquil north-end cove, sheltered from the open sea behind a headland and a tier of craggy sea stacks. Here, the water clears, making for good **fishing** from the rocks.

Colimilla

A boat trip across the lagoon for super-fresh seafood at the village of Colimilla is a primary Barra pastime. While you sit enjoying a reasonably priced oyster cocktail, ceviche, or broiled whole-fish lunch or dinner, enjoy the breeze and gaze out on the mangrove-enfolded glassy expanse of the Laguna de Navidad. Far away, a canoe may drift silently, while white herons quietly stalk their prey. Now and then a launch will glide in and deposit its load of visitors, or a fisherman will head out in the opposite direction.

One of the pleasantest Colimilla vantage spots is the **Restaurant Susana** (open daily 8-8), whose broad palapa extends out into the lagoon. Take mosquito repellent, especially if you're staying for dinner. Launches routinely ferry up to six passengers to Colimilla from the Barra lagoonside docks for $10 roundtrip. Tell them when you want to return, and they'll pick you up.

Playa De Cocos

A trip to wild, breezy Playa de Cocos, hidden just behind the Cerro San Francisco headland south of Barra, makes an interesting afternoon

Seafood palapas wait at Colimilla's lagoonside for visitor-filled boats from Barra de Navidad.

outing, especially when combined with the trip to Colimilla. A wide, golden-sand beach curves miles southward, starting beneath a cactus-dotted jungly headland. The beach, although broad, is steep, with waves that break strongly right on the sand. Although swimming is hazardous, fishing off the rocks and beachcombing are delights here. A feast of driftwood and multicolored shells—olives, small conches, purple-striated clams—litters the sand, especially on an intimate, spectacular hidden cove, reachable by scampering past the waves at the cliff bottom. For more details, see "Trailer Parks and Camping" below.

To get to Playa de Cocos, walk uphill to the road above the La Colimilla restaurants. Head left (east) for about a quarter mile. Turn right at the palm-lined boulevard and continue along the golf course about a mile and a quarter to the beach beneath the tip of the Cerro San Francisco headland.

You can also drive there by turning off Highway 200 at the "Ejido La Culebra" sign at Km 51 a few miles south of Barra. Follow the road about six miles, passing a golf course, to the beach and headland marked by the end of the asphalt and beginning of brick pavement.

Playa Coastecomate

Playa de Cocos has its exact opposite in Playa Coastecomate (Koh-ah-stay-koh-MAH-tay), tucked behind the ridge rising beyond the north edge of Melaque. The dark, fine-sand beach curves along a cove on the rampart-rimmed big blue **Bahía de Coastecomate.** Its very gentle waves and clear waters make for excellent swimming, windsurfing, snorkeling, and fishing from the beach itself or the rocks beneath the adjacent cliffs. A number of palapa restaurants along the beach serve seafood and drinks.

The Coastecomate beachside village itself, home for a number of local fisherfolk and a few North Americans in permanently parked RVs, has a collection of oft-empty bungalows on the hillside, a small store, and about three times as many chickens as people.

For lodging, try the bungalows, or see Hotel Costa Sur under "Melaque Hotels" below. To get there, drive, taxi, or bus via Transportes Cihuatlán to the Melaque turnoff from Highway 200. There, a dirt side road marked "Hotel Costa Sur" heads north, winding for two miles over

the ridge through pasture and jungly woodland to the beach. If you're walking, allow an hour, and take your sun hat, insect repellent, and water.

Barra-Melaque Hike

You can do this four-mile stroll either way, but starting from Barra with the sun behind you, the sky and the ocean will be at their bluest best. Take insect repellent, sunscreen, and a hat. At either end, enjoy lunch at one of the seaside restaurants (see "Food" below). At the Melaque end you can continue walking north to the cove on the other side of town. The trail beneath the cliff leads to spectacular wave-tossed tidepools and rugged sea rocks at the tip of the bay. At the Barra end, you can hire a launch to Colimilla. End your day leisurely by taxiing or busing back to your hotel from the bus station at either end.

Bird And Wildlife Viewing

The wildlife-rich upper reaches of the Laguna de Navidad stretch for miles. Besides ordinary varieties of egrets, terns, herons, pelicans, frigate birds, boobies, ducks and geese, patient bird-watchers can sometimes snare rainbow flash-views of exotic parrots and bright tanagers and orioles.

As for other creatures, quiet, persistent observers are sometimes rewarded with man-grove-edge views of turtles, constrictors, crocodiles, coatimundis, raccoons, skunks, deer, wild pigs, ocelots, wildcats, and very rarely, a jaguar. The sensitivity and experience of your boatman-guide is, of course, crucial to the success of any nature outing. Ask at the little office of the **Sociedad Cooperativos de Servicios Turistico** (at 40 Av. Vera Cruz on the lagoon front, tel. 702-28) for a suitable person.

ACCOMMODATIONS

Barra Hotels

Whether on the beach or not, all Barra hotels (except the four-star Cabo Blanco) fall in the budget or moderate category. One of the best, the family-run **Hotel Sands,** offers a bit of class at very modest rates (Morelos 24, Barra de Navidad, Jalisco 48987, tel. 333-700-18). Two tiers of rooms enclose an inner courtyard lined

BARRA AND MELAQUE HOTELS

Barra and Melaque hotels, in order of approximate double-room price (area code 333)

BARRA HOTELS (postal code 48987)

Bungalows Karelia, Av. L. de Legazpi s/n, 701-87, $24
Hotel Bogavante, Av. L. de Legazpi s/n, 703-84, $24
Hotel Sands, Morelos 24, 700-18, $24
Hotel Delfín, Morelos 23, 700-68, $24
Hotel Tropical, Av. L. de Legazpi 96, 700-20, fax 701-49, $27
Hotel Barra de Navidad, Av. L. de Legazpi 250, 701-22, $30
Hotel Cabo Blanco, P.O. Box 31, 700-22, fax 701-68, $63

MELAQUE HOTELS (postal code 48980)

Villas Camino del Mar, Av. Francisco Villa 6, 702-07, $31
Posada Pablo de Tarso, Av. Gómez Farías 408, 701-17, $35
Bungalows Mallorca, Abel Salgado 133, 702-19, $33
Hotel Club Náutico, Av. Gómez Farías 1A, 707-70, fax 702-39, $60
Hotel Coco Club, Av. Gómez Farías s/n, 700-01, fax 703-82, $77
Hotel Costa Sur, P.O. Box 12, 701-35, $100

vacy) are the cleanest and most deluxe of Barra's moderate hotels. The Delfín's tour de force, however, is the cheery patio buffet where guests linger over the breakfast offered every morning ($3-5, open daily 8:30-10:30) to all comers. Overnight guests, like those of the Sands, must put up with the moderate nighttime noise of the disco half a block away. For maximum sun and privacy take one of the top-floor rooms, many of which enjoy lagoon views. The Delfín's 30 rooms rent for about $24 low season, higher after Christmas and before Easter, fans, a small pool, and parking; credit cards accepted.

On the beach a few blocks away, the comfortable, high-ceilinged rooms of the **Hotel Tropical,** by contrast, feel completely private (Av. L. de Legazpi 96, Barra de Navidad, Jalisco 48987, tel. 333-700-20, fax 333-701-49). A number of them have small balconies with panoramic ocean vistas. Downstairs, a small pool is wedged between the beach and a breezy seaview restaurant. Rates for the 57 rooms with fans run about $27 d; credit cards are accepted.

Sharing the same beachfront by the town plaza nearby, the white stucco three-story **Hotel Barra de Navidad** encloses a cool, leafy interior courtyard (Av. L. de Legazpi 250, Barra de Navidad, Jalisco 48987, tel. 333-701-22, 333-703-33). The seaside upper two floors of comfortable but not deluxe rooms enjoy palm-fringed ocean vistas from private balconies. An inviting pool-patio on one side and a dependable upstairs restaurant complete the picture. Rates for the 57 rooms with fans run $24 s, $30 d, $35 t; credit cards are accepted.

The budget prices and homey beachside porch of the **Hotel Bogavante** keep a steady stream of mostly North American and European budget travelers returning year after year (Av. L. de Legazpi s/n, Barra de Navidad, Jalisco 48987, tel. 333-703-84). Many of the rooms, some of which are spacious bungalows, enjoy

with comfortable sitting areas that open into a lush green garden of leafy vines and graceful coconut palms. A side corridor leads past a small zoo of spider monkeys, raccoons, and squawking macaws to a view of Barra's colorful lineup of fishing launches. On the other side, past the swim-up bar, a big curving pool and outer patio spreads to the placid edge of the mangrove-bordered Laguna de Navidad. The pool-bar (happy hour 4-6 p.m. daily in season) and the sitting areas afford inviting places to meet other travelers. The rooms, all with fans (but without hot water) are plain but clean. Light sleepers should wear earplugs or book a room in the wing farthest from the disco down the street, whose music thumps away till around two most nights. Their 43 rooms and bungalows rent from about $24 d low season, $29 high, bungalows (sleeping four) with kitchenettes run from about $50 low season, $60 high; credit cards accepted, parking.

Across the street, its loyal international clientele swears by the German family-operated **Hotel Delfín** (Morelos 23, Barra de Navidad, Jalisco 48987, tel. 333-700-68). Its four stories of tile-floored, balcony-corridor rooms (where curtains, unfortunately, must be drawn for pri-

ocean views and can accommodate up to three adults and two children. The kitchenettes are especially handy for families weary of the hassles and expense of eating out. The 14 rooms (eight of them with kitchens) rent for about $19 s, $24 d, and $29 t, add about 10% around Christmas and the week before Easter, monthly rates available, no pool, fans.

Bungalows Karelia, the Bogavante's downscale twin lodging next door, shares the same pleasant beachside porch (Av. L. Legazpi s/n, Barra de Navidad, Jalisco, 48987, tel. 333-701-87). The Karelia offers all-kitchenette bungalows, satisfactory for many young families and travelers who don't mind cleaning up a bit in exchange for budget rates. The 10 bungalows rent for about $24 d, $26 t; with fans.

Barra's only deluxe lodging, the peach-hued stucco-and-tile **Hotel Cabo Blanco,** is part of a vacation home development sprouting along the three marina-canals that branch from the lagoon about five blocks inland from the town (P.O. Box 31, Barrra de Navidad, Jalisco 48987, tel. 333-700-22, fax 333-701-68). Within its manicured garden-grounds, Hotel Cabo Blanco offers night-lit tennis courts, restaurants, bars, two pools, kiddie pools, and Barra's most deluxe sportfishing yachts-for-hire. The lodgings themselves, all air-conditioned, range from deluxe, pastel-decorated hotel doubles to fancy two-story, four-bedroom family villas. Bring your repellent; mosquitoes and gnats from the nearby mangroves seem to especially enjoy the Cabo Blanco's plush ambience. Tariffs for the 125 rooms run from about $63 d. Villas sleeping two to six range from about $75 to $160; with TV, phones, a discotheque, and many water sports; credit cards accepted.

Melaque Hotels

Melaque has many hotels and bungalows, most of them poorly designed and indifferently managed. They scratch along, nearly empty except during the Christmas and Easter holiday deluges when Mexican middle-class families must accept anything to stay on the beach.

There are, nevertheless, some notable exceptions. One of them is the well-kept, colonial-chic **Posada Pablo de Tarso** (named after the apostle Paul of Tarsus). This unique label, along with the many classy details, including art-decorated rooms and handcarved bedsteads and

doors, all surrounding a flowery beachside pool-patio, points to a labor of love. The only drawback lies in the motel-style corridor layout, which requires guests to pull the dark drapes for privacy (Av. Gómez Farías 408, San Patricio Melaque, Jalisco 48980, tel. 333-701-17 and 333-702-68). The 27 rooms and bungalows begin at about $35 d; a kitchen raises the tariff to about $43 d; with a/c, TV, phones; reserve through the owner at Justo Sierra 2354, Segundo Piso, Guadalajara, Jalisco, tel. 36-521-425, and 36-166-688.

Just as classy in its own way is the **Villas Camino del Mar,** whose owner doesn't believe in advertising (Av. Francisco Villa 6, Colonia Villa Obregon, P.O. Box 6, San Patricio Melaque, Jalisco 48980, tel. 333-702-07). One pair of signs in the humble beach neigborhood about a quarter mile on the Barra side of the town center furnishes the only clue that this gem of a lodging hides among the Melaque dross. A five-story white-stucco monument draped with fluted, neoclassic columns and hanging pedestals, the Camino del Mar offers a lodging assortment that varies from simple double rooms through deluxe suites with kitchenettes to a rambling penthouse. The upper three levels enjoy sweeping ocean views, while the lower two overlook an elegant blue pool-patio bar and shady beachside palm grove. The clientele is split between Mexican middle-class families who come for weekends year-round, and quiet Canadian and American couples who come to soak up the winter sun for weeks and months on end. Reserve early, especially for the winter. The 23 rooms and suites include comfortable ocean-view doubles for as little as $31, one-bedroom kitchenette suites, about $58, and deluxe two-bedroom, two-bath suites with kitchen, about $92, fans only, weekly and monthly rates much lower.

If the Camino del Mar is full, try the **Bungalows Mallorca,** which shares the same golden sunset-view beach just one block away. While the Mallorca has spacious grounds, an inviting pool, and a beachside palm garden, its Motel 6-style room layout is about as unimaginative and un-Mexican as you can find south of Anchorage, Alaska. For groups and families used to providing their own entertainment and atmosphere, however, the kitchens and spacious (but dark) rooms of the Bungalows Mallorca may be just the ticket.

The owner, Luis Lomeli Suarez, furthermore, is a warmhearted elderly gentleman who probably would entertain any reasonable offer. The beach-side end units, with ocean-view balconies and jacuzzis, are the best. (Abel Salgado 133, Colonia Villa Obregon, P.O. Box 157, San Patricio Melaque, Jalisco 48980, tel. 333-702-19. The 24 two-bedroom bungalows with fans rent from about $33 d low-season to about $70 high-season quadruple with view balcony and jacuzzi. Discounts for weekly and monthly rentals.

If you prefer air-conditioning, privacy, a sea-view balcony, and a disco next door, you can have it right on the beach at the in-town **Hotel Club Náutico** (Av. Gómez Farías 1A, San Patricio Melaque, Jalisco 48980, tel. 333-707-70 and 333-707-66, fax 333-702-39. The deluxe rooms, in blue, pastels, and white, angle toward the ocean in tiers above the pool-patio along one side of the hotel. The upper-floor rooms nearest the beach are likely to be quietest and have the best views. The hotel also has a good beachside restaurant whose huge palapa both captures the cool afternoon sea breeze and frames the blue waters of the Bay of Navidad. The hotel's main drawback, however, is lack of space, being sandwiched into a long, narrow beachfront lot. The asking rate is a steep $60 d, low season, although they may accept less if they're empty; with a/c, TV, phones, parking, a travel agent, restaurant-bar; credit cards are accepted.

The adjacent ponderous pink **Hotel Coco Club** rambles for hundreds of yards along the north end of the Melaque beach (Av. Gómez Farías s/n, P.O. Box 8, San Patricio Melaque, Jalisco 48980, tel. 333-700-01, fax 333-703-82). Its bountiful buffets, open bars, and continuous activities, sports, and entertainment are popular with package groups of North Americans who come to enjoy a week of fun in the sun. The atmosphere, however, is institutional, and the building itself, with long concrete corridors, resembles a former Soviet People's hotel. The plain, but comfortable and private, rooms have air-conditioning and ocean-view balconies overlooking the palm-lined beachside pool-patio. For no extra charge guests can enjoy snorkeling, a gym, both high- and low-impact aerobics, kayaking, volleyball, tennis, windsurfing, croquet, Spanish language and dancing lessons, a miniclub for kids 4-12 and a nightly show-party

and a disco. The 236 rooms rent for about $55 per person per day, low-season double occupancy, $77 high, and about $80 low-season single occupancy, $125 high. Two children under 12 are free when accompanied by parents; a child over 12 with parent about $25 low season, $40 high; all meals and activities are included, credit cards are accepted; for reservations, contact the hotel or your travel agent.

The five-star **Hotel Costa Sur** on nearby Playa Coastecomate (see "Sights" above) offers a fancier, more personal alternative (P.O. Box 12, San Patricio Melaque, Jalisco 48980, tel. 333-701-35). Like a local-style Club Med, the Hotel Costa Sur's low-rise view villas spread like a mushroom garden in the jungly palm-forest hillside above the beach. Guests (mostly Canadians and American in winter, Mexicans in summer and holidays) enjoy all food and drinks, deluxe air-conditioned view rooms with cable TV, tennis courts, sailing, windsurfing, pedalboats, snorkeling, volleyball, and a large pool-patio right on the beach. Rates run about $75 per person per day, low-season double occupancy, $100 high; credit cards are accepted.

During the low summer-fall season, both the Hotel Coco Club and the Hotel Costa Sur may accept day guests for a set fee. Call them for details.

Trailer Parks And Camping

Barra-Melaque has one trailer park, **La Playa,** right on the beach in downtown Melaque (Av. Gómez Farías 250, San Patricio Melaque, Jalisco 48980, tel. 333-700-65). Although La Playa is a bit cramped and shadeless, long-timers nevertheless get their winter reservations in early for the choice beach spaces. The better-than-average facilities include a small store, fish-cleaning sinks, showers, toilets, and all hookups. The water is brackish; however, drink bottled. If the Melaque surf makes boat launching a bit tricky, you can use the ramp at the Hotel Cabo Blanco (see "Boat Launching" below). The 45 spaces rent for about $12 per day, $10 per day monthly.

Bear left on the dirt road past the north-end Melaque beach palapas and you will find an informal **RV-trailer park campground** with room for about 50 rigs and tents. The cliff-bottom lot spreads above a calm rocky cove, ripe for swimming, snorkeling, windsurfing, and fishing and enjoys a sweeping view of the entire Bay of Navidad. All spaces are usually full by Christmas and remain that way until March or April. The people are friendly, the price is certainly right, and the beer and water trucks arrive regularly throughout the season.

Wilderness campers will enjoy **Playa de Cocos,** a miles-long golden sand beach, accessible by launch from Barra to Colimilla, or by road the long way around (see "Sights" above). Playa de Cocos has an intimate hidden sandy cove, perfect for an overnight or a few barefoot days of birdwatching, shell collecting, beachcombing, and dreaming around your driftwood campfire. The restaurants at the village of Colimilla or the stores (by launch across the lagoon) in Barra are available for food and water. Mosquitoes, however, come out around sunset. Bring plenty of good repellent and a mosquito-proof tent.

FOOD

Breakfast And Snacks

An excellent way to start your Barra day is at the intimate palapa-shaded patio of the **Hotel Delfín** (Av. Morelos 23, tel. 700-68). While you dish yourself fruit and pour your coffee from their little countertop buffet, the cook fixes your choice of several kinds of eggs, from mushroom omelettes to spicy *huevos Mexicanos.* Their most popular dish, however, seems to be their luscious, tender banana pancakes (complete breakfast $3-5, open daily 8:30-10:30 a.m.).

Barra families seem to fall into two categories: those who sell food to sidewalk passersby, and those who eat the food. The three blocks of Av. Veracruz from Morelos to the city *jardín* (park) are dotted with tables which residents nightly load with hearty, economical food offerings, from tacos *de lengua* (tongue) and pork tamales to *pozole* Guadalajara and chiles rellenos. The wholesomeness of their menus is evidenced by their devoted followings of longtime neighbor and tourist customers.

Restaurants

(Complete Dinner Price Key: Budget = under $7, Moderate = $7-14, Expensive = more than $14.) One such family has built their sidewalk culinary skills into a thriving storefront business, the **Restaurant Pati,** at the corner of Vera Cruz and Jalisco (tel. 707-43, open daily 8 a.m.-11 p.m).

They offer the traditional menu of Mexican *antijitos*—tacos, quesadillas, tostadas—plus roast beef, chicken, and very tasty *pozole* soup. Budget.

Restaurant Ambar, Barra's fanciest eatery, stands beneath a luxuriously airy upstairs palapa diagonally across from the Pati (Av. Vera Cruz 101A, corner Jalisco, open daily 8-12 for breakfast, 5-10 for dinner, American Express accepted). Their unusual menu stresses light fare—eggs, fish, whole-wheat *(harina integral),* tortillas and bread. Besides a long list of sweet and nonsweet crepes, they feature a selection of seafood, vegetable salads, and Mexican plates that includes scrumptious chiles rellenos. Their wines, which include the good Baja California Cetto label, are the best in town. Moderate.

One of Barra's most entertainingly scenic restaurants is **Veleros,** right on the lagoon (Vera Cruz 64, open daily noon-10, credit cards accepted). If you happen to visit Barra during the full moon, don't miss watching its shimmering reflection from the palapa restaurant as it rises over the mangrove-bordered lagoon. An additional Veleros bonus is the fascinating darting, swirling school of fish attracted by the spotlight shining on the water. Finally comes the carefully prepared and served food, which you can select from a menu of shrimp, lobster, octopus, chicken, and steak entrees. Their brochettes are especially popular. Moderate.

For a change of scene, try **Restaurant Corales,** one block away, on the beach side of the sandbar, where guests enjoy a refreshing sea breeze every afternoon and a happy-hour sunset every evening (López de Legazpi 146, open daily noon-11, credit cards accepted). Besides an excellent fresh seafood selection, they feature popular pineapple chicken and succulent rib plates. Moderate.

Restaurant Pancho, three doors away at Legazpi 53 is one of Barra's original palapas, which old-timers can remember from the days when *all* Barra restaurants were palapas. The original Pancho, who has seen lots of changes in the old sandbar in his 80-odd years, still oversees the operation daily 8-8. Moderate.

Melaque has a pair of good beachside restaurants. **Restaurant El Dorado,** under the big beachside palapa in front of the Hotel Club Náutico, provides a cool breezy place to enjoy the beach scene during breakfast or lunch (Av. Gómez Farías 1A, tel. 707-70, open daily 8 a.m.-11 p.m., credit cards accepted). Service is crisp and the specialties are carefully prepared. Their live amplified lunch and dinner combo would be an asset except that they play loud enough to ruin most people's digestion. If enough people ask them to turn down the volume, they may eventually get the message. Stark lighting, along with the loud music, ruins the nights here, unfortunately.

One block along the beach toward Barra is the pleasantly picturesque little brick and tile **Restaurant Cesar and Charly** (Av. Gómez Farías on the beach across from the central bus terminal, tel. 706-99, open daily 7:30 a.m.-9 p.m.). The family owner-operators maintain an unusually extensive international menu with an extremely small kitchen by simply not giving up. If some ingredient is lacking, out the door some child will go with instructions to buy the required item. Within 15 minutes your selection will arrive, hot and home-cooked, from the kitchen.

SPORTS

Swimming, Surfing, And Bodysurfing
The roughest surf on the Bahía de Navidad shoreline is closer to Barra, the most tranquil closest to Melaque. Swimming is consequently best and safest toward the Melaque end, while, in contrast, the only good surfing spot is where the waves rise and roll in beside the Barra jetty. Bodysurfing and boogieboarding are best somewhere in between. Shops in Barra (see below) sell and rent surfboards and boogieboards.

Sailing And Windsurfing
Sailing and windsurfing are best near the Melaque end of the Bay of Navidad and in the Bay of Coastecomate nearby. The only equipment available for use, however, are the windsurfing outfits for guests only at the Hotels Coco Club (tel. 700-01) and Costa Sur (tel. 701-35), and Hobie Cats at the Costa Sur. Phone the hotels about a day membership if you want to participate.

Snorkeling And Scuba Diving
Snorkeling is good off the rocky headlands of both the bays of Navidad and Coastecomate. Both the Hotel Coco Club and Hotel Costa Sur organize tours for their guests to these spots. There are as yet no commercial scuba instructors in Barra or Melaque.

For other details on surfing, snorkeling, fishing, hiking, and walking, see the specific beaches under "Sights" in this chapter.

Tennis
The Hotels Coco Club and Costa Sur have tennis courts for guests and day members. Call the Hotel Cabo Blanco (tel. 700-22) about lessons or rentals of their courts.

Sportfishing
The captains of the Barra Boat Cooperative **Sociedad Cooperativa de Servicios Turistico** routinely take parties on successful marlin and swordfish hunts for about $100 per boat per day, including bait and tackle. Contact them at their lagoonside office at Av. Vera Cruz 40 (P.O. Box 43, Barra de Navidad, Jalisco 48987, tel. 333-702-28).

There are many other fish in the sea than deep-sea marlin and swordfish, both of which often make tough eating. Half-day trips (about $17/hour) arranged through the Sociedad Cooperativa de Servicios Turistico or others will typically hook several large dorado, albacore, snapper, or other delicious eating fish. Local restaurants will generally cook up a banquet for you and your friends for the price of the extra fish caught during such an outing.

Boat Launching
If you plan on mounting your own fishing expedition you can do it from the boat-launch ramp (at the end of Av. Pilipinas) near the Hotel Cabo Blanco. The fee (about $3.50 per day) covers parking your boat in the canal and is payable at the hotel desk (tel. 700-22).

Sports Equipment Sales And Rentals
Barra has two sports shops. The smallest, the **Farmacia Zurich** (on Legazpi right across Jalisco from the church, open daily 8-9) doubles by selling fishing lures, poles, and tackle, outboard motors, fins, snorkels, masks, surfboards, and boogieboards. They also rent surfboards and snorkel gear for very reasonable rates.

The other, **El Médico Fishing Nautic Sports** (Av. Vera Cruz 230, at Michoacán, tel. 708-08, open Mon.-Sat. 9-2 and 4-8, Sun. 9-2), has a lavish inventory of nearly everything. This often includes fishing poles, lures, and tackle, boogieboards and surfboards, snorkel gear, waterskis,

The antics of dwarfs, jugglers, and acrobats were common entertainments in pre-conquest Mexico.

outboard motors, tennis balls and racquets, and even an entire jet-ski boat.

EVENTS AND ENTERTAINMENT

Most entertainments in Barra and Melaque are informal and local. *Corridas de toros* (bullfights), however, are occasionally held during the winter-spring season at the bullring on Hwy. 200 across from the Barra turnoff. Local cowboys sometimes display their pluck in spirited *charreadas* (Mexican-style rodeos) in neighboring country villages. Check with your hotel desk or the Barra tourist information office (Calle Sonora, around the corner from the Hotel Tropical, tel. 701-00) for details.

Nightlife
The Bahía de Navidad **sunset** colors are enjoyed nightly at the bar happy hours at Hotel Tropical and its neighbors, Restaurant Corales and disco club Agarra La Barra. The same is true at the beachside Restaurant Dorado at Hotel Club Náutico in Melaque. You can prepare for this during the afternoons (Dec., Jan., and Feb., mostly) at the very congenial 4-6 happy hour around the swim-up bar at Barra's Hotel Sands (at Morelos 24, on the lagoon).

After dinner, huge speakers begin thumping away, lights flash, and the fogs ooze from the ceilings around ten at disco **El Galeón** (of the Hotel Sands, young local crowd) and **La Tanga**

(of the Hotel Coco Club in Melaque, mixed young-older local and tourist crowd). Their hours vary seasonally; call the Sands (tel. 700-18) and the Coco Club (tel. 700-01) for details. Another, less formal and very raucous disco bar is the neon-lit upstairs **Agarra La Barra** (a few doors from Hotel Tropical), where the speakers pound louder than the waves nightly from sunset to midnight.

SERVICES AND SHOPPING

Bank And Moneychanger
Barra and Melaque have one bank and one moneychanger between them. In Barra, the **Banco Somex** (Sinaloa at Vera Cruz, tel. 701-89) converts American (sorry, no Canadian) traveler's checks and cash Mon.-Fri. 10-11:30, closed weekends. For other business, they are open 9 a.m.-1:30 p.m., closed weekends.

The **Money Exchange Melaque** (Gómez Farías 27A across from the bus terminal, tel. 703-43) exchanges both American and Canadian traveler's checks and cash Mon.-Sat. 9-2 and 4-7, Sundays 9-2. Their tariff, however, amounts to a very steep three dollars per 100 above bank rate.

Post Office, Telegraph, And Telephone
Barra and Melaque each have a small **post office** (*correos*). The Barra office, on Guanajuato (at Mazatlán, two and a half blocks away from

the beach), is open Mon.-Fri. 8-1 and 3-6, closed weekends. The Melaque post office, on the *jardín* at López Mateos and Morelos, is open Mon.-Fri. 9-4, Sat. 9-12, closed Sundays.

The Barra **telegrafos,** which also handles money orders, is right at the Av. Vera Cruz corner of the *jardín* plaza (tel. 702-62, open Mon.-Fri. 9-3, closed weekends).

In Barra, the *larga distancia* (long distance telephone office, tel. 700-21 and 702-26, open Mon.-Sat 9-2 and 4-9, Sun. 9-2) is on beachfront Av. Legazpi a few doors from the Hotel Tropical. The area code for both Barra and Melaque is 333.

Travel Agents

For airplane tickets and other arrangements, contact **Agencia de Viajes Viacosta** in Barra on Av. Vera Cruz 204 (between Sinaloa and Guanajuato, tel./fax 702-58), open Mon.-Sat. 9-2 and 4-7, closed Sundays. In Melaque, contact the travel agency at the **Hotel Club Náutico,** Gómez Farías 1A, tel. 707-70, 707-66, and 707-76.

Shopping

There are no large markets, traditional or modern, in Barra or Melaque. There are a number of decently stocked **mini-supers** and *fruterias,* however. In Barra, try the government **Conasupo** (on Vera Cruz at the central plaza, open daily 9-9) and the **La Columena** fruit and grocery three doors away (open daily 7-10). (The Conasupo has a sign that they change Canadian money. If so, they are the only such place in Barra.)

In Melaque, nearly all grocery and fruit shopping takes place at the several good stores on main street **Av. San Patricio,** which runs away from the beach near the big microwave tower at the center of town.

Handcrafts

While Melaque has many stores crammed with humdrum commercial tourist curios, **Barra** has three unusual sources. The **Ambar** jewelry and crafts store (at Vera Cruz and Jalisco, beneath the tall palapa restaurant) has an unusual collection of silver, leather, textiles, and ceremonial crafts. Most outstanding of all is the lineup of one-of-a-kind fiesta masks and artifacts from Guerrero (open about 9-8 daily, American Express accepted).

One block away is the decidedly upscale (for Barra) **Tienda Oaxaca,** with racks of high-quality handmade and designer cottons, mostly from Oaxaca and Guadalajara. Not cheap, they are nevertheless marked at around half of what you would expect to pay in the U.S. or Canada for similar items (open daily 9-8:30, credit cards accepted).

Barra has a small **folk-crafts market** on the central plaza open daily 9-6. Most of the vendors seem to have brought the items from their own Pacific Mexico locales—which range from Sinaloa and Nayarit to Oaxaca and Guerrero. The Jalisco paper items especially, such as sculptures of human figures in local dress, and papier-mâché parrots—are bargainable for prices far below Manzanillo and Puerto Vallarta levels.

INFORMATION

Tourist Information Office

The small Barra-Melaque branch office of the Jalisco Department of Tourism is tucked away on Calle Sonora (tel./fax 333-701-00), around the corner from the Hotel Tropical. They distribute literature and answer questions during office hours (Mon.-Fri. 9 a.m.-7:30 p.m., Sat. 9-1).

Health And Police

In Barra, the government **Centro de Salud** clinic (corner Vera Cruz and Puerto de La Navidad, four blocks from the town square, no phone) has a doctor 24 hours a day. The Melaque Centro de Salud branch (Calle Gordiano Gaymar 10, off main beachside street Gómez Farías three blocks south of the big microwave tower) offers the same services, plus an ambulance, which can whisk emergency cases to Manzanillo when necessary.

For routine consultations, a number of Barra and Melaque doctors are available long hours at their own pharmacies. For example, in Barra, see Jose Quintero López, M.D. (on call 24 hours, tel. 703-16), evenings till ten at Farmacia Marcela, Av. Vera Cruz 69, around the corner from the bank.

Melaque's ambulance-equipped **paramedic** squad is on call and reachable on CB channel 9. **Police** are at the city office at 179 Vera Cruz by the central plaza, tel. 703-99. For the Melaque police headquarters, dial 700-80.

Books, Newspapers, And Magazines

The Barra **newsstand,** open daily 7 a.m.-9 p.m., at the corner of Vera Cruz and Michoacán, regularly stocks *Time, People, Life,* and the Mexico City *News* (which arrives around 1 p.m.) In Melaque, the **Librería Magnolia,** open daily 9-9, at Lopez Mateos 49F, on the central plaza, stocks the *News.*

Perhaps the best English-language lending library in all of Pacific Mexico is **Beer Bob's Book Exchange** on a Barra back street (61 Mazatlán, at Sinaloa). Thousands of well-used paperbacks, free for borrowing or exchange, fill the shelves. Chief librarian Bob (actually, Duane Renville, USN retired) manages his little gem of an establishment just for the fun of it. It is not a store, he says; just drop your old titles in the box and take away the equivalent from his well-organized collection. If you have nothing to exchange, simply return whatever you borrow before you leave town.

Ecology Group

The Grupo Ecologio de Cihuatlán maintains an ongoing save-the-turtles campaign. Some especially dedicated members have taken up residence at secluded local beaches in order to discourage poaching. Local leaders, who include teachers at the *preparatorio* in Cihuatlán and the *segundaria* in La Manzanilla, organize frequent antipoaching patrols among their friends, colleagues, and students. They are in-

Local chapters of Mexico's grassroots Partido Ecologista ("Ecology Party") are becoming increasingly influential in municipal elections.

terested in meeting visitors seriously interested in joining their efforts. For more information, contact the tourist information office (see above) in Barra.

GETTING THERE AND AWAY

By Air

Barra de Navidad is easily accessible to U.S. and Mexican destinations via the **Manzanillo** (officially the Playa de Oro) International Airport 18 miles (29 km) south. For detailed destination, arrival, and departure information, see "Getting There and Away" in the "Manzanillo" chapter.

By Car Or RV

Three highway routes access Barra de Navidad: from the north via Puerto Vallarta, from the south via Manzanillo, and from the northeast via Guadalajara.

From Puerto Vallarta, **Mexican National Highway 200** is all asphalt and in good condition along its 134-mile (216-km) stretch to Barra de Navidad. Traffic is generally light, and there are no long steep grades. Traffic may slow a bit as the highway climbs the 2,400-foot Sierra Cuale summit near El Tuito south of Puerto Vallarta, but the light traffic and the generally excellent road make safe passing relatively simple. Allow about three hours for this easy, very scenic trip either way.

From Manzanillo, the 38-mile (61-km) stretch of Hwy. 200 is nearly all country and all level. It's a snap in under an hour.

The same is not true, however, of the winding, 181-mile (291-km) route between Barra de Navidad and Guadalajara. From Plaza del Sol at the center of Guadalajara, follow the signs for Colima along the four-lane **Mexican National Highway 15** heading southwest. Nineteen miles from the city center, just after Hwy. 15 continues straight ahead for Morelia and Mexico City, turn right onto **Mexican National Highways 80 and 54** at a sign marked "Barra de Navidad" just after a sharp curve. Two miles farther, Hwy. 54 branches left to Colima; take the right branch, Mexican National Hwy. 80, to Barra de Navidad. From there, the narrow, two-lane, sometimes crowded, sometimes potholed road continues through a dozen little towns, over mountain grades, and around sharp curves for another 160 miles (258 km) to Melaque and Barra de Navidad. To be safe, allow at least six hours' driving time for the whole trip, either way.

By Bus

A number of regional bus lines cooperate in connecting Barra de Navidad and Melaque north with Puerto Vallarta, south with Cihuatlán, Manzanillo, and Lázaro Cárdenas, and northeast to Guadalajara. They arrive and leave so often (about every 15 minutes during the day) from the little Barra de Navidad station (on Av. Vera Cruz a block and a half past the central plaza, tel. 702-65, open daily 8 a.m.-10 p.m.) that they're practically indistinguishable from one another.

Of the bus lines, **Transportes Cihuatlán** and its sister line, **Autocamiones del Pacifico,** provide the most options: Super-first-class "Primera Plus" buses connect (three per day) with Guadalajara, Manzanillo, and Puerto Vallarta. In addition to this, Transportes Cihuatlán offers at least a dozen second-class buses per day in all three directions. These stop anywhere along the road where passengers wave them down.

All of the buses that stop in Barra also stop at the Melaque **Central de Autobuses** (on Gómez Farías at V. Carranza, tel. 700-03, open 24 hours).

Tres Estrellas de Oro (TEO) does not stop in Barra, however. It maintains its own small station in Melaque (at Gómez Farías 257, tel. 702-43). From there, TEO connects by first-class express north all they way with Tijuana twice a day, and east with Colima (continuing northeast to Guadalajara) once a day.

Note: All Barra de Navidad and Melaque bus departures are *salidas de paso,* meaning that they originate somewhere else. Reserved seats *(asientos reservados),* however, are generally available (with the possible exception of Christmas and Easter).

MANZANILLO AND INLAND TO COLIMA

MANZANILLO

Manzanillo (pop. around 100,000) is a small city tucked at the southern corner of a bay so broad it has room for a pair of five-mile-wide junior bays. From the north spreads the **Bahía de Santiago,** separated by the jutting Peninsula de Santiago from its twin **Bahía de Manzanillo** on the south.

Manzanillo's importance as a port has continued since the conquest. Even its name comes from its fortunate harborfront location, where *manzanillos*—trees whose poisonous yellowish red fruit resembles a small apple, or *manzanillo*—flourished beside the orginal wharves.

The splendid local fishing led to an unexpected bonus: flocks of visitors, drawn by Manzanillo's annual International Sailfish Tournament. During three days in 1957, for example, tournament participants brought in 336 sailfish. The word soon got around. The balmy winters and the golden sand beaches drew even more

visitors. By the 1980s, a string of small hotels, condos, and resorts lined Manzanillo's long, soft strands, providing jobs and opportunities in the previously sleepy bayside communities of Santiago and Salagua.

HISTORY

Before Columbus
One of the earliest records of Manzanillo comes from a story of Ix, king of ancient Coliman, now the state of Colima. The legend states that Ix received visits from Chinese trader-emissaries at a shore village, which became the present town of Salagua, on Tzalahua Bay (now the Bay of Manzanillo). It's not surprising that the dream of riches gained by trade propelled the Chinese across the Pacific hundreds of years before the Spanish conquest. The same goal drew Columbus across

the Atlantic, and pushed Hernán Cortés to this gateway to the Orient a generation later.

Conquest And Colonial Times

Cortés heard of the legend of the Chinese at Manzanillo Bay from the emperor of the Tarascan kingdom in Michoacán. With the riches of China tantalizingly within his grasp, Cortés sent his lieutenants to conquer Pacific Mexico, on whose sheltered beaches they would build ships to realize Columbus's old elusive quest.

In 1522, Gonzalo de Sandoval, under orders from Cortés, reconnoitered Manzanillo Bay, looking for safe anchorages and good shipbuilding sites. Before he left a year later, Sandoval granted an audience to local chieftains at the tip of the Santiago Peninsula, which to this day retains the name Playa la Audiencia.

Cortés himself visited Manzanillo Bay twice, in pursuit of a Portuguese fleet rumored to be somewhere off the coast. Cortés massed his forces at the northern bay of Manzanillo, which he christened Bahía de Santiago on July 24, 1535. Although Cortés's enemy failed to appear, the foreign threat remained. Portuguese, English, and French corsairs menaced Spain's galleons as they repaired, watered, and unloaded their rich cargoes for ten generations in Manzanillo and other sheltered Pacific harbors.

Independence

The hope generated by Independence in 1821 soon dissipated in the turbulent civil conflicts of the next half century. Manzanillo languished until President Porfirio Diaz's orderly but heavy-handed rule (1876-1910) finally brought peace. The railroad arrived in 1889; telephone, electricity, drainage, and potable water soon followed. During the 1950s and '60s the harbor was modernized and deepened, attracting ships from all over the Pacific and capital for new industries. Anticipating the demand, the government built a huge oil-fueled (but unfortunately smoky) generating plant, which powered a fresh wave of factories. By the 1970s, Manzanillo had become a major Pacific manufacturing center and port, providing thousands of local jobs in dozens of mining, agricultural, and fishing enterprises.

Recent Times

Although Mexican tourists had been coming to Manzanillo for years, international arrivals

Charming reminders of old Mexico await visitors who stroll Manzanillo's downtown lanes.

grew rapidly after the opening of the big Club Maeva and Las Hadas resorts in the 1970s. The new jetport north of town increased the steady flow to a flood; then came the 1980s, with Bo Derek starring in her fabulously successful movie *Ten,* which rocketed Las Hadas and Manzanillo to the stars among international vacation destinations.

SIGHTS

Getting Oriented

Long-timers know two Manzanillos: The old downtown, clustered around the south-end harborfront *jardín,* and the rest—greater Manzanillo—spread northerly along the sandy shores of **Manzanillo** and **Santiago Bays.** The downtown has the banks, the government services, and the busy market district, while most of the hotels, restaurants, and tourist businesses dot the northern beachfronts.

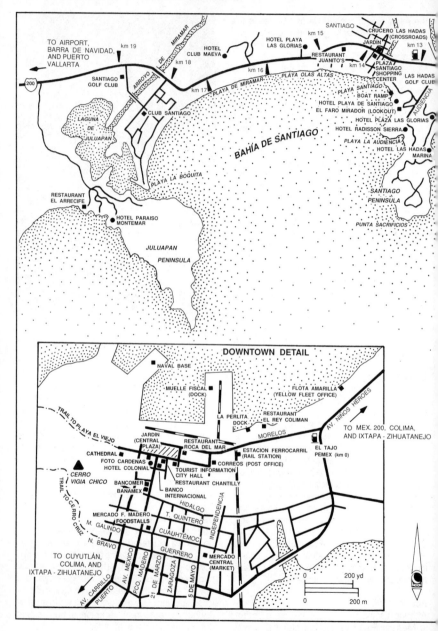

SANTIAGO

MIRAMAR

TO AIRPORT,
BARRA DE NAVIDAD,
AND PUERTO
VALLARTA

km 19

HOTEL
CLUB MAEVA

HOTEL PLAYA
LAS GLORIAS

km 15

CRUCERO LAS HADAS
(CROSSROADS)

JARDIN

km 13

km 18

RESTAURANT
JUANITO'S

km 14

PLAZA
SANTIAGO
SHOPPING
CENTER

200

DE

ARROYO

SANTIAGO
GOLF CLUB

km 16

PLAYA OLAS ALTAS

LAS HADAS
GOLF CLUB

km 17

PLAYA DE MIRAMAR

PLAYA SANTIAGO

AUDIENCIA

CLUB SANTIAGO

BOAT RAMP

LAGUNA
DE
JULUAPAN

HOTEL PLAYA DE SANTIAGO
EL FARO MIRADOR (LOOKOUT)

BAHÍA DE SANTIAGO

HOTEL PLAZA LAS GLORIAS

HOTEL RADISSON SIERRA

PLAYA LA AUDIENCIA

HOTEL LAS HADAS

PLAYA LA BOQUITA

MARINA

RESTAURANT
EL ARRECIFE

SANTIAGO
PENINSULA

HOTEL PARAISO
MONTEMAR

PUNTA SACRIFICIOS

JULUAPAN
PENINSULA

DOWNTOWN DETAIL

NAVAL BASE

MUELLE FISCAL
(DOCK)

FLOTA AMARILLA
(YELLOW FLEET OFFICE)

AV. NIÑOS HEROES

LA PERLITA
DOCK

RESTAURANT
EL REY COLIMAN

TRAIL TO PLAYA EL VIEJO

MORELOS

TO MEX. 200, COLIMA,
AND IXTAPA - ZIHUATANEJO

JARDIN
(CENTRAL
PLAZA)

RESTAURANT
ROCA DEL MAR

ESTACION FERROCARRIL
(RAIL STATION)

EL TAJO
PEMEX (km 0)

CATHEDRAL

CORREOS (POST OFFICE)

FOTO CARDENAS
HOTEL COLONIAL

TOURIST INFORMATION
CITY HALL

CERRO
VIGIA CHICO

BANCOMER
BANAMEX

RESTAURANT CHANTILLY

BANCO
INTERNACIONAL

TRAIL TO CERRO CRUZ

MERCADO F. MADERO
FOODSTALLS

HIDALGO

M. GALINDO

T. QUINTERO

N. BRAVO

CUAUHTEMOC

INDEPENDENCIA

GUERRERO

TO CUYUTLÁN,
COLIMA, AND
IXTAPA - ZIHUATANEJO

AV. MEXICO

FCO. MADERO

21 DE MARZO

ZARAGOZA

5 DE MAYO

MERCADO
CENTRAL
(MARKET)

AV. CARRILLO
PUERTO

0   200 yd

0   200 m

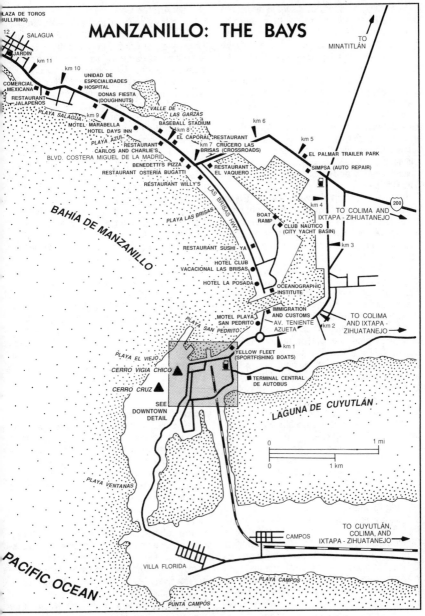

MANZANILLO: THE BAYS

PLAZA DE TOROS (BULLRING)

12 SALAGUA

JARDÍN

km 11

km 10

TO MINATITLÁN

COMERCIAL MEXICANA

RESTAURANT JALAPEÑOS

PLAYA SALAGUA

MOTEL MARABELLA

HOTEL DAYS INN

PLAYA AZUL

RESTAURANT CARLOS AND CHARLIE'S

BLVD. COSTERA MIGUEL DE LA MADRID

BENEDETTI'S PIZZA

RESTAURANT OSTERÍA BUGATTI

RESTAURANT WILLY'S

UNIDAD DE ESPECIALIDADES HOSPITAL

DONAS FIESTA (DOUGHNUTS)

VALLE DE LAS GARZAS

BASEBALL STADIUM

km 8

EL CAPORAL RESTAURANT

km 7 CRUCERO LAS BRISAS (CROSSROADS)

RESTAURANT EL VAQUERO

km 6

km 5

EL PALMAR TRAILER PARK

SIMPSA (AUTO REPAIR)

km 4

TO COLIMA AND IXTAPA - ZIHUATANEJO

200

BAHÍA DE MANZANILLO

PLAYA LAS BRISAS

LAS BRISAS HWY.

BOAT RAMP

CLUB NÁUTICO (CITY YACHT BASIN)

RESTAURANT SUSHI-YA

HOTEL CLUB VACACIÓNAL LAS BRISAS

HOTEL LA POSADA

OCEANOGRAPHIC INSTITUTE

km 3

IMMIGRATION AND CUSTOMS

AV. TENIENTE AZUETA

km 2

TO COLIMA AND IXTAPA - ZIHUATANEJO

MOTEL PLAYA SAN PEDRITO

PLAYA SAN PEDRITO

PLAYA EL VIEJO

CERRO VIGIA CHICO

CERRO CRUZ

SEE DOWNTOWN DETAIL

km 1

YELLOW FLEET (SPORTFISHING BOATS)

TERMINAL CENTRAL DE AUTOBUS

LAGUNA DE CUYUTLÁN

0   1 mi

0   1 km

PLAYA VENTANAS

CAMPOS

TO CUYUTLÁN, COLIMA, AND IXTAPA - ZIHUATANEJO

PACIFIC OCEAN

VILLA FLORIDA

PLAYA CAMPOS

PUNTA CAMPOS

© MOON PUBLICATIONS, INC.

Everything north of downtown is measured from the **El Tajo** junction (Km 0), marked by the downtown Pemex station. Here, along bayfront Av. Niños Héroes, the Barra de Navidad-Puerto Vallarta highway starts north just a few blocks from the *jardín.*

The highway curves past foothills and marshland, crossing the mirror-smooth waters of the **Valle de Las Garzas** ("Valley of the Herons") between Kms 5 and 7. The soaring white concrete sculpture at the traffic circle (Km 7) marks the *crucero* Las Brisas (or "suicide crossing" as known locally). Here, the Las Brisas Highway forks left, southward, through a neighborhood of condos, homes, and small hotels fronting **Playa Las Brisas.**

Back on the main highway, now the Boulevard Costera Miguel de la Madrid, continue north past the hotels and restaurants that dot the long **Playa Azul** beachfront. Just after the dusty little town *jardín* of **Salagua** around Km 11, a golf course and big white gate mark the Las Hadas *crucero* (crossing) at Km 12. There, Av. Audiencia leads uphill along the plush, condo-dotted **Santiago Peninsula,** flanked by the Las Hadas resort on its south side and Hotel Radisson Sierra on **Playa La Audiencia** on the north.

Back on the main road, continuing north, you pass the Pemex gas station at Km 13. Soon comes the Rio Colorado creek bridge, then the **Santiago** town *jardín* on the right, across from the restaurants, banks, and stores of **Plaza Santiago** shopping center (Km 13.5) on the left.

From there, traffic thins out, as you pass scattered beachfront condos along **Playa Olas Altas** (Km 15-16). Soon the **Club Maeva** spreads, like a colony of giant blue-and-white mushrooms, along the hill above **Playa de Miramar** at Km 17. Finally, another golf course and entrance gate at Km 19 mark the vacation-home community of **Playa Santiago.**

Getting Around

Visitors can easily drive, taxi (share to make it affordable), or bus to their favorite stops along Manzanillo's long shoreline. Dozens of **local buses** run along the highway through Las Brisas, Salagua, and Santiago (destinations marked on the windshields), all eventually returning to the downtown *jardín.* Fares (in pesos) run less than half a dollar. Hop on with a supply of small change and you're in business.

A Walk Around Downtown

A pair of busy north-south streets—**Av. Mexico** and **Av. Carrillo Puerto**—dominate the downtown. Avenida Carrillo Puerto traffic runs one way from the *jardín,* while Av. Mexico traffic does the reverse. The corner of Av. Mexico and Av. Juarez, adjacent to the *jardín,* is a colorful slice of old Mexico, crowded with cafes, curio shops, and street vendors. A dignified Porfirian kiosk presides nearby at the *jardín's* center, while, on the far side, bulging rail tank cars queue obediently along dockside Av. Morelos. In the distance, drab gray cutters and destroyer escorts line the **Base Naval** (BAH-say nah-VAHL) wharfs.

Walk a pair of blocks along Av. Juarez (which becomes B. Dávalos) past Av. Mexico to the cathedral, officially the **Parroquia Nuestra Señora de Guadalupe,** after Manzanillo's patron saint. Inside, four shining stained-glass panels flanking the main altar tell the story of Juan Diego and the miracle of the Virgin of Guadalupe.

During the first 12 days of December, a colorful clutter of stalls lines the streetfront, where families bring their children, girls in embroidered *huipiles* and *chinas poblanas* (skirts and blouses), and boys in sombreros and serapes. After paying their respects to the Virgin, they indulge in their favorite holiday foods, and get themselves photographed in front of a portrait of the Virgin. (See "Entertainment and Events" below for more details.)

Town Hills And Market

Steep knolls punctuate Manzanillo's downtown. Residents climb precipitous cobbled alleyways, too narrow for cars, to their small (yet luxuriously perched) homes overlooking the city. For an interesting little detour, follow one of the lanes that angle uphill off Av. Juarez past the end of the *jardín.*

An even steeper hill rises behind the cathedral—the brushy slope of **Cerro Vigia Chico**—where colonial soldiers kept a lookout for pirates. Above and beyond that towers the cross-decorated summit of **Cerro Cruz,** the highest point (about 1,000 feet) above the Bay of Manzanillo. Every May 3, *perigrinos* (pilgrims) climb to its summit. (See "Hikes" below.)

A Manzanillo downtown walk wouldn't be complete without including a stroll down Av.

Mexico, past a dozen old-fashioned little shops—*papelerías, farmacias, dulcerías, panaderías*—to the **Mercado** (turn left at Cuauhtémoc) at Calle Cinco de Mayo. Here you can wander among the mounds of bright produce, admire the festoons of piñatas, say a good word to the shrimp-sellers, and stop to listen to the harangue of a sidewalk politician or evangelist. (See "Shopping" below.)

BEACHES

Playa San Pedrito

Playa San Pedrito is Manzanillo's closest-to-downtown beach, a tranquil little strip of sand right on the harbor along Av. Teniente Azueta (which angles off Niños Héroes half a mile from the El Tajo junction Pemex station). The perfect Mexican Sunday beach, San Pedrito has lots of golden sand, seafood palapas, and a few big trees for shade. Although its very gentle waves are fine for swimming and windsurfing (with your own equipment) Playa San Pedrito is too close to the harbor for much good fishing or snorkeling.

Manzanillo Bay Beaches

From either the *jardín* or the Las Brisas *crucero*, ride a Las Brisas-marked bus to end-of-the-line Hotel La Posada at the southern end of **Playa Las Brisas.** From the jetty, which marks the entrance to the Puerto Interior ("Inner Harbor"), a hundred-foot-wide sand ribbon seems to curve north without end. It changes its name to **Playa Azul,** then **Playa Salagua** along its five-mile length, ending finally at Las Hadas at the base of the Santiago Peninsula. The beach, while wide, is also steep. The usually gentle waves break suddenly at the sand, allowing little chance for surfing, bodysurfing, or boogieboarding. Windsurfing (bring your own equipment) and surf fishing, however, are popular, as are snorkeling and scuba diving among the fish, which swarm around the corals and rocks of the south-end jetty.

A number of restaurants along the beaches provide refreshments. They include the Hotel La Posada and the Club Vacacional Las Brisas on Playa Las Brisas, Carlos and Charlie's and the big white Days Inn on Playa Azul, and Motel Marabella on Playa Salagua.

The Santiago Peninsula And Playa La Audiencia

One of Manzanillo's loveliest views is from **El Faro,** the white tower atop the Santiago Peninsula. At Las Hadas *crucero* (Km 12) turn onto the cobbled Av. Audiencia. Continue past the golf course to the top of the rise, turn right at Calle La Reyna, and keep winding upward to the summit. Although El Faro is the centerpiece of a serene condominium community atop the hill, they don't mind if you climb their tower.

The view is unforgettable. From the emerald ridge of the **Juluapan Peninsula** and the 4,000-foot (1,300-meter) **Cerro Toro** bull's hump on the north, the panorama sweeps past green sierras and the blue bays to the white downtown spread beneath the pyramid-peak of **Cerro Cruz** on the southern horizon. On the ocean side, due west, the **Hotel Radisson Sierra** rises above the diminutive sand ribbon of **Playa la Audiencia.**

Once an idyllic downscale cove, Playa la Audiencia is now dominated by the ultramodern gleaming white tower of the Hotel Radisson Sierra. Families nevertheless still come here on Sunday to play in the fine golden-black sand, drink coconut milk, eat tacos, and leave everything on the beach. The beach concessionaire, Promociones y Recreaciones Playa Audiencia, rents kayaks, windsurfing boards, waterskis, jet-ski boats, banana boats, and boogieboards right on the beach (daily 9-6; tel. 381-48). Instructors (see "Sports" below) from the hotel often guide **snorkeling** and **scuba diving** parties from the beach to the shoals on either side.

Santiago Bay Beaches

The beaches of Santiago Bay stretch for five golden miles north of the Santiago Peninsula to **La Boquita,** the lagoon-mouth beneath the Juluapan Peninsula's headland. The beaches are continuous variations of the same wide carpet of yellow, semicoarse sand.

First, at around Km 14, **Playa Santiago** reaches the Río Colorado creek, where it becomes **Playa Olas Altas.** Here, although the sand drops steeply into the surf, it levels out offshore, so the waves roll in gradually, providing excellent **surfing, bodysurfing,** and **boogieboarding breaks.**

Playa Miramar continues past Club Maeva, marked by the highway pedestrian overpass.

The beach itself is popular and cluttered with umbrellas, horses for rent, and vendors. The usually gentle surf is good for **bodysurfing** and **boogieboarding.** Concessionaires rent boogieboards for about $2 an hour.

Finally, at Club Santiago, the beach curves past a village of seafood palapas and fishing boats called **La Boquita** ("The Little Mouth"). The sand is wide, firm, and the surf is as tranquil as a huge kiddie pool. Offshore, a 200-foot wreck swarms with fish a few feet from the surface, excellent for **snorkeling** and **scuba diving.** On the other side of the beach, the **Laguna de Juluapan,** a wildlife-rich tidal wetland, winds along miles of forest-edged shallows and grassy marshes.

Hikes

The adventurous can seek out Manzanillo's many hidden corners, beginning right downtown. **Playa Viejo** is often missed, tucked in a little cove over the hill and accessible by path only. Wear walking shoes and a hat, and take your bathing suit, water, and a picnic lunch. Follow Calle Balbino Dávalos past the cathedral. Bear left up the narrow street and climb the steep concrete staircase (on the left) to the hilltop schoolyard. Continue down the other side along a wooded arroyo trail to the beach. The dark sand beach is strewn with shells and surf-rounded rocks. One dry, grassy spot for possible camping perches above the surf.

Also beginning from downtown, the steep trail to **Cerro Vigia Chico and Cerro Cruz** will challenge fit hikers. It leads to the top of the highest point in Manzanillo for breezy panoramic views of the city, bay, and ocean below. Allow about an hour and a half roundtrip for Cerro Vigia Chico, about twice that for the very steep continuation to Cerro Cruz (see below). Take plenty of water, and avoid midday heat by going early in the morning or late afternoon.

Head south along Av. Carrillo Puerto from the *jardín.* Notice the *sastrería* (tailor shop) Aguayo at no. 223 on the left-hand side, where the master tailor sews suits by hand. Turn the corner at the tortillería at Nícholas Bravo and head along the upward lane, past little hillside-perched houses. Ask the local people if you get lost. Ask "¿A Cerro Vigia, por favor?" They'll help keep you on the right track.

You'll know you've arrived when you see the white "Turquoise Radio" FM transmitter station atop the hill.

Cerro Cruz

Extra-fit hikers can gather breath and push ahead, along the steep, forested uphill path from "Turquoise Radio" to the summit of Cerro Cruz. There, a majestic panorama spreads below: from the Gibraltar-like headland of Juluapan in the north, past golden beaches, over the villa-studded Santiago Peninsula, past the white city to the huge expanse of the Laguna de Cuyutlán, where power stanchions leapfrog across the lagoon from the gargantuan, smoke-spewing seaside power plant.

ACCOMMODATIONS

Downtown Hotels

Near cafes, shopping, and transportation, Manzanillo's downtown is colorful and lively, but often noisy.

The **Hotel Colonial,** Manzanillo's best downtown hotel, is built around a dignified interior courtyard-restaurant. Dating from the 1940s, the Colonial is replete with old-fashioned touches—bright-hued tile staircases, stained-glass windows, and sentimental tile wall scenes. The rooms, although worn, have traditional high ceilings, hand-hewn leather chairs, and wrought-iron lamp fixtures. They open to shady, street-view corridors, lined with chairs for sitting. Try for a room on the relatively quiet Bocanegra Street side of the hotel (Bocanegra 28, at Av. Mexico, Manzanillo, Colima 28200, tel. 333-210-80, 333-211-34, 333-212-30). Their 38 rooms rent for about $20 s or d with fan, $22 with a/c; one block from the *jardín,* credit cards accepted.

If you prefer the beach, the **Motel Playa San Pedrito** offers a homey close-in alternative, right on popular Playa San Pedrito (Teniente Azueta 3, Manzanillo, Colima 28200, tel. 333-205-35). This unpretentiously Mexican family hotel rambles amidst a flowery garden, edged with colorful tropical plants and centering on a bubbling, blue swimming pool. A well-kept tennis court stands at one side, and beyond that, waves lap the sandy beach. With all those outdoor attractions, the plainness of the rooms and the dust in their corners matter

OWNING PARADISE

Droves of once-visitors have fled their northern winters and have bought or permanently rented a part of their favorite Pacific Mexico paradise. They happily reside all or part of the year in beachside developments that have mushroomed, especially in Mazatlán, Puerto Vallarta, Manzanillo, and Acapulco. Deluxe vacation homes, which foreigners can own through special trusts, run upward from about $50,000; condos begin at about half that. Timeshares, a type of rental, start at about $5,000.

Trusts

Past Mexican generations have feared (with some justification) that foreigners were out to buy their country. Present laws prohibit foreigners from having direct title to property within 30 miles (50 km) of a beachfront or within 60 miles (100 km) of a national border.

Mexican law, however, permits *fideicomisos*—trusts—which substitute for outright foreign ownership. Trusts allow you (as beneficiary) all the usual rights to the property, such as use, sale, improvement, and transfer, in exchange for paying an annual fee to a Mexican bank (the trustee), which holds nominal title to the property. Trust ownership has been compared to owning all the shares of a corporation, which in turn owns a factory. While not owning the factory in name, you have legal control over it.

Although some folks have been bilked into buying south-of-the-border equivalents of the Brooklyn Bridge, Mexican trust ownership is a happy reality for growing numbers of American, Canadian, and European beneficiaries who simply love Mexico.

Bienes raíces (real estate) in Mexico works a lot like in the U.S. and Canada. Agents work through multiple listings, show properties, assist negotiations, track paperwork, and earn commissions for sales completed. If you're interested in buying a Mexican property, work with one of the many honest and hard-working Mexican agents, preferably recommended through a reliable back-home firm.

Once you find a good property and have a written sales agreement in hand, your agent should recommend a notary *(notaria publica)* who, unlike a

U.S. notary public, is an attorney skilled and licensed in property transactions. A Mexican notary, functioning much as a title company does in the U.S., is the star actor in completing your transaction. The notary traces the title, ensuring that your bank-trustee legally receives it, making sure that the agreed-upon amounts of money get transferred between you, seller, bank, agent, and notary.

You and your agent should meet jointly with the notary early on to discuss the deal and get the notary's computation of the closing costs. For a typical trust-sale, closing costs (covering permit, filing, bank, notary, and registry fees) are considerable, typically about 8-10% of the sale amount. After that, you will continue to owe property taxes and an approximately one percent annual fee to your bank-trustee.

Time-sharing

Started in Europe, time-sharing has spread all over the globe. A time-share is a prepaid rental of a condo for a specified time period per year. Agreements usually allow you to temporarily exchange your time-share rental for similar lodgings throughout the world.

Your first contact with time-sharing will often be someone on a resort street corner who offers you a half-price tour for "an hour of your time." Soon you'll be attending a hard-sell session that offers you tempting inducements in exchange for a check written on the spot. The basic appeal is that your investment—say $10,000 cash for a two-week annual stay in a deluxe beach condo—will earn you a handsome profit if you decide to sell your rights sometime in the future. What they don't mention is that the interest that you could get for your $10,000 cash would go far toward renting an equally luxurious vacation condo every year without entailing as much risk.

And risk there is, because you would be handing over your cash for a promise only. Read the fine print. Shop around, and don't give away anything until you inspect the condo you would be getting and talk to others who have invested in the same time-share. It may be a good deal, but don't let them rush you into Paradise.

little. Request one of the *piso arriba* (upper-floor) rooms for privacy and sea views from a front balcony-corridor. The 33 fan-only rooms go for about $24 d, $27 t; with parking, and credit cards are accepted.

Las Brisas-Playa Azul Hotels

The swish of the waves on the sand, long walks at dusk, and good restaurants nearby summarize the attractions of the "passionate pink" **Hotel La Posada,** a durable jewel among Manzanillo's

MANZANILLO HOTELS

Manzanillo hotels, in order of increasing approximate double-room price (area code 333, postal code 28200)

Hotel Colonial, Bocanegra 28, 210-80, 211-34, $20

Hotel Playa de Santiago, P.O. Box 147, 300-55, fax 303-44, $24

Motel Playa San Pedrito, Teniente Azueta 3, 205-35, $24

Motel Parador Marabella, Km 8.5 Playa Azul (P.O. Box 554), 311-03, 311-05, $29

Club Vacacional Las Brisas, Av. L. Cárdenas 207, 320-75, 317-47, $31

Paraiso Montemar, Peninsula Juluapan, 317-11, 322-70, $50

Fiesta Mexicana-Days Inn, Blvd. Miguel de la Madrid Km 8.5 (P.O. Box 808), 321-80, (800) 325-2525, $58

Hotel La Posada, Av. L. Cárdenas 201, 318-99, $64

Club Maeva, P.O. Box 440, 301-41, fax 303-95, (800) GO-MAEVA, $73

Hotel Sierra Radisson Plaza, Av. La Audiencia 1, 320-00, fax 322-72, (800) 333-3333, $120

Las Hadas, P.O. Box 158, 300-00, fax 304-30, (800) 228-3000, $150

and comfortable but not deluxe, are on the beachside ocean-view upper floors. The 56 rooms and suites, all with kitchenettes, rent from about $31 d with fan, a/c available; with restaurant-bar, street parking, and credit cards accepted.

The **Hotel Fiesta Mexicana-Days Inn,** right on Playa Azul, appears as a big white box perched on the beach (Carretera Manzanillo-Santiago Km 8.5, Blvd. Miguel de la Madrid, P.O. Box 808, Manzanillo, Colima 28200, tel. 333-321-80). Inside, however, the rooms rise in tiers, which enclose a lovely patio with a meandering blue pool. On one side is a big restaurant with an ocean-vista veranda. The rooms are small-ish but comfortable, with TV, phones, and a/c. The rooms on the ocean side look out on sea views. Their 190 rooms rent for about $58 d, low-season promotions are sometimes available; with street parking and pool aerobics; credit cards are accepted; in the U.S. and Canada, reserve through the Days Inn toll-free number (800) 325-2525.

Not far away, the **Motel Parador Marabella** offers a breezy beachfront location at reasonable prices (Km 8.5 Playa Azul, P.O. Box 554, Manzanillo, Colima 28200, tel. 333-311-03, 311-05). All the ingredients seem to be in place—a small pool, rustling palms, a small bar-restaurant, sand and surf—for a tranquil Manzanillo week in the sun. The best rooms, on the upper floor of the two-story wing, have private balconies and sea views. Rates for the 60 rooms run about about $35 d with a/c, $29 with fan; with parking, and credit cards are accepted.

Santiago Peninsula Hotels

The Santiago Peninsula's sea-view villas, condo developments, and resorts for the rich and famous are luxuriously isolated, generally requiring a car or taxi to get anywhere.

Hotel Las Hadas is a self-contained city with a host of pleasurable amenities (P.O. Box 158,

small hotels (Av. Lázaro Cárdenas 201, P.O. Box 201, Manzanillo, Colima 28200, tel. 333-318-99). Every memorable detail—leafy potted plants, rustling palms, brick arches, airy beach-view *sala,* resplendent bay-view sunsets—adds to La Posada's romantic ambience. La Posada's clientele, mostly middle-aged North American winter vacationers, prefer the upstairs rooms, some of which have private balconies and sea views. Get your winter reservations in early. Rates for the 24 comfortable but non-deluxe rooms run about $64 d high season, some with a/c, including a big breakfast. Up to 30% low-season discounts are sometimes available. The hotel has a bar-cart, snack restaurant, good pool, street parking, and accepts credit cards.

A few doors north along the beach, the **Club Vacacional Las Brisas** likewise enjoys platoons of repeat customers (Av. L. Cárdenas 207, Fracc. Las Brisas, Manzanillo, Colima 28200, tel. 333-320-75, 333-317-47). Good on-site management keeps the garden manicured, the pool inviting, and the beach beyond the gate clean and golden. The best rooms, white-walled

Manzanillo, Colima 28200, tel. 333-300-00, fax 333-304-30). Las Hadas is so large that only a fraction of its rooms are near the sand, however. Most are a small hike to the beach. When guests finally get there, furthermore, they find no waves on the sheltered Las Hadas cove, and their views are further cluttered by the white Arabian-style tents of a regiment of fellow guests.

Las Hadas nevertheless offers plenty of interest, at extra charge: three restaurants, a sport-fishing marina, a sunset cruise, horseback riding, a golf course, a squadron of tennis courts, and a dozen aquatic sports. You'll have to do without parasailing, however. The approximately 300 luxurious white-and-blue motif suites, villas, and rooms rent from about $150 standard d to about $270 for a junior suite with breakfast and all amenities, including complete wheelchair access. For U.S. and Canada reservations, call Westin Hotels toll-free at (800) 228-3000.

On the other side of the peninsula, the shining white **Hotel Sierra** (officially the Hotel Radisson Sierra Plaza) towers futuristically above the gemlike Playa La Audiencia (Av. La Audiencia 1, Peninsula Santiago, Manzanillo, Colima 28200, tel. 333-320-00, fax 322-72). The hotel's large size, however, doesn't seem to bother the guests, whose activities focus upon the spreading ocean-view pool-patio. There, around the swim-up bar, drinks flow, music bounces, and water volleyball and polo fill the sunny days. No matter if guests tire of pool frolicking; every hotel corner, from the indulgent pastel-appointed rooms (each with sea-view balcony) to **Hidra,** the airy, rustic-chic restaurant-in-the-round, abounds with style. Bars offer nightly live music; fine crafts and designer clothes fill the boutiques, while hundreds of books and dozens of the latest U.S. magazines line the shop shelves. Rates for the 350 rooms run from about $120 d, depending upon season; with a/c, color cable TV, phones, mini-bars, all water sports, tennis, golf, wheelchair access, and credit cards accepted. For U.S. and Canada info and reservations, call the Radisson Hotels toll-free number (800) 333-3333.

Santiago Bay Hotels

The once-grand but now relatively humble '50s-genre **Hotel Playa de Santiago** on the south side of Santiago Bay nevertheless offers much for budget-conscious travelers (Balneario de Santiago s/n, Bahía de Santiago, P.O. Box 147, Santiago, Colima, tel. 333-300-55, 302-70, fax 303-44). Besides spacious, private balcony sea-view rooms overlooking the hotel's placid cove and beach, guests enjoy a palmy, seaside pool-sundeck, a tennis court, a boat ramp, and friendly management. Prices for the 105 rooms and suites run about $24 standard d, $28 deluxe d, and $50 for a split-level eight-bed apartment; phones, fans only; credit cards accepted.

The **Club Maeva,** Manzanillo's all-inclusive fun-in-the-sun colony, spreads for a white-washed quarter-mile on the hillside above Santiago Bay. Club Maeva (whose summer clientele is mostly Mexican, while Canadian and American during the winter), demonstrates the power of numbers. Its staff of 700 services upward of a thousand guests who enjoy a plethora of aquatic, field, court, and gym activities at no extra cost. Months would be needed to take full advantage of the endless sports menu, which includes pool scuba, snorkeling, tennis, horseback riding, volleyball, softball, aerobics, and basketball.

Besides sports, Club Maeva guests enjoy continuous open bar and restaurant service, nightly theme shows, a disco, a miles-long beach, sunning beside Latin America's largest pool, and a complete water-slide park.

Inclusive rather than exclusive, Club Maeva resembles a huge comfortable summer camp. Children are more than welcome, with a special 4- to 12-year-old miniclub. Club Maeva seems to offer options for everyone, such as table games—cards, backgammon, checkers, and chess—Spanish lessons, and a tranquil adults-only solarium and pool-bar.

The rooms, actually clusters of small villas, are an unusual luxurious-Spartan combination, snow white and royal blue with private view balconies and marble floors, but with no movable furniture. With the exception of stoves and refrigerators in some units, all shelves, cabinets, bed platforms, and seats are attractive but indestructible white concrete built-ins (P.O. Box 440, Manzanillo, Colima 28200, tel. 333-301-41, fax 303-95). The 550 rooms and suites rent for about $73 d, room only; all-inclusive plan runs about $88 per person, children 2-12 half price; with a/c, no phones or room TV; credit cards accepted. In the U.S. and Canada, call (800) GO-MAEVA for info and reservations.

Juluapan Peninsula Hotel

From atop its summit perch, the **Hotel Paraiso Montemar** overlooks Juluapan's rocky, windward shore. Originally built as condos for purchase, the many unsold units are managed as a hotel. Set in manicured, palmy hilltop grounds, with pool and clifftop palapa restaurant-bar, the Paraiso Montemar lives up to its name for those who enjoy luxurious solitude. The comfortably appointed stucco-and-tile units, clustered high above a panorama of blue sea, wave-washed cliffs, and hidden coves, enjoy the look and feel of romantic hideaway cottages. Paraiso Montemar's curse and blessing is isolation. A car is a must for shopping, sightseeing, and restaurants (Peninsula Juluapan, Manzanillo, Colima, tel. 333-317-11, 322-70). Rates for their 63 rooms and suites begin at about $50 d low season, $70 high, with a/c, cable TV, and phones; ask for a low-season extra discount. For reservations, write or call their Gualalajara agent: Paraiso Montemar, Tonallan 376, Ciudad del Sol, Guadalajara, Jalisco, tel. (36) 218-179 or (36) 213-546, fax (36) 227-026. Get there via the signed entrance road 2.3 miles (3.7 km) west from the Hwy. 200 turnoff at El Naranjo (Km 22), marked by a "Vida del Mar" sign.

Condominium Rentals

Many Manzanillo vacationers prefer condominiums. Owners often rent their units through agents who specialize in condo listings. Among the best organized is **Intercondos,** whom you can phone at (333) 329-04 or (333) 404-24 or write at P.O. Box 93, Santiago, Colima 28860. (You can also drop by their roadside office Mon.-Sat. at Km 14.5, north end of Santiago.) They rent condos, modest to luxurious, by the day, week, or month. Quality varies widely, however; advance as little deposit as possible on a sight-unseen rental. If it seems too good to be true, it probably is.

On the other hand, if you can't find the right condo for rent, you might look into buying one. Manzanillo's long, uncrowded beaches have many condos for sale, some for very reasonable prices.

Trailer Park And Camping

Guests at **El Palmar,** Manzanillo's only trailer park, enjoy 70 uncrowded, palm-shaded spaces right off the highway in the quiet Valle de las Garzas (Boulevard Costero Miguel de la Madrid Km 4.5, Manzanillo, Colima 28200, tel. 333-232-90). Amenities include a well-maintained pool, shaded club area, hot water, satellite TV, showers, and toilets. The managers are friendly and efficient. Stores, good restaurants, and beaches are within a short drive. Spaces rent for about $12 per day or $220 per month for two persons, all hookups included.

Camping

Condos, hotels, and restaurants have crowded out virtually all camping prospects along Manzanillo beaches. Authorities even discourage overnight RV parking in the remaining open space around Km 18 between Club Maeva and Club Santiago.

The closest good campsites are about a dozen miles north, three miles off Hwy. 200 at **Playa de Oro** (accessible by cobbled road from the signed turnoff near Km 31, five miles north of El Naranjo).

A land development turned sour, Playa de Oro has returned to the wild: an endless sandy beach with many drive-in sites, good for RVs and tents. The surf, while often not too rough, has some undertow; don't swim alone. Boogieboarding and surfing, however, are possible for cautious beginners and intermediates. Surf fishing is excellent, and the waves deposit carpets of shells and miles of driftwood, perfect for a week of beachcombing. You'll share the beach with a colony of sand crabs which, like a legion of arthropodic prairie dogs, jealously guard their individual sand-holes. Bring everything; the closest stores are in El Naranjo.

FOOD

Downtown Snacks And Foodstalls

The cluster of *fondas* (permanent foodstalls) of the **Mercado Francisco Madero** is the downtown mecca for wholesome homestyle cookery. Each *fonda* specializes in a few favorite dishes, which range from rich *pozole* and savory stewed pork, beef, or chicken to ham and eggs and whole grilled fish.

One of the favorites, the **Menudería Paulita** (open daily 5 a.m.-10 p.m.) is tended by a rollicking squad of women (off of Av. Mexico, at the F. Madero and Cuauhtémoc corner, five short blocks from the *jardín*). One of them enjoys the singular job of crafting and baking unending stacks of hot tortillas, which their mostly workingmen customers use to scoop up the last delectable morsels.

Besides sit-down meals, the same downtown neighborhood is a source of on-street desserts. These include *churros* (long doughnuts) and **pastries**, sold from carts late afternoons along Av. Mexico about four blocks from the *jardín*, and velvety ice cream from the **Bing** downtown branch (on the east end of the *jardín*).

North-end Breakfast And Snacks

Along the north-side highway, regulars flock nightly to tiny **Pepe's**, which specializes in mouth-watering barbecued beef, roast chicken, and pork loin tacos (around Km 8.5 Hwy. 200, beach side, open daily 7 p.m.-1 a.m.).

Folks who don't emerge too late from Pepe's will still be able to enjoy the main event at the nearby **Donas Fiesta** doughnut shop (Km 9

Doughnutlike deep-fried churros rank among downtown Manzanillo's most popular street snacks.

Hwy. 200, beach side, among the car rental agencies, open daily 7 a.m.-10 p.m., tel. 400-51). Besides her "All American" made-fresh doughnuts, the American proprietress also supplies creamy milkshakes, hot chocolate, and freshly ground hot coffee, all perfect prescriptions for homesick palates.

No local vacation would be complete without breakfast or lunch at **Juanito's**, Manzanillo's friendly refuge from Mexico (in Santiago, Km 13.5, a few blocks north of Santiago Plaza, open daily 8 a.m.-10 p.m., tel. 313-88). The longtime American expatriate owner features tasty, modestly priced hometown fare, such as ham and eggs any style, hotcakes, hamburgers, milkshakes, and apple pie. For a generation of repeat customers, Juanito's is home away from home, with satellite TV, *USA Today* for sale, a long-distance telephone, and bottomless cups of coffee.

Downtown Restaurants

(Complete Dinner Price Key: Budget = under $7, Moderate = $7-14, Expensive = over $14.) One of Manzanillo's prime people-watching cafes is the **Restaurant Chantilly** *(jardín* corner adjacent to City Hall; open daily except Saturday, 7 a.m.-10 p.m., tel. 201-94). The completely unpretentious Chantilly offers its mostly local clientele prompt service, an extensive economical menu, and long moments lingering over several varieties of *cafe espresso*. The *comida corrida* (five-course set lunch, $4.50) highlights many patrons' downtown day. Budget.

The dockside **Restaurant Rey Coliman**, one of the central district's few fancy eateries, specializes in romance. Candleglow, soft music, yachts swaying gently nearby, and glimmering harbor lights set the tone, while fresh oysters, shrimp, fish, lobster and meat dishes fill the tables. (Niños Héroes 411, on the seafront *malecón*, three blocks from the *jardín*, tel. 215-03, open daily 11-10, credit cards accepted). Moderate.

Sharing the same dockfront, **Restaurant Lychee** serves Chinese food that would be quite respectable even in San Francisco (Niños Héroes 397, open Mon.-Sat. noon-10, tel. 211-03). The mounds of crisp broccoli, bean sprouts, snow peas, and bok choy that enrich their dishes spell welcome relief for vegetable-hungry palates. Moderate.

Las Brisas Restaurants

Several popular restaurants cluster around the *crucero* Las Brisas intersection (marked by the traffic circle and sculpture) at Km 7. Foremost among them is **Osteria Bugatti**, which provides much more than its mere oyster house label suggests (open daily 1:30 p.m.-midnight, tel. 329-99, credit cards accepted). As much a nightclub as a restaurant, Bugatti's is where older folks go to remember the '40s and the young find out what they missed. The scene is certainly correct: couples swaying to live dance-floor swing and bebop, a platoon of tuxedo-attired waiters scurrying to and fro beneath glimmering chandeliers, and a strictly old-fashioned mayonnaise, boiled vegetable, meat, and spumoni menu. (Actually, it's a little better than that: You can get *ensalata* Caesar, good pastas, T-bone steak, pork chops, stuffed chicken, and fish fillet with your boiled vegetables.) Moderate.

Half a block but a world away is **Restaurant Vaquero**, Manzanillo's air-conditioned cowboy B-movie set (Crucero Las Brisas 19, tel. 316-54, open daily 2-11 p.m.). Its decor includes checkered tablecloths, wagon wheels, antelope-head wall trophies, rickety wood-frame windows and varnish-splashed plywood walls. The impression fits: an 1880s Sonora mining camp saloon-cafe, where teenage country waiters can manage little more than plopping plates onto your table and picking them up when you're finished. The cook outside hoists the ponderous steak-loaded iron grill to dump great shovels of charcoal into the fire below. You order your Vaquero steak by the kilogram—from two pounds on down. A "petite" half-pound (250-gram) T-bone or sirloin usually suffices. As an impression of the Wild West, Restaurant Vaquero seems correct. Historians tell us that the old cowboy joints were both seedy and expensive. (Vaqueros represents an improvement, however: it accepts credit cards.) Expensive.

Willy's nearby represents something altogether different again. Casual but elegant, Willy's airy, beachside terrace is *the* place to be seen in Manzanillo (two blocks down the Las Brisas Highway from the *crucero,* open daily 7 p.m.-midnight, reservations recommended, tel. 317-94). Owner Jean François LaRoche features a list of good but pricey designer appetizers, salads, seafood, meats, and desserts. Expensive.

The Las Brisas branch of the Mexican **Benedetti's Pizza** chain offers respectable Italian fare, good service, a friendly family atmosphere, and reasonable prices (open daily 2-11 p.m., tel. 315-92, next to Osteria Bugatti). Their salad plate (carrots, tomato, beets, mushrooms, lettuce, and hot bread, $2.25) is heaven for vegetable-starved budget travelers. Budget.

Good Asian food is hard to come by in Mexico. **Restaurant Sushi-ya,** however, does a creditable job of its Japanese-style offerings. Even its luxurious palapa roof creates an ambience not unlike traditional Japanese high-beamed wood interiors. Their excellent *gyoza* (Japanese pot stickers), slivered carrot and celery salad with *wasabi* horseradish sauce, teriyaki beef, and sticky rice seem small miracles in this pocket of Pacific Mexico. Moderate to expensive. Look for their sign on the left side about a mile and a half south along the Las Brisas Highway, a long block past the church; open Tues.-Thurs. 5-11, Fri.-Sun. 1-11, tel. 326-67.

Playa Azul-Salagua Restaurants

Restaurants dot the three-mile beach strip north of the *crucero* Las Brisas. One of the renowned is **Carlos and Charlie's,** the Manzanillo branch of late owner Carlos Anderson's goofy worldwide chain (Hwy. 200, Km 8, across from the baseball stadium, open Mon.-Sat. 1:30 p.m.-1 a.m. high season, call for low-season hours, tel. 311-50). The fun begins at the entrance where a sign announces: "Colima Bay Cafe, since 1800." Inside, the outrageous decorates the ceilings while a riot of photos—romantic, poignant, sentimental, and brutal—covers the walls. Meanwhile, the waiters (who, despite their antics, are gentle sorts) entertain the customers. The menu, with items such as "Moo," "Peep," and "Pemex," cannot be all nonsense, since many of them, such as Oysters 444, TBC Salad, and their tangy barbecued ribs, are delicious. Moderate to expensive.

A sensational hors d'oeuvre and salsa plate draws customers year-round to **Restaurant Jalapeños** (at Km 10.5, a quarter mile south of Comercial Mexicana, open daily 5 p.m.-midnight, no phone). Don't eat lunch if you want to fully appreciate it: a giant platter piled with hot, fresh chips, a trio of savory salsas, a plate of crisp pickled chiles, and a bowl of scrumptious refried beans. This comes automatically, all before the salads and entrees (try the luscious all-fresh cheese chiles rellenos, for example). Since you can't possibly have room for dessert, order a Sexy Coffee instead.

ENTERTAINMENT AND EVENTS

El Caporal

One of Manzanillo's unmissable entertainments starts quietly at around 1 p.m. at El Caporal, a big palapa restaurant-bar specializing in *botanas* (Mexican-style hors d'oeuvres). As soon as you order a drink, the *botanas*—small plates of ceviche, beans, pickled vegetables, and guacamole—begin to flow. By three o'clock, mariachis begin strumming away, more bottles pop open, and more *botanas* arrive. By four, the place is usually packed; if you stay till six you'll probably need someone to stuff you into a taxi home. El Caporal is behind the Superior beer distributor at the Km 8 post, open daily noon-7, tel. 322-10.

Sunsets, Strolling, And Sidewalk Cafes

Playa Las Brisas and Playa Azul provide the best vantage for viewing Manzanillo's often spectacular **sunsets.** For liquid refreshment and atmosphere to augment the natural light show, try one of the romantic beachside spots, such as **Hotel La Posada, Restaurant Willy's, Carlos and Charlie's** and the **Hotel Days Inn.** (Sunset views from the plush terraces at Santiago Peninsula and Bay hotels, such as Las Hadas, Sierra, and Club Maeva are unfortunately obstructed by intervening headlands.)

Las Hadas provides an out, however. Their trimaran sloop *Aguabundo* departs daily from the hotel marina (at 4:15) and the downtown La Perlita dock (at 5:00) for a *crucero de atardecer* (sunset cruise). The $27 per-person tariff includes open bar. For tickets, contact the hotel, tel. 300-00, or their La Perlita dock office, tel. 207-26, open daily 9-2 and 4-6, or a travel agent, such as Agencia Bahías Gemelas, tel 310-00.

Early evenings are great for enjoying the passing parade around the downtown *jardín.* Relax over dessert and coffee at bordering sidewalk cafes, such as **Chantilly,** (corner Av. Mexico, closed Sat.) or **Roca del Mar** (east side of *jardín,* next to Bing ice cream).

North of downtown, the **Salagua** (Km 11.5) and **Santiago** (Km 14) village plazas offer similar, even more *tipica,* sidewalk diversions.

Movies

After strolling a few times around the downtown *jardín,* you might enjoy taking in a movie at the adjacent **Cine Bahía.** Their double-bill programs ($1.25, beginning at 4:00) often combine an American sleeper with European art-erotica. In Santiago, the **Cine Plaza Santiago** (behind the Plaza Santiago shopping center) screens first-run Mexican and U.S. films ($1.40, beginning at 4:15, closed Thursdays). Across the highway, by the Santiago *jardín,* the **Cine Marisol** offers similar programs ($1.40, beginning at 4:00, closed Wednesdays).

Fiestas

Manzanillo's biggest parties are **Carnaval,** celebrated late Feb. or early March and the **Fiesta de Guadalupe** (Dec. 1-12). Manzanillo

BRUCE WHIPPERMAN

Many small shrines to the Virgin of Guadalupe appear in Manzanillo neighborhoods prior to December 12, the culminating day of the Virgin's fiesta.

Carnaval, similar to the grander Mazatlán affair, climaxes on Shrove Tuesday (six weeks, five days before Easter Sunday) with a parade of floats, bands, and masked merrymakers gyrating through the downtown streets.

The Fiesta de Guadalupe honors Manzanillo's (and all Mexico's) patron saint, the Virgin of Guadalupe. Shrines to the Virgin, with flower and food offerings beneath her traditional portrait, begin appearing everywhere, especially downtown, by the end of November. For 12 evenings beginning Dec. 1, floats parade and Indian-costumed dancers twirl around the *jardín*. Afternoons, people (women and girls, especially) proudly display their ancestry by dressing up in *huipiles, enredos,* and *fajas* and heading to the cathedral. Nearing their destination, they pass through lanes crowded with stalls offering *indígena* food, curios, toys, souvenirs of the Virgin, and snapshots of them beside the Virgin's portrait.

Sporting Events

Manzanillo hosts an occasional winter-season *corrida de toros* (bullfight) at either the Salagua or the El Coloma bullring (on Hwy. 200, four miles south of town). Watch for posters. For dates, call a travel agent or the downtown tourist information office (see "Information" below).

The local "magic hour of **baseball**" begins at 7:30 whenever the Manzanillo Atuneros (Tuna Fishermen) are in town. They play a spirited four-month schedule, beginning in October. If you see the stadium lights (on Playa Azul, next to the highway betweem Km 8 and Km 9), you'll know the faithful are gathering and the popcorn is hot ($3 per person; single games at 7:30; double-headers, usually Fridays at 6:00).

The renowned Manzanillo **International Sailfish Tournament** kicks off annually during the last half of November (for details, see "Sportfishing" below).

Maycol

Singer-instrumentalist Maycol wows audiences regularly at big local hotels and clubs, such as Ostería Bugatti and the Hotel Sierra. With fingers flying over half a dozen instruments from the piano to the saxophone and his velvety voice crooning dozens of tunes á la Frank Sinatra, Stevie Wonder, Nat King Cole (and even Dionne Warwick!), Maycol radiates such charisma that you think he is performing personally for you. (In fact, he will: for a private show for you and your friends, contact him or his wife Barbara at P.O. Box 726, Manzanillo, tel. 325-87.)

Tourist Shows

The **Club Maeva** hosts a lively Saturday **Mexican Fiesta,** including swirling dancers, mariachis, rope dance, and rooster fights. Other nights, they stage theme parties where guests become part of the entertainment: International Gala Night, a journey to the world's great cities; Brazilian Night, a glittering Rio de Janeiro Carnaval; and Wednesday amateur Night of the Stars, your chance to shine on the stage. Club Maeva parties, open to the public, begin with a big buffet at 8 p.m. and cost $25 per person, $12 for kids under 12; for reservations, phone 305-96, ext. 145.

Other clubs stage their own Mexican fiestas seasonally; for details, call Restaurant Oasis (on Playa Miramar in Club Santiago) or Hotel Playa de Oro (Thursdays, at Km 15.5, north of Santiago town, tel. 325-40).

Dancing And Discoing

The **Ostería Bugatti** offers cocktails, dining and live-music dancing nightly (at *crucero* Las Brisas, 1940s and '50s style, beginning around 8 p.m., tel. 329-99). The **Hotel Sierra** lobby-bar has live dance music (at Playa Audiencia, nightly 7-9, tel. 320-00). A poolside combo also plays for dancing at the **Restaurant Plazuela** of the Hotel Plaza Las Glorias on the Santiago Peninsula. (Get there by turning left at the sign half a mile uphill along Av. La Audiencia from *crucero* Las Hadas; reservations recommended, tel. 305-50, ext. 181.)

Discomania reigns regularly at a number of clubs along Hwy. 200. Call to verify hours, which vary with season. Some of the better spots, moving from south to north:

The very popular **Bar Felix** (on Playa Azul, Km 9) has relatively low volume, soft couches, and no cover, with two drinks required at $3 apiece. In season, lights begin gyrating daily except Mon. at 10:30, tel. 318-75.

At **Disco Oui,** (near Salagua Km 10, tel. 323-33, 313-03), loud heavy metal alternates with softer Latin-romantic. Lights begin around 10:30, music an hour later; about $8 cover.

Disco **Enjoy** (in Santiago, Km 15) patrons

gather in its soaring black-walled interior to watch weird Warhol-type videos and listen to medium-volume rock until midnight, when the lights begin whirling and the blasting begins in earnest. (About $8 cover, call 328-39 for info.)

The round, spacy interior of **Disco Solaris** (at Km 15.5, Hotel Playa Las Glorias) feels like a trip in a big flying saucer. Lights begin flashing, colored fogs descend, and music begins booming around 11:30 (about $7 cover, phone 325-40).

SPORTS

Walking And Jogging

All of the beaches of Manzanillo and Santiago bays are fine for walking. The sand, however, is generally too soft for jogging, except along the wide, firm, north-end **Playa de Miramar.** On the south side, the last mile of the no-outlet **Las Brisas Highway** asphalt serves as a relatively tranquil and popular jogging course.

Swimming, Surfing, And Bodysurfing

With the usual precautions, Manzanillo's beaches are generally safe for swimming, except on occasional days of high waves, when all but the most foolhardy avoid the surf. The safest swimming beaches are **Playa San Pedrito** and **Playa de Miramar** at the protected south and north ends, respectively.

The best surfing breaks occur along **Playa Olas Altas** ("High Waves Beach"), where, most any day, a sprinkling of surfers ride the swells a hundred yards offshore.

Bodysurfing and boogieboarding are much more common, especially on *playas* **Audiencia, Olas Altas,** and **Miramar,** where concessionaires often rent boogieboards. (See "Beaches" above.)

Sailing, Windsurfing, And Kayaking

Manzanillo's waters are generally tranquil enough for kayaking, but also windy enough for good sailing and windsurfing. A few concessionaires rent equipment at fairly hefty prices. At Playa de la Audiencia, the beach concessionaire, **Promociones y Recreaciones** (tel. 318-48), rents windsurfers ($18/hour plus $7 lesson) and kayaks ($18/hour) to any able body. At Las Hadas beachside, **Aquamundo** (tel. 300-00, ext. 759) rents small sailing outfits, wind-

surfers, and kayaks to Las Hadas guests and those of hotels Plaza Las Glorias, Club Maeva, Sierra, and Villa del Palmar.

Snorkeling And Scuba Diving

Manzanillo waters are generally clear. Visibility runs from about 30 feet onshore to 60-80 feet farther out. Manzanillo has three standout shore-accessible spots: the jetty rocks (depth 5-25 feet) at the south end of **Playa Las Brisas;** the shoals on both sides of **Playa de la Audiencia;** and the wrecked ('59 hurricane) frigate 200 yards off north-end **Playa La Boquita.** All of these swarm with schools of sponge- and coral-grazing fish.

The veteran YMCA-method certified dive instructor Susan Dearing operates **Underworld Scuba** from her poolside Hotel Sierra headquarters (tel. 320-00, ext. 85). With thousands of accident-free dives, Susan ranks among Pacific Mexico's best-qualified scuba instructors.

Susan and her assistants start you out with a free qualifying lesson at the pool. After enough free practice, they'll guide you in onshore dives (for about $40 for a two-hour outing, including one half-hour fully equipped dive). They guide experienced divers (bring your certificate) much farther afield, including super sites such as Roca Elefante at the Juluapan Peninsula's foamy tip.

Although Aguamundo at Las Hadas (which also services Club Maeva and guests of other hotels) has boats, scuba equipment, and experienced scuba guides, they have no certified instructors. Their guided scuba dives (often cluttered with tag-along snorkelers and spectators) are limited to certified scuba divers only.

Jet- And Waterskiing

At Playa de la Audiencia, jet-ski wave-runners and waterski towing are available at about $40 per half hour from the beach concessionaire **Promociones y Recreaciones** (tel. 318-48).

Aquamundo (tel. 300-00, ext. 759) at Las Hadas beach offers similar equipment and services to guests of hotels Las Hadas, Plaza Las Glorias, Club Maeva, Sierra, and Villa del Palmar.

Tennis And Golf

Manzanillo has no free public tennis courts. **Hotel Sierra,** however, rents its six superb courts to outsiders for $10 hourly during the day and $20 at night. Their teaching pro offers lessons for about $26 per hour. Most other large hotels, notably Club Maeva and Las Hadas, have many courts, but do not rent them to the public.

For tennis players on a budget the **Motel Playa San Pedrito,** the **Club Vacacional Las Brisas,** and the **Hotel Playa de Santiago** (see "Accommodations" above) each have a playable tennis court.

Manzanillo golfers enjoy two good golf courses. The nine-hole **Club Santiago** course (office just inside the Club Santiago gate at Highway 200, Km 19) is available for public use daily 8-5. The 18-hole greens fee runs about $33 (half that for nine holes), clubs rent for about $13 a set, and a golf cart about $30 ($20 for nine holes). Caddies work 18 holes for about $11 ($6 for nine holes). For information and reservations, phone the club at 303-70.

The renowned 18-hole **Las Hadas** course (at Km 12, Hwy. 200) is generally available only for Las Hadas (and Hotel Sierra, Plaza Las Glorias, and Club Maeva) guests. Fees vary. For specifics, check with your hotel desk.

Sportfishing

Manzanillo's biggest sportfishing operation is the **Flota Amarilla** ("Yellow Fleet"), whose many captains operate cooperatively through their association, Sociedad Cooperativa de Prestación de Servicios Turisticos Manzanillo. You can see their bright yellow craft anchored off their dockside office on Av. Niños Héroes, a long block east (away from downtown) of the El Tajo Pemex gas station.

Their five-person boats run about $130 for a day's billfish (marlin, sailfish) hunting, completely equipped with three fishing lines. Larger, plusher eight-person, six-line boats go for about $175, complete with ice and no-host bar. All of their boats are insured and equipped with CB radios and toilets. For information and reservations, call (333) 210-31, write Flota Amarilla-Soc. Coop. de P. de Servicios Turisticos Manzanillo, Av. Niños Héroes s/n, Manzanillo, Colima 28200, or drop into their dockside office.

The **Lori Fleet** captains, operating cooperatively through their Sociedad Cooperativa Playa Santiago, offer an alternative. Contact them in their office (tel. 313-23) on Hwy. 200, Km 8.5, next to Mariscos Barra de Navidad (or

call a travel agent, such as Agencia Bahías Gemelas, tel. 310-00).

Manzanillo sportsmen sponsor two annual **billfish tournaments** in early February and late November. Competing for automobiles as top prizes, hundreds of contestants ordinarily bring in around 300 big fish in three days. The complete entry fee runs about $430, which includes the farewell awards dinner. For more information, contact Fernando Adachi, tournament coordinator, at downtown Ferretería Adachi, Av. Mexico 251, tel. (333) 327-70 (or write the sponsors, the Deportivo de Pesca Manzanillo, P.O. Box 89, Manzanillo, Colima 28200).

Hopefully, sponsors of such tournaments will soon be able to devise competitions that will preserve, rather than wipe out, the species upon which their sport depends. Some progressive captains have seen the light and encourage their clients to release the fish when caught.

Yacht Berthing And Boat Launching

Las Hadas Hotel's excellent marina has about 100 berths (up to 80 feet) rentable for about $.40 per foot per day, including potable water and 110/220-volt electrical hookup. (Reservations recommended, especially during the winter; write Manager, Las Hadas Marina, P.O. Box 158, Manzanillo, Colima 28200, or phone tel. 333-300-00, fax 333-304-30.)

Las Hadas marina also has a boat ramp, available for a fee. Make arrangements before you arrive, however, or you might have to do some fast talking to get past the guard at the gate. At Hwy. 200 Km 12, follow Av. Audiencia past the hilltop, turn left at the Las Hadas sign. At the gate, the guard will direct you.

On the south end, you can either use the **Club Náutico** (Sailfish Tournament headquarters) boat ramp for about $7, or the impromptu ramp at the road's end for free. (At the end of the Las Brisas Highway, turn left at and follow the road in front of the Oceanographic Institute.)

At the north end, you can also use the **Hotel de Playa Santiago** ramp (tel. 302-55, fax 303-44) for a $5 fee. (From Hwy. 200, Km 13.5, just south of the Los Colorados creek bridge, turn and follow the side road along the peninsula's north shore to the hotel at road's end.)

SHOPPING

Markets And Downtown

Manzanillo's colorful, untouristed **Mercado Municipal** district clusters around the main market at Cuauhtémoc and Independencia (five short blocks along Av. Mexico from the *jardín*, turn left four blocks). Southbound "Mercado"-marked buses will take you right there.

Wander through the hubbub of fish stalls, piled with dozens of varieties, such as big, fresh-caught *sierra* (mackerel) or slippery *pulpo* (octopus). Among the mounds of ruby tomatoes, green melons, and golden papayas, watch for the exotic, such as *nopales* (cactus leaves) or spiny green *guanabanas,* the mango-shaped relative of the Asian jackfruit. On your way out, don't miss the spice stalls, with their bundles of freshly gathered aromatic cinnamon bark and mounds of fragrant dried *jamaica* flower petals (for flavoring *aguas* drinks).

Heading back toward the *jardín,* you might

Shrimp sellers display their fresh offerings near Manzanillo's central market.

look through some of the several of the *artesanías* (crafts shops) along **Av. Mexico** for Oaxaca black *barra* pottery, Tonalá papier-mâché animals and figurines, or Tlaquepaque glass. Don't be shy about bargaining. In this part of town, it's *la costumbre.* (For bargaining hints, see the main Introduction.)

Santiago Shopping

Every Saturday morning, folks gather for the **Santiago Market,** beneath *tianguis* (awnings) that spread along Av. V. Carranza, two blocks north of the town plaza. Although merchandise tends toward dime-store-grade clothes and hardware, it's worth a stroll if only for the color and the occasional exotica (wild fruits, antiques, bright for-sale parrots) that may turn up.

While you're there, check out some of the interesting folkcrafts shops that cluster in the same area. **Boutique Grivel** offers an unusually wide selection of quality folkcrafts from all over Mexico. Much loving care has obviously gone into the choosing and crafting of their many Oaxaca flower-embroidery dresses, animal-motif *huipiles,* and *chinas poblanas* blouses and skirts. Just name the handicraft—onyx, pottery, papier mâché, serapes, blankets, piñatas, silver—and they'll usually be able to show you a class assortment, priced to sell without bargaining. Boutique Grivel is on the north corner of the Plaza Santiago shopping center, across the highway from the town square; open Mon.-Sat. 9-8, Sun. 9-3, tel. 309-29.

Cross the highway and take a look inside **El Palacio de Las Conchas y Caracoles** shell emporium (open Mon.-Sat. 9-2 and 4-9, Sun. 9-2, tel. 302-60). Bring your shell book. Hosts of glistening, museum-quality specimens—iridescent silver nautiluses, luscious rose conches, red and purple corals—line a multitude of shelves. Purchase them (from $1000 on down) singly or choose from arrays of jewelry—necklaces, earrings, brooches, and rings.

For yet another unique selection, head a few blocks into Santiago's north side streets to **Centro Artesanal Las Primaveras** (two blocks from the highway at Juarez 40; open Mon.-Sat. 8-8, Sun. 8-2, tel. 301-73). There, scattered amidst a rambling, dusty clutter, many attractive handicrafts—blown glass, crepe flowers, pre-Columbian-motif pottery, leatherwork, papier-mâché clowns and parrots—languish, waiting for someone to rescue them.

Supermarket, Photo, And Health-food Stores

The Manzanillo branch of big **Comercial Mexicana** anchors the American-style Plaza Manzanillo shopping center at Km 11.5. They seemingly offer everything—from appliances and cosmetics to produce, groceries, and a bakery—spread along shiny, efficient un-Mexican aisles (open daily 9-9, tel. 300-05).

At the entrance to the same Plaza Manzanillo complex, drop off your film for quick finishing at up-to-date **Foto Sol.** They also sell popular films and stock some camera accessories (open daily 9-9, tel. 318-60).

Downtown, **Photo Studio Cárdenas** offers three-hour photo finishing, film, and some cameras and accessories (on the *jardín* at Balvino Dávalo 52, open 9:30-2 and 4:30-8:30, closed Sun., tel. 211-60). Their Santiago branch offers one-hour photo finishing (at the Plaza Santiago shopping center, Km 13.5, Hwy. 200, opposite the town *jardín,* tel. 307-85).

Manzanillo's health-food store, **Yacatecuhtli,** urges customers to "watch your health" with their yogurt, granola, natural vitamins, ginseng, alfalfa tablets, soy hamburger, and cheese (two locations: downtown, at Av. Mexico 249, open Mon.-Sat. 8 a.m.-10 p.m., Sun. 8-3 and 5-10; and in Santiago, across Hwy. 200 from the Plaza Santiago shopping center).

SERVICES

Money Exchange

The downtown **Banamex** (Banco Nacional de Mexico) exchanges both U.S. and Canadian traveler's checks and cash (open Mon.-Fri. 9-12, Av. Mexico 136, three blocks from the *jardín,* tel. 204-68). The **Bancomer** next door (Av. Mexico 122, tel. 228-88) does the same during the same hours. If they are too crowded, the **Banco Internacional,** one block from the *jardín,* changes U.S. traveler's checks and cash (across Av. Mexico from the Hotel Colonial, tel. 208-09, money exchange Mon.-Fri. 9:30-12). **Hint:** Avoid the Comermex bank on the *jardín;* they're much too slow.

Santiago has the only moneychangers outside of downtown besides hotels: **Banco Serfin** (U.S. traveler's checks and cash, Mon.-Fri. 10-12:45, tel. 309-41) and **Banco Internacional** (U.S. traveler's checks and cash, Mon.-Fri. 9:30-

12, tel. 303-81), both on the highway at Plaza Santiago.

American Express Agency

Although they don't cash American Express traveler's checks, **Agencia de Viajes Bahías Gemelas** (Twin Bays Travel Agency) sells them to card-carrying members for personal checks (usually up to $1000). As the official Manzanillo American Express office, they also perform the usual membership services and book air tickets, local tours, and hotel reservations (open Mon.-Sat. 9-2 and 4-6, at Hwy. 200 Km 9, next to Chrysler Motor, tel. 310-00, 310-53, fax 306-49). Agencia Bahías Gemelas also maintains a longer-hours Hotel Las Hadas branch (open Mon.-Sat 9-2 and 4-6, Sun. 10-12, tel. 300-00).

Post Offices, Telegraph, And Telephone

The downtown **Correos** (post office) is at the corner of Avs. Juarez and Cinco de Mayo, one long block (parallel to the waterfront) from the *jardín* (open Mon.-Fri. 8-7, Sat. 9-1).

Nearby **Telecomunicaciones,** the new high-tech telegraph office, sends telegrams, telexes, and fax messages. Open Mon.-Fri. 9-8, Sat. 9-12. *Giros* (money order) hours are shorter, however: Mon.-Fri. 9-1 and 3-5 only. In the Palacio Muncipal (city hall) on the *jardín,* bottom floor.

In **Santiago,** the post office and Telecomunicaciones (telegrams, telexes, faxes, and money orders) offices are together on side street Venustiano Carranza no. 2, across Hwy. 200 from Juanito's restaurant. Post office (tel. 411-30) hours are Mon.-Fri. 9-1 and 3-6, Sat. 9-1, while Telecomunicaciones hours are Mon.-Fri. 9-3.

Manzanillo's *larga distancia* (long-distance) telephone offices are conveniently spread from the downtown north along Hwy. 200. The most friendly is downtown **Caseta Telefónica del Rio** which, besides telephone, offers TV, breakfast, lunch, and dinner (Av. Mexico 336, daily 9 a.m.-10 p.m.). The Manzanillo area code is 333.

Efficient, computer-assisted **Computel** has three convenient locations: on the *malecón* (at Morelos 196, one block from the *jardín*), open daily 8 a.m.-10 p.m.; at *crucero* Las Brisas, open daily 8 a.m.-9:30 p.m.; and in Santiago, open Mon.-Sat. 7 a.m.-9:45 p.m., Sun. 9 a.m.-1 p.m. (next to Juanito's, which, incidentally, also offers long-distance service).

Immigration And Customs
Both **Migración** and the **Aduana** (Customs) occupy the upper floors of the **Edificio Federal Portuario** (Federal Port Building) on San Pedrito Beach, at the foot of Av. Teniente Azueta.

The cooperative, efficient Migración staff (third floor, open Mon.-Fri. 8-3 for business and around the clock for questions, tel. 200-30) can replace a lost tourist card. (Make a copy of it beforehand, just in case.)

Go to the Aduana (second floor, open Mon.-Fri. 8-3, tel. 200-87) if you have to leave Mexico temporarily without your car. In addition to your tourist card and all your car papers, bring a letter in Spanish signed by the person who will have custody of it. The letter should list your car's make, model, year, and ID number, its temporary location, and acknowledge the temporary transfer of custody. Make two copies of everything.

Consular Volunteer
Bill Le Coq volunteers his services as a semi-official U.S. consular officer. Reach him at his office in the **Edificio Tenisol** (formerly the Tenisol Hotel) bottom floor, at Club Santiago Mon.-Sat. from around nine till noon (Hwy. 200, Km 19, tel. 340-13).

Arts And Music Courses
Aleph Centro Cultural conducts a modest program of painting and dance (contemporary, jazz, and folkloric) classes for children and adults. They have no phone, but you can drop by their small cafe and gallery and talk with instructor-director Anna Cuevas during the day (Santiago Plaza shopping center nos. 17 and 18, Hwy. 200, Km 13.5, opposite the town *jardín*).

Auto Repairs
For competent car (especially European) repairs go to SIMPSA, a couple of blocks behind the Pemex station (Km 4.5 from downtown), tel. 247-55. Friendly German expatriate engineer Alfred Hasler and his lively crew of mechanics keep busy on cars when not occupied with ship and mine machinery.

INFORMATION

Tourist Information Offices
The efficient, helpful state-city **Turismo** (Tourist Information Office) downtown answers questions and dispenses an excellent compact fold-out Colima and Manzanillo map. For special questions or service, ask for the friendly director, Norma Rodriguez Espinosa. They are located at streetfront at the Palacio Municipal (city hall) on the *jardín* (tel. 200-00, open Mon.-Sat. 9-3 and 5-8).

The federal **Delegación de Turismo** (tourist office) on Playa Azul, more a regulatory agency than an information office, does answer questions, however (Hwy. 200, Km 9, next to Donas Fiesta, tel. 322-77, open Mon.-Fri. 9-3).

Hospital, Police, And Emergencies
In a medical emergency, call a taxi or **Cruz Roja** (Red Cross) at 200-96. Have them take you to **Hospital Santa Fe**, one of Manzanillo's respected private hospitals (at Hwy. 200, Km 9.5, tel. 325-12.) They have round-the-clock service, including a laboratory and several specialists on call (whom, of course, you can also visit for routine consultations).

For both medical consultations and a good pharmacy in Santiago, contact French-speaking **Joseph Cadet Jr., M.D.** at his office or his adjacent Farmacia Continental (next to Juanito's at Hwy. 200, Km 14.5; open Mon.-Sat. 10-2 and 5-8, pharmacy open Mon.-Sat. 9-2 and 4-9, tel. 382-86).

For **police** emergencies, call the **Preventiva Municipal** (tel. 210-04) in the city hall on the *jardín*.

Books, Newspapers, And Magazines
Revistas Saifer downtown (Av. Mexico 221, three and a half blocks from the *jardín*) stocks the Mexico City *News* and loads of American magazines, such as *Time, Life, Newsweek, Computer, Brides,* and *Ladies Home Journal* (open daily 6 a.m.-10:30 p.m., tel. 206-12).

Cervi Supermarket in Salagua usually stocks *USA Today* and the *News* newspapers, plus *People* and *Newsweek* magazines (near the Salagua signal corner, Hwy. 200, Km 11.5; open Mon.-Sat. 9-9, Sun. 9-2).

The *tabaquería* shop at **Hotel Sierra** (tel. 320-00) stocks U.S. newspapers, a big rack of U.S. magazines and many English-language paperbacks.

Pick up a copy of the *Manzanillo Guide,* an unusually good local tourist newspaper. Besides the ads, it lists local current events and entertainments, and has informative local history, archaeology, travel, and ecology feature articles.

Public Library
The Manzanillo **Biblioteca Municipal** (municipal library) is open Tues.-Sun. 8-1 and 4-8 on the third floor of the Palacio Municipal (city hall) on the *jardín* downtown.

GETTING THERE AND AWAY

By Air
The **Manzanillo airport,** officially the Playa de Oro International Airport (code ZLO), is 28 easy highway miles (44 km) north of downtown Manzanillo, and only about 20 miles (32 km) from most Manzanillo beachside hotels. In the other direction, the airport is 19 miles (30 km) south of Barra de Navidad.

The terminal itself is small for an international destination, with neither money exchange, hotel booking, nor tourist information booths. The terminal nevertheless has a few gift shops, snack stands, an upstairs restaurant, and a *buzón* (mailbox) just inside the front entrance.

Flights
Mexicana and **Aeromexico** flights each connect Manzanillo airport several times a week with Los Angeles (via Guadalajara) and Mexico City.

For reservations, contact the airlines' downtown offices: Aeromexico, at Av. Carrillo Puerto 107, tel. 212-67, 217-11; and Mexicana, Av. Mexico 382, tel. 210-09, 217-01, 219-72.

For flight information, call the airlines at their airport numbers: Aeromexico tel. 324-24; Mexicana 323-23.

Airport Arrival
With neither airport hotel booking service nor money exchange, you should fly into Manzanillo with a day's worth of pesos and a hotel reservation. If you don't, you'll be at the mercy of taxi drivers who love to collect fat commissions on your first-night hotel tariff.

After the usually cursory immigration and customs checks, independent arrivees have their choice of a car rental (see below) or **taxi tickets** from a booth just outside the gate. *Colectivo* (collective taxi-van) tickets run about $4.50 per

person to any Manzanillo hotel, while a *taxi especial* (individual taxi seating three, maybe four) runs about $12.

Colectivos head for **Barra de Navidad** and other northern points seasonally only. *Taxis especiales,* however, will take three passengers to Barra, Melaque, or Coastecomate for about $17 total (or to Hotel Los Angeles Locos, $35, hotels El Tecuán and Costa Careyes, $54, or Chamela-El Super, $57).

No public buses service the Manzanillo airport. Strong, mobile travelers on tight budgets could save many pesos, however, by hitching or hiking the five miles to Highway 200 and flagging down one of the frequent north or southbound second-class buses (fare about $2 to Barra or Manzanillo). Don't try it at night, however.

As for airport **car rentals,** the gang's all there: Avis (tel. 301-90), National (tel. 306-11), Budget (tel. 314-45), and Hertz (at Hotel Sierra tel. 320-00 or Hotel Las Hadas tel. 333-300-00). **Hint:** Unless you don't mind paying upwards of $50 per day, shop around for your car rental by toll-free 800 numbers at home *before* you leave.

Airport Departure
Save money by sharing a taxi (which shouldn't run more than $15) to the airport with fellow departing hotel guests. Always establish the taxi fare before you get into the taxi. If the driver insists on too much, hail another taxi.

Since airport authorities accept neither credit cards nor traveler's checks, save enough dollars or pesos to pay your **$12 international departure tax.** If you've lost your tourist card and don't have a duplicate, be prepared to pay a departure fine of around $20. (You might be able to squeeze by without a fine if you have a copy of your lost tourist card and a police report of the loss.)

By Car Or RV
Three main highway routes connect Manzanillo with the outside world: From the north via Puerto Vallarta and Barra de Navidad, from the northeast via Guadalajara and Colima, and from the southeast via Ixtapa-Zihuatanejo and Playa Azul (Lázaro Cárdenas).

From the north, Mexico National Highway 200 glides 172 smooth asphalt miles (276 km) from Puerto Vallarta via Barra de Navidad. Few steep grades or much traffic slow progress along this foothill-, forest-, and beach-studded route. Allow about four hours to or from Puerto Vallarta, about one hour to or from Barra.

The safety and ease of the new Guadalajara-Colima *autopista* (combined National Highways 15, 54, and 110) more than compensate for the tolls. Head southwest from the Glorietta Minerva circle in Guadalajara along Hwy. 15 for around 27 miles (45 km) until Acatlán de Juarez, and take the Hwy. 54 fork south for Colima. Later connect with Hwy. 110, bypassing Colima and continuing south to just before Tecomán, where Hwy. 200 splits off right, northwest, to Manzanillo. Figure about four and a half driving hours for this easy, 192-mile (311-km) trip, either way.

The same cannot be said for the winding 243 miles (390 km) of coastline Hwy. 200 between Zihuatanejo and Manzanillo. Keep your gas tank filled; the scenic but sparsely populated 150-mile stretch from Playa Azul to the Colima border has no gas stations. Allow a full eight-hour day, in broad daylight, either way. Don't try it at night.

By Bus

Several bus lines serve Manzanillo from the **Central Camionera** (Central Bus Terminal) at Hidalgo and Aldama (about a mile from the downtown El Tajo Pemex south along the Colima highway). The well-organized terminal has a long-distance telephone, left-luggage lockers, and a number of shops where savvy passengers stock up with food and water.

The separate ticket offices line up along one side of the terminal. All departures listed below are local *(salidas locales)* unless noted as *salidas de paso*. Choose first class whenever you can; its service, speed, and *asientos reservados* (reserved seats) far outweigh the small additional ticket cost. The bus lines divide roughly into north-south and east-west categories:

North-South Bus Lines

Transportes Cihuatlán (tel. 200-03) and its three small associated lines provide Manzanillo's most frequent service north and northeast. Their primera-plus (super-first-class) buses connect with Puerto Vallarta directly three times a day and Guadalajara (via Melaque and Autlán) twice. Many other first- and second-class buses follow the same routes, the second-class ones stopping everywhere.

Autotransportes Sur de Jalisco (tel. 210-03) second-class buses connect hourly 'round the clock with Guadalajara via Colima. Three buses per day also connect south with the Playa Azul junction and Lázaro Cárdenas.

Transportes Norte de Sonora (tel. 204-32) first-class *salidas de paso* connect with Puerto Vallarta, Mazatlán and Tijuana northbound (three per day), and Colima southbound (three per day). Three daily first-class *salidas locales* connect south with the Playa Azul junction and Lázaro Cárdenas.

Tres Estrellas de Oro (tel. 201-35) first-class buses connect north with Puerto Vallarta, Mazatlán, and Tijuana (three per day), and south with Playa Azul junction and Lázaro Cárdenas (one per day). First-class buses connect with Guadalajara, and east with Mexico City (three per day).

East-West Buses

Autobuses de Occidente (tel. 201-23) primera-plus and first-class buses (19 per day) connect 'round the clock with Mexico City through Michoacán via Pátzcuaro. Many second-class buses connect daily with subsidiary Michoacán destinations of Apatzingan, Zamora, Uruapan, and Morelia.

Flecha Amarilla (tel. 202-10) primera-plus buses connect direct with Mexico City (one per day) and Guadalajara (eight per day). First-class buses (about a dozen a day) connect with Mexico City through Colima and Michoacán destinations of Minatatlan, Colima, Zamora, Salamanca, Irapuato, and Morelia.

By Train

President Porfirio Diaz's once-plush 19th-century passenger service which carried Guadalajara's elite to frolic on Manzanillo's beaches has deteriorated to a pair of scruffy second-class diesels that chug opposite ways daily between Guadalajara and Manzanillo via Colima.

Train **no. 92** departs Guadalajara daily (Guadalajara-Manzanillo fare $1.50) at 9 a.m., arriving in Manzanillo at around 6:15 p.m. Meanwhile, train **no. 91** departs Manzanillo at 6 a.m., arriving in Colima at around 8 a.m., continuing to Guadalajara, where it arrives around 2:15 p.m.

In Guadalajara, passengers continuing east can immediately board the connecting first-class sleeper *El Tapatío* and arrive in Mexico City the following morning (or get off en route at Morelia, where the next day they can board a Pátzcuaro-Lázaro Cárdenas-bound train.)

Guadalajara train passengers continuing north can board the first-class coach **Estrella** the next day at 8:15 a.m., headed for Tepic (3 p.m. arrival), Mazatlán (6 p.m. arrival), and Mexicali (4 p.m. succeeding day arrival) at the U.S. border.

Colima dogs

BOB RACE

INLAND TO COLIMA

From atop their thrones of fire and ice high above the Valley of Colima, legends say that the gods look down upon their ancient domain. The name "Colima" itself echoes the tradition: from the Nahuatl "Colliman" *(colli* = ancestors or gods, and *maitl* = domain of).

Approaching from Manzanillo, visitors seldom forget their first view of the sacred mountains of Colima: the dignified, snowcapped 14,220-foot (4,335-meter) Nevado de Colima, above his fiery, tempestuous younger brother, the 13,087-foot (3,990-meter) Volcán de Colima. The heat from that heavenly furnace rarely reaches down the green slopes to the spring-fed valley, however. There the colonial city invites coastal visitors to its more temperate (1,400-foot) heights for a refreshing change of pace.

HISTORY

Before Columbus
Although Colima (pop. 180,000) is the smallish capital of a diminutive agricultural state, it is much more than a farm town. Visitors can enjoy the residents' obvious appreciation of their arts and their history—twin traditions whose roots may extend as far south as Ecuador and Peru and as far west as the Gulf coast's mystery-shrouded monument builders, the Olmecs.

Colima's museums display a feast of ceramic treasures left behind by the many peoples—Nahua, Tarascan, Chichimec, Otomi—who have successively occupied the valley of Colima for over 3,000 years. Much more than mere utilitarian objects, the Colima pottery bursts with whimsy and genius. Acrobats, musicians, and dancers frolic, old folks embrace, mothers nurse, and most of all, Colima's

hieroglyph of Colima

famous dogs scratch, roll, snooze, and play in timeless canine style, as if they could come alive at any moment.

Conquest And Colonization
By 1500, the ruler of Colima, in order to deter his aggressive Tarascan neigbors to the north, had united his diminutive kingdom with three neighboring coastal provinces. This union, now known as the Chimalhuacan Confederation, did not prevail against Spanish horses and steel, however. Many local folks take ironic pride that Colima is one of Mexico's earliest provinces. Their ancestors fell to the swords of conquistador Gonzalo de Sandoval and his 145 soldiers, who, in an anticlimax to their bloody campaign, founded the city on July 25, 1523.

Two years later, Cortés appointed his nephew, Francisco Cortés de Buenaventura, mayor and head of a settlement of about 100 Spanish colonists and 6,000 *indígena* tributaries.

Cortés himself, in search of Chinese treasure in the Pacific, repeatedly visited Colima on his way to and from the Pacific coast during the 1530s, most notably during January 1535, en route to his exploration of Baja California.

Scarcely a generation after the route to the Orient was finally discovered in the 1560s, the Spanish king bypassed Colima by designating Acapulco as the prime Pacific port. This, along with a series of disasters—earthquakes, volcanic eruptions, hurricanes, and pirates—kept Colima in slumber until President Porfirio Diaz built the railroad to the beaches and new port of Manzanillo during the 1880s.

Modern Times
The destructive 1910-17 Revolution and the hard economic times of the 1930s kept Colima quiet until the 1950s, when burgeoning mining, Pacific Rim shipping, fishing, and tourism brought thousands of new jobs. Manzanillo became a major port and manufacturing center, boosting Colima to a government and university headquarters and trading hub for the bounty (meat, hides, milk, fruit, vegetables, copra, sugar) of rich valley and coastal plantations, farms, and ranches.

COLIMA

LIBRAMIENTO A GUADALAJARA

TO COLIMA VOLCANES AND GUADALAJARA

54

UNIVERSITY OF GUADALAJARA

MOTEL CANDLES

HOTEL MARÍA ISABEL

BLVD. CAMINO REAL

AV. DE LOS INSURGENTES

TO COLIMA REGIONAL FAIRGROUND

CENTRAL CAMIONERA (BUS STATION)

TO GUADALAJARA

0.2 mi

0.2 km

LIBRAMIENTO A MANZANILLO

TO MANZANILLO AND IXTAPA - ZIHUATANEJO

AV. FELIPE SEVILLA DEL RIO

TO COMALA, LAGUNA CARRIZALILLO AND LAGUNA LA MARIA

IGNACIO SANDOVAL

EJERCITO NACIONAL

MUSEUM OF THE CULTURE OF THE WEST (ARCHAEOLOGY)

GALLARDO

ALDAMA

E. CARRANZA

PEDRO GALVAN

IGNACIO ALLENDE

ZARAGOZA

FCO. I. MADERO

HIDALGO

MORELOS

BRAVO

RESTAURANT CROTOS

AV. NIÑOS HÉROES

HOSPITAL CIVIL

GRAL. NUÑEZ

FILOMENO MEDINA

VICENTE GUERRERO

PALACIO FEDERAL (POST OFFICE AND TELEGRAPH)

AV. REY COLMAN

20 DE NOVIEMBRE

AV. DE LOS MAESTROS

MUSEO DE MASCARA Y DANZA (MASK AND DANCE)

OBREGÓN

POLICIA (POLICE STATION)

RESTAURANT FONDA SAN MIGUEL

CONSTITUCIÓN

ESTACIONAMIENTO (DOWNTOWN PARKING)

CAFE CISNES

PLAZA TORRES QUINTERO

TURISMO (TOURIST INFO.)

PLAZA NUÑES

BANAMEX (BANK)

HOTEL AMERICA

REVOLUCION

ESTACION FERROCARRIL (RAILROAD STATION)

P. SUAREZ

MATAMOROS

CORREGIDORA

V. CARRANZA

NIGROMANTE

ARTESANÍAS (CRAFTS)

HOTEL CEBALLOS

JARDIN DE LIBERTAD

MUSEO DE HISTORIA

PALACIO DE GOBIERNO (STATE GOVT.)

CATEDRAL

ABASOLO

VICTORIA

REFORMA

AV. CORONEL A. BRIZUELA

TO MANZANILLO

MACLOVIO HERRERA

HOSPITAL CENTRO MEDICO

IGLESIA DE LA SALUD

BOMBEROS (FIRE STATION)

MERCADO CONSTITUCIÓN (MARKET)

DEGOLLADO

TO VILLA DE ALVAREZ AND COMALA

DR. MIGUEL GALLARDO

TORRES QUINTERO

MOCTEZUMA

IGLESIA SAN JOSE

TO LO DE VILLA AND COQUIMATLÁN

© MOON PUBLICATIONS, INC.

At Colima's downtown Jardín de Libertad, a charro waits to join the procession of revelers that heads to the festival of Villa Alvarez daily for two weeks February 7-23.

IN-TOWN SIGHTS

Getting Oriented

Colima's central district is a simple, one-mile square. The street grid runs north-south (north, toward the volcanoes; south, toward the coast) and east-west. Nearly all sights are reachable by a few minutes' walk or short taxi ride from the central plaza, the **Jardín de Libertad.**

A Walk Around Downtown

An ambience of refined prosperity—fashionable storefronts, shady portals, and lush, manicured greenery—blooms in the blocks that spread from Jardín de Libertad. The landmark **Catedral** and **Palacio de Gobierno** statehouse stand side by side on Av. Constitución, bordering the *jardín.* For a colonial town, the buildings are not old, having replaced the original earthquake-weakened colonial-era structures generations ago. The hub of commercial and community activities, a number of local celebrations begin from the *jardín.* The mayor shouts the Grito de Dolores (independence cry, evening of Sept. 15), and crowds celebrate the Fiesta de Villa Alvarez (Feb. 7-23). (See "Entertainment and Events" below.)

Other landmarks dot the portals around the square. First, as you move counterclockwise from the cathedral, comes the renovated **Hotel Ceballos,** corner of Constitución and Av. Francisco I. Madero. At the succeeding corner (Madero and north-south Av. V. Carranza) rises

the **Palacio Municipal** (city hall). And finally, on the south side, stands the state and city **Museo de Historia** on Av. 16 de Septiembre, corner of Constitución.

Step into the museum (open Tues.-Sat. 10-2 and 4-6, Sun. 5-8, tel. 29-228) for excellent examples of Colima's famous pre-Columbian pottery and a good bookstore offering a number of excellent local art, history, and picture-guidebooks.

Back outside, cross over to the Palacio de Gobierno, stroll through its big, open front door and enjoy the calm, classic elegance of the cloistered inner patio. Continue out the other side and into Colima's second square, named after **Torres Quintero** (1866-1934), a beloved Colima teacher whose statue decorates the tree-shaded park.

For information and an excellent Colima map and English-language touristic services guide, stroll around the corner to the federal-state **Turismo** information office half a block east at 75 Hidalgo, the street bordering the south side of Jardín Quintero. Ask for the *mapa* and the *Guia de Servicios Turísticos.*

Double back to the Jardín de Libertad corner of Constitución and Madero and explore the little block-long **Andando Constitución** pedestrian mall, one of Colima's charming little corners. Here you will find several interesting shops, a good Italian restaurant, and, at the far end, a friendly coffee-break cafe and a good crafts store with a bountiful selection of reasonably priced folkcrafts. These include fine ceramic reproductions of Colima's dogs. (For more details, turn ahead to the "Food" and "Shopping" sections.)

Two Good Museums

For more excellent regional crafts, continue along Constitución four blocks north to Aldama, then east a block and a half to the **Museo de Culturas Populares**. Besides a folk-art sales shop (pottery, gourds, baskets, a loom, glassware) and several intriguing displays of masks (don't miss the scary horned crocodile-man) and ceremonial costumes, you can often watch potters and other artisans at work in the little house to the right of the museum entrance on Aldama. (The museum, the full name of which is Museo Universitario de Culturas Populares Maria Teresa Pomar, is located at Avs. Aldama and 27 de Septiembre; open Mon.-Sat. 9-2 and 4-7, tel. 268-69.)

The prime repository of Colima's archaeological treasures is the landmark **Museo de Culturas del Occidente** (Museum of Cultures of the West, open daily 9-5). Taxi along the diagonal street E. Carranza to side street Ejercito Nacional, about a mile from the town center. Inside the modern building, a spiral walkway leads you past artifact-illustrated displays of the history of Colima and surrounding regions. The exposition climaxes on the top floor with choirs of delightful classical Colima figurines: musicians tapping drums and fingering flutes, dancers circling, wrestlers grappling, and hosts of animals, including the all-time favorites, Colima dogs.

OUT-OF-TOWN SIGHTS

The valley and mountainsides surrounding the city offer a variety of scenic diversions, from relaxing in colonial villages and camping on sylvan mountainsides to exploring tombs, examining petroglyphs, and descending into limestone caverns.

Northside Foothill Country: Comala And Lakes Maria And Carrizalillos

Head out the Comala road toward the foothills northwest of the city, where your first reward will be ever-closer views of the volcanoes. **Comala** town, nestling above a lush stream val-ley about six miles from Colima, has always been a local Sunday favorite. Here, cares seem to float away in the orange-scented air around the plaza. Mariachis stroll every afternoon and restaurants (try Los Portales right on the plaza) serve *botanas* (appetizers) free with drinks (which should include at least one obligatory glass of local *ponche* fruit wine).

The road winding uphill past Comala leads past green pastures and groves through the village of Cofradia de Suchitán. Soon the road divides. Take the left fork and continue down a jungly, lava-cliffed canyon to ex-hacienda **San Antonio** about 20 miles (32 km) from Colima. Here, water gurgles from the ancient aqueduct, the stone chapel stands intact, and a massive gate and wall, like a medieval keep, still protect the inhabitants from long-forgotten marauders.

A gravel road continues uphill from San Antonio a few miles farther to the mountainside Shangri-La **Ejido La Maria**. Past a gate (where you pay a small admission to park), a walking trail downhill leads past tidy vegetable fields to the idyllic shoreline of natural **Laguna La Maria**. Here, weekend and holiday visitors enjoy creekside picnicking and camping beneath the spreading boughs of a venerable lakeside grove. At other times, walk-in campers often enjoy nearly complete solitude. (Bring everything, including water-purifying tablets, insect repellent, and tents for possible rain, especially during the summer.) The 4,000-foot (1,200-meter) elevation produces usually balmy days and mild nights.

For noncampers, the *ejido* (communal farm) offers five clean bungalows on the hillside above the lake, with complete kitchens (bring your food), flush toilets, and hot water for about $30 per night. Additionally, self-contained RVs can park hereabouts for a fee. Given the general friendliness of the local *ejido* folks, visitors who enjoy the outdoors by day and mountain stillness by night could spend a very enjoyable few days at Laguna La Maria.

Centro Turistico Carrizalillos ("Little Reeds") offers yet another outdoor possibility. Back at the fork, two miles uphill past Cofradio de Suchitán, head right. After about two more miles, follow the driveway off to the right. The Carrizalillos campsites spread for about a mile around the circumference of an oak-studded ridge that encloses a small natural lake. The few dozen developed campsites (picnic tables, water, pit

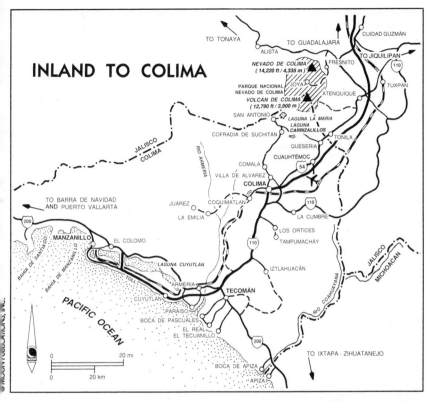

INLAND TO COLIMA

toilets), some suitable for small-to-medium RVs, rent for about $4 a day. A rustic view restaurant occupies a lakeside hilltop and a dozen housekeeping cabins overlook the lake. (The cabins may be in usable shape; the tariff is about $14 for two; take a look before paying.) In season, horses ($14/hour) and boats ($4/hour) are available. Given the magnificent mountain and valley views, the blue lake (if the water level is up), and the fresh air, Carrizalillos might be just right for a cool, restful change of pace.

The Volcanoes

Although taller by 1,200 feet, Nevado ("Snowy One") de Colima is far quieter than his younger brother, Volcán de Colima, one of the world's most active volcanoes. The **Volcán de Colima** has erupted dozens of times since the conquest, continuously belching a stream of smoke and ash and frequently burping up red-hot boulders. The government seals the access road when a serious eruption is imminent.

If you want a close-up look at Volcán de Colima, check with the federal-state tourism office (75 Hidalgo, downtown Colima, tel. 243-60 and 283-60) for advice, pack everything you're going to need, and head out along Hwy. 54 northeast of Colima. Drive a high-clearance truck or van or ride a second-class bus from the Central Camionera Bus Station (see "Getting There and Away" below). Pass Tonila (19 miles, 30 km from Colima) to a dirt turnoff road 36 miles (58 km) out. There, head left toward the mountain. The Volcanic National Park boundary is a bumpy 17 miles (27 km) farther. How far you can go after that depends upon the authorities.

The approach to the much quieter **Nevado de Colima** is considerably more certain. The clear dry winter months, when the views and the weather are the best, are the Colima climbers season of choice. The ascent, which begins at La Joya hut at around the 11,000-foot level, is not particularly difficult for experienced, fit hikers. The trail starts out leading for an easy hour to the microwave station at the tree line. Then it continues for a few hours of steep walking, except for a bit of scrambling at the end. Ice is a possibility all year around, however, so carry crampons and ice axes and be prepared to use them. Climbers often sleep overnight at La Joya, get an early morning start, and arrive at the summit before noon.

To get to Nevado de Colima, drive a jeep, pickup, or rugged, high-clearance van. Head out northeast along Hwy. 54 past Tonila toward Ciudad Guzmán. Fifty-two miles (83 km) from Colima, where Hwy. 54 heads to Guzmán, fork left toward Tonaya instead. Six miles past that, turn left at a dirt road at the sign marked Fresnito. It's 23 very rough miles (37 km) farther to La Joya. Pack up everything—winter sleeping bags, alpine equipment, water, and food—that you'll need.

Southern Excursion: Tampumachay

The valley of Colima has a number of important archaeological sites, one of the most accessible and scenic of which is near the village of Los Ortices, eight miles south of Colima city.

The **Centro Turistico Tampumachay,** a shady green miniresort, accommodates visitors with a modest five-room hotel, two swimming pools, a restaurant, and a camping area. Developed originally by archaeologist Fidencio Perez of Colima, the present owners continue his policy of careful custodianship of the nearby ruins.

The archaeological zone spreads along both edges of a deep, rocky gorge about a mile south of the hotel. The staff leads visitors on tours of the brushy, cactus-dotted cliffside plateau. Paths wind past intriguing animal- and human-motif petroglyph-sculptures and descend into tombs littered with grave pottery and human bones. Guides point out the remains of an unexcavated ceremonial platform on the opposite side of the canyon. (The tombs and petroglyphs are well preserved, since local people, fearing dire ghostly consequences, generally leave the site alone.)

Other local excursions include exploration of a limestone cave a couple of miles past the archaeological zone and hikes down into the gorge by a trail near the hotel. The Tampumachay resort itself is a lovely, tree-shaded garden, with artifact-dotted paths, a rope bridge, view gazebos, and pool-decks perfect for snoozing. Reservations are probably not necessary except during holidays (Centro Turistico Tampumachay, Los Ortices, Colima, tel. 331-472-25; five plain, clean fan-only rooms, about $24 d). Campsites for tents and RVs are also available.

Getting There: Eight miles (13 km) south of Colima city, follow the Los Ortices turnoff road from Highway 110. Watch carefully for the small hotel sign on the highway. More signs on the side road direct you about three more miles to Tampumachay.

ACCOMMODATIONS

Untouristed Colima has, nevertheless, a sprinkling of hotels. Some are city-style, downtown near the central plaza, and others are motel-style, in the suburbs.

Downtown Hotels

Many business travelers stay at **Hotel America,** three blocks from the city center. Outside, the facade is colonial; inside a two-story warren of rooms hides among a maze of glass-and-steel tropical terrariums. The rooms are spacious, carpeted, and comfortable. Lack of a pool is partially compensated by a sauna (use of which is limited to mornings, however). One of Hotel America's plusses is its good restaurant, where patrons enjoy snappy service and tasty food at reasonable prices. At Morelos 162, Colima, Colima 28000, tel. 331-295-96 and 331-203-66. Their 70 rooms rent for about $50 s, $60 d, with TV, a/c, phones, and parking; credit cards are accepted, and there is limited lower-level wheelchair access.

Hotel Ceballos, right on the central plaza, offers a more economical alternative. Although recently renovated, the hotel retains its high ceilings and graceful turn-of-the-century ambience. They offer two grades of accommodations: tastefully decorated, clean, and comfortable air-conditioned rooms, and slightly worn fan-only "economico" rooms. During hot weather especially, the a/c rooms are worth the price difference (Portal Medillin 12, Colima, Colima

28000, tel. 331-244-44). Rates for the 63 rooms run about $17 economy s or d, $24 deluxe with a/c; credit cards accepted, parking.

Suburban Hotels
Hotel Maria Isabel, a motel about a mile from the city-center, appeals to families and RV and car travelers. The double-story room tiers line a long parking lot edged on one side by a lawn and tropical foliage. A large pool and (mediocre) airy restaurant occupy one side near the entrance. The rooms come in economy and deluxe versions. The economy are very plain, the deluxe have tonier decor. Both have air-conditioning and TV. Although the Maria Isabel is attractive enough at first glance, general cleanliness and service leave something to be desired (Blvd. Camino Real at Av. Felipe Sevilla del Rio, Colima, Colima 28010, tel. 331-264-64 and 331-262-62). The 90 rooms go for about $20 economy s, $30 d; $24 and $33 deluxe; credit cards accepted, parking.

Neighboring **Hotel Los Candiles** avoids the usual cluttered motel parking lot atmosphere by putting the swimming pool-patio at the center and the cars off to the side. An attractive tropical garden-style hotel is the result. The rooms, in economy (fan only) and deluxe (a/c) options are clean, comfortable, and tastefully furnished (Blvd. Camino Real 399, Colima, Colima 28010, tel. 331-232-12). The 60 rooms rent for about $27 economy s or d, $45 deluxe; credit cards accepted, with TV and a restaurant.

FOOD

Breakfast And Snacks
A good place to start out the day is the restaurant at the **Hotel America** (open daily at seven for breakfast, dinner served till ten; Morelos 162, tel. 295-96.), where the servers greet you with hot coffee and a cheery "Buenos dias." The menu affords plenty of familiar fare, from fresh eggs any style to pancakes and fruit, at reasonable prices.

After a few hours among the downtown sights, the small sidewalk cafe **Cisnes** near Jardín de Libertad is just the place to enjoy a bite and watch the passing scene (at the end of Andando Constitución, the pedestrian-mall continuation of Av. Constitución, open Mon.-Sat. 8-3 and 4-10).

Restaurants
(Complete Dinner price key: Budget = under $7, Moderate = $7-14, Expensive = over $14.) **Livorno's** serves good pizza and other Italian specialties, complete with atmosphere, on Andando Constitución, right off Jardín de Libertad (open Tues.-Sun. noon-11 p.m., credit cards accepted). Livorno's is one of the few spots for a late snack downtown. Moderate.

The popularity of **Restaurant Fonda San Miguel** is due to its good regional food, refined ambience, and very correct service (open daily 7:30-6, 129 Av. 27 de Septiembre, near corner of Allende, tel. 448-40). Patrons enjoy shady seating beneath a hacienda roof beside a sunsplashed fountain-patio. Although they serve good breakfasts, the house specialties are Colima regional lunch and early dinner dishes, such as Pepena roast beef in sauce and Tatemado roast pork. Vegetable lovers, on the other hand, order their excellent tomato, onion, and avocado salad. Moderate.

Crotos Grill, near the eastern edge of downtown, is another local favorite, partly due to its airy, tropical setting. Lush vines hang from huge trees nearby, a big-beamed red-tile roof canopy soars overhead, and piano music plays softly in the background. Waiters move briskly about, serving delectable house specialties such as Parrillada (grill) for two, Sopa de Croto, or Ostiones de Chef (open daily 8 a.m.-1 a.m., Calz. Pedro A. Galvan 207, tel. 494-94; follow Av. Morelos from the city center east about a mile to wide Calzado Galvan, where Crotos will be one block south, downhill, across the street). Moderate to expensive.

ENTERTAINMENT AND EVENTS

Local folks compensate for the lack of nightlife by whooping it up during Colima's three major local festivals. Don't miss them if you happen to be in town.

For nine days beginning Jan. 23, people celebrate the **Fiesta de La Virgen de La Salud,** which climaxes on Feb. 2. The church (Iglesia de La Salud) neighborhood near Avs. Gallardo and Corregidora blooms with colorful processions and food and crafts stalls, and the church plaza resounds with music, folk dancing, and fireworks.

Ever since 1820, the Villa de Alvarez (a suburb a few miles northwest of the city center), has staged **Fiesta Charrotaurina,** a 10-day combination rodeo-bullfight-carnival. The celebration wouldn't be as much fun if the Villa de Alvarez people stayed to themselves. Every day, however, between Feb. 7 and 23 around noon, a troupe of Villa de Alvarez musicians, cowboys, cowgirls, papier-mâché bulls, and a pair of *mojigangos* (giant effigies of the Colima governor and spouse) assemble on Colima's downtown Jardín de Libertad. The music begins, the *mojigangos* start whirling, and a big crowd of bystanders follows them back to Villa de Alvarez.

Visitors who miss the Virgen de La Salud in January can get in on the similar **Fiesta de San Jose,** which culminates on March 19 in the westside neighborhood of the Iglesia de San Jose (corner Quintero and Suarez), with food, regional dancing, religious processions, and fireworks.

Toy horses-on-a-stick appeared among the Mexicans not long after the conquest.

ERIN DWYER

SHOPPING

Two good downtown sources sell reproductions of Colima's charming pre-Columbian animal and human figurines.

The state-operated **Casa de Las Artesanias** near Jardín de Libertad stocks a number of locally made figurines, plus shelves of handicrafts gathered from all over Mexico, such as sombreros, *huipiles,* serapes, toys, and Christmas decorations. Other local items include Colima coffee beans, regional cuisine cookbooks, and coconut candy (Av. Zaragoza and Andando Constitución, open Mon.-Fri. 10-2 and 5-8, Sat. 10-2, tel. 447-90).

If you prefer to buy your figurines directly from the artisan, go to the **Museo de Culturas Populares,** four blocks north of the *jardín.* The potters work in the little house to the right of the museum entrance on Av. Aldama. If no artisan is available, the museum shop inside sells figurines, plus many other folkcrafts, both local and national (Avs. Aldama and 27 de Septiembre, open Mon.-Sat. 9-2 and 4-7, tel. 268-69).

SERVICES AND INFORMATION

Money Exchange
The **Banamex** downtown branch (at Hidalgo 90, across from the Tourist Office, tel. 209-16 and 298-20) exchanges U.S. currency and traveler's checks Mon.-Fri. 9-12.

Post Office And Telephones
The main **Correos** (post office) is open Mon.-Fri. 9-2 and 4-6, Sat. 9-12 in the Palacio Federal on Plaza Nuñez (corner Madero and Nuñez) about six blocks east of the Jardín de Libertad.

The Farmacia Colima (on Jardín de Libertad, across Madero from the cathedral) operates a *larga distancia* (long-distance) telephone daily 8:30 a.m.-9:30 p.m. Colima's area code is 331.

Tourist Information Office
The efficient and helpful staff of the **Oficina de Turismo** (tourist office) at Hidalgo 75, two blocks east of Jardín de Libertad, answers questions and offers a good Colima brochure map and a bilingual tourist services guide (open Mon.-Fri. 9-1 and 3-6, tel. 243-60 and 283-60).

Hospital, Police, And Emergencies

The respected private hospital, **Centro Medico** at Maclovio Herrera 140, a quarter-mile north of Jardín de Libertad (tel. 240-44, 240-45, and 240-46), has emergency service and many specialists on 24-hour call.

The **Farmacia Colima** (open 8:30 a.m.-9:30 p.m., tel. 200-31 and 255-37), on the Jardín de Libertad, offers a large stock of medicines and drugs.

The **Caberca Policia** (police headquarters), tel. 218-01, is near the corner of Aldama and Barreda, four blocks north of Jardín de Libertad.

For **fire** emergencies, call the *servicio bomberos* (fire station), tel. 258-58, at the corner of Nigromante and Alvarez, three blocks from Jardín de Libertad.

Newsstand

English newspapers and magazines are rare in Colima. The newsstand next to the Hotel Ceballos stocks the English-language Mexico City *News,* however.

GETTING THERE AND AWAY

By Car Or RV

The Manzanillo-Colima combined Highways 200 and 110 *autopista* makes Colima safely accessible from Manzanillo in an hour. From Manzanillo, follow the *cuota* (toll) Hwy. 200 (34 miles, 54 km) southeast to the Hwy. 110 junction near Tecomán. Branch north, continuing on 110 for another 25 miles (40 km) to Colima. (See Manzanillo "Getting There and Away" above for highway routes from Guadalajara and Zihuatanejo.)

By Bus

Several excellent first-class bus lines, such as **Tres Estrellas de Oro** (tel. 284-48, 284-99), **Omnibus de Mexico** (tel. 290-50, 471-90), and **Autobuses de Occidente** (tel. 205-08, 481-79), provide frequent connections to Manzanillo to the south and Guadalajara to the north. All of these operate out of the big Nueva Central Camionera on the Hwy. 110 *libramiento* (bypass) east of town.

By Train

The Colima train station is at the end of Av. Medellin in the southern suburbs, about a mile from the town center. Reservations are not generally necessary. Simply buy tickets at the station prior to departure. One Guadalajara-bound second-class diesel coach departs daily around 8 a.m.; one similar Manzanillo-bound train departs in the opposite direction daily around 3 p.m. Call the ticket office, tel. 292-50, to verify times.

SOUTH TO IXTAPA-ZIHUATANEJO AND INLAND TO PÁTZCUARO

ALONG THE ROAD TO PLAYA AZUL

Heading southeast out of Manzanillo, the Mexican Pacific coast highway winds for 200 miles, hugging the shorelines of two states. First, it follows the southern Colima coast, well known for its beaches, surf, and abundant fresh seafood. After that, however, the road pierces the little-traveled wild coast of Michoacán.

That last lonely Michoacán coastal link was completed in 1984. Local people still remember when, if they wanted to travel to Manzanillo, they had to walk half the way. What they saw along the path is still there: mountainsides of great vine-draped trees and seemingly endless pearly, driftwood-strewn beaches, fringed by verdant palm groves and enfolded by golden sandstone cliffs. From ramparts high above the foaming surf, gigantic headlands seem to file in procession along the shore and fade into the sea-mist a thousand miles away. Along the highway, coatimundis peer from beneath bushes, iguanas scurry along the shoulder, and a rainbow of blossoms—yellow, red, pink, and violet—blooms from the roadside.

HISTORY

Before Columbus

The great Rio Balsas, whose watershed includes Michoacán and five other Mexican states, has repeatedly attracted outsiders. Some of the first settlers to the Rio Balsas basin came thousands of years ago, from perhaps as far away as Peru. They left remains—pottery, of unmistakable Andean influence—and their language, roots of which remain in the *indígena* dialects of highland Michoacán.

The major inheritors of this ancient Andean heritage became known as the Tarascans. They founded a powerful Michoacán empire, centered at highland Lake Pátzcuaro, which rivaled the Aztec empire at the time of the conquest.

Although the Tarascans were never subdued by the Aztecs, they quickly fell prey to the Spanish conquistadores, who were also drawn to the River Balsas. In search of the riches of the Southern Sea (as the Pacific was known to him), Hernán Cortés sent his captains Juan Rodriguez and Ximón de Cuenca to the mouth of the Rio Balsas, where they founded the Villa de La Concepción de Zacatula in 1523. But, like all the early Pacific ports, Zacatula was abandoned in favor of Acapulco by 1600.

The Michoacán-Colima coast slumbered until the 1890s, when the railroad arrived at the reawakened port of Manzanillo. En route, the train stopped at Cuyutlán, a village of salt harvesters, who soon became prosperous by lodging and feeding droves of rich Guadalajara seashore vacationers.

Neighboring coastal Michoacán had to wait for the dust of the 1910-17 Revolution to settle before getting its own development project. Again the Rio Balsas drew outsiders. Dam builders came to harness the river's hydropower to make steel out of a mountain of Michoacán iron ore. In succession came the new port, Lázaro Cárdenas, the railroad, the dam, then finally the huge Las Trucas (curiously, "The Trout") steel mill. Concurrently, Playa Azul, Michoacán's planned beach resort on the Pacific, was developed nearby.

The new facilities, however, never quite lived up to expectations. Although a few ships and trains still arrive, and some tourists come weekends and holidays, Lázaro Cárdenas and Playa Azul drowse fitfully, dreaming of their long-expected awakening.

CUYUTLÁN

Little Cuyutlán (pop. about 2,000) is heaven for lovers of nostalgia and tranquility. No raucous hangouts clutter its lanes, no rock music bounces from its few cafes. Sun, sand, and gentle surf are its prime amenities. Rickety wooden walkways lead across its hot dark sands to a line of beachfront umbrellas, where you can rent a chair for the day, enjoy the breeze, and feast on the offerings of seaside seafood kitchens.

Virtually all of Cuyutlán's hotels, restaurants, and services lie along a single street: Hidalgo, which runs from the *jardín* (on the Manzanillo-Armería road) a few blocks, crossing Av. Veracruz at the hotel corner and ending at the beachfront *malecón*.

The shady, cobbled side streets of Cuyutlán invite impromptu exploring. Near the beach, lanes lead past weathered wooden houses and palapas (some for rent). On the inland side of the *jardín* near the rail station, kerosene lamps flicker at night through the walls of bamboo village houses. The station itself is an antique out of the Porfirian age, with cast-iron benches and original filigreed columns still supporting its moss-streaked, gabled platform roof. Nearby, hulking wooden (exotically unusual in Mexico) salt warehouses line an earthen street. Those ancient repositories are reminders of the 300-year tradition of salt harvesting at the edges of nearby Cuyutlán lagoon.

The Green Wave

Cuyutlán's latter-day claim to fame is the mysterious Green Wave, which is said to occasionally rise offshore and come crashing down from a height of 20, 30, or even 50 feet. (The later at night the story is told, it seems, the greater the height.)

The source of the Green Wave's color is also a mystery, although some local aficionados speculate that an offshore algae bloom might be responsible.

Although several faithful still carefully scan the horizon (during the most-likely month of May), few folks seem to remember when the last Green Wave rolled shoreward. Some suggest that the 1978 local earthquake may have shifted the ocean bottom and quieted the Green Wave (temporarily, at least). The Hotel Morelos, at the corner of Hidalgo and Vera Cruz, displays, in addition to its lobby gallery of James Dean and Marilyn Monroe photos, a snapshot of an alleged 20-foot Green Wave by local photographer and enthusiast Eduardo Lolo.

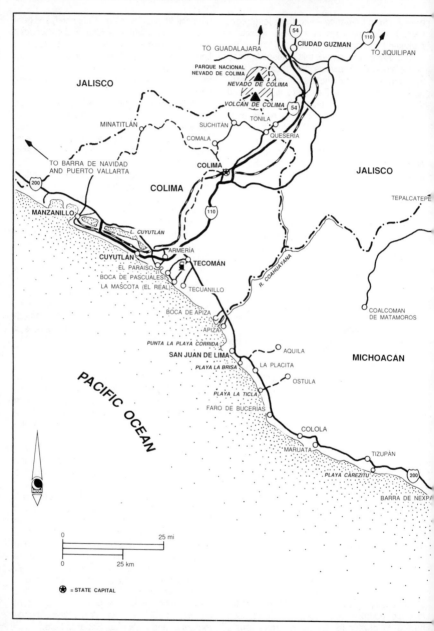

SOUTH
TO IXTAPA -
ZIHUATANEJO
AND INLAND
TO PÁTZCUARO

MICHOACAN

SIERRA MADRE DEL SUR

© MOON PUBLICATIONS, INC.

Beach Activities

Cuyutlán's wide and seemingly endless beach invites a number of activities and sports. The nearly level offshore slope produces little undertow, so wading and swimming conditions are ideal. The waves, which roll in gradually, are fine for boogieboarding, bodysurfing, and all levels of surfing, depending on the size of the swells. Bring your own surfboard (although boogieboard rentals are available on the beach). Shells become more common the farther you stroll away from the few picked-over blocks of beach.

As for fishing, the shallow slope decreases the chances for successful surf-casts. Best hire or launch your boat (easy in calm weather) and head to the happy fishing grounds beyond the waves.

Cuyutlán Accommodations

The **Hotel Morelos,** founded in the 1890s, continues Cuyutlán's turn-of-the-century tradition with a long (quaintly downhill-sloping) lobby festooned with plastic flowers and green Grecian columns. Although the family-run restaurant serves hearty local-style food, some of the rooms are dark and dank. Look at several before moving in (Hidalgo 185, Cuyutlán, Colima 28350, tel. 332-418-10, local ext. 107). The Morelos's 36 rooms rent for about $10 s, $17 d, $22 t, with hot water and fans.

Across Av. Veracruz stands the equally venerable but plainer **Hotel Fenix,** whose patrons likewise enjoy an open-air street-level restaurant. Although many of the rooms, scattered along upstairs corridors, are clean and airy, they tend toward the scruffy and have no hot water (Hidalgo 201, Cuyutlán, Colima 28350, tel. 332-418-10, local ext. 147). Rates for the 17 rooms with fan run about $7 per person.

Hotel Posada San Miguel, across Hidalgo from the Morelos, has bright, comfortable upstairs rooms that open onto a shady sitting porch overlooking the street (Av. Hidalgo, Cuyutlán, Colima 28350, tel. 332-418-10, local ext. 135). The eight rooms run about about $9 per person, with hot water and fans.

Fourth choice goes to Cuyutlán's newest and biggest, **Hotel Ceballos,** fronting the beach at the foot of Hidalgo. Inside, the cavernous atrium-lobby more resembles a bus station than a hotel. At night, guests sit watching a huge TV that echoes over the entire lobby. But that needn't bother you, especially if you rent one of the many Spartan but clean rooms, which, on the oceanfront side, enjoy private, breezy sea-view balconies. The Ceballos is open seasonally, Dec. 15-May 31 only (Veracruz no. 10, Cuyutlán, Colima 28350, tel. 332-418-10, local ext. 101). Their 80 rooms rent for about $18 per person with hot water and some fans. Try bargaining for a discount during times of low occupancy, such as weekdays and January and February.

Camping And RV Parking

Although Cuyutlán has no established campground, dirt roads lead to miles of open beach, good for camping or parking, on both sides of town. (Be careful of soft sand, however.) Cuyutlán, being a generally friendly, upright country place, will ordinarily present no security problem. If in doubt, however, don't hesitate to ask local shopkeepers. Say, "¿Es bueno acampar aca?"

Food

Besides the good Hotel Morelos restaurant and its rival at the Hotel Fenix across the street, the main good Cuyutlán eateries are the many seafood vendors, whose semipermanent umbrella-covered establishments do big business on holidays and weekends. Quality of the fare—oyster cocktails, grilled or boiled shrimp and lobster, and fried fish—is generally excellent, since many of them depend on loyal repeat customers.

Shopping, Services, And Information

Most of Cuyutlán's businesses are spread along Hidalgo between the beach and the *jardín.* For **groceries,** try Abarrotes Camacho or Abarrotes Baby, at 120 and 114 Hidalgo, respectively. Nearby also is the **Farmacia Carmen,** open daily 9-2 and 4-9. Across the street at 144 Hidalgo the *preventiva* (police) are on duty 'round the clock. Downhill, a block from the *jardín,* Manzanillo direction, is the **Centro de Salud** (health center), open routinely till 5 p.m., but only in emergencies after that.

Getting There And Away

By car or RV from Manzanillo, follow the Hwy. 200 *cuota* (toll) branch superhighway 17 miles (28 km) to Cuyutlán. Or, for a more scenic alternative, follow main street Av. Carrillo Puerto past the *jardín* through downtown Manzanillo and continue along the west end of placid Laguna Cuyutlán. This route curves past the power plant, through miles of *ciruela* orchards, then along a breezy barrier dune and wild beach, eventually joining the toll highway before Cuyutlán. (At one point, upon crossing a narrow estuary bridge, the highway asphalt joins with the railroad track. Don't forget to look for the train before starting across.)

Manzanillo taxis take passengers to Cuyutlán for about $20, one way. If this is too expensive, local **buses** connect with Cuyutlán every half hour until around 8 p.m. from Armería (transfer point on Hwy. 200, half an hour by bus from Manzanillo's Central Camionera bus station.)

Second-class diesel coach **no. 91** leaves Manzanillo every morning at around 6 a.m., arriving in Cuyutlán around 6:30, then continuing to Colima and Guadalajara. In the opposite direction, **no. 92** arrives at Cuyutlán from Guadalajara and Colima around 4:40 p.m. and continues to Manzanillo.

SOUTH COLIMA BEACHES

El Paraiso

El Paraiso (pop. 1,000), just seven miles south of Cuyutlán, is popular on Sundays and holidays with families, who fill the dozen beachfront seafood palapas lining the bumpy main street. El Paraiso's long strand (which extends for miles on both sides) is similar to Cuyutlán's: hot, dark sand and generally gentle, rolling surf, with little or no undertow, excellent for safe wading, swimming, bodysurfing, boogieboarding, and surfing.

The good beach and seafood accounts for the success of the **Hotel Paraiso** and restaurant, which perches above the surf at the south end (left as you arrive) of the beachfront street. Many of the hotel's plain but clean rooms enjoy the same airy oceanfront vista as their popular restaurant. The adjacent pool and sun deck is yet another reason for spending a day or two there. The 54 rooms (none with hot water, however) rent from about $23 d, $30 t; credit cards are accepted. Reserve, especially during holidays and weekends, by writing the hotel at Playa Paraiso, Armería, Colima 28300, or calling their agent in Tecomán, tel. (332) 406-07.

Boca De Pascuales, El Real, Tecuanillo, And Boca De Apiza

Although none of this quartet of downscale beachside palapa heavens has an acceptable hotel, local folks know them well for their gentle surf, abundant seafood, and wide-open spaces for tent and RV camping. Drivers can access them along good paved roads from Hwy. 200. For bus travelers, Tecomán central plaza is the point of departure for local buses, which run frequently until around 6 p.m. After that, take a taxi.

Boca de Pascuales, eight paved miles (13 km) from Hwy. 200, is literally the *boca* (mouth) of the Armería River, whose waters (which began on the snowy slope of Nevado de Colima) widen to a broad estuary. Here, they nourish schools of fish and flocks of seabirds—pelicans, cormorants, herons—which dive, swoop, and stalk for fry in the river mouth lagoon. Fishermen wade in and catch the very same prey with throw-nets.

The beach itself is broad, with semicoarse gray sand. The waves roll gradually shoreward over a near-level, sandy shelf, and recede with little or no undertow. Consequently, swimming, boogieboarding, and bodysurfing are relatively safe, and surfing is not uncommon. Lots of driftwood litters the sandbar, and several rentable fishing *lanchas* lie pulled up along the beach. A quarter-mile lineup of seafood *ramadas* (semitemporary flat palm-thatch roofs) provide shade and food for the local families who crowd in on Sundays and holidays. Get there from Hwy. 200 heading south, just before Tecomán. Follow the signed turnoff road about eight miles to the beach, turn right and continue a quarter mile past the *ramadas* to the lagoon and sandbar.

For more lovely beach and surf, head from Boca de Pascuales along the two miles of beachfront road to El Real (marked La Mascota on some maps). The paved road passes a file of hurricane-battered shoreline homes, separated by open spaces, good for camping or RV parking (if you don't mind occasional company). Ask if it's okay before setting up camp. (Bring all of your supplies, including water; the few stores along this stretch are meagerly stocked.)

Three or four restaurants (notably, the popular En Ramada Boca de Rio) dot the two miles to El Real. There, a few more more rustic seafood *ramadas* crowd the corner where the road heads back about seven miles (11 km) to Hwy. 200 at Tecomán.

For Tecuanillo, head seaward at the paved Hwy. 200 turnoff road a mile and a half south of the Tecomán (south end) Pemex station. Continue about six miles to the roadside ponds of the La Granja restaurant just before the beach. About six acres of ponds supply loads of *langostinas* (prawns) and *pargo* for on-the-spot consumption—broiled, boiled, ranchera, garlic, diabla, ceviche—any way you prefer, $4-8 (open Tues.-Sun. noon to six).

Besides its long, wide beach and good surf fishing, visitors to the hamlet of Tecuanillo enjoy the protection of some of the few official lifeguards on the south Colima coast. The friendly staff of the small road's-end naval detachment volunteers for the duty. They don't mind, since the beach is nearly empty except for weekends and holidays. Tecuanillo is a good tenting or RV parking spot for lovers of seafood and solitude who appreciate the added security of the nearby naval detachment. Beach palapa restaurants and a local store can supply food and drinks and the village has a water supply.

Boca de Apiza, at the mouth of the Coahuayana River (which forms the Colima-Michoacán border), has surfing potential, driftwood, and possible tenting spots next to a wild, mangrove jungle-lined beach. Get there by following Colima Hwy. 185, the signed, paved turnoff road about 21 miles (34 km) south of Tecomán. About three miles from the highway, past a mangrove channel, the road splits. Ahead is a beach with some informal camping spots; left about a mile the dry-weather-only dirt road dead-ends at a second beach, where powerful surfing waves rise sharply and break both left and right.

Although the fishing hamlet of Apiza is in Michoacán, it's barely so, being just south of the Rio Coahuayana. It's reachable by the paved side road one mile south of the river bridge. A dozen seafood *ramadas,* complete with tables and hammocks, spread along the road's end 2.5 miles from the highway. The long dark-sand beach spreads seemingly without limit on the south side, while on the other, a bamboo-hut village spreads quaintly along the boat-lined estuary bank. With a store for supplies, tenters and self-contained RV campers could fish, beachcomb, and bodysurf here for a month of Sundays.

Tecomán Services

Tecomán (pop. 50,000), on Hwy. 200, 37 miles (59 km) southeast of Manzanillo, three miles south of the Colima (Hwy. 110) junction, is south Colima's service center. All services are on or near the Hwy. 200 through-town main street.

For **money exchange,** try Banamex (López Mateos and Hidalgo, tel. 433-57) or Banco Serfin (Medellin 240, tel. 4-19-96). For a **doctor,** go to 24-hour emergency hospital Sanatorio Santa Fe (Allende and Medellin, tel. 427-43). The **Correos** (post office) is at Guerrero 1 (tel. 419-39). The Computel **long-distance telephone** and public fax is at Mina and Progreso (tel. 438-99).

Bus stations are maintained by Autobuses del Occidente at Progreso 628 (tel. 407-95), Tres Estrellas de Oro at Marquez 695 (tel. 405-77), and Autotransportes Colima (local second-class) at Cinco de Mayo 125 (tel. 411-04). **Gasoline** including Magna unleaded is at the north-end Pemex on Hwy. 200, a mile from the town *jardín.*

NORTHERN MICHOACÁN BEACHES

Adventure often draws travelers along the thinly populated, pristine northwestern Michoacán coast. Without telephones and electricity, most people live by natural rhythms. They rise with the sun, tend their livestock, coconuts, and papayas, take shady siestas during the heat of the day, and watch the ocean for what the tides may bring.

Outsiders often begin to enjoy the slow pace. They stop at little beaches, sit down for a soda beneath a *ramada,* ask about the fishing, the waves, and stroll along the beach. They wander, picking up shells and driftwood and saying hello to the kids and fisherfolk along the way. Charmed and fully relaxed, they sometimes linger for months.

On The Road

If **driving,** fill up with unleaded Magna Sin gas at the Tecomán (north side) Pemex (or the Playa Azul Pemex if traveling in the opposite direction.) The road runs 165 miles (267 km) between them with only a few stores selling leaded regular from drums. If you're driving south, read your odometer mileage at the Rio Coahuayana bridge (Hwy. 200, Km 231) at the

Colima-Michoacán border. (The kilometer markers, incidentally, begin with zero at the junction near Playa Azul, thus giving the distance directly from that point.) In such undeveloped country, road mileage will help you find and remember your own favorites among Michoacán's dozens of lovely beach gems.

Bus travelers enjoy the best connections at Manzanillo Central Camionera bus station, Armería, or Tecomán in the northwest, or Lázaro Cárdenas or La Mira (near Playa Azul) in the southeast. Bus lines, such as Autotransportes Sur de Jalisco, Transportes Norte de Sonora, and Flecha Amarilla, run a few daily first-class local departures from both Manzanillo and Lázaro Cárdenas. Second-class Autotransportes Galeana buses run from the same terminals approximately hourly during the day, stopping everywhere and giving adventurers the option of getting off wherever they spot the palmy little heaven they've been looking for.

San Juan De Lima

Although its number of hotels has recently doubled from two to four, San Juan de Lima (or Alima; residents say it doesn't matter) is small and sleepy. A scattering of small houses with neither phones nor good store, San Juan de Lima's popularity comes from its long, creamy sand beach, framed between a pair of rocky headlands. Very surfable breakers roll in gently from about 50 yards out and recede with little undertow. All beach sports are safe, except during the fall hurricane season, when the waves are 10 or 15 feet tall and surfers are as common as coconuts.

Fishing is probably best off the rocks at the sheltered north-end beach, **Playa La Punta Corrida,** where the very gentle waves allow easy boat launching. (Be on your guard for soft sand, however.) The same spot appears ripe for RV or tent camping. For access, see "Getting There" below.

Accommodations: The side-by-side hotels **Parador** and **Miramar,** each with about 10 rooms and its own sea-view palapa restaurant, manage to stay open all year. Mutual rivalry keeps their standards and prices on an approximate par. About $14 gets you a very plain but clean bare-bulb room with toilet and shower (sorry, no hot water). Try bargaining; you may be able to do better.

The Hotel Parador (the one on the right) has the largest and most popular palapa in town. The family who runs it takes special pride in the cooking, which invariably includes the fresh catch of the day. They're friendly, and the view from their shady tables is blue and breezy.

Getting There: San Juan de Lima is at Km 211, 12 miles southeast of the Colima border. Get to the north-end beach via the dirt road at Km 212.5 south of town. After a third of a mile (one-half km), follow the left fork. Continue past the oceanography station at mile 1.6 (Km 2.6) to the beach a half mile farther.

Playa La Brisa

At Km 206, 16 miles south of the Colima line, the highway climbs a headland, where a roadside *mirador* (viewpoint) affords a look southeast. Far below, a foam-bordered white strand curves from a little palm grove, past a lagoon to a distant misty headland. This is Playa La Brisa, where, beneath the little grove, the Renteria-Alvarez family members manage their miniature utopia.

Their shady grove is made for either tent or self-contained RV camping. People often ask them how much they charge. "Nothing," they say. "As long as you have a little lunch or dinner in our palapa here, stay as long as you like."

On the very broad beach beyond the grove, the waves roll in, breaking gradually both right and left. With little or no undertow, the surf is good for swimming, boogieboarding, and bodysurfing. Furthermore, taking your clue from the name "La Brisa," you know that windsurfing is frequently good here, too.

Additionally, the lagoon a mile down the beach affords opportunities for wildlife viewing, aided by your own kayak or portable rubber boat. Fishing is also often rewarding either from the rocks beneath the headland, or by boat (your own or local *panga*) launched from the beach. Get there by following the dirt road at Km 205 at the base of the hill one mile to the palm grove.

La Placita Services

The dusty town of La Placita (pop. 5,000), at Km 199 four miles south of La Brisa, has groceries, a small hotel (the Reina, next to the bridge), pharmacies (on the highway at the central plaza), and a government Centro de Salud (health center, on the street that borders the south edge of the plaza). La Placita has no phones, however. The closest telephone (and only one for another hundred miles south) is at Ranchito, at Km 222, 14 miles northeast.

Playa La Ticla

The broad, gray-white sands of La Ticla attract visitors—mostly surfers—for two good reasons: its big, right-breaking rollers, and an ice-cream van, which arrives daily at three. The specialties are fruit-flavored ices, which many La Ticla visitors seem to plan their day around.

Besides the surfing waves, a clear, sandy-banked river, fine for freshwater swimming, divides the beach in two. The town has both stores and a Centro de Salud (health center). The beach has plenty of room for RV parking and tents and would seem fine for camping. Unfortunately, however, drugs have led to problems, such as a gunpoint robbery during the early '90s. Check locally to see if things have improved.

Getting There: Turn off at the signed road at Km 173, 36 miles from the Colima border. At mile 1.7 (Km 2.7), follow the left, more-traveled fork; at the village basketball court, jog right, then left. Continue to the beach at mile 2.2 (Km 3.5).

Faro De Bucerías

Idyllic perfectly describes Faro de Bucerías: a crystalline yellow-sand crescent, clear blue waters, protected by offshore islets. The name Bucerías ("Divers") suggests what local people already know: that Faro de Bucerías is a top snorkeling location. Favorable conditions, such as minimal local stream runoff and a nearly pure silica-sandstone shoreline combine to produce unusually clear water. Chance has even intervened to make it better, in the form of a wreck beside the offshore Morro Elefante (Elephant Bluff) islet, where multicolored fish swarm amongst the corals.

Several petite sandstone bays and beaches dot the coast around the main beach, Playa de Faro de Bucerías, which has all the ingredients for a relaxing stay. The beach itself is a lovely half-mile arc, where the waves rise and crash immediately at the water's edge and recede with strong undertow. Wading is nevertheless safe and swimming ideal in a calm south-end nook, protected by a rocky, tidepool-laced outcropping.

For food and accommodations, beachside palapas serve seafood during holidays, while the **Parador Turistico** restaurant-campground on the northwest side of the bay serves visitors on a daily basis. You set up your tent or park your RV (sorry, motor homes are probably too big to get in) beneath their beachfront camping *ramada* for $1 per person per night, showers included.

This is a heaven for fresh seafood lovers. Local divers (marked by their floating offshore inner tubes) bring up daily troves of octopi, conches, clams, oysters, and lobsters, which you can purchase on the spot and have cooked in the restaurant. If you prefer, catch your own from the rocks or hire a local fisherman to take you out for half a day.

For more local diversions, you can poke around in tidepools or climb to the white lighthouse *(faro)* which perches atop the southeast rocky point. Another day you can walk in the opposite direction and explore little Playa Manzanilla and other hidden coves beyond the stony northeast headland.

Getting There: A big sign at Km 173 marks the Faro de Bucerías turnoff, 36 miles (58 km) from the Colima border. At the village, at mile 1.9 (Km 3.0), turn right (toward the dune) and and continue 100 yards to the Parador Turistico at the north end of the beach.

Playa Maruata

This unique seaside refuge has formed where a mountain river tries to empty into the sea but is partially blocked by a pair of big rocks. Sand has collected, so the rocks appear as islands in sand rather than water. The ocean has worn away sea tunnels, which surging waves penetrate, pushing air and water, gushing and spouting onto the shore. At times, a dry sand beach builds up next to the rocks, where campers can build an evening fire and be soothed to sleep by the gurgling, booming, and whistling lullaby of Maruata.

Besides plenty of beach for camping, the Nahua-speaking *ejido* (cooperative) owners of Playa Maruata run a pair of good palapa restaurants beneath the sleepy beachfront grove and maintain a few shady palm-frond *ramadas* on the sand for visitors. During the popular winter season, several tenters and self-contained RVers usually camp there. Water is scarce, so bring a supply if you plan to join them.

The lagoon provides a sheltered anchorage and a rest for fishermen at Maruata.

Maruata visitors enjoy three distinctly different beaches. On the northwest, right-side, thunderous, open-ocean breakers (advanced surfing) pound a long, steep beach. A small middle beach, protected between the rocks, has oft-swimmable (with caution) water. The southeast, left-side beach, is long and sheltered by the sea rocks, enclosing a shallow rivermouth lagoon. Its usually gentle waves are generally safe for wading, swimming, and boat launching. In addition, snorkeling off the rocks is often very good during the winter-spring dry season.

Getting There: Playa Maruata is 50 miles (80 km) southeast of the Colima line at Km 150. Just past a big bridge, the dirt turnoff road descends steeply from the northbound lane and crosses *under* the bridge. At the airstrip, bear left and follow for about a hundred yards and turn right at a wide gravel road, heading through the village. Continue through a stream (low water only) to the palm grove and beach. (If, on the other hand, you want to fly in, the airstrip is smooth asphalt and about half a mile long.)

Playa Carezitu

At Km 94, a rough lane angles sharply down from the highway past a house or two to Playa Carezitu, a crescent of yellow sand, enfolded by sandstone cliffs. Big rolling surfable breakers rise in the middle of the bay, while tranquil billows lap the sand on the sheltered northwest end. The beach arcs a few hundred yards past scattered shoreline rocks, ducking around a cliff corner to another longer beach that curves a mile to a south-end headland. Snorkeling and fishing (by either surf or rock casting) appear promising, while shells, driftwood, and a even a volleyball net enrich the beach possibilities. On one side, a semipermanent food palapa is set up to serve holiday visitors.

Playa Carezitu might be good for at least a pleasant afternoon, perhaps more. Temporary palm-thatch *ramadas,* apparently ready for new camper-occupants, stand on the beach. The entrance track, while too steep and rough for big RVs, is negotiable in dry weather by jeeps, pickups, and high-clearance vans. Be prepared with food and drinking water, however.

Barra De Nexpa

While well known as one of Pacific Mexico's best surfing beaches, Barra de Nexpa's appeal is not limited to surfers. Don Gilberto, the grandfatherly founder of this pocket utopia, will gladly tell you all about it (in Spanish, of course). As more people arrived, facilities were added. First, Don Gilberto built palapas (now rentable at $2 per person), a well, and showers. Then he built a restaurant (which his son now runs). Next, an informal RV and tenting park spread along the palmy shoreline of the adjacent freshwater lagoon. Finally, a line of Robinson Crusoe-like rustic beach houses sprouted along the sandbar.

Don Gilberto's enterprise grew, but the natural setting remained unchanged. The breakers (10-footers are common) still roll in, often curling into tubes, to the delight of both surfers and surf-watchers. Nexpa's big waves, however,

Rustic beach houses at Barra de Nexpa are popular accommodations, especially during the fall surfing season.

need not discourage waders and swimmers, who splash and paddle in the freshwater lagoon instead. Beachcombers savor many hours picking through driftwood and shells while birdwatchers enjoy watching dozens of species preen, paddle, stalk, and flap in the lagoon. And finally, when tired of all of these, everyone enjoys the hammocks, which seem to hang from every available Nexpa post and palm.

At the height of the fall-winter season, when lots of surfers and campers crowd in, the atmosphere is generally communal and friendly. At the palapa restaurant, on the beach, or in the shade beneath the palms and the *ramadas,* you won't lack company.

Getting There: At Km 56, 109 miles (175 km) southeast of the Colima border, follow the unmarked dirt road, which curves sharply, following an uphill slope. It continues, bumping and winding downhill about half a mile to the beach. (The road appears negotiable by all cars and RVs except motor homes. If in doubt, do a preliminary run.)

Caleta De Campos
Caleta de Campos (pop. around 4,000) is at the signed turnoff at Km 50, 112 miles (181 km) southeast of the Colima border. Sometimes called Bahía de Bufadero ("Blowhole"), Caleta de Campos is the metropolis and service center for this corner of Michoacán. Although it has a sandy beach beside a blue bay, the beach is a haven primarily for commercial fishing launches rather than visitors. Fishing *pangas*

(launches) may be rented on the beach. A half-day excursion (about $50) typically returns with 50 pounds of *huachinango* (snapper), *cabrilla* (sea bass), *sierra* (mackerel), *robalo* (snook) and *atún* (tuna). Anyone can launch a boat on the bay's protected northwest end, provided a strong truck is available to lug it up the steep beach-access road.

Caleta's one **hotel,** the Yuritza, perches on the hill above the beach. Plain but clean, the Yuritza is fine for an overnight stay. A big yard within the fenced hotel compound can also accommodate large RVs. Reserve by writing the hotel, address simply Caleta de Campos, Michoacán. Their 19 rooms rent for $11 s, $14 d, and include fans and baths, but lack hot water.

The good **Torta-Burger** *lonchería* occupies the corner across from the hotel. Their *liquados,* tortas, hamburgers, and ham and eggs taste delicious after a hard day riding the waves.

Most of Caleta's stores and institutions are scattered along its single main street, which leads from the highway. There you'll find a *larga distancia* (long-distance) telephone office (tel. 601-92), a *farmacia,* a grocery, and a *centro de salud* (health center) on a side street nearby.

Buses stop frequently at the highway turnoff. They include Galeana first- and second-class (running between Manzanillo and Lázaro Cárdenas), Flecha Roja (running to and from Zihuatanejo), and Galeana microbuses (running to and from Lázaro Cárdenas). Drivers will generally let you off anywhere along the highway you request.

PLAYA AZUL

It's easy to see how Playa Azul ("Blue Beach") got on the map of Pacific Mexico. The beach is long and level, the sand is yellow and silky. The waves roll in slowly, swish gently, and stop, leaving wet, lazy arcs upon the sand. At sunset, these glow like medallions of liquid gold.

Around Town

Playa Azul (pop. 5,000) is a small town on a big beach with a mile of palapa seafood restaurants. Three bumpy streets, Carranza, Madero, and Independencia, parallel the beachfront *malecón* walkway. Much of the activity clusters on or near a fourth street (actually a dirt lane), Aquiles Serdán, which bisects the other three and ends at the *malecón*. Here the atmosphere—piquant aromas of steaming *pozole* and hot tacos, the color of mounds of papayas and tomatoes, the language and laughter of the people—is uniquely and delightfully Mexican.

Beach Activities

The Playa Azul beach is good for just about everything. The waves, big enough for surfing as they break far offshore, roll shoreward, picking up boogieboarders and bodysurfers along the way, finally rippling around the ankles of waders and splashers at the sand's edge. Concessionaires rent chairs, umbrellas, boogieboards, but not surfboards. The weekend crowds keep the beach relatively free of shells and driftwood, although pickings will be better farther out along the beach (which stretches many miles in either direction.)

Eating is another major Playa Azul beach occupation. Fruit vendors stroll the sand, offering luscious cut pineapple, watermelon, and mangos-on-a-stick, while semipermanent beach stands and dozens of *malecón* restaurants offer fresh *cocktel de ostión* (oyster cocktail, $4), *langostina al gusto* (prawns any style, $6), and *langosta al vapor* (steamed lobster, $10).

ACCOMMODATIONS

Playa Azul has half a dozen hotels, one with a trailer park. Three of them stand out. One block from the beach, the triple-tiered main building of the **Hotel Playa Azul and Trailer Park** surrounds a lovely pool-patio of tall palms, rubber trees, and big-leafed vines. A spacious blue swimming pool curves artfully in the middle, while the bar and restaurant are tucked beneath a soaring beamed palapa on one side. The shady patio invites quiet relaxation; other rooms offer TV and ping-pong. Families especially enjoy the hotel's water-slide minipark (beachside, behind the main building past the trailer park).

The 55 rooms, spacious and comfortable but not luxurious, come in economy and standard versions. Economy rooms (with fan only, on the ground floor by the parking lot) rent for about $16 s and $21 d; standard rooms go for about $21 and $26 with fan only; add about $10 for a/c; parking is available, credit cards are accepted and there is limited wheelchair access.

The trailer park, with about a dozen spaces cramped behind the hotel, is nevertheless popular, since guests have access to hotel facilities. Spaces (up to about 30 feet) rent for about $15 per day with all hookups, including power for air-conditioning, toilets, and hot showers. Discounts for lower power and weekly and monthly stays are available. Contact the hotel for reservations, which are mandatory for the trailer park during the winter (Av. V. Carranza s/n, Playa Azul, Michoacán 60982, tel. 753-600-88 and 753-600-93, fax 753-600-92.

The **Hotel Maria Teresa,** three blocks south of Aquiles Serdán and three short blocks from the beach, stands within an airy garden compound, with parking on one side and an attractive palapa restaurant and sunny pool patio tucked on the other. Their discotheque, Playa Azul's only one, rocks Fridays and Saturdays 4-9 p.m. If you desire tranquility, however, request a room on the relatively *tranquilo* wing farthest from the disco (Av. Independencia 626, Playa Azul, Michoacán 60982, tel. 753-600-05 and 753-601-50). Their 42 comfortable, near-deluxe rooms, all with TV, phones, and a/c, rent for about $21 s, $26 d, and $31 t; credit cards accepted, limited wheelchair access.

Playa Azul's cheaper accommodations lack hot water, a serious defect for many winter vacationers. One good budget lodging *with* hot water, however, is the **Hotel Costa de Oro**, on Madero, one block east of Serdán, two blocks from the beach. Av. F. Madero s/n, Playa Azul, Michoacán 60982, tel. (753) 600-86. Their 14 rooms, Spartan but clean, rent from about $14 d.

FOOD

Avenida Aquiles Serdán (at the Hotel Playa Azul corner) offers several possibilities. The friendly **Super del Centro** grocery has a little bit of everything, from cheese and milk to mops and *espirales mosquitos* (mosquito coils). Open daily 7:30 a.m.-9 p.m.

Next door, open Fri., Sat., and Sun. evenings 6-10 only, a family fires up the gas at their **Cenaduría Lupita.** Their steaming tacos—of *res* (roast beef), *chorizo* (spicy sausage), and *lengua* (tongue)—wrapped in hot tortillas and spiced with piquant salsas make perfect appetizers.

For an equally tasty second course, step down Serdán past the corner of Madero and take a streetside table at **Restaurant Galdy** (open daily 7 a.m.-11 p.m.). The all-woman cadre of cooks and waitresses tries harder than anyone in town, especially with hearty *pozole* (soup), *pierna* (roast pork), and *platos mexicanos* (combination plates).

For dessert, step back to the Madero corner to **Frutería Berenice** for a succulent selection of fruit (open daily 6:30 a.m.-9 p.m.). Local mangos (spring, early summer), pineapple, and *platanos* (bananas) will be familiar, but *guanabanas* (green and scaly, like an artichoke) and *ciruelas* (yellow and round, like a plum) probably will not.

To top everything off, cross Serdán to the **panadería** and pick up some cake, cookies, or *donas* (open Mon.-Sat. 7 a.m-10 p.m.).

ENTERTAINMENT AND SHOPPING

Playa Azul's evening entertainment begins with sunset, views of which are unobstructed year-round. The effect is doubly beautiful, for the sky's golden glow is reflected from both the ocean and Playa Azul's shoreline swaths of flat wet sand. Sunset is also an excellent time for joggers and walkers to take advantage of the cool sea breeze and Playa Azul's level, firm sand.

Playa Azul's one regular dance spot, the discotheque at the Hotel Maria Teresa, on Independencia three blocks east of Aquiles Serdán, is open Fri. and Sat. 4-9 p.m.

The tourist market, marked by the awnings stretched over Aquiles Serdán next to the Hotel Playa Azul, has several stands that offer beach balls, T-shirts, and bathing suits. Some of the more common crafts, such as painted ceramic animals and papier-mâché, may be available also.

SERVICES AND INFORMATION

Playa Azul has only a few services. Go to Lázaro Cárdenas (see below), 14 miles (22 km) southeast along Hwy. 200, for what Playa Azul lacks.

The town **doctor,** Horacio Soto-Mayor, has an office (phoneless) next to the Pemex gasoline station at the highway entrance to town. If he's closed and it's an emergency, take a taxi to the Centro de Salud (tel. 500-04) in La Mira (five miles, at the Hwy. 200 and Hwy. 37 intersection). If they're closed, continue to the General Hospital in Lázaro Cárdenas.

For routine drugs and medications, try the **Farmacia Dios,** corner of Independencia and Aquiles Serdán (open Mon.-Sat. 9-9, Sun. 9-2 and 5-8, tel. 601-85).

The *larga distancia* (long-distance telephone) office is on Independencia, one block west of Aquiles Serdán.

GETTING THERE AND GETTING AWAY

By car or RV, paved Hwy. 200 connects Playa Azul with Manzanillo in the northwest (195 miles, 314 km). Although the route is in good condition and lightly traveled most of the way, its twists and turns through rugged oceanside canyons and along spectacular shoreline ridges make considerably slow going. Allow at least seven hours for safety. Fill up with gasoline as you start out, since the last available Magna Sin unleaded heading southeast is in Tecomán, about 167 miles (269 km) from the Playa Azul Pemex, which also stocks Magna Sin.

Between Playa Azul and Ixtapa-Zihuatanejo in the southeast, the route is relatively short and straight, although trucks sometimes slow progress. Allow two and a half hours for the 76-mile (122-km) trip.

With Pátzcuaro and central Michoacán in the north, Highways 37 and 14 connect with Playa Azul over 191 miles (307 km) of winding mountain highway. Although paved all the way, this route—through fertile valleys and over pine-shadowed crests—is potholed in places and occasionally congested. Allow at least seven hours for safety. Magna unleaded gasoline is only available at Arteaga, Nueva Italia, and Uruapan, so keep filled. (As for "bandidos," stick to the main highway for security. Many mountain folks cultivate marijuana and opium. They're understandably suspicious of wandering strangers.)

Upon bus arrival, ask your driver to drop you at the Hwy. 200 Playa Azul junction (three miles from Playa Azul, two miles from La Mira), where a taxi or local minivan can take you the rest of the way.

For bus departure from Playa Azul, go to La Mira (five miles by local minivan or taxi) and wait at the intersection of Highways 200 and 37. Although most Manzanillo-, Pátzcuaro-, and Zihuatanejo-bound buses stop at La Mira, reserved seats are only available from the Lázaro Cárdenas stations. See "Lázaro Cárdenas and Along the Road to Ixtapa-Zihuatanejo" below.

INLAND TO PÁTZCUARO

The high road from Playa Azul leads to Pátzcuaro (pop. 70,000), a city brimming with inspirations. Pine- and cedar-brushed mountains ring it; an islet-studded lake borders it. Its air is fresh and clean and the sky always seems blue. Visitors come from all over the world to wander through narrow colonial lanes, buy fine copperware and cloisonné, and gaze at grand, mystery-shrouded monuments of long-forgotten emperors.

HISTORY

Before The Conquest

The valley and lake of Pátzcuaro, elev. 7,500 feet (2,100 meters), have nurtured civilizations for millennia. The Tarascans, whose king, Tariácuri, rebuilt the city during the 1370s, were the last and the greatest. To them the lake and surrounding grounds were sacred: the door to their land of the ancestors. They chose the venerated foundation stones of already-ancient temples as the new city's cornerstones, marking the symbolic door to the land of the dead: *tza-capu-amúcutin-pátzcuaro*, the "stone door where all changes to blackness." The last part of that original name remains in use today.

The founders of Pátzcuaro did not call themselves Tarascans. This was from the Spanish label, meaning "son-in-law." Before the conquest, Pátzcuaro people called (and still call) themselves the Purépecha (poo-REH-peh-chah). After the Spanish arrived in 1521, they increasingly applied their own label as they intermarried with the Pátzcuaro people.

Prior to the conquest, the Valley of Pátzcuaro was the center of a grand Purépecha empire, which extended beyond the present-day borders of the state of Michoacán. Local folk are still proud that their ancestors were never subjects of the Aztecs, whose armies they defeated and slaughtered by the tens of thousands on the eve of the conquest.

Conquest And Colonization

As Cortés approached the Valley of Mexico, the jittery Aztec emperor Moctezuma sent ambassadors to Tzintzuntzán (seen-soon-SAHN), the Purépecha capital on the shore of the lake a dozen miles northwest of Pátzcuaro. The ambassadors implored King Zuangua, known by his imperial title *caltzonzin,* to send an army to help repel Cortés. The *caltzonzin* refused, hastening Moctezuma's downfall and perhaps his own.

The first Spaniards, a few seemingly harmless travelers, wandered into the Valley of Pátzcuaro in 1521. The smallpox they unwittingly brought, however, was far from harmless. Zuangua soon succumbed to the ugly disease, along with tens of thousands of his subjects.

The Spanish military threat, in the person of conquistador Cristóbal de Olid and 70 mounted

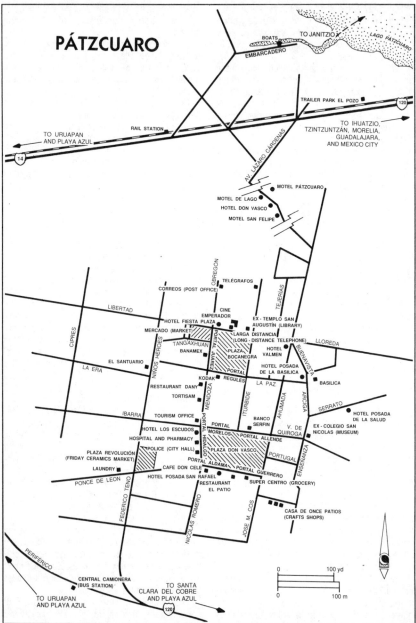

PÁTZCUARO

TO JANITZIO

LAGO PÁTZCUARO

BOATS
EMBARCADERO

TRAILER PARK EL POZO

120

TO URUAPAN
AND PLAYA AZUL

RAIL STATION

14

AV. LAZARO CÁRDENAS

TO IHUATZIO,
TZINTZUNTZÁN, MORELIA,
GUADALAJARA,
AND MEXICO CITY

MOTEL PÁTZCUARO

MOTEL DE LAGO
HOTEL DON VASCO
MOTEL SAN FELIPE

OBREGÓN

CORREOS (POST OFFICE)

TELÉGRAFOS

TEJERÍAS

LIBERTAD

CINE
EMPERADOR

HOTEL FIESTA PLAZA

EX - TEMPLO SAN
AUGUSTÍN (LIBRARY)

CIPRES

MERCADO (MARKET)

TANGAXHUAN

NIÑOS HÉROES

PORTAL JUAREZ

LARGA DISTANCIA
(LONG - DISTANCE TELEPHONE)

BUENAVISTA

LLOREDA

BANAMEX

PLAZA
BOCANEGRA

HOTEL
VALMEN

LA ERA

EL SANTUARIO

KODAK

PORTAL

REGULES

HOTEL POSADA
DE LA BASÍLICA

LA PAZ

BASÍLICA

RESTAURANT DANY

MENDOZA

ITURBIDE

AHUMADA

ARCIGA

SERRATO

TORTISAM

HOTEL POSADA
DE LA SALUD

IBARRA

TOURISM OFFICE

PORTAL

BANCO
SERFIN

V. DE
QUIROGA

EX - COLEGIO SAN
NICOLAS (MUSEUM)

HOTEL LOS ESCUDOS

PORTAL HIDALGO

MORELOS

PORTAL ALLENDE

HOSPITAL AND PHARMACY

ENSENANZA

PORTUGAL

PLAZA REVOLUCIÓN
(FRIDAY CERAMICS MARKET)

POLICE (CITY HALL)

PLAZA DON VASCO

PORTAL ALDAMA

PORTAL GUERRERO

LAUNDRY

CAFE DON CELE

PONCE DE LEON

FEDERICO TENO

HOTEL POSADA SAN RAFAEL

RESTAURANT
EL PATIO

SUPER CENTRO (GROCERY)

NICOLAS ROMERO

JOSE M COS

CASA DE ONCE PATIOS
(CRAFTS SHOPS)

PERIFERICO

TO URUAPAN
AND PLAYA AZUL

CENTRAL CAMIONERA
(BUS STATION)

TO SANTA
CLARA DEL COBRE
AND PLAYA AZUL

120

0   100 yd

0   100 m

N

© MOON PUBLICATIONS, INC.

soldiers, 200 foot soldiers, and thousands of Indian allies, arrived at Tzintzuntzán in 1522. As the new *caltzonzin,* Tangaxoan II, fled to Uruapan, Olid quickly appropriated the imperial treasure and the gold and jewels from the temples. After a short resistance, Tangaxoan II pledged his homage to Cortés and was soon baptized, accepting the Christian name of Pedro. By 1526, most of his subjects had followed suit.

Peace reigned, but not for long. Cortés was called back to Spain, and the gold-hungry opportunist, Nuño de Guzmán, took temporary control in Mexico City. In late 1528, Guzmán had the *caltzonzin* tortured and killed. The Spanish royal government, alarmed by Guzmán's excesses, sent an official panel, called the Second Audiencia, to replace him. Guzmán, one jump ahead of them, cleared out in command of a battalion of like-minded adventurers, hell-bent to find another Tenochtitlán in western Mexico. They pounced upon the Purépecha, burning, raping, and pillaging in the Valley of Pátzcuaro.

Vasco De Quiroga

The Purépecha fortunes began to improve, however, when Father Vasco de Quiroga, a member of the Second Audiencia, arrived in 1533. At the age of 63, he began his life's work on the shore of Lake Pátzcuaro. Through his kindness, compassion, and tireless energy, Don Vasco gained the confidence of the Purépecha. He immediately established a hospital for the care of the poor. Named Santa Fe de la Laguna, it still stands by the lakeshore.

Appointed bishop in 1538, Don Vasco moved the episcopal seat from Tzintzuntzán to Pátzcuaro, which had already become the provincial government headquarters. Pressing ahead, he immediately began the College of San Nicolas. Its features became the model for many more: a hospital for the care of the poor, a school to educate young Tarascans, and a seminary for training bilingual Tarascan priests.

Pátzcuaro's rich handicrafts heritage is partly due to Don Vasco. He moderated the Tarascans' *encomienda* obligations so that they had time to become self-sustaining on their communal and individual plots. Many entire villages became centers of specific skills and trades. Such traditions remain: Santa Clara turns out fine copperware; Tzintzuntzan, furniture. Other valley communities produce elaborate baskets,

delicate lacquerware, and handsome saddles.

Don Vasco toiled until his death in 1565 at the age of 95. Pátzcuaro people still adore him. Children often leave flowers at the foot of his statue in the plaza at the very heart of the city.

IN-TOWN SIGHTS

Getting Oriented

From the good bishop's tree-shaded bronze image in the main **Plaza Don Vasco de Quiroga,** the city spreads out along half a dozen north-south and east-west main streets. **Av. Mendoza** runs from the northwest plaza corner one long block north to the city's second square, **Plaza Gertrudis Bocanegra,** named for the city's renowned Independence heroine. The **market** spreads from the northwest side of Plaza Bocanegra, while past the south end, Av. La Paz runs uphill (east) two blocks to the **basilica.**

Back at the main plaza's northeast corner, a second main thoroughfare, **Av. Ahumada,** runs north, becoming Av. Lázaro Cárdenas, the main highway-access route. It continues about two miles to the east-west Uruapan-Morelia highway and the railroad station. Crossing the railroad tracks at the station, a branch road leads about a mile north to the **Lake Pátzcuaro** embarcadero, from where boats depart for Janitzio and other islands.

Getting Around

Virtually everything downtown is within a few blocks of the Plaza Don Vasco de Quiroga. For trips out of the city, however, hail a taxi or ride a white *colectivo* van from in front of the Hotel Los Escudos (Ibarra and Mendoza plaza corner) to the Central Camionera (main bus station) on the *periférico* boulevard on the west side of town.

A Walk Around Old Pátzcuaro

The natural place to start is at the center of the main plaza, beneath the statue of the revered Don Vasco de Quiroga (1470-1565). As first bishop of Pátzcuaro (see "History" above) he reversed the despair and destruction wrought by the conquistadores.

Colonial buildings, some dating back to the 17th century, rise behind the portals that spread

The facade of the Colegio San Nicolas (1540), a cherished national treasure, graces a quiet Pátzcuaro street corner.

BRUCE WHIPPERMAN

around the square. The portals are themselves named and localize individual addresses (such as the Hotel Los Escudos, Portal Hidalgo 73).

Walk east, uphill, one block to Pátzcuaro's oldest building, the former **Colegio San Nicolas,** begun by Don Vasco in 1540. Pass inside beneath its quaint three-bell Spanish classic facade to the venerable inner garden. Now called the Museo de Arte Popular (open Tues.-Sat. 9-7, Sun. 9-3, tel. 210-29), its portaled corridors lead past rooms filled with fine regional crafts. In a rear courtyard, be sure to see the stairstep foundations of the original Tarascan temple, exposed on the hillside. Turn around and inspect a wall inscribed with the marks of prisoners counting the days.

As you exit the museum, glance left at the curious little doorway emerging from the outside uphill lane. Behind that door, Pátzcuaro people say, is an aqueduct that Don Vasco built to supply the poor with water during times of drought.

Walk ahead past the big courtyard and church on the left, along Calle Enseñanza. After two blocks, turn right, downhill, to the former Dominican Convent of Santa Catarina de Sena, known popularly as the **Casa de Once Patios** ("House of Eleven Patios") on the left. Most of its inner labyrinth of gardens, corridors, and rooms is restored and open to the public. Dozens of artisans have set up display-workshops where they paint, weave, polish, and carve handicrafts for sale (open daily 9-2 and 4-7; see "Shopping," below, for details).

Return past the former Colegio San Nicolas and continue two blocks along Calle Arciga to the big **Basilica Maria Immaculada de la Salud,** begun by Don Vasco during the mid-16th century. In addition to Don Vasco's tomb, the basilica is noted for its four-century-old main altar image of the Virgin, made according to a pre-Columbian recipe of cornstalk paste and orchid glue.

Follow diagonal Av. Buenavista downhill and continue a block along Lloreda to the former monastery, **Ex-Templo San Augustín,** now the *biblioteca* (public library), at the northeast corner of Plaza Bocanegra (open Mon.-Fri. 9-7, Sat. 9-1). The library's main attraction is its huge mural, the first by Juan O'Gorman, completed in 1942. In this panorama of the history of the Valley of Pátzcuaro, O'Gorman is nearly as critical of the Tarascans' slaughtering of 30,000 Aztec prisoners as of Nuño de Guzmán (scowling like a demon in armor) as he tortures the last *caltzonzin* (emperor). All is not lost, however, as O'Gorman shows the murdered emperor's niece, Erendira, riding out (and becoming the first Native American to ride a horse) to warn the people. Don Vasco, the savior, appears at the bottom, assuring a happy ending as he brings utopia to Pátzcuaro.

The librarian has a Spanish copy of the mural guide, signed by O'Gorman, who appears with his wife at the mural's left side. The library also has a respectable book collection, including many Spanish-language reference works and several shelves of English language fiction and nonfiction.

JANITZIO

An excursion to the island of Janitzio (hah-NEET-seeoh) is *de rigueur* in Pátzcuaro. The breezy launch trip takes about half an hour. Waves splash, spray, and rock the bow; gulls wheel above the stern as the pyramidal volcanic island-village of Janitzio grows upon the horizon. The Janitzio villagers believe themselves to be the purest of the Purépecha. Only the young speak Spanish; the old (some of whom have never visited the mainland) hold fast to their language and traditional ways.

Fishing for the tasty Pátzcuaro *pescado blanco* (whitefish) is the major Janitzio occupation. Overfishing, however, has unfortunately reduced the famous *mariposas* (butterfly nets), which Don Vasco introduced long ago, to mere cere-

monial objects. Long, cumbersome nets are now needed for the increasingly meager catches. The price (about $10) of a succulent whitefish platter (the specialty of the dozen-odd embarcadero restaurants) has inflated beyond the reach of most Pátzcuaro families.

Fortunately, however, government and local cooperative conservation measures show promise of eventually replenishing the whitefish population. Meanwhile, the *mariposas* come out for display only during tourist-show regattas on weekends and holidays.

A steady procession of handicrafts shops lines the steep lane that winds to the island's summit. Although most items (baskets, masks, papier-mâché, lacquerware, cottons and woolens) are cheap and common, some unusual buys await those willing to look and bargain.

At the top, the still more isolated islets of Tecuen, Yuñuen, and La Pacanda dot the lake's northern reaches, while in the opposite direction, the city of Pátzcuaro basks at the foot of a distant pine-tufted green sierra. If you have the energy, climb to the tip-top of the colossal José Maria Morelos statue, lined inside with a continuous mural of scenes from the fiery Independence hero's life.

Getting to Janitzio: If you're driving, head downhill (north) a couple of miles along Av. Lázaro Cárdenas and turn left at the Uruapan-Morelia highway. Within a few hundred yards, turn right at the road crossing the rail tracks at the rail station. After about half a mile, bear right at a fork, and soon you'll see the parking lot (about $1). If you're not driving, taxi or ride the white *colectivo* VW van (about $.60, from the corner by the Hotel Los Escudos on Plaza Don Vasco, or the Mercado corner, Plaza Bocanegra) to the embarcadero. Return boat tickets, available from a dock-front booth, cost about $2. The last return boat leaves the island at 6 p.m.

IHUATZIO

Pre-Columbian ruins dot the Pátzcuaro Valley. Most remain unexcavated grassy mounds except the most famous: Ihuatzio (ee-WAHT-seeoh) and Tzintzuntzán, both near the lakeshore northeast of the city.

Pátzcuaro dominated the valley during the latter-1300s golden-era reign of King Tariácuri.

Eerie local-style masks are common sale items in Janitzio shops.

ERIN DWYER

IHUATZIO ARCHAEOLOGICAL ZONE

WALL-CAUSEWAY
WALL-CAUSEWAY
WALL-CAUSEWAY

OBSERVATORY

RECONSTRUCTED
PYRAMIDS

YACATAS

KING'S CAUSEWAYS

PARADE
GROUND

AREA OPEN
TO THE PUBLIC

PARKING

TO PÁTZCUARO

0   150 yd
0   150 m

© MOON PUBLICATIONS, INC.

When he died the valley was divided between his younger son and his nephews, Hiripan and Tangaxoan (ancestor of Tangaxoan II, the last Tarascan emperor). According to Vasco de Quiroga's 16th-century narrative, *Relación de Michoacán,* squabbling broke out among the heirs. Hiripan won out, and, by 1400, had concentrated power at Ihuatzio.

Exploring Ihuatzio
The remains of Ihuatzio, literally, "Place of the Coyotes," spread over a rectangular area about half a mile long by a quarter mile wide. Nearly all ruins are mound-dotted unexplored fields, closed to the public. The open part, the so-called **Parade Ground,** is about the size of four football fields and enclosed by a pair of ceremonial stepped-wall raised causeways. These lead toward a pair of hulking truncated pyramids which tower above the Parade Ground's west end. These, Ihuatzio's most prominent structures, lost nearly all of their original stone sheathing to colonial construction projects, although a remnant appears on the right pyramid's face as you approach from the Parade Ground.

Climb carefully (the steps are steep) to the top for a view of the surrounding unexcavated ruins.

Along the Parade Ground's north and south sides, notice the **King's Causeways,** a pair of long stepped mounds, presumably used as the *caltzonzin's* ceremonial approach road.

About a quarter mile due south rises another mound, which marks the **Observatory,** a mysterious 100-foot-wide cylindrical structure whose name merely represents an educated guess about its possible function. In nearly the same direction as the Observatory, but much closer, stands the rubbly mound of the **yácatas,** three half-cylindrical truncated pyramids, whose original forms are unrecognizable due to repeated ransackings. Their shapes, however, are certain, due to a number of other excavated local examples, most notably, Tzintzuntzán, five miles to the north. (The Ihuatzio site is open daily about 9-4; entry fee about $2, no facilities except a lavatory; don't forget your hat and drinking water.)

TZINTZUNTZÁN

Ihuatzio's power waned during the 1400s, gradually giving way to nearby Tzintzuntzán("Place of the Hummingbirds"). Within a generation, Tzintzuntzán became the hub of an expanded Tarascan empire, which included nearly all of present Michoacán and half of Jalisco and Guanajuato. When the Spanish arrived in 1521, authority was concentrated entirely in Tzintzuntzán, an imperial city whose population had swelled to perhaps as much as 100,000.

The present town (pop. 5,000) a dozen miles northeast of Pátzcuaro is a mere shadow of its former glory. The Great Platform, although long abandoned, still towers, in proud relief, on the hill above the dusty modern town.

Exploring The Archaeological Site

The entire archaeological zone (of which the Great Platform occupies a significant but very small area), spreads over nearly three square miles. The excavated part, open to the public, comprises only a fiftieth of the total, being confined within a rectangle perhaps 500 yards long and half that in width. Visitors approach the rear of the Great Platform from the east through a grassy park. They first see the Great Platform spreading from right (north) to left, with the town and lake below the far front side.

The Great Platform is singularly intriguing, because of its five side-by-side **yácatas:** massive, semicylindrical ceremonial platforms. The yácatas are built of huge cut basalt (lava) stones, like a giant child's neat stacks of black building blocks. When the Spanish arrived, a temple to the legendary god-king Curicaueri perched upon the yácata summit.

Although the Great Platform itself was purely ceremonial in function, excavations in outer portions of the zone reveal that imperial Tzintzuntzán was an entire city, housing all classes from kings to slaves. Within the city, people lived and worked according to specialized occupations—farmers, artisans, priests, and warriors. Most experts agree that such urban organization required a high degree of sophistication, including excess wealth, laws and efficient government, and a reliable calendar.

Tzintzuntzán grew through a number of stages from its founding around A.D. 900. Excavations beneath the Great Platform masonry reveal earlier yácatas overlaid, like layers of an onion, above earlier constructions with similar, but smaller, features. (Look, for example, at the archaeological test hole between Yácatas 4 and 5.)

Other intriguing structures dot the Great Platform. **Entrance ramps,** apparently built as boat-traffic terminals, appear beneath the Great Platform's 20-foot-high stepped retaining wall. (Records reveal that, at the time of the conquest, lake waters lapped beaches at the foot of these ramps.)

The Palace, a group of rooms surrounding an inner patio, stands about a hundred yards northeast of the first yácata. Because thousands of human bones and an altar were found here, some archaeologists speculated that it may have been a ceremonial depository for the remains of vanquished enemies.

About 75 yards in front of yácatas 4 and 5 is Building E, a puzzling L-shaped group of rooms. Although archaeolgists speculate that they may have been storerooms or granaries, excavations, curiously, revealed no entrances.

The site is open daily about 9-5; facilities include a picnic park and lavatories. Entry fee is about $3; bring your hat and drinking water.

BRUCE WHIPPERMAN

A sample of the huge selection of colonial-style woodcrafts for sale at Tzintzuntzán carver's shops.

TO TOWN, LAKE, AND PÁTZCUARO

FORMER LAKE LEVEL RAMP

RUBBLE

BLDG. A

BLDG. C

5

BLDG. D

RUBBLE

4

3

THE YÁCATAS

FORMER LAKE LEVEL RAMP

2

THE PALACE

PARKING

BLDG. E

GREAT PLATFORM

RUBBLE

1

TZINTZUNTZÁN ARCHAEOLOGICAL ZONE

0   50 yd

0   50 m

© MOON PUBLICATIONS, INC.

Modern Tzintzuntzán

The buildings the Spanish colonials erected still stand at the far (west) end of the town park (which spreads from the crafts stalls bordering the Hwy. 120-main street.) Clustered at the park's far end you will find the **Franciscan monastery and church.** Inside the church are several paintings and murals dedicated to the Señor de Rescate, whose festival the townspeople celebrate with Purépecha music and regional dances. The adjacent monastery, dedicated to Santa Anna, is known for its plateresque facade and courtyard, containing some of the world's oldest olive trees (which somehow survived the royal ban on olive trees in Mexico).

Back on the main street, handicrafts stores and shops offer some unusual woodwork. Especially noteworthy are the **Artesanias Lupita** and the warren of shops behind it. Wander among their riots of wood—giant masks, baskets, headboards, cabinets—where you can select from a potpourri of pre-Columbian, Gothic, baroque, and neoclassic motifs.

Getting To Ihuatzio And Tzintzuntzán

Drive Hwy. 120 from Pátzcuaro northeast (Morelia direction) about five miles (eight km) to the signed Ihuatzio turnoff. Turn left and continue about two more miles to a signed road on the right, which bumps for about another mile to the site parking lot. For Tzintzuntzán, continue about five miles on the highway past Ihuatzio to the right fork, which leads to the ruins on the hill above the highway.

By bus, from the Pátzcuaro Central Camionera (main bus station, south side of town) ride either the Ihuatzio or Tzintzuntzán blue-and-white *urbano* buses. Tell the driver "ruinas" and, at Ihuatzio, the driver will drop you within a mile of the site. At Tzintzuntzán, the driver will stop on the highway fork to the ruins (or, if you're lucky, at the ruins parking lot a quarter mile farther on).

ACCOMMODATIONS

Downtown Hotels

Pátzcuaro visitors enjoy a number of good, reasonably priced colonial-decor hotels clustered near the plazas. Because of the mild, dry climate, rooms generally have neither air-conditioning nor central heating. Fans and *chimeneas* (fireplaces, a cozy winter plus) are sometimes available, however.

The family-managed **Hotel Los Escudos,** right on the plaza, is a longtime Pátzcuaro favorite (Portal Hidalgo 73, Pátzcuaro, Michoacán 61600, tel. 454-201-38 and 454-212-90). Its rooms rise in three tiers around a cool, serene inner patio, wrapped in wrought iron, tile, and bright greenery. The homey, dark-paneled rooms come with lacey curtains, wood floors, and fireplaces (wood included). The wood-paneled cafe downstairs, one of Pátzcuaro's favorite meeting places, is a good spot for lingering over dessert with friends or a good book after a hard day on the lake. The hotel's 30 rooms rent for about $20 s and $27 d, with TV, parking, and credit cards accepted. Reservations, recommended any time, are mandatory weekends and holidays.

Hotel Posada San Rafael, on the adjacent plaza-front block, offers a second-choice alternative (Portal Guerrero, Plaza Vasco de Quiroga, Pátzcuaro, Michoacán 61600, tel. 454-207-70 and 454-207-

79). Greatly expanded during the 1980s from an original colonial mansion core, its 104 rooms spread along three stories of corridors facing a narrow inner parking courtyard. While the parked cars detract, the neocolonial decor—traditional tile, big-beamed ceilings, and hand-carved oak doors—lend a touch of charm. The paneled rooms, with throwrugs, wood floors, and fluffy curtains, if not deluxe, are at least clean and comfortable. Hot-water hours, however, are limited to 7-11 mornings and 6:30-9:30 evenings. Rates run about $17 s, $22 d, $27 t; no fireplaces; credit cards not accepted.

The **Hotel Fiesta Plaza** on Plaza Bocanegra is a 1990 newcomer among Pátzcuaro hotels (Plaza Bocanegra 24, Pátzcuaro, Michoacán 61600, tel. 454-225-15, 454-225-16). A former landmark colonial mansion, the hotel's three tiers of comfortable rooms enfold a fountain-decorated inner patio. Their restaurant, convenient for breakfast, spreads into the patio, while just outside the door the colorful Plaza Bocanegra hubbub—the market, the movie theater, a dozen taco stands, bus and minivan traffic—buzzes from morning to midnight. (Guests who require relief, however, should pick an upper-tier room away from the street.) Rooms rent for about $18 s, $23 d, $28 t; with TV, phones, and parking; credit cards accepted.

PÁTZCUARO HOTELS

Pátzcuaro hotels, in order of increasing double room price (area code 454, postal code 61600)

DOWNTOWN

Hotel Valmen, Lloreda 34, 211-61, $10
Hotel Posada de la Salud, Av. Serrato 9, 200-58, $13
Hotel Posada San Rafael, Portal Guerrero, 207-70, 207-79, $22
Hotel Fiesta Plaza, Plaza Bocanegra 24, 225-15, 225-16, $23
Posada de la Basilica, Arciga 6, 211-08, $23
Hotel Los Escudos, Portal Hidalgo 73, 201-38, 212-90, $27

AV. LÁZARO CÁRDENAS MOTELS

Motel del Lago, Av. L. Cárdenas 509, 214-71, $10
Motel San Felipe, Av. L. Cárdenas 321, 212-98, $23
Motel Pátzcuaro, Av. L. Cárdenas 506, 207-67, $23
Hotel Don Vasco, Av. L. Cárdenas 450, 202-27, fax 202-62, $62

Hotel **Valmen** (corner of Lloreda and Ahumada) two blocks up the street, offers a budget alternative (Lloreda 34, Pátzcuaro, Michoacán 61600, tel. 454-211-61). Plants and attractive tile soften the Valmen's otherwise Spartan (to the point of being un-Mexican) ambience. Two tiers of plain but tidy rooms, with hot showers, spread around the interior patio. Avoid the street noise by choosing an interior room. Rates run about $7 s, $10 d, $14 t.

Guests at the very popular **Posada de la Basilica** (on Arciga, one block farther uphill, across from the basilica) enjoy a very attractive view restaurant (Arciga 6, Pátzcuaro, Michoacán 61600, tel. 454-211-08). The panorama (also visible from the hotel's adjoining patio) of colonial city, lake, and mountains adds a bit of luxury to the hotel's authentically colonial atmosphere. The rooms, furnished in hand-carved, hand-woven and hand-wrought 17th-century chic, add even more. The 11 rooms, all with hot water, run about $18 s, $23 d, and $28 t; six rooms have fireplaces; reservations are generally necessary.

The **Hotel Posada de la Salud** (on the basilica's south side) is especially popular with female basilica visitors (Av. Serrato 9, Pátzcuaro, Michoacán 61600, tel. 454-200-58). The 15 plain but very clean rooms spread around a sunny, conventlike courtyard. The typical guest, while not saintly, is at least probably in bed reading by nine at the latest. Rooms rent for about $10 s, $13 d, and $16 t; reservations recommended, especially during religious holidays, such as the Fiesta de la Virgen de La Salud (first two weeks in Dec.) and Semana Santa (week preceding Easter Sunday).

Avenida Lázaro Cárdenas Hotels

A number of acceptable motel-style accommodations cluster along Av. Lázaro Cárdenas, about half a mile from the Uruapan-Morelia Highway.

The **Motel del Lago** is just a few blocks from the highway (Av. L. Cárdenas 509, Pátzcuaro, Michoacán 61600, tel. 454-214-71). The budget choice of families with wheels, the del Lago's 12 brick units surround a central parking area garden, bordered by leafy avocado, rubber, and peach trees. Although the cottages have fireplaces (wood $2 extra) and hot water, they're plain, a bit worn, and could be cleaner. The

prices are right, however. Rooms run $8 s, $10 d, and $12 t; credit cards accepted and limited wheelchair access.

Cross Av. Lázaro Cárdenas to **Motel Pátzcuaro,** a homey cluster of a dozen cottages, set half a block back from the road. Owned and operated by longtime lovers of Pátzcuaro, Obdulia and Arturo Pimentel Ramos, the units are attractively furnished in rustic browns, knotty-pine paneling, and brick fireplaces. The grassy grounds spread past a swimming pool (not maintained in winter) and a tennis court to an acre of tent and RV (self-contained only) sites on the adjacent gentle hillside. A kitchen is available for use of guests. The cottages rent for about $18 s, $23 d, and $27 t. Tent and RV guests pay about $3 per person per night. The cottages are often filled; it's best to make reservations: Av. L. Cárdenas 506, Pátzcuaro, Michoacán 61600, tel. 454-207-67; limited wheelchair access.

· Guests of the sprawling 103-room resort-style **Hotel Don Vasco** enjoy neocolonial decor, comfortable, high-beamed rooms, spreading lawns, quiet patio nooks, a chapel, a big pool, tennis, billiards, bowling, a bar, and a fancy restaurant (Av. Lázaro Cárdenas 450, Pátzcuaro, Michoacán 61600, tel. 454-202-27, fax 454-202-62). The rooms in the newer wing are large and luxurious, with private garden-view balconies. Rooms begin at about $53 s, $62 d; with TV, phones, electric heat, seasonal discotheque, credit cards accepted, parking, and limited wheelchair access to lower floors.

A more economical alternative is the **Motel San Felipe,** a few blocks uphill (Av. L. Cárdenas 321, Pátzcuaro, Michoacán 61600, tel. 454-212-98). Behind the roadside restaurant, 11 motel-style cottages surround a patio parking lot. Clean, comfortable, and carpeted, the units have colonial-style wrought-iron fixtures and brick fireplaces. The rooms rent for about $17 s, $23 d, and $31 for three or more; credit cards accepted, limited wheelchair access.

RV And Camping Park

Visitors who enjoy staying near the lakeside opt for **Trailer Park El Pozo** ("The Well"). Watch for the sign on the highway about a mile in the Morelia direction past the Av. Lázaro Cárdenas intersection. The 20 spaces spread downhill in a grassy park about a quarter mile from the reed-lined lakeshore. The friendly, family-run park provides all hookups, a picnic table with each space, some shade, toilets, and hot showers for about $10 per day (longer-stay discounts available). Tenters are also welcome, at about $3 per person. While reservations are not necessary year-round, it's best to call or write ahead of time for weekends and holidays: Trailer Park El Pozo, P.O. Box 142, Pátzcuaro, Michoacán 61600, tel. (454) 209-37.

FOOD

Breakfast And Snacks

A good spot to start out the day is **Restaurant Dany** at Mendoza 30 (the street connecting the west sides of Plazas Don Vasco and Bocanegra). Although they serve good food all day (8 a.m.-10 p.m. daily), the American breakfast ($4) in their shiny upstairs section tastes especially good on a crisp Pátzcuaro morning.

For quick cooling energy during the heat of the day, try the no-name *nevería* (ice-cream stand) in front of the Hotel Los Escudos on Plaza Vasco de Quiroga. Their fruit ices (like sherbet) are so popular that you may have to wedge your way in. Just point to what you want. (Don't worry, their offerings are pure; they depend on repeat customers. Open daily 9-6.)

For a hot pick-me-up, on the other hand, try a cup of freshly ground Michoacán mountain-grown coffee at **Cafe de Uruapan Don Cele** (open daily except Wed. 9-2 and 4-8) beneath Portal Aldama at the adjacent corner of the plaza. They also sell fresh-roasted beans for around $2 per pound ($4 per kilo).

At night at the market corner of Plaza Bocanegra, a very professional lineup of taco stands steams with hearty offerings. Among the best is **Tacos Rápido,** run by Jorge, whose fingers fly as if they could wrap a thousand *chorizo* (spiced sausage), *res* (roast beef), *pastor* (roast pork or beef), and *lengua* (tongue) tacos a night.

For a late snack, go to **Tortisam** at Mendoza 12 (between Plazas Vasco de Quiroga and Bocanegra). Juicy hamburgers, hot dogs, tortas, French fries, and malts plus lots of friendly cheer are the secret to the success of the paradoxically young proprietor Viejo ("Old") Sam. Open 10 a.m.-11 p.m. daily, tel. 224-06.

Restaurants

Pátzcuaro has a sprinkling of good, moderately priced restaurants, nearly all on or near the Plaza Vasco de Quiroga.

At the **Cafeteria Los Escudos** (Hotel Los Escudos, northwest plaza corner of Mendoza and Ibarra), conversation and cafe espresso sometimes seem as important as the menu. A broad list of regional (try the taco soup) and international favorites keeps customers satisfied. Open daily 8 a.m.-9:30 p.m., tel. 201-38; credit cards accepted.

Whitefish is the house specialty at the **Restaurant El Patio** (at 19 Plaza Vasco de Quiroga, near the Hotel Posada San Rafael), where soft music, muted lighting, and tasteful handicraft decor set the tone. Despite the mostly tourist clientele, many are longtime repeat customers (who know to start out with the excellent Tarascan soup). Open daily 8 a.m.-9:30 p.m, tel. 204-84; credit cards accepted.

Romantics congregate at the restaurant of the **Hotel Posada de la Basilica** (on Arciga, opposite the basilica). They enjoy Pátzcuaro's famous whitefish and wine (ask for Cetto label sauvignon blanc) while feasting on the gleaming view of the old city, the lake, and the mountains beyond. Open daily 8 a.m-9 p.m., tel. 211-08; credit cards not accepted.

ENTERTAINMENT AND EVENTS

Pátzcuaro's one unmissable entertainment is the famous **Viejecitos** ("Little Old Men") dance. Said to have been invented during the early colo-

The dance of the Viejicitos ("Little Old Men") is a popular Pátzcuaro tradition.

nial period to mock the conquerors, a troupe of men put on wrinkle-faced masks and *campesino*-style dress and dance as if every stumbling step were about to send them to the hospital. Hotels, such as the Don Vasco (tel. 202-27), often stage regular dance shows in season.

Local people celebrate a number of fiestas and holidays. During the first two weeks in December, dance, music, processions, fireworks, and foodstalls fill Pátzcuaro streets and plazas in celebration of the **Fiesta de la Virgen de La Salud,** the city's patron saint.

Later, Semana Santa (the pre-Easter week) festivities climax on **Viernes Santa** (Good Friday), when townsfolk carry big Christ-figures through the packed downtown streets.

Finally, on November 2, Pátzcuaro (and many neighboring towns) stage Mexico's most spectacular **Dia de los Muertos** ("Day of the Dead") festivals. Crowds converge on the *panteón* (cemetery) on the old Morelia road (a half mile northeast of the basilica, take a taxi) with loads of food offerings and decorations for the graves of their beloved deceased. They keep the candles burning next to the tombstones all night, illuminating their ancestors' return path to feast and rejoin the family once again.

The big movie house and theater **Cine Emperador** screens Mexican and American movies and stages occasional concerts and cultural events. Drop by (north end of Plaza Bocanegra, next to the Hotel Fiesta Plaza) and check the schedule.

SHOPPING

The Valley of Pátzcuaro is rich in handicrafts. Visitors need only travel to the **Mercado** (which extends a long block, beginning at the Plaza Bocanegra) to find good examples. Copperware from the village of Santa Clara de Cobre and woolens are among the most plentiful and bargainable items. (For bargaining hints, see the main Introduction.)

In the fish stalls, you'll see mounds of Pátzcuaro whitefish (at about $2 a kilo); and farther on, among the piles of produce, unusual fruits from around Uruapan (such as the brown, sour-tasting *mamey* and the greenish-pink *anona*—creamy, like a Southeast Asian custard apple).

For a uniquely rich selection of fine handicrafts, don't miss the former convent, **Casa de Once Patios,** one block east, one block south of the Plaza Don Vasco de Quiroga. In a dozen separate shops, artisans paint, carve, weave, and polish excellent work for sale. In the *local de paja* (straw shop), for example, workers fashion Christmas decorations—candy canes, trees, wreaths, bells—entirely of strands of colored straw. Nearby, the *local de cobre* (copper shop) displays shelves and cases of brilliant copper and silver plates, vases, cups, and jewelry.

Although other *locales* craft and display fine furniture, textiles, papier-mâché, and masks, the climax comes in the *local de laca,* with lacquerware so fine it rivals the rich cloisonnés of Europe and Asia. In the especially fine shop of the brothers Alozo Meza, artisans finish wares in a myriad of animal, human, and floral motifs in sizes and complexities to fit every pocketbook. Open daily 9-2 and 4-7.

On Fridays the small plaza, **Jardín Revolución,** blooms with ceramics from all over

Anona *fruits (foreground) for sale at the Pátzcuaro market.*

Michoacán (corner Ponce de Leon and Tena, one block west of the Plaza Don Vasco de Quiroga).

Grocery Store And Camera Shop
The **Super Centro** *abarrotería* grocery-liquor at Plaza Vasco de Quiroga 120, near the Hotel Posada San Rafael, conveniently stocks a little bit of everything (open daily 8:30-3 and 5-8:30, tel. 208-47).

The local Kodak dealer is at Plaza Bocanegra 21 (tel. 216-45) on the plaza's south side. Besides a fair stock of film and photo equipment they offer 24-hour color, three-day transparency, and five-day black-and-white photofinishing services (open Mon.-Fri. 9-2 and 4-8, and Sat.-Sun. 9-2, tel. 216-45).

INFORMATION AND SERVICES

Although the **Michoacán Tourism Office** is supposed to supply maps and answer questions, your hotel desk clerk will probably be more helpful. If you ask to see the *jefe* (chief, say HAY-fay), however, you may get a satisfactory response. They're located at Av. Ibarra 2, corner Av. Mendoza, on the Plaza Don Vasco de Quiroga (open Mon.-Sat. 9-2 and 4-7, tel. 212-14).

Banamex changes U.S. traveler's checks and cash Mon.-Fri. 9-1 at their Plaza Bocanegra (Portal Juarez, west side) headquarters (tel. 215-50, 210-31).

The **Clínica del Centro** provides 24-hour emergency medical service (gynecologist, surgeon, pediatrician, and internist on call). Their pharmacy (the El Portal, open 10-2 and 5-7) and adjacent hospital are located right on the Plaza Don Vasco de Quiroga at Portal Hidalgo 76, three doors from the Hotel Los Escudos.

For **police** emergencies, contact the *preventiva* (tel. 200-04 and 218-89) in the Palacio Municipal (city hall), next to the Clínica del Centro.

The **Correos** (post office, tel. 201-28) is open Mon.-Fri. only 9-2 and 4-6 at Obregon 13, one block north of the Plaza Bocanegra.

For computer-assisted *larga distancia* (long-distance telephone) and public fax, go to Com-

putel, on the Plaza Bocanegra next to the Cine Emperador movie house.

GETTING THERE AND AWAY

By Car Or RV
North-south National Highways 14 and 37 connect Pátzcuaro with the Pacific-coast Hwy. 200 at Playa Azul. The 192-mile (307-km) scenic but winding and sometimes potholed route requires around seven hours of careful driving. Fill with gasoline, especially unleaded. Magna Sin is available only at Uruapan, Nueva Italia, and Arteaga en route.

In the opposite direction, National Hwy. 120 connects with the state capital Morelia (in an hour and a half), where Hwy. 15 connects with Mexico City (in about eight hours).

By Bus
From the south-side **Central Camionera,** a number of lines, such as first-class Ruta de Paraiso and Tres Estrellas de Oro and second-class Galeana, connect with the Pacific coast destinations of La Mira (five miles from Playa Azul) and Lázaro Cárdenas, where buses connect farther to Zihuatanejo and Manzanillo. Tres Estrellas de Oro and Autobuses del Occidente connect to north and east destinations of Guadalajara, Morelia, and Mexico City.

By Train
Pátzcuaro lies on the rail line connecting Lázaro Cárdenas on the Pacific coast to Morelia. A northbound first- and second-class coach train departs Lázaro Cárdenas daily around noon, arriving at Pátzcuaro about 9 p.m. and Morelia about an hour and a half later. The opposite train departs Morelia daily around 6 a.m., arriving at the Pátzcuaro rail station around 7 a.m. It continues (via Uruapan and Nueva Italia), arriving at Lázaro Cárdenas at about 4 p.m. (Verify schedules and buy tickets at the station, tel. 208-03, just off the highway at the north side of town. Take a taxi, $2.)

Train connections may be made in Morelia for Mexico City, Guadalajara, Manzanillo, Mazatlán, and the U.S. border.

LÁZARO CÁRDENAS AND ALONG THE ROAD TO IXTAPA-ZIHUATANEJO

The new industrial port city of Lázaro Cárdenas, named for the Michoacán-born president (served 1934-39) famous for expropriating American oil companies, is Michoacán's Pacific transportation and service hub. Most of its businesses, including banks, bus stations, hotels, and restaurants, are clustered along Av. Lázaro Cárdenas, the main ingress boulevard, about three miles from its Hwy. 200 intersection.

SERVICES

Money Exchange

Banamex, at Av. L. Cárdenas 1646, tel. 220-20, exchanges U.S. dollar traveler's checks (Mon.-Fri. 9-12). If they're too crowded, try **Banco Serfin,** Av. L. Cárdenas 2082, four blocks down the street. Nearby, **Casa de Cambio** (money exchange) Las Truchas, at L. Cárdenas 1750, tel. 244-37, changes both U.S. and Canadian money (Mon.-Fri. 9-2 and 4-7, Sat. 9-2).

Hospitals, Post Office, And Telecommunications

The **General Hospital** is at Comonfort 202, tel. 226-42; the private hospital, Sanatorio Ramos, tel. 213-67, is on Av. Corregidora at Allende, not far from its intersection with Av. L. Cárdenas.

The **Correos** (post office) is on Av. N. Bravo, tel. 205-47; the **Telecomunicaciones** (telegraph, telephone, and public fax) is nearby at N. Bravo and Guerrero, tel. 202-73. **Computel,** the computer-assisted long-distance telephone and fax agency, operates daily all day at the Galeana bus station at 1810 L. Cárdenas, tel. 248-02.

Bus Terminals

A pair of long-distance bus terminals serves Lázaro Cárdenas. The northern terminal serves north- and northwest-connecting (Pátzcuaro and Manzanillo) passengers; the other, southeast-connecting (Zihuatanejo- and Acapulco-bound) passengers.

From the northern terminal, at 1810 Av. L. Cárdenas (tel. 202-62), Galeana and Ruta Paraiso

first- and second-class local-departure buses connect daily north with Uruapan, Pátzcuaro, and Morelia. Additionally, several more Galeana first- and second-class departures connect northwest with Manzanillo and intermediate points. Tres Estrellas de Oro (tel. 204-26) first-class buses also stop, en route between Manzanilo and Zihuatanejo. Besides these, Flecha Amarilla provides three daily first-class connections with Manzanillo, operating out of a small terminal at 1686 L. Cárdenas, next to Banamex.

The southeast terminal is at F. Madero 15 at Carranza (tel. 211-71), behind the northern terminal, two blocks from Av. L. Cárdenas. From there, first-class Flecha Roja local departures connect hourly during the day with Zihuatanejo and Acapulco. Similarly, first-class Auto Transportes Sur de Cuauhtémoc (a subsidiary of Estrella Blanca) local departures connect with Zihuatanejo, Acapulco, and intermediate points.

Trains

A combined first- and second-class coach train departs Lázaro Cárdenas daily at noon, northbound for Uruapan, Pátzcuaro, and Morelia, arriving in Pátzcuaro at 9 p.m. The opposite train departs Morelia at around 6 a.m., Pátzcuaro at around 7:30, arriving in Lázaro at 4 p.m. Call the station, tel. 228-36, for information. (Chinameca Viajes, tel. 237-99, a travel agent that also sells train tickets, may be more helpful.) Since you're saving so much money by train (tickets are only $11 first class to Pátzcuaro), have a taxi take you to the train station, which is on the outskirts of town.

At Morelia, train connections to Mexico City and Guadalajara (and thence Manzanillo, Mazatlán and the U.S. border) are available.

ALONG THE ROAD TO IXTAPA-ZIHUATANEJO

It's hard to remain unimpressed as you cross over the **Rio Balsas Dam** for the first time. The dam, which marks the Michoacán-Guerrero state boundary, is huge and hulking. Behind it a grand lake mirrors the Sierra Madre mountains, while on the opposite side, Mexico's greatest river spurts from the turbine exit gates hundreds of feet below. The river's power, converted into enough electric energy for millions of light bulbs, courses up great looping transmission wires, while the spent river meanders toward the sea.

On The Road
The middle of the dam (Hwy. 200, Km 103 north of Zihuatanejo) is a good point at which to reset your odometer. Your odometer and the kilometer markers may be your best way to find the several little hideaways between the Rio Balsas and Zihuatanejo.

As for bus travelers, having gotten aboard at La Mira or Lázaro Cárdenas (or Zihuatanejo, if traveling northwest), ask the driver to let you down at your destination.

Playas Atracadero And Los Llanos
Both of these little havens are especially for shellfish lovers who yearn for their fill of swimming, surfing, splashing, fishing, and beachcombing. Atracadero is the less frequented of the two. The several beach palapa restaurants operate seasonally only. (Crowds must gather sometimes, however: one of the palapas has a five-foot pile of oyster shells!) Another thing is certain; the local folks supplement their diet with plenty of iguanas, judging from the ones boys offer for sale along the road.

The beach sand itself is soft and gray. The waves, with good surfing breaks, roll in from far out, arriving gently on the beach. Boat launching would be easy during calm weather. Little undertow menaces casual swimmers, bodysurfers, or boogieboarders. Lots. of driftwood and shells—clams, limpets, snails—cover the sand. The beach extends for at least three miles past palm groves on the northwest. A fenced grove and house with pigs occupies the southeast. Although tenters could find camping space, RVers would be hard-pressed. Bring your own food and water.

To get to Playa Atracadero, turn off at Km 64, 24 miles (39 km) from the Rio Balsas and 40 miles from Zihuatanejo. Bear left all the way, 1.7 miles (2.8 km) to the beach.

At Los Llanos ("The Plains"), the day climaxes when the oyster divers bring in their catches

around 2:30. They combine their catches into big 100-pound (45-kg) bags, which wait for trucks to take them as far as Mazatlán. On the spot, one dozen in a cocktail go for between $3 and $4. (On the other hand, if you prefer to shuck your own oysters, you can buy them unshucked for $2 a dozen.) The divers also bring in octopus and lobsters, which, broiled and served with fixings, sell for about $7 for an average one-pounder. You can also do your own fishing via rentable (offer $15/hour) beach *pangas,* which go out daily and routinely return with three or four 20-pound fish.

The beach itself is level far out, with rolling waves fine for surfing, swimming, boogieboarding, and bodysurfing. There's enough driftwood and shells for a season of beachcombing. The beach spreads for hundreds of yards on both sides of the road's end. Permanent palapa restaurants supply shade, drinks, and seafood. Beach camping is common and popular, especially during the Christmas and Easter holidays. Other times, you may have the whole place to yourself. A north-end grove provides shade for camping. Bring your own food and water (although the small store at the highway village may help add to your supplies).

To get to Los Llanos, at Km 40, 39 miles (63 km) southeast of the Rio Balsas and 25 miles northwest of Zihuatanejo, turn off at the village of Los Llanos. (Notice the pharmacy at the highway and the gasoline for sale about one-tenth of a mile farther on.) At two-tenths of a mile, turn right just before the basketball court, and continue another 2.5 miles (4 km) to the beach.

Playa Majagua, Playa Troncones, And Dewey's Dew-Drop Inn
This pair of palmy nooks basks on a pristine coastal stretch, backed by a jungly, wildlife-rich hinterland.

Playa Majagua, at Km 32.5 north of Zihuatanejo, is a fishing hamlet with palmy shade, stick-and-wattle houses, and about half a dozen hammock-equipped *ramadas* scattered along the beach. One of the *ramadas* is competently run by a friendly family who call it Restaurant Los Angeles. Camping is safe and welcomed by local folks (although space, especially for RVs, is limited). Water is available, but campers should bring purifying tablets and food.

The beach curves from a rocky south-end point, past a lagoon (of Rio Lagunillas) miles northwest past shoreline palm and acacia forest. The sand is soft and dark yellow, with mounds of driftwood but few shells. Waves break far out and roll in gradually, with little undertow. Fine left-breaking surf rises off the southern point. Boats are easily launchable (several *pangas* lie along the beach) during normal good weather.

To get to Playa Majagua, turn off at the sign just south of the Rio Lagunillas bridge, at Km 32.5, 44 miles (70 km) southeast of Rio Balsas, 20 miles northwest of Zihuatanejo. Continue 2.9 miles to the beach.

Nearby Playa Troncones has a little bit of everything: shady seafood *ramadas* on the left as you enter from the highway; next, a half-mile beach with several spots to pull off and camp. At the southern end, a lagoon spreads beside a pristine coral-sand beach, which curls around a low hill toward a picture-perfect little bay. A small store can supplement your food. Water is available.

That's just the beginning. Troncones has **Dewey's Dew-Drop Inn** nearby. Owners Dewey and Carol McMillan began operating their small retreat in the late 1980s. Guests enjoy a clean room with bath and breakfast in their modern beach house, a small patio restaurant, plenty of shade, quiet, and opportunities for delighting in the outdoors. Guests swim, surf, body-surf, and boogieboard the waves, and jog and beachcomb along the sand. Wildlife—fish, whales, dolphins, and swarms of herons, boobies, egrets, and cormorants—abounds in the ocean and in nearby lagoons.

Their six rooms rent from $30 d with breakfast. Discounts are negotiable for long stays. Write them for reservations (mandatory during the winter) at P.O. Box 37, Zihuatanejo, Guerrero 40880. They close June, July, and August.

Get to Playa Troncones by following the signed, paved turnoff 2.2 miles to the Playa Troncones beachfront *ramadas*. Turn left for the camping spots and main part of the beach; turn right for Dewey's, which is almost half a mile farther along a beachfront forest road. (From Dewey's, the car-negotiable dry-weather track continues about a mile and a half along the beach to Playa Majagua.)

CATHY CARLSON

IXTAPA-ZIHUATANEJO
AND SOUTH TO ACAPULCO

IXTAPA-ZIHUATANEJO

The Costa Grande, the "Big Coast," of the state of Guerrero angles 200 miles southeast from the Rio Balsas to Acapulco. Before the highway came in the 1960s, this was a land of corn, coconuts, fish, and fruit. Although it's still that, the road added a new ingredient: a trickle of visitors seeking paradise in Zihuatanejo, a sleepy fishing village on a beautiful bay.

During the 1970s, planners decided to try to create the best of all possible worlds by building Ixtapa, a luxurious resort on a pearly beach five miles away. Now, Ixtapa-Zihuatanejo's clear, rich waters, forested eco-sanctuaries, pearly little beaches, pristine offshore islets, good food, comfortable hotels, and friendly local folks offer visitors the ingredients for memorable stays any time of the year.

HISTORY

Zihuatanejo's azure waters attracted attention long before Columbus. Local legend says that the Tarascans (whose emperor ruled from now-Michoacán and who were never subject to the Aztecs) built a royal bathing resort on Las Gatas Beach in Zihuatanejo Bay.

That was sometime around 1400. People had been attracted to the Costa Grande much earlier than that: Archaic pottery has been uncovered at a number of sites, left by artists who

hieroglyph of Zihuatanejo ("the Place of Women")

IXTAPA - ZIHUATANEJO

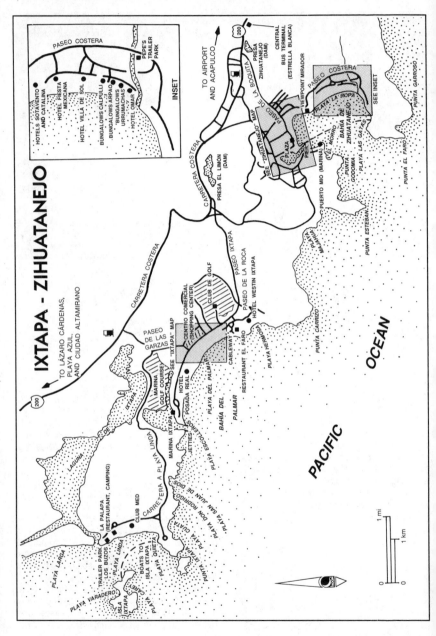

lived and died as long as five thousand years ago. Later, around 1000 B.C., the Olmecs (famous for their monumental Gulf Coast sculptures) came and left their unmistakable stamp on local ceramics. After them came waves of settlers, including the barbaric Chichimecs ("Drinkers of Blood"), the agricultural Cuitlatecs, and an early invasion of Aztecs, perhaps wandering in search of their eventual homeland in the Valley of Mexico.

None of those unsophisticated peoples were a match for the armies of Tarascan emperor Hiripan, who, during the late 1300s invaded the Costa Grande and established a coastal province, headquartered at Coyuca, between Zihuatanejo and present-day Acapulco.

Three generations later, however, the star of the Aztec emperor Tízoc was rising over Mexico. His armies invaded the Costa Grande and pushed out the Tarascans. By 1500 the Aztecs ruled the coast from their own capital at Zihuatlán, the "Place of Women" (so named because local society was matriarchal), not far from present-day Zihuatanejo.

Conquest And Colonization
Scarcely months after Hernán Cortés conquered the Aztecs, he sent an expedition to explore the "Southern Sea" and hopefully find a route to China. In November 1522 Captain Juan Alvarez Chico set sail with boats built in Tehuantepec and reconnoitered the coast to the Rio Balsas, planting crosses on beaches, claiming the land for Spain.

An oft-told Costa Grande story says that when Chico was exploring at Zihuatanejo, he looked down on the round tranquil little bay, lined with flocks of sea birds and women washing clothes in a freshwater spring. His Aztec guide told him that this place was called Zihuatlán. When Chico described the little bay, Cortés tacked *"nejo"* ("little") on to the name, giving birth to "Zihuatlanejo," which later got shortened to the present Zihuatanejo.

Cortés, encouraged by the samples of pearls and gold which Chico brought back, sent out other expeditions. Villafuerte established a shipyard and town at Zacatula at the mouth of the Balsas in 1523. Then, in 1527, Captain Alvaro Saavedra Cerón set sail for China from Zihuatanejo Bay. Not knowing any details of the Pacific Ocean and its winds and currents, it is not surprising that (although he did arrive in the Philippines), Saavedra Cerón failed to return to Mexico. A number of additional attempts would be necessary until finally, in 1565, Father André de Urdaneta coaxed the Pacific to give up its secret and returned, in triumph, from the Orient.

By royal decree, Acapulco became Spain's sole port of entry on the Pacific in 1561. Except for an occasional galleon (or pirate caravel) stopping for repairs or supplies, all other Pacific ports, including Zihuatanejo, slumbered for hundreds of years.

Zihuatanejo was one of the last to wake up. The occasion was the arrival of the highway from Acapulco during the 1960s. No longer isolated, Zihuatanejo's headland-rimmed aqua bay a attracted a small colony of paradise-seekers.

Zihuatanejo had grown to perhaps 5,000 souls by the late '70s when FONATUR, the government tourism-development agency, decided that Ixtapa ("White Place," for its brilliant sand beach five miles north of Zihuatanejo) was a perfect site for a world-class resort. Investors agreed, and the infrastructure—drainage, roads, and utilities—was installed. The jetport was built, hotels rose, and by the '90s the distinct but inseparable twin resorts of Ixtapa and Zihuatanejo (combined pop. 70,000) were attracting a steady stream of Mexican and foreign vacationers.

SIGHTS

Getting Oriented
Both Ixtapa and Zihuatanejo are small and easy to know. Zihuatanejo's little **Plaza de Armas** town square overlooks the main beach, **Playa Municipal,** just beyond the palm-lined pedestrian walkway, **Paseo del Pescador.** From the plaza looking out toward the bay, you are facing south. On your right is the **Muelle** (Moo-AY-yay) Pier, and on the left, the bay curves along the outer beaches Playas la Ropa, la Madera, and finally las Gatas beneath the far Punta El Faro ("Lighthouse Point").

Turning around and facing inland (north), you see a narrow waterfront street, **Juan Alvarez** running parallel to the beach past the plaza, crossing the main business streets (actually tranquil shady lanes) **Cuauhtémoc** and **Guerrero.** A third street, busy **Benito Juarez,** one block to the right of Guererro, conducts traffic several blocks

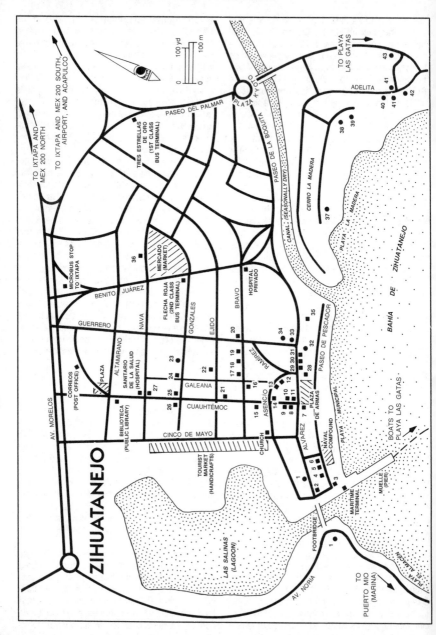

ZIHUATANEJO

1. Hotel Tres Marias (two locations)
2. Equipos y Embarcaciones (sporting goods)
3. Sociedad Cooperativa Teniente Azueta (sportfishing)
4. Sirena Gorda
5. Servicios Sociedad Cooperativa Juarez (sportfishing)
6. Servicios Turísticos Aquaticos (sportfishing)
7. Casa Marina
8. bank
9. money exchange
10. Ruby's Jewelry
11. Zihuatanejo Scuba Center
12. Librería Byblos (books)
13. Restaurant-Bar Victor y Paco
14. Super El Dorado
15. Al Andaluz Expresso
16. money exchange
17. Restaurante Tamales y Atoles "Any"
18. Galería Maya
19. Chamber of Commerce
20. Deportes Naútico (sporting goods)
21. Cafetería Nova Zelandia
22. Restaurant Los Braseros
23. Hotel Imelda
24. bakery
25. Laundry Super Clean
26. Super Foto La Palma
27. Laundry Disney
28. city hall
29. police
30. Migración (immigration)
31. Cerámicas Tonalá
32. Hotel Avila
33. Hotel Susy
34. Posada Citlali
35. Archaeology Museum
36. Super El Globo
37. Bungalows Pacifico
38. Bungalows Allec
39. Hotel La Madera
40. Hotel Palacio
41. Hotel Villas Miramar
42. Hotel Irma
43. Bungalows Milagro

to and from the shore, passing the market and intersecting a second main street, Av. Morelos. There, a right turn will soon bring you to Hwy. 200 and, within five miles, Ixtapa.

Nearly everything in Ixtapa lies along one three-mile-long boulevard, **Paseo Ixtapa,** which parallels the main beach, hotel-lined **Playa del Palmar.** Heading westerly from Zihuatanejo, you first pass the Club de Golf Ixtapa, then the big Sheraton on the left, followed by a succession of other high-rise hotels. Soon come the **Zona Comercial** shopping malls and the **Paseo de las Garzas** corner on the right. Turn right for either Hwy. 200 or the outer beaches, Playas Cuata, Quieta, Linda, and Larga. At Playa Quieta, boats continue to heavenly Isla Ixtapa.

If, instead, you had continued straight ahead back at the Paseo de las Garzas corner, you would have soon reached the **Marina Ixtapa** condo development and yacht harbor.

Getting Around

In downtown Zihuatanejo, shops and restaurants are within a few blocks' walking distance of the plaza. For the beaches, walk to La Madera, take a taxi ($2) to La Ropa, and a launch from the pier ($2) to Las Gatas. For Ixtapa, ride one of the very frequent microbuses, which leave from the market (or the bus station across the street). A taxi ride between Ixtapa and Zihuatanejo runs about $4. In Ixtapa itself, walk, or ride the microbuses that run along Paseo Ixtapa. For the Ixtapa outer beaches, take a taxi, about $4.

Museum

The small Museo Arqueologia de la Costa Grande (on the beachfront side of Alvarez, near the Guerrero corner) details the archaeological history of the Costa Grande (open Tues.-Sun. 10-6). Maps, drawings, small dioramas, and artifacts (many donated by local resident and innkeeper Anita Rellstab) illustrate the development of local cultures, from early hunting and gathering to agriculture and, finally, urbanization by the time of the conquest.

Around Zihuatanejo Bay

Ringed by forested hills, edged by steep cliffs, and laced by rocky shoals, Zihuatanejo Bay would be beautiful even without its beaches. Five of them line the bay. On the west side is narrow, tranquil Playa el Almacén ("Warehouse Beach"), mostly good for fishing from its nearby rocks. Moving past the pier toward town comes the colorful, bustling **Playa Municipal.** Its sheltered waters are fine for wading, swimming, and boat launching (which fishermen, their motors buzzing, regularly do) near the pier end.

Sun, Sand, And Tranquility
For a maximum of sun and serenity, walk (away from the pier) along Playa Municipal past the usually dry creek outlet that marks the beginning of **Playa la Madera.** After a hundred yards you reach the beginning of **Cerro la Madera,** the hill above the beach. A short, steep path leads over a rise to the sand beyond. (If you prefer, have a taxi take you to Playa la Madera, about $2.)

Playa la Madera ("Wood Beach"), once a loading point for lumber, is about 200 yards long and decorated with rocky nooks and outcroppings. The sand is fine and gray-white. Swells that enter the facing bay entrance break suddenly in two- or three-foot waves, which roll in gently and recede with little undertow. La Madera's calm waters are good mostly for child's play and easy swimming. Bring your mask and snorkel for glimpses of fish in the usually clear waters. A pair of beachside restaurant-bars, La Bocana and La Madera, serve drinks and snacks.

Zihuatanejo Bay's favorite resort beach is **Playa la Ropa** ("Clothes Beach"), a mile-long crescent of yellow-white sand washed by oft-gentle billows. The beach got its name centuries ago from the apparel that once floated in from an offshore Chinese wreck. From the bay's best *mirador* (viewpoint) at the summit of **Paseo Costera,** the La Ropa approach road, the beach sand, relentlessly scooped and redeposited by the waves, appears as a nearly endless line of half-moons.

On the 100-foot-wide beach itself, vacationers bask in the sun, jet-ski beetles buzz beyond the breakers, rental sailboats ply the waves, and windsurf outfits recline on the sand. The waves, generally too gentle and quick-breaking for surf sports, break close-in and recede with little undertow. Joggers come out mornings and evenings. Restaurants at the several beachfront hotels provide food and drinks.

Isolated **Playa las Gatas,** ("Cats Beach"), reachable on foot or easily by launch from the town pier, lies sheltered beneath the south-end Punta el Faro headland. Once a walled-in royal Tarascan bathing pool, the beach got its name from a species of locally common, small, whiskered nurse sharks. Generally calm and quiet, often with super-clear offshore waters, Playa las Gatas is a jumping-off spot for dive trips headed for prime local snorkeling grounds.

Ixtapa Beaches
Ixtapa's 10 distinct beaches lie scattered like pearls along Ixtapa's dozen miles of creamy, azure coastline. Moving from the Zihuatanejo direction **Playa Hermosa** comes first. The elevators of the super-luxurious clifftop Hotel Westin Ixtapa make access to the beach very

A rental windsurfer rests on Zihuatanejo Bay's Playa la Ropa.

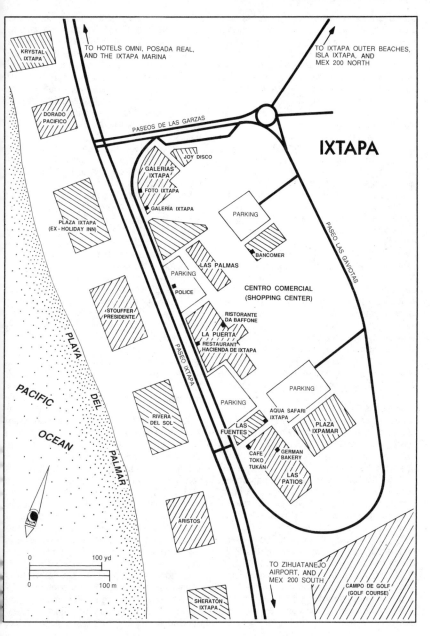

convenient. At the bottom you'll find a few hundred yards of seasonally broad white sand, with open-ocean (but often gentle) waves usually good for most water sports except surfing. Good beach-accessible snorkeling is possible off the shoals at either end of the beach. Extensive rentals are available at their beachfront aquatics shop. A poolside restaurant serves food and drinks. Hotel access is only by car or taxi.

For a sweeping vista of Ixtapa's beaches, bay, and blue waters, ride the **cable tramway** (open daily 7-7) to El Faro restaurant (open daily 8 a.m.-noon and 6-10 p.m.) at the south end of Ixtapa's main beach, Playa del Palmar.

Long, broad, and yellow-white, **Playa del Palmar** could be called the "Billion-dollar Beach" for the investment money it attracted to Ixtapa. The confidence seems justified. The broad strand stretches for three gently curving miles. Even though it fronts the open ocean, protective offshore rocks, islands, and shoals keep the surf gentle most of the time. Here, most of the sports are of the high-powered variety—parasailing ($10), jet- and waterskiing ($25), banana-boating ($5)—although boogieboards are rentable for $5 an hour on the beach.

Challenging **surfing** breaks sometimes roll in off the jetty at **Playa Escolleros**, at Playa del Palmar's far west end. Bring your own board, however. (For surfboard sales and rentals, see under "Sports" below.)

Ixtapa Outer Beaches

Ixtapa's outer beaches spread among the coves and inlets a few miles northwest of the hotel zone. Drive or taxi along the Paseo de las Garzas (left turn just past the shopping mall), then left again after less than a mile. After the Marina Golf Course, the road turns toward the shoreline, winding past a pair of hidden beach gems, **Playa San Juan de Dios** and **Playa Don Rodrigo.**

More easily accessible, however, is **Playa Cuata,** ahead one mile (bear left at the fork) before road's-end at Playa Quieta. Cream-yellow and nestling between rocky outcroppings, Playa Cuata has oft-gentle waves with correspondingly moderate undertow for good swimming, bodysurfing, and boogieboarding. Snorkeling and fishing are equally good around nearby rocks and shoals. (Bring your own food and drinks, however.)

Back at the main road fork, continue north past the rambling Club Med about another mile to the end of the pavement at **Playa Linda.** Here, an open-ocean yellow-sand beach extends for miles. Flocks of sandpipers and plovers skitter at the surf's edge; pelicans and cormorants dive offshore, while gulls, terns, and boobies skim the wavetops. Driftwood and shells decorate the sand beside a green-tufted palm grove, which seems to stretch endlessly north.

The friendly **La Palapa** beach restaurant (200 yards by dirt road past the pavement's end) offers beer, sodas, and seafood, plus showers and free parking and camping beneath their grove. Neighboring Stables Rudolfo provides horseback rides at about $15 per hour. Despite the stable-associated flies, this informal campground is kept secure and clean by a savvy management, who regularly attract a small colony of RV- and tent-camping customers.

The flat, wide beach has (sometimes powerful) rollers often good for surfing. Boogieboarding and bodysurfing (with caution, don't try it alone) are also possible here. Surf fishing likewise yields catches, especially of *lisa* (mullet), which locals have much more success netting than hooking.

Playa Quieta And Isla Ixtapa

Not-to-be-missed Isla Ixtapa is reachable by boat from Playa Quieta ("Quiet Beach"), a place that lives up to its name. A ribbon of fine yellow sand arcs around a smooth inlet dotted by a regatta of Club Med kayaks and sailboats plying the water. A few sunbathers and families laze on the sands, while several palapas beneath the shoreline trees offer rentals, food, and drinks.

Every few minutes a boat heads from the beach dock to mile-long Ixtapa Island offshore (daily 9-5, $2 roundtrip). Upon arrival, you can soon discover the secret to the preservation, despite crowds of visitors, of the island's pristine beaches, forests, and natural underwater gardens. "No trash here," the palapa proprietors say. "We bag it up and send it back to the mainland."

It shows. Great fleshy green orchids and bromeliads hang from forest branches, multicolored fish dart among offshore rocks, shady native acacias hang lazily over the shell-decorated sands of the island's little beaches. Boats from Quieta arrive at **Playa Cuachalatate** (koo-ah-chah-lah-TAH-tay), the island's most popular beach, named for a local tree, whose bark relieves liver ailments. Many visitors stay all day, enjoying splashing, swimming, and eating fresh fish, shrimp, and clams cooked at any one of a dozen palapas. Visitors also enjoy the many sports rentals: waterskis, banana rides, boats for fishing, aquatic bicycles ($25/hour), snorkel gear ($5/hour), and kayaks ($7/hour).

For a change of scene, follow the short path over the west-side (right as you arrive) forested knoll to **Playas Varadero and Carey** on opposite flanks of an intimate little isthmus. Varadero's yellow-white sand is narrow and tree-shaded, its waters are calm and clear. Behind it lies Playa Carey, a steep coral-sand beach fronting a rocky blue bay. Named for the sea-tur-tle species, Playa Carey is a magnet for beach lovers, snorkelers, and the scuba divers who often arrive by boat to explore the waters around the coral reef just offshore.

Scuba diving is so rewarding here that the Escuela de Buceos ("Diving School") Oliverio maintains headquarters near the west end of Playa Cuachalatate. Others in Ixtapa and Zihuatanejo (see "Sports" below) are better equipped to provide the same services, however.

ACCOMMODATIONS

Zihuatanejo's hotels divide themselves by location and (largely by price) between downtown and Playas La Madera-La Ropa.

IXTAPA-ZIHUATANEJO HOTELS

Ixtapa-Zihuatanejo hotels, in order of approximate high-season double room price (area code 753, postal code 40880)

ZIHUATANEJO DOWNTOWN

Hotel Tres Marias (old branch), Noria 4, Col. Lázaro Cárdenas, 421-91, 425-91, $23
Posada Citlali, Guerrero 3, 420-43, $27
Hotel Susy, Guerrero and Alvarez, 423-39, $27
Hotel Tres Marias (new branch), end Alvarez, 421-91, 425-91, $28
Hotel Avila, Alvarez 8, 420-10, $40

ZIHUATANEJO PLAYAS MADERA AND LA ROPA

Bungalows Milagro, Av. Marina Nacional s/n, 430-45, $25
Hotel Palacio, Av. Adelita (P.O. Box 57), 420-55, $25
Bungalows Allec, Cerro la Madera, 420-02, $40
Hotels Sotavento and Catalina, P.O. Box 2, 420-32, 420-24, fax 429-75, $40
Hotel Fiesta Mexicana, Playa la Ropa, 437-76, 436-36, $47
Bungalows Pacifico, Cerro la Madera (P.O. Box 12), 421-12, $50
Hotel Villas Miramar, Av. Adelita (P.O. Box 211), 421-06, 426-16, $55
Hotel Villa del Sol, P.O. Box 84, 422-39, 432-39, fax 427-58, U.S. (800) 223-6510, Canada (800) 424-5500, $180

IXTAPA

Hotel Posada Real, Paseo Ixtapa s/n, 316-25, 317-45, fax 318-05, (800) 528-1234, $91
Hotel Sheraton Ixtapa, Paseo Ixtapa s/n, 318-58, fax 324-38, (800) 325-3535, $127
Hotel Dorada Pacifico, Paseo Ixtapa s/n (P.O. Box 15), 320-25, $140
Hotel Krystal Ixtapa, Paseo Ixtapa s/n, 303-33, fax 302-16, (800) 231-9860, $143
Hotel Westin Ixtapa, Paseo de la Roca (P.O. Box 97), 321-21, fax 307-51, (800) 228-3000, $187

IXTAPA OR ZIHUATANEJO?

Your choice of local lodging sharply determines the tone of your stay. Zihuatanejo still resembles the colorful seaside village that visitors have enjoyed for years. Fishing *pangas* decorate its beachside, while *panaderías, taquerís,* and *papelerías* line its narrow shady lanes. Many of its hotels—budget to moderate, with Spartan but clean fan-only rooms—reflect the tastes of the bargain-conscious travelers who "discovered" Zihuatanejo during the 1960s.

Ixtapa, on the other hand, mirrors the fashion-wise preferences of new-generation Mexican and international vacationers. A broad boulevard fronts your Ixtapa hotel, while on the beach side, thatch-shaded chairs on a wide strand, a palmy garden, blue pool, and serene outdoor restaurant are yours to enjoy. Upstairs, your air-conditioned room—typically in plush pastels, with private sea-view balcony, marble bath, room service, and your favorite TV shows by satellite—brings maximum convenience and comfort to a lush tropical setting.

Actually, you needn't be forced to choose. Split your hotel time between Ixtapa and Zihuatanejo and enjoy both worlds.

Zihuatanejo Downtown Hotels

Starting on the west side near the beach, begin at the **Hotel Tres Marias**, which has two branches. The old hotel is across the lagoon-mouth by footbridge from the end of Paseo Pescador (Noria 4, Colonia Lázaro Cárdenas, Zihuatanejo, Guerrero 40880, tel. 753-421-91, 753-425-91). Its longtime popularity derives from its low prices and the colorful lagoon-front boat scene, visible from porches outside of some of its 25 rooms. Otherwise, it's a strictly bare-bones place, without even hot water. Rooms rent for about $18 s, $23 d, and $31 t, with fan.

Guests at the **new branch** of the Hotel Tres Marias (near the end of Alvarez) nearby enjoy a few more amenities and a long-popular restaurant downstairs. A few of the 18 rooms have air-conditioning and/or private balconies looking out on the usually quiet street below. Being close to the pier, the new branch is popular with fishing parties. Newcomers might pick up some local fishing pointers around the tables after dinner. Same address and phone as old hotel above; rooms go for about $23 s, $28 d or t,

with hot water and fans; add about $6 for a/c.

A few blocks east on Alvarez is the **Hotel Avila,** downtown Zihuatanejo's only beachfront hostelry. Popular for its location rather than its management, which seems to be content with the dirt in the corners, the Avila has 27 rooms, some of which enjoy luxurious private-terrace bay views. Try for an upper-floor beachside room, while avoiding those that front the noisy street (Juan Alvarez 8, Zihuatanejo, Guerrero 40880, tel. 753-420-10). Rooms rent from about $40 s or d with fan only, $47 with a/c; with TV, phones, and hot water; credit cards accepted.

Hotel Susy, corner of Guerrero across the street, has three tiers of rooms surrounding a shady inner patio. The seven upper-floor bayside rooms have private view balconies. Inside corridors unfortunately run past room windows, necessitating closing curtains for privacy, a drawback in these fan-only rooms. Avoid traffic noise by requesting an upper-floor room away from the street (Guerrero and Alvarez, Zihuatanejo, Guerrero 40880, tel. 753-423-39). The 20 clean but very plain rooms go for about $20 s, $27 d, including fans and hot water.

A better choice next door is the popular **Posada Citlali,** built in a pair of triple tiers, which rise around a shady, plant-decorated inner courtyard. The 20 plain, rather small but clean rooms are all thankfully removed from direct street noise. Guests on the upper floors enjoy less corridor traffic and consequently more privacy. Reservations are mandatory during the high winter season and strongly recommended at other times (Av. Guerrero 3, Zihuatanejo, Guerrero 40880, tel. 753-420-43). Rates run $20 s, $27 d, with hot water and fans.

Zihuatanejo Playa La Madera
And Playa La Ropa Hotels

The other half of Zihuatanejo's lodgings spreads along Playas la Madera and la Ropa on the east side of the bay. Several of them cluster on Cerro la Madera, the bayside hill just west of town. Due to Zihuatanejo's one-way streets (which fortunately direct much noisy traffic away from downtown) getting to Cerro la Madera is a bit tricky. The key is **Plaza Kyoto,** the traffic circle-intersection of Paseo de la Boquita and Paseo del Palmar a quarter mile east of downtown. (If you're driving, follow the small "Zona Hotelera" signs.) At Plaza Kyoto, head across the canal bridge and turn right at the first street. Straight ahead another block Av. Adelita, the address of several Playa la Madera hotels, runs along the base of Cerro la Madera.

By location, moving eastward, start at **Bungalows Pacifico,** the labor of love of longtime local resident Anita Rellstab. Superlatives can only describe what her guests enjoy: six spacious, comfortable, art-decorated hillside apartments with broad bay-view patios and complete furnishings, including kitchenettes and daily maid service. Anita herself, an amateur archaeologist, ecologist, and community leader, is a friendly, forthright, and knowledgeable hostess.

Flower-bedecked and hammock-draped, Anita's retreat is ideal for those seeking quiet relaxation. No matter for lack of a pool; lovely Playa la Madera is a short walk down the leafy front slope. Get your reservations in early, especially for winter (Cerro la Madera, Calle Eva Samano de Lopez Mateos, P.O. Box 12, Zihuatanejo, Guerrero 40880, tel. 753-421-12). The apartments rent for $50 d, $60 t; with hot water, fans only, and street parking; monthly discount possible during the May 1-Dec. 1 low season; get there via the short street uphill from Av. Adelita.

Along the same rustic-scenic hilltop street, **Bungalows Allec** guests enjoy luscious bay views from their private balconies. Comfortable but not luxurious, the 12 light, clean apartments have hot water and fans. Six of the apartments are very large, sleeping up to six, with completely equipped kitchenettes. The others are small but cozy doubles. No pool, but Playa la Madera is a just a few steps downhill (Cerro la Madera, Calle Eva Samano de Lopes Mateos, Zihuatanejo, Guerrero 40880, tel. 753-420-02). The kitchenette apartments go for about $70 low season, $100 high; the smaller doubles go for about $30 low, $40 high. Monthly low-season discounts may be available; street parking.

Downhill on Av. Adelita is the family-run **Hotel Palacio,** a beachfront maze of rooms connected by meandering, multilevel walkways. Room windows along the two main tiers face corridor walkways, where curtains must be drawn for privacy. Upper units fronting the quiet street avoid this drawback, however. The rooms themselves are plain but clean and comfortable, with fans and hot water. Guests enjoy a small but very pleasant bay-view pool-sun deck, which

perches above the waves at the hotel beachfront (Playa la Madera, Av. Adelita, P.O. Box 57, Zihuatanejo, Guerrero 40880, tel. 753-420-55). The 25 rooms rent for about $18 s, $25 d, $30 t; street parking.

The **Hotel Villas Miramar** next door clusters artfully around gardens of pools, palms, and leafy potted plants. The gorgeous, manicured layout makes maximum use of space, creating both privacy and intimacy in a small setting. The designer rooms have high ceilings, split levels, built-in sofas, and large, comfortable beds. The street divides the hotel into two different but equally lovely sections, each with its own pool. The restaurant, especially convenient for breakfast, is in the shore-side section, but still serves guests who sun and snooze around the luxurious, beach-view pool-patio garden on the other side of the street (Playa la Madera, Av. Adelita, P.O. Box 211, Zihuatanejo, Guerrero 40880, tel. 753-421-06, 753-426-16). The 16 rooms rent for about $48 d low season, $55 high; with phones and a/c; and credit cards accepted; additional discounts may be available during May-June and Sept.-Oct. low seasons.

Nearby, a couple of blocks off the beach, is the downscale but homey **Bungalows Milagro,** the project of local doctor Klaus Bührer and his wife Lucina Gomes. A haciendalike compound of cottages and apartments clustering around a shady pool, the Bungalows Milagro is winter headquarters for a cordial group of German longtime returnees. The friendly atmosphere and the inviting pool-garden account for the Milagro's success, rather than the plain but clean kitchenette lodgings, which vary in style from ramshackle-rustic to 1940s motel. Look at several before you choose (Playa la Madera, Av. Marina Nacional s/n, Zihuatanejo, Guerrero 40880, tel. 753-430-45). The 10 rooms rent, low season, for about $27 for three, $47 for six, a bit more during high season. Additional discounts may be negotiated for longer stays and fewer occupants; all with fans and parking; hot water in only five of the units.

About a mile farther along the road to Playa la Ropa, the twin **Hotels Sotavento and Catalina** perch together on a leafy hillside above La Ropa Beach. Good management by a savvy husband-wife owner team keeps the rambling complex healthy. The twin hotels contrast sharply. The Sotavento is a 70-room mod-style warren that stairsteps five stories down the hillside. Each floor of rooms opens to a broad, hammock-hung communal terrace overlooking the beach and bay. The Hotel Catalina's 30 cabañas, by contrast, lie scattered beneath shady hillside trees all the way down to the beach. A pair of restaurants, a mediocre breakfast-lunch cafeteria at the beach level, and a fancier dinner restaurant upstairs service the guests, many on vacation packages.

The Sotavento's rooms are '60s modern, clean and comfortable, opening on to the view terrace, with king- or queen-sized beds and ceiling fans. The Catalina's comfortably appointed tropical-rustic cabañas are more private, being separate units with individual view terraces and hammocks. At the bottom of the hill, the hotel aquatics shop offers sailing, windsurfing, snorkeling, and other rentals; those who want to rest enjoy chairs beneath the shady boughs of a beachside grove. The address is the same for both hotels: Playa la Ropa, P.O. Box 2, Zihuatanejo, Guerrero 40880, tel. (753) 420-32, (753) 420-24, fax (753) 429-75. Standard rooms rent during high season for $40 s or d, deluxe terrace suites $50, and deluxe bungalows $67. A few small "student" units rent for about $30; discounts possible May through mid-November; no pool, fans only, parking, credit cards accepted.

Half a dozen hotels and bungalow complexes spread along La Ropa Beach. The **Hotel Fiesta Mexicana** seems to be popular for nothing more than its stunning location right in the middle of the sunny beach hubbub. Its 60 rooms, in low-rise stucco clusters, while comfortable and air-conditioned, are (like the entire hotel) neither fancy nor particularly tidy. This, however, doesn't seem to bother the mostly North American winter clientele, who jet-ski, parasail, and boogieboard from the beach, snooze around the pool, and socialize beneath the palapa of the beachside restaurant. (Playa la Ropa, Zihuatanejo, Guerrero 40880, tel. 753-437-76, 753-436-36). Standard rooms rent from around $47 d high season; $70 for room with private view patio, $80 for deluxe. Low-season discount runs about 15%; parking; credit cards accepted.

German expatriate Helmut Leins sold out in Munich and came to create paradise on Playa la Ropa in 1978. The result is Playa la Ropa's luxury **Hotel Villa del Sol,** an exquisite beachside mini-Eden. A corps of well-to-do North American,

European, and Mexican clients return yearly to enjoy tranquility and the elegance of the Villa del Sol's crystal-blue pools, palm-draped patios, and classic palapas. The lodgings themselves are spacious, with shining floor tile, handcrafted wall art, tropical-canopy beds, and private hammock-hung patios. The plethora of extras includes a restaurant, bars, pools, night tennis courts, a newsstand, boutique, beauty salon, and meeting room for about 30 people (Playa la Ropa, P.O. Box 84, Zihuatanejo, Guerrero 40880, tel. 753-422-39, 753-432-39, fax 753-427-58). The approximately 50 accommodations begin at about $180 s or d high season, $144 low season, add $30 per person for mandatory meals high season. Super-plush options include more bedrooms and baths, ocean views, and jacuzzis for $400 and up; with a/c and parking; credit cards accepted. For U.S. reservations, call (800) 223-6510; in Canada, call (800) 424-5500.

Ixtapa Hotels

Ixtapa's dozen hotels line up in a luxurious strip between the beach and boulevard Paseo Ixtapa. Among the most reasonably priced is the Best Western **Hotel Posada Real** at the far west end. With a large grassy football field instead of tennis courts, the hotel attracts a seasonal following of soccer enthusiasts. Other amenities include three restaurants (one of them the attractive Los Cocos), two pools, and a disco. The 110 smallish rooms are clean and comfortable, but lack ocean views (Paseo Ixtapa s/n, Ixtapa, Guerrero 40880, tel. 753-316-25, 753-317-45, fax 753-318-05). Rooms rent for about $91 d, often with big discounts for longer stays. Kids under 12 are always free; with a/c, satellite TV, phones and parking; credit cards accepted. For info and reservations in the U.S. and Canada, call (800) 528-1234.

Nearer the middle of the hotel zone, the Mexican-owned **Krystal Ixtapa** towers over its spacious garden compound. Its innovative wedge design ensures an ocean view from each room. A continuous round of activities (such as a ping-pong tournament, handicrafts and cooking classes, and aerobics and scuba lessons) fills the days while buffets, Mexican fiestas, dancing, and discoing fill the nights. Unscheduled relaxation centers on the blue pool, where guests enjoy watching each other slip from the waterslide and duck beneath the waterfall all day. The 260 deluxe clean, and tastefully appointed rooms and suites have private view balconies, satellite TV, and phones (Paseo Ixtapa s/n, Ixtapa, Guerrero 40880, tel. 753-303-33, fax 753-302-16. Rooms rent from $143 d high season, about $90 low. Check for additional discounts through extended-stay or other packages. Extras include tennis courts, racquetball, an exercise gym, parking, and wheelchair access; credit cards accepted. For U.S. and Canada reservations, call toll-free (800) 231-9860.

If the Krystal is full, try the nearly-as-good **Hotel Dorado Pacifico** next door. Although fewer organized activities fill the day, three palm-shaded blue pools, water-slides, a swim-up bar, and three restaurant-bars seem to keep guests happy. Upstairs, the rooms, all with sea-view balconies, are tastefully appointed with sky-blue carpets and earth-tone designer bedspreads (Paseo Ixtapa s/n, P.O. Box 15, Ixtapa, Guerrero 40880, tel. 753-320-25). The 285 rooms rent from about $140 d high season, with a/c, phones, and TV; low season and extended-stay discounts may be available. Extras include tennis courts, parking, and wheelchair access; credit cards accepted.

The **Hotel Sheraton Ixtapa,** by the golf course at the east end of the beach, rises around a soaring lobby-atrium. A worthy member of the worldwide Sheraton chain, the Sheraton Ixtapa serves its mostly American clientele with complete resort facilities, including pools, all sports, an exercise gym, several restaurants and bars, cooking and arts lessons, nightly dancing, and a Fiesta Mexicana. The 332 rooms in standard (which enjoy mountain-view balconies only), deluxe, and junior suite grades, are spacious and tastefully furnished in designer pastels and include a/c, phones, and satellite TV (Paseo Ixtapa s/n, Ixtapa, Guerrero 40880, tel. 753-318-58, fax 753-324-38). Standard rooms run from about $80 d low season, $127 high; deluxe from about $100 d low season, $155 high; parking, credit cards accepted, and wheelchair access. In the U.S. and Canada, call Sheraton toll-free (800) 325-3535.

From the adjacent jungly hilltop, the **Hotel Westin Ixtapa** (formerly the El Camino) slopes downhill to the shore like a latter-day Mexican pyramid. The monumentally stark hilltop lobby, open and unadorned except for a clutch of huge stone balls, contrasts sharply with its surroundings. The hotel's severe lines immediately shift the focus to the adjacent jungle. The fecund forest aroma wafts into the lobby and terrace restaurant, where guests sit watching iguanas munch hibiscus blossoms in the nearby treetops.

The hotel entertains guests with a wealth of resort facilities, including pools, four tennis courts, a gym, aerobics, an intimate shoal-enfolded beach, restaurants, bars, and nightly live dance music. The standard rooms, each with its own spacious view patio, are luxuriously Spartan, floored with big designer tiles, furnished in earth tones and equipped with big TVs, small refrigerators, phones, and a/c. More luxurious options include suites with individual pools and jacuzzis (Paseo de la Roca, P.O. Box 97, Ixtapa, Guerrero 40880, tel. 753-321-21, fax 753-307-51). The 427 rooms begin at about $155 for a standard low-season double, $187 high, and run about twice that for super-luxury suites. June-October, bargain packages can run as low as $55 d per night, including buffet breakfast, tennis, and a local tour for two. In the U.S. and Canada, call Westin toll-free at (800) 228-3000.

Trailer Parks And Camping

Ixtapa-Zihuatanejo has two very basic trailer parks at opposite ends of the road. **Pepe's Trailer Park,** on the hillside road about 200 yards inland from the far end of Playa la Ropa, offers about 15 spaces for tenters or self-contained RVs (P.O. Box 272, Zihuatanejo, Guerrero 40880, no phone). The friendly on-site owners (in the house uphill) have built a little park out of their forested slope. Here, dogs bark and horses graze in adjacent leaf-fringed meadows, and local folks stroll by on the way to town and the beach. Their spaces, with electricity (inadequate for a/c, however), water, showers, and toilets, rent for about $12 for a trailer, $10 for a tent. It's filled only during the Christmas-New Year and Easter weeks; otherwise, you may have the place to yourself.

On north-end Playa Linda, RV camping and tenting possibilities include previously mentioned **La Palapa** and, a quarter mile along the dirt road extending north from there, **Trailer Park Los Buzos,** in a big, fenced, palm-edged lot. Beside beachcombing and surf-fishing heaven Playa Linda, Los Buzos offers camping and basic showers and toilets (but no electricity) for about $2 per night. The owner arrives every morning around eight, operates his downscale palapa restaurant, and leaves before sunset. He does a brisk business between Christmas and New Year and the week before Easter; other times a few RVs and tenters often remain, keeping each other company.

House, Apartment, And Condo Rentals
Zihuatanejo residents sometimes offer their condos and homes for temporary lease through agents. Among the better known is **Elizabeth Williams,** a longtime local realtor. Contact her at P.O. Box 169, Zihuatanejo, Guerrero 40880, tel. (753) 426-06, fax (753) 447-62, for a list of possible rentals.

The local **Century 21** real estate affiliate also handles rentals. Contact them at their main office in Zihuatanejo at Av. Marina Nacional 71G, tel. (753) 440-10, fax (753) 435-46.

FOOD

Snacks, Bakeries, And Breakfasts
For something cool in Zihuatanejo, stop by the **Paletería y Nevería Michoacána** ice shop across from the plaza. Besides ice cream, popcorn, and safe *nieves* (ices) they offer delicious *aguas* (fruit-flavored drinks, $.50), which make nourishing, refreshing Pepsi-free alternatives.

The **Panadería Francesa** bakery, four short blocks up Cuauhtémoc from the beach, turns out a daily acre of fresh goodies, from *pan integral* (whole wheat) and black bread loaves to doughnuts and rafts of Mexican-style cakes, cookies, and tarts. With coffee, chairs and tables (open daily 7 a.m.-9 p.m., tel. 427-42, on C. González, corner of Galeana, the lane paralleling Cuauhtémoc).

Tasty, promptly served breakfasts are the specialty of the downtown **Cafetería Nova Zelandia.** Favorites include hotcakes, eggs any style, fruit, juices, and espresso coffee. They serve lunch and supper also (open daily 8 a.m.-10 p.m.; on Cuauhtémoc, corner of Ejido).

For hot sandwiches and good pizza on the downtown beach, try the friendly **Cafe Marina.** Their shelves of books for lending or exchange are nearly as popular as their food (open Mon.-Sat. noon-10, closed May 1-July 31; on Paseo de Pescador, just west of the plaza).

A local vacation wouldn't be complete without dropping in to the **Sirena Gorda** ("Fat Mermaid") near the end of Paseo de Pescador across from the naval compound. Here the fishing crowd relaxes, trading stories after a tough day hauling in the lines. The other unique attractions, besides the well-endowed sea nymphs who decorate the walls, are tempting shrimp-bacon and fish tacos, juicy hamburgers, fish *mole,* and conch and cactus plates (open Thurs.-Tues. 7 a.m.-10 p.m., tel. 426-87).

In Ixtapa, the **Cafe Toko Tukán** offers a refreshing alternative to hotel breakfasts. White cockatoos and bright toucans on a leafy patio add an exotic touch as you enjoy the fare, which, besides the usual juices, eggs, hotcakes, and French toast, includes lots of salads, veggie burgers, and sandwiches (open daily 8 a.m.-10 p.m., on the west front corner of the Los Patios shopping complex, across the boulevard from Hotel Aristos, tel. 307-17).

The perfume wafting from freshly baked European-style yummies draws dozens of the faithful to the nearby **German Bakery,** brainchild of local long-timers Helmut and Esther Walter. He, a German, and she, an East Indian from Singapore, satisfy homesick palates with a continuous supply of scrumptious cinnamon rolls, pies, and hot buns (open daily 8-2, on the inner patio, upper floor of the Los Patios shopping complex, tel. 303-10).

Restaurants
(Complete Dinner Price Key: Budget = under $7, Moderate = $7-$14, Expensive = more than $14.) Local chefs and restaurateurs, long accustomed to foreign tastes, operate a number of good local restaurants, mostly in Zihuatanejo (where, in contrast to Ixtapa, most of the serious eating occurs *outside* of hotel dining rooms).

In Zihuatanejo, all trails seem to lead to cafe **Al Andaluz Expresso,** on Cuauhtémoc a block from the plaza (open daily 8 a.m.-11 p.m., tel. 438-50, credit cards accepted). Here the atmosphere is refined but friendly and the food familiar and good, including pastrami, corned beef, lean ham, Texas steak, Denver sandwiches, deli-type salads and pickles, cheeses, hot beef with gravy, and good pastries and coffee. Moderate.

Around the corner, from sidewalk tables along its mall-like streetfront, the **Restaurant-Bar Victor y Paco** extends beneath a tastefully decorated and softly lit palapa (open daily noon-11:30, Pedro Ascencio 10, near the corner of Cuauhtémoc, tel. 420-72, credit cards acccepted). Opening for lunch and continuing through a happy hour, Victor y Paco specializes in dinner. Service is crisp, and the house specialties, including *mole* chicken, red snapper *(huachinango zihua)* and octopus *(pulpo costeña)* are delicious. Moderate.

Zihuatanejo has a pair of good, genuinely local-style restaurants in the downtown area. **Tamales y Atoles "Any,"** Zihuatanejo's clean, well-lighted place for Mexican food, is the spot to find out if your favorite Mexican restaurant back home is serving the real thing (open daily noon-10, at Nicolas Bravo 33, between Cuautémoc and Guerrero). Tacos, tamales, quesadillas, enchiladas, chiles rellenos, and such goodies are called *antijitos* in Mexico. At Tamales y Atoles "Any," they're savory enough to please even demanding Mexican palates. Budget to moderate.

Restaurant Los Braseros, on the next street away from the beach, is similarly authentic and popular (open daily 4 p.m.-1 a.m., at Ejido 21, between Cuauhtémoc and Guerrero, tel. 448-58). Waiters are often busy after midnight even during low season serving around seven kinds of good tacos and specialties such as "Gringa," "Porky," and "Azteca" from a menu it would take about three months of dinners (followed by a six-month diet) to fully investigate. Moderate.

Ixtapa restaurants have to be exceptional to compete with the hotels. One such, the **Belle Vista** *is* in a hotel, being the Westin Ixtapa's view-terrace cafe (open daily 7 a.m.-11 p.m.; call ahead to reserve a terrace-edge table, tel. 321-21, credit cards accepted). Breakfast is the favorite time to watch the antics of the iguanas in the adjacent jungle treetops. These black, green, and white miniature dinosaurs crawl up and down the trunks, munch flowers, and sunbathe on the branches. The food and service, incidentally, are quite good. Moderate to expensive.

The **Hacienda de Ixtapa,** right on the boulevard across from the Hotel Stouffer Presidente, offers good food and service in an airy patio setting (open daily 7 a.m.-11 p.m., tel. 306-02, credit cards accepted). Fruit plate, eggs any style, and hotcakes breakfasts run about $2

each, while fish fillet ($6), T-bone ($9), and lobster ($14) dinners are similarly reasonable and tasty. Moderate.

Those hankering for Italian-style pastas and seafood head to **Ristorante Da Baffone,** at the back side of the La Puerta shopping complex on the Paseo Ixtapa (open daily about noon to midnight, during high season, call for reservations, tel. 311-22). Here, Mediterranean-Mex decor covers the walls while marinera-style shrimp and clams with linguini, calimari, ricotta and spinach-stuffed canelloni, and glasses of chianti and chardonnay load the tables. Moderate-expensive.

Other Ixtapa restaurants, also popular for their party atmosphere, are described below.

ENTERTAINMENT AND EVENTS

In Zihuatanejo, visitors and residents content themselves mostly with quiet pleasures. Afternoons, they stroll the beachfront or the downtown shady lanes and enjoy coffee or drinks with friends at small cafes and bars. As the sun goes down, however, folks head to Ixtapa for its sunset vistas, happy hours, shows, clubs, and dancing.

Sunsets
Sunsets are tranquil and often magnifient from the **Restaurant-Bar El Faro,** which even has a cableway (south end of the Ixtapa beach, open 7-7) leading to it. Many visitors stay to enjoy dinner and the relaxing piano bar (open daily around 5:30-10; reservations recommended winter and weekends, tel. 310-27; drive or taxi via the uphill road toward the Westin Ixtapa at the golf course; at the first fork, head right for El Faro).

For equally brilliant sunsets in a lively setting, try either the lobby-bar or Belle Vista terrace restaurant of the **Westin Ixtapa.** Lobby-bar happy hour runs from 6 to 7; live music begins around 7:30. (Drive or taxi, following the signs, along the uphill road at the golf course, following the signs to the crest of the hill just south of the Ixtapa beach.)

Sunset Cruises
Those who want to experience a sunset party at sea ride the trimaran *Rainbow,* which leaves from the Zihuatanejo pier around 5 p.m. daily, re-

turning around 8:00. The tariff runs about $40 per person, including buffet and open bar. Book tickets through a hotel travel agent or contact the launch cooperative, Teniente Azueta, at tel. 420-56 (or stop by their office at the foot of the Zihuatanejo pier).

A smaller sailboat, piloted by Sailboats of the Sun, leaves for a sunset open-bar party from the Puerto Mio dock (about half a mile from town, at the end of the road that curves around the western, right-hand side of Zihuatanejo Bay). The two-and-a-half-hour cruise costs about $20 per person, including open bar. Call Puerto Mio (tel. 420-95) for more information. (They also run an all-day cruise to Ixtapa Island, including open bar, snorkeling, and lunch on the island for about $40 per person.)

Tourist Shows

Ixtapa hotels regularly stage **Fiesta Mexicana** extravaganzas, which begin with a sumptuous buffet and go on to a whirling skirt-and-sombrero folkloric ballet. Afterward, the audience usually gets involved with piñatas, games, cockfights, dancing, and continuous drinks from an open bar. In the finale, fireworks often boom over the beach, painting the night sky in festoons of reds, blues, and greens.

Entrance, usually open to public, runs about $30 per person, with kids under 12 usually half price. Shows at the **Krystal Ixtapa** (Monday, tel. 303-33), the **Dorado Pacifico** (Tuesday, tel. 320-25), and the **Sheraton** (Wednesday, tel. 318-58) are among the most popular. Call ahead for confirmation and reservations.

Clubs And Hangouts

Part restaurant and part wacky night spot, the **Restaurant-Bar Cocos** at Ixtapa's Hotel Posada Real offers hamburgers and seafood in a Robinson Crusoe-chic setting. Patrons recline in ceiling-hung chairs, while waiters try to outdo each other's zany tricks, and lively (but not too loud) tropical music bounces out of the speakers (open daily 7 a.m.-11 p.m.).

Next door, **Carlos and Charlie's** is as wild and as much fun as all of the other Carlos Anderson restaurants from Puerto Vallarta to Paris. Here in Ixtapa you can have your picture taken on a surfboard in front of a big wave for $3, or have a fireman spray out the flames from the chili sauce on your palate. You can also enjoy

the food, which, if not fancy, is innovative and tasty. Loud rock music ($10 minimum) goes on from about 10 p.m. to about 4 a.m. during the winter season. (The restaurant serves daily from noon to midnight, tel. 300-85; about half a block on the driveway road west past the Hotel Posada Real.)

Dancing And Discoing

Nearly all Ixtapa hotel lobbies blossom with dance music from around seven during the high winter season. Year-round, however, good medium-volume groups usually play for dancing nightly at the **Westin Ixtapa** (tel. 321-21), the **Sheraton** (tel. 318-58), and the **Krystal** (tel. 303-33) lobby bars from around 7:30 to midnight.

Christine, Ixtapa's big-league discotheque, offers fantasy for a mere $10 cover charge. From about 10 p.m., the patrons warm up by listening to relatively low-volume rock, watch videos, and talk while they can still hear each other. That stops around 11:30, when the fogs descend, the lights begin flashing, and the speakers boom forth their 200-decibel equivalent of a fast freight roaring at trackside. (At the Hotel Krystal, call 303-33, ext. 429, to verify times.)

SPORTS

Walking And Jogging

Zihuatanejo Bay is strollable from the Playa la Madera all the way west to Puerto Mio. A relaxing half-day adventure could begin by taxiing to the Hotel Irma (Av. Adelita, on Playa la Madera) for breakfast. Don your hats and follow the stairs down to Playa la Madera and walk west toward town. At the end of the Playa la Madera, detour right via the narrow path over the big beachside rock and down to the main town beach. Past the pier and across the lagoon bridge, head left along the bayside road to **Puerto Mio** for a drink at the hotel cafe and perhaps a dip in their pool. (Allow three hours, including breakfast, for this two-mile walk; do the reverse trip during late afternoon for sunset drinks or dinner at the Irma.)

Playa del Palmar, Ixtapa's main beach, is good for similar strolls. Start in the morning with breakfast at the Restaurant-Bar El Faro (open daily 6-11 a.m., 6-10 p.m., tel. 310-27) atop the hill at the south end of the beach. Ride the cableway or walk downhill. With the sun at your back, stroll the beach, stopping for refreshments at the hotel pool-patios enroute. The entire beach stretches about three miles to the marina jetty, where you can often watch surfers challenging the waves and where taxis and buses return along Paseo Ixtapa. Allow about four hours, including breakfast. The reverse walk would be equally enjoyable during the afternoon. Time yourself to arrive at the El Faro cableway about half an hour before sundown to enjoy the sunset over drinks or dinner. (Get to El Faro by driving or taxiing via Paseo de la Roca, which heads uphill off the Zihuatanejo road at the golf course. Follow the first right fork to El Faro.)

Adventurers who enjoy ducking through underbrush and scrambling over rocks might enjoy exploring the acacia forest and pristine beaches of the uninhabited west side of **Isla Ixtapa.** Take water, lunch, and a good pair of walking shoes. (For Isla Ixtapa access, see under "Sights" above. Your exploration should begin at the far end of Playa Varadero.)

Joggers often practice their art either on the smooth, firm sands of Ixtapa's main beachfront or on Paseo Ixtapa's sidewalks. Best avoid crowds and midday heat by jogging early mornings or late afternoons. For even better beach jogging, try the flat, firm sands of uncrowded **Playa Quieta** about three miles by car or taxi northwest of Ixtapa. Additionally, mile-long **Playa la Ropa** can be enjoyed by early morning and late afternoon joggers.

Golf And Tennis
Ixtapa's 18-hole, professionally designed **Campo de Golf** is open to the public. In addition to its manicured, 6,898-yard course, patrons enjoy full facilities, including pool, restaurant, pro shop, lockers, and tennis courts. Greens fee runs $32, cart $25, club rental $15, caddy for $8 18 holes ($5 for nine), and golf lessons, $23 an hour. Play goes on daily around 6 a.m.-4:30 p.m. The clubhouse (P.O. Box 105, Zihuatanejo, Guerrero, 40880, tel. 310-30) is off Paseo Ixtapa, across from the Sheraton. No reservations are accepted; morning golfers, get in line early during the high winter season.

Ixtapa has nearly all of the local **tennis** courts, all of them private. The Campo de Golf (see above) has some of the best. Rentals run about $7 per hour during the day and $8.50 nights.

Reservations (tel. 310-30) may be seasonally necessary. A pro shop rents and sells equipment. Teaching professional Luis Valle offers lessons for about $17 per hour.

Several hotels also have tennis courts, equipment, and lessons. Call the **Sheraton** (tel. 318-58), **Omni** (tel. 300-03), **Dorado Pacifico** (tel. 320-25), **Krystal** (tel. 303-33), and the **Westin Ixtapa** (tel. 321-21) for rental information.

Horseback Riding
Stables Rudolfo on Playa Linda (see under "Ixtapa Outer Beaches" above) rents horses for beach riding daily for about $16 per hour. Travel agencies and hotels offer the same (for considerably higher prices, however).

Swimming, Surfing, And Bodysurfing
Calm Zihuatanejo Bay is fine for swimming but too calm for surfing, bodysurfing, and boogieboarding (except marginally at Playa la Ropa.)

Heading northwest to more open coast, waves improve for bodysurfing and boogieboarding along Ixtapa's main beach **Playa del Palmar**, while usually remaining calm and undertow-free enough for swimming beyond the breakers. As for surfing, good breaks sometimes rise off the jetty at Playa Escolleros at the west end of Playa del Palmar.

Along Ixtapa's outer beaches, swimming is great along very calm Playa Quieta, while surfing, bodysurfing, and boogieboarding are correspondingly good (and hazardous) in the sometimes mountainous surf of Playa Larga farther north. (See "Sights" above for more beach details.)

Snorkeling And Scuba Diving
Clear offshore waters (sometimes up to 100-foot visibility during the Nov.-May dry season) have drawn a steady flow of divers and nurtured professionally staffed and equipped dive shops. Good snorkeling and scuba spots, where swarms of multicolored fish graze and glide among rocks and corals, lie just offshore, accessible from Playa las Gatas, Playa Hermosa, and Playa Carey (on Isla Ixtapa). (For access details and beach snorkeling prospects, see various beach headings under "Sights" above.)

Many operators take parties for offshore **snorkeling** excursions by boat. On Playa la

Ropa, contact the aquatics shop at the foot of the hill beneath Hotel Sotavento. Playa las Gatas, easily accessible by boat for $2 from the Zihuatanejo pier, also has a scuba shop and snorkel and excursion boat rentals. In Ixtapa, similar services are available at beachside shops at the **Westin Ixtapa, Sheraton, Krystal,** and seasonally at other hotels.

Other even more spectacular offshore sites, such as Morros de Potosi, El Yunque, Bajo de Chato, Bajo de Torresillas, Piedra Soletaria, and Sacramento, are safely accessible with the help of professional guides and instructors only.

Two local dive shops stand out. In downtown Zihuatanejo, marine biologist-instructor Juan M.B. Avila coordinates his **Zihuatanejo Scuba Center** (open Thurs.-Tues. 8:30 a.m.-8:00 p.m. at Cuauhtémoc 3, Zihuatanejo, Guerrero 40880, tel. 421-47). Licensed for instruction through both PADI (Professional Association of Dive Instructors) and NAUI (National Association of Underwater Instructors), Avila is among Pacific Mexico's best-qualified professional instructors. Aided by loads of state-of-the-art equipment and several experienced assistants, his shop has accumulated a long list of repeat customers.

Avila's standard resort dive package, including a morning pool instruction session and an afternoon offshore half-hour dive, runs about $65 per person complete. Other services for beginners include open-water certification (one week of instruction, $350) and more rigorous PADI or NAUI certification (price negotiable). For certified divers (bring your certificate), Avila offers night, shipwreck, deep-water, and marine-biology dives at more than three dozen coastal sites.

In Ixtapa, **Aqua Safari Ixtapa** is well equipped and equally professional. A partnership of American Joe Wattels and Mexican PADI-licensed instructor Eduardo "Lalo" Loaizia Michel, Aqua Safari Ixtapa offers one-day resort dive-training and open-water certification for beginners, and wreck and deep-water dives for the experienced. They're located upstairs in the Centro Comercial Los Fuentes shopping complex, opposite end of the corridor from the Cafe Toko Tukán (open 9 a.m.-6 p.m. at local no. 10, Centro Comercial Los Fuentes, Ixtapa, Guerrero 40880, tel. 753-324-15; for U.S. and Canada information, call Joe Wattels in Eugene, Oregon, at 503-485-0928).

Sailing, Windsurfing, And Kayaking

The tranquil waters of Zihuatanejo Bay, off Ixtapa's Playa del Palmar, and the quiet strait off Playa Quieta (see "Sights" above) are good for these low-power aquatic sports. Shops on Playa la Ropa in Zihuatanejo Bay and in front of Ixtapa hotels, such as the Westin Ixtapa, the Sheraton, and the Krystal, rent small sailboats, sailboards, and sea kayaks hourly.

Fishing

Surf or rock casting with bait or lures, depending on conditions, is generally successful in local waters. Have enough line to allow casting beyond the waves (about 50 feet out on Playa la Ropa, 100 feet on Playa del Palmar and Playa Linda).

The rocky ends of *playas* la Ropa, la Madera, del Palmar, and Cuata on the mainland, and Playa Carey on Isla Ixtapa are also good for casting. (For details and access, see "Sights" above.)

For deep-sea fishing, you can launch your own boat (see below) or rent one. *Pangas* (fishing launches) are available for rent from individual fishermen on the beach, the boat cooperative (see below) at Zihuatanejo pier, or aquatics shops of the Hotel Sotavento on Playa la Ropa or the Hotels Westin Ixtapa, Sheraton, Krystal, and others on the beach in Ixtapa. Rental for a seaworthy *panga,* including tackle and bait, should run $20-25 per hour, depending upon the season and your bargaining skill. An experienced boatman can help you and your friends hook, typically, six or eight big fish, which local restaurants are often willing to serve a small banquet for you in return for your extra fish.

Big-game Sportfishing

Zihuatanejo has long been a center for billfish (marlin and swordfish) hunting. Most local captains have organized themselves into cooperatives, which visitors can contact either directly or through town and hotel travel agents. Trips begin around 7 a.m. and return 2-3 p.m. Fishing success depends on seasonal conditions. If you're not sure of prospects, go down to the Zihuatanejo pier around 2:30 and see what the boats are bringing in. During good times they often return with one or more big marlin or swordfish per boat (although captains are increasingly asking that billfish be set free after the battle has been won). Although fierce fighters, the sinewy billfish do not make the best eating. Boats typically bring in two or three other large fish, such as *dorado* (dolphin fish or mahimahi), yellowfin tuna, and roosterfish, all more highly prized for the dinner table. Marlin, and especially swordfish, are often discarded after the pictures are taken.

The biggest local sportfishing outfitter is the blue-and-white fleet of the **Sociedad Cooperativa Teniente Azueta**, named after the naval hero Lieutenant José Azueta. You can see many of their several dozen boats bobbing at anchor adjacent to the Zihuatanejo pier. Arrangements for fishing parties can be made through hotel travel desks or at their office (open daily 6-6, tel. 420-56) at the foot of the pier. The largest 36-foot boats, with four or five lines for a day's fishing, go out for about $250. Twenty-five-foot boats with three lines run about $120 per day.

The smaller (18-boat) **Servicios Sociedad Cooperativa Juarez** tries harder by offering similar boats for lower prices. Their 36-foot boats for six start around $200; their 25-foot for four, about $100. Contact them at their office across from the naval compound near the end of Paseo de Pescador (open daily 9 a.m.-6 p.m, tel. 437-58).

Next door, the private **Servicios Turísticos Aquaticos** also provides boats and captains for similar prices (open daily 9 a.m.-6 p.m., tel. 441-62).

Prices quoted by providers often (but not necessarily) include fishing licenses, bait, tackle, and amenities such as beer, sodas, ice, and on-board toilets. Such details should be pinned down (ideally by seeing the boat) before putting your money down.

Sportfishing Tournament

Twice a year, usually in May and December, Zihuatanejo fisherfolk sponsor a Tourneo de Pez Vela (swordfish tournament), with prizes for the biggest catches of swordfish, marlin, and other varieties. Entrance fee runs around $450, and the prizes usually include a new Dodge pickup, cars, and other goodies. For information, contact the local sportfishing cooperative, Sociedad Cooperativa Teniente José Azueta, Muelle Municipal, Zihuatanejo, Guerrero 40880, tel. (753) 420-56.

Marinas And Boat Launching

Marina Ixtapa, at the north end of Paseo Ixtapa, offers excellent boat facilities. The slip charge runs about $.33 per foot per day, subject to a minimum of about $11 per day. This includes use of the boat ramp, showers, pump-out, electricity, trash collection, mailbox, phone, fax, and satellite TV. Contact them for reservations and info by writing Marina Ixtapa, Ixtapa, Guerrero 40880, or calling them at (753) 321-00 or (753) 301-00, or fax (753) 305-13.

The smooth, gradual Marina Ixtapa **boat ramp,** free to the public, is on the right-side street leading to the water, just before the marina condo complex.

Puerto Mio, Zihuatanejo's small private boat harbor at the end of the western curve of Zihuatanejo Bay, rents boat slips for about $.44 per foot per day. The fee includes toilets, water, electricity, and use of their swimming pool, showers, and adjacent restaurant. The usefulness of Puerto Mio's boat-launching ramp is reduced, however, by its rapid drop-off. Although they state that minimum contract slip-rental period is for six months, they may negotiate if they have extra space (P.O. Box 387, Paseo del Morro, Playa del Almacén, Zihuatanejo, Guerrero 40880, tel. 753-427-40, 753-436-24, 753-437-45).

Sports Equipment Shops

Deportes Naúticos Adidas, corner of N. Bravo and Guerrero in downtown Zihuatanejo, sells snorkel equipment, boogieboards, tennis rackets, balls, and a load of other general sporting goods (open Mon.-Sat. 10-2 and 4-8, tel. 444-11).

Equipo and Embarcaciones, at the pier end of Alvarez, has a more specialized stock of equipment, including fishing tackle, fins and snorkels, waterskis, jet-ski boats, and surfboards (open Mon.-Sat. 9-2 and 4-7, tel. 432-29).

SHOPPING

Zihuatanejo

Every day is market day at the Zihuatanejo **Mercado** (on Av. Benito Juarez, four blocks from the beach). Behind the piles of leafy greens, round yellow papayas, and huge gaping sea bass, don't miss the sugar and spice stalls. There you will find big, raw brown sugar cones,

Fresh fruit is among the big bargains at the Zihuatanejo mercado.

RICK F. WHIPPERMAN

thick golden homemade honey, mounds of fragrant jamaica petals, crimson dried chiles, and forest-gathered roots, barks, and grasses sold in the same pungent natural forms as they have been for centuries.

For more up-to-date merchandise nearby, go to the **Super El Globo** on the side street next to the market (open Mon.-Sat. 8 a.m.-7:30 p.m., Sun. 8-3, tel. 427-40). Although dark and disorganized (air compressors next to baby toys next to dog food), they stock most of what people need, including Cocoa Puffs, Canada Dry, Nucoa, spaghetti, and J & B scotch.

For convenience shopping, the **Super El Dorado,** one block from the beach, is one of the only stores in downtown Zihuatanejo with much food (open daily 9-2 and 4-9, tel. 427-25).

Handicrafts

Zihuatanejo shoppers enjoy a good, reasonable handicrafts selection, available from both a tourist market and a sprinkling of good downtown shops.

The **tourist market** stalls display a flood of crafts brought by families who come from all parts of Pacific Mexico. Their goods—delicate Michoacán lacquerware, bright Tonalá birds, gleaming Taxco silver, whimsical Guerrero masks, rich Guadalajara leather—spread for blocks along Av. Cinco de Mayo on the downtown west side. Compare prices; and although bargaining here is customary, the glut of merchandise makes it a one-sided buyer's market,

with many sellers barely managing to scrape by. If you err in your bargaining, kindly do it on the generous side.

Prominent among **downtown shops** is the **Casa Marina,** a family project of community leader Helen Krebs Posse. She and her adult children and spouses separately own and manage stores in the complex, just west of the plaza.

Helen's store, the **Embarcadero,** on the lower floor, street side, has an unusually choice collection of woven and embroidered finery, mostly from Oaxaca. In addition to walls and racks of colorful, museum-quality traditional blankets, flower-embroidered dresses, and elaborate crocheted *huipiles,* she also offers wooden folk-figurines and a collection of intriguing masks.

Other stores in the Casa Marina complex include **La Zapoteca** on the bottom floor, specializing in weavings from Teotitlán del Valle in Oaxaca. Farther on and upstairs are El Jumil (silver and masks), Latzotil (Mayan art), El Calibria (leather), and the Cafe El Marina (pizza and used paperbacks). Local weavers demonstrate in the Embarcadero and La Zapoteca stores mornings and afternoons (open Mon.-Sat. 9-1 and 4-8, tel. 423-73, credit cards accepted).

Cerámicas Tonalá, a block east, on the opposite side of the plaza, has one of the finest Tonalá pottery collections outside of the renowned source itself (open Mon.-Sat. 9-2 and 4-8, credit cards accepted). Here, graceful glazed vases and plates, decorated in traditional plant and animal designs, fill the cabinets, while a menagerie of lovable owls, ducks, fish, armadillos, and frogs, all seemingly poised to spring to life, crowd the shelves.

A few steps up Cuauhtémoc, across from Banamex, **Ruby's Jewelry** offers an extensive gem, gold, and silver jewelry collection (open Mon.-Sat. 9-2:30 and 4-8:30, tel. 439-90, credit cards accepted). As with gold and precious stones, their silver prices are simply reckoned by weighing, at about $1 per gram. Their cases and cabinets of glittering earrings, chains, bracelets, and rings would be quite sufficient; but striking pieces by noted artists—arresting animal-human figures by Mario Gonzales; Jaime Barba's big, gleaming papier-mâché lions; amethyst, obsidian, agate, and silver Indian busts by Daniel Serrano—add a showy touch of class.

At **Galería Maya** nearby, friendly owners Olivia, Edith, and Tania have accumulated a multitude of one-of-a-kind folk curios from many parts of Mexico. Their wide-ranging, carefully selected collection includes masks, necklaces, sculptures, purses, blouses, *huipiles,* ritual objects, and much more (open Mon.-Sat. 10-2 and 5-9, tel. 446-06, at Nicolas Bravo 31, between Cuauhtémoc and Guerrero).

Guerrero basket

Ixtapa Shopping

Ixtapa's **Centro Comercialías Ixtapa** subcomplex is at the corner of Paseo Las Garzas. Here, the small **Galería Ixtapa,** right on the boulevard, offers an interesting collection of curios, handicrafts, and unique art-to-wear (open Mon.-Sat. 10-2 and 5-8).

Photography

In Zihuatanejo, one-hour photofinishing, popular film varieties, and some photo supplies are available at local Kodak dealer **Super Foto La Palma,** at the corner of Guerrero and Cuauhtémoc four blocks from the beach (open Mon.-Sat. 9-2 and 3:30-8, tel. 433-28).

One-hour develop-and-print, film, and a limited stock of supplies are also available in Ixtapa at **Foto Ixtapa** on Paseo Ixtapa, corner Paseo de las Garzas (open daily 9-8, tel. 314-36, in the Galería Ixtapa shopping complex).

SERVICES

Money Exchange

To change money in Zihuatanejo, go the **Banamex** (Banco Nacional de Mexico) a few doors up Cuauhtémoc from the plaza (open for money exchange Mon.-Fri. 9-11, tel. 421-81).

If the Banamex lines are too long, go next door to the **Casa de Cambio Ballestros** to change U.S., Canadian, French, German, Swiss, and other currencies and traveler's checks. For the convenience, they give you about three percent less for your money than Banamex (open daily 9-2 and 3-8).

In Ixtapa, change money at your hotel desk; or, for better rates, go to **Bancomer** in the El Portal complex behind the shops across the boulevard from the Hotel Stouffer Presidente (open for traveler's checks and currency exchange Mon.-Fri. about 9:30-11:30 a.m., tel. 305-64 and 306-24).

The local **American Express** branch in the Hotel Westin Ixtapa issues and cashes American Express traveler's checks and provides travel agency services to the public. For card-carrying members, they provide full money services, such as check-cashing. The travel agency is open Mon.-Sat. 8-6 and Sun. 8-12; money services hours are approximately 9-5 Mon.-Sat.; call for confirmation, tel. 308-53, fax 312-06).

Post And Telephone

The only **post office** serving both Zihuatanejo and Ixtapa is in Zihuatanejo at Cuauhtémoc 72, five blocks from the beach (open Mon.-Fri. 8-7, Sat. 9-1, tel. 421-92).

The small Maritime Terminal office on the Zihuatanejo pier sells stamps and has a mailbox, long-distance telephone, and public fax (open Mon.-Sat. 9-3).

Downtown Zihuatanejo's private *larga distancia* (long-distance) telephone office also changes both U.S. and Canadian currency and traveler's checks (open daily 8 a.m.-9 p.m., on Galeana, the lane parallel to Cuauhtémoc, corner of Bravo, tel. 428-00).

In Ixtapa, streetside public phone booths handle international long distance calls. For best rates, call collect. Dial * * 0 1 ("star-star-zero-one") for the English-speaking AT&T international operator. The Ixtapa-Zihuatenejo area code is 753.

Immigration And Customs

If you lose your tourist card, go to **Migración** on Alvarez behind the Zihuatanejo plaza-front Palacio Municipal (city hall). Bring your passport and some proof (such as your airline ticket, or a copy of your lost tourist permit) of the date you arrived in Mexico (open Mon.-Fri. 9-3 and 4-9, tel. 427-95).

The **Aduana** (customs) office is at the airport, off Hwy. 200 about seven miles south of Zihuatanejo (open daily 8-7, tel. 432-62). If you have to temporarily leave the country without your car, have someone fluent in Spanish call them about the required paperwork.

Laundries

In Zihuatanejo, do your laundry any hour of the day and night at **Laundry Disney** at Cuauhtémoc 39, five blocks from the beach. If, on the other hand, you haven't time to do it yourself, take it to **Laundry Super Clean** at Gonzales and Galeana, just off Cuauhtémoc, four blocks from the plaza (open Mon.-Sat. 8-8, tel. 423-47).

INFORMATION

Tourist Information Offices

The Ixtapa federal office of **Turismo** (open Mon.-Fri. 9-3 in the La Puerta shopping complex, across the boulevard from the Hotel Presidente) appears to function more as a regulatory agency rather than an information office. In Ixtapa, try the travel agent in your hotel lobby instead.

An excellent alternative local information source is the **Camara de Comercio** (chamber of commerce) in downtown Zihuatanejo. Friendly director Gilda Soberanis and her staff are ready and able to answer questions, suggest contacts, and provide whatever local maps and literature they have (open Mon.-Fri. 9-2 and 4-7, on Bravo, near corner of Guerrero, tel. 425-75).

Hospital, Police, And Emergencies

Zihuatanejo has good hospitals and doctors. For daytime medical office visits or 24-hour emergencies, go to the private **Sanitario de la Salud** (tel. 447-46) on the downtown corner of Cuauhtémoc and Nava. They have many on-call specialists, including dentists, and a 24-hour **pharmacy.**

Similar round-the-clock services in Zihuatanejo are available at the **Hospital Privado** of Dr. Arturo H. Montenegro (corner Juarez and Bravo, tel. 439-91 and 430-70).

Routine medicines and drugs are available at a number of pharmacies on Cuauhtémoc in downtown Zihuatanejo (such as the **Farmacia Zihuatanejo,** at Cuauhtémoc 10, one block from the plaza, tel. 420-30).

For medicines and drugs in Ixtapa, try your hotel shop, or call the **Farmacia Ixtapa** (in the shopping complex across from the Hotel Presidente, tel. 307-87).

For **police emergencies** in Ixtapa and Zihuatanejo, contact the *caberca de policía* headquarters in Zihuatanejo, on Calle Limón near the post office, tel. 420-40. You can also go directly to the *caseta de policía* on-duty police booth behind the Zihuatanejo plaza-front city hall, or the same in Ixtapa on the boulevard across from the Hotel Presidente.

Books, Newspapers, And Magazines

The best local English-language selection lines the many shelves in the bookshop of the **Hotel Westin Ixtapa.** Besides dozens of new paperback novels and scores of popular U.S. magazines, they stock *USA Today* and the *News* of Mexico City newspapers and a thoughtful selection of Mexico guides and books of cultural and historical interest (open daily 9-9).

The newsstand (open daily 8-8) on Zihuatanejo plaza is a source of some popular U.S. magazines, such as *Vogue, Time,* and *Sports Illustrated,* plus the newspapers *News* of Mexico (around 9 a.m.) and *USA Today* (after 11 a.m.). A similar small selection is available at the newsstand on Cuauhtémoc, two blocks from the plaza, corner of Ejido (open daily 8-7).

The friendly small Zihuatanejo bookstore **Librería Byblos,** despite its mainly Spanish inventory, does have a shelf of used English-language paperbacks. They also stock English-Spanish dictionaries and a good map of Guerrero (open Mon.-Sat. 10-3 and 5-10, Sun. 5-10 at Asencio 11, off Cuauhtémoc, one block from the plaza, tel. 422-81). More used paperbacks line the walls of friendly **Cafe Marina** adjacent to the beach just west of the plaza (open Mon.-Sat. noon-10 p.m., closed May 1-July 31).

The small Zihuatanejo **Biblioteca** (public library) also has some shelves of English-language paperbacks (open Mon.-Fri. 9-1 and 4-7, Sat. 9-2, Sun. 9-1, on Cuauhtémoc, at the little plaza five blocks from the beach).

Ecological Association And Humane Society
The grassroots **Asociación de Ecologistas** sponsors local cleanup, save-the-turtles, and other projects. The president, Jorge Luis Reyes (tel. 437-04), and a cadre of community leaders, including Anita Rellstab, owner of Bungalows Pacifico (tel. 421-12), and marine biologist Juan M. Barnard Avila, owner of Zihuatanejo Scuba Center are dedicated to preserving the Ixtapa-Zihuatanejo coast. Look for their new office on Cuauhtémoc near the library. They welcome volunteers to join their efforts.

Helen Krebs Posse is the guiding light of the **Sociedad Protectora de Animales,** which is working hard to establish a local center for the care of neglected and abandoned animals. Contact her at her shop, Embarcadero, just west of the Zihuatanejo plaza (tel. 423-73).

GETTING THERE AND AWAY

By Air
Three major carriers connect Ixtapa-Zihuatanejo directly with U.S. and Mexican destinations.

Aeromexico flights connect with **Houston** directly via Mexico City on Mondays, Wednesdays, and Fridays. Many other flights connect directly with Mexico City. For flight information, call 422-37; for reservations, phone 420-18.

Mexicana Airlines flights connect directly with **Los Angeles** via Guadalajara daily. For flight information, call 422-37; for reservations, tel. 322-08.

Delta Airlines flights connect directly with **Los Angeles** Wednesdays, Saturdays, and Sundays. For flight information and reservations, call 433-83.

Air Arrival And Departure
Ixtapa-Zihuatanejo is quickly accessible, only seven miles (11 km) north of the airport via Hwy. 200. Arrival is generally simple, if you come with a day's worth of pesos and hotel reservations. The terminal has no money exchange, information booth, or hotel-reservation service. It's best not to leave your hotel choice up to your taxi driver, for he will probably deposit you at the hotel that pays him a commission on your first night's lodging.

Transportation to town is usually by taxi or *colectivo* van. Tickets, good for anywhere in Ixtapa-Zihuatanejo, are available at booths near the terminal exit for about $6 per person for a *colectivo* or $18 for three persons in a taxi. Mobile **budget travelers** can walk the few hundred yards to the highway and flag down one of the frequent daytime Zihuatanejo-bound buses (very few, if any, of which continue to Ixtapa, however). At night, ride a *colectivo*.

Several major **car rentals** operate airport booths. Avoid problems and save money by negotiating your rental through the agencies' toll-free yellow-page 800 numbers before departure: Hertz (tel. 430-50; or at Hotel Ixtapa Plaza, tel. 310-66, ext. 300); Dollar (tel. 423-14; or at the Sheraton, tel. 318-58; Dorado Pacifico, tel. 320-25; Krystal tel. 303-33); Econo (tel. 443-50; Ixtapa Palace, tel. 305-30); Avis (tel. 429-32); and Budget (Zihuatanejo tel. 448-37, Ixtapa tel. 321-62, 321-88).

Departure is quick and easy if you have your passport, tourist permit (which was stamped on arrival), and $12 cash (or the equivalent in pesos) international departure tax. Departees who've lost their tourist permits can avoid trouble and a fine by either getting a duplicate at Zihuatanejo Immigration (see "Information" above) or (perhaps) by having a police report of the loss.

For last-minute postcards and shopping, the airport has a mailbox and a few gift shops.

By Car Or RV

Three routes, two easy and one difficult, connect Ixtapa-Zihuatanejo with Playa Azul and Michoacán to the northwest, Ciudad Altamirano and central Guerrero to the east, and Acapulco southeast.

Traffic sails smoothly along the 76 miles (122 km) of Hwy. 200, either way, between Zihuatanejo and Lázaro Cárdenas/Playa Azul. The same is true of the 150-mile (242-km) Hwy. 200 southern extension to Acapulco. Allow about two and a half hours to or from Playa Azul, four hours to or from Acapulco.

The story is much different, however, for the winding, lonely cross-Sierra Hwy. 134 (intersecting with Hwy. 200 nine miles north) between Zihuatanejo and Ciudad Altamirano. Rising along spectacular, jungle-clad ridges, the paved but sometimes potholed road leads over cool, pine-clad heights and descends to the Altamirano high valley after about 100 miles (160 km). The continuing leg to Iguala on the Acapulco-Mexico City highway is longer, about 112 miles (161 km), equally winding and often busy. For safety, allow about eight hours westbound and nine hours eastbound for the entire trip. Keep filled with gasoline, and be prepared for emergencies, especially along the Altamirano-Zihuatanejo leg, where no hotels and few services exist.

By Bus

Zihuatanejo's big, shiny long-distance **Central de Autobus** (central bus terminal) is on Hwy. 200, Acapulco-bound side, about a mile south of downtown Zihuatanejo. Travelers enjoy a restaurant-cafeteria, a public long-distance phone, left-luggage lockers, and a snack stand (but no food store). You'd best prepare by stocking up with water and goodies before you depart.

Estrella Blanca (EB, tel. 434-77), the major carrier, computer-coordinates its service with the service of its subsidiaries Flecha Roja (FR) and Transportes Cuauhtémoc. Tickets are available for all departures from computer-assisted agents. In total, they offer primera plus (infrequent, super-first-class, reserved), first-class (frequent, reserved), and second-class (very frequent, unreserved) service.

Most buses run along the Hwy. 200 corridor, connecting with Lázaro Cárdenas/Playa Azul and northwestern points, and with Acapulco and points south and east.

Dozens of primera-plus and first-class buses and many (every 20 minutes) second-class buses connect daily with Acapulco. Many of them continue to Mexico City. In the opposite direction, many primera-plus and first-class buses and second-class buses (at least one an hour) connect daily with Lázaro Cárdenas/Playa Azul and northwest points.

One first-class bus connects directly with the U.S. border (Nuevo Laredo) daily. One first-class bus connects northward with Michoacán (Morelia) via Ciudad Altamirano daily.

Major bus carrier **Estrella de Oro** (tel. 438-02) and its subsidiary lines offer competing long-distance service from their station on Paseo del Palmar, four blocks from Plaza Kyoto. Try them if you can't get satisfactory connections through Estrella Blanca.

ALONG THE ROAD TO ACAPULCO

Although the 150-mile (242 km) Zihuatanejo-Acapulco stretch of Hwy. 200 is smooth and easy, resist the temptation to hurry through. Your reward will be a string of bright little pearls—idyllic south-seas villages, miles of strollable, fishable beaches, wildlife-rich *esteros,* gorgeous small hotels, and a tranquil little beach resort on the hidden edge of Acapulco.

On The Road

If you're driving, mark your odometer at the Zihuatanejo southside Pemex, near Km 240 on Hwy. 200. (Or, if driving north, do the same at the Acapulco *zócalo* (old town square) Km Zero, and head out on the northbound coast road past Pie de la Cuesta. (See the Acapulco map.) Road mileages and kilometer markers are helpful in finding the paths to hidden little beaches.

Bus travelers, take a second-class bus from Zihuatanejo (or from Acapulco) Estrella Blanca Central de Autobus. Ask the driver to drop you at your chosen haven.

PLAYA LAS POZAS

This surf-fishing paradise is reachable via the Zihuatanejo airport turnoff road. The reward is a lagoon full of bait fish, space for RV or tent camping (be careful of soft sand), a wide beach, and friendly beachside palapa restaurants.

The beach itself is 100 yards wide, of yellow-white sand, and extends for miles in both directions. It has driftwood but not many shells. Fish thrive in its thunderous, open-ocean waves. Consequently, casts from the beach can routinely yield five- and 10-pound catches by either bait or lures. Local folks catch fish mostly by net, both in the surf and the nearby lagoon. During the June-Sept. rainy season, the lagoon breaks through the bar. Big fish, gobbling prey at the outlet, can be netted or hooked at the same spot themselves.

Camping is popular here on weekends and holidays. Other times you may have the place to yourself. As a courtesy, ask the friendly Netos family (who runs the best of the palapa restaurants) if it's okay.

Get there by following the well-marked airport turnoff road at Km 230. After one mile, turn right at the cyclone fence just before the terminal and follow the bumpy but easily passable straight level road 1.1 miles (1.8 km) to the beach.

BARRA DE POTOSÍ

Nine miles (15 km) south of Zihuatanejo, a sign points right to Barra de Potosí, a picture-perfect fishing hamlet at the sheltered south end of the Bahía de Potosí. After a few miles through green, tufted groves, the road parallels the bayside beach, a crescent of fine white sand, virtually undeveloped except for one hotel.

The **Hotel Condominios Barra de Potosí** perches right on the beach. With eight apartments (with hot water and fans), a pretty beachfront pool, palms, a bar, and a restaurant, it appears perfect for a tranquil week's rest. Reservations are probably necessary only during the post-Christmas and pre-Easter weeks; try writing for information at simply Barra de Potosí, Guerrero.

The surf is generally tranquil and safe for swimming near the hotel, although the waves, which do not roll but rather break quickly along long fronts, are not good for surfing.

The waves become even more tranquil at the south end, where a sheltering headland rises beyond the village and the lagoon. Beneath its swaying palm grove, the hamlet of Barra de Potosí (pop. about 1,000) has the ingredients for weeks of tranquil living. Several broad, hammock-hung palapa restaurants (here called *enramadas)* front the bountiful lagoon.

Home for swarms of birds and waterfowl and shoals of fish, the **Laguna de Potosí** stretches for miles to its far mangrove reaches. Adventure out with your own boat or kayak, or go with **Orlando,** who regularly takes parties out for fishing or wildlife-viewing tours.

Bait fish (caught locally with nets) abound in the lagoon. Fishing is fine for bigger catches (jack, snapper, mullet, mojarra) by boat or casts

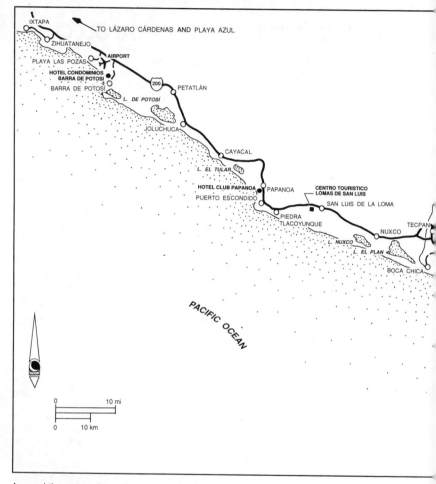

beyond the waves. Launch your boat easily in the lagoon, then head, like the local fishermen, past the open sandbar.

Camping is common by RV or tent along the uncrowded edge of the lagoon. Village stores can provide basic supplies.

Get there by taking the signed turnoff road at Km 225 (nine miles south of Zihuatanejo) just south of the Los Achotes River bridge. Continue along the good (trailer-accessible) dirt road for 5.5 miles (8.9 km) to the hotel and the village half a mile farther south.

PAPANOA

The small town of Papanoa (pop. 2,000) straddles the highway 47 miles (75 km) south of Zihuatanejo and 103 miles (165 km) north of Acapulco. Local folks tell the tongue-in-cheek story of its Hawaiian-sounding name. It seems that there was a flood, and the son of the local headman had to talk fast to save his life by escaping in a *canoa*. Instead of saying "Papa . . . canoa," the swift-talking boy shortened his plea to "Papa . . . noa."

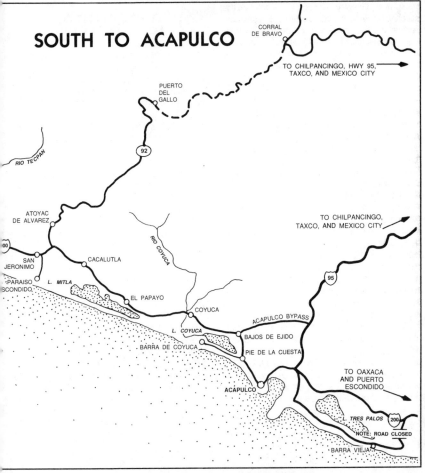

The town itself has a few snack restaurants, a pharmacy, groceries, and Estrella Blanca and Tres Estrellas de Oro first-class bus stops; also, a long-distance telephone, regular leaded gas for sale, and one resort-style lodging, the **Hotel Club Papanoa** (Papanoa, Guerrero 40907, tel. 742-704-50, local ext. 13).

Near the beach about a mile south of town, the hotel has about 30 large rooms, a restaurant, and a big pool set in spacious ocean-view garden grounds. The phone (local extension 13) often doesn't work, however. Intended to be

luxurious but now a bit scruffy around the edges, the hotel remains popular on weekends and holidays, but is nearly empty most other times. Rooms run about $33 s, $44 for two to four, with hot water and fans.

The hotel grounds adjoin the beach, **Playa Cayaquitos.** The wide, breezy, yellow-gray strand stretches for two miles, washed by powerful open-ocean rollers with good left and right surfing breaks. Additional attractions include surf fishing beyond the breakers and driftwood along the sand. Beach access is via the off-highway driveway just north of the hotel. At the beach, a parking lot borders a seafood restaurant. Farther on, the road narrows (but is still motor home accessible) through a defunct beachside home development, past several brush-bordered informal RV parking or tenting spots.

PIEDRA TLACOYUNQUE

At Km 150 (56 miles, 90 km from Zihuatanejo, 94 miles from Acapulco) a signed side road heads seaward to Piedra Tlacoyunque and the Carabelas Restaurant. One mile down the good dirt road, the restaurant appears, perching on a bluff overlooking a monumental sandstone rock, Piedra Tlacoyunque. Below, a wave-tossed strand, ripe for beachcombing and surf fishing, stretches for miles. Powerful breakers with fine right-hand surfing angles roll in and swish up the steep beach. For fishing, buy some bait from the net fishermen on the beach and try some casts beyond the billows crashing into the south side of the Piedra. Later, stroll through the garden of sea stacks on the north side. there you can poke among the snails and seaweeds in a big sheltered tidepool, under the watchful guard of the squads of pelicans roosting on the surrounding pinnacles.

At the **Carabelas Restaurant** on the bluff above, you can take in the whole breezy scene while enjoying the recommended catch of the day. For an overnight or a short stay, ask the restaurant owners if it's okay to park your (self-contained) RV in the restaurant lot or in the beach-level grove down below.

CENTRO TURISTICO LOMAS DE SAN LUIS

Little was spared to embellish this pretty haciendalike corner of a big mango, papaya, and coconut grove. It appears as if the owner, tiring of all work and no play, built a park to entertain his friends. Now, his project blooms with lovely swimming and kiddie pools, a big palapa restaurant, a smooth palapa-covered dance floor, a small zoo, basketball and volleyball courts, and an immaculate small hotel.

Ideal for an overnight or a respite from hard Mexico traveling, the five hotel rooms rent from about $27 with a/c and hot water, credit cards accepted. If you'll be arriving on a weekend or holiday, write them for a reservation: Centro Turistico Lomas de San Luis, Carretera Zihuatanejo-Acapulco, Km 142, San Luis de la Loma, Guerrero 40906.

They are located on the southbound side of the road near Km 142, 61 miles (98 km) south of Zihuatanejo, 89 miles north of Acapulco.

San Luis De La Loma

The pleasant little town of San Luis de la Loma (pop. 5,000) runs along a hilltop main street that angles off Hwy. 200 near Km 140. Besides a number of groceries and pharmacies, they have a Centro de Salud (health center), a *larga distancia* (long-distance telephone), a dentist, a clinical analysis lab, and a Somex bank (traveler's checks cashed Mon.-Fri. 9-11 a.m. on the main

Pelicans, tide pools, a garden of sandstone, and gourmet surf fishing attract adventurers to Playa Piedra Tlacoyunque.

square a quarter mile from the highway). First-class buses also stop and pick up passengers there on the highway.

BOCA CHICA

For the fun and adventure of it, visit Boca Chica, a beach village accessible by boat only. Here, camping is *de rigueur*, since even permanent residents are doing it. (It makes no sense to pour concrete on a sandbar where palm fronds are free and the next wave may wash everything away anyway.)

The jumping-off spot is near Km 98 (88 miles, 142 km south of Zihuatanejo, 61 miles north of Acapulco), where a sign marks the dirt road to Tetitlán (pop. 2,000). Pass through the town (long-distance phone, pharmacy, groceries) within three miles, and continue to road's end at Laguna Tecpan. Here, launches will ferry you across to the village on the sandbar about a mile across the lagoon. Bargain the *viaje redondo* (return-trip) price with your boatman before you depart (unless, of course you have your own kayak or boat).

On the other side, the waves thunder upon the beach and sand crabs guard their holes, while the village's four separate societies—people, dogs, pigs, and chickens—each go about their distinct business. Shells and driftwood decorate the sand, and surf fishing with bait from the lagoon couldn't be better.

Most visitors come for the eating only: super-fresh seafood charcoal-broiled in one of the dozen palapas along the beach. If, however, you plan to camp overnight, bring drinking water, a highly prized Boca Chica commodity.

During the summer rainy season, the Tecpan River, which feeds the lagoon, breaks through the bar. Ocean fish enter the lagoon, and the river current sometimes washes Boca Chica, palapas and all, out to sea.

PIE DE LA CUESTA

"Foot of the Hill," the translation of the name Pie de la Cuesta, well describes this downscale resort village. Tucked around the bend from Acapulco, between a wide beach and placid Laguna Coyuca, Pie de la Cuesta appeals to those who want the excitement that the big town offers and the tranquility it doesn't.

Laguna Coyuca, kept full by the sweet waters of the Río Coyuca, has long been known for its fish, birdlife, and tranquil, palm-lined shores. During the early 1400s, the Tarascans (who ruled from the Michoacán highlands) established a provincial capital near the town of Coyuca nearby. After the Aztecs drove out the Tarascans a century later (and the Aztecs in turn were defeated by the Spanish) Pie de la Cuesta and its beautiful Laguna Coyuca slumbered in the shadow of Acapulco.

Sights

Laguna de Coyuca is a large sandy-bottomed lake, lined by palms and laced by mangrove channels. It stretches 10 miles along the shoreline, west from Pie de la Cuesta, which occupies the southeast (Acapulco) side. The barrier beach-sandbar, wide Playa Pie de la Cuesta, separates the lagoon from the ocean. It extends a dozen miles west to the river outlet, which is open to the sea only during the rainy season. A road runs along the beach west the length of Laguna Coyuca to the tourist hamlet of Barra de Coyuca. There, palapas line the beach and serve seafood to busloads of Sunday visitors.

Playa Pie de la Cuesta, a seemingly endless, hundred-yard-wide stretch of yellow sand, is fine for surf fishing, beachcombing, jogging, and long sunset walks. Its powerful open-ocean waves are unsuited for either surfing or swimming, however. They break thunderously near the sand and recede with strong, turbulent undertow.

On the other side of the bar, the east end of Laguna Coyuca is an embarkation point for lagoon tours and center for waterskiing and jet-skiing. Among the best equipped of the shoreline clubs that offer powerboat services is the **Restaurant and Club de Skis Tres Marías.** Besides a pleasant lake-view shoreline palapa restaurant, they offer waterskiing at about $35/hour and jet-ski boats for about $50/hour.

If, however, you want to launch your own boat, you can do so easily at Club Tres Marias and others for about $10. The boat traffic (which confines itself mostly to midlagoon) does not deter **swimming** in the lagoon's clear waters. Slip on your bathing suit and jump in anywhere along the sandy shoreline.

Lagoon tours begin from several landings dotting the Pie de la Cuesta end of the lagoon. Half-day regular excursions (maximum 10 persons, about $14 apiece) push off daily at around

11 a.m., noon, and 1:30 p.m. Along the way, they pass islands with trees loaded with nesting cormorants, herons, and pelicans. In midlake, gulls dip and sway in the breeze behind your boat while a host of storks, ducks, avocets, and a dozen other varieties paddle, preen, and forage in the water nearby. Other times, your boat passes through winding channels hung with vines and lined with curtains of great mangrove roots. At midpoint, tours usually stop for a bite to eat at Isla Montosa. Here, roosters crow, pigs root, bougainvillea blooms, and a colony of fishing families live, unencumbered by 20th-century conveniences, beneath their majestic shoreline palm grove.

On another day, drive or ride one of the frequent buses that head from Pie de la Cuesta to **Barra de Coyuca** village at the west end of the lagoon. Along the way, you will pass several scruffy hamlets and a parade of fenced lots, some still open meadows where horses graze while others are filled with trees and big houses. Lack of potable water, local residents complain, is a continuing problem on this dry sandbar.

At road's end, 10 miles from Pie de la Cuesta, a few tourist stores, a platoon of T-shirt vendors, and hammock-equipped beach palapa restaurants serve holiday crowds. Boats head for tours from lagoonside, where patrons at the Restaurant Dos Vistas enjoy a double view of both beach and lagoon.

Accommodations And Food

Around a dozen basic bungalows, *casas de huéspedes* (guesthouses), and hotels line the Pie de la Cuesta's single beachside road. Competition keeps cleanliness high, management sharp, and prices low. They all cluster along a quarter mile of roadfront, enjoying highly visible location that extend directly to the beach. None of them have phones and few accept credit cards. Write for reservations, especially for the winter season and holidays. Shower water is generally room-temperature tepid. If heated, it's noted below.

In order of increasing price, first comes **Casa de Huéspedes Leonor,** which is very popular with a loyal cadre of Canadian winter returnees (63 Carretera Pie de la Cuesta, Guerrero 39900). They enjoy camaraderie around the tables of the palapa restaurant that occupies the beachside end of a large leafy parking-lot gar-

den. The several breezy more private upper-floor units are most popular. All ten rooms have two beds, showers, and fans, and rent for about $17 d daily, $14 monthly.

More picturesque rustic are the **Bungalows Maria Cristina,** nine units (six rooms, three kitchen-equipped bungalows) set between a streetside parking lot and a palmy beachside restaurant-garden. The very plain rooms, with toilets and showers, rent for about $17 d. The most charming of the bungalows is a big, breezy, and private upper-level unit sheltered beneath a thatched palapa roof for about $47. Negotiate for low-season and long-term discounts. (P.O. Box 607, Acapulco, Guerrero 39300.)

Guests at the **Hotel and Restaurant Casa Blanca** enjoy a tranquil, car-free tropical garden and restaurant and careful feminine management (P.O. Box 153, Acapulco, Guerrero 39300). The 10 very clean rooms, with ruffled bedspreads, toilets, and showers are a bargain at about $10 s, $17 d, $24 t. Discounts may be available for monthly rental.

Husband-wife (he Canadian, she Mexican) owner-managers account for the relaxed atmosphere of the new-age **Villa Nirvana** (302 Playa Pie de la Cuesta, P.O. Box 950, Acapulco, Guerrero 39300). Additional pluses include a big blue pool at the beach end of a lovely high-fenced garden. Cars park inside the fence. Rooms occupy two stories on one side of the garden, upper floors being more private. Rooms (two with hot water) rent for about $24 d, with fans. Discounts for monthly rentals run 15-20%.

At the top among Pie de la Cuesta accommodations is the **Hotel Club Puesta del Sol,** where guests enjoy a good restaurant, a blue pool, and a tennis court within spacious, sculpture-decorated garden grounds (P.O. Box 1264, Acapulco, Guerrero 39300). Tasty food from the kitchen of the amiable comanager and friendly hours spent around the restaurant tables account for the hotel's loyal North American, European, and Mexican clientele. The 24 Spartan but clean and tastefully furnished rooms are spread among two double-story buildings, one at beachfront. Rooms away from the beach run about $20 s or d; on the beach, $25 s or d; kitchen-equipped bungalows go for about $50 for four; all rooms have fans, warm-water showers, and include parking.

Trying hard to be luxurious is the **Ukae Kim Hotel Club de Playa y Ski** (Playa Pie de la Cuesta 336, Pie de la Cuesta, Guerrero 39900). Unfortunately, the builder crammed the 31 rooms into a small space, rendering them private but dark. Their brochure advertises massage, but when questioned they admit they don't have it. Amenities include a small but artful pool and palapa restaurant at the hotel's beachfront end. They also have a water-sports marina across the street, which provides waterskiing for $50 per hour. For maximum light, try for an upper, sea-front room. The clean, tastefully decorated rooms go for about $43 s or d; $60 for more luxury with jacuzzi; with hot water; credit cards accepted.

Pie de la Cuesta has two trailer parks. Most popular is the long-standing **Acapulco Trailer Park,** with about 60 palm-shaded lagoon- and beachside spaces with all hookups (P.O. Box 1, Acapulco, Guerrero 39300). A friendly atmosphere, good management, and many extras, including a good fence and gate keep the place full all winter. Facilities include a boat ramp, a store, a security guard, and clean restrooms and showers. Spaces rent (low season) for about $10 beach side, $9 lagoon side; one free day per week. Get your winter reservation in early.

Nearby is the **Trailer Park Quinta Dora,** with 36 spaces beneath a majestic lagoon-side grove (P.O. Box 1093, Acapulco, Guerrero 39300). With neither gate nor fence, however, security has been a problem here. Their 15 all-hookup spaces go for about $13 ($15 for a/c power) for two persons. Spaces without sewer rent for about $10. Camping runs $8. Discounts are available for long-term stays; with showers, toilets, and restaurant.

The **security guard** at the Acapulco Trailer Park is a reminder of former times, when muggings and theft were occurring with some frequency on Playa Pie de la Cuesta. Although bright new night lights on the beach and a local police station have greatly reduced the problem, local folks still warn against camping or walking on the beach at night.

As for **food,** most folks either do their own cooking, eat at their Pie de la Cuesta lodgings, or go into Acapulco. Of the very few eateries along the Pie de la Cuesta road, the best is the lakeview palapa of the Club de Skis Tres Marias (see above).

Information And Services

Nearly all services are concentrated twenty minutes away in Acapulco. Pie de la Cuesta does nevertheless have a small *policía* (police) station and a *larga distancia* (long-distance) telephone office (tel. 748-356-18) near the intersection of the Pie de la Cuesta road and the highway to Acapulco.

Getting There And Away

Pie de la Cuesta is accessible via the fork from Hwy. 200 near Km 10, 144 miles (232 km) southwest of Zihuatanejo. First-class buses drop passengers at the roadside, where they can either walk, taxi, or ride one of the very frequent Acapulco microbuses half a mile to the hotels.

From the same intersection, Acapulco is six miles (10 km) by car, taxi ($5), or local bus.

ACAPULCO AND INLAND TO TAXCO

ACAPULCO

All over Mexico and half the world, Acapulco (pop. 1,500,000) means merrymaking, good food, and palmy, wave-washed beaches. Despite 50 years of continuous development, its reputation is as deserved as ever. The many Acapulcos—the turquoise bay, edged by golden sands and emerald hills, the host of hotels, humble and grand, the spontaneous entertainments, the colorful market, and shady old town square—continue to draw millions of yearly visitors from all over the world.

HISTORY

Before Columbus
Despite its modern facade, Acapulco has been well known as a traveler's crossroads for at least a millennium. Its name comes from the Nahuatl (Aztec) words that mean "place of dense reeds."

The earliest-discovered local remains, stone metates and pottery utensils, were left behind by seaside residents around 2500 B.C. Much later, sophisticated artisans fashioned curvaceous female figurines, which archaeologists unearthed at Las Sabanas near Acapulco during the mid-20th century. Those unique finds added fuel to speculation of early Polynesian or Asian influences in Pacific Mexico as early as 1,500 years before Columbus.

Other discoveries, however, resemble artifacts found in highland Mexico. Although undoubtedly influenced by Tarascan, Mixtec, Zapotec, and Aztec civilizations and frequented by their traders, Acapulco never came under their direct control, but instead remained subject to local chieftains until the conquest.

hieroglyph of Acapulco

Conquest And Colonization

The Aztecs had scarcely surrendered when Cortés sent expeditions south to build ships and find a route to China. The first such explorers sailed out from Zacatula, near present-day Lázaro Cárdenas on the coast 250 miles northwest of Acapulco. They returned, telling Cortés of Acapulco Bay. By a royal decree dated April 25, 1528, "Acapulco and her land . . . where the ships of the south will be built . . . " passed directly into the hands of the Spanish Crown.

Voyages of discovery set sail from Acapulco for Peru, the Gulf of California, and to Asia. None returned from the across the Pacific, however, however, until Father Andrés de Urdaneta discovered the northern Pacific tradewinds, which propelled him and his ship, loaded with Chinese treasure, to Acapulco in 1565.

From then on, for more than 200 years, a special yearly trading ship, the *Nao de China,* the Manila Galleon, set sail from Acapulco for the Orient. Its return sparked an annual merchant fair, swelling Acapulco's population with traders jostling to bargain for the Manila Galleon's shiny trove of silks, porcelain, ivory, and lacquerware.

Acapulco's yearly treasure soon attracted marauders, too. In 1579, Francis Drake threatened, and in 1587, off Cabo San Lucas, Thomas Cavendish was the first to capture the Manila Galleon, the *Santa Anna.* The cash booty alone, 1.2 million gold pesos, severely depressed the London gold market.

After a Dutch fleet invaded Acapulco in 1615, the Spanish rebuilt their fort, which they christened Fort San Diego in 1617. Destroyed by an earthquake in 1776, the fort was rebuilt by 1783. But Mexico's War of Independence (1810-21)

stopped the Manila Galleon forever, sending Acapulco into a century-long slumber.

Modern Acapulco

In 1927, the government paved the Mexico City-Acapulco road; the first cars arrived on Nov. 11. The first luxury hotel, the Mirador, at La Quebrada, went up in 1933; soon airplanes began arriving. During the 1940s President Miguel Alemán (1946-52) fell in love with Acapulco and thought everyone else should have the same opportunity. He built new boulevards, power plants, and a superhighway. Investors responded with a lineup of high-rise hosteleries. Finally, in 1959, presidents Eisenhower and Adolfo López Mateos convened their summit conference in a grand Acapulco hotel.

Thousands of Mexicans flocked to fill jobs in the shiny hotels and restaurants. They built shantytowns, which climbed the hills and spilled over into previously sleepy communities nearby. The government responded with streets, drainage, power, and schools. By the 1990s more than a million people were calling Acapulco home.

SIGHTS

Getting Oriented

In one tremendous sweep, Acapulco curves around its big half-moon bay. Face the open ocean and you are looking south. West will be on your right hand, east on your left. One continuous beachfront boulevard, appropriately named the **Costera Miguel Alemán** (the "Costera," for short), unites old Acapulco, west of Parque Papagayo amusement zone, with new Acapulco, the lineup of big beach hotels that stretches around the bay to the Las Brisas condo headland. There, during the night, a big cross glows and marks the hilltop lookout, Mirador La Capilla, above the bay's east end.

On the opposite, old-town side of Parque Papagayo, the Costera curves along the palmy, uncluttered *playas* Hornos and Hamacas to the steamship dock. Here the Costera, called the *malecón* as it passes the *zócalo* (town square), continues to the mansion-dotted hilly jumble of **Peninsula de las Playas.**

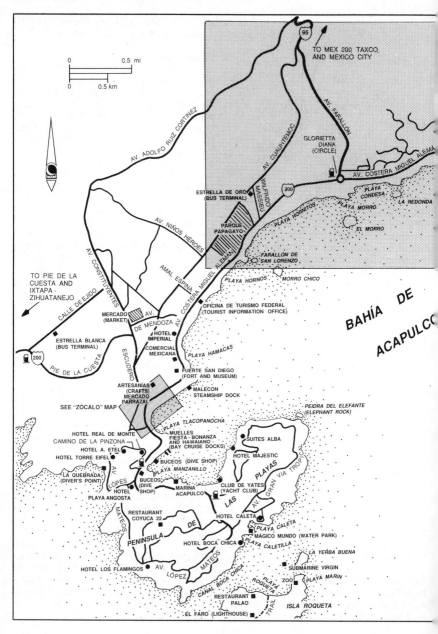

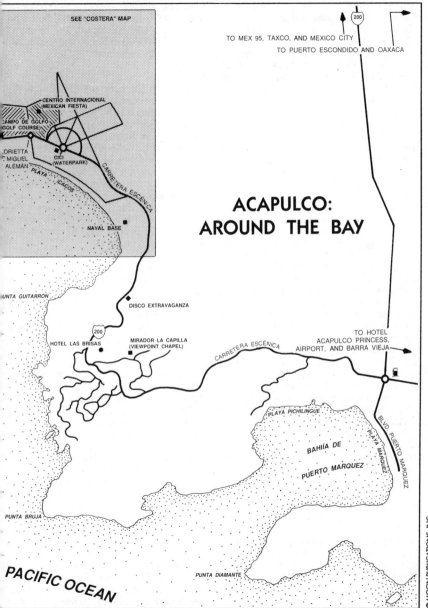

SEE "COSTERA" MAP

TO MEX 95, TAXCO, AND MEXICO CITY
TO PUERTO ESCONDIDO AND OAXACA

CENTRO INTERNACIONAL
(MEXICAN FIESTA)

CAMPO DE GOLFO
(GOLF COURSE)

GORIETTA
MIGUEL
ALEMÁN

CICI
(WATERPARK)

PLAYA ICACOS

CARRETERA ESCÉNICA

NAVAL BASE

ACAPULCO:
AROUND THE BAY

PUNTA GUITARRÓN

DISCO EXTRAVAGANZA

HOTEL LAS BRISAS

MIRADOR LA CAPILLA
(VIEWPOINT CHAPEL)

CARRETERA ESCÉNICA

TO HOTEL
ACAPULCO PRINCESS,
AIRPORT, AND BARRA VIEJA

PLAYA PICHILINGUE

BAHÍA DE
PUERTO MÁRQUEZ

BLVD PUERTO MÁRQUEZ

PLAYA MÁRQUEZ

PUNTA BRUJA

PUNTA DIAMANTE

PACIFIC OCEAN

© MOON PUBLICATIONS, INC.

Getting Around

Buses run nearly continuously along the Costera. Fare averages the equivalent of about $.20, rarely more than $.40. Bus routes—indicated by such labels as "Base" (BAH-say, the naval base on the east end), "Centro" *(zócalo),* "Caleta" (the beach, at the far west end), "Cine" (movie theater near the beach before the *zócalo),* "Hornos" (the beach near Parque Papagayo)—run along the Costera.

Taxis, on the other hand, cost between $2 and $5 for any in-town destination. They are not metered, so agree upon the price *before* you get in. If the driver demands too much, hailing another taxi often solves the problem.

A Walk Around Old Acapulco

In old Acapulco, traffic slows and people return to traditional ways. Couples promenade along the *malecón* dockfront, fishing boats leave and return, while in the adjacent *zócalo* families stroll past the church, musicians play, and tourists and businessmen sip coffee in the shade of huge banyan trees.

Start your walk beneath those *zócalo* trees. Under their pendulous air roots, browse the bookstalls, relax in one of the cafes; at night, watch the clowns perform, listen to a band concert, or join in a pitch-penny game. Take a look inside the mod-style **cathedral** dedicated to Our Lady of Solitude. Admire its angel-filled sky-blue ceiling and visit the Virgin to the right of the altar.

Outside, cross the boulevard to the *malecón* dockside; in midafternoon, you may see huge marlin and swordfish being hauled up from the boats.

Head out of the *zócalo* and left along the Costera past the steamship dock a few blocks to the 18th-century fort, **Fuerte San Diego,** atop its bayside hill (open Tues.-Sun. 10:30-4:30). Engineer Miguel Costansó completed the massive, five-pointed maze of moats, walls, and battlements in 1783.

Inside, galleries within the original fort storerooms, barracks, chapel, and kitchen illustrate local pre-Columbian, conquest, and colonial history. The excellent, unusually graphic displays include much about pirates (such as Francis Drake and John Hawkins, known as "admirals" to the English-speaking world); Spanish galleons, their history and construction; and famous visitors, notably Japanese Captain

Hasekura, who in 1613 built a ship and sailed from Sendai, Japan, to Acapulco; thence he continued overland to Mexico City, by sea to Spain, to the Pope in Rome, and back again through Acapulco to Japan.

La Quebrada

Head back to the *zócalo* and continue past the cathedral. After three short blocks to Av. López Mateos, continue uphill to the La Quebrada diver's point, marked by the big parking lot at the hillcrest. There, Acapulco's energy focuses five times a day (at 1 p.m and evenings hourly 7:30-10:30) as tense crowds watch the divers plummet more than a hundred feet to the waves below. (Admission is about $1.50, collected by the divers' cooperative. Performers average about $100 per dive from the proceeds.) The adjacent Hotel Plaza Las Glorias (the former Hotel Mirador) charges about $7 cover to view the dives from their terrace.

Old Town Beaches

These start not far from the *zócalo.* At the foot of the Fuerte San Diego, the sand of **Playa Hamacas** begins, changing to **Playa Hornos** ("Ovens") and continuing north a mile to a rocky shoal-line called Farallón de San Lorenzo. Hornos is the Sunday favorite of Mexican families, where boats buzz beyond the very tranquil waves, retirees stroll the wide, yellow sand, while vendors work the sunbathing crowd.

Moving south past the *zócalo* and the fishing boats, you'll find **Playa Tlacopanocha,** a petite strip of sand beneath some spreading trees. Here, bay-tour launches (see "Isla Roqueta" below) wait for passengers and kids play in the glassy water (which would be great for swimming if it weren't for the refuse from nearby fishing boats).

From there, cross the Costera and hop on a bus marked "Caleta" to gemlike **Playa Caleta** and its twin **Playa Caletilla** on the far side of the hilly pensinsula (named, appropriately, Peninsula de las Playas). With medium-coarse yellow sand and blue ripples for waves, Caleta and Caletilla are for people who want company. They are often crowded, sometimes nearly solid on Sundays. Boats offer banana-tube rides, and snorkel gear is rentable from beach concessionaires. Dozens of stalls and restaurants serve refreshments.

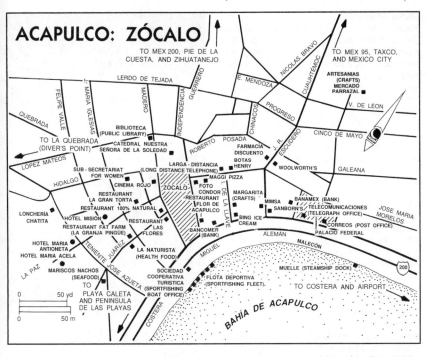

ACAPULCO: ZÓCALO

Magico Mundo water park, with an aquarium, museum, restaurant, water-slides, cascades, and more, perches on the little peninsula between the beaches (open daily 9-5, admission $5 adult, $3.50 child).

Isla Roqueta

A Roqueta Island ticket tout will often try to snare you as you get off the Caleta bus. The roundtrip, which runs around $4, is usually in a boat with a glass bottom, through which you can peer at the fish (as they peer back) in their aqua underwater world. On the other side, you can sunbathe on sunny little Playa Roqueta, have lunch at one of several beachside palapas, swim and snorkel, and quaff the thirst of the famous Roqueta beer-drinking burros (who are said to prefer Corona).

The burros are the island's sole inhabitants, except for the lighthouse keeper, for whom the burros haul supplies weekly. For those with the energy, the gradual lighthouse trail, only a few hundred yards long, begins at Playa Roqueta

(open Wed.-Mon., admission $1). Take drinks and a hat.

Other island attractions include a good small zoo in the shady mixed acacia-deciduous hillside forest above Playa Roqueta. Animals include many endangered local varieties, such as howler monkeys, jaguar, mountain lion, coatimundi, peccary, crocodile, and ocelot. Past the zoo hillcrest, a trail leads steeply downhill to tiny, secluded **Playa Marin,** where you can loll in the waves (which funnel into the narrow channel) to your heart's content. (Be prepared to avoid sunburn, however.)

A **boat tour** from Playa Tlacopanocha (see above) is another way to get to Isla Roqueta. The glass-bottomed boats *Maryvioli, Santa Maria,* and *Tequila* leave several times daily for hour-and-a-half tours (about $5 per person). Trips include viewing underwater life, shoreline vistas, the *Virgen Submarina* (a statue submerged in the Isla Roqueta channel), a stop on the island, and snorkeling. Beer and soft drinks are sold on-board.

Playa Angosta

Back on the mainland, you can visit another hidden beach nearby, Playa Angosta ("Narrow Beach"), the only Acapulco strand with an unobstructed sunset horizon. A breezy dab of a beach, sandwiched between a pair of sandstone cliffs, Angosta's ocean waves roll in, swishing upon the sand. A hotel palapa (see Hotel Playa Angosta under "Accommodations" below) occupies one side of the beach and a few fishing launches and nets are on the other. Swimming, bodysurfing, and boogieboarding are sometimes possible here, with caution; otherwise, Angosta is best for scenery and picnics.

New Town Beaches

These are the hotel-lined golden shores where affluent Mexicans and foreign visitors stay and play in the sun. They are variations on one continuous curve of sand. Beginning at the west end with **Playa Hornitos** (also known as Playa Papagayo), they continue, changing names from **Playa Morro** to **Playa Condesa** and finally, **Playa Icacos,** which curves and stretches to its sheltered east end past the naval base. All of the same semicoarse golden silica sand, the beaches begin with fairly broad 200-foot-wide *playas* Papagayo and Morro. They narrow sharply to under 100 feet at Playa Condesa, then broaden again to more than 200 feet along Playa Icacos.

Their surf is mostly very gentle, breaking in one- or two-foot waves near the sand and receding with little undertow. This makes for safe swimming within float-enclosed beachside areas, but it's too tranquil for bodysurfing, boogieboarding or surfing. Beyond the swimming floats, motorboats hurry along, pulling parasailors and banana-tube riders, while jet-ski boats cavort and careen over the swells.

Such motorized hubbub lessens the safety and enjoyment of quieter sports off most new town beaches. Sailboaters and windsurfers with their own equipment might try the remote, more tranquil east end of Playa Icacos, however.

Waterskiing, officially restricted to certain parts of Acapulco Bay, has largely moved to Coyuca Lagoon northwest of the city. Coyuca Lagoon has enough space for many good motorboat-free spots for sailboaters and windsurfers.

Beach palapas spread like a field of buttons on Playa Hornitos, as seen from the upper floors of the Hotel Ritz.

Rocky outcroppings along *playas* Papagayo, Morro, and Condesa add interest and intimacy to an already beautiful shoreline. The rocks are good for tidepooling and fishing by pole-casting (or by line, as locals do) above the waves.

Beaches Northwest Of Town: Pie De La Cuesta And Laguna Coyuca

For details on this downscale little resort and beautiful lagoon northwest of Acapulco, see the previous chapter. Get there from Acapulco by "Pie de la Cuesta"-marked buses, which leave frequently from the *zócalo* area (on Av. Escudero adjacent to Sanborn's and Woolworth's).

Beaches Southeast Of Town

Ride a "Puerto Marquez" or "Lomas" bus or drive along the Costera eastward. Past the naval base entrance on the right, the road climbs the hill, passing a number of panoramic bay viewpoints. After the Las Brisas condo-hotel complex, the road curves around the hill shoulder and heads downward past picture-perfect vistas of **Bahía Puerto Marquez.** At the bottom-of-the-hill intersection and gas station, a road forks right to Puerto Marquez.

The little bayside town is mainly a Sunday seafood and picnicking retreat for Acapulco families. Dozens of palapa restaurants line its motorboat-dotted sandy beach. One ramshackle hotel, at the far south end of the single main beachfront street, offers lodgings.

If you're driving, mark your odometer at the hill-bottom intersection and head east toward the airport. If traveling by bus, continue via one of the "Lomas" buses, which continue east from Acapulco about once an hour. About a mile farther, a turnoff road goes right to the Acapulco Princess and the Pierre Marquez hotels and golf course on **Playa Revolcadero.** (For hotel details, see under "Accommodations" below.)

Beach access is by side roads or by walking directly through the hotel lobbies. If you come by bus, hail a taxi from the highway to the Hotel Princess door for the sake of a good entrance.

Playa Revolcadero, a broad, miles-long yellow-white strand, has the rolling open-ocean billows that Acapulco Bay doesn't. The sometimes-rough waves are generally good for boogieboarding, bodysurfing, and even surfing near the rocks on the northwest end. Because of the waves and sometimes hazardous currents, the hotel provides lifeguards for safety. The Playa Revolcadero breeze is also brisk enough for sailing and windsurfing with your own boat or board. Some rentals may be available from the hotel beach concession.

Barra Vieja

About seven miles (11 km) from the Puerto Marquez traffic intersection, the Barra Vieja road forks right and heads along a breezy wild beach. About two miles from the fork, you will pass the Marparaiso Queen condo-hotel. The 100 two-bedroom luxury apartments surround a spacious pool-garden with beachside restaurant. Sleeping four, the air-conditioned kitchenette apartments rent for about $95. Filled with mostly Canadian clients during the winter, the apartments may be bargainable for less during slack periods. They have no phone; write them for reservations: Km 9.6, Carretera Barra Vieja, Acapulco, Guerrero.

About 18 miles (32 km) from the traffic intersection (11 miles from the fork) a sign marks Playa Encantada, an airy downscale beachside restaurant beside a big blue pool, garden, and large parking lot. The owner, Gloria Rioja de Reyes, and her manager-son invite visitors to park in their lot and set up tents on the beach. If they don't mention any fee, parking and tenting will probably be gratis if you eat a few meals in their restaurant. On the wide, breezy strand, the rolling waves, with ordinary precautions, would be good for boogieboarding, bodysurfing, and possibly surfing. The sun sets on an unobstructed horizon, and the crab-rich beach is good for surf fishing (or by boat if you launch during morning calm). Additionally, the firm, level sand is excellent for jogging, walking, and beachcombing. Tenters could set up comfortably and securely in the shade of the little beachside palm grove.

About a mile farther on, the stores (groceries and long-distance phone) and modest houses of fishing village Barra Vieja dot the roadside. Many seafood palapas line the beachside. The better among them include the upscale Beto's Condesa (with pool) and Gloria del Mar, with no pool. The latter is a family operation, run by a friendly woman who stretches out in a hammock reading her Bible when she has no customers.

Besides the beach, Barra Vieja visitors enjoy access to the big **Laguna Tres Palos** mangrove lagoon from the *estero* at the east end of town before the bridge. From there, boatmen take parties on fishing and wildlife-viewing excursions.

The road (which maps routinely show going through) ends about two miles farther east at scruffy Lomas de Chapultepec village.

ACCOMMODATIONS

Location largely determines the price and style of Acapulco hotels. In the old town, most hotels are either clustered around the *zócalo* or perched on the hillsides of Peninsula de las Playas. They are generally not on the beach and are cheaper and less luxurious. Most new town hotels, by contrast, lie mostly along the Costera Miguel Alemán right on the beach. Guests often enjoy numerous resort amenities

ACAPULCO HOTELS

Acapulco hotels, in order of increasing approximate high-season double-room price (area code 74, postal code 39300, unless otherwise noted)

ZÓCALO AND PENINSULA DE LAS PLAYAS HOTELS

Hotel Maria Acela, La Paz 19, 820-661, $14

Hotel Asturias, Quebrada 45, 836-548, $17

Hotel Playa Angosta, P.O. Box 88, 821-629, 822-785, (800) 33MEXICO, (800) ACAPULCO, $27

Hotel Misión, Felipe Valle 12, 823-643, $15

Hotel Maria Antioneta, Teniente Azueta 15, 825-024, $30

Hotel Misión, Felipe Valle 12, 823-643, $30

Hotel Torre Eifel, Inalambrica 110, 821-683, $30

Amuebalados Etel, Pinzona 92, 822-240, 822-241, $34

Hotel Caleta, Playa Caleta, 837-536, $50

Hotel Flamingos, P.O. Box 70, 820-690, 820-692, fax 839-806, $55

Hotel Majestic, Pozo del Rey 73, 834-710, 820-655, fax 821-614, $55

Hotel Boca Chica, Playa Caletilla s/n, 836-601, 836-741, $60

Suites Alba, Gran Via Tropical 35, 830-073, fax 838-378, $65

COSTERA HOTELS

Hotel del Valle, G. Gomez Espinosa 8 (P.O. Box C-14), 858-336, 858-388, $22

Hotel Sands, Juan de la Cosa 178, (P.O. Box 256), 891-748, fax 841-053, $50

Auto-Hotel Ritz, Wilfido Massieu s/n, (P.O. Box 157), 858-023, fax 855-647, $51

Romano Palace, Costera M. Alemán 130, 847-730, $55

Hotel Maris, Costera M. Alemán 59, 858-440, 858-492, $73

Maralisa Hotel and Beach Club, El Esclavo s/n, 856-677, fax 8-592-28, in U.S. (800) 223-6510, in Canada (800) 424-5500, $83

Hotel Fiesta Americana Condesa, Costera M. Alemán 1220, 842-828, (800) 1-FIESTA, $100

Ritz, Costero M. Alemán s/n, (P.O. Box 259), 857-544, 857-336, fax 857-076, (800) 237-7487, $116

Hyatt Regency, Costera M. Alemán 1, postal code 39860, 842-888, fax 643-087, (800) 233-1234, $192

Hotel Villa Vera and Racquet Club, Lomas del Mar 35, 840-333, 847-479, in U.S. (800) 223-6510, in Canada (800) 424-5500, $132

Acapulco Princess, Playa Revolcadero, (south of town on the airport road) 843-100, (800) 223-1818, $300

---

and luxury view rooms at correspondingly luxurious prices.

Many lodgings, however, defy categorization. Acapulco offers numerous choices to suit individual tastes and pocketbooks. In all cases, and especially in the luxury hotels, you can often save money by requesting low-season, package, and weekly or monthly discounts. For winter high-season lodgings, call or write for early reservations. (See the chart above for a listing according to price.)

Hotels Near The *Zócalo*

A number of clean, economical hotels cluster in the colorful neighborhood between La Quebrada and the *zócalo*. Among the most popular is the colonial-chic **Hotel Misión,** built in two stories around a plant-decorated patio, shaded by a spreading mango tree (Felipe Valle 12, Acapulco, Guerrero 39300, tel. 74-823-643; corner of La Paz, two blocks from the *zácalo*). When the mangos ripen in April guests get their fill of the perfumy fruit. The 24 attractively dec-

(top) One of Pacific Mexico's many varieties of pea family embellishes a hillside
near Barra de Navidad, Jalisco. (bottom) Any time is nap time poolside at the Hotel Bucanero in San Blas.
(photos by Bruce Whipperman)

(top left) shops on Paseo Isla Cuale, Puerto Vallarta; (top right) weaver using traditional backstrap loom, Puerto Vallarta; (bottom left) an Amuzgo Indian potter poses behind her goods near Pinotepa Nacional, Oax (bottom right) Florencio Gallardo, woodcarver of Huazolotitlán, Oaxaca (photos by Bruce Whipperman)

orated rooms rent for about $15 per person during the Nov.-Dec. and March-April high months, $12 otherwise; with fans, hot water, and parking.

One block farther along La Paz, the '60s-modern **Hotel Maria Antioneta** fronts the lively shop- and restaurant-lined Av. Azueta (Teniente Azueta 15, Acapulco, Guerrero 39300, tel. 74-825-024). The 34 plainly furnished but comfortable rooms are light and pleasant, especially on the upper floor. Most rooms are fortunately recessed along the leafy inner courtyard, away from street noise. Rates run about $15 per person, with hot water and fans.

A block away, on the quiet cul-de-sac end of Av. La Paz, stands the Spartan three-story **Hotel Maria Acela** (Av. La Paz 19, Acapulco, Guerrero 39300, tel. 74-820-661). Its family management lends a homey atmosphere more like a guesthouse than a hotel. The austerely furnished rooms, although clean, lack hot water. The 21 rooms rent for around $9 s, $14 d, with fan.

The **Hotel Asturias,** on Av. Quebrada a few blocks uphill from the zócalo, offers a relaxing atmosphere at budget rates (Quebrada 45, Acapulco, Guerrero 39300, tel. 74-836-548). Its two stories of plain but tidy rooms surround a plant-decorated pool-patio with chairs for sunning. Get an upper room for more light and privacy. Rates for the 15 rooms run about $12 s, $17 d, and $25 t year-round, with fans; four short blocks from the cathedral, between Ramirez and Ortiz.

A few blocks farther uphill, **Hotel Torre Eifel** rises above its hillside garden overlooking the La Quebrada diver's point tourist mecca (Inalambrica 110, Acapulco, Guerrero 39300, tel. 74-821-683). The 25 simply but comfortably furnished rooms rise in four motel-modern tiers above an inviting pool and patio. Guests in the uppermost rooms enjoy breezy sea views and a sunset horizon. Rooms rent for about $20 s, $30 d, and $40 t, with fans, hot water, and parking; at the corner of Av. Pinzona, one block uphill from the La Quebrada parking lot.

Two more blocks up winding Av. Pinzona, the Hotel **Amuebalados Etel** ("Ethel's Furnished Apartments") stands on the hillside above old Acapulco (Av. Pinzona 92, Acapulco, Guerrero 39300, tel. 74-822-240 and 74-822-241). Well managed by friendly owner Etel (great-granddaughter of renowned California pioneer John A. Sutter), the three-building complex stairsteps downhill to a luxurious view garden and pool. Its

airy hillside perch lends the Amuebalados Etel a tranquil, deluxe ambience unusual in such an economical lodging. Chairs and sofas in a small street-level lobby invite relaxed conversation with fellow guests. The primly but thoughtfully furnished and well-maintained rooms range from singles to multibedroom view apartments. The dozens of rooms and suites rent from about $14 per person low season, $17 high, with fans, a/c, and hot water. Completely furnished view apartments with kitchens go for about $80, with approximately 25% discount for monthly rentals, some parking, and credit cards accepted.

Peninsula De Las Playas Hotels

Many of these lodgings are spread along one continuous boulevard that winds through this plush hillside neighborhood. The boulevard starts as the Costera Miguel Alemán as it heads past the zócalo toward the peninsula. There it veers left as the Gran Via Tropical, rounding the peninsula clockwise. Passing Caleta and Caletilla beaches, the boulevard changes to Av. López Mateos and continues along the peninsula's sunset (southwest) side past Playa Angosta and La Quebrada diver's point before ending back in the zócalo neighborhood.

First along that path comes the big hillside **Hotel Majestic,** winter headquarters for crowds of youthful American, Canadian, and German vacationers (Av. Pozo del Rey 73, Acapulco, Guerrero 39300, tel. 74-834-710, 74-820-655, fax 74-821-614). Guests enjoy breezy bay views from the spacious grounds which spread downhill to a bayside beach club. Tennis, beach, and pool sports fill the days, while dining in the restaurants, theme parties, and disco dancing enliven the nights. The Spartan but comfortable tile-floored rooms come with a/c, cable TV, and telephones. The 210 rooms and suites rent from about $55 d high season, $45 low, credit cards accepted, with parking. Sports opportunities include windsurfing, kayaking, a gym, aerobics, and more.

A couple of blocks farther along Gran Via Tropical the multistory **Suites Alba** apartment-style complex rambles through its well-kept hilltop garden of palms and pools (Gran Via Tropical 35, Acapulco, Guerrero 39300, tel. 74-830-073, fax 74-838-378). The mostly Canadian and American middle-class guests enjoy many facilities, including a pair of pools, a jacuzzi, a restaurant, tennis courts, a minimart, and a downhill bay-

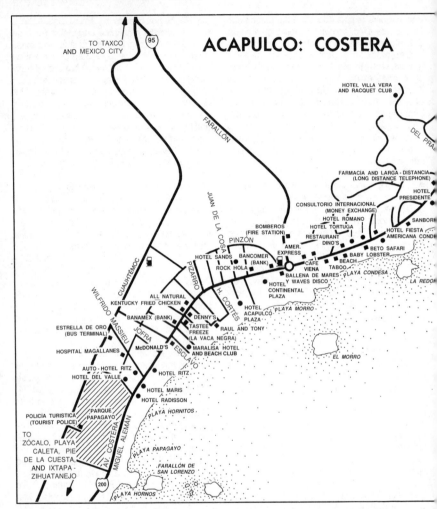

ACAPULCO: COSTERA

TO TAXCO
AND MEXICO CITY

95

FARALLÓN

HOTEL VILLA VERA
AND RACQUET CLUB

DEL PRA

FARMACIA AND LARGA - DISTANCIA
(LONG DISTANCE TELEPHONE)

HOTEL
PRESIDENTE

JUAN DE LA COSA

CONSULTORIO INTERNACIONAL
(MONEY EXCHANGE)

HOTEL ROMANO

BOMBEROS
(FIRE STATION)

HOTEL TORTUGA

RESTAURANT
DINO'S

SANBOR

PINZÓN

AMER.
EXPRESS

HOTEL FIESTA
AMERICANA COND

BETO SAFARI
BABY LOBSTER

HOTEL SANDS

BANCOMER
(BANK)

CAFE
VIENA

TABOO
BEACH

CUAUHTEMOC

ROCK HOLA

BALLENA DE MARES
Y WAVES DISCO

PLAYA CONDESA

LA REDO

PIZARRO

HOTEL
CONTINENTAL
PLAZA

PLAYA MORRO

H. CORTÉS

ALL NATURAL
KENTUCKY FRIED CHICKEN

HOTEL
ACAPULCO
PLAZA

WILFRIDO MASSIEU

BANAMEX (BANK)

DENNY'S

ESTRELLA DE ORO
(BUS TERMINAL)

JOFRA

TASTEE
FREEZE
(LA VACA NEGRA)

RAUL AND TONY

HOSPITAL MAGALLANES

McDONALD'S

ESCLAVO

MARALISA HOTEL
AND BEACH CLUB

EL MORRO

AUTO - HOTEL RITZ
HOTEL DEL VALLE

HOTEL RITZ

HOTEL MARIS

HOTEL RADISSON

PLAYA HORNITOS

POLICIA TURISTICA
(TOURIST POLICE)

PARQUE
PAPAGAYO

AV. COSTERA
MIGUEL ALEMAN

TO
ZÓCALO, PLAYA
CALETA, PIE
DE LA CUESTA,
AND IXTAPA -
ZIHUATANEJO

PLAYA PAPAGAYO

FARALLÓN DE
SAN LORENZO

200

PLAYA HORNOS

side beach club with its own saltwater pool. The comfortably furnished apartments have kitchenettes, a/c, and private garden-view balconies. The 292 apartments begin at about $65 d, $77 t, with discounts for monthly and low-season rentals; credit cards accepted, parking.

On the opposite side of the peninsula, guests at the **Hotel Boca Chica** enjoy views of Playa Caletilla on one hand and the green Isla Roqueta beyond an azure channel on the other (Playa Caletilla, Acapulco, Guerrero 39300, tel. 74-836-601, 74-836-741). The hotel perches on a rocky point, invitingly close to the clear aqua water from the pool deck and surrounding garden paths. The light, comfortably furnished rooms vary; if you have the option, look at two or three before you choose. Early reservations year-round are strongly recommended. Rates for the 45 rooms with phones and a/c run about $60 d; credit cards accepted, parking.

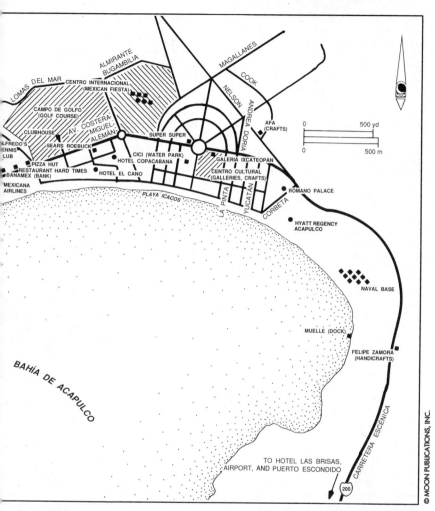

If you like the location but can't get into the Hotel Boca Chica immediately, try the second-choice **Hotel Caleta** on the other side of Playa Caleta nearby (Playa Caleta, Acapulco, Guerrero 39300, tel. 74-837-536, 74-837-538). There are 260 rooms from about $50 d with a/c, phones, parking, credit cards accepted; ask for a discount.

Hotel Flamingos, uphill about a mile along Av. López Mateos, is where oldsters reminisce

and youngsters find out who John Wayne, Johnny Weissmuller, and Rory Calhoun were (P.O. Box 70, Acapulco, Guerrero 39300, tel. 74-820-690 and 74-820-692, fax 74-839-806). Faded Hollywood photos decorate the open-air lobby walls, while nearby pathways wind through a hilltop jungle of palm, hibiscus, and spreading mangos. The rooms, several with private, ocean-view balconies, perch on a cliffside that plummets into foaming breakers hundreds of feet below. Soft evening guitar music in an open-air sunset view restaurant and a luxurious cliffside pool-patio complete the lovely picture. The 40 rooms, in standard, superior, and junior suite grades, run about $44, $55, and $66 d low season, respectively. Add about $10 for high season, $25 for an extra person. They also rent some bungalows with kitchenettes and a luxurious cliffside view house; with parking, some a/c; credit cards accepted.

Continue along Av. López Mateos to the once-presidential palace, now **Hotel Playa Angosta** (P.O. Box 88, Acapulco, Guerrero 39300, tel. 74-821-629 and 74-822-785). The hotel is a mecca for an informal club of Canadian and American returnees. They spend their days relaxing both at poolside and on the scenic little beach across the street. At night, many linger in friendly conversation around the hotel restaurant's tables and bar. The 31 rooms, in tiers around an inner patio, are charmingly decorated in stucco and pastels. Rooms vary; some have luxurious king-size beds, others private sunset ocean-view balconies. Rates run $20 s, $27 d with fan only, higher for a/c. For U.S. and Canada reservations, call toll-free 800-33MEXICO or 800-ACAPULCO.

Costera Hotels

With few exceptions, these hostelries line both sides of the busy beach boulevard, Costera Miguel Alemán. Hotels are either right on or just a short walk from the beach. By location, moving easterly from the Papagayo amusement park, first comes the economy **Hotel del Valle,** which shares its fortunate location with much more luxurious neighbors (G. Gomez Espinosa 8, P.O. Box C-14, Acapulco, Guerrero 39300, tel. 74-858-336 and 74-858-388). Two motel-style tiers of plain but clean single-bed rooms border a small but inviting pool-patio. On a side street away from the noisy boulevard, the del Valle is a tranquil winter headquarters for retirees and youthful budget travelers. The 20 rooms rent for $22 d with fan, $28 with a/c; with hot water.

Around the corner, three high-rise hotels occupy the Costera beachfront. After the towering Radisson, inappropriately cramped into a small lot, comes the more comfortably sized **Hotel Maris,** where guests get spacious rooms with private view balconies for surprisingly reasonable rates (Av. Costera M. Alemán 59, Acapulco, Guerrero 39300, tel. 74-858-440 and 74-858-492). Lobby-level amenities include a small pool above the beach club with bar and restaurant (where you may have to ask them to turn down the TV volume). No parking is available, however. Rates for the 84 rooms run about $50 d and $65 t low-season, $73 d and $92 t high; with a/c, TV, and phones.

Next door rises the midsize **Ritz,** a favorite of a generation of upper-class Mexican families (Costera M. Alemán, P.O. Box 259, Acapulco, Guerrero 39300, tel. 74-857-544, 74-857-336, fax 74-857-076). Past the plush lobby, you soon see why. An airy, broad palapa restaurant looks out on a beach and bay panorama, as Latin music plays softly in the background. Nearby a wooden walkway meanders over an intimate blue swimming pool. Live music plays nightly, while on weekends a riot of balloons and crepe festoons the plumy grove for a beachside fiesta. Upstairs, onyx floors and baths, pastel bedspreads and drapes, and private view balconies embellish the rooms. The 252 rooms and suites rent from about $86 d low season, $116 d high for standard rooms, with a/c, TV, and phones. Junior suites run about $20 more. For reservations in the U.S., phone (800) 237-7487; with parking and wheelchair access; credit cards accepted.

Across the street, the **Auto-Hotel Ritz** plugs along successfully in the shadow of its luxurious neighbor (Av. Wilfrido Massieu s/n, P.O. Box 157, Acapulco, Guerrero 39300, tel. 74-858-023, fax 74-855-647). Activity revolves around the verdant pool-patio, where a platoon of guests (many Canadian and European) are usually soaking up the sun. Upstairs, they enjoy tastefully appointed light-decor rooms and private balconies overlooking the patio's palmy jungle (or, from the top floor, the sea). The 103 rooms rent for about $51 d, $61 t high season, about $10 less during low; with a/c, restaurant, and parking; credit cards accepted.

Two blocks farther east, the low-rise **Maralisa Hotel and Beach Club** nestles among its big beachside condo neighbors (Enrique El Esclavo s/n, Acapulco, Guerrero 39300, tel. 74-856-677, fax 74-859-228). The Maralisa is a luxuriously simple retreat, where guests, after their fill of sunning beside the big palm-lined pool-patio, can walk a few steps for a jog or stroll along the beach. Later, they might dine in the hotel's beachside restaurant or go out for dancing in nearby resort hotels. Maralisa guests additionally enjoy access to the tennis courts and other plush amenities of the Hotel Villa Vera and Racquet Club uphill (see below). Many of the Maralisa's 90 comfortable rooms, tastefully decorated in whites and warm pastels, have private balconies. Standard rooms rent for about $50 d low season, $83 high; superior go for about $10 more. Two kids under 12 stay free; with a/c, TV, phones, and parking; credit cards accepted. For information and reservations in the U.S., call (800) 223-6510; in Canada, (800) 424-5500.

Several blocks farther east the low-rise **Hotel Sands** contrasts sharply with the monumental Acapulco Plaza across the boulevard (Calle Juan de la Cosa 178, P.O. Box 256, Acapulco, Guerrero 39300, tel. 74-891-748, fax 74-841-053). In addition to a pool-patio and restaurant next to the main '60s-modern building, the deceivingly spacious grounds encompass a shady green park in the rear that leads to an attractive hidden cabaña-enclosed garden. Of the main building rooms, the uppers are best, with private balconies and light, comfortable (even if a bit tattered and less than immaculate) furnishings. Cabaña guests, on the other hand, enjoy tasteful browns, tile decor, and big windows looking out into a leafy garden. Bungalows 1-8 are the most secluded. The 59 rooms and 34 cabañas run $50 d, $60 t high season, about $10 less low season. Additional 33% discounts for three-, six-, and nine-night stays are often available. All with a/c, cable TV, and phones; parking, squash courts, and jeep rental; credit cards accepted.

The super-luxury **Hotel Fiesta Americana Condesa** presides atop its rocky shoreline perch smack in the middle of new Acapulco (Av. Costera M. Alemán 1220, Acapulco, Guerrero 39300, tel. 74-842-828). Boulevard traffic roars nonstop past the front door and nightclubs rock all night nearby. By day, ranks of middle-American and Canadian vacationers sun on the hotel's spacious pool-deck and downstairs at its palapa-shaded beach club. Resort facilities include multiple restaurants and bars, nightly live music, shops, rentals, tennis, golf, and all aquatic sports. Rooms, most with private bay-view balconies, are furnished in luscious pastels, rattan, and designer lamps. Rooms rent from around $100 d, with a/c, TV, phones, parking, and full wheelchair access; credit cards accepted. In Canada and the U.S. call (800) 1-FIESTA for information and reservations.

In exclusive isolation several blocks uphill, guests at the **Hotel Villa Vera and Racquet Club** enjoy what seems like their own Acapulco country club (Lomas del Mar 35, Acapulco, Guerrero 39300, tel. 74-840-333, fax 74-847-479). Overlooking the entire city and bay, the hotel's dozens of bungalows nestle in a manicured garden around an elegant hillside pool and terrace restaurant. The lodgings, which range from one-room doubles to suites, are decorated in creams, pastels, and earth tones and tastefully appointed with handicrafts and one-of-a-kind wall art. No children admitted, however. Rates for the 80 rooms and suites run about $132 d low season, $198 high for superior grade; $165 and $237, respectively, for suite; with a/c, cable TV, phones, parking, clay tennis courts, massage, and sauna; credit cards accepted. For U.S. information and reservations, call (800) 223-6510; from Canada, (800) 424-5500. Get there via the street between the Pizza Hut and the golf course, continuing uphill at each fork. The Villa Vera gate will appear on the left after about a quarter mile.

Back on the Costera, many folks who want a reasonably priced ocean-view room a block from the beach go to the **Romano Palace,** (not to be confused with the Romano Days Inn). The youthful, mostly single clientele also likes the lively late-night bar and the big pool-deck where they can rest and recover during the day. The 279 light and comfortable rooms come with a/c, TV, and phones. (Costera M. Alemán 130, Acapulco, Guerrero 39300, tel. 74-847-730). Rooms rent for about $45 d low season, $55 high; parking available, credit cards accepted.

Next door rises the 20-story tower of the **Hyatt Regency Acapulco** everything resort, with spacious gardens, blue lagoon swimming pool, a Tarzan jungle waterfall, a squadron of personal beach palapas, restaurants, bars, nightly music till midnight, shops, all aquatic sports, and tennis and golf (Costera M. Alemán 1, Acapulco, Guerrero 39860, tel. 74-842-888, fax 74-843-087). The 690 rooms, all with private view balconies, are large and luxurious. Low season prices, furthermore, can be surprisingly reasonable. Standard rooms rent from about $83 d low season, $192 high, with a/c, cable TV, phones, parking, and full wheelchair access; credit cards accepted. For information and reservations in the U.S. and Canada, call (800) 233-1234.

Out-of-town Hotels

The sleepy **Pie de la Cuesta** resort village on placid Coyuca Lagoon (about six miles by road northwest from the Acapulco *zócalo*) has several reasonably priced beachside lodgings. Drive (see map, "Acapulco: Around the Bay"), taxi (about $5), or ride a Pie de la Cuesta-marked bus from Av. Escudero in front of Sanborn's and Woolworth's near the *zócalo*.

Past the southeast end of town near the airport, the showplace **Acapulco Princess** provides a plethora of resort facilities (including an entire golf course) spreading from luscious beachfront garden grounds (Playa Revolcadero, Acapulco, Guerrero 39300, tel. 74-843-100). Although the hotel centers on a pair of hulking neopyramids (1,019-room total), the impression from the rooms themselves is of super-luxury; from the garden it is of Eden-like jungle tranquility—meandering pools, gurgling cascades, strutting flamingos, swaying palms—which guests seem to soak up with no trouble at all. Rooms rent from about $200 d low season, $300 high; all facilities, all sports, full wheelchair access, credit cards accepted. From the U.S. and Canada, call (800) 223-1818 for information and reservations.

Trailer Parks And Camping

Although condos and hotels have replaced virtually all of Acapulco's in-town trailer parks, good prospects exist nearby. Among the best is the **Acapulco Trailer Park** right on the beach in Pie de la Cuesta resort village six miles by the coast highway northwest of the *zócalo*.

And although development and urbanization have likewise squeezed out in-town camping, possibilities exist in a pair of palm-shadowed beachside trailer parks in Pie de la Cuesta. Camping is also possible at Playa Encantada beach restaurant near Barra Vieja (see under "Sights" above).

FOOD

Breakfast And Snacks Near The *Zócalo*

For good breakfasts, try friendly **100% Natural,** a few steps off the *zócalo*. A branch of a family-owned local chain, they serve many egg favorites, pancakes, fruit, and wholesome bread (Juarez 2, open daily 7 a.m.-10 p.m.).

Sidewalk cafe **Maggi Pizza** on the opposite side of the *zócalo*, end of Carranza, beneath the big tree, is a friendly source of late-night snacks. You will have to be up late indeed to outlast the club of domino aficionados who seem to own the place.

Eat well for under $3 at **Lonchería Chatita,** where a friendly female kitchen squad serves mounds of wholesome, local-style specialties (open daily 8 a.m.-10 p.m., Av. Azueta, corner of Hidalgo). On a typical day, these may include savory chiles rellenos, rich *puerco mole de Uruapan, pozole* (savory hominy soup), or potato pancakes.

For something creamy and cool, go to **Bing** ice cream (open daily 9 a.m.-11 p.m.) one block from the *zócalo* toward the steamship dock.

Continue another block to **Sanborn's,** where you can escape the heat and enjoy home-style ham and eggs, hamburgers, roast beef, and apple pie, although prices are fairly high *(malecón* corner of Escudero, open daily 7:30-11).

Woolworth's, one block from the Costera, behind Sanborn's, also offers air-conditioned ambience and similar fare (at more reasonable prices).

Costera Breakfast And Snacks

Snack food concentrates in Acapulco, as in many places, around **McDonald's** (corner Esclavo and Av. Costera M. Alemán, just one block east of Hotel Ritz; open daily 9:30 a.m.-midnight; tel. 860-777). Except for breakfast, which they don't serve, you'll find everything from Chicken McNuggets to the Big Mac, priced about a third higher than back home.

For an interesting contrast, visit **Taco Tumbra** across the street from McDonald's (open Sun.-Thurs. 6 p.m.-2 a.m, Fri.-Sat. 6 p.m.-4 a.m.). Here, piquant aromas of barbecued chicken, pork, and beef and strains of Latin music fill the air. For a treat, order three of their delectable tacos, along with a refreshing fruit juice *(jugo,* HOO-go) or fruit-flavored *agua*.

ACAPULCO RESTAURANTS

Restaurants, in approximate ascending order of price:

ZÓCALO AND PENINSULA DE LAS PLAYAS RESTAURANTS

Lonchería Chatita, Azueta and Hidalgo, 8 a.m.-10 p.m., Mexican

100% Natural, *zócalo*, 7 a.m.-10 p.m., international

Maggi Pizza, *zócalo*, 7 a.m.-1 a.m., Italian

La Gran Torta, La Paz 6, 838-476, 8 a.m.-midnight, Mexican

Fat Farm (La Granja Pingüe), Juarez 10 at Felipe Valle, 835-339, 9 a.m.-10 p.m., international

Restaurant Flor de Acapulco, *zócalo*, 825-018, 7:30 a.m.-10:30 p.m., international-Mexican

Las Flores, *zócalo*, 839-463, Mon.-Sat. noon-midnight, Sun. 5-midnight, German-Mexican

Mariscos Nachos, Juarez and Azueta, 10 a.m.-9:30 p.m., seafood

Sanborn's, *malecón* and Escudero, 826-167, 7:30 a.m-11 p.m., international

Hotel Los Flamingos, Av. López Mateos s/n, 820-690, 8 a.m.-10:30 p.m., international

Coyuca 22, Coyuca 22, 823-468, 7-10:30 p.m., Nov. 1-Apr. 30, international

COSTERA RESTAURANTS

Taco Tumbra, Costera next to McDonald's, Sun.-Thurs. 6 p.m-2 a.m, Fri.-Sat. 6 p.m.-4 a.m., tacos

Tastee-Freeze (Vaca Negra), Costera next to Denny's, 8 a.m.-4 a.m., international

All Natural, Costera across from Denny's, open 24 hours, international

Cafe Viena, Costera by American Express, 8:30 a.m.-11 p.m., international

Restaurant Hard Times, Costera by the Pizza Hut, 840-064, Tues.-Sun. 6 p.m-midnight, international

Dino's, Costera, next to Hotel Tortuga, 840-037, 6-11:30 p.m., Italian

Raul and Tony, Calle H. Cortés, 852-051, 852-103, 8 a.m.-midnight, Cuban-international

La Cava, Hotel Ritz, Av. Costera M. Alemán and Wilfrido Massieu, 857-544, 6-11:30 p.m., international

---

About three blocks east, **Tastee-Freeze** nestles beneath its soaring concrete canopy (corner Costera M. Alemán and Sandoval, open daily 8 a.m.-4 a.m.). A pre-McDonald's mecca for homesick palates, Tastee Freeze (also known as Vaca Negra—"Black Cow"), serves from an extensive snack menu which includes beer ($1), foot-longs ($2), a big burger ($3), malts ($1), and loads of sundaes.

Denny's next door is a little bit of Council Bluffs, Seattle, and Denver all rolled into Acapulco. This is where, 'round the clock, you can have it all, especially breakfasts: blueberry pancakes, three-egg omelettes drowned in American cheese with hash browns, or the Grand Slam—two eggs, pancakes, sausage, bacon, toast and all the coffee you can drink.

All Natural, in 24-hour competition directly across the Costera from Denny's, offers appropriately contrasting fare: many veggie and fruit drinks (try the Conga—made of papaya, guava, watermelon, pineapple, lime, and spinach), several egg breakfasts, breads, sandwiches, tacos, and enchiladas.

Bob's Big Boy next door seems to try harder than everyone, with economy 'round-the-clock breafasts (fruit salad $2, hotcakes $1.50, eggs $2) and a host of hamburgers.

The diminutive **Cafe Viena,** a half mile farther along the Costera, offers still more options (on the Costera next to American Express, between the Diana Circle and the Hotel Fiesta Americana Condesa, open daily 8:30 a.m.-11 p.m.). You can start out with familiar egg and toast breakfasts, or enjoy sampling the strudels, bear claws, pies, and cakes, which friendly owner Sophia crafts in her small bakery upstairs. Weekend evenings at 7:00 patrons gather to enjoy piano melodies played on the baby grand, which spreads over a quarter of the tiny seating area.

Zócalo And Peninsula
De Las Playas Restaurants

(Complete Dinner Price Key: Budget = under $7, Moderate = $7-14, Expensive = more than $14.) Even though Acapulco has seemingly zillions of restaurants, only a fraction may suit your expectations. Some may be too raucous, others too expensive, and others too touristy. Although local restaurants come and go like the Acapulco breeze, a handful of solid longtime eateries continue, depending on a steady flow of repeat customers.

The **Restaurant Flor de Acapulco** on the *malecón* end of the *zócalo* has been a favorite of Acapulco regulars since soon after it opened way back in 1936 (open daily 7:30 a.m.-10:30 p.m., tel. 825-018). Although the food is good enough, meeting with friends or watching the world go by beneath an umbrella-shaded plaza-edge table is the first order of business here. Budget to moderate.

Food, by contrast, *is* the priority at the German **Restaurant Las Flores** directly across the plaza (*zócalo*, corner Juarez; open Mon.-Sat. noon-midnight, Sun. 5-midnight, tel. 839-463). Not that the *zócalo* views from the restaurant's open-air upper floors aren't interesting, but the old-Europe specialties, such as roast pork Dubrovnik, weinerschnitzel Vienna, and sauerbraten are too tasty to be ignored. Moderate.

Two blocks along the same street, the **Fat Farm** (La Granja Pingüe) would be unique even without the name (Juarez 10, at Felipe Valle, open daily 9 a.m.-10 p.m., tel. 835-339). It's a cooperative, run by graduates of a local orphanage. The relaxed atmosphere, service, and food are made to please. Breakfasts are the high point of many a long-timer's day. Fare also includes several flavors of ice cream and sandwiches (such as their giant tuna, $2.50). Budget.

La Gran Torta is a *zócalo* headquarters for hearty local-style food at local-style prices (La Paz 6, one block from the *zócalo*, open daily 8 a.m-midnight, tel. 838-476). Specialties here are tortas (big sandwiches), often of *pierna* (roast pork), *chorizo* (spicy sausage), or *pollo* (chicken) with tomato and avocado stuffed in a *bolillo* (French roll). Additional favorites include hearty *pozole*, (hominy and pork or chicken stew) on Thursdays and Fridays. Budget.

Good, reasonably priced seafood restaurants are unexpectedly hard to come by in Acapul-co. An important exception is the lineup of local-style seafood eateries along Av. Azueta three blocks from the *zócalo*. Located right where the boats come in, they get the freshest morsels first. Among the best and friendliest is **Mariscos Nachos,** where continuous patronage assures daily fresh shrimp, prawns, half a dozen kinds of fish, and lobster (big, $17, smaller, $10; corner Juarez and Azueta, open daily 10 a.m.-9:30 p.m. Moderate.

Many visitors' Acapulco vacations wouldn't be complete without a dinner at the luxurious clifftop restaurant at the **Hotel Flamingos** (Av. López Mateos s/n, open daily 8 a.m.-10:30 p.m., tel. 820-690, about a mile uphill, west from Playa Caleta). Here all the ingredients for a memorable evening—attentive service, tasty seafood, chicken, and meat entrees, airy sunset view, and soft strumming of guitars—come together. Moderate.

Coyuca 22 is both the name and the address of the restaurant so exclusive and popular that it manages to close half the year. The setting is a spacious hilltop garden, where tables spread down a open-air bay- and city-view terrace. Arrive early (around 6:45) to enjoy the postsunset sky light up and paint the city ever-deepening colors, ending in a deep rose as finally the myriad lights shimmer and stars twinkle overhead. After that, the food (specialties, such as prime rib and lobster tails) and wines seem like dessert. Expensive. Entrees run about $30. Open daily 7-10:30 p.m. from Nov. 1-April 30. Reservations are required, tel. 823-468 and 835-030; dress: elegant resort wear, coat not necessary.

Costera Restaurants

The Hotel Ritz's **La Cava** restaurant is a long-time favorite of serious eaters. Atmosphere—candlelight and roses, tuxedoed waiters and wine steward—enhances the enjoyment of their carefully prepared and presented specialties (Av. Costera M. Alemán and Wilfrido Massieu, open nightly 6-11:30, tel. 857-544). Start with a Caesar salad, continue with a cream of spinach soup, and end with a seafood pasta, such as clam linguini, all accompanied with a Baja California Cetto-label sauvignon blanc. Expensive. Reservations recommended.

Restaurant-nightclub **Raul and Tony,** right on the beach a few blocks farther east, specializes in romance, music, and Cuban food (Calle H. Cortés, Playa El Morro; open daily 8 a.m.-midnight, tel. 852-051, 852-103. They're especially proud of their daily *paella* and *picadillo*, which go quite well with the live Latin music that begins (in season) at 8:30 nightly. Moderate to expensive. *Comida* (lunch) runs from 1-6, dinner begins at six. Get there by following the street by Denny's to the beach.

The waiters at **Restaurant Hard Times** work as if hard times were about to descend (Av. Costera M. Alemán by the Pizza Hut, open Tues.-Sun. 6 p.m.-midnight, tel. 840-064). If you come in on a slow night, two or three of them will execute your orders like a squad of quarterbacks. This is the place if you want a salad bar or a five-course soup (with bread, butter, onions, cheese, and croutons). If you have any room after that, their long list of regular entrees and desserts will certainly suffice. The place is hard to miss because of the fire engine-red 1936 Ford V8 with blazing headlights parked in the doorway. Moderate.

One of the most atmospheric and palate-pleasing Italian restaurants is **Dino's**, on the Costera a block west of the Fiesta Americana Condesa (Costera M. Alemán, next to Hotel Tortuga; open daily 6-11:30 p.m., tel. 840-037). Here, guests can choose from a bay-view terrace in front or an intimate fountain patio in back. From the menu, they select among antipastos, salads, meats, and many seafood and meat pastas smothered in sauces, made with a flourish right at the table. Moderate to expensive.

ENTERTAINMENT AND EVENTS

Strolling And Sidewalk Cafes

The old *zócalo* is the best place for strolling and people-watching. Bookstalls, vendors, band concerts, and, weekend nights especially, pitchpenny games, mimes, and clowns are constant sources of entertainment. When you're tired of walking, take a seat at a sidewalk cafe, such as the Flor de Acapulco, and let the scene pass *you* by for a change.

Movies

A number of cinemas dot the Costera. The movies usually begin around 4:00 or 4:30. The second screening generally starts around 8:30 and finishes around midnight. From lower-brow to high, first comes the **Cine Variedades** (admission $1.70) at Mendoza and Cuauhtémoc, where visitors can enjoy viewing a double-whammy bill of Mexican and American action potboilers.

Farther up the scale is the **Cine Hornos** (admission $2, Nuñez de Balboa 10, tel. 851-731, on the Costera, corner of de Ulloa), which shows mostly American first-run action flicks. Next come the **Cine Rojo** (admission $3, on the *zócalo*, tel. 836-382) and the jointly owned **Cine Flamboyant** (admission $3, across the Costera from the Hotel Acapulco Plaza, tel. 847-502), which show first-run American action and drama.

Tourist Shows

The Mexican Fiesta, Acapulco's dance performance extravaganza, goes on Tues., Thurs., and Sat. at the sprawling Centro Internacional (formerly Convention Center) just east of the golf course. The all-Mexico sombrero and whirling-skirt folkloric dance show is highlighted by a replica performance of the wheeling Papantla flyers. Tickets, available from travel agents, can include either the show only ($17), the show and two drinks ($24), or the show, drinks, and buffet ($43, kids half price). The buffet begins around 7 p.m., followed by the performance at 8:15.

Sunsets

West-side hills block Acapulco Bay's sunset horizon. Sunset connoisseurs remedy the problem, however, by gathering at certain points on the Peninsula de las Playas, such as **La Quebrada, Playa Angosta,** and the cliffside restaurant and gazebo-bar of the **Hotel Flamingos** before sunset (or around 5:30).

Bay Cruise Parties

One popular way to enjoy the sunset and a party at the same time is by a cruise aboard either of the steel excursion ships ("yachts") *Bonanza* or *Hawaiano*. They leave from the pair of bayside docks on the Costera half a mile (toward the Peninsula de las Playas) from the *zócalo*. Both excursions leave about 4:30, return around 7:00, and include live music, dancing, and open bar. Tickets are available from travel agents or at the dock (*Bonanza* reservations tel. 831-803, *Hawaiano* tel. 821-217, 820-785) for about $18 per person, kids half price. They also offer mid-day *(paseo matutino*, 11-2, with snorkeling) and moonlight *(lunada*, 10:30 p.m.-1 a.m.) cruises for similar prices.

Bullfights

Bullfights are staged every Sunday at 5:30 at the arena near Playa Caletilla. Avoid congestion and parking hassles by taking a taxi. Get tickets through a travel agent or the ticket office, tel. 821-182, 839-561.

Dancing

Several of the Costera hotels have live groups for dancing at their lobby-bars. Moving east along the Costera, the best possibilities are the **Radisson** (tel. 855-596), **Ritz** (tel. 857-544), **Acapulco Plaza** (tel. 858-050), the **Fiesta Americana Condesa** (tel. 842-828), and the **Hyatt Regency** (842-888). Call to verify times.

Many restaurant-bars along the Costera have nightly dance music, both recorded and live. A pair of favorites of both longtime tourists and local people are the **Tropicana** (on beach side, across the Costera from Cine Hornos) and the **Copacabana** (on beach side, near corner of Amal Espina). Both have cocktails and live Latin (sometimes called "Tropical") music for dancing till around 3:00. Call ahead (Copacabana tel. 851-051, Tropicana tel. 853-050) to verify times.

A lively band also plays nightly at the restaurant-club **Paradise** in the Costera beach entertainment strip (see below) by the Hotel Fiesta Americana Condesa (on the Costera across from the Hotel Romano, tel. 845-988). Zany waiters, a lively, varied musical repertoire, and good-enough food all spell happy times at the Paradise.

Discotheques usually monitor their entrances carefully and are consequently safe and pleasant places for a night's entertainment (provided you either are either immune to the noise or bring earplugs). They open their doors around 10:00 and play relatively low- volume music and videos for starters until around 11:00, when fogs descend, lights flash, and the thumping begins, continuing sometimes till dawn. Admission runs from about $7 to $10 or more for the tonier joints.

Moving west to east along the Costera, first comes the **Isabelle** (corner of de Ulloa adjacent to the Cine Hornos), popular with a youngish local crowd. Past Papagayo Park, the club **Rock Hola** (corner de la Cosa, across from

the Acapulco Plaza Hotel) plays mostly '60s and '70s-style medium volume rock for a mixed crowd, beginning at 7:00.

Three blocks farther on, the neon of **La Ballena de Mares y Waves** disco is impossible to miss on the beach side of the Diana Circle. Very loud rap and video numbers entertain mostly young, mixed tourist and local patrons from about 9:30.

The next quarter mile, between the Diana Circle and the Fiesta Americana condesa, is nearly solid with clubs, hangouts, and discos. During peak seasons, the dancing crowds spill on to the Costera. Stroll along and pick out the style and volume that you like.

Among the clubs, **Beach** disco is the loudest, brashest, and most popular of all. For the entrance of $10 ($17 Wed., open bar included) the music and the lights go till dawn. Other neighboring discos, such as Taboo, Baby Lobster, Corona, Blackbeard's, and Beto Safari, while sometimes loud, are nevertheless subdued in comparison.

Reigning above all of Acapulco's lesser centers of discomania is **Extravaganza**, visible everywhere around the bay as the pink neon glow on the east-side Las Brisas hill. Go there, if only to look. (And call for a reservation beforehand, 847-164, or they won't let you in.) Inside, the impression is of ultramodern fantasy—a giant spaceship window facing outward on a galactic star carpet—while the music explodes, propelling you, the dancing traveler, through inner space. A mere $10 cover gets you through the door; inside, drinks are $5-10 while champagne runs $300 a bottle.

Child's Play

CICI (short for Centro Internacional de Convivencia Infantil) is the biggest of Acapulco's water parks. An aquatic paradise for families, CICI has acres of liquid games, where you can swish along a slippery toboggan run, plummet down a towering kamikaze slide, or loll in a gentle wave pool. Other pools contain performing whales, dolphins, and sea lions. Patrons also enjoy a restaurant, a beach club, and much more. CICI is on the east end of the Costera between the golf course and the Hyatt Regency; open daily 10-6, adult admission $7, kids $6, sea mammal performances occur at 12:30, 3:30, and 5:30.

Magico Mundo, Acapulco's other water park, is on the opposite side of town at Playa Caleta. For details, see "Sights" above.

SPORTS

Walking And Jogging

The most interesting walking in Acapulco is along the two-mile stretch of beach between the Hotel Fiesta Americana Condesa and the rocky point at Parque Papagayo. Avoid the midday heat by starting early for breakfast along the Costera (such as at Sanborn's, Av. Costera M. Alemán 1226, tel. 844-465, open from 7:30 a.m.) and walking west along the beach with the sun to your back. Besides the beach itself, you'll pass rocky outcroppings to climb on, tidepools to poke through, plenty of fruit vendors, and palapas to rest in from the sun. Bring a hat, shirt, and sunscreen and allow two or three hours. If you get tired, ride a taxi or bus back. (You can do the reverse walk just as easily after about 3:00 in the afternoon from Playa Hamacas just past the steamship dock after lunch (try the Flor de Acapulco) on the *zócalo.*

Soft sand and steep slopes spoil most **jogging** prospects on Acapulco Bay beaches. However, the green open spaces surrounding the Centro Internacional (formerly the Convention Center, just east of the golf course) provide a good in-town substitute.

Tennis And Golf

Acapulco's tennis courts are all private and mostly at the hotels. Try the **Acapulco Plaza** (tel. 859-050), **Fiesta Americana** (tel. 842-828), Villa Vera (tel. 840-333), **Presidente** (tel. 841-700), and the **Hyatt** (tel. 841-225). The Hyatt, for example, has five night-lit hard courts which, for visitors, rent for $16 per hour during the day and $21 at night. (If, however, you live in Acapulco, or play with someone who does, courts run only $5 by day and $10 by night.) Lessons by the in-house teaching pro cost about $25 an hour.

If you prefer clay courts, the **Hotel Villa Vera and Racquet Club** (see "Accommodations" above) has three of them for about $21 per hour by day and $24 by night.

One of the coziest places for tennis in town is **Alfredo's Tennis Club,** literally the home of former tennis champion Alfredo Millet. He has two night-lit courts, rentable for $10 per hour during the day, $20 at night, including towel, refreshment, and use of his swimming pool. Lessons run $50 an hour. At Av. Prado 29, tel. 840-004, 847-070; get there via Av. Deportes, next to the Pizza Hut. Go uphill one block, then left another to Alfredo's, at the corner of Prado.

If Alfredo is all booked up and you can't afford $20 an hour for a tennis court, call some of the less plush hotels with courts (See "Accommodations" above), such as the **Gran Motel Acapulco** (Costera near the Hotel Acapulco Plaza, tel. 855-437), **Las Hamacas** (tel. 837-709), Majestic (tel. 834-710), and **Suites Alba** (tel. 830-073).

The Acapulco **Campo de Golf** (tel. 840-781, 840-782), right on the Costera, is open daily to the public, first-come first-served, from 6:30 a.m. to 5:30 p.m. daily. (Exception: Wednesday after 1 p.m., the course is limited to foursomes.) Greens fee for 18 holes runs about $40, caddy $14, club rental $15.

Much more exclusive and better maintained is the Club de Golf at the hotels Acapulco Princess and Pierre Marques (tel. 842-000), about five miles past the southeast edge of town (see "Out-of-town Hotels" above). Here, the 18-hole greens fee runs $60 if you're a hotel guest and $80 if you're not. Caddies, carts, and club rentals are correspondingly priced.

Swimming, Surfing, Bodysurfing, And Boogieboarding

Acapulco Bay's tranquil (if not pristine) waters generally allow safe swimming from hotel-front beaches. The water is too tranquil for surf sports, however. Strong waves off open-ocean Playa Revolcadero southeast of the city often give good bodysurfing, boogieboard, and surfboard rides. The waves, however, can be dangerous. The Acapulco Princess on the beach provides lifeguards. Check with them before venturing in. Bring your own equipment; rentals may not be available.

Snorkeling And Scuba Diving

Although local water clarity is often not ideal, Acapulco does have at least one professional dive shop, the well-equipped **Escuela de Buceo Nautilus,** run by NAUI-licensed instructor Mario Trevino Diaz. Beginning training, including an easy local dive, runs about $40 per person. Open-water certification takes an average of five days and totals around $250 or $300. Trips to local sites for qualified divers (bring your certificate) run about $50, including equipment, boat, guide, and two full tanks. Additional options include night, wreck, and biological dives. Address: Priv. Garcia Moraga, local 2, Acapulco, Guerrero 39300, tel. 831-108, open daily 8-2 and 3-6. Diaz is located in the little park across the boulevard from the Pemex gas station on the Costera about half a mile toward the peninsula past the *zócalo*.

The best local snorkeling is off **Roqueta Island.** Closest access point is by boat from the docks at Playa Caleta (and Playa Tlacopanocha). Trips usually run about $20 per person for a two-hour snorkeling trip, equipment included. Snorkel trips can also be arranged through beachfront aquatics shops at hotels such as the Ritz, Acapulco Plaza, Fiesta Americana Condesa, and the Hyatt Regency.

Sailing And Windsurfing

Close-in Acapulco Bay waters are too congested with motorboats for tranquil sailing or windsurfing. Nevertheless, the beach concessionaire (FADAP, Fondo de Actividades Deportivas Aquaticos, tel. 840-909) at both the Acapulco Plaza and Hyatt Regency does rent (or take people sailing in) simple boats from $20 per hour.

Limited windsurfing is also possible at the Hotel Majestic beach club in the little sub-bay sheltered by the Peninsula de las Playas.

Outside of town, tranquil Laguna Coyuca on the coast about 20 minutes' drive northwest of the *zócalo* offers good windsurfing and sailing prospects.

Jet-skiing, Waterskiing, And Parasailing

Power sports are very popular on Costera hotel beaches. Concessionaires (recognized by their lineup of beached boats) operate from most big hotel beaches, notably at the Radisson, Ritz, Acapulco Plaza, Fiesta Americana Condesa, and the Hyatt Regency. Prices run about $60 per hour for jet-ski boats, $50 per hour for waterskiing, and $20 for a 10-minute parasailing ride.

Sportfishing

Fishing boats line the *malecón* dockside across the boulevard from the *zócalo*. Activity centers on the office (see *zócalo* map) of the 20-boat blue-and-white fleet run by **Sociedad Cooperativa Turisticas,** whose dozens of licensed captains regularly take visitors for big-game fishing trips. Although some travel agents may book you individually during high season, the Sociedad Cooperativa Turisticas office (tel. 821-099, open daily 8 a.m.-6 p.m.) rents only entire boats, including captain, equipment, and bait.

Rental prices and catches depend on the season. Drop by the dock after 2 p.m. to see what they are bringing in. During good times, boats might average one big marlin or sailfish apiece. Best months for sailfish *(pez vela)* are

Sailfish, which sportfishing boats frequently bring in at Acapulco's zócalo-front malecón, make tough eating and should be released when caught.

said to be November, December, and January; for marlin, February and March.

Big 40-foot boats with five or six fishing lines rent from about $150 per day. Smaller boats, with three or four lines and holding five or six passengers, rent from around $120 or less. All of the Cooperativa boats are radio-equipped, with toilet, life preservers, tackle, bait, and ice. Customers usually supply their own food and drinks. Although the Cooperativa is generally competent, look over the boat and check its equipment before putting your money down.

Sailfish and marlin are neither the only nor necessarily the most desirable fish in the sea. Competently captained *pangas* (motor launches) can typically haul in three or four large 20- or 30-pound excellent-eating *robalo* (snook), *huachinango* (snapper) or *atún* (tuna) in two hours just outside Acapulco Bay.

Such lighter boats are rentable from the cooperative for about $30 per hour or less from individual fishermen on Playa Hamacas (past the steamship dock at the foot of Fort San Diego).

Marina And Boat Launching

A safe place to launch or dock your boat is the new 150-slip **Marina Acapulco** on the Peninsula de las Playas's sheltered inner shoreline (Av. Costera M. Alemán 215, Fracc. Las Playas, Acapulco, Guerrero 39300, tel. 748-474-36 and 748-374-61). Boat launching runs about $34 per day. The slip rate is $12 per foot per month, including 110/220-volt power, potable water, pump-out, satellite disk TV connection, toilets, showers, ice, and access to the marina pool, restaurant, hotel, and repair facilities. Get there via the driveway past the suspension bridge over the Costera about a mile from the *zócalo*.

SHOPPING

Market

Acapulco, despite its modern glitz, has a very colorful traditional market, which is fun for strolling through even without buying anything. Vendors arrive here with grand intentions: mounds of neon-red tomatoes, buckets of *nopales* (cactus leaves), towers of toilet paper, and mountains of soap bars. As you wander through the sunlight-dappled aisles, past big gaping fish, bulging

rounds of cheese, and festoons of huaraches, don't miss Piñatas Amanda, one of the market's friendliest shops. You may even end up buying one of her charming paper Donald Ducks, Snow Whites, or Porky Pigs. The market is at the corner of Mendoza and Constituyentes, a quarter mile inland from Hornos Beach. Ride a "Mercado"-marked bus, or taxi.

Supermarkets And A Natural-food Store

In the *zócalo* area, **Woolworth's** is a good source of a little bit of everything at reasonable prices (on Escudero, corner of Morelos, behind Sanborn's; open daily 9:30 a.m.-8:30 p.m.). Their lunch counter, furthermore, provides a welcome refuge from the midday heat.

Comercial Mexicana, not far from the *zócalo,* is a big Mexican K mart, which, besides the expected film, medicines, cosmetics and housewares, also includes groceries and a bakery (on the Costera at Cinco de Mayo, around the curve from the *zócalo*, near Fort San Diego; open daily 9-9, tel. 835-449).

Super-Super, at the other end of town, is an American-style refuge from Mexico, even if only for its ice-cream-cool air-conditioning (on the Costera across from CICI water park; open daily 8 a.m.-11 p.m., tel. 846-961). Besides groceries and notions, its big newsstand carries loads of U.S. magazines, paperback novels, records, and some Mexico guides.

Back near the *zócalo,* **La Naturista de Acapulco,** one of Acapulco's few health stores, carries shelves of vitamins, plus alfalfa, anise, oats, soya, betel, and a host of other natural remedies (Juarez 15, corner of Valle, one block from the *zócalo;* open Mon.-Sat. 9 a.m.-7 p.m., tel. 823-262).

Photofinishing And Film

Foto Condor, right on the *zócalo,* does photofinishing and sells photo supplies and several popular film varieties (corner J. Carranza; open daily 8 a.m.-9 p.m., tel. 822-112).

One of the best-stocked photo shops in town is **Super Foto Economica,** on the Costera across from the Torre Acapulco condo tower (Costera M. Alemán 82, not far from Hotel Fiesta Americana Condesa, tel. 840-643 and 841-194). In addition to one-hour color service, they rent cameras and stock and develop professional films, including black-and-white and transparencies.

Handicrafts

Despite much competition, asking prices for Acapulco handicrafts are relatively high. Bargaining, furthermore, seldom brings them down to size. **Sanborn's,** two blocks from the *zócalo* (with another branch on the Costera a block from the Fiesta Americana Condesa), is a good starting point for comparison shopping, since their prices are both fixed and fairly reasonable (At Costera M. Alemán and Escudero; open daily 7:30 a.m.-11 p.m., with bookstore and restaurant, tel. 826-167). Sanborn's all-Mexico selection includes, notably, black Oaxaca *barra* pottery, painted gourds from Uruapan, Guadalajara leather, Taxco silver jewelry, colorful plates from Puebla, and Tlaquepaque pottery and glass.

With Sanborn's prices in mind, head one block toward the *zócalo* to **Margarita,** where, in the basement of the big old Edificio Oviedo, glitters an eclectic fiesta of Mexican jewelry (I. de la Llave and Costera M. Alemán, local 1; open Mon.-Sat. 9-9, Sun. 9-3, tel. 820-590, 825-240). Never mind if the place is empty; cruise-line passengers regularly fill the aisles. Here you'll be able to see artisans adding to the acre of gleaming silver, gold, copper, brass, fine carving, and lacquerware around you. Don't forget to get your free margarita (or soft drink) before you leave.

Another bountiful handicrafts source near the *zócalo* is the artisans' market **Mercado de Parrazal** (from Sanborn's, head away from the Costera a few short blocks to Vasquez de Leon and turn right one block). There, a big plaza of semipermanent stalls offers a galaxy of Mexican handicrafts: Tonalá and Tlaquepaque papier-mâché, brass, and pottery animals; Bustamante-replica eggs, masks, and humanoids; Oaxaca wooden animals and black pottery; Guerrero masks; and Taxco jewelry. Sharp bargaining is necessary, however, to cut the excessive asking prices down to size.

The new side of town has a number of interesting handicrafts sources. Along the Costera sidewalk bordering the shady Centro Cultural (galleries, library open Mon.-Sat. 9-2 and 4-7, and oft-closed museum) grounds, vendors pile tables with crafts. Among the most intriguing are the originals of Juan Silviera, who, with his wife, Blanca, has built a thriving business fashioning fanciful painted animals. Fluent in English

(he lived for years in Canada) and very well informed, Juan also leads private insider's-eye tours of Acapulco. If you miss him, call him at home, tel. 855-521.

The biggest crafts store in Acapulco, AFA (Artesanias Finas de Acapulco), is tucked a block off the Costera near the Hyatt Regency (on Horacio Nelson, corner of James Cook, tel. 848-039, 848-040, fax 842-448; open Mon.-Sat. 9 a.m.-7:30 p.m., Sun. 9-3). Although jewelry is their strong suit, they have a lot more from most everywhere in Mexico. Items include pottery, papier-mâché, lacquerware, onyx, and much leather, including purses, belts, and saddles.

Some of the most unusual of Acapulco's handicrafts come from the hillside store of **Felipe Zamora** (beside the highway, uphill between the Hyatt and Las Brisas hotels; open daily 10 a.m.-8 p.m., tel. 843-410). A virtual museum of odd art-for-furniture, Zamora's pieces include fantastic hewn driftwood tables, gigantic demon and gargoyle masks, pious antique madonnas, and rusted Singer sewing machines.

SERVICES

Money Exchange

In the *zócalo* neighborhood, go to the **Bancomer** (fronting the Costera, tel. 848-055) to change U.S. (9 a.m.-1:30 p.m.) or Canadian (11 a.m.-1:30 p.m.) cash or traveler's checcks. Although the lines at **Banamex** nearby (on the Costera two blocks from *zócalo* next to Sanborn's, tel. 883-720, 837-020) are usually longer, they exchange major currencies (including French, Spanish, British, German, Swiss, and Japanese) and have longer hours, Mon.-Fri. 9-1:30.

After hours near the *zócalo,* you can exchange most major currencies and traveler's checks at *casa de cambio* **Mimsa** (open Mon.-Fri. 9-5, Sat. 9-2, tel. 837-777) in the Edificio Oviedo, street level, across from Sanborn's. Their rates, however, run about $3 per hundred less than banks.

On the new side of town, change money at **Banamex** across from McDonald's (open Mon.-Fri. 9-5, tel. 859-020) or at the **Bancomer** Glorietta Diana (Diana Circle) office (open Mon.-Fri. 9-1 for U.S. currency and traveler's checks and 10:30-1 for Canadian, tel. 848-055).

After hours on the Costera, the **Consultorio International** (tel. 843-108) in Galería Picuda shopping center across from the Hotel Fiesta Americana Condesa exchanges currency and traveler's checks daily 9-9.

American Express Offices
The main Acapulco American Express branch (on the Costera between the Glorietta Diana and the Fiesta Americana Condesa), cashes and sells American Express traveler's checks, provides member financial services and travel agency services. Agency hours are Mon.-Fri. 9-6 and Sat. 9-1:30, although financial service hours may be shorter. Call 845-550 or 846-887 for details.

The American Express branch agency at the Hyatt Regency (tel. 842-888, ext. 682) provides similar services Mon.-Sat. 8-7.

Post, Telephone, And Telegraph
The Acapulco main *correos* (post office) is in the Palacio Federal across the Costera from the steamer dock three blocks from the *zócalo*. They provide Mexpost fast mail and philatelic services. (Mon.-Fri. 8-8, Sat. 9-1, tel. 822-083.) A **branch post and telegraph office** at the Estrella de Oro bus terminal (Cuauhtémoc and Massieu) is open Mon.-Fri. 9-8, Sat. 9-12.

Telecomunicaciones next to the main post office provides money order, telegram, telex, and fax services (Mon.-Fri. 9-6 and Sat. 9-12, tel. 822-622 and 822-621).

Near the *zócalo,* you can call *larga distancia* (long-distance) daily 8 a.m.-10 p.m. from the small office on J. Carranza at Calle de la Llave.

Round-the-clock long-distance telephone is available at **Larga Distancia Sendatur** (tel. 830-714) at the Estrella Blanca Central de Autobus (central bus terminal) at Ejido 47, about a mile northwest from the *zócalo* on the road to Pie de La Cuesta. The Acapulco area code is 74.

Immigration And Customs
If you lose your tourist card go to **Migratorios** (in the Palacio Federal next to the main post office) with proof of your identity and some proof (such as your passport, airline ticket, or a copy of your lost tourist card) of your arrival date in Mexico. If you try to leave Mexico without your tourist card, you may face trouble and a fine. Also re-port to Migratorios if you arrive in Acapulco by yacht.

The **Aduana** (customs, tel. 824-976 and 820-931) is likewise in the Palacio Federal. If you have to temporarily leave your car in Mexico, you must go to their superior office, the Secretaria de Hacienda (treasury) y Credito Publico (open Mon.-Fri. 8:30-1:30, corner of Capitan Amal Espina and Urdaneta, two blocks off the Costera at Playa Hornos, tel. 862-435 and 862-495) to execute the proper paperwork.

Consulates
Acapulco has several consulates. The U.S. consular officer, Bob Urbanek (Hotel Club del Sol mezzanine, tel. 856-600, ext. 7348), holds office hours Mon.-Fri. 10-2. He's a busy man, and asks that you kindly have your problem written down, together with a specific request for information or action.

The **Canadian** consul, Diane McLean de Huerta is also at the Hotel Club del Sol, tel. 856-621. For the **British** consul, Derek Gore, call 841-650 or 846-605 at the Hotel Las Brisas. Call the **German** consul, Mario Wichtendahl, at 841-860; the **Netherlands** consul is at the Hotel Presidente, tel. 841-800; the **French** at 841-710 and 823-394; and **Spanish** at 862-466.

INFORMATION

Tourist Information Office
The helpful federal Turismo information office staff answers questions and gives out whatever maps and information they may have at their office on the beach side of the Costera, corner of Amal Espina, across from Banamex (Av. M. Alemán 107, tel. 851-022, 851-304, and 851-178; open Mon.-Fri. 8-8, Sat.-Sun. 10-6).

Medical, Police, And Emergencies
If you get sick, see your hotel doctor or go to the **Hospital Magellanes,** one of Acapulco's most respected private hospitals, for either office calls or 'round-the-clock emergencies. Facilities include a lab, 24-hour **pharmacy,** and an emergency room with many specialists on call (at W. Massieu 2, corner of Colón, one block from the Costera and the Hotel Ritz; tel. 856-544, 856-597, 856-706).

For routine medications near the *zócalo*, go to the big **Farmacia Discuento** (discount pharmacy, tel. 820-804) open daily 8 a.m.-10 p.m., at Escudero and Carranza, across the street from Woolworth's.

For **police** emergencies, call the Policia Turistica station (tel. 850-490, 850-862, and 850-650) at the end of Av. Caminos, on the inland side of Papagayo Park.

In case of fire, call the *bomberos* (fire fighters), tel. 844-122, on Av. Farallon, one block off the Costera from the Glorietta Diana (Diana Circle).

Books, Newspapers, And Magazines

One of the best book sources in town is Sanborn's on the Costera (open 7:30 a.m.-11 p.m., tel. 844-467), ground floor of the Condo Estrella tower, one block from the Hotel Fiesta Americana Condesa. They stock hundreds of magazines, paperback novels, maps, Mexico guides, and coffee-table art and archaeological books. The *zócalo* branch (on the Costera across from the steamship dock, same hours) is equally good.

English-language international newspapers, such as the *News* of Mexico City, the *Los Angeles Times,* and *USA Today,* are often available in the large hotel bookshops, especially the Acapulco Plaza, Fiesta Americana Condesa, and the Hyatt Regency. On the other end of town, newsstands around the *zócalo* regularly sell the *News.*

A pair of Acapulco English-language newspapers keep abreast of local happenings. The Acapulco *Heat* (tel. 812-625) covers social events, Mexico travel, restaurants, and lists houses and apartments for sale or rent. Pick the *Heat* up at the Fat Farm restaurant or Super-Super grocery store.

The Acapulco *News* (tel. 834-068), the other local paper, covers political, business, and general news.

Public Library

The small, friendly Acapulco *biblioteca* (public library) is near the *zócalo* adjacent to the cathedral. Their collection, used mostly by college and high school students in their airy reading room, is nearly all in Spanish (at Madero 5, corner of Quebrada, open Mon.-Fri. 9-9, Sat. 9-8, tel. 820-388).

Guide And Language Instruction

Sculptor and art teacher Juan Silviera offers personalized tours of Acapulco for small groups (P.O. Box 112, Acapulco, Guerrero 39300, tel. 74-855-521). Personable and well informed, Silviera also speaks fluent English, having lived in Canada for many years. "They may pay whatever they want," he replies, when asked about his fee.

The long-established **Harmon Hall** school of languages offers Spanish instruction. Their four-week package includes 20 hours of intensive study and runs $180. (70 Costera M. Alemán, Fracc. Las Playas, Acapulco, Guerrero 39300, tel. 74-838-147).

Service Club And Women's Meeting

The **Friends of Acapulco** holds fund-raising fiestas and fashion shows to support the Acapulco Children's home and other local good works. Their members meet regularly for dinner at the Hotel Las Hamacas on Playa Hornos. Call for information at 850-255, or write P.O. Box C-54, Acapulco, Guerrero 39300.

The Guerrero state Sub Secretaria de Mujer ("Women's Sub-Secretariat") provides counseling and help for problems such as rape, domestic abuse, abandonment, and birth control at their small Acapulco office at Hidalgo 1, half a block from the *zócalo* (open Mon.-Fri. 9-3 and 6-9, tel. 826-311 and 822-525).

The sub-secretariat also sponsors a public meeting on the first Thursday of each month (at 6 p.m. at Fuerte de San Diego auditorium) where women meet and share their feelings, concerns, and ideas. Local leaders, such as Inez Huerta Pegueros, director of the Acapulco chapter of the nationwide Movimiento Social Contra la Violencia Sexual, often attend.

GETTING THERE AND AWAY

By Air

Several airlines connect the Acapulco airport (code-designated ACA, officially the Juan N. Alvarez International Airport) with U.S. and Mexican destinations.

Aeromexico flights connect directly with Houston (via Mexico City) four times weekly and with New York (via Mexico City) daily. For reservations, contact them at the Torre Acapul-

MEXICO CITY DRIVING LIMITS

In order to reduce smog and traffic gridlock, authorities have limited what cars can drive in Mexico City, depending upon the last digit of their license plates. If you violate these rules, you risk getting an expensive ticket: On Monday, no vehicle may be driven with final digits 5 or 6; Tuesday, 7 or 8; Wednesday, 3 or 4; Thursday, 1 or 2; Friday, 9 or 0. Weekends, all vehicles may be driven.

co (tel. 851-625 and 851-600) or Hotel Imperial (tel. 847-224 and 847-009). For flight information, call 840-085.

Delta Airlines flights connect daily with Dallas; others connect daily with Los Angeles, continuing to Portland. One additional Saturday flight connects weekly with Los Angeles. For reservations, call 840-797 and 840-716; for flight information, call 840-446.

Mexicana Airlines flights connect with Chicago daily and with Mexico City five times daily. For reservations, contact them at Torre Acapulco (tel. 841-215); for flight information, call 841-815.

American Airlines flights connect twice daily with Dallas. For reservations and flight information, call 841-179 or 841-244.

Continental Airlines charter flights connect several times weekly with Houston. For reservations, call 847-003; for flight information, cal 843-308.

Flights of Mexicana Airlines's subsidiary, **Aerocaribe**, connect with Oaxaca, Huatulco-Puerto Ángel, and Puerto Escondido four times weekly. For reservations, call 842-621; for flight information call 845-785; or call Mexicana (see above).

Canadian Holiday Airlines charter flights connect (mostly during the winter) with Toronto, Vancouver, and Calgary. For information, call their Acapulco agent at 846-554.

Air Arrival And Departure

After the usually perfunctory immigration and customs checks, Acapulco arrivees enjoy airport car rentals, efficient transportation for the 15-mile trip to town, and money exhange service (U.S. and Canadian cash and traveler's

checks, Mon.-Fri. 10 a.m-3 p.m.). If you'll be arriving after money-exchange hours or on weekends, change a day's worth of money before arrival.

Airport **car rental** agents usually include Hertz (tel. 858-947, 856-889), Avis (tel. 841-633, 842-581), National (tel. 848-234, 844-348), Budget (tel. 848-200, 859-050 ext. 3096), Economovil (tel. 842-828, 843-260), and SAAD jeep rentals (tel. 843-445, 845-325). You can ensure availability and often save money by bargaining with agencies via their national toll-free numbers prior to arrival.

Tickets for **ground transport** to town are sold by agents near the terminal exit. Options include collective GMC Suburban station wagon (about $5, kids half price) or microbus (about $2.50, kids half price), both of which deposit passengers at individual hotels. *Taxis especiales* (private taxis) run about $17 to a $30 maximum, depending on distance. Plush limousines go for between $21 and $38. GMC Suburbans can be hired "especial" as private taxis for about $32 for up to seven passengers.

On your **departure** day, save money by sharing a taxi with fellow departees. Don't get into the taxi until you settle the fare. (Having already arrived, you know what the airport ride should cost. If the driver insists on greed, hail another taxi.)

Simplify your departure by having $12 U.S. cash or its peso equivalent (they don't take traveler's checks or credit cards) for your international departure tax. If you lost your tourist card (which Immigration stamped upon your arrival), don't pass Go; rather return to Migratorios (see "Information" above) prior to your departure date.

The Acapulco air terminal building has a number of shops for last-minute handicrafts purchases, a *buzón* (mailbox) for postcards, long-distance telephones, and a restaurant.

By Bus

Major competitors **Estrella Blanca** and **Estrella de Oro** operate separate long-distance Centrales de Autobus (central bus terminals) on opposite sides of town.

Estrella Blanca (tel. 821-100, 823-691, 831-251) coordinates its service with subsidiary lines Flecha Roja, Lineas Unidas, Autotransportes

Cuauhtémoc, and Gacela at its big northwest-side terminal at Av. Ejido 47. The airy station is so clean you could sleep on the onyx floor and not get dirty; bring an air mattress and blanket. Other conveniences include inexpensive left-luggage lockers, food stores across the street, and a 24-hour *larga distancia*.

Scores of Estrella Blanca *salidas locales* (local departures) connect with destinations in three directions: northern interior, and Costa Grande (northwest) and Costa Chica (southeast) coastal destinations.

Most connections are first class or *primera plus* (super first class). Specific northern interior connections include Mexico City (dozens daily, some via Taxco), Toluca, Morelia via Chilpancingo and Altimirano (six daily), and Guadalajara (three daily).

Many first- (about 10 per day) and second-class (hourly) departures connect northwest with Costa Grande destinations of Zihuatanejo and Lázaro Cárdenas. Southeast Costa Chica connections, terminating in Puerto Escondido, include four first-class daily (one via Ometepec) and approximately one second-class connection per hour.

The busy, modern **Estrella de Oro** bus terminal on the east side (at Cuauhtémoc and Massieu, tel. 858-705) connects with Mexico City corridor (Chilpancingo, Iguala, Taxco, Cuernavaca) and northwest Costa Grande destinations. Services include left-luggage lockers ($4 per day), snack bars, food stores, restaurant, and *correos* (post) and *telegrafos* offices (on the outside upstairs walkway, west end, open Mon.-Fri. 9-8, Sat. 9-12).

Northwest Estrella de Oro connections include dozens of first and super first class with Mexico City and intermediate points. (Only a few, however, connect directly with Taxco.) Four departures connect daily with Costa Grande (three with Zihuatanejo, one only with Lázaro

Cárdenas). Estrella de Oro offers no Costa Chica (Puerto Escondido) connections southeast.

Car Or RV

Good highways connect Acapulco north with Mexico City, northwest with the Costa Grande and Michoacán, and southeast with the Costa Chica and Oaxaca.

The Mexico City Hwy. 95 *cuota* (toll) superhighway would make the connection via Chilpancingo easy (83 miles, 133 km, about two hours) if it weren't for the Acapulco congestion (see below). The uncluttered extension (125 miles, 201 km) to Cuernavaca via Iguala is a breeze in three hours. For Taxco, leave the superhighway at Iguala and follow the winding but scenic old Hwy. 95 cutoff 22 miles (35 km) northwest. From Cuernavaca, the over-the-mountain leg to Mexico City (53 miles, 85 km) would be simple except for Mexico City gridlock, which might lengthen it to two hours. Better allow at least seven hours for the entire 261-mile (420-km) Acapulco-Mexico City trip.

The Costa Grande section of Hwy. 200 northwest toward Zihuatanejo is generally uncluttered and smooth (except for a few narrow one-lane bridges). Allow about four hours for the 150-mile (242-km) trip.

The same is true for the Costa Chica stretch of Hwy. 200 southeast to Pinotepa Nacional (157 miles, 253 km) and Puerto Escondido (247 miles, 398 km total). Allow about four driving hours to Pinotepa, six total to Puerto Escondido.

Acapulco's most congested ingress-egress bottleneck is the over-the-hill leg of Hwy. 95 from the middle of town. You can bypass this by driving east along the Costera past Las Brisas as if you were heading to the airport. At the intersection near Puerto Marques (marked by a Pemex station), head north. When you reach Hwy. 200, head right for the Costa Chica, or left for Hwy. 95 and northern points.

INLAND TO TAXCO

As Acapulco thrives on what's new, Taxco (pop. 150,000) luxuriates in what's old. Nestling among forest-crowned mountains and decorated with monuments of its silver-rich past, Taxco now enjoys an equally rich flood of visitors who stop en route to or from Acapulco. They come to enjoy its fiestas and clear, pine-scented air and to stroll the cobbled hillside lanes and bargain for world-renowned silver jewelry.

And despite the acclaim, Taxco preserves its diminutive colonial charm *because* of its visitors, who come to enjoy what Taxco offers. They stay in venerable, family-owned lodgings, walk to the colorful little *zócalo,* where they admire the famous baroque cathedral, and wander among the awning-festooned market lanes just downhill.

HISTORY

The traditional hieroglyph representing Taxco shows athletes in a court competing in a game of *tlachtli* (still locally played) with a rubber ball. "Tlachco," the Nahuatl (Aztec-language) name representing that place (which had become a small Aztec garrison settlement by the eve of the conquest) literally translates as "Place of the Ball Game." The Spanish, more interested in local minerals than in linguistic details, shifted the name to Taxco.

Colonization

In 1524, Hernán Cortés, looking for tin to alloy with copper to make bronze cannon, heard that people around Taxco were using bits of metal for money. Prospectors hurried out, and within a few years they struck rich silver veins in Tetelcingo, now known as Taxco Viejo ("Old Taxco"), seven miles downhill from present-day Taxco. The Span-

hieroglyph of Taxco ("Place of the Ball Game")

ish Crown appropriated the mines and worked them with generations of *indígena* forced labor.

Eighteenth-century enlightenment came to Taxco in the person of Jose Borda, who, arriving from Spain in 1716, modernized the mine franchise that his brother had been operating. Jose improved conditions, began paying the miners, thereby increasing productivity and profits. In contrast to past operators, Borda returned the proceeds to Taxco, building the monuments that still grace the town. His fortune built streets, bridges, fountains, arches, and his masterpiece, the church of Santa Prisca (which included a special chapel for the miners, who before had not been allowed to enter the church).

Independence And Modern Times

The 1810-21 War of Independence and the subsequent civil strife reduced the mines to but a memory within a generation. They were nearly forgotten when William Spratling, an American artist and architect, moved to Taxco in 1929 and began reviving Taxco's ancient but moribund silversmithing tradition. Working with local artisans, Spratling opened the first cooperative shop, Las Delicias, which remains today.

Spurred by the trickle of tourists along the new Acapulco highway, more shops opened, increasing the demand for silver, which in turn led to the reopening of the mines. Soon silver demand outpaced the supply. Silver began streaming in from other parts of Mexico to the workbenches of thousands of artisans in hundreds of family- and cooperatively owned shops dotting the still-quaint hillsides of a new, prosperous Taxco.

SIGHTS

Getting Oriented

Although the present city, elev. 5,850 feet (1,780 meters), spreads much farther, the center of town encompasses the city's original seven hills, wrinkles in the slope of a towering mountain.

For most visitors, the downhill town limit is the Carretera Nacional (National Highway), named after John F. Kennedy. It contours along the hillside from **Los Arcos** ("The Arches") on

TAXCO

TO GRUTAS DE CACAHUAMILPA
XOCHICALCO, AND MEXICO CITY

LOS ARCOS

1

LA GARITA

2

3

PUENTE RAMONET (SHRINE)

HOSPITAL ESTATAL

6

IGLESIA DE CHAVARRIETA

JUAREZ

4

HOSPITAL
ESPECIALIDADES

BENITO

EX - CONVENTO
SAN BERNARDINO

5

7

CORREOS (POST OFFICE)

8

10

CASA BORDA (CITY HALL)

11

ZÓCALO

9

MUERTOS

12

13

CUAUHTÉMOC

PARROQUIA DE SANTA PRISCA

16

17

POLICIA
PREVENTIVA
(POLICE)

14   15

18   BANCO
CONFIA

20   J. R. DE ALARCON

BANCOMER
(BANK)

19

PLAZUELA DE SAN JUAN

LA VERACRUZ

22

TELÉGRAFOS

21

(AV. JOHN F. KENNEDY)

PILITA

SAN NICOLAS

IGLESIA DE
VERA CRUZ

TO CERRO HUIXTECA
(BUG FESTIVAL)

IGLESIA DE SANTÍSIMA

PARQUE GUERRERO

FLECHA ROJA
(LOCAL AND 2ND CLASS BUS TERMINAL)

IGLESIA DE SAN NICOLAS

SANTA ANA

LARGA - DISTANCIA
(LONG DISTANCE TELEPHONE)

ESTRELLA DE ORO
(1ST CLASS BUS TERMINAL)

MORELOS

HOSPITAL ALICIA

HOSPITAL SEGURO SOCIAL

CARRETERA NACIONAL

2

95

TO ACAPULCO

24

23

0   300 yd

0   300 m

© MOON PUBLICATIONS, INC.

TAXCO

1. Cableway to Hotel Monte Taxco
2. tourist information (two locations)
3. Hotel Borda
4. Biblioteca (Library) Taxco-Canoga Park
5. Cafe Gizmo
6. Hotel Posada de la Misión (Cuauhtémoc Mural)
7. Restaurant Taberna
8. Hotel Agua Escondida
9. Hotel Posada Los Castillo
10. Hotel Los Arcos
11. Casa Ayja (grocery)
12. Casa Humboldt (crafts)
13. Restaurant La Parroquia
14. Hotel Rancho Taxco Victoria
15. Restaurant El Adobe
16. Cine Ana Maria
17. Photo Tienda Misión
18. La Gruta (silver)
19. Casa Dominguez (bookstore)
20. Museo Spratling (Archaeology Museum)
21. Hotel Santa Prisca
22. market
23. Hotel Hacienda del Solar
24. Restaurant La Ventana de Taxco

the north (Mexico City) end of town about two miles, passing the Calle Pilita intersection on the south (Acapulco) edge of town. Along the *carretera,* immediately accessible to a steady stream of tour buses, lie the town's plusher hotels and many silver shops.

The rest of the town is fortunately insulated from tour buses by its narrow winding streets. From the *carretera,* the most important of them climb and converge, like bent spokes of a wheel, to the *zócalo* (main plaza). Beginning with the most northerly, the main streets are La Garita, Alarcón, Veracruz, Santa Ana, Morelos, and Pilita.

Getting Around

Although walking is Taxco's most common mode of transport, taxis go anywhere within the city limits for about $1.50 to $2. White *kombi* collective vans (fare about $.20) follow designated routes, marked on the windshields. Simply tell your specific destination to the driver. **Flecha Roja** second-class local buses leave frequently from their *carretera* terminal (near the corner of Santa Ana) for nearby destinations.

Around The *Zócalo*

All roads in Taxco begin and end on the *zócalo* at **Santa Prisca** church. French architect D. Diego Durán designed and built it between 1751 and 1758 with money from the fortune of silver king Don José Borda. The facade, decorated with pedestaled saints, arches, and spiraled columns, follows the baroque *churrigueresque* style (after Jose Churriguera, 1665-1725, the "Spanish Michaelangelo"). Interior furnishings include an elegant pipe organ, brought from Germany by boat and muleback in 1751, and several gilded side altars. The riot of interior elaboration climaxes in the towering gold-leaf main altar, which seems to drip with ornamentation in tribute to Saint Prisca, the Virgin of Guadalupe, and the Virgin of the Rosary, who piously preside above all.

Dreamy Bible-story paintings by Miguel Cabrera decorate a chamber behind the main altar, while in a room to the right, portraits of Pope Benedict IV, who sanctioned all this, and Manuel Borda, Santa Prisca's first priest, hang amongst a solemn gallery of subsequent padres.

Outside, landmarks around the plaza include the **Casa Borda,** visible (facing away from the church facade) on the right side of the *zócalo.* This former Borda family town house, built concurrently with the church in typical baroque colonial style, now serves as the Taxco city hall.

Heading from the church steps, you can continue downhill in either of two interesting ways. If you walk left immediately downhill from the church, you reach the lane, Calle Los Arcos, running alongside and below the church. From there, reach the **market** by heading right before the quaint archway over the street, down the winding staircase-lane, where you'll soon be in a warren of awning-covered stalls.

If, however, you head right from the church steps, another immediate right leads you beside the church along legendary **Calle de los Muertos** ("Street of the Dead"), named partly because of the many workmen who died constructing the church.

Continuing downhill, you'll find **Museo Guillermo Spratling** fronting the little plaza behind the church. On the main and upper floors, the National Institute of Archaeology displays intriguing carvings and ceramics (including unusual phallic examples), such as a ball-game ring, animal masks, and a priestly statuette, with knife in one

Santa Prisca church, built in 1758 with profits from Taxco's silver mines, remains the center of town activities.

hand, human heart in the other. Basement-floor displays interestingly detail local history from the Aztecs through William Spratling. The museum is open Tues.-Sat. 10-5, Sun. 9-3, tel. 216-60.

Back outside, one block down Alarcón (the downhill extension of Calle Muertos), stands **Casa Humboldt,** named after the celebrated geographer (who is said to have stayed only one night, however).

Other In-town Sights
A short ride, coupled with a walk circling back to the zócalo, provides the basis for an interesting half-day exploration. Taxi or ride a kombi to the Hotel Posada de la Misión, where the **Cuauhtémoc Mural** glitters on a wall near the pool. Executed by renowned muralist Juan O'Gorman with a riot of pre-Columbian symbols—yellow sun, pearly moon (including rabbit), snarling jaguar, writhing serpents, fluttering eagle—the mural glorifies Cuauhtémoc, the last Aztec emperor. Cuauhtémoc, unlike his uncle

Moctezuma, tenaciously resisted the conquest, but was captured and later executed by Cortés in 1524. His remains were discovered not long ago in Ixcateopan, about 24 miles away by local bus or car. Follow the fork from the carretera about two miles south of town. In Ixcateopan, a small museum and memorial document and enshrine the remains.

Continue your walk a few hundred yards along the carretera (Mexico City direction) from the Hotel Posada de la Misión. There, a driveway leading right just before the gas station heads to the Hotel Borda grounds. Turn left on the road just after the gate and you'll come to an antique brick smelter chimney and cable-hung derrick. These mark an inactive **mineshaft** that descends to the mine-tunnel honeycomb thousands of feet beneath the town. (The mines are still being worked from another entrance, but for lead rather than silver. You can see the present-day works from the hilltop of the Hotel Hacienda del Solar on the south edge of town.)

Now, return to the carretera, cross over and stroll the **Calle la Garita** about a mile back to the zócalo. Of interest along the way (see map) are the **Iglesia de Chavarrieta,** the **Biblioteca (library) Taxco-Canoga Park,** and the **ex-Convento San Bernardino,** where across the street you can stop in at the **Cafe Gizmo** for a drink or snack.

Farther on, a block before the zócalo, pause to decipher the colored stone mosaic of the **Taxco Hieroglyph** which decorates the pavement in front of the Correos (post office).

Cableway To Hotel Monte Taxco
On the north side of town, where the carretera passes beneath Los Arcos ("The Arches"), a cableway above the highway lifts passengers to soaring vistas of the town on one side and ponderous, pine-studded mesas on the other (open daily 7:30 a.m.-7 p.m.; one-way tickets about $1.70, kids half price; return by taxi if you miss the last car). The ride ends at the Hotel Monte Taxco, where you can make a day of it golfing, horseback riding, playing tennis, eating lunch, and sunning on the panoramic-view pool deck.

Town Vistas
You needn't go as far afield as the Hotel Monte Taxco to get a good view of the city streets and houses carpeting the mountainside. Vistas depend not only on vantage point but time of day,

TLATCHTLI: THE BALL GAME

Basketball fever is probably a mild affliction compared to the enthusiasm of pre-Columbian crowds for *tlatchtli,* the ball game played throughout (and still played in some parts of) Mesoamerica. Contemporary accounts and latter-day scholarship have led to a partial picture of *tlatchtli* as it was

played centuries ago. Although details varied locally, the game's basis was a hard natural rubber ball, which players batted back and forth across a center dividing line with leg-, arm-, and torso-blows.

Play and scoring was vaguely similar to tennis. Opponents, either individuals or small teams, tried to smash the ball past their opponents into scoring niches at the opposite ends of an I-shaped, sunken court. Players could also garner points by forcing their opponents to make a wild shot that bounced beyond the court's retaining walls.

Courts were often equipped with a pair of stone rings fixed above opposing ends of the center dividing line. One scoring variation awarded immediate victory to the team who could manage to bat the *tlatchtli* through the ring.

Like tennis, players became very adept at smashing the ball at high speed. Unlike tennis, however, the ball was solid and perhaps as heavy as a baseball. Although protected by helmets and leather, players were usually bloodied, often injured, and sometimes even killed from opponents' punishing *tlatchtli*-inflicted blows. Matches were sometimes decided like a boxing match, with victory going to the opponent left standing on the court.

As with everything in Mesoamerica, tradition and ritual ruled *tlatchtli.* Master teachers subjected initiates to rigorous training, prescribed ritual, and discipline not unlike those of a medieval monastic brotherhood.

Potential rewards were enormous, however. Stakes varied in proportion to a contest's ritual significance and the rank of the players and their patrons. Champion players could win fortunes in gold, feathers, or precious stones. Exceptional games could result in riches and honor for the winner, and death for the loser, whose heart, ripped from his chest on the centerline stone, became food for the gods.

---

since the best viewing sunshine (which frees you from squinting) should come generally from *behind.* Consequently, spots along the highway (more or less *east* of town), such as the pool-patios of the **Hotel Posada de la Misión** and the **Hotel Borda** provide good morning views, while afternoon views are best from points west of town, such as the restaurant balcony at (or the hilltop of) the **Hotel Rancho Taxco Victoria.**

SIGHTS OUT OF TOWN

The monumental duo, the Grutas de Cacahuamilpa caves and the ruins of ancient Xochicalco combine for an interesting day-trip. Don't get started too late; the Grutas are 15 miles (25 km) north (Mexico City direction) of town and Xochicalco is 25 miles (40 km) farther.

Grutas De Cacahuamilpa

They're worth the effort, however. The Grutas de Cacahuamilpa are one of the world's great caverns. Forests of stalagmites and stalactites, in myriad shapes—Pluto the Pup, the Holy Family, a desert caravan, asparagus stalks, cauliflower heads—festoon a series of gigantic limestone chambers. The finale is a grand, 30-story hall that meanders for half a mile, like a fairyland in stone. The caves are open daily; hourly three-mile, two-hour walking tours in Spanish are included in the $3 admission and begin at 10 a.m. A few gift shops sell souvenirs; snack bars supply food.

Getting There: *Kombi* collective vans go hourly, beginning at 8:30 a.m., from the Flecha Roja bus station on the *carretera* to the caves for a one-way fare of about $1.25. By car, get to the caves via Hwy. 95 north from Taxco; after 10 miles (16

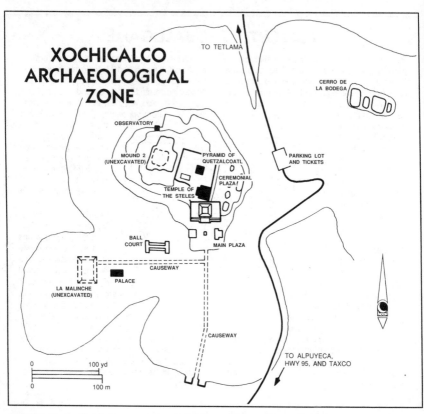

km) from the northside Pemex station, fork left onto Hwy. 55 toward Toluca. Continue five more miles (eight km) and turn right at the signed Cacahuamilpa junction. After a few hundred yards, turn right again into the entrance driveway.

Xochicalco

Xochicalco (soh-shee-KAHL-koh), an hour farther north, although little publicized, is a fountainhead of Mesoamerican legend. The ruin itself spreads over a half a dozen terraced pyramid hilltops above a natural lake-valley, which at one time sustained a large population. Xochicalco flowered during the late-classic period around A.D. 800, partly filling the vacuum left by the decline of Teotihuacan, the previously dominant Mesoamerican classic city-state. Some archaeologists speculate that Xochicalco at its apex was the great center of learning, known in legend as Tamanchoan, where astronomer-priests derived and maintained calendars and where the Queztalcoatl legend was born.

Exploring the Site: Walk about 100 yards directly west, uphill, from the parking lot, where the **Pyramid of Quetzalcoatl** ("The Plumed Serpent") rises on the hilltop. Vermilion paint remnants hint of its original appearance, which was perhaps as brilliant as a giant birthday cake. In bas-relief around the entire base a serpent writhes, intertwined with personages, probably representing chiefs or great priests. Above these are warriors, identified by their helmets and *atlatl,* or lance-throwers.

Most notable, however, is one of Mesoamerica's most remarkable sculptures, to the left of the staircase. It shows the 11th week sign, *ozomatli*

ozomatli (monkey), being pulled by a hand (via a rope) to join with the fifth week sign, *calli* (house). Latter-day scholars generally interpret this as describing a calendar correction that resulted from a grand conclave of chiefs and sages from all over Mesoamerica, probably at this very spot.

About 150 feet south rises the **Temple of the Steles,** so named for three large stone tablets found beneath the floor. They narrate the events of the Quetzalcoatl legend, wherein Quetzalcoatl (discoverer of corn and the calendar) was transformed into the morning star (the planet Venus) and who continues to rule the heavens as the brightest star and the Lord of Time.

About 100 yards farther south, the **Main Plaza** was accessible to the common people via roads from below. This is in contrast to the sacrosanct **Ceremonial Plaza** nearby. A faintly visible causeway once connected the yet-unexplored La Malinche pyramid, 200 yards to the southwest, with the Ceremonial Plaza.

That causeway passed the **Ball Court,** which is strikingly similar to ball courts as far away as Toltec Tula in the north and Mayan Copan, in Honduras far to the south. On the opposite side of the causeway from the Ball Court lies the **Palace,** a complex marked by many rooms with luxury features such as toilet drainage, fireplaces, and steam baths.

On the opposite side of the complex is the **Observatory,** a room hollowed into the hill and stuccoed and fitted with a viewing shaft for timing the sun and star transits essential for an accurate calendar.

Get to Xochicalco by continuing past the Grutas (see directions above) driveway entrance. Continue northeast via Hwy. 160 toward Alpuyeca. After 25 miles (40 km) from the caves, a signed road heads left uphill to the Xochicalco ruins, which are open daily 10-5. Admission runs about $3.50, Sundays and holidays free. Since caretakers shoo all visitors out by 5 p.m., arrive early enough to allow a couple of hours to explore the ruins. Bring food, drinks, a hat, and comfortable walking shoes.

ACCOMMODATIONS

Taxco's inexpensive and moderately priced hotels cluster in the colorful *zócalo* neighborhood, while the deluxe lodgings are scattered mostly along the *carretera*. The dry, temperate local climate relegates air-conditioning, ceiling fans, and central heating to frills offered only in the most expensive hotels. All of the hotel recommendations below have hot water and private baths, however.

Taxco's only *zócalo*-front hostelry, the **Hotel Agua Escondida,** stands on the diagonally opposite corner from the church (Calle Guillermo Spratling 4, Taxco, Guerrero 40200, tel. 762-207-26, 762-207-36). A multilevel maze of hidden patios, rooftop sun decks and dazzling city views, the Agua Escondida has dozens of clean, comfortable rooms. The name, which translates as "Hidden Water," must refer to its big swimming pool, which is tucked away in a far rooftop corner. Rooms vary; if you have the choice, look at several. Try to avoid the oft-noisy streetfront rooms. If you don't mind climbing, some of the upper-floor rooms have airy, penthouse views. The 76 rooms run about $27 s, $34 d, and $37 t, with limited parking; credit cards accepted.

On Alarcón just downhill behind the Agua Escondida, a pair of former colonial mansions, now popular hotels, face each other across the street. The **Hotel Los Arcos,** the homier of the two, has 28 comfortable rooms in tiers around an inviting fountain patio and restaurant (J. Ruiz de Alarcón 2, Taxco, Guerrero 40200, tel. 762-218-36). Rooms rent for about $18 s, $22 d.

The **Hotel Posada Los Castillo** across the street is small and intimate, with plants, carved wood, paintings, and sculptures gracing every wall and corner (J.R. Alarcón 7, Taxco, Guerrero 40200, tel. 762-213-96, 762-234-71). Rooms, in neocolonial decor, are clean and comfortable. The owners also run a nearby silver boutique, whose displays decorate the downstairs lobby. The 14 rooms rent for about $16 s, $23 d, and $29 t, with credit cards accepted.

Heading past the opposite side of the plaza, follow Cuauhtémoc to the Plazuela de San Juan and the adjacent **Hotel Santa Prisca** (Cena Obscura 1, P.O. Box 42, Taxco, Guerrero 40200, tel. 762-200-80, 762-209-80). A tranquil, dignified old hostelry built around a perfumy garden of orange trees, its off-lobby dining room shines with graceful details, such as beveled glass, a fireplace, blue-white stoneware and ivy-hung portals. Its tile-decorated rooms, in two tiers around the garden just outside, are clean and comfortable. Rooms go for about $28 s and $37 d, with parking; credit cards accepted.

Continue along the hill another two blocks past Plazuela de San Juan to the **Hotel Rancho Taxco Victoria,** which rambles, in a picturesque state of decay, along its view hillside (Carlos J. Nibbi 5 and 7, Taxco, Guerrero 40200, tel. 762-202-10, 762-200-10). Built sometime back in the 1920s, the hotel usually slumbers on weekdays, reviving on weekends and holidays. (Actually, it's two hotels in one—the Victoria uphill and the Rancho Taxco, neglected and returning to the earth across the road downhill.) The better-maintained Victoria, however, is replete with rustic, old-world extras—hand-hewn furniture, whitewashed stucco walls, riots of bougainvillea, a spreading view garden—plus a big pool and a relaxed restaurant and bar where guests enjoy the best afternoon vista in town. Some of the spacious, comfortable rooms have luxurious view balconies. Standard-grade rooms run about $28 s, $37 d, and $49 t; deluxe for $35 s, $40 d, with parking; credit cards accepted.

From a distance, the **Hotel Borda** off the *carretera* downhill, appears to be the luxury hotel it once was (Cerro de Pedregal, P.O. Box 83, Taxco, Guerrero 40200, tel. 762-200-25, 762-202-25, fax 762-206-17). Lackluster management, however, detracts from the hotel's magnificent assets—a grand vista, spacious garden, luxurious pool-patio shaded by great, vine-draped trees. Check to see if your room is clean and in working order before you move in. The 110 rooms rent for about $43 s, $50 d, and $60 t, with restaurant, bar, live music nightly, and parking; credit cards accepted.

The **Hotel Posada de la Misión** decorates a hillside nearby (Cerro de la Misión 32, Taxco, Guerrero 40200, tel. 762-200-63, 762-205-33, fax 762-221-98). Its guests, many on group tours, enjoy cool, quiet patios, green gardens, plant-lined corridors, a sunny poolpatio, and a view restaurant. Many of the luxurious rooms have panoramic city views; some have fireplaces. All rooms have color TV and phones. Rooms rent for about $90 s, $100 d with breakfast, Christmas-New Year's prices higher; with parking, credit cards accepted. Just off the *carretera,* 200 yards south of the Pemex gas station.

The luxuriously exclusive **Hotel Hacienda del Solar** spreads over a tranquil hilltop garden on the south edge of town (P.O. Box 96, Taxco, Guerrero 40200, tel. 762-203-23). Guests in many of the 22 airy and spacious rooms enjoy private patios, fireplaces, and panoramic valley and mountain views. Rooms, in standard, deluxe, and junior suite versions, vary individually but are all artfully furnished with appointments including hand-woven rugs, colorful tile, paintings, and folk art. The standard rooms share a spacious living area near the lovely view pool-patio; deluxe and junior suite rooms have huge beds and deep tile bathtubs. Other amenities include a view restaurant, the Ventana ("Window") de Taxco, and a cocktail lounge. Adults 22 years and over only, however. Rooms for two go for about $68 standard, $91 deluxe, and $115 junior suite. During certain busy seasons, meals may be required with rentals, which will consequently rise to about $140, $164, and $188.

Vacationers who want resort amenities stay at the **Hotel Monte Taxco,** atop a towering mesa accessible by either a steep road or cableway from the highway just north of town (Lomas de Taxco, Taxco, Guerrero 40200, tel. 762-213-00, 762-213-01, fax 762-214-28). On weekends, the hotel is often packed with wellheeled Mexico City families, whose kids play organized games while their parents enjoy the panoramic poolside view or play golf and tennis. The 156 deluxe rooms, many with view balconies, rent from about $93 d, with a/c, phones, and TV; facilities include restaurants, a piano bar, disco, parking, a gym, sauna, spa, ninehole golf course, and tennis courts; credit cards accepted; in Canada and the U.S. call (800) 929-9394 for info and reservations.

FOOD

Stalls And Snacks

The score of *fondas* (foodstalls) atop the *artesanías* (ar-tay-sah-NEE-ahs) handicrafts section of the market is Taxco's prime source of wholesome country-style food. The quality of their fare is a matter of honor for the proprietors, since, among their local patrons word of a little bad food goes a long way. It's very hard to go wrong, moreover, if your selections are steaming hot and made fresh before your own eyes (in contrast, by the way, to most restaurant and hotel fare).

You can choose from a potpourri that might include steaming bowls of *menudo* or *pozole,* or maybe plates of pork or chicken *mole,* or *molcajetes* (big stone bowls) filled with steaming meat and broth and draped with hot nopal cactus leaves.

Stalls offering other variations appear evenings on the *zócalo.* A family sells tacos and *pozole,* while another, which labels itself La Poblana, arrives in a truck and offers French-fried bananas, *churros,* and potato chips fried on the spot until about 10:30 p.m., next to the church.

Restaurants

(Complete Dinner Price Key: Budget = under $7, Moderate = $7-14, Expensive = more than $14.) Of the *zócalo* restaurant options, the upstairs **La Parroquia,** a half block from the church steps, ranks among the best (open 8:30 a.m.-10 p.m., tel. 230-96, credit cards accepted). The front balcony tables are ideal perches for the view or watching the parade below while enjoying a good breakfast, lunch, or dinner. Moderate.

Two blocks downhill from the *zócalo,* just past the post office, **La Taberna** restaurant offers tasty light lunches and dinners in a cool, intimate patio setting (Juarez 12; open daily 1 p.m.-midnight, tel. 252-26; credit cards accepted). The friendly European owner's specialties include pastas (spinach lasagna, clam linguini), salads, desserts, and wines. Moderate to expensive.

A block on the opposite side of the *zócalo,* overlooking Plazuela de San Juan, the Mexican-style **Restaurant El Adobe** is a good place for breakfast or lunch while sightseeing or shopping (Plazuela de San Juan 13, opposite Bancomer; open daily 8 a.m.-11 p.m, tel. 214-16). For breakfast, you can enjoy juice, eggs, and hotcakes; for lunch, hamburgers, tacos, enchiladas, and guacamole. Budget to moderate.

A classy spot where you can enjoy the view, a swim, and lunch after seeing the Cuauhtémoc Mural is the adjacent **Restaurant El Mural** (at the Hotel Posada La Misión on the *carretera,* see "Accommodations" above; open daily for breakfast 7-9:30, lunch 1-3:30, dinner 7-11). If the place is packed with tours, however, have a

drink, enjoy the mural, and go somewhere else. Expensive.

For good food in an elegant view setting, go to **Restaurant La Ventana de Taxco** at the Hotel Hacienda del Solar two blocks off the highway, south end of town (open daily for breakfast 8:30-10:30, lunch 1-4:30, and dinner 7-11, when the whole town appears like a shimmering galaxy through the windows; reservations recommended, tel. 205-87). Their mostly Italian and Mexican specialties include salads, lasagna, scallopini, saltimbocca, *mole* chicken, enchiladas, and wines. Expensive; figure about $30 per person.

ENTERTAINMENT, EVENTS, AND SPORTS

Around The *Zócalo*

Taxco people mostly entertain each other. Such spontaneous diversions are most likely around the *zócalo,* which often seems like an impromptu festival of typical Mexican scenes. Around the outside stand the monuments of the colonial past, while on the sidewalks sit the *indígenas* who come in from the hills to sell their onions, tamales, and pottery. Kids run between them, their parents and grandparents watching, while young men and women flirt, blush, giggle, and jostle one another until late in the evening.

Three restaurant-bars on the side adjacent to the church provide good perches for viewing the hubbub. Visitors can either join the locals at **Bar Serta,** on the church corner, or take a balcony seat and enjoy the bouncy music with the mostly tourist crowd at **Bar Paco** next door. For more tranquility, head upstairs to **Restaurant La Parroquia** a few steps farther on.

For a glimpse of a different slice of Taxco life, head downhill on Alarcón a half block past the Casa Borda (city hall). There, at a no-name video parlor, a dozen boys are usually honing their reflexes in nonstop bashing of electronic skinheads and extraterrestrials (although three vintage manual table-soccer games remain the most popular).

Dancing And Discoing

Seasonally and on weekends the larger hotels have music for evening dining and dancing. Call the hotels Borda (tel. 200-25, 202-25), Posada de la Misión (tel. 200-63, 205-33), and the Monte

MIK MELLINS

Taxco people celebrate their festival of the jumil *(a type of grasshopper), on the first Monday after the Nov. 2 Day of the Dead.*

Taxco (which also has a discotheque, tel. 200-63, 205-33) for details.

Festivals

Many local fiestas provide the excuses for folks to celebrate, starting on January 17 and 18, with the Festival of Santa Prisca. On the initial day, kids and adults bring their pet animals for blessing at the church. The next day, pilgrims arrive at the *zócalo* at dawn and sing *Mañanitas* in honor of the saint, then head for folk dancing inside the church.

During the year Taxco's many neighborhood churches celebrate their saints' days (such as Chavarrieta, March 4; Veracruz, the four weeks before Easter; San Bernardino, May 20; Santísima Trinidad, June 13; Santa Ana, July 26; Asunción, Aug. 15; San Nicolas, Sept. 10; San Miguel, Sept. 19; San Franscisco, Oct. 4; and Guadalupe, Dec. 12) with food, fireworks, music, and dancing.

Religious fiestas climax during Semana Santa (Easter week), when, on Jueves and Viernes Santa (Thursday and Friday before Easter), cloaked penitents proceed through the city, carrying gilded images and bearing crowns of thorns.

On the Monday after the Nov. 2 Dia de los Muertos (Day of the Dead), Taxco people head to pine-shaded **Parque Huixteco** atop the Cerro Huixteco behind town to celebrate their unique **Fiesta de los Jumiles.** In a ritual whose roots

are lost in pre-Columbian legend, people collect and feast on *jumiles* (small crickets)—raw or roasted—along with music and plenty of beer and fixings. Since so many people go, transportation is easy. Ask a taxi or *zócalo* van driver or your hotel desk clerk for details.

Sports

Since most local people go everywhere by foot, walking Taxco's streets and side lanes seems to always lead somewhere interesting. And since all roads return to the *zócalo*, getting lost is rarely a problem.

The Hotel Monte Taxco (tel. 213-00, 213-01; for access, see "Sights" above) has **horses** ready for riding, three good **tennis** courts, and a **nine-hole golf course** available for fee use by nonguests. Informal *sendas* (hiking paths; ask directions from the horse-rental man) branch from the horse paths to the surrounding luscious pine- and cedar-forested mesa country. Take sturdy shoes, water, and a hat.

SHOPPING

Market

Taxco's big market day is Sunday, when the town is loaded with people from outlying villages selling produce and live animals. The market is located just downhill from Los Arcos, the lane that runs below the right side of the *zócalo* church (as you face that church). From the lane, head right before the arch and down the staircase. Soon you'll be descending through a warren of market stalls. Pass the small Baptist church on Sunday and hear the congregation singing like angels floating above the market. Don't miss the spice stall, **Yerbería Castillo,** piled with the intriguing wild remedies collected by owner Elvira Castillo and her son Teodoro.

Farther on you'll pass mostly scruffy meat stalls but also some clean juice stands, such as **Liquados Memo** (open daily 7 a.m.-6 p.m.), where you can rest with a delicious fresh *zanahoria* (carrot), *toronja* (grapefruit), or *sandia* (watermelon) juice.

Before leaving the market, be sure to ask for *jumiles* (hoo-MEE-lays), live crickets that are sold in bags for about a penny apiece, ready for folks to pop them into their mouths.

If *jumiles* don't suit your taste, you may want to drop in for lunch at one of the *fondas* (foodstalls, see "Food" above) above the market's *artesanías* (handicrafts) section.

Handicrafts

The submarket Mercado de Artesanías (watch for a white sign above an open area by the staircase) offers items for mostly local consumption, such as economical belts, huaraches, wallets, and inexpensive silver chains, necklaces, and earrings.

As you head out for tonier shops, don't miss the common but colorful and charming ceramic cats, turtles, doves, fish, and other figurines that local folk sell very cheaply. (If you buy, bargain—but not too hard—for the people are poor and have often traveled far.)

Nearby, one block downhill on Alarcón past the church, the state of Guerrero runs a handicrafts exposition in the **Casa Humboldt** (Alarcón 6, open Mon.-Sat. 10-2 and 4-8.) Included in the many reasonably priced (but indiscriminately selected) items are masks, furniture, and ceramics.

BUYING SILVER AND GOLD

One hundred percent pure silver is rarely sold because it's too soft. Silver (which comes from all over Mexico to be worked by Taxco's hundreds of silver shops) is nearly always alloyed with 7.5% copper to increase its durability. Such pieces, identical in composition to sterling silver, should have ".925" stamped on their back sides. Other, less common grades, such as "800 fine" (80% silver) should also be stamped.

If silver is not stamped with the degree of purity, it probably contains no silver at all and is an alloy of copper, zinc, and nickel, known by the generic label "alpaca," or "German silver."

Some shops determine silver jewelry prices simply by weighing, which typically translates to about $1 per gram. If you want to find if the price is fair, ask the shopkeeper to weigh it for you.

People prize pure gold partly because, unlike pure silver, it does not tarnish. It nevertheless is rarely sold pure (24-karat) but, for durability, is alloyed with copper. Typical purities, such as 18-karat (75%) or 14-karat (58%), should be stamped on the pieces. If not, chances are that they contain no gold at all.

Masks are the prime attraction at the **D'Avila Ofebres** shop on Plazuela de San Juan just past the end of Cuauhtémoc (Plazuela de San Juan 7, in the courtyard in front of the Cine Ana Maria across from Bancomer; open daily 9-9, tel. 211-08). Hundreds of masks from all over Guerrero—stone and wood, antique and new—line the walls like a museum. All of the many motifs, ranging from black men puffing cigarettes and blue-eyed sea goddesses to inscrutable Aztec gods in onyx and grotesque lizard-humanoids are priced to sell.

Silver Shops

Good silver shops cluster around the *zócalo* and downhill on the highway. Perhaps the favorite of all is the friendly, family-owned **Los Castillo** on the little plaza downhill behind the Hotel Agua Escondida (Plazuela de Bernal 10, open daily 9-1 and 3-7, tel. 206-52 and 219-88, credit cards accepted). Run by the industrious and prolific Castillo family, the shop offers a big variety at reasonable prices. Here you can watch silversmiths at work, and, unlike at many shops, can bargain a bit.

One of the more interesting silver shops, if for only a look around, is **La Gruta,** on Cuauhtémoc between the *zócalo* and Plazuela de San Juan (Cuauhtémoc 10, open Mon.-Sat. 10-8, Sun. 10-4, tel. 206-95, credit cards accepted). Inside, plaster stalagmites hang above small mountains of silver-decorated quartz crystals.

Enough silver stores for a week of shopping line the *carretera* John F. Kennedy downhill (*carretera* JFK 28, across from Hotel Posada de la Misión, open Mon.-Sat. 9 a.m.-7:30 p.m.). The original shop, **Las Delicias,** begun by William Spratling in cooperation with local silversmiths in 1931, is still a good place to buy silver, especially if you're looking for more elaborate pieces, set with semiprecious turquoise and lapis lazuli.

A Camera Store And A Grocery

Unusually well-stocked **Tienda la Misión,** half a block from the *zócalo,* offers many cameras, lenses, accessories, and much Kodak film, including professional Vericolor 120, Tri-X Pan, Plus-X, and Ektachrome (Cuauhtémoc 6, open Mon.-Sat. 9-2 and 4-8, Sun. 9-2, tel. 201-16). They also do photocopying, including enlargement and reduction.

A grocery store, **Casa Ayja,** a rarity in silver-rich Taxco, three blocks down Juarez from the *zócalo,* stocks a bit of everything, including wines, cheeses, and milk on its clean, well-organized shelves and aisles (Benito Juarez 7, open daily 9-10, tel. 203-64).

SERVICES AND INFORMATION

Money Exchange
Banks near the *zócalo* are Taxco's best source of pesos. **Banco Confia** (tel. 202-37), at the *zócalo* corner of Cuauhtémoc, changes U.S. currency and traveler's checks Mon.-Fri. 9-12. Likewise do **Banco Somex** and **Bancomer** (tel. 202-87, 202-88, Mon.-Fri. 10-12:30), a few doors farther along Cuauhtémoc.

Post, Telephone, And Telegraph
The **Correos** (post office, tel. 205-01), at Juarez 6, three blocks downhill from the *zócalo,* is open weekdays and Saturday mornings. **Telecomunicaciones** (tel. 248-85), in the same building, offers telegraph, money order, long-distance, and public fax services. The Taxco area code is 762.

Medical And Police
Taxco has a pair of respected private hospitals, both on the *carretera.* The **Clínica de Especialidades** (specialties, tel. 211-11) at the highway curve called "Manguito" has a 24-hour emergency room, pharmacy (tel. 245-00), and many specialists on call. The similar **Clínica Privado Alicia** (tel. 230-12) offers the same services at the corner of San Miguel across from the government Seguro Social hospital.

For routine drugs and medicines, go to one of many local pharmacies, such as **Farmacia Lourdes** (open 8 a.m.-10 p.m., tel. 210-66) at Cuauhtémoc 8, half a block from the *zócalo.*

Tourist Information Offices
Taxco has two tourist information offices, both beside the highway at opposite ends of town, open daily approximately 9 a.m.-2 p.m and 3-7 p.m. The knowledgeable and English-speaking officers readily answer questions and furnish whatever maps and literature they may have. The north office (tel. 207-98) is next to Pemex at the Av. La Garita corner. The south office is about a quarter mile south of the south-end Pemex station.

For **police** emergencies, contact the *policia* (tel. 200-07) at the city hall on the *zócalo* or at the substation on the side street below the *carretera* near the corner of Alarcón.

Books, Magazines, And Newspapers
English books and newspapers are hard to find in Taxco. Nevertheless, the bookstore **Casa Dominguez** does stock *Newsweek, Time, Life, Vogue,* and *Sports Illustrated* and sometimes a U.S. newspaper or two. They are open daily 9-2 and 4:30-8 on the Los Arcos lane adjacent and below the church.

GETTING THERE AND AWAY

By Car Or RV
National Highway 95 provides the main connection south with Acapulco in a total of about 167 miles (269 km) of easy driving via Iguala, accessible to/from Taxco via the winding, 22-mile (36-km) old Hwy. 95 cutoff. Allow about five hours' driving time for the entire Taxco-Acapulco trip, either direction.

Highway 95 also connects Taxco north via Cuernavaca with Mexico City, a total of about 106 miles (170 km). All driving except the 20-mile (32 km) leg of old Hwy. 95 north of Taxco is by the Hwy. 95 superhighway. Congestion around Mexico City lengthens the driving time to about three hours in either direction.

Authorities limit driving your car in Mexico City according to the last digit of your license plate (see p. 327).

Hwy. 55 provides an alternate northern connection between Taxco and **Toluca.** The road, although paved and in good condition for the 74 miles (119 km), is narrow and winding. Allow at least two hours driving, either direction.

By Bus
The competing lines **Flecha Roja** (tel. 201-31, highway corner near Veracruz) and **Estrella de Oro** (tel. 206-48, highway corner of Pilita) operate out of separate terminals on the *carretera.* Although both have many daily connections north with Mexico City and south with Acapulco via Iguala and Chilpancingo, Flecha Roja additionally provides many first- and second-class connections with local and intermediate destinations.

THE COSTA CHICA AND INLAND TO OAXACA

In reality, the Costa Chica, the "Little Coast," which includes Guerrero south of Acapulco and the adjoining coast of Oaxaca, isn't so small after all. Highway 200, heading out of the Acapulco hubbub, requires 300 miles to traverse it. Traffic thins out, passing scattered groves, fields, and villages along the Costa Chica southern bulge, where the coast curves, like the belly of a dolphin, to its most southerly point near Puerto Ángel.

In the main resorts of the Costa Chica—Puerto Escondido, Puerto Ángel, and Bahías de Huatulco—the beaches face south, toward the Mar del Sur, the Pacific Ocean. On the other hand, if travelers head inland, they go north, over the verdant, jungle-clad Sierra Madre del Sur and into the Valley of Oaxaca, the *indígena* heartland of southern Mexico.

To about a million Oaxacan native peoples, Spanish is a foreign language. Many of them (Zapotecs, Mixtecs, and a score of smaller groups) live in remote mountain villages, subsisting on corn and beans as they always have,

with neither electricity, sewers, schools, nor roads. Those who live near towns often speak the Spanish they have learned by coming to market. In the Costa Chica town markets you will brush shoulders with them—mostly Mixtecs, Amusgos, and Chatinos—men sometimes in pure-white cottons and women in colorful embroidered *huipiles* over wrapped, hand-woven skirts.

Besides the *indígenas,* you will often see Afro-Mexicans—*morenos,* "brown ones"—known as Costeños because their isolated settlements are near the coast. Descendants of African slaves imported hundreds of years ago, the Costeños subsist on the produce from their village gardens and the fish they catch.

Costa Chica Indians and Costeños have a reputation for being unfriendly and suspicious. If true in the past (although it's certainly less so in the present), they have had good reason to be suspicious of outsiders, who (in their view) have been trying to take away their land, gods, and lives for 300 years.

Communication is nevertheless possible. Your arrival, for the residents of a little mountain or shoreline end-of-road village, might be the event of the day. People are going to wonder why you came. Smile and say hello. Buy a soda at the store or palapa. If kids gather around, don't be shy. Draw a picture in your notebook. If a child offers to do likewise, you've succeeded.

ALONG THE ROAD TO PUERTO ESCONDIDO

If driving from Acapulco, mark your odometer at the traffic circle where Highways 95 and 200 intersect over the hill from Acapulco. If, on the other hand, you bypass that congested point via the Acapulco airport road, set your odometer to zero when you get to Hwy. 200, then add three miles (five km). Mileages and kilometer markers along the road are sometimes the only locators of turnoffs to hidden villages and palmy little beaches.

Fill up with gas before starting out in Acapulco. After that, both regular and Magna Sin (unleaded) are available at Pinotepa Nacional (157 miles, 253 km), Puerto Escondido (247 miles, 398 km), and near Puerto Ángel (291 miles, 469 km).

If you're going by bus, ride one of the several daily first-class buses from the **Estrella Blanca** terminal in Acapulco. (Or either ride a second-class bus from the Estrella Blanca terminal at Cuauhtémoc 97 in Acapulco, or simply wave one down on the road.)

PLAYA VENTURA

Three miles east of the small town of Copala, 77 miles (Km 123) from Acapulco, a road-side sign points toward Playa Ventura. Four miles down a good dirt road (which a truck-bus from Copala traverses regularly) you arrive at Ventura village. From there, a mile-long golden-sand beach arcs gently east. Past a lighthouse, the beach leads to a point, topped by a stack of granite rocks, known locally as Casa de Piedra ("House of Stone").

Playa Ventura can provide nearly everything for a restful day or week in the sun. Several good tenting or RV (maneuverable medium rigs, vans, or campers) spots sprinkle the inviting, outcropping-dotted shoreline. Shady palapas set up by former campers stand ready for rehabilitation and reuse by new arrivees.

Surf fishing (with net-caught bait fish) is fine from the beach, while *pangas* go out for deep-sea catches. Good **surfing** breaks angle in from the points, and, during the rainy season, the

Oxcarts—slow but dependable and cheap—still do their part in rural Pacific Mexico.

(top left) Plaza de Armas, Guadalajara; (top right) Hotel Radisson Sierra, Manzanillo;
(bottom) village church decorations near La Salina, Guerrero (photos by Bruce Whipperman)

(top) bringing in the catch at Rincón de Guayabitos, Nayarit;
(bottom) cooking tortillas atop a traditional adobe stove (photos by Bruce Whipperman)

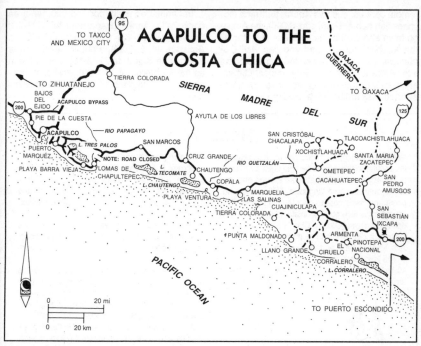

behind-the-beach lagoon is good for fishing, shrimping, and wildlife viewing. (Bring your kayak or inflatable raft.)

The palm-lined beach stretches southeast for miles. Past the picturesque Casa de Piedra outcropping, an intimate, palapa- and *panga*-lined sandy cove curves invitingly to yet another palmy point, Pico del Monte. Past that lies still another, even more pristine cove and beach.

Food And Accommodations

Besides the village store, food is available at a number of beach palapa restaurants, foremost of which is the **Restaurant-Cabaña Perez.** If anyone dispels the rumor that Costeño folks are unfriendly, it's the hospitable father-son team of Bulmaro and Luis Perez, who have put together the modest beginnings of a little retreat. Bulmaro and Luis invite visitors to park in their small lot, where they offer a friendly word, showers, and a bit of palmy shade for nothing more than the price of a meal at their restaurant. "If more people come," Luis says, "maybe we can build some hotel rooms."

SAN MARCOS, OMETEPEC, AND CUAJINICULAPA

A few larger towns along the road can provide a number of essential services. Thirty-six miles (58 km) east of Acapulco, **San Marcos** (pop. 10,000, tel. area code 745) has a bank (Banamex, tel. 300-36), Seguro Social (health center, tel. 303-39), pharmacies (El Rosario, tel. 300-08), a motel (Le Carma Inn, tel. 300-37, 20 rooms around a small pool-patio), and post, telephone, and telegraph offices.

Ometepec, a couple of hours' drive farther east, is accessible via a 10-mile paved road, which branches off Hwy. 200 at a well-marked intersection 110 miles (175 km) from Acapulco. Besides being an important service center, Ometepec (elev. 2,000 feet) enjoys a cooler climate, drawing crowds of native peoples, notably Amusgos, from outlying villages to its big morning market. Many local buses follow dirt and gravel roads from Ometepec to more remote centers, such as **Xochistlahuaca** (so-chees-tlah-hoo-AH-kah, pop. 3,000), the Amusgo town about 30 miles northeast. Not far off the Xochistlahuaca road you can visit **Cochoapa,** the partially excavated archaeological site where a number of very ancient Olmec-style stelae and sculptures have been unearthed. Ask around for a local guide.

In Ometepec itself (pop. 15,000, tel. area code 741), banks (Banamex, tel. 201-22; Somex, tel. 201-13), a private hospital (De la Amistad, tel. 202-24), a public health center (Centro de Salud, tel. 202-16), hotels (such as the Montero, tel. 201-00), and post, telephone, and telegraph offices provide essential services.

THE MIXTECS

Sometime during the 1980s, the Mixtecs regained the population they had at the time of the conquest—of about 350,000. Of that total, around one-third speak only their own language. Their villages and communal fields spread over tens of thousands of square miles of remote mountain valleys north, west, and southwest of Oaxaca City. Their homeland, the Mixteca, is divided into three distinct regions: Mixteca Alta, Mixteca Baja, and the Costera.

The **Mixteca Alta** centers in the mountains about 100 road miles north of Oaxaca City, in the vicinity of small towns such as San Juan Bautista Cuicatlán, on Hwy. 131, and Jocotipac and Cuyamecalco, several

Compare this pre-Columbian Mixtec birth scene with the Huichol birth scene on p. 116.

miles along local branch roads from the highway.

Mixteca Baja communities, such as San Miguel El Grande, San Juan Mixtepec, and Santiago Juxtlahuaca, dot the western Oaxaca mountains and valleys in a broad region centering roughly on Tlaxiaco on Hwy. 125.

In the **Costera,** important Mixtec communities exist in or near Pinotepa Nacional, Huaxpaltepec, and Jamiltepec, all on Hwy. 200 in southwestern Oaxaca.

The Aztec-origin name Mixtecos ("People of the Clouds") was translated directly from the Mixtecs' name for their own homeland: Áunyuma ("Land of the Clouds"). The Mixtecs' name for themselves, however, is Nyu-u Sabi ("People of the Rain").

When the conquistadores arrived in Oaxaca, the Mixtecs were under the thumb of the Aztecs, who, after a long, bitter struggle, had wrested control of Oaxaca from combined Mixtec-Zapotec armies in 1486. The Mixtecs naturally resented the Aztecs, whose domination was transferred to the Spanish during the colonial period, and, in turn, to the mestizos during modern times. The Mixtecs still defer to the town Mexicans, but they don't like it. Consequently, many rural Mixtecs, with little state or national consciousness, have scant interest in becoming Mexicanized.

In isolated Mixtec communities, traditions still rule. Village elders hold final authority, parents arrange marriages through go-betweens, and land is owned communally. Catholic saints are thinly disguised incarnations of old gods such as Tabayukí, ruler of nature, or the capricious and powerful *tono* spirits, which lurk everywhere.

In many communities, Mixtec women exercise considerable personal freedom. At home and in villages, they often still work bare breasted. And while their men get drunk and carry on during festivals, women dance and often do a bit of their own carousing. Whom they do it with is their own business.

Back on Hwy. 200, **Cuajiniculapa** (Kwah-hee-nee-koo-LAH-pah), pop. 10,000, tel. area code 741, 125 miles (199 km) from Acapulco, also has a Banamex (tel. 400-11), a *centro de salud* (health center, tel. 401-42), a pharmacy (Nueva, tel. 402-07), a very basic hotel (Marin, tel. 400-11), and post, telephone, and telegraph offices.

Cuajiniculapa is a major market town for the scattering of Costeño communities, such as San Nicolas (pop. 5,000, eight miles south), along the beach road (at Km 201) to Punta Maldonado, the local fishing port.

PINOTEPA NACIONAL

Pinotepa Nacional (pop. about 25,000; 157 miles, 253 km, east of Acapulco, 90 miles, 145 km, west of Puerto Escondido) and its neighboring communities comprise an important indigenous region. Mixtec, Amusgo, Chatino, and other peoples stream into town for markets and fiestas in their traditional dress, ready to combine business with pleasure. They sell their produce and crafts—pottery, masks, handmade clothes—at the market, then later get tipsy, flirt, dance, and perhaps even engage in a bit of carousing.

The Name
So many people have asked the meaning of their city's name that the town fathers wrote the explanation on a wall next to Hwy. 200 on the east side of town. Pinotepa comes from the Aztec-language words *pinolli* (crumbling) and *tepetl* (mountain); thus "Crumbling Mountain." The second part of the name came about because, during colonial times, the town was called Pinotepa Real (Royal). This wouldn't do after Independence, so the name became Pinotepa Nacional, reflecting the national consciousness that emerged during the 1810-21 struggle for liberation.

The Mixtecs, the dominant regional group, disagree with all this, however. To them, Pinotepa has always been Ñií Yu-uku ("Place of Salt"). Only within the town limits do the Mexicans (mestizos), who own most of the town businesses, outnumber the Mixtecs. The farther from town you get, the more likely you are to hear people conversing in the Mixtec language,

a complex tongue that relies on many subtle tones to make meanings clear.

Market
Hwy. 200, called Av. Porfirio Diaz in town, is Pinotepa's one main business street. It passes the main market (behind the big secondary school) on the west side and continues about a mile to the town plaza, the *zócalo.*

Despite the Pinotepa market's oft-exotic goods—snakes, iguanas, wild mountain fruits, forest herbs and spices—its people, nearly entirely Mixtec, are its main attraction, especially on the big Wed. and Sun. market days. Men wear pure-white loose cottons, topped by a woven straw hat. Women wrap themselves in their lovely striped purple, violet, red, and navy blue *pozahuanco* sarong-like skirts. Many women carry a polished tan *ticara* gourd bowl atop their heads, which, although it's not supposed to be, looks like a whimsical hat. Older women (and younger ones with babies at their breasts) go bare-breasted with only their white *huipile* draped over their chests for as a concession to mestizo custom. Others wear an easily removable *mandil,* a light cotton apron-halter above their *pozahuanco.* A number of women can ordinarily be found at any given time selling beautiful handmade *pozahuancos.*

Festivals
Although the Pinotepa Wednesday and Sunday markets are big, they don't compare to the week before Easter (Semana Santa). People get ready for the finale with processions, carrying the dead Christ through town to the church each of the seven Fridays before Easter. The climax comes on Good Friday (Viernes Santa), when a platoon of young Mixtec men portray the Jews (Judíos) by painting their bodies white, intoning ancient Mixtec chants, and shooting arrows at Christ on the cross. On Saturday, the people mournfully take the Savior down from the cross and bury him, and on Sunday gleefully celebrate his resurrection with a riot of fireworks, food, and folk dancing.

Although not as spectacular as Semana Santa, there's plenty of merrymaking, food, dancing, and processions around the Pinotepa *zócalo* church on July 25, the day of Pinotepa's patron, St. Santiago.

Accommodations And Food

The motel-style **Hotel Carmona,** on Hwy. 200 about three blocks west of the central plaza, offers three stories of clean, nonfancy rooms, a big pool-sun deck, and a passable restaurant. For festival dates, make advance reservations (Av. Porfirio Diaz 127, Pinotepa Nacional, Oaxaca 71600, tel. 954-322-22). The 50 rooms run about $18 s, $23 d, $27 t; for a/c-equipped kitchenette suites, add $10-15; credit cards accepted.

If the Carmona is full, there are a couple of more basic hotels in town you can take a look at: **Hotel Marisa,** Av. Juarez 134, tel. (954) 321-01; and **Hotel Tropical,** Av. 3 Poniente and Progreso, tel. (954) 320-10.

Campers enjoy a tranquil spot on the Rio Arena about two miles east of Pinotepa. Continue east past the river bridge a few hundred yards to a pumphouse, where a dirt track forks down to the riverbank. You will often find neighbors—in RVs or tents—set up on the riverside beneath Restaurant La Roca a few hundred yards down the smooth stream (which is very good for kayaking).

For **food,** Pinotepa has at least two recommendable restaurants. East of town is the country-club-style **Bora Bora,** beyond the arch and uphill, just across the street from the westernmost Pemex gas station (moderately priced outside palapa dining, open daily till about 9).

For a nighttime snack, try the very clean and friendly family run **Burger Bonny** (at the southeast corner of the main plaza, open daily 5-11 p.m.). Besides six varieties of the best hamburger on the Costa Chica, they offer tortas, nachos, French fries, hot dogs, microwave popcorn, fruit juices, *liquados,* and milkshakes at very reasonable prices.

Services

For **money exchange,** go to either the Bancomer (U.S. traveler's checks and cash, 10 a.m.-1:30 p.m., tel. 326-44) on main street Porfirio Diaz about two blocks west of the central plaza, or the Banco Somex (tel. 323-63) around the corner.

The **Correos** (post office, tel. 322-64) is by the bus station, about two blocks west and across the street from Bancomer. The **Telegrafos** (telegraph office) is on the central plaza, and is open Mon.-Sat. 9-1 and 3-5 for money orders and 9-9 for telegrams. There is also a *larga distancia* (long-distance) telephone office on the central plaza.

For a **doctor,** go to the Clínica Rodriguez at 503 N. Aguirre Palancares, tel. 323-30, one block north of the central plaza. Get routine medications at one of several town **pharmacies,** such as Farmacia Jesus on the central plaza.

Getting There And Getting Away

By **car or RV,** Hwy. 200 connects west to Acapulco (157 miles, 253 km) in an easy four hours driving time. The 90-mile (145-km) eastward continuation to Puerto Escondido can be done safely in about two and a half hours. Additionally, the 229-mile (368-km) Hwy. 125-Hwy. 190 route connects Oaxaca and Pinotepa Nacional. Although winding most of the way, the road is in good condition and generally uncongested. It's safely driveable from Oaxaca in about seven hours; add an hour for the 5,000-foot climb the opposite way.

Three long-distance **bus** lines connect Pinotepa Nacional with destinations north, east, and west. **Estrella Blanca** and subsidiary Flecha Roja have several daily first- and second-class *salidas de paso* (buses passing through) departures from their station (tel. 322-54) on Porfirio Diaz about three blocks west of the *zócalo.*

The smaller lines **Fletes y Pasajes** and **Estrella del Valle** have no station. Their buses depart daily, however, one block north of the central plaza on side street Aguirre Palancares. Fletes y Pasajes buses connect daily with Oaxaca via Hwys. 125 and 190. Estrella de Valle buses also connect with Oaxaca, but in the opposite direction: first east to Puerto Escondido, then continuing north over the Sierra to Oaxaca via Hwy. 131. Inquire with the drivers for tickets and times.

EXCURSIONS NORTH OF PINOTEPA

Yet another exciting time around Pinotepa is during **Carnaval** when nearby communities put on big extravaganzas. Pinotepa Don Luis, sometimes known as Pinotepa Chica, ("Little Pinotepa," about 15 miles by side road northeast of Pinotepa Nacional), is famous for wooden masks the people make for their big Carnaval festival. The celebration usually climaxes on the Sunday before Ash Wednesday, when everyone seems to be in costume and a corps of performers gyrates in the traditional dances: Paloma ("Dove"), Tigre ("Jaguar"), Culebra ("Snake"), and Tejón ("Badger").

Pinotepa Don Luis bubbles over again with excitement during Semana Santa, when the faithful carry fruit- and flower-decorated trees to the church on Good Friday, explode Judas effigies on Saturday, and celebrate by dancing most of Easter Sunday.

The festival year at Pinotepa Don Luis begins early, on Jan. 20, with the uniquely Mixtec festival of San Sebastian. Village bands blare, fireworks pop and hiss, and penitents crawl, until the finale, when dancers whirl the local favorite dance, Las Chilenas.

San Juan Colorado, a few miles north of Pinotepa Don Luis, usually appears as just another dusty little town until Carnaval, when its festival rivals that of its neighbors. Subsequently, on Nov. 29, droves of Mixtec people come into town to honor their patron, San Andres. After the serious part at the church, they celebrate with a cast of favorite dancing characters such as Malinche, Jaguar, Turtle, and Charros (cowboys).

Amusgo Country

Cacahuatepec (pop. about 3,000, on Hwy. 125 about 25 miles north of Pinotepa) and its neighboring community San Pedro Amusgos are important centers of the Amusgo people. Approximately 20,000 Amusgos live in a roughly 30-mile-square region straddling the Guerrero-Oaxaca border. Their homeland includes, besides the above towns, Xochistlahuaca, Zacoalpán, and Tlacoachistlahuaca on the Guerrero side.

The Amusgo language is linguistically related to Mixtec (although it's unintelligible to Mixtec speakers). Before the conquest, the Amusgos were subject to the numerically superior Mixtec kingdoms until the Amusgos were conquered by the Aztecs in 1457, and later by the Spanish.

Now, most Amusgos live on as subsistence farmers, supplementing their diet with occasional fowl or small game. Amusgos are best known to the outside world for the lovely animal-, plant-, and human-motif *huipiles,* which Amuzgo women always seem to be hand-embroidering on their doorsteps.

Although **Cacahuatepec** enjoys a big market each Sunday, that doesn't diminish the importance of its big Easter weekend festival and the day of Todos Santos (All Saints' Day, Nov. 2) and Day of the Dead, Nov. 2, when, at the cemetery, people welcome their ancestors' return to rejoin the family.

San Pedro Amusgos celebrations are among the most popular regional fiestas. On June 29, the day of San Pedro, people participate in religious processions, and costumed participants dressed as Moors and Christians, bulls, jaguars, and mules dance before crowds of men in traditional whites and women in beautiful heirloom *huipiles.* Later, on the first Sunday of October, folks crowd into town to enjoy the traditional processions, dances, and sweet treats of the fiesta of the Virgen de la Rosario ("Virgin of the Rosary").

Even if you miss the festivals, San Pedro Amusgos is worth a visit to buy *huipiles* alone. Two or three shops sell them along the main street through town. Look for the sign of **Trajes Regionales Elia,** the little store run by Elia and Edin Guzmán (tel. 955-300-45). Besides dozens of beautiful embroidered garments, they stock a few Amusgo books and offer friendly words of advice and local information. (Edin has traveled in the U.S. and understands some English.)

EXCURSIONS EAST OF PINOTEPA

For 30 or 40 miles east of Pinotepa, where road kilometer markers begin at zero again near the central plaza, Hwy. 200 stretches through the coastal Mixtec heartland, intriguing to explore, especially during festival times. The population of San Andres Huaxpaltepec, about 10 miles east of Pinotepa, sometimes swells from about 4,000 to 20,000 or more during the three or four days before the day of Jesus the Nazarene (the fourth Friday before Good Friday). The entire town becomes a spreading warren of shady stalls, offering everything from TVs to stone metates. (Purchase of a corn-grinding metate, which, including stone roller, sells for about $25, is as important to a Mixtec family as a refrigerator is to an American. Mixtec husband and wife usually examine several of the concave stones, deliberating the pros and cons of each before deciding.)

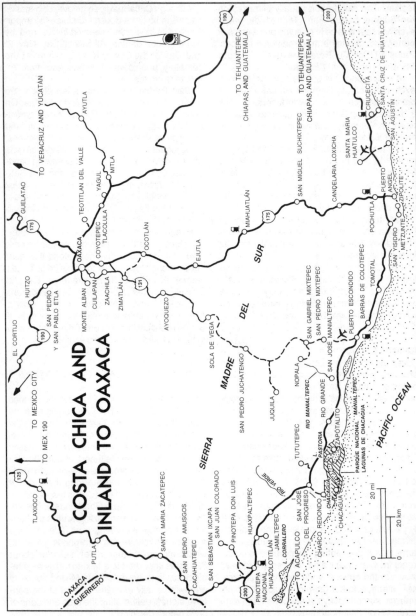

COSTA CHICA AND INLAND TO OAXACA

The Huaxpaltepec (oo-wash-pahl-tay-PAYK) Nazarene fair is typical of the larger Oaxaca country expositions. Even the highway becomes a lineup of stalls; whole clans camp under the trees; and mules, cows, and horses wait patiently around the edges of a grassy trading lot, as men discuss prices. (The fun begins when a sale is made, and the new owner tries to rope and harness his bargain steed.)

Even sex is for sale within a quarter of very tightly woven no-see-through grass houses, patrolled by armed guards. (Walking through, you may notice that, instead of the usual women, one of the houses offers men, dressed in low-cut gowns, lipstick, and high-heeled shoes.)

Huazolotitlán Masks

Huazolotitlán (pop. about 3,000) nearby has several woodcarvers who craft excellent masks. Among them is Florencio Gallardo, whose house is on the left just before the town-edge creek-bottom, Arroyo Barrio. Florencio often can be found working in his woodchip-littered front-yard palapa, fashioning a handsome wooden owl or fierce jaguar mask. Specializing in human likenesses, Florencio will carve a mask or sculpture of anyone of whom he has a photo. His fee begins at around $35. For more examples, visit other carvers nearby, such as José Luna, Lázaro Gómez, and the master Idineo Gómez.

Huazolotitlán (ooah-shoh-loh-teet-LAN), is about two miles via the graded gravel road that forks south uphill from Hwy. 200 in Huaxpalte-pec. Ride the local truck or bus, or hire a taxi for $2-3.

Santiago Jamiltepéc

About 18 miles (at Km 30) east of Pinotepa is the hilltop town of Santiago Jamiltepéc (hah-meel-teh-PEC, for short). Two-thirds of its 20,000 inhabitants are Mixtec. A grieving Mixtec king named the town in memory of his infant son, Jamilly, who was carried off by an eagle from this very hilltop.

The market, while busy most any day, is biggest and most colorful on Thursdays. The town's main fixed-date festivals are celebrated on Sept. 1, Jan. 1, and Feb. 15. In addition, Jamiltepéc celebrates its famous pre-Easter (week of Ramos) festival, featuring neigborhood candlelight processions accompanied by 18th-century music. Hundreds of the faithful bear elaborate wreaths and palm decorations to the foot of their church altars.

Jamiltepéc is well worth a stop if only to visit the handicrafts shop, **Yu-uku Cha-kuaa** ("Hill of Darkness"), of Santiago de la Cruz Velasco. Personable Santiago runs his shop, one of the few such local outlets, because the government cluster of shops (Centro Artesanal de la Costa, on the highway) closed down, victim of a dispute over control. The local Mixtec artisans wanted to manage their own handicrafts sales, while the Jamiltepéc branch of the INI (Instituto Nacional Indigenista), preferred to manage instead. The Mixtecs stuck together and refused to bring their handicrafts, closing the government operation.

Some of those crafts—masks, *huipiles,* carvings, hats—occupy the shelves and racks in Santiago's small store, which he keeps open till 7:00 or 8:00 each night except Sundays and holidays (on main street Av. Principal at Franciso Madero, by Seguro Social, the government health clinic). If you don't want to miss him, write Santiago a letter at his shop, Av. Principal, Barrio Grande, Sec. 5, Jamiltepéc, Oaxaca 71700.

LAGUNAS DE CHACAGUA NATIONAL PARK AND VICINITY

The Lagunas de Chacagua National Park spreads for about 20 miles of open-ocean beach shoreline and islet-studded, jungly lagoons midway between Pinotepa Nacional and Puerto Escondido. Tens of thousands of birds in a host of species fish the waters and nest in the mangroves of the two main lagoons, Laguna Pastoría on the east side, and Laguna Chacagua on the west.

The fish and wildlife of the lagoons, long harvested by local people, are in a state of recovery. Commercial fishing is strictly licensed. A platoon of Marines patrols access roads, shorelines, and the waters themselves, making sure that catches are within legal limits. Crocodiles were hunted out during the 1970s, but the government is trying to restore them with a hatchery on Laguna Chacagua.

For most visitors, mainly Mexican families on Sunday outings, access is by boat, except for one rugged road. (See details below.) From east-side Zapotalito village, the local fishing cooperative offers full- and half-day boat excursions to

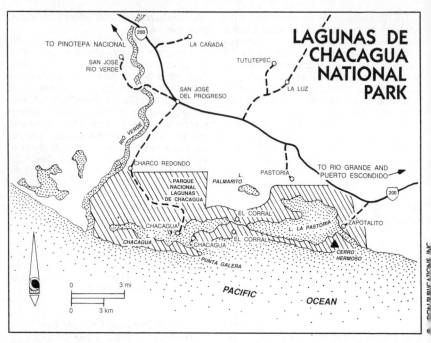

LAGUNAS DE CHACAGUA NATIONAL PARK

the beaches, Playa Hermosa, on the east side and Playa Chacagua on the west.

Exploring Lagunas De Chacagua

Zapotalito, on the eastern shore of Laguna Pastoría, is the sole easy access point to the Lagunas de Chacagua. Get there from the turnoff at Km 82, 51 miles from Pinotepa and 41 miles from Puerto Escondido. A sign visible from the Pinotepa direction reads "Zapotalito" and "Cerro Hermoso," while another, from the Puerto Escondido direction, reads "Chacagua." (Local buses run from Rio Grande all the way to Zapotalito on the lagoon, while second-class buses from Puerto Escondido and Pinotepa Nacional will drop you on the highway.)

From the Zapotalito landings, the fishing cooperative, Sociedad Cooperativa Turistica Escondida, enjoys a monopoly for transporting visitors on the lagoons. The boatmen used to make livings fishing; now they mostly ferry tourists. (Having specialized in fishing, they are generally neither wildlife-sensitive nor wildlife-knowledgeable.) Canopied powerboats, seating about

ten, make long, full-day trips for about $50 per boat. (Cheaper half-day excursions go to nearby Playa Hermosa at the mouth of Laguna Pastoría for a couple of hours' beach play and snorkeling—if you bring your own snorkeling gear.)

The full-day destination, Playa Chacagua, about 14 miles distant, unfortunately necessitates a fast trip across the lagoon. It's difficult to get them to slow down. They roar across broad Laguna Pastoría, scattering flocks of birds ahead of them. They wind among the islands, with names such as Scorpios ("Scorpion"), Venados ("Deer"), or Culebra ("Snake"), sometimes slowing for viewing multitudes of nesting pelicans, herons, and cormorants. They pick up speed again in the narrow jungle channel between the lagoons, roaring past idyllic, somnolent El Corral village, and break into open water again on Laguna Chacagua.

The **crocodile hatchery** is at Chacagua village on the west side of the lagoon, home to about two dozen local Costeño families, a shabby hotel, and a pair of lagoonside palapa restau-

LAGUNAS DE CHACAGUA ALTERNATIVES

Few roads penetrate the thick tropical deciduous forest surrounding the lagoons. Well-prepared adventurers, however, could try to thumb a ride or drive a rugged high-clearance vehicle along the very rough 18-mile forest (dry season only) track to Chacagua village from San Jose del Progreso (on Hwy. 200, 36 miles, 58 km, from Pinotepa Nacional) to Chacagua village. Before setting out, check with local residents or storekeepers about safety and road conditions.

If you have a boat or kayak, you could try launching your own excursion on Laguna Pastoría. The Cooperativa members, being both poor and jealous of their prerogatives, may ask you for a "launching fee," whether they're entitled to it or not.

Some of the islands in Laguna Pastoría are high and forested, and might be bug-free enough during the dry Nov.-Feb. months for a relaxing few days of wilderness camping, kayaking, and wildlife-viewing. You might be able to pay a boatman to drop you at your choice of islands and pick you up at a specified later time. Take everything, especially drinking water and insect repellent.

rants. Past the rickety crocodile caretaker's quarters are a few enclosures housing about a hundred crocodiles segregated according to size, from hatchlings to six-foot-long toothy green adults.

The tour climaxes at the west half of Chacagua village across the estuary. Here, palms line the placid lagoon, shading the **Hotel Siete Mares** ("Seven Seas") bamboo tourist cabañas. The hotel, a quiet rustic tropical resort, offers a small restaurant, showers and toilets, a few cabins (rent negotiable from about $15, depending upon season), and a beautiful beach a short walk away.

Playa Chacagua is lovely *because* of its isolation. The unlittered golden-white sand, washed by gently rolling waves, seems perfect for all beach activities. You can snorkel off the rocks nearby, fish in the breakers, and surf the intermediate breaks that angle in on the west side. A few palapas provide food and drinks, and, for beachcombers, wildlife viewers,

and backpackers (who bring their own water), the breezy, jungle-backed beach spreads for 10 miles both ways.

Rio Grande

Rio Grande (pop. about 5,000, tel. area code 954), a few miles east of the Lagunas Chacagua, is a transportation, supply, and service point for the region. They have several *abarroterías* (groceries), a bank (Bancomer, tel. 325-30), a pharmacy (Josafat Figueroa Cuevas, local tel. 26) a doctor (Galvo Marco Martinez, local tel. 8), a *larga distancia* (long-distance) telephone (tel. 324-50), and a hotel.

The **Hotel Santa Monica** (Av. Puebla, Rio Grande, Oaxaca 71830, local tel. 124), on the north side of the highway in the center of town, has 22 rooms in two floors, encircling a spacious parking courtyard. With fans, toilet, and hot water, the rooms rent for about $9 s, $13 d. (They're not too clean, but will do for a night.)

The friendly, family-run restaurant across the street provides good cheer and hearty meals daily from around 7 a.m. to 10 p.m.

LAGUNA MANIALTEPEC

Sylvan, mangrove-fringed Laguna Manialtepec, about 10 miles west of Puerto Escondido, is a repository for a trove of Pacific Mexico wildlife. Unlike Lagunas de Chacagua, Laguna Manialtepec is relatively deep and fresh most of the year, except occasionally during the rainy season when its main source, the Rio Manialtepec, breaks through its sandbar and the lagoon becomes a tidal estuary. Consequently lacking a continuous supply of ocean fish, Laguna Manialtepec has been left to local people, a few Sunday visitors, and its wildlife.

Laguna Manialtepec abounds with birds. Of the hundreds of species that frequent the lagoon, 40 or 50 are often spotted in a morning outing. Among the more common are the olivaceous cormorant and its relative, the *anhinga;* and herons, including the tricolored, green-backed, little blue, and the black-crowned night heron. Other common species include ibis, parrots, egrets, and ducks, such as the Muscovy and the black-bellied whistling duck. Among the most spectacular are the huge great blue herons, while the most entertaining are the northern *jacanas,* or lily walkers, who scoot across lily pads as if they were the kitchen floor.

Lagoon tours are best arranged through travel agencies in Puerto Escondido. Although most of these advertise "ecotours," the most genuine is **Hidden Voyages Ecotours,** led by Canadian ornithologist Michael Malone and arranged through the very competent travel agency Turismo Rodemar (see "Sights out of Town" in the "Puerto Escondido" section below).

La Alejandria

Laguna de Manialtepec is ripe for kayaking, boating, and camping along its shoreline. Bring plenty of repellent, however. Alternatively, RV and tent campers can settle in for a few days in one of a number of shady restaurant compounds along the shore. Among the friendliest and best

organized of these is the little family-run pocket paradise of La Alejandria, near the Km 125 marker about 10 miles from Puerto Escondido.

La Alejandria spreads along its hundreds of yards of lakefront, shaded by palms and great spreading trees. It's so idyllic that the "Tarzan" TV series picked La Alejandria for its film setting, adding a rustic lake tree house, complete with rope bridges, to the already-gorgeous scene.

La Alejandria rents about six RV spaces with electricity and water for about $8, and three dilapidated-rustic cabins with shower and toilet for about $18. (Take a look first; the owner says he's going to fix them up.) Camping spaces go for about $7. The homey centerpiece restaurant-bar, screened-in from bugs, gleams with a generation of care, reminiscent of a venerable East African safari lodge.

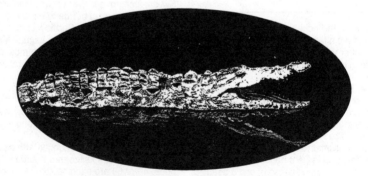

ERIN DWYER

Through public education and the assistance of the government crocodile nursery at Chacagua village, caimanes (crocodiles) may once again hunt in wild Costa Chica lagoons.

PUERTO ESCONDIDO

Decorated by intimate coves, sandy beaches, and washed by jade-tinted surf, Puerto Escondido enjoys its well-deserved popularity. Despite construction of a jet airport in the 1980s, Puerto Escondido remains a place where everything is within a short walk, no high-rise blocks anyone's sunset view, and moderately priced accommodations and good food remain the rule.

Puerto Escondido, "Hidden Port," got its name from the rocky Punta Escondida, which shelters its intimate half-moon cove, which perhaps would have remained hidden if local farmers had not discovered that coffee thrives beneath the cool forest canopy of the lush seaward slopes of the Sierra Madre del Sur. They began bringing their precious beans for shipment when the port of Puerto Escondido was established in 1928.

When the coast highway was pushed through during the 1960s, Puerto Escondido's then-dwindling coffee trade was replaced by a growing trickle of vacationers, attracted by the splendid isolation, low prices, and high waves. With some of the best surfing breaks in North America, a permanent surfing colony soon got established. This led to more nonsurfing visitors, who, by the 1990s, were enjoying the comfort and food of a string of small hotels and restaurants lining Puerto Escondido's still-beautiful but no longer hidden cove.

SIGHTS

Getting Oriented
Puerto Escondido (pop. around 30,000) seems like two small towns, separated by Hwy. 200, which runs along the bluff above the beach. The upper town is where most of the local folks live and go about their business, while in the town below the highway, most of the tourist restaurants, hotels, and shops spread along a single, mile-long beachfront street, **Av. Pérez Gasga.**

Av. Pérez Gasga runs east-west, mainly as a pedestrian mall, where motor traffic is allowed only before noon. Afternoons, the *cadenas* (chains) go up, blocking cars at either end.

Beyond the west-end *cadena,* Pérez Gasca leaves the beach, winding uphill to the highway, where it enters the upper town at the *crucero,* Puerto Escondido's only signaled intersection. From there, Pérez Gasga continues into the upper town as Av. Oaxaca, National Hwy. 131.

Getting Around
In town, walk or take a taxi, which should run no more than $2 to anywhere.

For longer local excursions, such as Lagunas Manialtepec and Chacagua (westbound) and as far as Pochutla (near Puerto Ángel) eastbound, ride one of the very frequent *urbano* microbuses that stop at the *crucero.*

BEACHES AND ACTIVITIES

Puerto Escondido bayfront begins at the sheltered rocky cove beneath the rocky lighthouse point, Punta Escondida. The shoreline continues easterly along Playa Principal, the main beach, curving southward at Playa Marineros and finally straightening into long, open-ocean Playa Zicatela. The sand and surf change drastically, from narrow sand and calm ripples at Playa Principal to a wide beach pounded by gigantic rollers at Zicatela.

Playa Principal
Playa Principal is where Mexican families love to frolic on Sundays and holidays and sun-starved winter vacationers doze in their chairs and hammocks beneath the palms. The sheltered west side is very popular with local people who arrive afternoons with nets and haul in small troves of silvery fish. The water is great for wading and swimming, clear enough for casual snorkeling but generally too calm for anything else in the cove. A few hundred yards east around the bay, however, the waves are generally fine for bodysurfing and boogieboarding, with a minimum of undertow. Although not a particularly windy location, windsurfers do occasionally practice their art here (with their own equipment). Fishing is fine off

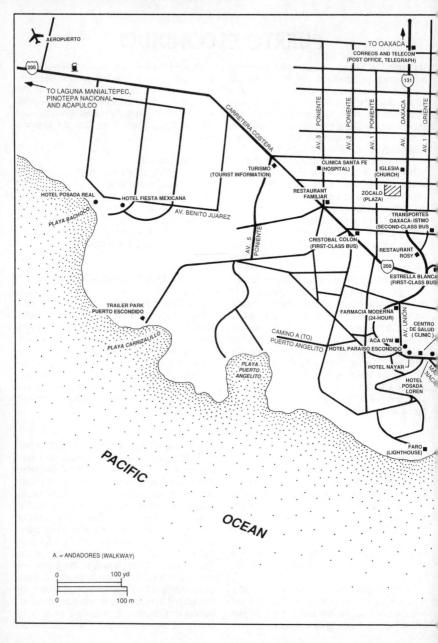

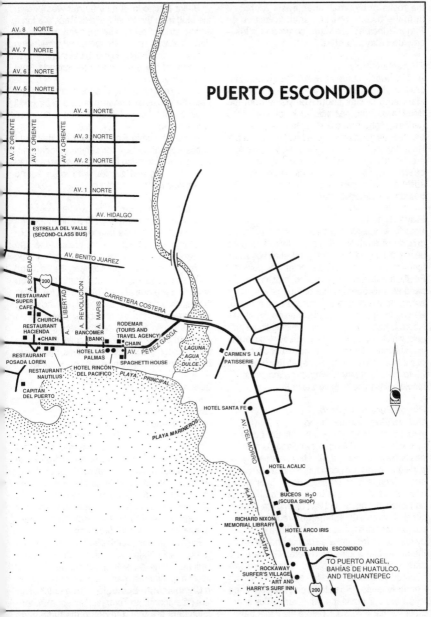

PUERTO ESCONDIDO

AV. 8 NORTE
AV. 7 NORTE
AV. 6 NORTE
AV. 5 NORTE
AV. 4 NORTE
AV. 3 NORTE
AV. 2 NORTE
AV. 1 NORTE
AV. HIDALGO

AV. 2 ORIENTE
AV. 3 ORIENTE
AV. 4 ORIENTE

ESTRELLA DEL VALLE
(SECOND-CLASS BUS)

AV. BENITO JUAREZ

A. SOLEDAD
200
CARRETERA COSTERA
RESTAURANT
SUPER
CAFE
CHURCH
RESTAURANT
HACIENDA
CHAIN
A. LIBERTAD
A. REVOLUCION
A. MARIS
BANCOMER
(BANK)
RODEMAR
(TOURS AND
TRAVEL AGENCY)
CHAIN
AV. PEREZ GASGA
LAGUNA
AGUA
DULCE
CARMEN'S LA
PATISSERIE
RESTAURANT
POSADA LOREN
HOTEL LAS
PALMAS
HOTEL RINCON
DEL PACIFICO
SPAGHETTI HOUSE
PLAYA PRINCIPAL
RESTAURANT
NAUTILUS
CAPITAN
DEL PUERTO

PLAYA MARINEROS

HOTEL SANTA FE

AV. DEL MORRO

HOTEL ACALIC

BUCEOS H₂O
(SCUBA SHOP)

RICHARD NIXON
MEMORIAL LIBRARY
HOTEL ARCO IRIS
PLAYA ZICATELA
HOTEL JARDIN ESCONDIDO

TO PUERTO ANGEL,
BAHIAS DE HUATULCO,
AND TEHUANTEPEC

ROCKAWAY
SURFER'S VILLAGE
ART AND
HARRY'S SURF INN

200

© MOON PUBLICATIONS, INC.

the rocks or by small boat, easily launched from the beach. Shells, generally scarce on Playa Principal, are more common on less-crowded Playa Zicatela.

Playa Marineros

As the beach curves toward the south, it increasingly faces the open ocean. Playa Marineros begins about 100 yards from the "Marineros," the eastside rocky outcroppings (whose jutting forms are supposed to resemble visages of grizzled old sailors) in front of the Hotel Santa Fe. Here the waves, while rough, are not always fatal. Swimmers beware; appearances can be deceiving. Intermediate surfers practice here, as do daring boogie-boarders and bodysurfers.

Playa Zicatela

Past the Marineros rocks you enter the hallowed ground of **surfers,** Playa Zicatela. The wide beach, of fine, golden-white sand, stretches south for miles to a distant cliff and point. The powerful Pacific swells arrive unimpeded, crashing to the sand with awesome, thunderous power. Both surfers and nonsurfers congregate year-round, waiting for the renowned Escondido "pipeline," where grand waves curl into whirling liquid tunnels, which expert surfers skim through like trains in a subway. At such times, the watchers on the beach outnumber the surfers by as much as 10 or 20 to one. Don't try surfing or swimming at Zicatela unless you're expert at both.

Playas Puerto Angelito, Carrizalillos, and Bachoco

About a mile west of town, the picture-postcard blue little bays of Puerto Angelito and Carrizalillos nestle beneath the seacliff. Their sheltered gold-and-coral sands are perfect for tranquil picnicking, sunbathing, and swimming. Here, **snorkeling and scuba diving** are tops, among shoals of bright fish that graze and dart among the close-in coral shelves and submerged rocky outcroppings. Get there by launch from Playa Principal, by taxi, or on foot (take a sun hat and water) by the street that angles from Pérez Gasga uphill across from the Hotel Nayar. Continue a few hundred yards and angle left again at Camino a Puerto Angelito ("Road to Puerto Angelito") and follow the trail down the cliff. Carrizalillos is another quarter mile west, before the trailer park.

Playa Bachoco, a mile farther west, down the bluff from the Hotel Posada Real, is a long, scenic strip of breeze-swept sand, with thunderous waves and correspondingly menacing undertow. Swimming is much safer in the inviting pool of the adjacent Hotel Posada Real beach club.

If you're strong, experienced, and can get past the waves **snorkeling** is said to be good around the little surf-dashed islet a hundred yards offshore.

Although Playa Bachoco's rock-sheltered nooks appear inviting for camping, local people don't recommend it, because of occasional *rateros* (thugs and drunks) who roam Puerto Escondido beaches at night.

Trouble In Paradise

Occasional knifepoint robberies and muggings have marred the once-peaceful Puerto Escondido nighttime beach scene. Walk alone and you invite trouble, especially along the unlit stretch of Playa Principal between the east end of Pérez Gasga and the Hotel Santa Fe. (If you have dinner alone at the Hotel Santa Fe, avoid the beach by returning by taxi or walking along the highway to Pérez Gasga back to your hotel.)

Fortunately, such problems seem to be confined to the beach. Visitors are quite safe on the Puerto Escondido streets themselves, often more so than on their own city streets back home.

Beach Hikes

You can stroll as far out of town along on Playa Zicatela as you want, in walks ranging from an hour to a whole day. Take a sun hat, a shirt, drinks, and snacks if you plan on walking more than a mile (past the last restaurant) down the beach. Your rewards will be the acrobatics of surfers challenging the waves, rafts of shore-birds, and occasional finds of driftwood and shells. After about three miles you will reach a cliff and a sea arch, which you can scamper through at low tide to the beach on the other side, **Playa Barra de Colotepec.**

Playa Barra de Colotepec's surf is as thunderous as Zicatela's and the beach even more pristine, being a nesting site for sea turtles. About a quarter mile past the point you will come to **Campamento Ecologio Ayuda Las Tortugas** ("Campamento Tortugas," for short), where volunteers are trying to get to the turtle eggs

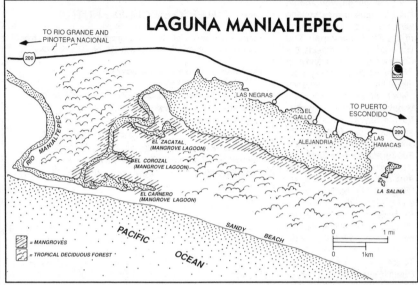

LAGUNA MANIALTEPEC

TO RIO GRANDE AND
PINOTEPA NACIONAL

LAS NEGRAS

EL GALLO

TO PUERTO
ESCONDIDO

RIO MANIALTEPEC

LA ALEJANDRIA

LAS HAMACAS

EL ZACATAL
(MANGROVE LAGOON)

EL COROZAL
(MANGROVE LAGOON)

EL CARNERO
(MANGROVE LAGOON)

LA SALINA

PACIFIC OCEAN

SANDY BEACH

= MANGROVES

= TROPICAL DECIDUOUS FOREST

© MOON PUBLICATIONS, INC.

before the poachers do. (See "Trailer Parks and Camping" below.)

Playa Barra de Colotepec continues for another mile to the jungle-fringed lagoon of the Rio Colotepec, where hosts of birds and wildlife, both common and rare, paddle and preen in the clear, fresh water.

You could break this eight-mile roundtrip into a pair of more leisurely options: Hike A could cover Zicatela only. On Hike B you could explore Barra de Zicatela and the Laguna de Colotepec by driving, taxiing, or busing straight to Campamento Tortugas: From Hwy. 200 about three miles south of town, turn off, or have the local microbus drop you, at the signed side road. After about half a mile, follow the left fork to the campground and Playa Barra Colotepec.

Beach Boat Tours

Travel agencies and the local boat cooperative, Sociedad Cooperativa Punta Escondida, offer trips for parties of several passengers to a number of beautiful local bays, including Carrizalillo and Puerto Angelito (see above), plus Manzanillo, Puesta del Sol, and Coral. The minimum hour-and-a-half trip runs about $40 for an entire (eight-person) boat. Trips can be extended

(at about $25 per additional hour) to your heart's content of beach picnicking, snoozing, and snorkeling.

SIGHTS OUT OF TOWN

Whether you go escorted (see "Tours" below) or independently, outings away from the Puerto Escondido resort can reveal rewarding glimpses of flora and fauna, local cultures, and idyllic beaches seemingly half a world removed from the Pérez Gasga tourist hubbub.

To the west of Puerto Escondido are the festivals, markets, and handicrafts of Mixtec towns and villages around Jamiltepéc and Pinotepa Nacional. For wildlife lovers and beachgoers there are the jungly lagoons and pristine strands of the Laguna de Manialtepec and Parque Nacional Lagunas de Chacagua. (For details, see above.)

Also on the west side, the **Aguas Termales Atotonilco** hot springs, a Chatino Indian sacred site, provides an interesting focus for a day's outing. The jumping-off point is the village of San José Manialtepec, about half an hour by bus or car west of Puerto Escondido.

At the village, you should hire someone to show you the way, up the semiwild canyon of the Rio Manialtepec. The trail winds along cornfields, beneath forest canopies and past Chatino villages. Finally you arrive at the hot springs, where a clear bathtub-sized rock basin bubbles with very hot (bearable for the brave), clear, sulfur-smelling water. **Get there** by driving or busing to the Hwy. 200 turnoff for San José Manialtepec, around Km 116, just east of the Rio Manialtepec. Village stables provide horses and guides to the hot springs. (Actually, it's a very easy two-mile walk, except in times of high water on the river, which the trail crosses several times.)

Tours

Puerto Escondido agencies conduct outings to all of the above and more. Among the very best are the **Hidden Voyages Ecotours** of the Canadian husband-wife team of Michael Malone and Joan Walker. Working through the competent Turismo Rodemar Travel Agency (Av. Pérez Gasga 906, P.O. Box 122, Puerto Escondido, Oaxaca 71980, tel. 207-34), ornithologist Michael and artist-ecologist Joan lead unusually informative beach, lagoon, and mountain tours seasonally from late fall through Easter. In addition, they also offer a sunset lagoon wildlife and beach excursion, plus a two-day trip to Nopala, center of Chatino culture, including a coffee plantation in the cool Sierra Madre del Sur mountain jungle. Their trips ordinarily run about $40 per day per person.

ACCOMMODATIONS

The successful hotels in Puerto Escondido are appropriate to the town itself: small, reasonably priced, and near the water. They dot the beachfront from Playa Zicatela around the bay and continue up Av. Pérez Gasga to the highway. Most are either on the beach or within a stone's throw of it (which makes sense, because it

---

PUERTO ESCONDIDO HOTELS

Puerto Escondido hotels, in ascending order of approximate high-season double-room price (area code 958, postal code 71980)

Rockaway Surfer's Village, del Morro s/n, Playa Zicatela, 206-68, $18

Rincón del Pacífico, Pérez Gasga 900, 200-56, 201-93, $22

Hotel Posada Loren, Pérez Gasga 507, 200-57, $27

Hotel Nayar, Pérez Gasga 407, 201-13, 203-19, $27

Hotel Arco Iris, del Morro s/n, Colonia Marinero, 204-32, $27

Hotel Las Palmas, Pérez Gasga s/n, 202-30, 203-03, $40

Hotel Paraiso Escondido, Calle Union 1, 204-44, $51

Santa Fe, Calle del Morro, Playa Marinero, (P.O. Box 96), 201-70, 202-66, fax 202-60, $55

---

seems a shame to come all the way to Puerto Escondido and not stay where you can soak up the beauty).

Downhill along Pérez Gasga from the *crucero,* is the **Hotel Paraiso Escondido** on a short side street to the left (Calle Union 1, Puerto Escondido, Oaxaca 71980, tel. 958-204-44). A tranquil colonial-chic refuge, the hotel abounds in unique artistic touches—Mixtec stone glyphs, tiny corner chapels, stained glass, and old-world antiques—blended into the lobby, corridors, and patios. The two levels of rooms nestle around a lovely view pool and restaurant patio. The rooms themselves are large, with view balconies and designer tile bathrooms, wrought-iron fixtures, and handcrafted wooden furniture. Very popular with North American and German winter vacationers; get reservations in early. Their 24 rooms rent from about $42 s, $51 d, with a/c, pool, kiddie pool, and parking, but *no* credit cards are accepted.

Just downhill is the motel-style **Hotel Nayar,** spreading from its inviting pool-patio past the reception to a viewpoint restaurant (Pérez Gasga 407, Puerto Escondido, Oaxaca 71980, tel. 958-201-13 and 958-203-19). Its spacious and comfortable (but Spartan) air-conditioned rooms have private balconies, many with sea views. A potentially beautiful hotel, the Nayar suffers from lackluster management. This often results in sullen desk personnel, dirt in the corners, torn drapes, and bare-bulb lighting. The

Nayar's 36 rooms run about $18 s, $20 d, $23 t low season, and $23, $27, and $33 high.

The more popular **Hotel Posada Loren,** downhill half a block farther, is as good as it first appears, from its leafy pool-patio and its private balcony view rooms to its rooftop sun deck (Av. Pérez Gasga 507, Puerto Escondido, Oaxaca 71980, tel. 958-200-57). Intelligent clerks staff the desk while *camaristas* scrub the rooms spotless every day. (They also assiduously spray with DDT; tell them "no DDT" if you'd prefer they didn't.) The rooms spread through two three-story buildings; the front building rooms have better views. Reserve a *cuarto con vista* if you want a view room. Reservations are often necessary, especially in the winter. The 24 basic but comfortable rooms rent for about $18 s, $20 d, $23 t low season; $23, $27, and $33 high; with parking, fans, and some a/c; credit cards accepted.

Right on the beach amidst the tourist-mall hullabaloo is the longtime favorite, **Hotel Las Palmas** (Av. Pérez Gasga s/n, Puerto Escondido, Oaxaca 71980, tel. 958-202-30, 958-203-03). Its main plus is the palmy, vine-strewn patio where you can sit for breakfast every morning, enjoy the breeze, and watch the boats, the birds, and families frolicking in the billows. The big drawback, besides sleepy management and no pool, is lack of privacy. Exterior walkways pass the room windows, which anyone can see through. Closing the curtains unfortunately makes the (fan-only) rooms very dark and hot. This doesn't bother the legions of return customers, however, since they spend little time in their rooms anyway. Tariffs for the 40 smallish rooms run about $32 s, $40 d, and $48 t, rather high without a pool; phones, no parking, credit cards accepted.

The **Rincón del Pacífico** next door offers about the same, but for significantly lower prices (Av. Pérez Gasga 900, Puerto Escondido, Oaxaca 71980, tel. 958-200-56, 958-201-93). The two tiers of clean, comfortable rooms enfold a shady patio that looks out onto the lively, lovely beachfront. As at the Hotel Las Palmas above, a stay in one of their glass-front rooms feels like life in a fishbowl. This is nevertheless a very popular hotel. Reserve early. Rates for the 28 rooms run about $22 s or d, $27 t; four suites with TV and a/c rent for about $37 s or d; with a restaurant, but no parking or pool; credit cards accepted.

Puerto Escondido's class-act hostelry is the newish **Hotel Santa Fe,** built in graceful neocolonial style, appealing to both Mexican and foreign vacationers (Calle del Morro, Playa Marinero, Puerto Escondido, P.O. Box 96, Puerto Escondido, Oaxaca 71980, tel. 958-201-70, 958-202-66, fax 958-202-60). With curving staircases, a palm-shaded pool-patio, and flower-decorated walkways, the Santa Fe achieves an ambience both intimate and luxuriously private at the same time. Its restaurant, furthermore, is outstanding (see "Food" below). The rooms are spacious, comfortable, and thoughtfully appointed with handpainted tile, rustic wood furniture, and regional handicrafts. Get your reservation in early. Their 50 rooms rent for about $45 s or d, $55 t, low season, and $55 and $65 high; with TV, a/c, phones and parking; credit cards accepted.

Farther south on Calle Morro, which runs along Playa Zicatela is the **Hotel Arco Iris** (Calle del Morro s/n, Colonia Marinero, Puerto Escondido, Oaxaca 71980, tel. 958-204-32). A flowery, shady green garden surrounds the hotel, leading to an attractive pool-patio. For those who love sunsets, sand, and waves (and don't mind their sometimes insistent pounding), one of the spacious, simply furnished top-floor view rooms might be just right. The Arco Iris's proximity to the famous Puerto Escondido "pipeline" draws both surfers and surf-watchers to the second-floor restaurant La Galera, which seems equally ideal for wave-watching at breakfast and sky-watching at sunset. The rates for the 26 rooms run about $23 s, $27 d; suites with kitchen, about $33 d, $40 t; with fans and parking.

Farther along Playa Zicatela is the very tidy **Rockaway Surfer's Village,** a fenced-in cluster of about 15 clean, concrete-floored bamboo-and-thatch cabañas (Calle del Morro, Playa Zicatela, Puerto Escondido, Oaxaca 71980, tel. 958-206-68). Spacious and fan-equipped, they sleep about four and have private showers and toilets, mosquito nets, and shady, hammock-hung front porches. An attractive, leafy pool-patio occupies the center, while the manager's cabaña, offering beach, surfing, and snorkeling rentals and supplies stands to one side. (For equipment rental details, see "Sports" below.) Cabaña rentals run about $9 per person per night; weekly or monthly discounts are possible; parking.

Trailer Parks And Camping

Trailer Park Puerto Escondido occupies a breezy lot overlooking little blue Carrizalillo Bay on the west side of town. Their acre of around 100 spaces blooms with green grass during the popular winter season, when dozens of Canadians and Americans pull in and stay for two or three months. The congenial company, all hookups, a large swimming pool, clean showers and toilets, some shaded spaces, and good fishing keep them returning. Figure on paying about $12 per day, discounts available for monthly rentals. Get there from Hwy. 200, about half a mile west of the *crucero,* via the dirt road across (on the ocean side) from the big white Rancho El Pescador; after about a quarter mile, diagonal right about another quarter mile to the trailer park (Puerto Escondido, Bahía Carrizalillo, Oaxaca 71980, tel. 958-200-77).

Campamento Ecologio Ayuda Las Tortugas

For safety reasons, local people do not recommend camping in isolated spots along Puerto Escondido beaches. The Campamento Ecologio Ayuda Las Tortugas ("Help the Turtles Ecological Campground") solves this problem by providing a safe camping place on a pristine beach.

Engineer Jorge Gutierrez, who works in Oaxaca City, thought something ought to be done to save the turtles of Barra de Colotepec. He bought the land, dug a well, equipped it with an old-fashioned windmill, and recruited volunteers to build and maintain a campground.

Now, his volunteers maintain the campground when Jorge has to be in Oaxaca. They welcome visitors to stay free at one of the several shaded campsites and help (they need donations of food and supplies) with their efforts. They have had some success keeping the turtle eggs from poachers, having released hundreds of hatchlings which they and other volunteers personally saved.

"I have no official permission to do this," Jorge says. "The government could kick us out of here at any time." He hopes, however, that more volunteers and visitors will add fuel to the flickering little ecological flame he's started on Playa Barra de Colotepec.

FOOD

Breakfast And Snacks

Mornings you can smell the aroma of Carmen's **La Patisserie** along Playa Marinero (open Mon.-Sat. 7 a.m.-8 p.m., on the little street that heads toward Playa Marinero from Hwy. 200, just past the bridge). Follow the fragrance to the source, a small homey shop with a few tables for savoring the goodies. Before noon you'll usually find owner Carmen Arizmendi in the kitchen or behind the counter; afternoons, however, you'll often glimpse her swimming across the bay.

Right in the middle of the Av. Pérez Gasga bustle, **Cafe Il Capuchino** is a gathering place for tourists and local folks who enjoy good desserts and coffee with their conversation (open daily 8 a.m-11 p.m.). Furthermore, the best homesickness remedy in town is their apple pie, a slice of which enables you to endure a minimum of one more hard week on the local beaches.

Restaurant Super Cafe means just that: super local mountain-grown coffee and whole beans (open Mon.-Sat. 7 a.m.-9 p.m, Sun. till 1 p.m.). Super Cafe would enjoy more business if it weren't so hard to find, but therein lies the charm: an airy, vine-draped view retreat, only blocks (but seemingly miles removed) from the busy beach scene. Friendly, family-run Super Cafe specializes in *cafe con leche* (coffee with steamed milk), omelettes, and local favorites such as chiles rellenos mole and tamales Oaxaqueños. Get there by following Andando Soledad, the lane that leads uphill from the Pérez Gasga west-end chain. After a block, by the church, head left along the narrow walkway between the houses.

Uphill, on Av. Oaxaca above the *crucero,* local people flock to **Restaurant Rosy.** A *cenaduría* (evening-only eatery), Rosy specializes in tasty barbecued pork, beef, or chicken *(puerco, res,* or *pollo)* tacos and *pozole* (rich hominy stew, topped with onions and roast chicken or pork.) Open daily 4-10 p.m.

Restaurants

(Complete Dinner Price Key: Budget = under $7, Moderate = $7-14, Expensive = more than $14.) Most of Puerto Escondido's reliable restaurants line Av. Pérez Gasga, beginning near the west *cadena* (chain). The major exception is **Restaurant Familiar,** Puerto Escondido's locally popular whole-food restaurant above the highway. The family owners are serious about their indigenous heritage, having decorated their restaurant walls with handcrafted ceremonial art while offering traditional unprocessed grains, including in-house whole-wheat bread, tortillas, and yogurt. Their specialty is a hearty five-course afternoon *comida,* including soup, pasta, entree, dessert, and tea or coffee for about $5. Their à la carte menu specializes in local delicacies, such as banana-leaf-wrapped tamales Oaxaqueños (open Mon.-Sat. 8-8, on Calle 1 Norte, near corner of Hwy. 200, three blocks west of the *crucero).* Budget.

Downhill on Pérez Gasga, just outside the west chain, is the streetside patio of **Restaurant Hacienda y Sardina de la Plata,** formerly two restaurants now combined into one (Av. Pérez Gasga 512, tel. 203-28, open daily 7:30 a.m-11 p.m., credit cards accepted). The present establishment is the brainchild of Barcelona-born owner-chef Fernando de Abascal López, who enjoys orchestrating a unique seafood repertoire. His list includes Catalan specialties such as Txanguro de Jaiva (snails, shrimp, and octopus in a white sauce), or Mero a la Sol (a sea bass feast for a party of four to 10). Besides such exotica, he also serves plenty of good pasta, steaks, lobster, Mexican plates, and breakfasts. Moderate.

Just inside the chain, the beachside **Restaurant Posada de Loren** specializes in brochettes of jumbo shrimp, fish, steak, and lobster (Av. Perez Gasga s/n, tel. 204-48, open daily 3-11 p.m., credit cards accepted). The Loren's palm-shaded, beach-view tables are especially pleasant for a late lunch or early dinner, when the beach activity—men fishing with nets and lines, kids digging, pelicans diving, cormorants bobbing, boats scurrying—is at its colorful best. Moderate.

The upstairs palapa of the nearby **Restaurant Nautilus** affords a cool, palm-fringed bay view that makes even a simple lunch seem luxurious (open daily 8 a.m.-midnight, credit cards accepted). Furthermore, the European owner-chef adds the adventure of sushi, smoked ham with melon, and vegetables Hindu style to an already eclectic list of salads, pastas, and seafoods. Moderate.

Near the east end of the Pérez Gasga mall, the **Restaurant Perla Flameante** offers good food, incense, new-age jazz, and a beach view from beneath a big, cool palapa (open daily 7 a.m.-11 p.m., no credit cards). The friendly, conscientious staff take pride that they make everything in-house, from the mayonnaise to the potato chips that come with their big fish burger. Fish fillets rule their menu. The varieties, such as sierra, tuna, yellowtail, and mahimahi, are exceeded only by the number of styles—Cajun, teriyaki, wine and herbs, pepper-mustard, butter and garlic, orange—in which they are served. Budget to moderate.

If you have dinner at the restaurant of the **Hotel Santa Fe,** you may never go anywhere else (on Av. del Morro, east side of the bay, tel. 201-70, open daily 7:30 a.m.-11 p.m.). Savory food, impeccably served beneath a luxurious palapa and accompanied by softly strumming guitars, brings travelers from all over the world. Although everything on their menu is good, they are proudest of their Mexican favorites, such as rich tortilla soup, bountiful plates of chiles rellenos, or succulent snapper, Veracruz style. Moderate to expensive.

At the far end of Av. del Morro on Zicatela Beach is friendly **Art and Harry's Surf Inn,** named after the Canadian expatriate owners' grandfathers (open daily, noon till about 10 p.m.). The restaurant, a big, breezy, upper-floor palapa, is best around sunset when patrons enjoy Frisbee golf (see "Sports" below) and more unobstructed sunsets per year than any other palapa in Puerto Escondido. Personable co-owner Patty Mikus keeps customers coming with her fresh salads, soups, and tasty (honey, garlic, teriyaki, Hawaiian, or marinera) fish plates.

ENTERTAINMENT AND EVENTS

Sunsets And Happy Hours

Many bars have sunset happy hours, but not all of them have good sunset views. Since the Oaxaca coast faces south (and the sun sets in the west), bars along eastside Zicatela Beach, such as the Hotel Santa Fe, Hotel Arco Iris, and Art and Harry's are only ones which can offer unobstructed sunset horizons.

Strolling Pérez Gasga

Strolling the Péerez Gasga mall is Puerto Escondido's prime after-dinner entertainment. By around 9:00, however, people get weary of walking and (since there are few benches) begin sitting on the curb and sipping bottles of beer near the west-end chain. (If you don't drink, however, you could probably qualify for a curbside spot with a beer bottle filled with water.)

The main attraction of this curb-sitting is watching other people sitting on the curb, while listening to the music that blasts nightly from the tiny open-air bars **Mr. Magoo's** and **Bar Coco** 50 feet away. The music is so loud that little can be gained except hearing impairment by actually taking a seat in the bars themselves.

Those who prefer to dance with their music go to some of the few **discotheques** in town. Most popular are the Disco Paraiso at the Hotel Fiesta Mexicana (tel. 201-15, above Playa Bachoco) and the La Bahía (with a bay view) in town above the highway, three blocks east of the *crucero).*

Festivals

Puerto Escondido pumps up with a series of fiestas during the low-season (but excellent for vacationing) month of November. Scheduled "Fiestas de Noviembre" events invariably include surfing and usually sportfishing, culinary, and beauty contests.

If instead you hanker for the old-fashioned color of a traditional fiesta, take a day-trip one hour west of Puerto Escondido to enjoy a fiesta at one of the small towns around Pinotepa Nacional.

SPORTS

Walking, Jogging, Gym, And Tennis

Playa Zicatela is Puerto Escondido's most interesting walking course. (See "Beach Hike" above.) Early mornings, before the heat and crowds, are good for jogging along the level section of Av. Pérez Gasga. Calle del Morro on Playa Zicatela is good for jogging anytime it isn't too hot.

The **Aca Gym**, at Union 102, up the staircase from Hotel Paraiso Escondido, has a roomful of standard exercise equipment. Single visits run about $3.30, one-month passes about $23 (open Mon.-Fri. 7-2 and 4-9, Sat. 7-2 and 4-7, tel. 200-17).

One of the better night-lit **tennis** courts in town available for public rental is at the Hotel Fiesta Americana. Call 201-15 for details.

Surfing, Snorkeling, And Scuba Diving

Although surfing is *de rigueur* for the skilled in Puerto Escondido, beginners often learn by bodysurfing and boogieboarding first. Boogieboards and surfboards are for sale and rent ($7/day) at a number of shops along Pérez Gasga, such as **Central Surf** (open daily 9-2 and 5-9:30), two doors from the Hotel Palma Real. On Playa Zicatela, **Rockaway Surfer's Village** rents surfboards ($7/day) and boogieboards ($5/day) and sells related supplies.

Beginners practice on the gentler billows of Playa Principal and adjacent Playa Marinero (see above) while advanced surfers go for the awesome waves of Playa Zicatela, which regularly slam foolhardy inexperienced surfers onto the sand with backbreaking force.

Clear blue-green waters, coral reefs, and droves of multicolored fish make for good local **snorkeling and diving**, especially in little Puerto Angelito and Carrizalillo bays (see "Beaches And Activities" above) just west of town. A number of Av. Pérez Gasga stores sell serviceable amateur-grade snorkeling equipment.

Friendly Jorge Perez Bravo, a PADI-certified dive guide, runs **Buceos H2O** out of his small shop on Av. del Morro about a quarter mile past the Hotel Santa Fe. He outfits and guides parties on local trips for a minimum of about $40 per person per dive, boat and equipment included.

Sportfishing

Puerto Escondido's offshore waters abound with fish. Launches go out mornings from Playa Principal and routinely return with an assortment including big tuna, mackerel, snapper, sea bass, and snook. The sheltered west side of the beach is calm enough to easily launch a mobile boat with the help of usually willing beach hands.

The local **Sociedad Cooperativa Punta Escondida,** which parks its boats right on Playa Principal, regularly takes fishing parties of three or four out for about $23 an hour, including bait and tackle. Additionally, travel agencies, such as Turismo Rodemar (Av. Pérez Gasga 905, tel. 207-34), arrange such trips at about the same prices.

SHOPPING

Market And Handicrafts
As in most Mexican towns, the place to begin your Puerto Escondido shopping is at the local **Mercado** (on Av. 10 Norte one block west of the electric station on Av. Oaxaca). Although produce occupies most of the space, a number of stalls at the south end offer authentic handicrafts. These include Guerrero painted pottery animals, San Bartolo Coyotepec black pottery, and beautiful *huipiles* from San Pedro Amusgos and Pinotepa Nacional.

Back downhill on Av. Pérez Gasga, the prices increase along with the selection. **Chimali** stands out among its several neighbor stalls at the corner of uphill lane Andador Revolución. Look over their intriguing assortment of masks from Guerrero, which include jaguar, devil, and scary human-animal lizard and snake motifs. Notable also is their black San Bartolo pottery and the endearing multicolored animals—fish, cats, ducks—from Iguala and Zitlala in Guerrero.

One short block west, a similar stall-cluster lines Andador Marisol, where the little **Meli** shop has an interesting selection of authentic *huipiles* from Amusgos, Huazolotitlán, Oaxaca, and Mitla.

Groceries And Photography
Abarrotes Lupita, a fairly well-stocked grocery, offers meats, milk, ice, and vegetables. In addition, it stocks maps and a number of English-language publications, such as the *News* of Mexico City and magazines such as *Time, Life,* and *Newsweek* (open daily 10 a.m.-11 p.m., on the inland side of Gasga, outside of the east-end chain).

Foto Express Figueroa, on Gasga next to Turismo Rodemar, offers fast photofinishing services, Kodak color print and slide film, and a moderate stock of accessories, including point-and-shoot cameras (open daily 9:30-2 and 4:30-8, tel. 205-26).

SERVICES

Money Exchange
Bancomer, in the middle of the Gasga tourist zone, changes U.S. and Canadian cash and traveler's checks Mon.-Fri. 9-12. (Across from Hotel Rincón del Pacifico, tel. 204-11.) After hours, the small *casa de cambio* (money exchange) office across the street changes a larger range of foreign currencies for a correspondingly larger fee (open Mon.-Sat. 9-2 and 5-8, tel. 205-92, across from Farmacia Cortés).

Post, Telegraph, And Telephone
The **Correos** (post office) and **Telegrafos** are side by side on Av. 7 Norte, corner Av. Oaxaca, seven blocks into town from the *crucero.* The post office is open Mon.-Fri. 8-7, Sat. 9-1; the Telegrafos, which has public fax (tel. 958-202-32) is open Mon.-Fri. 9-1 and 3-7 (9-1 and 3-5 for money orders), Sat. 9-12.

More conveniently located on Pérez Gasga, a *larga distancia* (long-distance telephone office) is open long hours (Mon.-Sat. 9 a.m.-10 p.m., Sun. 9 a.m.-1 p.m.) across from the Farmacia Cortés. The Puerto Escondido area code is 958.

INFORMATION

Tourist Information Office
The friendly, well-informed Oficina de Turismo provides a very clear map handout, which, besides an overall state highway map, has detailed maps of Puerto Escondido, Puerto Ángel, Bahías de Huatulco, and Oaxaca City and its environs (open Mon.-Fri. 9-2 and 5-8, tel. 201-75, at Calle 5 Poniente and Hwy. 200, in the little office on the beach side of the highway about four long blocks west of the *crucero).* The staff, especially the director Elisabeth Weber and her English-speaking assistant Marco Antonio Zavala, are unusually conscientious and knowledgeable.

Hospital, Police, And Emergencies
For medical emergencies, go to the 24-hour **Hospital Santa Fe,** which has an internist, pediatrician, gynecologist, and a dental surgeon on call. For more routine consultations, office hours are Mon.-Fri. 9-2 and 4-8, Sat. 9-2 (three blocks west of the *crucero,* uphill from the highway on Calle 3 Poniente between Calles 2 and 3 Norte).

The government health clinic, **Centro de Salud** (tel. 201-20), is on Av. Pérez Gasga, just uphill from the Hotel Loren.

A couple of good pharmacies, including the 24-hour **Farmacia La Moderna** (tel. 205-49) on Gasga a block below the *crucero,* and **Farmacia Cortés** (open 8-2 and 5-10, tel. 201-12)

BRUCE WHIPPERMAN

Mark Wilkinson, friendly founder of Puerto Escondido's Richard Nixon Memorial Library.

on the Pérez Gasga mall, can fill prescriptions and supply many common over-the-counter remedies.

For **police** emergencies, call 201-11, or go to the headquarters in the Agencia Municipal on Pérez Gasga across from the Hotel Posada Loren.

Books, Magazines, Newspapers, And Library
The excellent book, office, and engineering supplies store **Acuario Comercial** on Pérez Gasga has a very well-stocked magazine rack. Scores of popular U.S. magazines from *Surf* and *Guns* to *Vogue* and *Time, Life,* and *Newsweek* fill the shelves (open Mon.-Sat. 8:30-2 and 4-7, tel. 201-25, just uphill from Hotel Nayar).

One of the few outlets of any English-language newspaper is the Abarrotes Lupita, on Perez Gasga, outside the east-end chain. The *News* from Mexico City usually arrives in the early afternoon.

The **Richard Nixon Memorial Library,** project of friendly American expatriate Mark Wilkinson,

has a few hundred volumes of used paperback books for sale or trade. Mark is usually present from 12-5 daily at his library-home on Av. del Morro, next to Buceos H20 on Playa Zicatela.

GETTING THERE AND AWAY

By Air
The small jetport, officially the Aeropuerto Puerto Escondido, (code-designated PXM), is just off the highway a mile west of town. Only a plain waiting room with check-in desks, the airport has no services save a small snack bar. *Colectivo* (collective taxi) to hotels in town runs $2 per person. With a minimum of luggage, however, arrivees can walk a block to the highway and flag down a local microbus to the town highway stop. Arrive with a hotel in mind, unless you prefer letting your taxi driver choose one, where he will probably collect a commission for depositing you there.

The international **departure tax** is $12 or its Mexican peso equivalent. If you lose your tourist card, avoid trouble or a fine by going to Turismo for help *before* your day of departure.

A few regularly scheduled airlines connect Puerto Escondido with other Mexican destinations.

Mexicana Airlines flights (tel. 204-22, 200-98) connect daily, except Tues., with Mexico City.

Aero Morelos flights (local agent, Turismo Rodemar, tel. 207-34, 207-37) connect with Oaxaca and Huatulco daily.

Aerocaribe flights (tel. 209-97, 203-89) connect with Oaxaca and Acapulco daily.

Puerto Escondido is also accessible via the Puerto Ángel-Huatulco airport, one hour away by road. See "Getting There And Getting Away" in the "Bahías de Huatulco" section below.

By Car Or RV
National Highway 200, although sometimes winding, is generally smooth and uncongested between Puerto Escondido and **Acapulco,** 247 miles (398 km) west. Allow about eight hours' driving time. Regular gasoline is available at three or four towns along the way; Magna Sin unleaded is available in Pinotepa Nacional.

Traffic sails between Puerto Escondido and **Puerto Ángel,** 44 miles (71 km) apart, in an easy hour. (Actually, Pochutla is immediately on the highway; Puerto Ángel is six miles downhill from the junction.) **Santa Cruz de Huatulco** is an easy 22 miles (35 km) farther east.

To or from **Oaxaca City,** all-paved National Hwy. 175 connects at Pochutla junction with Hwy. 200 via its winding but spectacular 148-mile (238-km) route over the pine-clad Sierra Madre del Sur. The route, which rises 7,000 feet through Chatino and southern Zapotec Indian country, can be chilly in the winter, and has few services along the lonely 100-mile middle stretch. Take water and blankets, and be prepared for emergencies. Allow about eight hours from Puerto Escondido, seven hours the other way.

By Bus

Five long-distance bus lines serve Puerto Escondido; two of them are first class. **Estrella Blanca** (tel. 204-27, 200-86, the station-lot on Av. Oaxaca just uphill from the *crucero)* buses travel the Hwy. 200 Acapulco-Huatulco route. More than a dozen daily *salidas de paso* come through en route both ways between Acapulco and Pochutla and Huatulco (Crucecita). Three additional evening buses pass through, connecting with Mexico City via Acapulco.

Cristobal Colón, the other first-class bus line (tel. 202-84, small station on the highway, uphill side, two blocks west of the *crucero)* covers the south coast, beginning in Puerto Escondido, connecting all the way to San Cristobal las Casas in Chiapas. Intermediate destinations include Pochutla, Huatulco (Crucecita), Salina Cruz, and Tuxtla Gutierrez. At Pochutla, passengers can transfer to Oaxaca-bound buses. Several departures per day connect with all of the above destinations.

The best-organized second-class bus line is **Autobuses Oaxaca-Istmo** (tel. 203-92), on Hidalgo one block east of Av. Oaxaca, corner of 1 Oriente. Several daily local departures connect Puerto Escondido with Oaxaca via Salina Cruz on the Isthmus of Tehuantepec. Intermediate destinations include Pochutla and Huatulco (Crucecita).

Camiones Oaxaca Pacifico (tel. 202-22, on Hidalgo, corner of 3 Oriente) provides more or less the same second-class service and covers the same Isthmus route as Autobuses Oaxaca-Istmo above.

Finally, for a real backcountry bus adventure, ride one of the scruffy red machines of **Autobuses Estrella Roja del Sureste** to Oaxaca. Traversing some of Mexico's most undeveloped mountain country via gravel Hwy. 125, they depart daily from the dusty lot at Calle 10 Norte and Av. Oaxaca, adjacent to the Mercado.

MIKE WELLINS

PUERTO ÁNGEL

During his presidency in the 1860s, Oaxaca-born Benito Juarez shaped many dreams into reality. One such dream was to better the lot of his *indígena* brethren in the isolated south of Oaxaca by developing a port for shipping lumber and coffee that they could harvest in the lush Pacific-slope jungles of the Sierra Madre del Sur. The small bay of Puerto Ángel, directly south of the state capital, was chosen, and by 1870 it had become Oaxaca's busiest port.

Unfortunately, Benito Juarez died a year later. New priorities and Puerto Ángel's isolation soon wilted Juarez's plan and Puerto Ángel lapsed into a generations-long slumber.

In the 1960s, Puerto Ángel was still a sleepy little spot connected by a single frail link—a tortuous cross-Sierra dirt road—to the rest of the country. Adventure travelers saw it at the far south of the map and dreamed of a south-seas paradise. They came and were not disappointed. Although that first tourist trickle has grown steadily, it's only enough to support the sprinkling of modest lodgings and restaurants that now dot Puerto Ángel's tranquil, little blue bay.

SIGHTS

Getting Oriented

Puerto Ángel is at the southern terminus of Hwy. 175, about six miles (nine km) downhill from its intersection with Hwy. 200. It's a small place, where nearly everything is within walking distance along the beach, which a rocky bayfront hill divides into two parts: **Playa Principal,** the main town beach, and sheltered west-side **Playa Panteón,** the tourist favorite. A scenic boulder-decorated shoreline *andador* (walkway) connects the two beaches.

A graded dirt road winds west from Playa Panteón along the coastline a couple of miles to **Playa Zipolite,** lined by a colony of rustic hammock-and-bamboo beachfront cabañas, popular with an international cadre of budget-minded seekers of heaven on earth. Continuing west, the road passes former turtle-processing village beaches of **Playa San Augustino** and **Playa Metzunte.** From there it goes on another four miles, joining with Hwy. 200 at San Yisidro village at Km 198.

The major local service and transportation center is **Pochutla** (pop. 20,000), a mile north along Hwy. 175 from its Hwy. 200 junction.

Getting Around

Microbuses run frequently between Pochutla and Puerto Ángel from about 7 a.m. to 9 p.m., stopping at the Hwy. 200 intersection. Some buses continue on to Zipolite and Metzunte from Boulevard Uribe, Puerto Ángel's main bayfront street. Taxis also routinely make runs between Puerto Ángel and either Zipolite or Pochutla for about $3 or $4.

Playas Principal, Panteón, And Estacahuite

Playa Principal's 400 yards of wide golden sand decorate most of Puerto Ángel's bayfront. Waves can be strong near the pier, where they often surge vigorously onto the beach and recede with some undertow. Swimming is more tranquil at the sheltered west end toward Playa Panteón. The bay's clear waters are good for casual snorkeling around rocks on both sides.

Sheltered Playa Panteón is Puerto Ángel's sunning beach, lined with squadrons of beach chairs and umbrellas in front of beachside restaurants. **Playa Oso** ("Bear Beach") is a little dab of sand beside a rugged seastack beyond Playa Panteón, fun to swim to or walk to from the road above the beach. Follow the uphill dirt road behind Restaurant Leyvis y Vicente about 200 yards to a blue metal gate. Go through, pass the house—if the occupants are there, ask if it's okay to pass—and carefully descend the steps and steep trail down to Playa Oso.

Playa Estacahuite, just outside the opposite (east) side of the bay, is actually two beaches in one: a pair of luscious coral-sand nooks teeming with fish grazing the living reef just offshore. (Don't put your hands in crevices. A moray eel may mistake your finger for a fish and bite.) A pair of palapa restaurants perched picturesquely above the beaches provide food and drinks. Get there in less than a mile by taxi or on foot via the dirt road that forks right off the highway about 400 yards uphill from beachfront Boulevard Uribe.

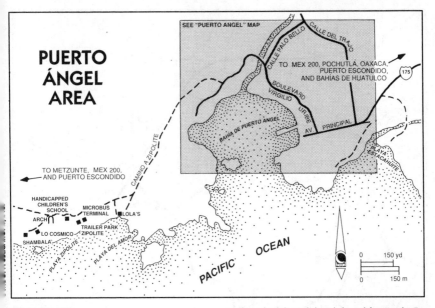

PUERTO ÁNGEL AREA

SEE "PUERTO ANGEL" MAP

TO MEX 200, POCHUTLA, OAXACA, PUERTO ESCONDIDO, AND BAHIAS DE HUATULCO

CALLE PALO BELLO

CALLE DEL TRAJO

BOULEVARD VIRGILIO URIBE

AV. PRINCIPAL

BAHIA DE PUERTO ANGEL

PLAYA ESTACAHUITE

175

CAMINO A ZIPOLITE

TO METZUNTE, MEX 200, AND PUERTO ESCONDIDO

HANDICAPPED CHILDREN'S SCHOOL
MICROBUS TERMINAL
ARCH
LOLA'S
LO COSMICO
TRAILER PARK ZIPOLITE
SHAMBALA
PLAYA ZIPOLITE
PLAYA DEL AMOR

PACIFIC OCEAN

0   150 yd
0   150 m

Playa Zipolite

Playa Zipolite is a wide, mile-long strand of yellow-white sand enfolded by headlands and backed by palm groves. It stretches from the intimate little cove and beach of **Playa del Amor** tucked on its east side to towering seacliffs rising behind the new-age **Shambala.**

Good surfing notwithstanding, Zipolite's renown stems from its status as one of the very few (if not the only) nude beaches in Mexico. Bathing *au naturel,* practiced nearly entirely by visitors and a few local young men, is tolerated only grudgingly by local people, many of whose livelihoods depend on the nudists. If you're discreet and take off your clothes at the more isolated west end, no one will appear to mind (and women will avoid voyeuristic attentions of Mexican boys and men).

Visitors' nude sunbathing habits may have something to do with the gruffness of some local people. Many of them probably prefer their former occupations in turtle fishing rather than serving tourists (who often seem to be in short supply compared to the battalion of beachfront palapas competing for their business).

Most Zipolite visitors stay in the palm-shaded trailer park or in one of the score of hammock-equipped stick-and-thatch beachfront cabaña hotels. Often with fans and outside cold-water showers and privies, cabañas rent for about $10 double per night. Although many are indifferently managed, some, such as Lola's, Lo Cosmico, and Shambala (see "Accommodations" below), are outstanding.

Playas San Augustinillo And Metzunte

About a mile west of Zipolite, a wide, mile-long, yellow-sand beach curves past the village of San Augustinillo. On the open ocean but partly protected by offshore rocks, its surf is much like that of Zipolite, varying from gentle to rough, depending mostly upon wind and offshore swells. Small village groceries and beachside palapa restaurants supply food and drinks to the occasional Zipolite overflow and local families on weekends and holidays. **Fishing** is excellent, either in the surf, from nearby rocks, by rented *panga,* or your own boat launched from the beach. Beach camping is customary, especially at a pull-in roadside ramada at the east, Zipolite, end of the beach.

Remnants of the local turtle industry can be found at the rusting former processing factories on Playa San Augustinillo (west end) and Playa

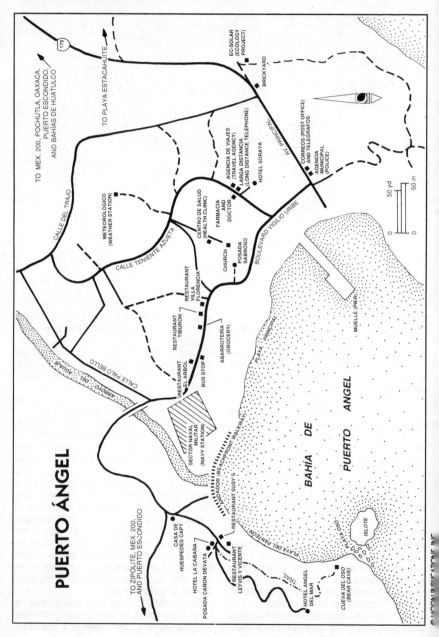

PUERTO ÁNGEL

TO MEX. 200, POCHUTLA, OAXACA, PUERTO ESCONDIDO, AND BAHÍAS DE HUATULCO

TO PLAYA ESTACAHUITE

CALLE DEL TRAJO

EC-SOLAR (ECOLOGY PROJECT)

BRICKYARD

AGENCIA DE VIAJES (TRAVEL AGENCY)

LARGA DISTANCIA (LONG DISTANCE TELEPHONE)

HOTEL SORAYA

AV. PRINCIPAL

CORREOS (POST OFFICE) AND TELEGRAFOS

AGENCIA MUNICIPAL (POLICE)

METEOROLÓGICO (WEATHER STATION)

CALLE TENIENTE AZUETA

CENTRO DE SALUD (HEALTH CLINIC)

FARMACIA AND DOCTOR

RESTAURANT VILLA FLORENCIA

CHURCH

POSADA SABROSO

BOULEVARD VIGILIO URIBE

RESTAURANT TIBURON

ABARROTERÍA (GROCERY)

ARROYO DEL AGUAJE

CALLE PALO BELLO

RESTAURANT EL ARBOL

BUS STOP

MUELLE (PIER)

SECTOR NAVAL MILITAR (NAVY STATION)

ANDADOR (BEACHFRONT WALKWAY)

PLAYA PRINCIPAL

BAHÍA DE PUERTO ÁNGEL

RESTAURANT SUSY'S

PLAYA DEL PANTEÓN

ISLOTE

PLAYA DEL OSO

TRAIL

TO ZIPOLITE, MEX. 200, AND PUERTO ESCONDIDO

CASA DE HUESPEDES CAPY

HOTEL LA CABAÑA

POSADA CAÑON DEVATA

RESTAURANT LEYVIS V VICENTE

HOTEL ANGEL DEL MAR

CUEVA DEL OSO (BEAR CAVE)

50 yd

50 m

0

Metzunte two miles farther west. The former turtle plant (follow the side road, east end of the beach) at Metzunte lives on as a **turtle hatchery,** where visitors can see hatchlings swim in tanks overlooking the beach where their ancestors once swarmed.

The half-mile-long yellow-sand Metzunte Beach, like San Augustinillo, is semisheltered and varies from tranquil to rough. Fishing is likewise good, camping (as a courtesy, ask if it's okay) is customary, and local stores and seafood palapa restaurants sell basic supplies and food.

ACCOMMODATIONS

Puerto Ángel Hotels: Around The Bay

Although none of Puerto Ángel's dozen-odd lodgings are directly on the beach, all except one are within a stone's throw of it. The successful ones have given their legion of savvy repeat customers what they want: clean, basic accommodations in tranquil, television-free settings where Puerto Ángel's natural isolation and tropical charm set the tone for long, restful holidays.

Moving west around the bay from the pier, first comes the motel-style **Hotel Soraya,** perched on the bluff above Playa Principal (Priv. José Vasconcelos 2A, Puerto Ángel, Oaxaca 70902, no phone). Well managed by a personable woman owner, the hotel includes a restaurant with an airy bay view, fine for bright morning breakfasts and sunset-glow dinners. Outside, two tiers of Spartan but light and comfortable rooms enclose a parking-patio. Although some rooms have a/c, the fan-only ones are generally better. Rent on the upper tier for more privacy. The 32 rooms rent for about $20 s, $22 d, $27 t, credit cards accepted.

Heading around the curve of the bay to the Playa Panteón ("Cemetery") neighborhood, you'll find one of Puerto Ángel's best budget lodgings, **Casa de Huéspedes Capy,** sitting on the bay-view hillside by the road fork to Zipolite (Playa Panteón, P.O. Box 44, Puerto Ángel, Oaxaca 70902). Rooms, in two tiers with views toward Playa Panteón, are basic but clean with fans and cold-water private baths. Good family management, however, is the Capy's strong suit. This shows especially in the shady view restaurant, Arcely, where good food in a friendly atmosphere encourages guests to linger, reading or talking, for hours. The 10 rooms rent for about $7 s, $12 d or t.)

The unusually well-kept **Hotel Cabaña** downhill is just a few steps from Playa Panteón (Playa Panteón, Calle Pedro Sainz de Barada, Puerto Ángel, Oaxaca 70902, tel. 958-400-26). Past the lobby is a verdant, plant-decorated patio, while upstairs, guests enjoy chairs and shady tables on a breezy bay-vista sun deck. Marble shines in the baths and the floors of the 23 comfortable, very clean rooms, some with private view balconies. Several beachfront restaurants are conveniently nearby. Rooms rent for $27 s or d, $40 t, credit cards accepted.

Tucked in the leafy canyon a hundred yards uphill from the beach is **Posada Cañon Devata,** life-project of local ecological leaders Mateo and Suzanne Lopez (P.O. Box 74, Pochutla, Oaxaca 70900, rooms rent from about $14, bungalows $27, with fans and parking). Artists Mateo and Suzanne (he's Mexican, she's American) have become an example to local people, having reforested their originally denuded canyon property over a period of several years. They gradually added on land, so that their now-lush arroyo encompasses an entire watershed-ecosystem.

Their accommodations, a multiroom lodge and several luxury-rustic detached bungalows, dot the slopes of their sylvan jungle retreat. All are comfortably furnished and thoughtfully decorated with handicrafts and Mateo's expressive primitivist oil paintings.

Their restaurant (see "Food" below) serves all-organic fruits and vegetables and whole-wheat bread and tortillas, while their gift shop, Sueños de Amusgo, (see "Shopping" below), offers one-of-a-kind handicrafts, including many Amusgo *huipiles* and a gallery of Mateo's paintings.

Atop the hill via the adjacent steep road, the **Hotel Ángel del Mar** offers a sharply contrasting style of lodging (Puerto Ángel, Oaxaca 70902, tel. 958-403-97, local 6. Rates for the 31 rooms run from about $23 s, $30 d low-season). Guests enjoy a big open-air dining room, swimming pool, and large light rooms with private balconies looking down upon a panoramic bay vista. Mornings, guests can enjoy sunrise over the bay and evening sunsets over the ocean. Tired management, however, has unfortunately contributed to sometimes mediocre food, unresponsive desk staff, dusty halls, and rusty fixtures. During high season, meals may be included in the price, which consequently rise by about $25 per person; with TV and parking; credit cards accepted.

Zipolite Accommodations

Zipolite's line of rustic (bring your own towel and soap) lodgings starts at **Lola's** on the east end of the beach (Playa Zipolite, Puerto Ángel, Oaxaca 70902). The friendly, elderly owner continues her decades-long good management of her thatch-shaded restaurant and beach cabañas. For customers who hanker for a bit better lodging, Lola has broken new ground with Zipolite's first modern-standard units, a pair of shiny new rooms with hot water and ceiling fans.

The scene at Lola's resembles a miniresort, with the restaurant right on the beach, where guests enjoy late breakfasts, stroll out for swims, read thick novels, and kick back and enjoy convivial conversation with their mostly North American and European fellow vacationers. Cabañas rent for about $9 d with fan, toilet, and shower, the more deluxe rooms for about $18.

The **Lo Cosmico** cabañas nestle on a cactus-dotted rocky knoll at the opposite end of the beach (Playa Zipolite, Puerto Ángel, Oaxaca 70902). White spheres perched on their thatched roof peaks lend a mystical Hindu-Buddhist accent to the cabañas' already picturesque appearance. In the restaurant on the rise you're likely to find Regula and Antonio, Lo Cosmico's European-Mexican husband-wife owners. Regula manages the restaurant, specializing in a dozen varieties of tasty crepes, while Antonio supervises the hotel. Their hillside and beach-level cabañas are clean, candle-lit, and equipped with hammocks and concrete floors. Showers and toilets are outside. Cabañas rent for about $5 per person.

Shambala, on the adjacent forested hillside, is as it sounds—a tranquil Buddhist-style retreat (Puerto Ángel, Playa Zipolite, Oaxaca 70902). Shambala's driving force is the friendly owner-community leader, Gloria Esperanza Johnson, who arrived in Zipolite by accident in 1970 and decided to stay, eventually adopting Mexican citizenship. She built the place from the ground up, gradually adding on until now about 100 cabañas, a macrobiotic beach-

view restaurant, and a spiritual center occupy her hilltop. Shambala is a quiet, alcohol-free haven for lovers of reading, sunbathing, hiking, yoga, and meditation. It sits atop an enviable few acres at the edge of a pristine hinterland. Adjacent cactus-studded cliffs plummet spectacularly to surf-splashed rocks below, while trails fan out through lush tropical deciduous forest. The very simple candle-lit thatched concrete-floored cabañas with hammocks rent for about $5 per person. Toilets and showers are shared.

Get to both Shambala and Lo Cosmico by turning from the main road onto the dirt driveway near the arch at Zipolite's west end. Bear right at the first fork, then left at the next for Lo Cosmico, right for Shambala.

Trailer Parks And Camping

The **Zipolite Trailer Park** has about 50 parking or camping spaces beneath a shady, tufted grove near the middle of Playa Zipolite. A spirit of camaraderie often blooms among the tents and assorted RVs of travelers from as far away as the Klondike, Kalispell, and Khabarovsk. About $4 gets you a space for two, including showers and toilets (no hookups).

One of Zipolite's best tenting spots is the forested hilltop behind **Shambala.** The friendly owner, Gloria Johnson, would probably allow you to use her showers and toilets for a small fee.

FOOD

(Complete Dinner Price Key: Budget = under $7, Moderate = $7-14, Expensive = more than $14.) For a small place, Puerto Ángel has good food, starting with a pair of respectable eateries in side-by-side competition right on the main beachfront street. The Italian born owner-chef of the **Villa Florencia** specializes in antipasti, salads, and meat and seafood pastas (open daily 8 a.m.-11 p.m.). Like a good country Italian restaurant, service is crisp; presentations are attractive. Their modest wine list includes some good old-country imports, and the cappuccino is probably the best on the Costa Chica. Moderate.

Next door, the **Restaurant Tiburón** ("Shark") tries just as hard, specializing in a list of daily seafood specials, such as New Orleans jambalaya, scallops Margarita, and Veracruz-style red snapper (open daily 8 a.m.-11 p.m.). Moderate.

For a homey change of pace, get in on the family-style dinner at the macrobiotic restaurant at the **Posada Cañon Devata.** Their fare is all fresh, organic, and high in vegetables and grains and low in meat. Reserve for the 7 p.m. dinner by early afternoon. Moderate. (See "Accommodations" above for more info).

Four or five restaurants line Playa Panteón. Here, the main attraction is the beach scene rather than the food. **Susy's** and **Leyvis y Vicente** seem to be the best of the bunch; fish will generally be the best choice (make sure it's fresh; open seasonally about 8 a.m.-9 p.m.).

Zipolite also has some good eating places. For hearty macrobiotic-style fare and a breezy beach view, go to the restauraurant at **Shambala** (see "Accommodations" above) at the west end of Playa Zipolite. Personable owner Gloria Johnson runs a very tidy kitchen, which serves good breakfasts, soups, salads, and sandwiches (open daily 8 a.m.-8 p.m.). No alcohol, however.

Regula, the European co-owner of **Lo Cosmico** on the knoll just east of Shambala, cooks from a similar macrobiotic-style menu, although she specializes in several variations of crepes, including egg, meat, cheese, and vegetable (open daily from around 8 a.m. to 6 p.m.).

ENTERTAINMENT AND SPORTS

Puerto Ángel's entertainments are mostly spontaneous. If anything exciting is going to happen, it will most likely be on the beachfront Boulevard Uribe where people tend to congregate during the afternoon and evenings. A small crowd may accumulate in the adjacent restaurant Villa Florencia for talk, TV, coffee, or something from the bar.

Sunset-watchers get their best chance from the unobstructed hill perch of the **Hotel Ángel del Mar,** where the bar and restaurant can provide something to enliven the occasion if clouds happen to block the view.

The same spot provides music for dancing at their discotheque during the highest seasons, most likely between Christmas and New Year and the week before Easter.

For more excitement, head to Puerto Escondido (see the previous section) for more and livelier entertainments.

Jogging, Swimming, And Surfing
"Holey" streets, rocky roads, and lack of grass sharply curtail Puerto Angel **jogging** prospects. The highway, however, which runs gradually uphill from near the pier, does provide a continuous, more or less smooth surface. Confine your jogging, however, to early morning or late afternoon, and take water. **Swimming** provides more local exercise opportunities, especially in the sheltered waters off of Playa Panteón.

Bodysurfing, boogieboarding, and surfing are sometimes rewarding, depending on wind and swells, off Playa Zipolite. Be careful of undertow, which is always a threat, even on calm days at Zipolite. If you're inexperienced, don't go out alone. Alcohol and surf, moreover, don't mix. On rough days, unless you're an expert, forget it. Bring your own board; few, if any, rentals are available.

Sailing And Windsurfing
If you have your own carryable boat or windsurfing gear, sheltered Playa Panteón would be a good place to put it into the water, although the neighboring headland may decrease the available wind. Calm mornings at Playas Zipolite, San Augustinillo, or Metzunte (see above), with more wind but rougher waves, might also be fruitful.

Snorkeling And Scuba Diving
Rocky shoals at the edges of Puerto Ángel Bay are good for casual snorkeling. Playa Estacahuite (see above), on the open ocean just beyond the bay's east headland, is even better. Best bring your own equipment. If you don't, you can rent a snorkel and mask from Vicente, at his restaurant, Leyvis y Vicente, on Playa Panteón, for about $3 an hour.

Vicente likewise takes experienced **scuba** divers to local sites for about $40 per person for a one-tank dive, basic equipment furnished.

Beginners who want to learn diving contact the well-equipped and certified dive instructors of **Buceos Triton** dive shop 45 minutes' drive south in Santa Cruz de Huatulco. (See "Sports" in the "Bahías de Huatulco" section below for details.)

Fishing

The bayfront pier is the best place to bargain for a boat and captain to take you and your friends out on a fishing excursion. Prices depend on season, but you can figure on paying about $30 an hour for a boat for four or five persons with bait and two or three good rods and reels. During a three-hour outing a few miles offshore, a competently captained boat will typically bring in three or four big, good-eating *robalo* (snook), *huachinango* (snapper), *atún* (tuna), or pompano. If you're uncertain about what's biting, go down to the dock around 2:00 or 3:00 in the afternoon and see what the boats are bringing in.

Vicente, of Leyvis y Vicente restaurant on Playa Panteón, also takes out fishing parties of up to six persons for around $30 an hour, bait and tackle included. You can also arrange fishing trips through the **travel agent** in the office across the street from the doctor and pharmacy on Av. Teniente Azueta, just uphill from Uribe.

SHOPPING

Market

The biggest local market spreads along the Pochutla main street, Hwy. 175, about seven miles from Puerto Ángel, one mile inland from the Hwy. 200 junction. Mostly a place for looking rather than buying, throngs of vendors from the hills line the sidewalks, even crowding into the streets, to sell their piles of onions, mangos, forest herbs, carrots, cilantro, and jicama.

Groceries

Little-bit-of-everything store **Super Alex,** with branches in both Zipolite and on the beachfront Boulevard Uribe in Puerto Ángel, sells cheese, milk, bread, some vegetables, and other essentials.

Handicrafts

Sueños ("Dreams") **de Amusgos,** at Posada Cañon Devata (see "Accommodations" above) is one of the Costa Chica's most interesting handicrafts shops. Owners Suzanne and Mateo López have assembled a quality collection of Amusgo, Mixtec, and Chatino crafts, including many fine hand-crocheted *huipiles* from San Pedro de Amusgos.

SERVICES AND INFORMATION

Money Exchange

Bancomer in the center of Pochutla (corner main street Lázaro Cárdenas and Av. 3A Norte, tel. 400-63) changes U.S. dollar traveler's checks and Canadian cash Mon.-Fri. 9-10 a.m. Call to confirm hours.

Post, Telephone, Telegraph, And Travel Agent

The Puerto Ángel **Correos** (post office) and **Telegrafos** stand side by side at the Agencia Municipal (city hall) at the foot of Hwy. 175. The Correos is open Mon.-Fri. 9 a.m.-4 p.m, the Telegrafos, Mon.-Fri. 9 a.m.-3 p.m.

The Puerto Ángel *larga distancia* (long-distance) telephone office (tel. 958-403-97, 403-98, 403-99) is on Av. Teniente Azueta, just uphill from Uribe. Hours are Mon.-Sat. 9 a.m.-2 p.m. and 5-10 p.m. The Puerto Ángel area code is 958.

Puerto Ángel's only *agencia de viajes* (travel agency) arranges tours and fishing trips and sells reserved air and bus tickets at the small office on Azueta next door to the *larga distancia.*

Medical And Police

Puerto Ángel's respected private **doctor,** Dr. Constancio A. Juarez, holds consultation hours (Mon.-Sat. 7 a.m.-2 p.m. and 5-9 p.m.) and also runs the **pharmacy** on Av. Teniente Azueta across from the *larga distancia.*

Otherwise, go to the government **Centro del Salud** (health clinic) on the hill behind the church. (Go up Azueta a long curving block, go left at the first corner, and continue another block to the health center.)

For **police emergencies,** go to the Agencia Municipal, next to the post office at the foot of Hwy. 175.

Ecological Projects

Community leaders, such as Suzanne and Mateo López, owners of Posada Cañon Devata, and Gloria Esperanza Johnson, owner of Shambala in Zipolite, are trying to awaken local awareness of ecological issues. Suzanne and Mateo, by restoring their entire canyon ecosystem property, and Gloria, by spearheading efforts to prevent the deforestation of coastal lands, hope to serve as examples of the benefits that simple efforts can yield.

In parallel but separate action, **EC-Solar,** the semiprivate ecological "Peace Corps," has established a local headquarters up the off-highway side road just past the concrete brickyard two blocks from the bay. They are working with local *campesinos* to build environmentally appropriate solutions to village sewage, water, health, and agricultural problems.

GETTING THERE AND AWAY

By Air

Scheduled flights to Mexican destinations connect daily with airports at **Huatulco,** 19 miles (30 km), or **Puerto Escondido,** 44 miles (71 km) by road from Puerto Ángel. For details see "Getting There and Away" in the "Puerto Escondido" and "Bahías de Huatulco" sections of this chapter.

By Car Or RV

Good roads connect Puerto Ángel to the west with Puerto Escondido and Acapulco, north with Oaxaca, and east with the Bahías de Huatulco and Tehuantepec.

Highway 200 connects westward with Puerto Escondido in an easy 44 miles (71 km), continuing to Acapulco in an additional seven hours (247 miles, 398 km) of driving. In the opposite direction Bahías de Huatulco (actually Crucecita) is a quick 22 miles (35 km). The continuation to Tehuantepec stretches another 92 miles (148 km), or around two additional hours' driving time.

To **Oaxaca** north, paved but narrow and winding National Hwy. 175 connects 148 miles (238 km) over the Sierra Madre del Sur from its junction with Hwy. 200 at Pochutla. The road climbs to 7,000 feet through cool (chilly in winter) pine forests and hardscrabble Chatino and Zapotec Indian villages. Fill up with gas in Pochutla (Magna Sin unleaded is available only at the Pemex at the north edge of town), carry water and blankets, and be prepared for emergencies. The first gas station and services are in Miahuatlán, 90 miles north. Allow about seven driving hours from Puerto Ángel to Oaxaca, about six in the opposite direction.

By Bus

A number of first- and second-class bus lines in Pochutla connect to points north, east, and west. The three separate stations cluster less than a mile from the Hwy. 200 junction along Hwy. 175, the main street into Pochutla (before the town center near the taxi stand).

About 10 first-class **Gacela** buses (tel. 403-80, a subsidiary of Estrella Blanca) per day connect with Puerto Escondido, continuing to Acapulco. They also connect east (about 14 per day) with Bahías de Huatulco destinations of Crucecita and Santa Cruz de Huatulco. One super-first-class bus per day connects with Mexico City.

All first-class **Cristóbal Colón** buses (tel. 402-74) connect east with Crucecita (six per day). One bus per day connects with Tehuantepec, continuing to San Cristóbal las Casas in Chiapas. Three buses connect north with Oaxaca via Tehuantepec; one bus daily connects with Puebla and Mexico City. Two buses connect daily west with Puerto Escondido.

Frequent second-class service is offered by **Autobuses Estrella del Valle** and **Autobuses Oaxaca Pacifico,** connecting with Oaxaca, Crucecita, Puerto Ángel, and Puerto Escondido.

BAHÍAS DE HUATULCO

The nine azure Bays of Huatulco decorate a couple of dozen miles of acacia-plumed rocky coastline east of Puerto Ángel. Between the bays, the ocean joins in battle with jutting, rocky headlands, while in their inner reaches the ocean calms, caressing diminutive crescents of coral sand. Inland, a thick hardwood forest seems to stretch in a continuous carpet to the Sierra.

Ecologists shiver when they hear that these bays are going to be developed. FONATUR, the government tourism development agency, says however, that it has a plan. Relatively few (but all upscale) hotels will occupy the beaches; other development will be confined to a few inland centers. The remaining 70% of the land will be kept as pristine ecological zones and study areas.

Although this story sounds sadly familiar, FONATUR (which developed Ixtapa and Cancún) seems to have learned from its experience. Up-to-date sewage treatment is being installed *ahead of time;* logging and homesteading have been reversed, and soldiers patrol the beaches, stopping turtle poachers. If all goes according to the plan, the nine Bahías de Huatulco and their 100,000-acre forest hinterland will be both a tourist and ecological paradise, in addition to employing thousands of local people, when complete in 2020. If this Huatulco dream ends as well as it has started, Mexico should take pride while the rest of the world should take heed.

HISTORY

Long before Columbus, the Huatulco area was well-known to the Aztecs and their predecessors. The name itself, from Aztec words meaning "land where a tree is worshipped," reflects one of Mexico's most intriguing legends—of the Holy Cross of Huatulco.

When the Spanish arrived on the Huatulco coast, the local Indians showed them a huge cross that they worshipped at the edge of the sea. A contemporary chronicler, Ignacio Burgoa, conjectured that the cross had been left by an ancient saint—maybe even the Apostle Thomas—some 15 centuries earlier. Such speculation notwithstanding, the cross remained as the Spanish colonized the area and established headquarters and a port, which they named San Agustín, at the westernmost of the Bays of Huatulco.

Spanish ports and their treasure-laden galleons from the Orient attracted foreign corsairs—Francis Drake in 1579 and Thomas Cavendish in 1587. Cavendish arrived at the bay now called Bahía Santa Cruz, where he saw the cross that the Indians were worshipping. Believing that it was the work of the devil, Cavendish and his men tried to chop, saw, and burn it down. Failing at all of these, Cavendish looped his ship's mooring ropes around the cross, and with sails unfurled, tried using the force of the wind to pull it down. Frustrated, he finally sailed away, leaving the cross of Huatulco still standing beside the shore.

In 1612, Bishop Juan de Cervantes managed to bring the cross (or a part of it) to the cathedral in Oaxaca. With a piece cut from that, he made a copy of the original, which the faithful still venerate at the main altar on each Friday of Lent.

SIGHTS

Getting Oriented

With no road to the outside world, the Bahías de Huatulco remained virtually uninhabited and undeveloped until 1982, when coastal Hwy. 200 was pushed through. A few years later, Huatulco's planned initial kernel of infrastructure was complete, centering on the brand-new residential-service town, Crucecita (pop. 10,000), and nearby Santa Cruz de Huatulco boat harbor and hotel village on Bahía Santa Cruz.

The Bays of Huatulco embellish the coastline both east and west of Santa Cruz. To the east, a paved road links Bahías Chahue, Tangolunda, and Conejos. To the west lie Bahías El Organo, El Maguey, and Cacaluta, all road-accessible from Santa Cruz. Isolated farther west are Bahías Chachacual and San Agustín, with no road from Santa Cruz (although a good dirt road runs to San Agustín from Hwy. 200 near the airport).

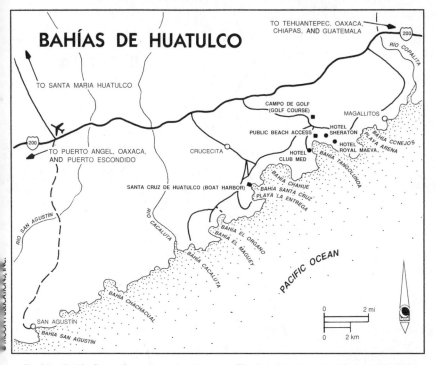

BAHÍAS DE HUATULCO

Besides Bahía Santa Cruz, the only other bay of Huatulco that has been extensively developed is Tangolunda, five miles east. Its golf course, small restaurant-shopping complex, and three resort hotels (Club Med, Sheraton, and Club Maeva) have been fully operational since the late 1980s.

Getting Around

Frequent public **microbuses** connect Crucecita and Bahías Santa Cruz, Chahue, and Tangolunda. Taxis make the same trips for about $3 by day, $4 at night. No public transportation is available to the other bays. Taxi drivers might take you for a look at west-side bays El Organo, El Maguey, and Cacalute for about $20 roundtrip from Crucecita or Tangolunda, perhaps $10 to Bahía Conejos.

For an extended day-trip to all eight road-accessible bays, figure on $50 for either a taxi or a rental car. (Call Dollar at the Sheraton, tel. 100-38, ext. 787, or Budget in Crucecita at Octillo and Jazmín, tel. 700-34, 700-10.)

The local boat cooperative runs launches from the Santa Cruz harbor. With the possible exception of Sundays and holidays, they rent only complete boats for up to about 10 people. Full-day excursions run about $120, while drop-off runs to the nearest beach are about $10; to the more remote, around $30.

Tours offer another alternative. Agents organize groups for local boat or land excursions. A six-hour sunning, swimming, and snorkeling trip to a couple of Bahías de Huatulco beaches, for example, runs around $20. Trips to Puerto Ángel, Puerto Escondido, and wildlife-rich lagoons go for $40-60 per person. Contact a travel agent, such as Servicios Turisticos del Sur (Sheraton Hotel, tel. 100-55, ext. 784; or Hotel Castillo, tel. 705-72, in Santa Cruz).

Crucecita And Santa Cruz

Despite its newness **Crucecita** ("Little Cross," pop. about 10,000) resembles a traditional Mexican town, with life revolving around a central

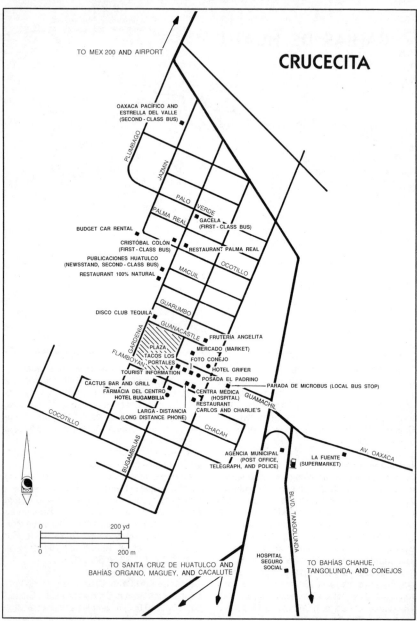

CRUCECITA

TO MEX 200 AND AIRPORT

OAXACA PACÍFICO AND
ESTRELLA DEL VALLE
(SECOND - CLASS BUS)

PLUMBAGO

JAZMÍN

PALO VERDE

PALMA REAL

GACELA
(FIRST - CLASS BUS)

BUDGET CAR RENTAL

CRISTÓBAL COLÓN
(FIRST - CLASS BUS)

RESTAURANT PALMA REAL

OCOTILLO

PUBLICACIONES HUATULCO
(NEWSSTAND, SECOND - CLASS BUS)

RESTAURANT 100% NATURAL

MACUIL

GUARUMBO

DISCO CLUB TEQUILA

GARDENIA

GUANACASTLE

FRUTERIA ANGELITA

PLAZA

MERCADO (MARKET)

TACOS LOS
PORTALES

FOTO CONEJO

FLAMBOYAN

HOTEL GRIFER

TOURIST INFORMATION

POSADA EL PADRINO

CACTUS BAR AND GRILL

PARADA DE MICROBUS (LOCAL BUS STOP)

FARMACIA DEL CENTRO

CENTRA MEDICA
(HOSPITAL)

HOTEL BUGAMBILIA

GUAMACHIL

LARGA - DISTANCIA
(LONG DISTANCE PHONE)

RESTAURANT
CARLOS AND CHARLIE'S

COCOTILLO

CHACAH

BUGAMBILIAS

AV. OAXACA

AGENCIA MUNICIPAL
(POST OFFICE,
TELEGRAPH, AND POLICE)

LA FUENTE
(SUPERMARKET)

BLVD. TANGOLUNDA

N

MOON

0   200 yd

0   200 m

HOSPITAL
SEGURO
SOCIAL

TO SANTA CRUZ DE HUATULCO AND
BAHÍAS ORGANO, MAGUEY, AND CACALUTE

TO BAHÍAS CHAHUE,
TANGOLUNDA, AND CONEJOS

plaza and market nearby. Crucecita is where the people who work in the Huatulco hotels, businesses, and government offices live. Although pleasant enough for a walk around the square and a meal in a restaurant, it's nothing special—mostly a place whose modest hotels and restaurants accommodate business travelers and weekenders who can't afford the plush hotels near the beach.

The two deluxe hotels and the few travel-oriented businesses of **Santa Cruz de Huatulco** (on Bahía Santa Cruz about two miles from Crucecita) cluster near the boat harbor. Fishing and tour boats come and go; vacationers sun themselves on the tranquil, yellow-sand **Playa Santa Cruz** (beyond the restaurants adjacent to the boat harbor), while T-shirt and fruit vendors and boatmen hang around the quay watching for prospective customers. After the sun goes down, however, tourists quit the beach for their hotels, workers return to their homes in Crucecita, leaving the harbor and streets empty and dark.

Exploring The Bays Of Huatulco
Isolation has left the Huatulco waters blue and unpolluted, the beaches white and clean. Generally, the bays are similar: deciduous (green July-Feb.) forested rocky headlands enclosing generally steep, soft yellow-coral sand crescents. Water is clear and good for snorkeling, scuba diving, sailing, kayaking, and windsurfing during the often-calm weather. Beaches, however, are typically steep, causing waves to break quickly near the sand, unsuitable for bodysurfing, boogieboarding, or surfing.

The six undeveloped Huatulco bays have no water nor much shade, since they're so pristine that even coconut palms haven't gotten around to sprouting there. When exploring, bring food, drinks, hats, sunscreen, and mosquito repellent. When camping (which is permitted everywhere except Tangolunda) bring everything.

East Side: Chahue, Tangolunda, And Conejos
Bahía Chahue, about a mile from Santa Cruz, is wide, blue, and forest-tufted, with a steep yellow dune growing to a huge pile, as if scooped up by a tipsy giant at the east end. Chahue, the site of a new Holiday Inn, is nevertheless uncrowded even on weekends and holidays and nearly empty the rest of the time.

About four miles farther east is the breezy and broad **Bahía Tangolunda.** Although hotels front much of the beach, a signed public access road borders the western edge of the golf course (turn right just east of the Club Med road). Except for its east end, the Tangolunda beach is steep and the waves often break quickly right at the sand. Palapa restaurants at the beach serve food and drinks; or if you prefer, stroll a quarter mile for refreshments at the luxurious poolside beach clubs of the Sheraton and Club Maeva resorts.

Over the headland about two miles farther, **Punta Arena** ("Sand Point") a forested thumb of land, juts out into wide **Bahía Conejos.** Three separate steep beaches spread along the inner shoreline. The main entrance road arrives at high-duned Playa Punta Arena. Playa Tejoncito ("Little Badger") is beyond the rocks far to the right; Playa Conejos ("Rabbits") is to the left on the other side of Punta Arena. A few palm-frond *ramadas* for shade and a saltwater flush toilet lavatory occupy the Playa Punta Arena dune. Trees behind the dunes provide a few shady spots for RV or tent campers. A stable (see "Sports" below) takes visitors on horseback rides along a trail that heads east from there.

Beyond tiny **Magallitos** fishing village, less than a mile farther on, a long broad, beach with oft-powerful surfing rollers (novices beware) stretches for at least a mile east. Beach palapas serve drinks and very fresh seafood. A lagoon behind the village (bring your kayak) appears ripe for wildlife viewing.

West Side: Playa Entrega And Bahías El Organo, El Maguey, Cacaluta, And San Agustín
Playa Entrega is a little dab of sand slipped into the west side of Bahía Santa Cruz. It is the infamous spot where, on January 20, 1831, Vicente Guerrero, president and Independence hero, was brought ashore in custody of archvillain Francisco Picaluga and sent to be murdered in Oaxaca a few months later.

Quarter-mile-long Playa Entrega is the ideal Sunday beach, with calm clear water and clean yellow sand. Swimming and kayaking, and often snorkeling, sailing, and windsurfing possibilities are excellent. Some trees provide shady spots for tenting and RV camping. No facilities exist except for seasonal and holiday food and drink stands.

Get there via the main street, Bulevar Benito Juarez, which passes the Santa Cruz boat harbor. Continue west past the Hotel Binneguenda (mark your odometer) on the right. After a few hundred yards, the road curves left and follows a small valley uphill. Atop the hill, a third of a mile (one-half km) past the hotel, follow the fork. Within another mile you'll pass a wave-tossed cove below on the right. Continue and you'll see Playa Entrega edging the bay to the left. Bear left downhill to the beach at 2.9 miles (4.6 km).

If, instead of the left fork to La Entrega, you follow the right fork you'll be headed for the Bahías El Organo, El Maguey, and Cacaluta. **El Organo** is first; after about half a mile from the fork, look for a rough dirt trail to the left. The beach is isolated, intimate, and enfolded by rocky shoals on both sides. Some trees behind the dune provide shade.

Continuing straight ahead, the road forks again (about 1.3 miles from the hotel). Head left to El Maguey, right to Cacaluta. The sandy crescent of **El Maguey** is bordered by tidepools tucked beneath forested headlands. Facing a protected fjordlike channel, the Maguey beach is virtually waveless and fine for swimming, snorkeling, diving, windsurfing, and sailing. It would be a snap to launch a boat here for fishing in the bay. During weekends and holidays, picnickers arrive and banana towboats and *aguamotos* (mini-motorboats) buzz the beach and bay. Although camping is possible, room is limited.

Bahía Cacaluta, two miles past the El Maguey fork, spreads along a mile-long, heart-shaped beach, beckoningly close to a cactus-studded offshore islet. Swimmers beware, for waves typically break powerfully, surging upward and receding with strong undertow. Many shells—limpets and purple- and brown-daubed clams—speckle the beach. Surf fishing prospects, either from the beach itself or from rocks on either end, appear excellent. Although the sand directly behind the beach is too soft for vehicles, some space exists farther back for RV parking and camping. Tenters could have their pick anywhere along the dune.

Bahía Chachacual, past the Rio Cacaluta about four miles farther west, is a sand-edged azure nook accessible only via forest trails.

Bahía San Agustín, by contrast, is well known and reachable (taxi $2) by the dirt road just west of the airport, across the highway from the fork to Santa Maria Huatulco. After about seven miles along a firm track, accessible by all but the bulkiest RVs, bear right to the modest village of palapas at the bay's sheltered west end. From there, the beach stretches eastward along a mile of forest-backed dune. Besides good swimming, sailing, windsurfing, shell-collecting, and fishing prospects, San Agustín also has a number of behind-the-dune spots (follow the left fork shortly before the road's end) for RV and tent camping. Beachside palapas can, at least, supply seafood and drinks and maybe some basic groceries.

ACCOMMODATIONS

In Huatulco, as in other resorts, hotels on the beach are the most expensive. Crucecita's hotels are cheapest; Tangolunda's are most expensive, while the Santa Cruz hotels are in between.

Most of the **Crucecita** lodgings are near the central plaza. The **Grifer,** at Guamachil and Carrizal, would be nothing special in most resorts of Pacific Mexico, but in hotel-poor Huatulco, it is often full (P.O. Box 159, Crucecita, Oaxaca 70980, tel. 958-700-48). Three tiers of nondescript modern rooms enclose a TV-dominated atrium; a passable street-level restaurant is convenient for breakfast. The 16 rooms rent for $27 s or d, with ceiling fans, no credit cards.

Across Guamachil in mid-block, the **Posada el Padrino** offers small, plain but clean a/c rooms on the two floors above its good street-level restaurant. (Calle Guamachil, Lote 15 MZ 17 SECT, Crucecita, Oaxaca 70980, tel. 958-700-60). (See "Food" below.) The eight rooms rent for about $23 s or d, $30 t; only Mexican credit cards are accepted.

The **Hotel Suites Bugambilias,** at the southeast plaza corner, offers a more deluxe, family-run alternative (corner Flamboyan and Bugambilias, P.O. Box 289, Crucecita, Oaxaca 70980, tel. 958-703-90, 958-700-18). The rooms, although clean and comfortable, have motel-style walkways passing their windows, decreasing privacy. Rates for the 20 rooms run about $27 s, $34 d, $44 d, with fan and TV; credit cards are accepted.

Santa Cruz Hotels

A block from the beach in Santa Cruz, first choice goes to the **Hotel Binneguenda.** Neocolonial arches, pastel stucco walls, and copper and ceramics handicrafts decorate the interiors while in the adjacent leafy patio, guests sun themselves around the pool (Benito Juarez 5, Santa Cruz de Huatulco, Oaxaca 70900, tel. 958-700-77, fax 958-702-84). In the restaurant, the customers seem as well fed and satisfied as the waiters are well trained and attentive. Upstairs, the colonial-modern-decor rooms are spacious, comfortable, and equipped with phones, TV, and a/c. Rates for the 75 rooms run about $67 s or d, $77 t, with parking; credit cards accepted.

Hotel Castillo Huatulco down the street a couple of blocks amounts to a poor second choice, unless you can get in for prices substantially less than the Binneguenda (Benito Juarez, P.O. Box 354, Santa Cruz de Huatulco 70980, tel. 958-701-26, 958-702-51, fax 958-701-31). Loosely managed and often noisy, with recorded salsa music thumping away in the bar, its 106 rooms, although comfortable, are crowded into a smaller space than the Binneguenda's 75. They are nevertheless popular with families on weekends and holidays but nearly empty (and perhaps bargainable) during quieter seasons. High-season rates run from about $66 s or d, $77 t, with phones, TV, a/c, pool, parking, tennis court; credit cards accepted.

Tangolunda Luxury Resorts

Three big hotels spread along the Tangolunda shoreline. The Club Med dominates the sheltered western side-bay, with four stacklike towers that make the place appear as a big ocean liner. The smaller Sheraton and Club Royal Maeva stand side by side on the bay's inner recess next to the golf course.

The emphasis of all three resorts is on facilities, including multiple pools, bars, and restaurants, music, discos, shows, and sports such as tennis, golf, sailing, kayaking, windsurfing, snorkeling, diving, and swimming. Additional services include shops, baby-sitting, children's clubs, and arts and crafts instruction.

In contrast to the Sheraton, which operates in usual hotel style, the Club Royal Maeva and Club Med rates include everything—all food, sports, lessons, and entertainment. Their cuisine, although tasty and bountiful, is not fancy. The atmosphere resembles a big upscale summer camp, with hosts of options, even for those who want to do nothing.

The **Sheraton Huatulco** is a generic (but worthy) member of the worldwide chain (Paseo Benito Juarez, Bahía Tangolunda, Oaxaca 70989, tel. 958-100-55, 958-100-05, 958-100-39). Rooms are comfortable, deluxe, and decorated in soothing pastels, with private bay-view balconies, phones, cable TV, and a/c. Rates for its 360 rooms and suites begin at $116 s, $121 d high season, $90 s, $95 d low. For information and reservations from the U.S. and Canada, call Sheraton toll-free at (800) 325-3535.

If you're activity-oriented, you'll likely get more for your money at either the Club Med or the Royal Maeva. The 300-room Maeva is very well managed and smaller; consequently it's likely to be more personalized than the sprawling 554-room Club Med. Accommodations in both are luxurious, with phones, cable TV, and private bay-view balconies.

Packages at the **Club Med** vary according to season, but begin at about $750 per week ($108 per day) per person double occupancy, plus $70-100 in "membership" fees. Child (6-11) rates run about $600 per week. High season rates run nearly double that. Call (800) CLUBMED for information and reservations in the U.S. and Canada.

Club Maeva double-occupancy rates run about $110 per adult per day low season, $135 high, two kids free with parents. For information and reservations in the U.S. and Canada, call (800) GOMAEVA.

Trailer Parks And Camping

In Santa Cruz, the **Trailer Park Mangos** rents about 30 spaces in a shady mango grove about a quarter mile east (toward Tangolunda) of the Hotel Castillo. The sparse facilities include toilets, showers, and electricity but no sewer hookup. RVs pay $12 daily, tenters about $3 per person. When the place is empty, (which is most of the time) you could probably bargain for a much better rate.

Authorities generally permit **camping** at all of the Bahías de Huatulco except Tangolunda. For details, see "Exploring the Bays of Huatulco" above. You also might save time by checking with FONATUR (see "Information" below) for any access changes or recommendations. The soldiers who guard the beaches against turtle poachers and squatters also make camping much more secure. They usually welcome a kind word and maybe a cool drink as a break from their lonely and tedious vigil.

FOOD

Aside from the Tangolunda hotels, nearly all good Huatulco eateries are near the **Crucecita plaza.**

Breakfast And Snacks
For inexpensive home-style cooking, try the *fondas* at the Crucecita *mercado,* between Guamachil and Guanacastle, half a block off the plaza.

The *mercado* stalls are good for fresh fruit during daylight hours, as is the **Frutería Angelita** (open daily 6 a.m.-8 p.m.), just across Guanacastle.

Also nearby, the **Panadería San Alejandro on Flamboyan** (on the east side of the market) offers mounds of fresh baked goodies (daily 6 a.m.-10 p.m.).

The crowds will lead you to Crucecita's best-bet snack shop, **Los Portales Taco and Grill**, corner of Guamachil and Bugambilias, right on the plaza. Breakfasts, besides a dozen styles of tacos, Texas chili (or, as in Mexico, *frijoles charros*—"cowboy beans"), and barbecued ribs are their specialties. Beer is less than a dollar (open daily 24 hours, tel. 700-70).

Restaurants
Equally successful is **Restaurante Rancho el Padrino,** on the bottom floor of the Posada el Padrino on Guamachil, half a block from the plaza. Wall art, folkcrafts, and quiet conversation set the tone, while tasty country specialties fill the tables. Try their Oaxacan-style tamales, or *botanas Oaxaqueñas*—cheese, sausage, pork, beef, and guacamole snacks, for example (open Tues.-Sun. 8 a.m.-11 p.m., Mon. 1-11 p.m., tel. 700-60).

Restaurant Palma Real, away from the square, does well on nearly exclusively local patronage. Good service and careful preparation are the key to the tasty soup, seafood, pasta, and meat menu (open daily 7 a.m.-10 p.m.; on Gardenia four blocks from the plaza, corner of Ocotillo, tel. 706-71).

The local edition of the **Carlos and Charlie's** worldwide chain is on Carrizal, corner of Flamboyan. Late owner Carlos Anderson's formula of tasty specialties, outrageous decor, brash music, and zany waiters is a safe bet to brighten the evening of visitors who want a party. Hours vary seasonally, call 700-05.

ENTERTAINMENT

Hangouts And Discos
Huatulco entertainments center on the Crucecita plaza. Although the hubbub quiets down during low seasons, some spots are reliable amusement sources year-round. The **Cactus Bar and Grill,** on the Flamboyan side of the plaza, livens up with videos, music, and the antics of its "Cucharachas" and "Muppets" nightly 7 p.m.-3 a.m.

On the other hand, you can get swept up nightly in your own high-volume disco fantasy across the plaza at **Tequila** (8 p.m.-4 a.m.).

In Santa Cruz, lights flash, fogs descend, and customers gyrate to the boom-boom at **Magic Circus** disco in the old Marlin Hotel on Calle Mitla two blocks behind Banamex off the main boulevard. Admission (from around 10 p.m.) runs about $10. Call 700-37 or 700-18 to confirm.

Hotel Music And Dancing
The **Sheraton** in Tangolunda is the most reliable source of hotel nightlife. Live music plays before dinner (about 6-8) in the lobby-bar, guests dance to a live Latin band in the Banquet Salon (about $30 with dinner, $7 without), and decorations overflow at theme-night parties (Italian, French, Mixteca, Chinese, about $25 per person with dinner). Call 100-55, 100-05, or 100-39 for details and reservations.

SPORTS

Walking, Jogging, Tennis, And Golf
Huatulco's open spaces and smooth roads and sidewalks afford plenty of walking and jogging

opportunities. One of the most serene spots is along the Tangolunda Golf Course mornings or evenings. Also, an interesting **trail** takes off from the stables at Bahía Conejos (see "Horseback Riding" below).

If you're planning on playing lots of **tennis,** best check into either the Club Maeva or the Club Med, which have good courts and instructors. Otherwise, the Hotels Sheraton (tel. 100-55, 100-05, 100-39 and Castillo (tel. 701-26, 958-702-51) and the Tangolunda Golf Course (tel. 100-37 and 100-59) have tennis courts. Call for rental information.

The breezy green **Tangolunda Golf Course** (tel. 100-37 and 100-59), designed by the late architect Mario Chegnan Danto, stretches for 6,851 yards down Tangolunda Valley to the bay. The course starts from a low building complex (watch for dirt road entrance) off the Santa Cruz-Tangolunda highway across from the sewage plant. Greens fee runs about $26, cart $26, club rental $13, caddy $12. (The tennis courts, maintained by the same government corporation that owns the golf course, are next to the clubhouse on the knoll at the east side of the golf course.)

Horseback Riding

Rancho Caballo del Mar at Bahía Conejos guides horseback trips along the ocean-view forest trail which stretches from their corral to the eco-preserve zone by the Río Copalita. The four-mile tour, which costs about $40 per person, returns via Magallitos shoreline village for swimming and lunch. Adventurers can also walk the same four-mile roundtrip in around three hours. Take a hat, water, and a bathing suit, and start early (around 8:00) or late (around 3:00) to avoid the midday heat.

Swimming, Snorkeling, And Diving

Swimming is ideal in calm corners of the Bahías de Huatulco. Especially good swimming beaches are at Playa Entrega in Bahía Santa Cruz and Bahía el Maguey (see "Sights" above). Generally clear water makes for rewarding **snorkeling** off the rocky shoals of all of the Bays of Huatulco. Local currents and conditions, however, can be hazardous. Novice snorkelers should go on trips accompanied by strong, experienced swimmers or professional guides (see below). Bring your own equipment; gear purchased locally will be expensive at best and unusable at worst.

Huatulco snorkelers and divers enjoy the services of well-equipped and professional **Buceos Triton** dive shop at the Hotel Castillo in Santa Cruz (open daily 9-2, 4-7, tel. 700-51, 701-26, 701-53). Owner and certified instructor Enrique La Clette has had extensive training in France, the U.S., and Mexico City. He starts novices out with a pool mini-course, followed by a three-hour ($50) trip in a nearby bay. Snorkelers go for about $20, with good equipment furnished.

Buceos Triton's PADI open-water certification course takes about five days and runs about $300, complete. After that, you are qualified for more advanced tours, which include local shipwrecks, night dives, and marine flora, fauna, and ecology tours.

La Clette's interests reach much deeper than the commercial. A marine biologist by training, he is a leader in the local ecological association that watchdogs FONATUR's Huatulco development work. (See "Information" below.)

Fishing And Boat Launching

The local boat cooperative **Sociedad Servicios Turisticos Costa Oaxaqueña** takes visitors out for fishing excursions from the Santa Cruz boat quay. Their prices are high for what they offer, however. For a launch with only two lines and bait, they want $40 an hour, although during low seasons you may be able to bargain them down to a more digestible tariff. More reasonable prices might be obtainable by asking around among the fishermen at Santa Cruz, or at minivillages San Agustín and Magallitos (see "Sights" above).

You can leave the negotiation up to a travel agent, who will arrange a fishing trip for you and your friends. You'll stop afterward at a beachside palapa, which will cook up a feast with your catch. Save money by bringing your own tackle. Rates for an approximately three-hour trip run about $85 without tackle, $170 with. Contact an agent such as Servicios Turisticos del Sur (at the Sheraton tel. 100-55, ext. 784; or Hotel Castillo, tel. 705-72; or on the Crucecita plaza, tel. 700-46) for reservations.

Some of the Huatulco bays offer easy boat-launching prospects, especially at the protected beaches of La Entrega, Bahía el Maguey, and San Agustín.

SHOPPING

Market And Handicrafts

Crucecita has a small traditional market (officially the Mercado Tres de Mayo) off the plaza between Guanacastle and Guamachil. Although produce, meats, and clothing occupy most of the stalls, a few offer Oaxaca handicrafts. Items include black *barra* pottery, hand-crocheted Mixtec and Amusgo *huipiles,* wool weavings from Teotitlán del Valle, and whimsical duck-motif wooden bowls carved by an elderly, but sharp-bargaining, local gentleman.

Steep rents and lack of business force many local silver, leather, art and other handicraft shops to hibernate until tourists arrive in December. The few healthy shops with good selections cluster either around the Crucecita plaza, the Santa Cruz boat quay, or in the Tangolunda shopping complex adjacent to the Sheraton (or in the hotel itself). Prices are generally high, however.

BRUCE WHIPPERMAN

A woodcarver displays his unique wares in the Crucecita market.

Supermarket, Laundry, And Photo Supplies

The supermarket **La Fuente** in Crucecita on east-side Av. Oaxaca offers a large stock of groceries, an ice machine, and a little bit of everything else (open daily 6 a.m.-9 p.m., a block east of the Pemex station, tel. 700-22).

Take your washing to the **Lavandería M and M** next door to the supermarket (open Mon.-Sat. 8 a.m.-9 p.m.).

For film and quick develop-and-print, go to **Foto Conejo,** just off the Crucecita plaza, across Guamachil from the market. Besides a photo-portfolio of the Bays of Huatulco, the friendly owner stocks supplies, point-and-shoot cameras, and Kodak, Fuji, and Konica slide and print film (open Mon.-Sat. 9 a.m.-8 p.m., tel. 700-54).

SERVICES

Money Exchange

Huatulco banks are on the Benito Juarez main street in Santa Cruz, corner of Pochutla. **Banamex** (tel. 702-66) exchanges both U.S. and Canadian traveler's checks Mon.-Fri. 9-3; **Bancomer** across the street (tel. 703-85) does the same Mon.-Fri. 9-12.

Post, Telegraph, And Telephone

The Huatulco Correos (post office) and Telegrafos stand side by side in the Agencia Municipal (across the east-side Blvd. Tangolunda from the Pemex station in Crucecita). Post office (tel. 798-99) hours are Mon.-Fri. 9-1 and 3-6, Sat. 9-1; Telegrafos (tel. 708-94) is open Mon.-Fri. 9-1 and 3-6, Sat. 9-12. *Larga-distancia* service is available in Crucecita on Flamboyan. The area code for Bahías de Huatulco is 958.

Immigration And Customs

Both Migración and the Aduana are at the Huatulco airport. If you lose your tourist card, avoid trouble or a fine at departure by presenting Migración with proof of your date of arrival (an airline ticket, or preferably a copy of your lost tourist card) at least a day before your scheduled departure.

Medical And Police

Among the best of Huatulco private hospitals is **Central Médica** (at Flamboyan 5, tel. 701-04, 706-87, and 707-34) in Crucecita half a block from the plaza. They have lots of diagnostic equipment, a 24-hour emergency room, and several specialists on call.

Alternatively, you can go to the **Centro de Salud** (tel. 704-03) public health clinic next door, or the big **Seguro Social** hospital (tel. 701-24, 702-64, and 703-83) on the boulevard to Tangolunda a quarter mile south of the Pemex gas station.

For routine medications, Crucecita has many pharmacies, such as **Farmacia del Centro** (tel. 702-32, plaza corner of Flamboyan and Bugambilias) beneath the Hotel Bugambilias.

For **police** emergencies, call the Crucecita *policia* (tel. 702-10) in the Agencia Municipal behind the post office across the Tangolunda boulevard from the Pemex *gasolinera*.

INFORMATION

Tourist Information Offices

Three information offices serve Huatulco visitors. In downtown Crucecita, a small private office (on Guamachil just off the plaza) answers questions. The local federal tourist information office (tel. 100-32) is on the road into Tangolunda just before the shopping complex. If the preceding are seasonally closed, try the FONATUR office (National Tourism Development and Promotion, tel. 700-30, 702-47, 702-62, open Mon.-Fri. 9-3 and 5-7), on the boulevard to Tangolunda, right side, heading beachward from the Pemex station.

Newspapers And Magazines

The bookshop at the Sheraton (tel. 100-55) in Tangolunda stocks English-language paperback novels, Mexico art and guidebooks, newspapers, such as *USA Today,* and many magazines.

In Crucecita, the small **Publicaciones Huatulco** newsstand and bus station sells the English-language *News* of Mexico City (open daily 6 a.m.-9 p.m., corner of Gardenia and Macuil, three blocks north of the plaza).

Ecology Association

Local ecologists and community leaders monitor Huatulco's development through their **Asociación Pro Desarrollo y Sociocultural y Ecologios de Bahías de Huatulco.** Association President, marine biologist Enrique La Clette and his associates are working earnestly to assure the government's plan—that 70% of Huatulco will remain pristine—continues in force as development proceeds. One of their initial victories was to dissuade Club Med from dumping its raw sewage into Tangolunda Bay. Enrique, who is friendly and fluent in English, enjoys talking to fellow ecologists. Drop into his dive shop Buceos Triton (tel. 700-51, 701-26, 701-53) at the Hotel Castillo in Santa Cruz.

GETTING THERE AND AWAY

By Air

The Huatulco airport (officially the Aeropuerto Internacional Bahías de Huatulco, code-designated HUX) is just off Hwy. 200 eight miles (13 km) west of Crucecita and 19 miles (31 km) east of Puerto Ángel. The terminal is small, with only check-in booths, a snack bar, and a few trinket shops.

Current regularly scheduled flights connect only with domestic destinations:

Mexicana Airlines flights connect twice daily with Mexico City. For flight information, call 702-23 or 702-43; for reservations, tel. 102-28 or 102-08.

Aeromexico flights connect once daily with Mexico City. For flight information and reservations, call 103-29 or 103-36.

Aeromorelos flights connect daily with Oaxaca. For flight information, call 702-72; for reservations, call 100-55, ext. 784.

Aerocaribe flights connect twice daily with Puerto Escondido, Oaxaca, and Acapulco. For flight information and reservations call 702-25.

Arrival is usually simple. Since the terminal has no money-exchange counter, come loaded with sufficient pesos to last until you can get to the bank in Santa Cruz. After the typically quick immigrations and customs checks, arrivees have a choice of efficient ground transportation to town. Agents sell tickets for collective "ichivan" vans or GMC Suburbans to Crucecita or Santa Cruz (about $7) or the Sheraton, Club Maeva, or Club Med (for about $8). A private *taxi especial* for three, possibly four passengers, runs about $23. Prices to Puerto Ángel are about double these.

Mobile travelers on a budget can walk the couple of blocks from the terminal to Hwy. 200

and catch one of the frequent public **micro-buses** headed either way to Crucecita (east, left) or the Pochutla (Puerto Ángel) junction (west, right).

If a Budget **car rental** agent is not inside the terminal to meet you, call them at their main office in Crucecita (tel. 700-10, 700-19, 700-34).

By Car Or RV.

Paved highways connect Huatulco east with Tehuantepec, west with Puerto Ángel and Puerto Escondido, and north with Oaxaca.

Highway 200, the east-west route, runs an easy 72 miles (113 km) to Tehuantepec, connecting with Mex. 190 northwest with Oaxaca, and continuing east to Chiapas and the Guatemala border. In the opposite direction, the route is equally smooth, connecting with Puerto Escondido in 66 miles (106 km) continuing to Acapulco in a long 273 miles (440 km). Allow about an hour and a half to Tehuantepec, the same to Puerto Escondido, and to Acapulco, a full eight hours' driving time, either direction.

Highway 175, the cross-Sierra connection north with Oaxaca, although paved, is narrow and winding, with few services for the lonely 80-mile stretch between its junction with Hwy. 200 at Pochutla (22 miles west of Crucecita) and Miahuatlán in the Valley of Oaxaca. The road climbs to 7,000 feet into pineclad, winter-chilly Chatino and Zapotec country. Be prepared for emergencies. Allow eight hours northbound, seven hours southbound, for the entire 170-mile (273-km) Huatulco-Oaxaca trip.

By Bus

Two first-class and two second-class bus lines connect Huatulco with destinations east, west, and north. They depart from small separate terminals in Crucecita scattered along Calle Gardenia north of the plaza.

Cristóbal Colón first-class buses (corner of Ocotillo, tel. 702-61) connect west with **Puerto Escondido** (four per day). Buses also connect east with Tehuantepec, continuing to Oaxaca (two per day) and Mexico City via Puebla (one per day).

Gacela first-class buses (corner of Palo Verde, tel. 701-03) connect 10 times daily west with **Acapulco via Puerto Escondido,** one continuing to Mexico City.

About six second-class **Oaxaca-Istmo** buses connect by the long Salina Cruz-Tehuantepec route with Oaxaca daily from their station (newsstand Publications Huatulco, corner of Macuil).

Three second-class **Estrella del Valle** and **Autobuses Oaxaca-Pacífico** buses connect daily with **Oaxaca via Pochutla** (from Jazmin, corner Sabali, nine blocks north of the plaza, tel. 701-93).

INLAND TO OAXACA

Valley of Oaxaca is really three valleys, which diverge, like the thumb, index finger, and middle finger of a hand, from a single strategic point. Aztec conquerors called that spot Huaxyacac (yoo-AHSH-yah-kahk, "Point of the Calabash,") Hill for a forest of gourd-bearing trees, which once carpeted its slopes. The Spanish, who founded the city at the foot of the hill, shifted that name to more-pronounceable Oaxaca.

The people of the Valley of Oaxaca, walled by mountains from the rest of Mexico, both enjoy and suffer from their long isolation. They are poor but proud inheritors of rich traditions that live on despite 300 years of Spanish occupation.

A large proportion of Oaxacans are pure Indian and speak one of a dozen different tongues. Significant numbers speak no Spanish at all. Even in and around Oaxaca city itself they make up a sizable fraction of the people. Far out in the country, they *are* the people. Mostly speaking the Zapotec or Mixtec languages, they harvest their corn for tortillas, their maguey for *pulque* and *aguardiente* (fire water). They spin their wool, hoe their vegetables, then go to market and sit beside their piles of blankets and mounds of onions, wondering if their luck is going to change.

HISTORY

Before Columbus
Evidence of human prehistory litters the river-bottoms and hillsides of the Valley of Oaxaca. Cave remains not far from the ancient city-state of Mitla tell of hunters who lived there as long as 8,000 years ago. Several thousand years later,

hieroglyph
of Oaxaca

their descendants, heavily influenced by the mysterious Olmecs of the Gulf coast, were carving gods and glyphs on stone monuments in the Valley of Oaxaca. Around 600 B.C., people speaking a Zapotec mother tongue, similarly influenced by the Olmecs, founded Monte Albán on a mountaintop above the present city of Oaxaca.

Monte Albán ruled the Valley of Oaxaca for more than a millennium, climaxing as a sophisticated metropolis of perhaps 40,000, controlling a large and populous area of southern Mexico and enjoying diplomatic and trade relations with distant kingdoms. But, for reasons unknown, Monte Albán declined to a shadow of its former glory by A.D. 1000.

Mixtec-speaking people filled the vacuum. They took over Monte Albán, using it mostly as a burial ground. Their chiefs divided up the Valley of Oaxaca and ruled from separate feudalistic city-states, such as Mitla, Yagul, Matatlán, and Zaachila, for hundreds of years.

The Mixtecs in turn gave way to the Aztecs whose invading warriors crossed the mountains and threatened Oaxaca during the 1450s. In 1486 the Aztecs established a fort on the hill of Huaxyacac (now called El Fortín), overlooking the present city of Oaxaca. They ruled their restive Zapotec and Mixtec subjects for barely a generation, however. On November 21, 1521, conquistador Francisco de Orozco and his soldiers replaced them on the hill of Huaxyacac scarcely four months after the Spanish tide had flooded the Aztecs' Valley of Mexico homeland.

Conquest And Colonization
Spanish settlers began arriving soon after the conquistadores. At the foot of the hill of Huaxyacac, they laid out their town, which they christened Antequera after the old Spanish Roman city. Soon, however, the settlers came into conflict with Cortés, whom the king had named marquis of the Valley of Oaxaca, and whose entire valley domain surrounded the town. Townspeople had to petition the queen of Spain for land on which to grow vegetables: they were granted a one-league square in 1532.

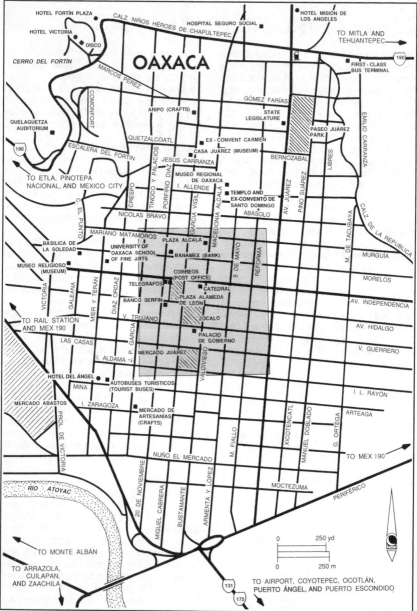

For hundreds of years, Cortés's descendants reigned, the church grew fat, the colonists prospered, and the Indians toiled—in cane and corn, in cattle pastures and silk mulberry groves.

Independence, Reform, And Revolution

In contrast to its neighbors in the state of Guerrero, conservative Antequera was a minor, grudging player in the (1810-21) War of Independence. But as the *insurgente* tide swept the country, local nationalist fervor switched the city's name back to the original Mexican Oaxaca.

By the 1850s, times had changed. Oaxacans were leading a new national struggle. Benito Juarez, a pure Zapotec *indígena,* was rallying liberal forces in the civil War of the Reform against the oligarchy that had replaced colonial rule. Born in Guelatao, northeast of the valley, Juarez at age 12 was an orphan sheepherder. A Catholic priest, struck by the boy's intelligence, brought him to the city as a servant and taught him Spanish in preparation for the priesthood.

Benito became a lawyer instead. He hung out his shingle in Oaxaca, first as a defender of the poor, then state legislator, governor, chief justice, and finally the president of Mexico. In his honor, the city's official name was again changed—to Oaxaca de Juarez—in 1872.

In 1861, after winning the three-year civil war, Juarez's Reformista forces had their victory snatched away. France, taking advantage of the United States's preoccupation with its own civil war, invaded Mexico and installed an Austrian Hapsburg prince as Emperor Maximilian of Mexico.

It took Juarez five years to prevail against Maximilian and his conservative Mexican backers. Although Maximilian and Juarez paradoxically shared many of the same liberal ideas, Juarez had Maximilian executed after his defeat and capture in 1867. Juarez bathed Mexico in enlightenment as he promulgated his "Laws of the Reform" (which remain essentially in force). Although the country rewarded him with re-election, he died of exhaustion in 1871.

Another *indígena*-descent Oaxacan, General Porfirio Diaz, vowed to carry Juarez's banner. Diaz, the hero who defeated the French in the battle of Puebla on "Cinco de Mayo" (May 5) of 1862, was elected president in 1876. "No Reelección" was his campaign cry. He subsequently ruled Mexico for 34 years.

Under Diaz's "Order and Progress," Mexico was modernized at great human cost. As railroads, factories, and mines mushroomed, property ownership increasingly became concentrated among rich Mexicans and their foreign friends. Smashed protest marches, murdered opposition leaders, and rigged elections returned Diaz to office time and again.

But not forever. The revolt that ousted Diaz in 1910 has, in theory, never ceased. Now, the PRI, the Institutional Revolutionary Party, presides over a uniquely imperfect Mexican form of democracy. Under three generations of PRI rule, Oaxaca *indígenas'* lives have improved gradually. Although *indígena* families now go to government health centers and more of their children attend government rural schools, the price for doing so is to become less *indígena* and more Mexican. Although the government's INI (National Indigenous Institute) claims to represent *indígenas'* welfare, its director always seems to be a Spanish-speaking mestizo member of the PRI.

Times in the Valley of Oaxaca have nevertheless gotten better. When tens of thousands of Zapotec and Mixtec men, women, and children parade in the Oaxaca *zócalo* on May 1 to protest the assassination of their leaders, the thousands of police on hand do not interfere.

CITY SIGHTS

Getting Oriented

The streets of Oaxaca (pop. 300,000, elev. 5,110 feet, 1,778 meters) still run along the same simple north-south grid that city fathers laid out in 1529. If you stand at the center of the old *zócalo* and look out toward the **Catedral** across the Av. Hidalgo, you will be looking north. Diagonally left, to the northwest, you'll see the smaller plaza, **Alameda de León,** and directly beyond that, in the distance, the historic hill of Huaxyacac, now called **Cerro del Fortín.**

Along the base of that hill the Pan American Hwy. (National Hwy. 190) runs generally east-west through the northern suburbs. Behind you (although you can't see it from the *zócalo)* the **Periférico** peripheral boulevard loops around the town's south end. There it passes the yawning but oft-empty wash of the **Rio Atoyac** and

DOWNTOWN OAXACA

MARIANO MATAMOROS

EX - CONVENT SANTA CATALINA
(HOTEL STOUFFER PRESIDENTE)

MURGUÍA

PLAZA ALCALÁ

TOURIST INFORMATION
BOOTH

MUSEO RUFINO
TAMAYO

BANAMEX (BANK)

CASA DE CORTÉS
(CITY MUSEUM)

BIBLIOTECA (PUBLIC LIBRARY)

AV. MORELOS

SAN FELIPE NERI
(CHURCH)

PALACIO DE
LAS GEMAS
(HANDICRAFTS)

TURISMO (INFORMATION)

PASTELERÍA
(PASTRY SHOP)

HOTEL ANTONIO'S

TELEGRAFOS
CORREOS (POST OFFICE)

CATEDRAL

AV. INDEPENDENCIA

TEATRO ALCALÁ

PLAZA ALAMEDA
DE LEÓN

LIBRERÍA CRYSTAL

HOTEL MONTE ALBÁN
FARMACIA HIDALGO

HOTEL MARQUES
DEL VALLE
MONEY EXCHANGE

AMERICAN EXPRESS

RESTAURANT EL MESÓN

FOTO FIGUEROA

BANCO
SERFIN

HOTEL
SEÑORIAL

HOTEL REAL
DE ANTEQUERA

AV. HIDALGO

RESTAURANT
ASADOR VASCO

ZÓCALO

RESTAURANT
AMARANTOS

EXPRESS KOLOR
CAFÉ JARDÍN

VALERIO TRUJANO

CAFÉ TERRANOVA

RESTAURANT
LOS DANZANTES

COMPANIA JESUS
(CHURCH)

PALACIO DE GOBIERNO

COMERCIAL DEPORTIVA
(SPORTING GOODS)

LIBRERÍA UNIVERSITARIA
(BOOKS)

SAN AGUSTÍN
(CHURCH)

V. GUERRERO

HOTEL GALA

LAS CASAS

CRISTOBAL COLON

MERCADO JUAREZ

0   100 yd
0   100 m

I. ALDAMA

I. L. RAYÓN

© MOON PUBLICATIONS INC

street names: MARIANO MATAMOROS, M. ALCALÁ, REFORMA, TINOCO Y PALACIOS, PORFIRIO DIAZ, GARCIA VIGIL, VALDIVIESO, 5 DE MAYO, 20 DE NOVIEMBRE, MIGUEL CABRERA, BUSTAMANTE, ARMENTA Y LÓPEZ, M. FIALLO

the sprawling **Mercado Abastos** market and second-class bus terminal on the southwest. Beyond that, if you find a clear vantage point you'll see the hill of **Monte Albán** looming 1,000 feet (450 meters) above the southwest horizon.

A Walk Around Town

The venerable restored downtown buildings, and the streets, some converted to traffic-free malls, make a delightful strolling ground for dis-

covering traditional Mexico at its best. The *zócalo* itself sometimes seems to be a place in slow, leisurely motion, perfect for sitting at one of many sidewalk cafes and watching the world float by. Officially Jardín Juarez, the *zócalo* was laid out in 1529. Its portals, clockwise from the west side, are named Flores, Clavería, Juarez, and Mercaderes.

Prominent off the *zócalo's* north side is the cathedral that replaced the 1550 original, demolished by an earthquake in 1696. Finished in 1733, the present cathedral is distinguished by its Greek marble main altar, where a polished Italian bronze Virgin of the Ascención presides piously over the faithful.

Continue behind the cathedral north along the tranquil **Andador de Macedonio Alcalá** pedestrian mall, named after the composer of the Oaxacan hymn "Dios Nunca Muere" ("God Never Dies"). Paved with Oaxaca green stone in 1985 and freed of auto traffic, the mall connects the *zócalo* with a number of distinguished Oaxaca monuments.

Among them is the **Teatro Alcalá** (head right one block from the back of the cathedral along Independencia). Christened by a 1909 opening performance of *Aida,* the Alcalá houses a treasury of Romantic-era art. Above the foyer, a sumptuous marble staircase rises to a bas-relief medallion allegorizing the triumph of art. Additionally, there is a gallery of the paintings of Miguel Cabrera (1695-1768), a Zapotec Indian who rose to become New Spain's renowned baroque painter (open 10-2 and 4-8 at 900 Independencia, tel. 629-69).

Continuing north along the Alcalá street mall, you soon pass the **Casa de Cortés,** now the city history museum, at number 202 (open Wed.-Mon. 8-8, tel. 684-99).

Detour right again at Murgia one block to the **ex-Convento de Santa Catalina,** the second-oldest convent in New Spain, founded in 1576. Although the quarters of the first initiates were spare, the convent grew into a sprawling chapel and cloister complex decorated by fountains and flower-strewn gardens. Juarez's reforms drove out the sisters in 1862; the building has since served as city hall, school, and movie theater. Now, it stands beautifully restored (note the native-motif original murals) as the Hotel Stouffer Presidente.

Return to the mall and continue another block to Oaxaca's pride, the **Templo and ex-Convento de Santo Domingo.** Begun in 1531 by Dominican friars, the church sank to the status of a mere stable during the 1860s' anticlerical War of Reform. Times, however, changed, and restoration began in the 1950s. Inside, Santo Domingo glows with a wealth of art. Above the antechamber spreads the entire genealogical tree of Saint Dominic, starting with Mother Mary and weaving through a score of noblemen and women to the saint himself over the front door.

Continuing inside, the soaring, Sistine Chapel-like nave glitters with saints, cherubs, and Bible-story paintings. The altar climaxes in a host of cherished symbols—the Last Supper, sheaves of grain, loaves and fishes, Jesus and Peter on the Sea of Galilee—in a riot of gold leaf.

Next door, the regional **Museo de Oaxaca** occupies the restored ex-convent. Upstairs rooms exhibit major artifacts, including the turquoise skull and the solid gold masks recovered from Monte Albán Tomb 7 (open daily 10-6, tel. 629-91).

Head west one block (along Carranza, off Alcaló across from the museum) to 609 Garcia Vigil and the **Casa de Juarez** museum. Here are the documents and personal effects of Benito Juarez, in the house where he lived with his benefactor, Padre Antonio Salanueva. (Open Tues.-Sun. 7-7).

Sights West And South Of The *Zócalo*

The **Museo Arte Prehispanico de Rufino Tamayo** (on Morelos, two blocks west and north of the *zócalo)* displays artist Rufino Tamayo's brilliant collection of pre-Columbian artifacts (503 Morelos, between Palacios and Diaz, open Mon. and Wed.-Sat. 10-2 and 4-7, Sun. 10-3, tel. 647-50). Displays include hosts of animal motifs—Colima dogs, parrots, ducks, snakes—whimsically crafted into polychrome vases, bowls, and urns.

Continue three blocks west, past the University of Oaxaca School of Fine Arts and the airy Plaza of Dances, to the baroque **Basilica de Nuestra Señora de la Soledad.** Inside, the Virgin of Solitude, the patron of Oaxaca, stands atop the altar with her five-pound solid golden crown, encrusted with 600 diamonds.

Step into the **Religious Museum** at the downhill side of the church, rear end. A host of objects of adornment—shells, paintings, jewelry—crowd cabinets, shelves, and aisles of musty rooms. Large stained-glass panels tell of the images of Jesus and the Virgin that arrived miraculously in 1620, eventually becoming Oaxaca's patron symbols (open Mon.-Sat. 10-3, tel. 675-66).

The traditional **Juarez Market** occupies the one-block square that begins just one block south of the *zócalo.* Stroll around there for fun and perhaps a bargain in the honeycomb of traditional leather, textile, and clothing stalls. (See "Shopping" below for more details.)

ACCOMMODATIONS

Oaxaca offers a wide range of good hotels. Air-conditioning is not particularly necessary in temperate Oaxaca, although hot-water showers (furnished by all hotels listed below) feel especially comfy during cool winter evenings. The less expensive hotels are generally near the colorful, traffic-free *zócalo*. With one exception, Oaxaca's plush, resort-style hostelries dot the northern edge of town. See the chart below for hotels listed in order of price.

Hotels Near The *Zócalo*

Along with an enviable *zócalo* location, **Hotel Señorial** guests enjoy clean rooms, efficient management, a reliable restaurant, and a small swimming pool (Portal de Flores 6, Oaxaca, Oaxaca 68000, tel. 951-639-33, fax 951-636-68). The hotel's only drawback is that its many interior rooms have louvered (non-soundproof) windows on hallways and communal air shafts. This, combined with the hard, shiny vinyl floors, result in noise that can't be shut out. Light sleepers, bring earplugs, especially on weekends and holidays, when the popular Señorial will be brimming. The 107 rooms rent for about $25 s, $29 d, $35 t, with TV and parking; credit cards are *not* accepted.

The **Hotel Antonio's,** although not right on the *zócalo,* is only two blocks away on Independencia at Diaz, a block from the cathedral (Independencia 601, Oaxaca, Oaxaca, 68000, tel. 951-672-27). This newly renovated, authentically colonial small hotel offers colorful streetfront ambience, a restaurant, friendly management, and more than a bit of old Mexico charm within its quiet inner courtyard. Rooms are thoughtfully decorated, comfortable, and very clean. The 15 rooms rent for about $18 s, $23 d, and $27 t; parking included.

On the leafy Alameda de León square just off the *zócalo* stands the also-popular **Hotel Monte Albán** (Alameda de León 1, Oaxaca, Oaxaca 68000, tel. 951-627-77). The hotel centers on a big patio-restaurant that hosts folk-dance shows nightly 8:30-10:00. During the first evening this could be understandably exciting, but after a week you might feel as if you were living in a three-ring circus. The 20 rooms, which surround the patio in two tiers are genuinely colonial, with soaring beamed ceilings, big bedsteads, and the requisite few cockroaches per room. (When a cockroach was pointed out, the bellman promptly crushed it underfoot and nudged it into a corner with the toe of his shoe.) Rates, which run about $37 d, $44 t, are high for such an ordinary, although nicely located, hotel; credit cards accepted.

For a better choice, head for the old standby, the **Hotel Marques del Valle** on the north side of the *zócalo* (Portal Clavería, P.O. Boxes 13 and 35, Oaxaca, Oaxaca 68000, tel. 951-636-77, 951-634-74, fax 951-699-61). Once Oaxaca's best, the hotel appears to have faded into middle age. The chandelier-hung lobby now seems cramped, while massive wrought-iron fixtures cast

---

OAXACA HOTELS

Oaxaca hotels, in ascending order of approximate double room price (area code 951, postal code 68000, unless otherwise noted)

Hotel Antonio's, Independencia 601, 672-27, $23

Hotel Real de Antequera, Hidalgo 607, 640-20, 646-35, $23

Hotel Señorial, Portal de Flores 6, 639-33, fax 636-68, $29

Hotel Monte Albán, Alameda de León 1, 627-77, $37

Hotel Gala, Bustamante 103, 422-51, 413-05, fax 636-60, $37

Hotel Marques del Valle, Portal Clavería (P.O. Box 13), 636-77, 634-74, fax 699-61, $39

Hotel Misión de los Angeles, Calz. Porfirio Díaz 102, postal code 68050, 515-00, 516-80, $68

Hotel Fortín Plaza, Av. Venus 118, Colonia Estrella, postal code 68040, 577-77, fax 513-28, $70

Hotel Victoria, Km 545 Carretera Panamericana, postal code 68070, 526-33, fax 524-11, $83

Stouffer Presidente, Cinco de Mayo 300, 606-11, fax 607-32, (800) 468-3571, $140

gloomy nighttime shadows through the soaring, balconied central atrium. The 96 rooms, however, retain their original 1940s polish, with shiny handcrafted cedar furniture and marble-finished baths. Deluxe rooms have TV, carpets, and some balconies looking out on to the zócalo. Standard rooms rent for about $36 s, $39 d, while deluxe go for $50 d; with restaurant-bar and credit cards accepted.

Just half a block east on Hidalgo, the **Hotel Real de Antequera** offers a good location at a modest price (Hidalgo 607, Oaxaca, Oaxaca 68000, tel. 951-640-20 and 951-646-35). An older hotel built around an atrium-courtyard, the Real de Antequera's 29 rooms, although not deluxe, are comfortable and very clean. Some even have luxurious onyx-tiled bathrooms. Noise echoing upstairs may at times be a problem; try for one of the quieter rooms away from the street along the hallway leading away from the central atrium. Rates run about $18 s, $23 d, and $27 t; credit cards accepted; with fans.

The '80s-mod **Hotel Gala,** on Bustamante half a block south of the zócalo's southeast corner, is for those who want comfortable, modern-standard deluxe accommodations at relatively moderate prices (Bustamante 103, Oaxaca, Oaxaca 68000, tel. 951-422-51, 951-413-05, fax 951-636-60). Rooms, although tastefully decorated and carpeted, are small. Get one of the quieter ones away from the street. The 36 rooms rent for about $29 s, $37 d, and $45 for junior suite; with phones, TV, fans, a restaurant; credit cards are accepted, but there is no parking.

Oaxaca's classiest hotel, the Stouffer Presidente, occupies the lovingly restored ex-Convent Santa Catalina, four blocks north of the zócalo (Calle Cinco de Mayo 300, Oaxaca, Oaxaca 68000, tel. 951-606-11, fax 951-607-32). Flowery hidden courtyards, massive arched portals, soaring beamed ceilings, a big blue pool, impeccable bar and restaurant service combine to create a refined but relaxed old-world atmosphere. Rooms are large, luxurious, and exquisitely decorated with antiques and folkcrafts and furnished with modern-standard conveniences. If street noise is likely to bother you, get a room away from bustling Calles Abasolo and Cinco de Mayo. Rates run about $140 s or d, $170 t; with phones and TV, but parking not included; credit cards accepted. For information and reservations in the U.S. and Canada, call the Stouffer toll-free number, (800) 468-3571.

Northside Luxury Hotels

Three upscale suburban hostelries dot the north side of Hwy. 190. The **Hotel Victoria,** choicest of the three, spreads over a lush hillside garden of panoramic vistas and luxurious resort ambience (Km 545, Carretera Panamericana, Oaxaca, Oaxaca 68070, tel. 951-526-33, fax 951-524-11). The '50s-style lobby extends from an upstairs view bar downhill past a terrace restaurant to a flame tree and jacaranda-decorated pool-patio. As for rooms, the best ones are in the newer view wing detached from the lobby building. There, the junior suites are spacious, comfortable, and luxuriously appointed, with double-sized bathrooms and private view balconies. The 150 rooms, bungalows, and junior suites rent for about $83, $103, and $125 d, respectively; with TV, phones, a/c, tennis court, disco, handicrafts shop, and parking; credit cards accepted.

The **Hotel Fortín Plaza,** next to the highway two blocks downhill, is hard to miss, especially at night (Av. Venus 118, Colonia Estrella, Oaxaca, Oaxaca 68040, tel. 951-577-77, fax 951-513-28). Its blue-lit six-story profile tops everything else in town. The hotel offers the usual modern facilities—restaurant-bar, pool, disco, and parking—in a compact, attractively designed layout. Upstairs, guests enjoy deluxe, clean, and comfortable rooms with private view balconies (whose tranquility is reduced, however, by considerable highway noise). Room rates run about $55 s, $70 d, and $83 t, with phones, TV, and parking; credit cards accepted.

Hotel Misión de Los Angeles, half a mile farther east (on the prolongation of Juarez) rambles like a hacienda through a spreading oak-and acacia-dotted garden-park (Calz. Porfirio Diaz 102, Oaxaca, Oaxaca 68050, tel. 951-515-00, fax 951-516-80). With an ambience akin to an elite suburban junior college, the hotel conducts cooking, language, and cultural classes and arranges bus tours of ruins, crafts villages, and markets. If you tire of all the activity, kick back beside the big pool or enjoy a set or two of tennis. The rooms and suites are spacious and comfortable, with big garden-view windows or balconies. Upper rooms are quieter and more private. The 162 rooms and suites rent from about $68 d for standard, $106 d for suite; with phones, parking, disco, restaurant, and a folkloric performance; credit cards accepted.

Trailer Parks And Camping

Oaxaca has a pair of reliable trailer and camping parks; one, the **Oaxaca,** is at the far northeast side of town on Violeta (north several blocks from the big Hwy. 190 intersection four blocks east of the bus station). Their 100 all-hookup spaces include showers, toilets, laundromat, recreation hall, a fence, and a night watchman (900 Violeta, Oaxaca, Oaxaca 68000, tel. 951-527-96). Spaces rent for about $13 per night, with discounts for extended stays. Pets okay.

The newer **Rosa Isabel** trailer park is on Hwy. 190 past the Mexico City side of town in the Loma del Pueblo Nuevo suburb. They have all hookups, toilets, showers, and a recreation hall, with a tennis and sports club nearby (Km 539, Carretera Nacional, Colonia Loma del Pueblo, Oaxaca, Oaxaca 68000, tel. 951-607-70). The 70 spaces rent for about $10 a night, with discounts for extended stays.

FOOD

Snacks And Foodstalls

During fiestas, snack stalls along Hidalgo at the cathedral-front Alameda de León square abound in local delicacies. Choices include *clayudas,* giant crisp tortillas loaded with avocado, tomato, onions, and cheese, and *empanadas de amarillo,* huge tacos stuffed with cheese and red salsa. For dessert, have a *bonuelo,* a crunchy, honey-soaked wheat tortilla.

At nonfiesta times, you can still fill up on the sizzling fare of taco, torta, hamburger, and hot dog (eat 'em only when hot) stands that set up in the same vicinity.

For sinful desserts, go to the **Pasteleria** (pastry shop) at Morelos and Reforma, three blocks northeast of the *zócalo* (open Mon.-Sat. 8 a.m.- 9 p.m., Sun. noon-7 p.m.).

Cafes And Restaurants

Oaxaca visitors enjoy many good eateries right on or near the *zócalo.* Besides the interesting passing scene, the *zócalo-* front sidewalk cafes usually offer passable, and in some cases quite good, food and service. They all are open long hours, from about 8 a.m. to midnight, and serve from very recognizable standard menus.

The better cafes, clockwise around the *zócalo,* are the Jardín (southwest corner), the Marques (north side), the Amarantos (northeast corner), and the Terranova (southeast corner). Of these, the best are the **Amarantos** (four stars for service and fresh, appetizingly presented food) and the **Terranova** (where entrees are made to order, and the service is as crisp as the salads).

Serious-eating long-timers return to **El Asador Vasco** restaurant on the second-floor balcony above the Jardín (Portal Flores 11, tel. 697-19; open daily 1-11:30 p.m.). The menu specializes in hearty Basque-style country cooking: salty, spicy, and served among the decor of a medieval Iberian manor house. Favorites include fondues (bean, sausage, and mushroom), garlic soup, salads, veal tongue, oysters in hot sauce, and the *carnes asadas* (roast meats) house specialties. Prices tend to be high; expect to pay about $20 per person.

For a tasty meal or snack, try **La Casita** around the corner (on Hidalgo at the Alameda de León). You can order either a hearty *comida corrida* multicourse lunch or one of their tasty "mystery" offerings, such as tortilla, "cat," or "nothing" soup (Hidalgo 612, tel. 629-17; open daily 1-6 p.m. only).

Also on Hidalgo, just past the *zócalo's* opposite (south) side, the intimate and friendly little **El Mesón** specializes in a lunch buffet (Hidalgo 805, tel. 627-29; open daily 8 a.m. till midnight). For about $4, diners select from fresh fruit, salads, chili beans, and several entrees, including roast beef and pork, chicken, *moles,* tacos, tamales, and enchiladas.

Double your Mexican food vocabulary in one night at **Restaurant Los Danzantes** one block west of the *zócalo.* Regulars enjoy Oaxaca favorites such as *amarillo* (spicy meat stew), *ejotes* (green beans, many styles), and *chichillo* (beef in dark mole). The house super-special is Botanas Oaxaqueñas, a huge plate of snacks, including *chapulines* (small grasshoppers), chiles rellenos, guacamole, chorizo (spiced sausage), and more (corner 20 Noviembre and Trujano, tel. 668-80; open daily 10 a.m.-11 p.m.).

ENTERTAINMENT, EVENTS, AND SPORTS

Around The Zócalo

The Oaxaca zócalo, years ago relieved of traffic, is ideal ground for spontaneous diversions. A concert or performance seems to be going on nearly every evening. When it isn't, you can run like a kid over the plaza, bouncing a 10-foot-long *aeroglobo* into the air. (Get them from vendors in front of the cathedral.) If you're in a sitting mood instead, watch the world go by from a zócalo sidewalk cafe. Later, take in the folk-dance performance at the Hotel Monte Albán on the adjacent Plaza Alameda de León (nightly 8:30-10, about $4).

Fiestas

There seems to be a festival somewhere in the Valley of Oaxaca every week of the year. Oaxaca's wide ethnic diversity explains much of the celebrating. Sixteen languages, in hundreds of dialects, are spoken within the state. Authorities recognize around 500 distinct regional costumes. Each of the groups celebrates its own traditions.

All of this ethnic ferment focuses in the city during the July **Lunes de Cerro** festival. Known in pre-Hispanic times as the Guelaguetza (gay-lah-GAY-tzah, "Offering"), tribes reunited for rituals and dancing in honor of Centeotl, the god of corn. The ceremonies, which climaxed with the sacrifice of a virgin who had been fed hallucinogenic mushrooms, were changed to tamer mixed Christian-Indian rites by the Catholic Church. Lilies replaced marigolds, the flower of death, and saints sat in for the indigenous gods.

Now, for the weeks around the two Mondays following July 16, the Virgin of Carmen day, Oaxaca is awash with Indians in costume from all seven traditional regions of Oaxaca. The festivities, which include a crafts and agricultural fair, climax with dances and ceremonies at the Guelaguetza auditorium on the Cerro del Fortín hill northwest of the city. Entrance to the events runs about $5; bring a hat and sunglasses. Make hotel reservations months ahead of time. For more information, write the local tourist information office (see "Information" below) or call the auditorium office at 678-33.

Note: If the first Monday after July 16 happens to fall on July 18, the anniversary of Juarez's death, the first Lunes del Cerro shifts to the following Monday, July 25.

On the Sunday before the first Lunes del Cerro, Oaxacans celebrate their history and culture at the Plaza de Danzas adjacent to the Virgen de la Soledad church. Events include a big sound, light, and dance show and depictions in tableaux of the four periods of Oaxaca history.

Besides the usual national holidays, Oaxacans celebrate a number of other locally important fiestas. March 21, the first day of spring, kicks off the **Flower Games** ("Juegos Florales"). Festivities go on for 10 days, including crowning of a festival queen at the Teatro de Alcalá, poetry contests, and performances by renowned artists and the National Symphony.

On the second Monday in October, residents of Santa Maria del Tule venerate their ancient tree in the **Lunes del Tule** festival. Locals in costume celebrate with rites, folk dances, and feats of horsemanship beneath the boughs of their beloved great cypress.

Oaxaca people venerate their patron, the Virgin of Solitude, Dec. 16-18. Festivities, which center on the Virgin's basilica (on Independencia six blocks west of the zócalo), include fireworks, dancing, food, and street processions of the faithful bearing the Virgin's gold-crowned image decked out in her fine silks and satins.

For the Fiesta of the Radishes (Rábanos) on Dec. 23, celebrants fill the Oaxaca zócalo, admiring displays of plants, flowers, and figures crafted of large radishes. Ceremonies and prizes honor the most original designs. Foodstalls nearby serve traditional delicacies, including *buñuelos* (honey-soaked fried tortillas), plates of which traditionally get thrown into the air before the evening is over.

Oaxaca people culminate their Posada week on **Nochebuena** (Christmas Eve) with candle-lit processions from their parishes, accompanied by music, fireworks, and floats. They converge on the zócalo in time for a midnight cathedral Mass.

Folkloric Dance Shows

If you miss the Lunes del Cerro festival, some localities stage smaller Guelageutza celebrations year-round. So do a number of hotels. Days may change, so call ahead to confirm: Hotel

Stouffer Presidente (tel. 606-11; Fridays, $30 show with dinner, not including drinks), Hotel Misión de los Angeles (tel. 515-00; daily, free to watch, dinner at regular prices), Hotel Fortín Plaza (tel. 577-77).

Nightlife

When lacking an official fiesta, you can create your own at a number of nightspots around town.

The big hotels are most reliable for **live dance music.** Call to confirm programs: Stouffer Presidente (tel. 606-11), Victoria (tel. 526-33), Fortín Plaza (tel. 501-00), and Misión de los Angeles (tel. 515-00).

The Victoria, Misión de los Angeles, and Misión San Felipe hotels also operate **discotheques** separate from their lobby-bar entertainment. Call them for details.

Sports

For **jogging,** try the public **Ciudad Deportiva** ("Sports City") fields on the west side of Hwy. 190 about two miles north of the town center.

For an invigorating in-town **walk,** climb the **Cerro del Fortín** hill. Your reward will be a breezy city, valley, and mountain view. The key to getting there through the maze of city streets is to head to the **Escalera del Fortín** (staircase), which will lead you conveniently to the instep of the hill. For example, from the northeast *zócalo* corner walk north along the Alcalá mall (see "Sights" above). After five blocks, in front of the Santo Domingo church, turn left onto Allende, continue four blocks to Crespo and turn right. After three blocks, you'll see the staircase on the left. Continue uphill, past the Guelaguetza open-air auditorium, to the road (Nicolas Copernicus) heading north to the **Planetarium.** After that, enjoying the panorama, you can keep walking along the hilltop for at least another mile. Take a hat and water. The roundtrip from the *zócalo* is a minimum of two miles; the hilltop rises only a few hundred feet. Allow at least a couple of hours.

Swimmers do their thing at **Balneario La Bamba,** about 2.5 (four km) south of town along Hwy. 175 toward the airport. The pool is open daily 10-5, tel. 409-25. Serious lap swimmers should choose days and hours in order to avoid crowds.

For **tennis,** stay at either the Hotel Victoria or the Misión de los Angeles (see "Accommoda-

tions" above), which have courts. Otherwise, call the Club de Tenis Brenamiel (tel. 418-15 and 698-24, Km 539.5 on Hwy. 190, about three miles north of the center of town) and see if they'll accommodate you.

A pretty fair general **sporting goods** selection is available at Comercial Deportiva Antequera store a block east of the *zócalo* (Guerrero 207 between Armenta y Lopez and Fiallo; open Mon.-Sat. 9-2 and 4-8, tel. 403-83).

SHOPPING

Market And Groceries

The traditional town market, **Mercado Juarez,** covers the entire square block just one block south of the *zócalo.* Although the hundreds of stalls offer everything, cotton and wool items—such as dresses, *huipiles,* woven blankets, and serapes—are among the best buys. Despite the festoons and piles of merchandise, bargains are there for those willing to search them out.

The Juarez Market got so crowded that the city built a bigger one—the **Mercado Abastos**—which sprawls beside the Periférico southwest of the city. The main market day is Saturday, when folks can find everything the Juarez has, and in even greater quantities (which also means you may have to dig harder through lots of cheap items to find what you're looking for).

For simple, straightforward **grocery shopping,** stop by Abarrotes Lonja on the *zócalo* next to the Hotel Señorial (open 8 a.m.-9:30 p.m. daily).

Handicrafts

Oaxaca is famous for handicrafts. Among them are *huipiles,* the most common from San Pedro de Amusgos; wool blankets, carpets, and serapes from Teotitlán del Valle; embroidered cotton "wedding dresses," originally from San Antonino, near Ocotlán; pottery—black from San Bartolo Coyotepec and green from Atzompa; carved animals from Arrazola; mescal, and some masks. If you somehow can't make it to the source villages (see "Around the Valley of Oaxaca" below), try the Juarez and Abastos markets or the sprinkling of tourist shops along the Alcalá street mall north of the *zócalo.*

Shoppers serious about getting the most for their money can get prices in perspective at the government-run **Mercado de Artesanías** three blocks south and three blocks west of the *zócalo*. Although it lacks Juarez Market's colorful bustle, the Mercado de Artesanías has a little bit of everything in relatively uncrowded displays. The fixed prices, although often a bit high, provide a good yardstick. They're open Mon.-Sat. 9-2 and 4-8, corner of Zaragoza and Garcia.

Shops North of the *Zócalo*: Head north along the Alcalá mall from the northeast corner of the *zócalo*. Soon comes **Yalalag,** among the biggest and most expensive of Oaxaca's handicrafts stores. Quality is high, and selection, from all over Oaxaca and much of Mexico, is extensive (Alcalá 104; open Mon.-Sat. 9-1 and 4:30-8, tel. 621-08).

The **Palacio de las Gemas** (corner of Morelos and Alcalá), although specializing in semiprecious stones and jewelry, has much more, including a host of charming handpainted tinware Christmas decorations, Guerrero masks, and pre-Columbian reproductions in onyx and turquoise (open Mon.-Sat. 10-2 and 4:30-8:30, tel. 695-96).

The store in the **Museo de Oaxaca** at M. Alcalá 202 has a small but good-quality all-Oaxaca selection, including *huipiles,* masks, and weavings (open Mon.-Sat. 8-8.).

Walk one block west to **Artesanías Cosijo** on Garcia Vigil 202 for a big selection of Guerrero masks, carved animals, and some Aguilar sisters pottery (G. Vigil 202; open Mon.-Sat. 9-1 and 4-8, tel. 614-00).

Back on Alcalá, the **Plaza Alcalá** across the street from the Museo de Oaxaca has a number of shops, including bookstore **Dante** on the second floor. Their select assortment includes guides, maps, cookbooks, histories, posters, postcards, records, and cassettes (Alcalá 307; open daily 9-7).

Creart Artesanías, at the Alcalá corner of Murguía, has a quality selection of stoneware, pottery, Arrazola wooden animals, and masks (open Mon.-Sat. 11-2 and 5-8, tel. 614-87).

Rewards await shoppers who are willing to walk the several blocks more to the state-run **ARIPO** (Artesanías y Industrias Populares de Oaxaca) at 809 Garcia Vigil, one block north of the Juarez Museum. There, masks, wedding dresses, carved animals, ceramics, and tinware fill the rooms. Prices vary: cheap on some items and high on others (open Mon.-Sat. 9:30-7, Sun. 9-1, tel. 413-54).

Camera And Photo
Downtown has a pair of good camera shops. **Foto Figueroa,** one block west of the *zócalo,* well stocked with Kodak film and accessories, offers quick develop-and-print (Hidalgo 516, corner 20 de Noviembre; open Mon.-Sat. 9-1:30 and 7-7:30, tel. 637-66).

Express Kolor, half a block down 20 de Noviembre, is even better stocked, with scores of point-and-shoot cameras and many Minolta, Vivitar, and Olympus accessories. They also stock Konica, Fuji, Kodak, and Agfa films in color and black-and-white, both roll and sheet (20 de Noviembre 225; open Mon.-Sat. 9-2 and 4-8, tel. 614-92).

SERVICES

Money Exchange
Several banks dot the downtown area. **Banamex** (tel. 687-15, corner Morelos and Diaz), has generally the longest hours, changing U.S. cash and traveler's checks Mon.-Fri. 9-11:30 and 4-5. If Banamex is too crowded, try **Bancomer,** at Vigil and Morelos, tel. 606-02, 606-75. Otherwise, go to **Banco Confia,** one block from the *zócalo* (corner Hidaldo and 20 de Noviembre, tel. 609-13, 642-18), or its next-door neighbor, **Banco Serfin** (tel. 611-00).

After bank hours, go **Casa de Cambio Internacional de Divisas** (tel. 633-99) on the Alcalá street mall, just north of the *zócalo,* behind the cathedral. Although they pay about two percent less than banks, they change many major currencies and traveler's checks (open Mon.-Sat. 8-8, Sun. 8-5, tel. 633-99).

The local **American Express** agency operates an efficient, full-service office right at the *zócalo's* northeast corner. They cash Amercian Express traveler's checks for about a dollar per hundred less than banks (Viajes Mexico Istmo y Caribe, Valdiviesio 2, tel. 627-00, 629-19, fax 674-75; open Mon.-Sat. 9-1 and 4-7, money service hours shorter).

Post, Telephone, And Telegraph
The Oaxaca **Correos** (post office) is across from the cathedral at the corner of the Alameda de León square and Independencia (open Mon.-Fri. 9-8, Sat. 9-1, tel. 62661).

Telegrafos (tel. 649-02) at the next corner (Independencia and 20 de Noviembre) offers money orders, telephone, and public fax. Hours are Mon.-Fri. 9-8 (money orders 9-1:45 and 2-6) and Sat. 9-1 (money orders 9-12). The Oaxaca area code is 951.

Consulates
The U.S. Consul (tel. 430-54) holds hours Mon.-Fri. 9-2 at Alcalá 201, three blocks north of the zócalo. The Consular Corps of Oaxaca (which includes representatives from Canada, U.K., Germany, and France) handles business at offices at Hidalgo 817, Suite 5, tel. 656-00.

Language Courses
The **Instituto de Comunicación y Cultura,** in offices at 307 Alcalá, second floor, offers Spanish courses for visitors. The minimum is one week for $75. Class begin each Monday. They also arrange homestays with Mexican families. Contact director Yolanda Garcia, tel. (951) 634-43, fax (951) 632-65 during regular office hours, or (951) 627-52 Sundays.

The **Universidad Autonoma de Benito Juarez** also offers courses (class size four, for $200 per month) and homestays. Contact them through the director at Independencia and Alcalá, Oaxaca, Oaxaca 68000, tel. (951) 638-70.

INFORMATION

Tourist Information
Oaxaca **Turismo** runs an efficient, very helpful office at the corner of Cinco de Mayo and Morelos two blocks north, one block east from the zócalo. The friendly staff distributes a good state-city map (open Mon.-Sat. 9-8:30, tel. 648-28).

Medical, Police, And Emergencies
For well-equipped 24-hour emergency care and medical consultations, go to **Diagnostica Medica,** at Durango 245 in Colonia Roma, tel. (951) 208-6568. Otherwise, try the government **Hospital Seguro Social** (emergency tel. 528-53, consultation 520-33) on Hwy. 190 (Calz. Héroes de Chapultepec) between Juarez and Alcalá. Alternately, **Clinica de Urgencias Médicas,** a small private clinic, has competent doctors and long hours (Armenta y Lopez 700, six blocks south of the zócalo, tel. 617-73).

For routine medicines and drugs, go to one of many pharmacies, such as the **Farmacia Hi-**

dalgo, corner 20 de Noviembre and Hidalgo, one block west of the zócalo (tel. 655-57 and 644-59, open Mon.-Sat. 9 a.m.-10 p.m. and Sun. 9-2 and 6-9).

For **police** emergencies, call the **Dirección de Seguridad,** tel. 627-26 (at Aldama 108, just north of the zócalo). For fire, call the **bomberos** (fire fighters), tel. 622-31.

Books, Newspapers, Magazines, And Library
One of the best bookstores in town is **Librería Universitaria** at Guerrero 104, half a block east of the zócalo. They have English paperbacks, both used and new, a number of Indian language dictionaries, and guides, cookbooks, art, and history books (open Mon.-Sat. 9:30-2 and 4-8, tel. 642-43).

Librería Crystal, at Valdivieso 116, behind the cathedral, just north of the zócalo, also has a selection of guides, maps, history, and coffee-table art books (open Mon.-Sat. 9-8).

The daily English-language News of Mexico City is available late mornings at stands around the zócalo. Some U.S. newspapers and magazines may be available at the shop in the **Hotel Stouffer Presidente** (Cinco de Mayo, corner Murguía, tel. 606-11).

Pick up a copy of the informative monthly, the Oaxaca Times, at your hotel or at the publisher, the Instituto de Comunicación y Cultura (tel. 634-43) at 307 Alcalá, second floor. The newspaper prints cultural and historical features, tourist hints, and a list of local events.

The **Biblioteca** (public library), in a lovingly restored ex-convent, is worth a visit, if only for its graceful, cloistered Renaissance interiors and patios (open Mon.-Sat. 10-2 and 4-8, corner of Morelos and Alcalá, two blocks north of the zócalo).

GETTING THERE AND AWAY

By Air
The Oaxaca airport (code-designated OAX) has several daily flights that connect with Mexican destinations.

Mexicana Airlines flights connect four times daily with Mexico City. Three of these flights depart Mexico City early enough to allow same-day connections to Oaxaca from many U.S. destinations. For flight information and reservations, call 684-14 or 657-96.

Aeromexico flights connect twice daily with Mexico City. For flight information and reservations, call 637-65 or 610-66.

Aerocaribe flights connect once daily with Tuxtla Gutierrez in Chiapas, and once daily with Bahías de Huatulco, Puerto Escondido, and Acapulco. For information and reservations, call 593-24 or 622-47.

One **Aerovias Oaxaqueñas** flight connects daily with Puerto Escondido. For reservations, call their office (Armenta y Lopez 209) at tel. 638-33 or 676-89; for flight information, call the airport at 616-00.

Aviacsa connects once daily (except Sun.) with Chiapas, Tabasco, and Yucatán destinations of Tuxtla Gutierrez, Villahermosa, Mérida, and Cancún. For information and reservations, call 318-09 or 318-01.

The Oaxaca airport is not large, with few services other than a few shops and car rentals. Since there is no money-exchange agency, arrive with enough pesos to last until you can get to a bank.

Arrival transportation for the six-mile trip into town is easy. Fixed-fare collective taxi tickets run about $3 per person ($6 to north-side Hotels Misión de los Angeles, Fortín Plaza, and Victoria). For the same trip, a *taxi especial* (private taxi) ticket runs about $10 for three persons. No public buses run between the airport and town.

Car rental agents operating at the Oaxaca Airport are Budget (tel. 503-30, tel. 652-52 airport, and tel. 606-11 ext. 172 Hotel Presidente), Dollar (tel. 663-29), and Hertz (tel. 624-34).

On **departure,** save enough dollars or pesos for your $12 international departure tax (which may be collected at Mexico City). If you lose your tourist card, best contact the helpful **Turismo** information office downtown (Cinco de Mayo and Morelos, open Mon.-Sat. 9-8:30, tel. 648-28) for assistance *before* your planned day of departure.

By Car Or RV

Paved (but long and winding) roads connect Oaxaca south with Puerto Ángel, southwest with Pinotepa Nacional, northwest with Mexico City, and southeast with Tehuantepec.

South to **Puerto Ángel,** narrow **National Hwy. 175** connects along 148 winding miles (238 km) over the Sierra Madre del Sur to its junction with Hwy. 200 at Pochutla (thence six miles to Puerto Ángel). The road climbs to 7,000 feet through winter-chilly pine forests and Chatino and Zapotec villages. Fill up with Magna Sin unleaded gas at the last-chance Mihuatlán Pemex heading south; carry water and blankets and be prepared for emergencies. Allow about six driving hours from Oaxaca to Puerto Ángel, about seven in the opposite direction.

The 229-mile (368-km) **Hwy. 190-Hwy. 125** route connects Oaxaca southwest with **Pinotepa Nacional.** Although winding most of the way, the generally uncongested road is smooth and safely driveable from Oaxaca in about seven driving hours, add an hour for the 5,000-foot climb in the opposite direction.

The 350-mile (564-km) winding **Hwy. 190-160** Oaxaca-Cuernavaca-Mexico City route requires two days for safety. Under the best of conditions, driving time runs 12 hours either way. Take it easy and stop over en route. (Make sure that you arrive in Mexico City on a day when your car is permitted to drive. See p. 327.)

The relatively easy 157-mile (252-km) Oaxaca-Tehuantepec **Hwy. 190** route requires around five hours either way. From there, roads connect east to Chiapas, Yucatán and Guatemala, or northwest along the coast with Bahías de Huatulco and Puerto Ángel.

By Bus

Autobuses de Oriente and **Cristóbal Colón,** Oaxaca's first-class carriers, operate out of the big modern terminal on Hwy. 190 (Calz. Héroes de Chapultepec 1036 at Carranza) on the north side of town.

Autobuses de Oriente (tel. 517-03 and 509-03) offers many connections northwest along the Hwy. 190 corridor; dozens daily with Mexico City, four with Puebla, and two with Veracruz.

Cristóbal Colón (tel. 512-48 and 512-14), on the other hand, connects northeast with Villahermosa, southeast with Tehuantepec, Chiapas, and Guatemala, and south (via Hwys. 190 and 200) with Bahías de Huatulco, Pochutla-Puerto Ángel, Puerto Escondido, and Pinotepa Nacional.

A swarm of second-class buses runs from the **Central Camionera Abastos** by the Periférico, prolongation of Trujano, southeast side of town.

Cooperative bus lines **Oaxaca-Istmo** (tel. 629-08) connects with Tehuantepec and Pochutla-Puerto Ángel via the Isthmus route. **Autotransportes Oaxaca-Pacifico** (tel. 691-03) travels the Hwy. 175 route north-south between Oaxaca and Pochutla-Puerto Ángel. Both lines connect along coastal Hwy. 200 with Bahías de Huatulco and Puerto Escondido.

For a backcountry adventure, ride **Estrella Roja del Sureste** (tel. 606-94), whose first- and second-class buses connect along bone-jangling, partly-paved Hwy. 131 north-south directly with Puerto Escondido. From there, they make coastal connections with Pochutla-Puerto Ángel, Bahías de Huatulco, and Pinotepa Nacional.

By Train
Although they're sometimes painfully slow, trains connect Oaxaca (via Puebla) with Mexico City, and thence with most of Pacific Mexico. (See "Pacific Mexico By Train" map in the main Introduction.)

One Mexico-City-bound train departs daily at the station on Calz. Madero about a mile and a half west of downtown. Service, very cheap, is by first- and second-class coach only, with restaurant. Call the station at 622-53 for departure information and prices.

AROUND THE VALLEY OF OAXACA

Oaxaca offers much of interest—archaeological sites, crafts villages and weekly markets—outside the city. Valley market towns each have their market day, when local color is at a maximum and prices are at a minimum. Among the choices, starting on the east side (see "Valley of Oaxaca" map) are Teotitlán del Valle (half an hour east, Saturday), Tlacolula (one hour east, Sunday), Ocotlán (half an hour south, Friday), Zaachila (half an hour southwest, Thursday), Zimatlán (one hour southwest, Wednesdays), and San Pedro y San Pablo Etla (half an hour northeast, Wednesdays).

These market visits can be conveniently combined with stops at handicrafts villages, ruins (notably Mitla, on the east side, and Monte Albán, west) and other sights along the way.

Getting Around The Valley Of Oaxaca

Although droves of second-class buses from the Abastos terminal run everywhere in the Valley of Oaxaca, it would take you a month touring that way. It's better to rent a car (call Hertz, tel. 654-78; Dollar, tel. 663-29; or Automovilista Rojo, tel. 664-22) or ride one of the several reasonably priced tour buses that leave daily from the Hotel del Ángel (tel. 666-33, 601-99) corner of Mier y Terán and Mina, six blocks southwest of the *zócalo*. Many other hotels also have such tour arrangements. See your desk clerk.

EAST SIDE:
EL TULE, TEOTITLÁN DEL VALLE, MITLA, AND TLACOLULA.

Enough attractions lie along this route for days of exploring. For example, you could visit El Tule and the Saturday Teotitlán market, continuing for an overnight at Mitla. Next morning, explore the Mitla ruins for a couple of hours, then return, spending the afternoon at the Sunday market at Tlacolula along the way.

El Tule is a gargantuan Mexican cypress *(ahuehuete)*, probably the largest tree in Latin America and maybe the world. Its gnarled, house-size trunk divides into a forest of elephantine limbs that rise to festoons of bushy

branches reaching 15 stories overhead. The small town Santa Maria del Tule, nine miles (14 km) east of the city on Hwy. 190, seems built around the tree. A crafts market, a church, and the town plaza, where residents celebrate their El Tule with a fiesta on October 7, all surround the beloved 2,000-year-old living giant.

Teotitlán del Valle, nine miles farther, at the foot of the Sierra, means "Place of the Gods" in Nahuatl; before that it was known as Xa Quire, or "Foot of the Mountain," by the Zapotecs who settled it around A.D. 1000. Dominican missionaries introduced the first sheep, whose wool, combined with local skills, results in the fine serapes, carpets, and blankets that seem to fill every shop in town.

Nearly every house is a minifactory where people card, spin, and dye wool, often using traditional hand-gathered cochineal, indigo, and moss dyes. Every step of wool preparation is laborious; pure water is even a chore—families typically spend two days a week collecting it from mountain springs. The weaving, on traditional hand looms, is the easy part.

The best day to visit Teotitlán is on market day Saturday, when your choices will be manifold. You can visit shops of masters such as Isaac Vasquez or humbler but excellent shops, such as that of Reynaldo Sosa, who markets the work of the Mujeres Tejedoras ("Women Weavers") cooperative at Juarez 4 near the market. Finally, you can select from the the hosts of bright displays at the market itself, by the church, end of Juarez.

The best weaving is generally the densest, typically packing in about 20 strands per inch; ordinary weaving uses about half that. Please

hieroglyph of Teotitlán

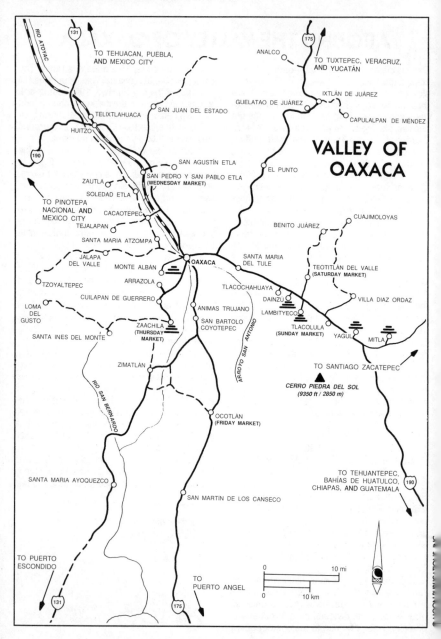

Weaving is but the climax of the laborious processes that include growing, shearing, washing, carding, spinning, and dyeing wool.

don't bargain too hard. Even the best prices typically bring the weavers less than a dollar an hour for their labor.

The Zapotecs who founded **Tlacolula** (24 miles, 38 km, from Oaxaca) around A.D. 1250 called it Guichiibaa ("Town of Heaven"). Besides its Sunday market, its 1523 chapel, Señor de Tlacolula (with a headless St. Paul), and its adjacent 1531 church, Tlacolula is famous for mescal. Get a good free sample at friendly **La Favorita** shop (on main street Juarez no. 9) as you head toward the market. Besides a pet monkey and many hand-embroidered Amusgo *huipiles* and Teotitlán weavings, La Favorita offers mescal in 20 flavors, 10 for women and 10 for men.

MITLA

Mitla is but the last (although best known) of the famous series of ruins east of Oaxaca city. For energetic explorers, Dainzú (15 miles, 24 km), Lambityeco (18 miles, 28 km), and Yagul (28 miles, 45 km) are all worth a visit.

Mitla, however, about 31 miles (50 km) east of Oaxaca, is a "must" for Valley of Oaxaca sightseers. Mitla (Liobaa in Zapotec, the "Place of the Dead") flowered late, reaching a population of perhaps 10,000 during its apex around A.D. 1350. It remained occupied and in use for generations after the conquest.

During Mitla's heyday several feudalistic, fortified city-states vied for power in the Valley of Oaxaca. Concurrently, Mixtec-speaking people arrived from the north, perhaps under pressure from Aztecs and others in central Mexico. Evidence suggests that these Mixtec groups, in interacting with the resident Zapotecs, created the unique architectural styles of late cities such as Yagul and Mitla. Archaeologists believe, for example, that the striking *greca* (Greek-like) frets that honeycomb Mitla facades result from the Mixtec influence.

Exploring The Site

In a real sense, Mitla lives on. The ruins coincide with the present town of San Pablo Villa de Mitla, whose main church actually occupies the northernmost of five main groups of monumental ruins. Virtually anywhere archaeologists dig within the town they hit remains of the myriad ancient dwellings, plazas, and tombs that connected the still-visible landmarks.

Of the five ruins clusters, the best preserved is the fenced-in Columns Group. Its exploration requires about an hour. The others—the Arroyo and Adobe groups beyond an arroyo, and the South Group across the Mitla River—are rubbly, unreconstructed mounds. The North Group has suffered due to past use by the local parish. Evidence indicates that the Adobe and South groups were ceremonial compounds, while the

hieroglyph of Mitla ("Place of the Dead")

Arroyo, North, and Columns groups were palaces.

The public entrance to the Columns Group leads from the parking lot, past a tourist market and through the gate (open daily 9-5, admission $3). Inside, two large patios, joined at one corner, are each surrounded on three sides by elaborate apartments. A shrine occupies the center of the first patio. Just north of this stands the **Palace of Columns,** the most important of Mitla's buildings. It sits atop a staircase, inaccurately reconstructed in 1901.

Inside, a file of six massive monolithic columns supported the roof. A narrow "escape" passage exits out the right rear side to a large patio enclosed by a continuous narrow room. The purely decorative *greca* facades, which required around 100,000 cut stones for the entire complex, embellish the walls. Remnants of the original red and white stucco that lustrously embellished the entire complex hide in niches and corners.

Walk south to the second patio, which has a similar layout. Here, the main palace occupies the east side, where a passage descends to a tomb beneath the front staircase. Both this and another tomb beneath the building at the north side of the patio are intact, preserving their original crucifix shapes. (The guard, although he is not supposed to, may try to collect a tip for letting you descend.) No one knows who and what were buried in these tombs, which were open and empty at the time of the conquest.

The second tomb is similar, except that it contains a stone pillar called the Column of Life; by embracing it, legend says, you will learn how many years you have left.

The Church Group (notice the church domes) on the far side of the Palace of Columns is worth a visit. Builders used the original temple stones to erect the church here. On its north side is a patio leading to another interior patio surrounded by another *greca* fret-embellished palace.

Museum And Accommodation

The University of the Americas (Mexico City) houses an excellent Oaxaca artifact collection at the **Frissell Museum,** just west of the Mitla town plaza.

Hotel La Zapoteca, just south of the Mitla River bridge, has a good homey restaurant and clean, reasonably priced lodgings, okay for an overnight (Cinco de Febrero 8, Mitla, Oaxaca

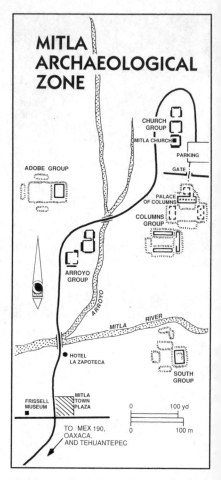

MITLA ARCHAEOLOGICAL ZONE

70430, tel. 956-200-82 or 956-201-80, local 26). The 20 rooms with bath rent for about $14 s, $18 d, $27 t with hot water and parking.

SOUTH SIDE: SAN BARTOLO COYOTEPEC, AND OCOTLÁN DE MORELOS

These crafts towns make a nice pair to visit on Ocotlán's Friday market day. Coyotepec ("Hill of the Coyote") on Hwy. 175, 14 miles (23 km)

south of the city, is famous for its pottery and its August 24 festival, when masked villagers, costumed half-man, half-woman in tiaras, blond wigs, tin crowns, and velvet cloaks dance in honor of their patron, San Bartolo.

Their pottery, the renowned black *barra* sold all over Mexico, is available at a number of cottage factory-shops (watch for signs) along off-highway (east side) Juarez Street. Now-elderly **Dona Rosa** is the most famous of local potters who pioneered the technique of crafting lovely big round jars without a potter's wheel. With their local clay, Dona Rosa's descendants and neighbor families regularly turn out acres of glistening black plates, pots, bowls, trees of life, and fetching animals for very reasonable prices. (Figure on about $25 for a pearly three-gallon vase, and perhaps $2 for a cute little black rabbit.)

Ocotlán ("Place of Pines"), 26 miles, 42 km south of Oaxaca, has the equally interesting trio of shops run by the **Aguilar sisters**, Irene, Guillerma, and Josefina. Watch for the signs about a quarter mile, Oaxaca side, from the town plaza. Their creations include a host of fanciful figures in clay: vendors with big ripe strawberries, green and red cactus, goats in skirts, and bikini-clad blondes.

Your main Ocotlán attraction (unless you're lucky enough to arrive during the May 18 fiesta) will be the big Friday market. Hint: Since markets are best in the morning, make Ocotlán your *first* Friday stop.

SOUTHWEST SIDE: ARRAZOLA, CUILAPAN, AND ZAACHILA

This excursion is best on Thursday, when you can begin fresh in the morning at the big weekly market and ruins in Zaachila, then head back to the ex-Convent Santiago Aposto near Cuilapan, continuing toward town for a visit to see the animals being crafted in Arrazola village.

Get there by tour bus or by car by heading toward Monte Albán (look for the big road sign) west over the Atoyac River from the Periférico at the south edge of town. Just after crossing the bridge fork left (south) from the Monte Albán road on to the Zaachila road.

Your destination is the Zaachila town plaza-market about 10 miles south of Oaxaca. Like Mitla, **Zaachila** overlies the ruins of its ancient namesake city, which rose to prominence after the decline of Monte Albán. Although excavations have uncovered many Mixtec-style remains, historical records nevertheless list a number of Zapotec kings who ruled Zaachila as a virtual Zapotec capital. On the eve of the conquest, a Mixtec noble minority, however, dominated the Zapotec-speaking inhabitants, whose leaders the Mixtec warriors had sent fleeing for their lives to Tehuantepec.

The big forested hill that rises north of the plaza-market is topped by a large, mostly unexplored pyramid. Several unexcavated mounds and courtyards dot the hill's north and south flanks. The site parking lot and entrance gate are adjacent to the colonial church just north of the plaza.

In 1962, archaeologist Roberto Gallegos uncovered a pair of unopened tombs beneath the summit of the Zaachila pyramid. They yielded a trove of polychrome pottery, gold jewelry (including a ring still on a left hand), and jade fan handles. Tomb 1, which is open for public inspection, descends via a steep staircase to an entrance decorated with a pair of cat-motif heads. On the antechamber walls a few steps farther on are depictions of owls and a pair of personages (perhaps former occupants) inscribed respectively with (month-week) name-dates 5 Flower and 9 Flower. Do not miss (take

*carved wooden
rabbit from
Arrazola,
Valley of Oaxaca*

a flashlight) the bas-reliefs on the tomb's back wall, which depict a man whose torso is covered with a turtle shell and another whose head is emerging from a serpent body.

Hint: The narrow tomb staircase is negotiable only by a few persons at a time and often requires an hour for a tour bus crowd to inspect it. Rather than wasting your market time standing in line, go downhill, stroll around the market, and return when the line is smaller. Drivers, arrive early, around nine, to avoid Thursday tour bus crowds.

Cuilapan de Guerrero, a few miles north toward Oaxaca, is known for its elaborate unfinished ex-Convent of Saint Santiago (visible from the highway) where President Guerrero was executed in 1831. Although begun in 1535, the cost of the basilica and associated monastery began to balloon. In 1550, King Phillip demanded humility and moderation of the builders, whose work was finally ended by a 1570 court ruling. The extravagances—soaring, roofless basilica, magnificent baptismal font, splendid Gothic cloister, and elaborate frescoes—remain as national treasures.

Arrazola (turn west onto signed Hwy. 145 a few miles farther north, or about five miles south of the Atoyac River Bridge) is the source of the intricately painted fanciful wooden creatures that are increasingly turning up in shops all over Mexico and foreign countries.

Few, if any, signs direct visitors to the workshops. Turn right after a few miles at Calle Obregon (just past the basketball court) and start looking around near the top of the hill. Although every family along the street seems to craft its own variations, **Pepe Santiago** and his Santa's workshop of craftspersons seems to have the edge. Inside the Santiago compound (on the left just before the hilltop), men saw and carve away, while a cadre of young women painstakingly add riots of painted brocade to whimsical dragons, gargoyles, armadillos, giraffes, rabbits, and everything in between.

NORTHEAST OF TOWN: MONTE ALBÁN AND ETLA

Monte Albán is among Mesoamerica's most regal and spectacular ruined cities. The original name is lost in antiquity. "Monte Albán" was probably coined by a local Spaniard because of its resemblance to a similarly named Italian hill town.

Monte Albán's people cultivated corn, beans, squash, chiles, and fruits on the hillsides and adjacent valleys, occasionally feasting on meat from deer, small game, and perhaps (as other ancient Mexicans) domesticated dogs. Tribute from surrounding communities directly enriched Monte Albán's ruling classes, and, by extension, its artisans and farmers.

Monte Albán reigned for least 1,200 years, between 500 B.C. and A.D. 750, as the capital of the Zapotecs and the dominant force between Teotihuacán in the Valley of Mexico and the Maya empires of the south.

Archaeologists have organized the Valley of Oaxaca's history from 500 B.C. to the conquest in five periods, known as Monte Albán I through V. Over those centuries, the hilltop city was repeatedly reconstructed, with new walls, plazas, and staircases which, like peels of an onion, now overlie earlier construction.

Remains from Monte Albán Period I (500 B.C.-A.D. 0) reveal an already advanced culture, with gods, permanent temples, a priesthood, writing, numerals, and a calendar. Sharply contrasting house styles indicate a differentiated, multilayered society. Monte Albán I ruins abound in graceful polychrome ceramics of uniquely Zapotec style.

Concurrent Olmec influences have also been found, notably in the buildings known as the **Danzantes** ("Dancers"), decorated with unique, Negroid-appearing personages on bas-reliefs, similar to those unearthed along the Veracruz and Tabasco coasts.

Monte Albán II people (A.D. 0-300), by contrast, came under heavy influence from Chiapas and Guatemala in the south. They built strange, ship-shaped buildings, such as Monte Albán's Building J, and left unique remains of their religion, such as the striking jade bat-god now on display in the Anthropology Museum in Mexico City.

Monte Albán reached its apex during Period III (A.D. 300-800), attaining a population of perhaps 40,000 in an urban zone of about three square miles, which spread along hilltops (including the El Gallo and Atzompa archaeological sites) west of the present city of Oaxaca.

Vigorous Period III leaders rebuilt the main hilltop complex as we see it today. Heavily influ-

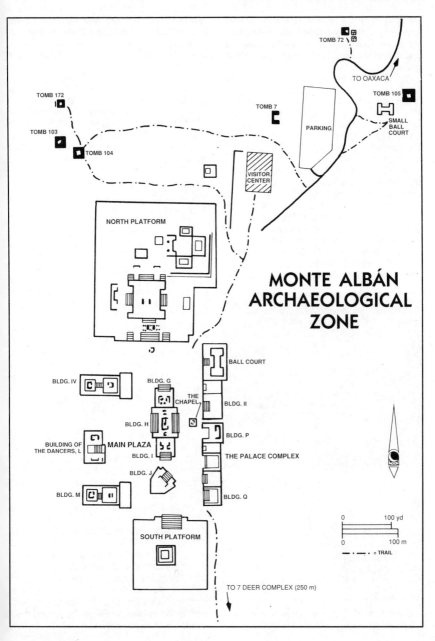

MONTE ALBÁN
ARCHAEOLOGICAL
ZONE

TOMB 72

TO OAXACA

TOMB 105

SMALL
BALL
COURT

PARKING

TOMB 7

TOMB 172

TOMB 103

TOMB 104

VISITOR
CENTER

NORTH PLATFORM

BALL COURT

BLDG. IV

BLDG. G

THE CHAPEL

BLDG. II

BLDG. H

BLDG. P

BUILDING OF
THE DANCERS, L

MAIN PLAZA

BLDG. I

THE PALACE COMPLEX

BLDG. J

BLDG. M

BLDG. Q

SOUTH PLATFORM

0   100 yd

0   100 m

—·—·— = TRAIL

TO 7 DEER COMPLEX (250 m)

enced by the grand Teotihuacán styles, the buildings were finished with handsome sloping staircases, corniced walls, monumental carvings, ball courts, and hieroglyph-enscribed stelae depicting gods, kings, and heroic scenes of battle.

By A.D. 750, however, few foreign influences were continuing to enrich Monte Albán's uniquely Zapotec pottery styles. Quality declined until they seemed like mere factory copies. Concurrently, the Zapotec pantheon expanded to a horde of gods, as if mere numbers could protect the increasingly isolated Valley of Oaxaca from the outside world.

In A.D. 800, Monte Albán, mysteriously cut off from the rest of Mesoamerica, was declining in population and power. By A.D. 1000, the city was nearly abandoned. The reasons, whether drought, disease, or revolt and consequent loss of the (necessarily imported) water, wood, salt and food supplies, remain an enigma.

During Periods IV and V, Mixtec peoples from the north invaded the Valley of Oaxaca. They warred with valley Zapotecs, and despite their relatively small numbers, became a ruling class in a number of Valley city-states. The blend of Mixtec and Zapotec art and architecture sometimes led to new forms, especially visible at the west-valley sites of Yagul and Mitla.

Monte Albán, meanwhile, although abandoned, was not forgotten. It became both a refuge and a venerated burial place. In times of siege, local people retreated within the walls of a fortress built around Monte Albán's South Platform. At other times, Mixtec nobles opened tombs and reused them as burial vaults right down until the eve of the conquest.

Exploring Monte Albán

Visitors to Monte Albán enjoy a panoramic view of green mountains rising above the checkerboard of the Valley of Oaxaca. Monte Albán is fun for a picnic; or, alternatively, it is an auspicious place to perch atop a pyramid above the grand Main Plaza, etched by lengthening afternoon shadows, and contemplate the ages.

As you enter past the Visitor Center, north is on your right, marked by the grand **North Platform,** topped by clusters of temples. The **Ball Court** will soon appear below on your left. Twenty-foot-high walkways circumscribe the sunken "I"-shaped playing field. To ensure true bounces, builders spread smooth stucco over all surfaces, including the slopes on opposite sides (which, contrary to appearances, did not seat spectators). This, like all Oaxacan ball courts, had no stone ring (for supposed goals), but rather four mysterious niches at the court's opposite "I"-end corners.

The **Main Plaza,** 1,000 feet long and exactly two-thirds that wide, is aligned along a precise north-south axis. Probably serving as a market and civic-ceremonial ground, the monumentally harmonious Main Plaza was the Zapotec "navel" of the world.

Monte Albán's oldest construction, of the **Danzantes** (surmounted by newer Bldg. L, on the west side of the plaza between Buildings M and IV) dates from Period I. Its walls are graced with a host of personages, known commonly as the *danzantes,* (dancers) from their oft-contorted postures—probably chiefs, vanquished by Monte Albán's armies. Their headdresses, earplugs, bracelets, and necklaces mark them among the nobility, while glyphs around their heads identify each individual.

BRUCE WHIPPERMAN

Ocotlán's Aguilar sisters specialize in whimsical, one-of-a-kind pottery pieces.

Building J (circa A.D. 0), one of the most remarkable in Mesoamerica, stands nearby in mid-plaza at the foot of the South Platform. Speculation has raged since excavators unearthed its arrow-shaped base generations ago. It is not surprising that Alfonso Caso, Monte Albán's principal excavator, theorized that it was an astronomical observatory. In the mind's eye, it seems like some fantastic ocean (or space?) vessel, being navigated to some mysteriously singular southwest destination by a ghostly crew oblivious of its worldly, earthbound brother monuments.

The **South Platform,** especially during the late afternoon, affords Monte Albán's best vantage point. Starting on the right-hand, Palace complex side, **Bldg. II** has a peculiar tunnel on its near side, covertly used by priests for privacy or perhaps some kind of magical effect. South of that stands Building P, an undistinguished, albeit multiroom palace.

The South Platform itself is only marginally explored. Looters have riddled the mounds on its top side. Its bottom four corners were embellished by fine bas reliefs, two of which had their engraving *intentionally buried* from view. You can admire the fine sculpture and yet-undeciphered Zapotec hieroglyphs on one of them, along with others, at the South Platform's plaza-edge west side.

Still atop the South Platform, turn southward, where you can see the 7 Deer complex, a few hundred yards away, labeled for the name-date inscribed on its great lintel.

Turning northward again, look just beyond Building J, to Buildings G, H, and I at plaza-center, erected mostly to cover a rocky mound impossible to remove without the then-unavailable dynamite. Between these buildings and the Palace complex on the right stands the small **Chapel** where the remarkable bat-god jade sculpture was found.

On Monte Albán's northern periphery stand a number of tombs which, when excavated, yielded a trove of artifacts, now mostly housed in museums. Walking west from the Northern Platform's northeast base corner, you will pass Mound X on the right. A few hundred yards farther comes the **Tomb 104** mound, presided over by an elaborate ceramic urn representing Cojico, the Zapotec god of rain. Just north of this is **Tomb 172,** with the skeletons and offerings left intact.

Heading back along the northernmost of the two paths from Tomb 104, you will arrive at **Tomb 7** a few hundred feet behind the Visitor Center. Here, around 1450, Mixtec nobles removed the original 8th-century contents and reused the tomb, burying a deceased dignitary and two servants for the netherworld. Along with them they left a fabulous treasure in gold, silver, jade, alabaster, turquoise, now mostly visible at the regional Museo de Oaxaca. (See "City Sights" above.)

A few hundred feet toward town on the opposite side of the road from the parking lot is a trail, leading past a small ball court to the Cerro de Plumaje ("Hill of Plumage"), site of **Tomb 105.** A magnificent entrance door lintel, reminiscent of those at Mitla, welcomes you inside. Past the patio, descend to the mural-decorated tomb antechamber. Inside the cruciform tomb itself, four figures walk in pairs toward a great glyph, flanked by a god and goddess, identified by their name-dates.

Visitor Center And Getting There
The Monte Albán Visitor Center has a small museum, cafe, information counter, and good store, with many books—guides, histories, art, folklore—on Mesoamerica. One of the most useful archaeological guides is Ignacio Bernal's *Official Guide of the Oaxaca Valley,* which includes Monte Albán, Cuilapan, Zaachila, Dainzu, Lambityeco, Yagul, and Mitla. Also covering the same territory, but in more depth, is *Oaxaca, the Archeological Record* by archaeologist Marcus Winter.

Get to Monte Albán either by driving (follow the big "Monte Albán" sign on the Periférico, end of Cabrera) over the Rio Atoyac bridge. Bear right after the bridge, and continue about four miles (six km), bearing uphill, to the summit. By bus, either go by tour from your hotel or downtown Hotel del Ángel daily (six blocks from the zócalo, corner Ordaz and Mina, tel. 666-33, 601-99), or take one of the very frequent Monte Albán buses from the Abastos terminal (on the Periférico, end of Trujano).

Monte Albán is open daily from 10 a.m., closing promptly at 5 p.m.

Etla
The untouristed, very colorful Wednesday market at Etla (officially San Pedro y San Pablo

Etla) northeast of Oaxaca could be visited either separately or in coordination with a visit to Monte Albán. Although Etla's market invariably has stalls overflowing with its famous white cheese, vendors offer much other old-fashioned merchandise. (How would you like, for example, some fresh sheepskins, burro pack-frames, green Atzompa pottery, or red Oaxaca tamales?)

Preferably visit the market in the forenoon, and Monte Albán in the midafternoon. Arrive at Monte Albán around 2:30 to allow enough leisure to tour the ruins before the closing at 5 p.m. **Getting to Etla:** By car, head north along Hwy. 190 about nine miles (15 km) from the city center, turn left just before the Pemex station. San Pablo y San Pedro Etla is about half a mile from the highway. By bus, ride one of the many "Etla" buses from the Abastos second-class terminal, or a tour bus.

mask with unusual monkey mascot motif

BOB RACE

BOOKLIST

Some of these books are informative, others are entertaining, and all of them will increase your understanding of Mexico. Some are easier to find in Mexico than at at home, and vice versa. Take some of them along on your trip. If you find others that are especially noteworthy, let us know. Happy reading.

HISTORY

Calderón de la Barca, Fanny. *Life in Mexico, with New Material from the Author's Journals.* New York: Doubleday, 1966. Edited by H.T. and M.H. Fisher. An update of the brilliant, humorous, and celebrated original 1913 book by the Scottish wife of the Spanish Ambassador to Mexico.

Casasola, Gustavo. *Seis Siglos de Historia Grafica de Mexico* (Six Centuries of Mexican Graphic History). Mexico City: Editorial Gustavo Casasola, 1978. Six fascinating volumes of Mexican history in pictures, from 1325 to the present.

Díaz del Castillo, Bernal. *The True Story of the Conquest of Mexico.* Garden City: Doubleday, 1956. Trans. by Albert Idell. A soldier's still-fresh tale of the conquest from the Spanish viewpoint.

Garfias, Luis. *The Mexican Revolution.* Mexico City: Panorama Editorial, 1985. A concise Mexican version of the 1910-1917 Mexican Revolution, the crucible of present-day Mexico.

León-Portilla, Miguel. *The Broken Spears: The Aztec Account of the Conquest of Mexico.* New York: Beacon Press, 1962. Provides an interesting contrast to Díaz del Castillo's account.

Meyer, Michael, and William Sherman. *The Course of Mexican History.* New York: Oxford University Press, 1991. An insightful, 700-plus page college textbook in paperback. A bargain, especially if you can get it used.

Reed, John. *Insurgent Mexico.* Fast-moving (but not unbiased) description of the 1910 Mexican Revolution by the reporter famed for his

reporting of the subsequent 1917 Russian Revolution. Reed, memorialized by the Soviets, was resurrected in the 1981 film biography *Reds.*

Simpson, Lesley Bird. *Many Mexicos.* Berkeley: The University of California Press, 1962. A much reprinted, fascinating broad-brush version of Mexican history.

Spores, Ronald. *The Mixtecs in Ancient and Colonial Times.* Norman, OK: University of Oklahoma Press, 1984. Authoritative background for visitors to Oaxaca.

Whitecotton, Joseph. *The Zapotecs.* Norman, OK: University of Oklahoma Press, 1977. An examination of the dominant Oaxacan native group's history and culture from prehistory to the present.

UNIQUE GUIDE AND TIP BOOKS

Franz, Carl. *The People's Guide to Mexico.* Santa Fe: John Muir, 1990. An entertaining and insightful A to Z general guide to the joys and pitfalls of independent economy travel in Mexico.

Freedman, Jacqueline, and Susan Gerstein. *Traveling Like Everybody Else.* Adama Books. Your handicap needn't keep you at home.

Rogers, Steve, and Tina Rosa. *The Shopper's Guide to Mexico.* Santa Fe: John Muir, 1989. A well-written guide to shopping in Mexico, with emphasis on handicrafts. Includes the Pacific Coast resorts, plus Guadalajara, Pátzcuaro, and Oaxaca.

Weisbroth, Ericka, and Eric Ellman. *Bicycling Mexico.* New York: Hunter, 1990. These intrepid adventurers cover Pacific Mexico from

Puerto Vallarta to Acapulco, Pinotepa Nacional to Puerto Ángel, and highland Oaxaca, Michoacán, and Jalisco.

Werner, David. *Where There Is No Doctor*. Palo Alto: Hesperian Foundation (P.O. Box 1692, Palo Alto, CA 94302). How to keep well in the backcountry.

Wheeler, Maureen. *Traveling With Children*. Hawthorn, Victoria, Australia: Lonely Planet Publications. In the third world, some people have good trips *because* they bring the kids.

Whitman, John. *The Best Mexican Travel Tips*. New York: Harper and Row, 1986. Thousands of ways to save money, time, and trouble in Mexico.

FICTION

Fuentes, Carlos. *Where the Air is Clear*. New York: Farrar, Straus and Giroux, 1971. The seminal work of Mexico's celebrated novelist.

Jennings, Gary. *Aztec*. New York: Atheneum, 1980. Beautifully researched and written monumental tale of lust, compassion, love, and death in pre-conquest Mexico.

Peters, Daniel. *The Luck of Huemac*. New York: Random House, 1981. An Aztec noble family's tale—of war, famine, sorcery, heroism, treachery, love, and finally disaster and death—in the Valley of Mexico.

Porter, Katherine Ann. *The Collected Stories*. New York: Delacorte, 1970.

Rulfo, Juan. *The Burning Plain*. Austin: University of Texas Press, 1967. Stories of people torn between the old and new in Mexico.

Traven, B. *The Treasure of the Sierra Madre*. New York: Hill and Wang, 1967. *Campesinos, federales, gringos,* and *indígenas* all figure in this famous modern morality tale set in Mexi-

co's rugged outback. Only the most famous of the mysterious author's many novels of oppression and justice set in Mexico's jungles.

PEOPLE AND CULTURE

Berrin, Kathleen. *The Art of the Huichol Indians*. Lovely, large photographs and text by a symposium of experts provides a good interpretive introduction to Huichol art and culture.

Lewis, Oscar. *Children of Sanchez*. New York: Random House, 1961. Poverty and strength in the Mexican underclass, sympathetically described and interpreted by renowned sociologist Lewis.

Meyerhoff, Barbara. *Peyote Hunt: the Sacred Journey of the Huichol Indians*. Ithaca: Cornell University Press, 1974. A description and interpretation of the Huichol's religious use of mind-bending natural hallucinogens.

Riding, Alan. *Distant Neighbors: A Portrait of the Mexicans*. New York: Random House Vintage Books. Rare insights into Mexico and Mexicans.

Wauchope, Robert, Editor. *Handbook of Middle American Indians, Volumes 7 and 8*. Austin: University of Texas Press, 1969. Authoritative surveys of important Indian-speaking groups in northern and central (vol. 8) and southern (vol. 7) Mexico.

FLORA AND FAUNA

Goodson, Gar. *Fishes of the Pacific Coast*. Stanford: Stanford University Press, 1988. Over 500 beautifully detailed color drawings highlight this pocket version of all you ever wanted to know about the ocean fishes (including common Spanish names) from Alaska to Peru.

Leopold, Starker. *Wildlife of Mexico*. Berkeley: University of California Press. Classic, illustrated layman's survey of common Mexican mammals and birds.

Mason, Charles T. and Patricia B. *A Handbook of Mexican Roadside Flora.* Tuscon: University of Arizona Press, 1987. Authoritative identification guide, with line illustrations, of all the plants you're likely to see in Pacific Mexico.

Morris, Percy A. *A Field Guide to Pacific Coast Shells.* Boston: Houghton Mifflin, second edition 1966. The compleat beachcomber's Pacific shell guide.

Novick, Rosalind, and Lan Sing Wu. *Where to Find Birds in San Blas, Nayarit.* Second edition 1988. (Order through the authors at 178 Myrtle Court, Arcata CA 95521, tel. 707-822-0790.)

Pesman, M. Walter. *Meet Flora Mexicana.* Delightful anecdotes and illustrations of hundreds of common Mexican plants. Published around 1960, now out of print.

Peterson, Roger Tory, and Edward L. Chalif. *Field Guide to Mexican Birds.* Boston: Houghton Mifflin, 1973. With hundreds of Peterson's crisp color drawings, this is a must for serious birders and vacationers interested in the life that teems in Pacific Mexico's wild beaches and lagoons.

Wright, N. Pelham. *A Guide to Mexican Mammals and Reptiles.* Mexico City: Minutiae Mexicana, 1989. Pocket-edition lore, history, descriptions and pictures of commonly seen Mexican animals.

ARCHITECTURE, ARTS AND CRAFTS

Baird, Joseph. *The Churches of Mexico.* Berkeley: University of California Press. Mexican colonial architecture and art, illustrated and interpreted.

Cordrey, Donald and Dorothy. *Mexican Indian Costumes.* Austin: University of Texas Press, 1968. A lovingly photographed, written, and illustrated classic on Mexican Indians and their dress, emphasizing textiles.

Covarrubias, Miguel. *Indian Art of Mexico and Central America.* New York: Knopf, 1957. A timeless work by the renowned interpreter of *indígena* art and design.

Martinez Penaloza, Porfirio. *Popular Arts of Mexico.* Mexico City: Editorial Panorama, 1981. An excellent, authoritative, pocket-sized exposition of Mexican art.

GLOSSARY

Many of these words have a social-historical meaning; others you will not find in the usual English-Spanish dictionary.

alcalde — a mayor or municipal judge

audiencia — one of the royal executive-judicial panels sent to rule Mexico during the 16th century

ayuntimiento — either the town council or the building where it meets

cabercera — head town of a municipal district, or headquarters in general

cabrón — literally a cuckold, but more commonly bastard, rat, or S.O.B., sometimes used affectionately, however.

cacique — a chief or boss

campesino — a country person; a farm worker

caudillo — a dictator or political chief

charro — cowboy

chingar — literally, to "rape," but also the universal Spanish "f" word, the equivalent of "screw" in English

Churrigueresque — a Spanish Baroque architectural style that was incorporated into many Mexican colonial churches, named after Jose Churriguera (1665-1725)

cientificos — President Porfirio Diaz's technocratic advisers

colectivo — a collective taxi or microbus that picks up and deposits passengers along a designated route

colegio — a preparatory school or junior college

colonia — a suburban subdivision-satellite of a larger city

Conasupo — a government store that sells basic foods at subsidized prices

criollo — an all-Spanish descent person born in the New World

curandero(a) — an Indian medicine man (or woman)

damas — ladies, as in "ladies room"

de lujo — deluxe

encomienda — a colonial award of tribute from a designated Indian district

indígena — a country person of all-Indian descent who speaks his or her native tongue

estación ferrocarril — railroad station

finca — a farm

fraccionimiento — a city sector or subdivision

fuero — the former right of clergy to be tried in separate ecclesiastical courts

gachupine — "one who wear spurs"; a derogatory term for a Spanish-born colonial

gente de razón — "people of reason"; whites and mestizos in colonial Mexico

gringo — a once-derogatory but now commonly used term for North American whites

grito — an impassioned cry, as in Hidalgo's Grito de Dolores

hacienda — a large landed estate; also the government treasury

hidalgo — a nobleman; called honorifically by "Don" or "Doña"

licencado — an academic degree, (abbrev. Lic.) approximately equivalent to a bachelor's degree

machismo, macho — an exaggerated sense of maleness, or a person who holds such an opinion of himself

mestizo — a person of mixed Indian-European descent

milpa — an Indian farm plot, usually of corn

mordida — slang for a bribe; a "little bite"

Pemex — acronym for Petróleos Mexicanos, the national oil corporation

peninsulares — the Spanish-born ruling colonial elite

peones — poor wage-earners, usually country Indians

plan — a political manifesto, usually by a leader or group consolidating or seeking power

pronunciamiento — a declaration of rebellion by an insurgent leader

Porfiriato — the 34-year (1876-1910) ruling period of President-dictator Porfirio Diaz

puta — whore, bitch, or slut

pueblo — a town or people

quinta — a villa or country house

quinto — the royal "fifth" tax on treasure and precious metals

rurales — a former federal country police force created to fight *bandidos*

vaquero — cowboy

vecindad — neighborhood

zócalo — town plaza or central square

ENGLISH-SPANISH MINI-DICTIONARY

A profitable route to learning Spanish in Mexico is to refuse to speak English. Prepare yourself (instead of watching the in-flight movie) with a basic word list in a little pocket notebook. Use it to speak Spanish wherever you go.

Basic And Courteous

Courtesy is very important to Mexican people. They will appreciate your use of some basic expressions. (Note: The upside-down Spanish question mark merely warns the reader of the query in advance.)

hello — *hola*

How are you? — *¿Como está usted?*

very well, thank you — *muy bien, gracias*

okay, good — *bueno*

not okay, bad — *malo, feo*

and you? — *¿y usted?*

(Note: Pronounce *Y*, the Spanish "and," like English "ee," as in "keep.")

thank you very much — *muchas gracias*

please — *por favor*

You're welcome. — *De nada.*

Just a moment, please. — *Momentito, por favor.*

How do you say . . . in Spanish? — *¿Como se dice . . . en español?*

excuse me (when you're trying to get attention) — *excúseme, con permiso*

excuse me (when you've made a boo-boo) — *lo siento*

good morning — *buenos dias*

good afternoon — *buenas tardes*

good evening — *buenas noches*

Sir (Mr.), Ma'am (Mrs.), Miss — *Señor, Señora, Señorita*

What is your name? — *¿Como se llama usted?*

pleased to meet you — *con mucho gusto*

My name is . . . — *Me llamo . . .*

Would you like . . . ? — *¿Quisiera usted . . . ?*

Let's go to . . . — *Vamanós a . . .*

I would like to introduce my . . . — *Quisiera presentar mi . . .*

wife — *esposa*

husband — *marido, esposo*

friend — *amigo (male), amiga (female)*

sweetheart — *novio (male), novia (female)*

son, daughter — *hijo, hija*

brother, sister — *hermano, hermana*

father, mother — *padre, madre*

see you later (again) — *hasta luego (la vista)*

goodbye — *adiós*

yes, no — *sí, no*

I, you, he, she — *yo, usted, él, ella*

we, you (pl.), they — *nosotros, ustedes, ellos*

Do you speak English? — *¿Habla usted inglés?*

Getting Around

If I could use only two Spanish phrases, I would choose "excúseme," followed by "¿Donde esta . . . ?".

Where is . . . ? — *¿Donde está . . . ?*

the bus station — *la terminal autobús*

the bus stop — *La parada autobús*

the taxi stand — *el sitio taxi*

the train station — *la terminal ferrocarril*

the airport — *el aeropuerto*

the boat — *la barca*

the bathroom, toilet — *el baño, sanitorio*

men's, women's — *de hombres, de mujeres*

the entrance, exit — *la entrada, la salida*

the pharmacy — *la farmacia*

the bank — *el banco*

the police, police officer — *la policía*

the supermarket — *el supermercado*

the grocery store — *la abarrotería, bodega*

the laundry — *la lavandería*

the stationery (book) store — *la papelería (librería)*

the hardware store — *la ferretería*

the (long distance) telephone — *el teléfono (larga distancia)*

the post office — *los correos*
the ticket office — *la oficina boletos*
a hotel — *un hotel*
a cafe, a restaurant — *una café, un restaurante*
Where (Which) is the way to . . . ? — *¿Donde (Cuál) está el camino a . . . ?*
How far to . . . ? — *¿Qué tan lejos a . . . ?*
How many blocks? — *¿Quantas cuadras?*
(very) near, far — *(muy) cerca, lejos*
to, toward — *a*
by, through — *por*
from — *de*
the right, the left — *la derecha, la izquierda*
straight ahead — *derecho, directo*
in front — *en frente*
beside — *al lado*
behind — *atrás*
the corner — *la esquina*
the stoplight — *la semafora*
a turn — *una vuelta*
right here — *aquí*
somewhere around here — *acá*
right over there — *allí*
somewhere over there — *allá*
street, boulevard, highway — *calle, bulevar, carretera*
bridge, toll — *puente, cuota*
address — *dirección*
north, south — *norte, sur*
east, west — *oriente, poniente*

Doing Things

Verbs are the key to getting along in Spanish. They employ mostly predictable forms and come in three classes, which end in ar, er, and ir, respectively:

to buy — *comprar*
I buy, you (he, she, it) buys — *compro, compra*
we buy, you (they) buy — *compramos, compran*

to eat — *comer*
I eat, you (he, she, it) eats — *como, come*
we eat, you (they) eat — *comemos, comen*

to climb — *subir*
I climb, you (he, she, it) climb — *subo, sube*
we climb, you (they) climb — *subimos, suben*

Got the idea? Here are more (with irregularities marked in bold).

to do or make — *hacer*
I do or make, you (he she, or it) do or make — ***hago,*** *hace*
we do or make, you (they) do or make — *hacemos, hacen*

to go — *ir*
I go, you (he, she, or it) goes — ***voy, va***
we go, you (they) go — ***vamos, van***

to have — *tener* (regular except for ***tengo,*** I have).
to come — *venir* (regular except for ***vengo,*** I come).
to give — *dar* (regular except for ***doy,*** I give).
to love — *amar*
to swim — *nadar*
to walk — *andar*
to work — *trabajar*
to want — *desear*
to read — *leer*
to write — *escribir*
to repair — *reparar*
to arrive — *llegar*
to stay — *quedar*
to look — *mirar*

Spanish has two forms of to be: use *estar* when speaking of location ("I am at home." *"**Estoy** en casa."*) and *ser* for state of being ("I am a doctor." *"**Soy** doctor."*). *Estar* is regular except for ***estoy,*** I am. *Ser* is very irregular:
to be — *ser*
I am, you (he, she, it) is — ***soy, es***
we are, you (they) are — ***somos, son***

At The Station And On The Bus

I'd like a ticket to . . . — *Quisiera un boleto a . . .*
first (second) class — *primera (segunda) clase*
roundtrip — *ida y vuelta*
how much? — *¿cuanto cuesta?*
reservation — *reservación*
reserved seat — *asiento reservado*
seat number . . . — *número asiento . . .*
baggage — *equipaje*
Where is this bus going? — *¿Donde va este autobús?*
What's the name of this place? — *¿Como se llama este lugar?*
Stop here, please! — *¡Pare aquí, por favor!*

Eating Out

A *restaurante* (rays-tah-oo-RAHN-tay) generally implies a fairly fancy joint, with prices to match. The food and atmosphere, however, may be more to your liking at any one of several other types of eateries (in approximate descending order of price): *comedor, café, fonda, lonchería, jugería, taquería.*

I'm hungry. — *Tengo hambre.*
I'm thirsty — *Tengo sed.*
menu — *menú*
order — *orden*
soft drink — *refresco*
coffee, cream — *café, crema*
tea — *te*
sugar — *azúcar*
drinking water — *agua pura,* or *potable*
bottled carbonated water — *agua mineral*
bottled uncarbonated water — *agua sin gas*
glass — *vaso*
beer — *cerveza*
dark — *obscura*
draft — *de barril*
wine — *vino*
white, red — *blanco, tinto*
dry, sweet — *seco, dulce*
cheese — *queso*
snack — *antijo, botana*
daily special — *comida corrida*
fried — *frito*
roasted — *asada*
barbecued — *al carbón*
breakfast — *desayuno*
eggs — *huevos*
boiled — *tibios*
scrambled — *revueltos*
bread — *pan*
sweet roll — *pan dulce*
toast — *pan tostada*
oatmeal — *avena*
bacon, ham — *tocino, jamón*
salad — *ensalada*
lettuce — *lechuga*
carrots — *zanahoria*
tomato — *tomate*
oil — *aceite*
vinegar — *vinagre*
lime — *limón*

mayonnaise — *mayonesa*
fruit — *fruta*
mango — *mango*
watermelon — *sandía*
papaya — *papaya*
banana — *plátano*
apple — *manzana*
orange — *naranja*
fish — *pescado*
shrimp — *camarones*
oysters — *ostiones*
clams — *almejas*
octopus — *pulpo*
squid — *calamare*
meat (without) — *carne (sin)*
chicken — *pollo*
pork — *puerco*
beef, steak — *res, bistec*
the check — *la cuenta*

At The Hotel

In the resorts of Pacific Mexico, finding a reasonably priced hotel room (except during the high-occupancy weeks after Christmas and before Easter) usually presents no major problem.

Is there . . . ? — *¿Hay . . . ?*
an (inexpensive) hotel — *un hotel (económico)*
an inn — *una posada*
a guesthouse — *una casa de huéspedes*
a single (double) room — *un cuarto sencillo (doble)*
with bath — *con baño*
shower — *ducha*
hot water — *agua caliente*
fan — *abanico, ventilador*
air-conditioned — *aire acondicionado*
double bed — *cama matrimonial*
twin beds — *camas gemelas*
How much for the room? — *¿Cuanto cuesta el cuarto?*
dining room — *comedor*
key — *llave*
towels — *toallas*
manager — *gerente*
soap — *jabón*
toilet paper — *papel higiénico*
swimming pool — *alberca, piscina*
the bill, please — *la cuenta, por favor*

At The Bank
The oft long lines, short hours, and miniscule advantage in exchange rate of *el banco* sometimes make a nearby private *casa de cambio* a very handy alternative:

money — *dinero*
money-exchange bureau — *casa de cambio*
I would like to exchange traveler's checks. — *Quisiera cambiar cheques de viajero.*
What is the exchange rate? — *¿Cuál es el cambio?*
How much is the commission? — *¿Cuanto cuesta el comisión?*
Do you accept credit cards? — *¿Aceptan tarjetas de credito?*
money order — *giro*
teller's window — *caja*
signature — *firma*

Shopping
Es la costumbre in Mexico that the first price is never the last. The custom of bargaining often transforms shopping from a perfunctory chore into an open-ended adventure. Bargain with humor, and be prepared to walk away if the price is not right.

How much does it cost? — *¿Cuanto cuesta?*
too much — *demasiado*
expensive, cheap — *caro, barato (económico)*
too expensive, too cheap — *demasiado caro, demasiado barato*
more, less — *mas, menos*
small, big — *chico, grande*
good, bad — *bueno, malo*
smaller, smallest — *mas chico, el mas chico*
larger, largest — *mas grand, el mas grande*
cheaper, cheapest — *mas barato, el mas barato*
What is your final price? — *¿Cual es su último precio?*
Just right! — *¡Perfecto!*

Telephone, Post Office
In much of Pacific Mexico, long distance connections must be made at a central long-distance office, where people sometimes can sit, have coffee or a *refresco,* and socialize while waiting for their *larga distancia* to come through:

long distance telephone — *teléfono larga distancia*

I would like to call . . . — *Quisiera llamar a . . .*
station to station — *a quién contesta*
person to person — *persona a persona*
credit card — *tarjeta de credito*
post office — *correos*
general delivery — *lista de correos*
letter — *carta*
stamp — *estampilla*
postcard — *tarjeta*
aerogram — *aerogramo*
air mail — *correo aereo*
registered — *registrado*
money order — *giro*
package, box — *paquette, caja*
string, tape — *cuerda, cinta*

Formalities
Although crossing into Mexico is relatively easy, it is among the most foreign of destinations — more so than either India or Japan.

border — *frontera*
customs — *aduana*
immigration — *inmigración*
tourist card — *tarjeta de turista*
inspection — *revisón*
passport — *pasaporte*
profession — *professión*
marital status — *estado civil*
single — *soltero*
married, divorced — *casado, divorciado*
widowed — *viudado*
insurance — *seguros*
title — *títul*
driver's license — *licencia de manejar*
fishing, hunting, gun license — *licencia de pescar, cazar, armas*

At The Pharmacy, Doctor, Hospital
For a third-world country, Mexico provides good health care. Even small Pacific Mexico towns have a basic hospital or clinic.

Help me please. — *Ayudeme por favor.*
I am ill. — *Estoy enfermo.*
Call a doctor. — *Llame un doctor.*
Take me to . . . — *Lleve me a . . .*
hospital — *hospital, sanatorio*
drugstore — *farmacia*
pain — *dolor*
fever — *fiebre*
headache — *dolor de cabeza*

stomacheache — *dolor de estómago*
burn — *quemadura*
cramp — *calambre*
nausea — *náusea*
vomiting — *vomitar*
medicine — *medicina*
antibiotic — *antibiótico*
pill, tablet — *pastilla*
aspirin — *aspirina*
ointment, cream — *pomada, crema*
bandage — *venda*
cotton — *algodón*
sanitary napkins (use brand name)
birth control pills — *pastillas contraceptivos*
contraceptive foam — *espuma contraceptiva*
diaphragm (best to carry an extra)
condoms — *contraceptivas*
toothbrush — *cepilla dental*
toothpaste — *crema dental*
dentist — *dentista*
toothache — *dolor demuelas*

At The Gas Station
gas station — *gasolinera*
gasoline — *gasolina*
leaded, unleaded — *plomo, sin plomo*
full, please — *lleno, por favor*
gas cap — *tapón*
tire — *llanta*
tire repair shop — *vulcanizador*
air — *aire*
water — *agua*
oil (change) — *aceite (cambio)*
grease — *grasa*
My . . . doesn't work. — *Mi . . . no sirve.*
battery — *batería*
radiator — *radiador*
alternator, generator — *alternador, generador*
tow truck — *grúa*
repair shop — *taller mechánico*
tune-up — *afinación*
parts store — *refraccionería*

Numbers And Time
zero — *cero*
one — *uno*
two — *dos*
three — *tres*
four — *cuatro*
five — *cinco*
six — *seis*
seven — *siete*

eight — *ocho*
nine — *nueve*
10 — *diez*
11 — *once*
12 — *doce*
13 — *trece*
14 — *catorce*
15 — *quince*
16 — *dieciseis*
17 — *diecisiete*
18 — *dieciocho*
19 — *diecinueve*
20 — *veinte*
21 — *veinte y uno*, or *veintiuno*
30 — *treinta*
40 — *cuarenta*
50 — *cincuenta*
60 — *sesenta*
70 — *setenta*
80 — *ochenta*
90 — *noventa*
100 — *ciento*
101 — *ciento y uno*, or *cientiuno*
200 — *doscientos*
500 — *quinientos*
1,000 — *mil*
10,000 — *diez mil*
100,000 — *cien mil*
1,000,000 — *un milión*
1993 — *mil novecientos noventa y tres*
one-half — *medio*
one-third — *un tercio*
one fourth — *un cuarto*

What time is it? — *¿Que hora es?*
It's one o'clock. — *Es la una.*
It's three in the afternoon. — *Son las tres de la tarde.*
It's 4 a.m. — *Son las cuatro de la manana.*
six-thirty — *seis y media*
a quarter till eleven — *un cuarto hasta once*
a quarter past five — *un cuarto después cinco*

Monday — *lunes*
Tuesday — *martes*
Wednesday — *miércoles*
Thursday — *jueves*
Friday — *viernes*
Saturday — *sábado*
Sunday — *domingo*

January — *enero*
February — *febrero*
March — *marzo*
April — *abril*
May — *mayo*
June — *junio*
July — *julio*
August — *agosto*
September — *septiembre*
October — *octubre*
November — *noviembre*
December — *diciembre*

last Sunday — *domingo pasado*
next December — *diciembre próximo*
yesterday — *ayer*
tomorrow — *mañana*
an hour — *una hora*
a week — *una semana*
a month — *un mes*
a week ago — *hace una semana*
after — *después*
before — *antes*

A LITTLE SPANISH

Your Pacific Mexico adventure will be more fun if you use a little Spanish. Mexican folks, although they may smile at your funny accent, will appreciate it nevertheless. Your halting efforts break the ice and transform yourself from a foreign stranger to a potential friend.

Spanish commonly uses 30 letters—the familiar English 26, plus four straightforward additions: ch, ll, ñ, and rr, which are explained in "Consonants," below.

Vowels

Once you learn them, Spanish pronunciation rules (in contrast to English) don't change. Spanish vowels generally sound softer than in English: (Note: The capitalized syllables below receive stronger accents.)

Pronounce *a* like ah, as in hah: *agua* AH-gooah (water), *pan* PAHN (bread), *casa* CAH-sah (house).

Pronounce *e* like ay as in may: *mesa* MAY-sah (table), *tela* TAY-lah (cloth), and *de* DAY (of, from).

Pronounce *i* like ee as in need: *diez* dee-AYZ (ten), *comida* ko-MEE-dah (meal), and *fin* FEEN (end).

Pronounce *o* like oh as in oh: *peso* PAY-soh (weight), *ocho* OH-choh (eight), and *poco* POH-koh (a bit).

Pronounce *u* like oo as in cool: *uno* OO-noh (one), *cuarto* KOOAHR-toh (room), *usted* oos-TAYD (you).

Accent

The rule for accent, the relative stress given to syllables within a given word, is straightforward.

If a word ends in a vowel, an *n*, or an *s*, accent the next-to-last syllable; if not, accent the last syllable.

Pronounce *gracias* GRAH-seeahs (thank you), *orden* OHR-dayn (order), and *carretera* kah-ray-TAY-rah (highway).

Otherwise, accent the last syllable: *venir* vay-NEER (to come), *ferrocarril* fay-roh-cah-REEL (railroad), and *edad* ay-DAHD (age).

For practice, apply the accent (vowel, n, or s) rule for the vowel-pronunciation examples above. Try to accent the words correctly without looking at the "answers" to the right.

Exceptions to the accent rule are always marked with an accent sign: (á, é, í, ó, or ú), such as *teléfono* tay-LAY-foh-noh (telephone), *jabón* hah-BON (soap), *rápido* RAH-pee-doh (rapid).

Consonants

Seventeen Spanish consonants: *b, d, f, k, l, m, n, p, q, s, t, v, w, x, y, z* and *ch* are pronounced almost as in English; *h* occurs, but is silent — not pronounced at all.

As for the remaining seven (*c, g, j, ñ, ll, r, and rr*) consonants pronounce *c* "hard," like k as in keep: *coche* KOH-chay (car, auto), Tepic Tay-PEEK (capital of Nayarit state). Exception: Before *e* or *i*, pronounce *c* as an English s, as in sit: *cerveza* sayr-VAY-sah (beer), *encima* ayn-SEE-mah (atop).

Before *a, o, u,* or a consonant, pronounce *g* "hard," as in gift: *gato* GAH-toh (cat), *hago* AH-goh (I do, make). Otherwise, pronounce *g* like h as in hat: *giro* HEE-roh (money order), *gente* HAYN-tay (people).

Pronounce *j* like an English h, as in has: *jueves* HOOAY-vays (Thursday), *mejor* may-HOR (better).

Pronounce *ll* like y, as in yes: *toalla* toh-AH-yah (towel), *ellos* AY-yohs (they, them).

Pronounce ñ like ny, as in canyon: *año* AH-nyo (year), *señor* say-NYOR (Mr., sir).

The Spanish *r* is lightly trilled, with tongue at the roof of your mouth like the British r in very ("vehdy," like a very light d.) Pronounce *r* like a very light English d, as in ready: *pero* PAY-doh (but), *tres* TDAYS (three), *cuatro* KOOAH-tdoh (four).

Pronounce *rr* like a Spanish *r*, but with much more emphasis and trill. Let your tongue really flap.

INDEX

Page numbers in **boldface** indicate the primary reference. *Italicized* page numbers indicate information in captions, callouts, charts, or maps.

ABOUT THE AUTHOR

The lure of travel drew Bruce Whipperman away from a twenty-year physics teaching career during the early 1980s. The occasion was a trip to Kenya, which included a total solar eclipse and a safari. He hasn't stopped traveling since.

With his family grown, he has been free to let the world's wild, beautiful corners draw him on: to the ice-clawed Karakoram, the Gobi Desert's trellised oases, pink palaces of Rajastan, Japan's green wine country, Bali's emerald terraces, and now, Pacific Mexico's velvet beaches and tradition-rich highland valleys.

Bruce has always pursued his travel career for the fun of it. He started with slide shows and photo gifts for friends. Others wanted his photos, so he began selling them. Once stranded in Ethiopia, he began to write. In 1983, the *San Francisco Examiner* published his first travel story—of Singapore's Raffles Hotel.

Ten years later, after dozens of magazine and newspaper feature stories, the *Pacific Mexico Handbook* became his first book. Travel, after all, is for returning home; and that coziest of journeys always brings a tired but happy Bruce back to his friends, son, daughter, and sweetheart Linda Reasin in Berkeley, California.

For him, travel writing heightens his awareness and focuses his own travel experiences. He always remembers what a Nepali Sherpa once said, "Many people come, looking, looking; few people come, see."

Bruce invites the *Pacific Mexico Handbook's* readers likewise to "come see"—and discover and enjoy—this palmy, exotic land with a fresh eye and renewed compassion.

MOON HANDBOOKS—THE IDEAL TRAVELING COMPANIONS

Open a Moon Handbook and you're opening your eyes and heart to the world.
Thoughtful, sensitive, and provocative, Moon Handbooks encourage an intimate
understanding of a region, from its culture and history to essential practicalities. Fun to
read and packed with valuable information on accommodations, dining, recreation, plus
indispensable travel tips, detailed maps, charts, illustrations, photos, glossaries, and
indexes, Moon Handbooks are ideal traveling companions: informative, entertaining,
and highly practical.

To locate the bookstore nearest you that carries Moon Travel Handbooks or to order
directly from Moon Publications, call: (800) 345-5473, Monday-Friday, 9 a.m.-5 p.m. PST.

THE PACIFIC/ASIA SERIES

BALI HANDBOOK   by Bill Dalton
Detailed travel information on the most famous island in the world. 428 pages.   **$12.95**

BANGKOK HANDBOOK   by Michael Buckley
Your tour guide through this exotic and dynamic city reveals the affordable and accessible
possibilities. Thai phrasebook. 214 pages.   **$10.95**

BLUEPRINT FOR PARADISE: How to Live on a Tropic Island   by Ross Norgrove
This one-of-a-kind guide has everything you need to know about moving to and living
comfortably on a tropical island. 212 pages.   **$14.95**

FIJI ISLANDS HANDBOOK   by David Stanley
The first and still the best source of information on travel around this 322-island archipelago.
Fijian glossary. 198 pages.   **$11.95**

INDONESIA HANDBOOK   by Bill Dalton
This one-volume encyclopedia explores island by island the many facets of this sprawling,
kaleidoscopic island nation. Extensive Indonesian vocabulary. 1,000 pages.   **$19.95**

JAPAN HANDBOOK   by J.D. Bisignani
In this comprehensive new edition, award-winning travel writer J.D. Bisignani offers to
inveterate travelers, newcomers, and businesspeople alike a thoroughgoing presentation of
Japan's many facets. 800 pages.   **$22.50**

MICRONESIA HANDBOOK: Guide to the Caroline, Gilbert, Mariana, and Marshall Islands
by David Stanley
Micronesia Handbook guides you on a real Pacific adventure all your own. 345 pages.   **$11.95**

NEW ZEALAND HANDBOOK   by Jane King
Introduces you to the people, places, history, and culture of this extraordinary land. 571 pages.
$18.95

OUTBACK AUSTRALIA HANDBOOK   by Marael Johnson
Australia is an endlessly fascinating, vast land, and *Outback Australia Handbook* explores the cities and towns, sheep stations, and wilderness areas of the Northern Territory, Western Australia, and South Australia. Full of travel tips and cultural information for adventuring, relaxing, or just getting away from it all. 355 pages.   **$15.95**

PHILIPPINES HANDBOOK   by Peter Harper and Evelyn Peplow
Crammed with detailed information, *Philippines Handbook* equips the escapist, hedonist, or business traveler with thorough coverage of the Philippines's colorful history, landscapes, and culture. 587 pages.   **$12.95**

SOUTHEAST ASIA HANDBOOK   by Carl Parkes
Helps the enlightened traveler discover the real Southeast Asia. 873 pages.   **$16.95**

SOUTH KOREA HANDBOOK   by Robert Nilsen
Whether you're visiting on business or searching for adventure, *South Korea Handbook* is an invaluable companion. Korean glossary with useful notes on speaking and reading the language. 548 pages.   **$14.95**

SOUTH PACIFIC HANDBOOK   by David Stanley
The original comprehensive guide to the 16 territories in the South Pacific. 740 pages.   **$19.95**

TAHITI-POLYNESIA HANDBOOK   by David Stanley
All five French-Polynesian archipelagoes are covered in this comprehensive guide by Oceania's best-known travel writer. 235 pages.   **$11.95**

THAILAND HANDBOOK   by Carl Parkes
Presents the richest source of information on travel in Thailand. 568 pages.   **$16.95**

THE HAWAIIAN SERIES

BIG ISLAND OF HAWAII HANDBOOK   by J.D. Bisignani
An entertaining yet informative text packed with insider tips on accommodations, dining, sports and outdoor activities, natural attractions, and must-see sights. 347 pages.   **$11.95**

HAWAII HANDBOOK   by J.D. Bisignani
Winner of the 1989 Hawaii Visitors Bureau's Best Guide Award and the Grand Award for Excellence in Travel Journalism, this guide takes you beyond the glitz and high-priced hype and leads you to a genuine Hawaiian experience. Covers all 8 Hawaiian Islands. 879 pages.   **$15.95**

KAUAI HANDBOOK   by J.D. Bisignani
Kauai Handbook is the perfect antidote to the workaday world. Hawaiian and pidgin glossaries. 236 pages.   **$9.95**

MAUI HANDBOOK   by J.D. Bisignani
"No fool-'round" advice on accommodations, eateries, and recreation, plus a comprehensive introduction to island ways, geography, and history. Hawaiian and pidgin glossaries. 350 pages. **$11.95**

OAHU HANDBOOK by J.D. Bisignani
A handy guide to Honolulu, renowned surfing beaches, and Oahu's countless other diversions. Hawaiian and pidgin glossaries. 354 pages. **$11.95**

THE AMERICAS SERIES

ALASKA-YUKON HANDBOOK by Deke Castleman and Don Pitcher
Get the inside story, with plenty of well-seasoned advice to help you cover more miles on less money. 384 pages. **$13.95**

ARIZONA TRAVELER'S HANDBOOK by Bill Weir
This meticulously researched guide contains everything necessary to make Arizona accessible and enjoyable. 505 pages. **$14.95**

BAJA HANDBOOK by Joe Cummings
A comprehensive guide with all the travel information and background on the land, history, and culture of this untamed thousand-mile-long peninsula. 356 pages. **$13.95**

BELIZE HANDBOOK by Chicki Mallan
Complete with detailed maps, practical information, and an overview of the area's flamboyant history, culture, and geographical features, *Belize Handbook* is the only comprehensive guide of its kind to this spectacular region. 263 pages. **$14.95**

BRITISH COLUMBIA HANDBOOK by Jane King
With an emphasis on outdoor adventures, this guide covers mainland British Columbia, Vancouver Island, the Queen Charlotte Islands, and the Canadian Rockies. 381 pages. **$13.95**

CANCUN HANDBOOK by Chicki Mallan
Covers the city's luxury scene as well as more modest attractions, plus many side trips to unspoiled beaches and Mayan ruins. Spanish glossary. 257 pages. **$12.95**

CATALINA ISLAND HANDBOOK: A Guide to California's Channel Islands
by Chicki Mallan
A complete guide to these remarkable islands, from the windy solitude of the Channel Islands National Marine Sanctuary to bustling Avalon. 245 pages. **$10.95**

COLORADO HANDBOOK by Stephen Metzger
Essential details to the all-season possibilities in Colorado fill this guide. Practical travel tips combine with recreation—skiing, nightlife, and wilderness exploration—plus entertaining essays. 422 pages. **$15.95**

COSTA RICA HANDBOOK by Christopher P. Baker
Experience the many wonders of the natural world as you explore this remarkable land. Spanish-English glossary. 700 pages. **$19.95**

IDAHO HANDBOOK by Bill Loftus
A year-round guide to everything in this outdoor wonderland, from whitewater adventures to rural hideaways. 275 pages. **$12.95**

JAMAICA HANDBOOK   by Karl Luntta
From the sun and surf of Montego Bay and Ocho Rios to the cool slopes of the Blue Mountains, author Karl Luntta offers island-seekers a perceptive, personal view of Jamaica. 213 pages. **$12.95**

MONTANA HANDBOOK   by W.C. McRae and Judy Jewell
The wild West is yours with this extensive guide to the Treasure State, complete with travel practicalities, history, and lively essays on Montana life. 393 pages.   **$13.95**

NEVADA HANDBOOK   by Deke Castleman
Nevada Handbook puts the Silver State into perspective and makes it manageable and affordable. 400 pages.   **$14.95**

NEW MEXICO HANDBOOK   by Stephen Metzger
A close-up and complete look at every aspect of this wondrous state. 375 pages.   **$13.95**

NORTHERN CALIFORNIA HANDBOOK   by Kim Weir
An outstanding companion for imaginative travel in the territory north of the Tehachapis. 800 pages.   **$19.95**

OREGON HANDBOOK   by Stuart Warren and Ted Long Ishikawa
Brimming with travel practicalities and insiders' views on Oregon's history, culture, arts, and activities. 461 pages.   **$15.95**

PACIFIC MEXICO HANDBOOK   by Bruce Whipperman
Explore 2,000 miles of gorgeous beaches, quiet resort towns, and famous archaeological sites along Mexico's Pacific coast. Spanish-English glossary. 428 pages.   **$15.95**

TEXAS HANDBOOK   by Joe Cummings
Seasoned travel writer Joe Cummings brings an insider's perspective to his home state. 483 pages.   **$13.95**

UTAH HANDBOOK   by Bill Weir
Weir gives you all the carefully researched facts and background to make your visit a success. 445 pages.   **$14.95**

WASHINGTON HANDBOOK   by Dianne J. Boulerice Lyons and Archie Satterfield
Covers sights, shopping, services, transportation, and outdoor recreation, with complete listings for restaurants and accommodations. 433 pages.   **$13.95**

WYOMING HANDBOOK   by Don Pitcher
All you need to know to open the doors to this wide and wild state. 495 pages.   **$14.95**

YUCATAN HANDBOOK by Chicki Mallan
All the information you'll need to guide you into every corner of this exotic land. Mayan and Spanish glossaries. 391 pages. **$14.95**

THE INTERNATIONAL SERIES

EGYPT HANDBOOK by Kathy Hansen
An invaluable resource for intelligent travel in Egypt. Arabic glossary. 522 pages. **$18.95**

MOSCOW-ST. PETERSBURG HANDBOOK by Masha Nordbye
Provides the visitor with an extensive introduction to the history, culture, and people of these two great cities, as well as practical information on where to stay, eat, and shop. 260 pages. **$13.95**

NEPAL HANDBOOK by Kerry Moran
Whether you're planning a week in Kathmandu or months out on the trail, *Nepal Handbook* will take you into the heart of this Himalayan jewel. 378 pages. **$12.95**

NEPALI AAMA by Broughton Coburn
A delightful photo-journey into the life of a Gurung tribeswoman of Central Nepal. Having lived with Aama (translated, "mother") for two years, first as an outsider and later as an adopted member of the family, Coburn presents an intimate glimpse into a culture alive with humor, folklore, religion, and ancient rituals. 165 pages. **$13.95**

PAKISTAN HANDBOOK by Isobel Shaw
For armchair travelers and trekkers alike, the most detailed and authoritative guide to Pakistan ever published. Urdu glossary. 478 pages. **$15.95**

STAYING HEALTHY IN ASIA, AFRICA, AND LATIN AMERICA
by Dirk G. Schroeder, Sc D, MPH
Don't leave home without it! Besides providing a complete overview of the health problems that exist in these areas, this book will help you determine which immunizations you'll need beforehand, what medications to take with you, and how to recognize and treat infections and diseases. Includes extensively illustrated first-aid information and precautions for heat, cold, and high altitude. 200 pages. **$10.95**

MOONBELTS

Made of heavy-duty Cordura nylon, the Moonbelt offers maximum protection for your money and important papers. This all-weather pouch slips under your shirt or waistband, rendering it virtually undetectable and inaccessible to pickpockets. One-inch-wide nylon webbing, heavy-duty zipper, one-inch quick-release buckle. Accommodates traveler's checks, passport, cash, photos. Size 5 x 9 inches. Black. **$8.95**

> **New travel handbooks may be available that are not on this list.**
> **To find out more about current or upcoming titles,**
> **call us toll-free at (800) 345-5473.**

IMPORTANT ORDERING INFORMATION

FOR FASTER SERVICE: Call to locate the bookstore nearest you that carries Moon Travel Handbooks or order directly from Moon Publications:

(800) 345-5473 • **Monday-Friday** • **9 a.m.-5 p.m. PST** • **fax (916) 345-6751**

PRICES: All prices are subject to change. We always ship the most current edition. We will let you know if there is a price increase on the book you ordered.

SHIPPING & HANDLING OPTIONS: 1) Domestic UPS or USPS first class (allow 10 working days for delivery): $3.50 for the first item, 50 cents for each additional item.

Exceptions:
- **Moonbelt** shipping is $1.50 for one, 50 cents for each additional belt.
- Add $2.00 for same-day handling.
- UPS 2nd Day Air or Printed Airmail requires a special quote.
- International Surface Bookrate (8-12 weeks delivery):
  $3.00 for the first item, $1.00 for each additional item. Note: Moon Publications cannot guarantee international surface bookrate shipping.

FOREIGN ORDERS: All orders that originate outside the U.S.A. must be paid for with either an International Money Order or a check in U.S. currency drawn on a major U.S. bank based in the U.S.A.

TELEPHONE ORDERS: We accept Visa or MasterCard payments. Minimum order is US$15.00. Call in your order: (800) 345-5473, 9 a.m.-5 p.m. Pacific Standard Time.

ORDER FORM

Be sure to call (800) 345-5473 for current prices and editions or for the name of the bookstore nearest you that carries Moon Travel Handbooks • 9 a.m.–5 p.m. PST
(See important ordering information on preceding page)

Name: _____Date: _____

Street: _____

City: _____Daytime Phone: _____

State or Country: _____Zip Code: _____

QUANTITY	TITLE	PRICE

Taxable Total_____

Sales Tax (7.25%) for California Residents_____

Shipping & Handling_____

TOTAL_____

Ship: ☐ UPS (no PO Boxes)   ☐ 1st class   ☐ International surface mail

Ship to: ☐ address above   ☐ other _____

_____

Make checks payable to: **MOON PUBLICATIONS, INC.** P.O. Box 3040, Chico, CA 95927-3040 U.S.A. We accept Visa and MasterCard. **To Order**: Call in your Visa or MasterCard number, or send a written order with your Visa or MasterCard number and expiration date clearly written.

Card Number: ☐ **Visa**   ☐ **MasterCard**

☐ ☐ ☐ ☐   ☐ ☐ ☐ ☐   ☐ ☐ ☐ ☐   ☐ ☐ ☐ ☐

Exact Name on Card: _____

expiration date:_____

signature_____

FA/93

THE METRIC SYSTEM

1 inch	= 2.54 centimeters (cm)
1 foot	= .304 meters (m)
1 mile	= 1.6093 kilometers (km)
1 km	= .6124 miles
1 fathom	= 1.8288 m
1 chain	= 20.1168 m
1 furlong	= 201.168 m
1 acre	= .4047 hectares
1 sq km	= 100 hectares
1 sq mile	= 2.59 square km
1 ounce	= 28.35 grams
1 pound	= .4536 kilograms
1 short ton	= .90718 metric ton
1 short ton	= 2000 pounds
1 long ton	= 1.016 metric tons
1 long ton	= 2240 pounds
1 metric ton	= 1000 kilograms
1 quart	= .94635 liters
1 US gallon	= 3.7854 liters
1 Imperial gallon	= 4.5459 liters
1 nautical mile	= 1.852 km

To compute centigrade temperatures, subtract 32 from Fahrenheit and divide by 1.8. To go the other way, multiply centigrade by 1.8 and add 32.

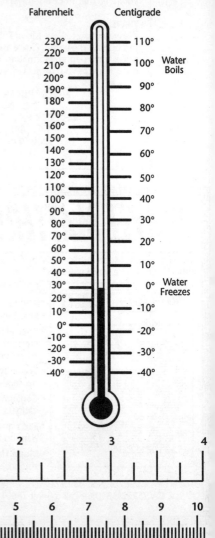